Samuel Johnson

BOOKS BY JEFFREY MEYERS

BIOGRAPHY

A Fever at the Core: The Idealist in Politics

Married to Genius

Katherine Mansfield

The Enemy: A Biography of Wyndham Lewis

Hemingway

Manic Power: Robert Lowell and His Circle

D. H. Lawrence

Joseph Conrad

Edgar Allan Poe: His Life and Legacy

Scott Fitzgerald

Edmund Wilson

Robert Frost

Bogart: A Life in Hollywood

Gary Cooper: American Hero

Privileged Moments: Encounters with Writers

Wintry Conscience: A Biography of George Orwell

Inherited Risk: Errol and Sean Flynn in Hollywood and Vietnam

Somerset Maugham

Impressionist Quartet: The Intimate Genius of Manet and Morisot,
    Degas and Cassatt

Modigliani

CRITICISM

Fiction and the Colonial Experience

The Wounded Spirit: T. E. Lawrence's *Seven Pillars of Wisdom*

A Reader's Guide to George Orwell

Painting and the Novel

Homosexuality and Literature

D. H. Lawrence and the Experience of Italy

Disease and the Novel

The Spirit of Biography

Hemingway: Life into Art

BIBLIOGRAPHY

T. E. Lawrence: A Bibliography

Catalogue of the Library of the Late Siegfried Sassoon

George Orwell: An Annotated Bibliography of Criticism

EDITED COLLECTIONS

George Orwell: The Critical Heritage

Hemingway: The Critical Heritage

Robert Lowell: Interviews and Memoirs

The Sir Arthur Conan Doyle Reader

The W. Somerset Maugham Reader

EDITED ORIGINAL ESSAYS

Wyndham Lewis: A Revaluation

Wyndham Lewis *by Roy Campbell*

D. H. Lawrence and Tradition

The Legacy of D. H. Lawrence

The Craft of Literary Biography

The Biographer's Art

T. E. Lawrence: Soldier, Writer, Legend

Graham Greene: A Revaluation

SAMUEL JOHNSON

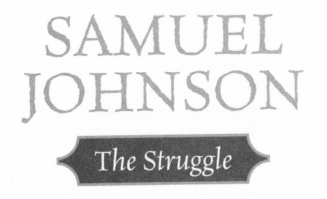

The Struggle

JEFFREY MEYERS

BASIC
BOOKS

A MEMBER OF THE PERSEUS BOOKS GROUP
NEW YORK

Books published by Basic Books are available at special discounts for bulk purchases in the United States by corporations, institutions, and other organizations. For more information, please contact the Special Markets Department at the Perseus Books Group, 2300 Chestnut Street, Suite 200, Philadelphia, PA 19103, or call (800) 810-4145 extension 5000, or e-mail special.markets@perseusbooks.com.

Designed by Linda Harper

Library of Congress Cataloging-in-Publication Data
Meyers, Jeffrey.
Samuel Johnson : the struggle / Jeffrey Meyers.
    p. cm.
  Includes bibliographical references and index.
  ISBN 978-0-465-04571-6
  1. Johnson, Samuel, 1709–1784. 2. Great Britain—Intellectual life—18th century.
  3. Authors, English—18th century—Biography. 4. Lexicographers—Great Britain—Biography.
  5. Intellectuals—Great Britain—Biography. I. Title.

PR3533.M49 2008
828'.609—dc22
[B]

2008012302

10 9 8 7 6 5 4 3 2 1

FOR JAMES SALTER

CONTENTS

ILLUSTRATIONS

ILLUSTRATIONS IN INSERT

1. *Michael Johnson,* engraving by Edward Francis Finden, c.1830—Samuel Johnson Birthplace Museum, Lichfield

2. *Samuel Johnson* by Sir Joshua Reynolds, 1756–57—National Portrait Gallery, London

3. *David Garrick* by Thomas Gainsborough, 1770—National Portrait Gallery

4. *Elizabeth Johnson,* artist unknown—Houghton Library, Harvard University

5. *Bennet Langton,* artist unknown—Samuel Johnson Birthplace Museum

6. *Giuseppe Baretti,* after Sir Joshua Reynolds, 1773—National Portrait Gallery

7. *Samuel Johnson* by Sir Joshua Reynolds, 1769—Houghton Library, Harvard University

ILLUSTRATIONS IN TEXT

ACKNOWLEDGMENTS

I have used four sources of new material on Johnson: the James Clifford archive, the Donald Greene archive, the Rothschild collection and the Hyde collection. James Clifford did not live to write the third and final volume of his life of Johnson. I am grateful to Columbia University for information from his vast archive. Clifford's pupil Donald Greene, the greatest Johnson scholar of the twentieth century, also planned to write the life of Johnson. Greene's son, Richard, kindly sent me his father's archive and allowed me to study it at home. Loren and Frances Rothschild, with characteristic generosity, invited me to stay with them in Los Angeles while reading their superb collection of Johnson books, letters and manuscripts. I have studied the great Donald and Mary Hyde collection, which was made available to scholars at Harvard University in June 2006. These archives provided many illuminating yet unpublished contemporary descriptions of Johnson.

I was also able to use Bruce Redford's complete, five-volume edition of Johnson's *Letters* (1992–94) and Roger Lonsdale's superb four-volume edition of *The Lives of the Poets* (2006). I am grateful to Lynda Mugglestone and Lucie Walker for help during my research at Pembroke College, Oxford, and to the curators of the Samuel Johnson Birthplace Museum in Lichfield and Dr. Johnson's House in Gough Square, London. Mary and Howard Berg in Cambridge and Liz Hodgkin in the Cotswolds provided splendid hospitality.

I wrote my first dissertation and first three articles on Johnson, who has remained a lifelong interest. I've profited from friendships with several distinguished Johnsonians who helped illuminate the complexities of his character. I knew John Wain in London and Oxford when he was writing his biography of Johnson (1974). I learned a great deal from stimulating conversations with my friend Dr. Bernard Meyer, who wrote several incisive psychoanalytical essays on Johnson. Morris Brownell, my classmate in graduate school at Berkeley, offered decades of valuable advice and encouragement. Paul Alkon gave me many books on Johnson and the eighteenth century, and sharpened my ideas in our talks.

Other friends also gave crucial help with this book: John Abbott, Katherine Bucknell, Robert DeMaria, Trevor Howard-Hill and William Pritchard answered queries. Gerald Caplan advised me about the law, Nora Crook about Frank Barber in Jamaica, Christian Kopff about Roman history, Francis Martin about private collections and Martin Postle about Reynolds' paintings. Beryl Bainbridge discussed her novel about Queeney Thrale; Keith Crook lent me his dissertation on Johnson; John Burke sent me his book. Emma Butterfield of the National Portrait Gallery was particularly helpful with the photographs. My wife, Valerie—born a few miles from Lichfield—helped with the research in England and America, and compiled the index. She, Paul Alkon and Frederick Crews read and improved each chapter.

No species of writing seems more worthy of cultivation than biography, since none can be more delightful or more useful, none can more certainly enchain the heart by irresistible interest, or more widely diffuse instruction to every diversity of condition.

—SAMUEL JOHNSON, *RAMBLER 60*

INTRODUCTION
THE STRUGGLE

Samuel Johnson—moralist, poet, essayist, critic, dictionary maker, conversationalist and larger-than-life personality—had a formidable intellect and a passion for ideas. A man of humble background, he used his great mind and dominant character to overcome his physical defects, complete ambitious literary projects, and gain acceptance and honors. He also had a compassionate heart and a heroic capacity for suffering. He endured constant pain, long years of profound depression and two decades of failure. Ford Madox Ford called him "the most tragic of all our major literary figures."

Johnson struggled with disease from the moment of his birth to his final fight. From infancy he was blind in one eye and deaf in one ear. In childhood he had tubercular lesions on his neck and smallpox that left scars on his face; from early manhood he suffered from convulsive tics and twitches. Reflecting on the contrast between his mind and body and striving for control of his life, Johnson asserted, "There are perhaps very few conditions more to be pitied than that of an active and elevated mind, labouring under the weight of a distempered body." His struggle to overcome his disabilities suggests Nietzsche's aphorism "what does not destroy us makes us stronger."[1]

Born in straitened circumstances, but keenly aware of his genius, Johnson was alienated from his elderly parents. Physically repulsive and

1

slovenly in dress and habits, by nature indolent and melancholy, he experienced humiliating poverty at Oxford and left without a degree. He had a perennially unsatisfied craving for love and sympathy, and as a young man contracted a bizarre and sexually frustrating marriage to a much older woman. After her death, despite uncommonly strong sexual passions, he remained celibate for more than thirty years.

Johnson was a mass of contradictions: lazy and energetic, aggressive and tender, melancholic and humorous, commonsensical and irrational, comforted yet tormented by religion. In his life and work he exalted virtue, propagated knowledge and alleviated suffering. The miserable, the victimized and the oppressed always had a claim on his compassion. His social ideas were progressive and humane. He strongly opposed vivisection and foxhunting, debtors' prisons, Negro slavery and the exploitation of native people from India to America. He gave generously to beggars and homeless children, rescued prostitutes, secured clothing for French prisoners of war and defended criminals who had been condemned to hang. For decades he supported a household of pathetic, impoverished and contentious dependents. But these charitable acts could not dispel his overwhelming guilt and fear of eternal damnation.

Despite his physical disabilities, Johnson was unusually tall and strong, with immense vitality and great physical courage. His character and manners were aggressive, and he saw life itself as a perpetual contest. James Boswell compared Johnson's continual attempts to control the demons of his mind to the efforts of a Roman gladiator in the Colosseum. He fought "the wild beasts of the Arena . . . ready to be let out upon him. After a conflict, he drove them back into their dens; but not killing them, they were still assailing him." Johnson's description of himself at Oxford defined his essential qualities: poor, bitter, angry, violent and combative; challenging his superiors, dominating others by his brains and his talent. He told Boswell, "I was mad and violent. It was bitterness which they mistook for frolick. I was miserably poor, and I thought to fight my way by my literature and my wit; so I disregarded all power and all authority." "The gradations of a hero's life," he believed, "are from battle to battle, and of an author's from book to book."[2]

Johnson, a literary hero, battled from book to book and struggled against formidable obstructions. His violence and surprising athletic feats were essential outlets for his frustration, his anger and his sexual passion. When one publisher urged him to work faster on the catalogue of Sir Robert Harley's vast library, he knocked him down. When another pressured him to produce more copy for the *Dictionary of the English Language* and threatened to cut off his funds, he adopted a military metaphor and a typically combative stance: "my citadel shall not be taken by storm while I can defend it, and if a blockade is intended, the country is under the command of my batteries." He described the inevitable limitations of his edition of Shakespeare's plays as if he'd been battling the text itself: "from many [passages], after all my efforts, I have retreated, and confessed the repulse."

Johnson's mental problems forced him to live in a state of siege. He hoped "always to resist, and in time to drive [away]" the black dog of melancholy. Failure to prepare for death, he believed, "is to sleep at our post at a siege, but to omit it in old age, is to sleep at an attack."[3] His battles lasted till the very end and there was never any possibility of surrender. "Time cannot always be defeated," he bravely claimed, "but let us not yield till we are conquered." During his final illness, he again insisted, though greatly weakened, "I will be conquered; I will not capitulate," and went down with all guns firing. Johnson believed that "to strive with difficulties and to conquer them, is the highest human felicity."

Johnson always enjoyed a fight. When he traveled to Plymouth with Joshua Reynolds in August 1762, he became embroiled in a quarrel between the old and new parts of town. He resolutely took the side of the established town and, violently partisan, derided the dockers of the recently built area as upstarts and aliens. When the dockers, destitute of water, petitioned their rivals for a share of the precious commodity, Johnson zealously exclaimed: "No, no! I am against the *dockers*; I am a Plymouth man. Rogues! Let them die of thirst. They shall not have a drop!" He urged the gentle author Fanny Burney to topple a rival from her literary eminence. He even encouraged discord in his own household. Inciting a half-reformed prostitute to defend herself against the intimidating blind poetess Anna Williams, he cried: "At her again, Poll! Never flinch, Poll."[4] In the last year of his life, at the age of seventy-five, he started a riot to protest a cancelled display of fireworks.

In the nineteenth century, when Johnson was generally out of favor, two emotionally troubled writers identified with his sufferings and paid tribute to his noble character. Thomas Carlyle asked, "shall we not say, of this great mournful Johnson, that he guided his difficult confused existence wisely; led it *well*, like a right-valiant man?" John Ruskin called him "a man entirely sincere, and infallibly wise."[5] Johnson's lifelong struggle against overwhelming disadvantages was inspired by a belief that his superior intellect was a gift from God and that he was obliged to use it to the fullest extent.

Boswell's monumental *Life of Johnson* and private journals are the most authoritative sources of information about Johnson. But he devotes only one-fifth of his book to the first fifty-five years of Johnson's life and four-fifths to his last twenty years. He had an extraordinary ability to record Johnson's talk and bring him uncannily to life, and through him we know Johnson as a living, breathing man. Yet even Boswell was unaware of crucial aspects of Johnson's history, and deliberately suppressed some sensitive but revealing sexual material. He did not know that Johnson wrote a substantial part of Robert Chambers' Oxford law lectures. Apart from a few entries that he secretly transcribed in Johnson's house, Boswell had not read Johnson's private diaries. He certainly did not know Johnson's "secret far dearer to him than his life."

Boswell could not have known the quite shocking entry of 1775 in the Reverend Thomas Campbell's *Diary of a Visit to England in 1775*, which was not published until 1947. Johnson almost never used obscenities and condemned those who did. But the chaste widower was certainly thinking of himself when—according to his lifelong friend, the actor David Garrick—he was asked to name the greatest pleasure in life. Instead of mentioning religious devotion or intellectual conversation, convivial company, foreign travel or literary fame, Johnson said that the first pleasure was "fucking & the second was drinking. And therefore he wondered why there were not more drunkards, for all could drink tho' all could not fuck."

Since Johnson's wife had been dead for more than thirty years when Boswell's *Life of Johnson* was published in 1791, and he had no children or blood relatives who might protest, Boswell was unusually free to write whatever he wished. He was astonishingly frank about recording intimate details in his own journals. But he felt obliged to draw a discreet veil around certain aspects of Johnson's life that he did know about but felt would detract from his friend's prestige and dignity.

Johnson's covert sexual life was far more interesting than Boswell's own frantic fornication and punitive doses of clap. But Boswell listed under the Latin heading *tacenda* (unmentionable) a great many incidents that make Johnson more vulnerable and more human. As the editor of Boswell's correspondence observed: "[His] treatment of those materials which deal with Johnson's weaknesses, real and alleged—his indolence, his oddities and asperity of manner, his excesses in eating and drinking, his profanity and bawdy, his sexual lapses, his intellectual narrowness and prejudice, his use of drugs, his insanity—all of these subjects appear among the unused sources, and seem to compose themselves into a pattern of editorial suppression."[6]

When Boswell did discuss these delicate matters, he tended to sanitize them. Johnson's learned friend Bennet Langton told Boswell, who was assiduously gathering material for the *Life of Johnson*, that when Johnson's play *Irene* was staged at Garrick's playhouse, he used "to go occasionally to the green room of Drury Lane Theatre where he was much regarded by the Players and was very easy and facetious with them." Harmless enough, so far. But the real interest of this anecdote is the effect these uninhibited, scantily clad actresses had on the impressionable Johnson. Boswell recorded, but did not publish, Johnson's confession to Garrick that he was sorely tempted by these young beauties: "I'll come no more behind your scenes David; for the silk-stockings and white bubbies of your actresses excite my genitals." Another version of this confession, which Garrick told the radical MP John Wilkes, was that "the silk stockings and white bosoms of your actresses do make my genitals to quiver." This pulsating vibrato is decorously and moralistically tamped down in the *Life*, where both "bubbies" and "genitals" disappear. Using Latinate diction, Boswell makes him more moral and "Johnsonian": "Johnson at last denied himself this amusement, for considerations of rigid [a nice pun] virtue; saying, 'I'll come no more behind your scenes, David; for the silk stockings and white bosoms of your actresses excite my amorous propensities.'"[7] The effect is to mock the sexual urges of a respectable man, rather than allow us to see the misery of his sexual frustration.

I have profited from previous biographies of Johnson, but also differ from them in significant ways. James Clifford's first two volumes (1955 and 1979)—heavily reliant on the discoveries of A. L. Reade—are extremely academic, adhere to a rigid chronology and try to cover every event in Johnson's life. I sometimes depart from strict chronology to narrate major themes and try to emphasize not the events of his life, but what they mean. Walter Jackson Bate's biography (1977) is also academic and sometimes stretches credulity with dubious psychoanalytic theories. John Wain's life (1974) is more readable, but he confessed "there is no research in this book," which lacks endnotes to substantiate his argument. All these books were published 30 or more years ago. I have benefited from the great contributions to Johnson scholarship since then.

A crucial issue in Johnson's life concerns his use of padlocks, chains and whips, first discovered by Katharine Balderston in 1949. Hester Thrale loyally kept this matter secret, and contemporary biographers like Sir John Hawkins, James Boswell and Arthur Murphy knew nothing about it. Joseph Wood Krutch's modern biography (1944) appeared before Balderston published her essay. Despite the overwhelming evidence of Johnson's darkest secret, his modern biographers have not been able to reconcile his obsession with their exalted image of the great moralist and stern philosopher. Preferring to keep Johnson safely on a pedestal, they've consistently refused to face the implications of Balderston's discovery. James Clifford's unfinished life stopped before this episode occurred, and his biography of Hester Thrale (revised in 1968) completely ignored the issue. Christopher Hibbert (1971) was cautious and indecisive. Though Hester had said "do not quarrel with your Governess for not using the Rod enough," Hibbert wrote, in an awkward style that expressed his own uneasiness: "whether or not the rod was actually used, whether or not

Johnson's fantasies [*sic*] about manacles and fetters were erotic and masochistic in their nature, it is impossible now to say."

John Wain devoted an entire chapter to "The Padlock." But he, too, with an unconvincing "absolutely certain," shied away from the inevitable conclusion: "if one thing can be taken as absolutely certain, it is that Hester did *not* engage in any degrading sexual activity with Johnson." The psychoanalytic Walter Jackson Bate was most likely to be receptive to Hester's comment that a woman's power to tie and whip a man like Johnson was "*literally* and *strictly* true." Yet Bate maintained: "not only is the 'evidence' so slender and disconnected as to come close to nonexistence, but it flies in the face . . . of both psychological probability and practical good sense." In 1979 the psychoanalyst Bernard Meyer criticized Bate for denying the obvious: "in the face of rather compelling evidence to the contrary, [Bate] has spared no effort to rescue Johnson from any suspicion of deviant behavior, specifically in the form of *bondage* and related perversions." Robert DeMaria (1993), following the well-worn path, repeated Bate's denial and concluded that Johnson's whipping by Mrs. Thrale was merely a lighthearted frolic: "there is no convincing evidence that [Johnson's "jest"] was realized in anything beyond polite behaviour and a kind of country-house theatrical life."[8] Biographers, like lawyers, should be required to take a course in evidence. I believe Johnson's secret life adds to rather than detracts from his greatness. It makes his character more complex and tormented, his struggle more extreme, his achievement more impressive.

Samuel Johnson: The Struggle, published to commemorate the 300th anniversary of his birth, places him in the social and historical context of eighteenth-century England. It describes his circle of London friends, each one preeminent in his profession—the politician Edmund Burke, the painter Sir Joshua Reynolds, the biographer James Boswell, the author Oliver Goldsmith, the historian Edward Gibbon, the actor David Garrick, the novelist Fanny Burney—perhaps the most brilliant concentration of genius in English history. This book also reveals how Johnson's greatest works—*The Vanity of Human Wishes,* the *Rambler,* the *Dictionary of the English Language, Rasselas,* the edition of Shakespeare's works, the *Journey to the Western Islands of Scotland* and especially his late masterpiece *The Lives of the Poets*—evolved from his tormented character.

This book offers several new interpretations of Johnson's life and works: his reasons for leaving Oxford; his ability to become a lawyer without a university degree; his relations with women, marriage and sexual life; his intimacy with Hester Thrale; his tendency to tears; his hostility to Jonathan Swift; the paternity of his servant Francis (Frank) Barber; the similarities between Shakespeare's life and his own; the meaning of *The Vanity of Human Wishes*; his wife's influence on the heroine of *Irene*; the parallels between Shakespeare's Falstaff and Boswell; and Johnson's impact on five major writers of the nineteenth and twentieth centuries.

1

LICHFIELD LAD
1709–1728

I

Samuel Johnson took inordinate pride in his birthplace. In a satiric jab at the nearby industrial center that would soon eclipse his native town, he defiantly said, "we are a city of philosophers: we work with our heads, and make the boobies of Birmingham work for us with their hands." Lichfield, in the English Midlands, 120 miles northwest of London, was a cathedral town, a military garrison and a major market. When Johnson first brought James Boswell there, he indulged in two of his favorite pastimes, Scot-bashing and Boswell-bashing, and exclaimed, "I turned him loose at Lichfield, my native city, that he might see for once real civility: for you know he lives among savages in Scotland, and among rakes in London."

Johnson could also be quite critical of Lichfield, and emphasized its benighted state in a letter to his intimate friend Hester Thrale. Referring to Fanny Burney's acclaimed novel, he wrote, "the name of Evelina had never been heard at Lichfield, till I brought it. I am afraid my dear Townsmen will be mentioned in future days as the last part of this nation that was civilised." He insisted that the inhabitants of Lichfield were "the most sober, decent people in England," but also (using "decent" in a quite different sense) remembered that "all the *decent* people in Lichfield got drunk every night, and were not the worse thought of."[1]

Lichfield, meaning "field of the dead," was named for martyred Christians and produced some martyrs of its own. The last man to be condemned for heresy in England was burned in the marketplace in 1612. The essayist Joseph Addison, whose father had been dean of the fourteenth-century, red sandstone, twin-spired cathedral, had attended the same grammar school as Johnson. At the beginning of the eighteenth century the town had a population of about 4,000. London then had 675,000; but the next largest cities—Bristol, Norwich and Liverpool—all had fewer than 30,000.

Located in the valley of the Trent, Lichfield manufactured cloth, leather and coaches. It held annual fairs, with high-stakes cockfighting and savage bear-baiting, and inns packed with drunken revelers. There was no street lighting until the late 1730s, and at night people walked warily through the dark town. The historian John Brewer provides a lively description of the place:

> Lichfield was a typical English cathedral town, its genteel social life centred on the families of clerics and ecclesiasts in the cathedral close. . . . They fraternized with Lichfield's lawyers, doctors, traders and prosperous merchants, and with the squirearchy whose houses were not far from the city. In the early eighteenth century Lichfield was the social and cultural centre of the west Midlands; even as it was eclipsed by the growing industrial city of Birmingham, it remained a lively town, with a theatre (first opened in 1736), several booksellers and printers, a cathedral lending library of 3,000 literary, philosophical, scientific and religious books, an annual music festival on St. Cecilia's Day, and a busy social calendar tied to the Lichfield races. In the winter there were private subscription balls and large public dinners. . . . The most important cultural figure was [the physician, botanist and author] Erasmus Darwin, the grandfather of the more famous Charles.

Johnson's struggling shopkeeping family stood outside this elite circle of clergymen, attorneys and squires.

Johnson was a close contemporary of Benjamin Franklin, whom he once met, and of Frederick the Great of Prussia, whose biography he wrote. Johnson's long life extended from the High Tory reign of Queen Anne through the loss of the American colonies and the Gordon Riots under King George III. In 1709, the year he was born, the young Alexander Pope published his *Pastorals*, Addison and Richard Steele brought out the first issue of the *Tatler* (a precursor of Johnson's *Rambler*) and Parliament enacted the first copyright law, from which Johnson would later benefit. In the battle of Poltava in the Ukraine that year, Peter the Great defeated Charles XII of Sweden, whom Johnson in a famous passage would use to exemplify the vanity of human wishes.

In his autobiographical writings, Johnson retrospectively emphasized his humble origins to show how hard he had to struggle in his youth. He said, in a characteristically balanced sentence, that a cousin who became a curate was the only relative "who ever rose in fortune above penury or in character above neglect." Though he was respectful of rank and zealous to maintain the social hierarchy, his own family was undistinguished, and he hardly knew who his grandfather was. His grandparents, in fact, had died before he was born, but a small family legacy enabled his elderly parents to complete their house, expand their business and get a boost in life.

His father, Michael Johnson, the son of a small farmer, was born in Cubley, Derbyshire, in 1657. He grew up in Lichfield and attended the town's excellent grammar school. From the age of sixteen to twenty-four he was apprenticed to a London bookseller in St. Paul's Churchyard, and in 1681 he returned home to start his own business. Even taller and stronger than his son, Michael liked riding around the countryside with books in his saddlebags or his cart, selling them to bibliophiles who lived in rural areas. He set up a stall in distant towns on market days, and traveled as far as Scotland and Ireland. He himself published and sold a dozen medical tracts or sermons by local clergymen. A Lichfield dignitary praised the scholarly Michael, who "worked with his head," by stating that "he propagates learning all over this diocese, and advanceth knowledge to its just height; all the Clergy here are his Pupils, and suck all they have from him."[2] In a similar fashion, Samuel Johnson would later ghostwrite sermons for clergymen and propagate knowledge throughout the country.

In 1706, when the forty-nine-year-old Michael married the thirty-seven-year-old Sarah Ford, who came from a superior family with wealthy connections, he built a house in the market square of Lichfield. The ten rooms, with attic and cellar, housed his family as well as the shop where he sold and bound books. According to one of his advertisements, Michael sold "shop-books, pocket-books, 'fine French prints, for stair-cases and large chimney pieces,' maps, large and small . . . as well as general literature, while 'to please the ladies' are added a 'store of fine pictures and paper hangings.'"

In 1709 he completed his house and started a tanning and parchment factory on the outskirts of town. A popular figure, he was elected sheriff, or mayor, of Lichfield. He continued to rise in civic affairs, and became a magistrate and member of the town council in 1712, and senior bailiff in 1725. With a fine intellect, considerable energy and solid knowledge of books, Michael soon became well known throughout the Midlands. But as his civic career prospered, his business gradually lost momentum. He was weak on finance, failed to develop or even sustain his trade and got no help from his wife, who did not share his love of books. When he grew older and could no longer travel, his business sharply declined. He was fined for creating a muck heap and indicted for tanning without having served an apprenticeship. He was unable to repair his tannery, which had fallen down from neglect, but he continued—with pointless yet pathetic compulsion, since anyone could enter from the rear—to lock the front door every night. His parchment business finished him off. No wonder that Sarah adopted "a constant attitude of querulous complaint" while Michael radiated "a general sensation of gloomy wretchedness."[3] Sam's boyhood and youth were marked by his father's slow descent.

Recalling the late, unhappy marriage of his ill-matched parents and of St. Paul's adage "It is better to marry than to burn," Johnson asserted that "a man of sense and education should meet a suitable companion in a wife. . . . He did not approve of late marriages. . . . [But] even ill assorted marriages were preferable to cheerless celibacy." Sarah thought she'd married beneath her, and criticized her husband's business failures, but did nothing to encourage his success. As Johnson wrote of this depressing, discontented household: "My father and mother had not much happiness from each other. They seldom conversed; for my father could not bear to talk of his affairs; and my mother, being unacquainted with books, cared not to talk of anything else. Had my mother been more literate, they had been better companions. She might have sometimes introduced her unwelcome topick with more success, if she could have diversified her conversation. Of business she had no distinct conception; and therefore her discourse was composed only of complaint, fear, and suspicion." When things went badly, as they usually did, Sarah reminded Michael that she came from a superior family, that she was used to better treatment and that she would insist on entertaining her friends with expensive cups of tea.

Johnson, who paradoxically combined a scrupulous attention to veracity with a tendency to wild exaggeration, once claimed, while disparaging his own family, that one of his uncles had been hanged. Neither the zealous researcher A. L. Reade nor anyone else has ever found evidence of this hanging. If it had taken place, it would surely have influenced Johnson's vehement opposition to capital punishment for minor crimes.

The one strong branch in the family tree was his uncle Andrew Johnson. This powerful fellow, while managing a ring for boxers and wrestlers in Smithfield, London, for a whole year, was never thrown or conquered. In those days boxing "matches were fought with bare knuckles and very few rules. Contestants could do anything they liked to each other as long as it was above the belt."[4] They could seize their opponent by the throat, throw him to the ground and use tactics more often employed in wrestling. Andrew taught Sam how to attack and defend himself in boxing, and Sam later justified this violent sport, which accustomed men to painful blows and to the sight of their own blood. It was a great thing for the son of a scholarly, mild-mannered, hen-pecked father to have an uncle who was a famous fighter.

II

Johnson, born on September 18, 1709, when the forty-year-old Sarah was well past the usual time for bearing a first child, came close to dying at birth. The surgeon, uncle of Sam's future classmate and lifelong friend Edmund Hector, was surprised that the frail infant had actually drawn breath and survived the ordeal. Soon afterwards, Sam suffered his first serious illness. "My mother," he wrote, "had a very difficult and dangerous labour, and was assisted by George Hector, a man-midwife of great reputation. I was born almost dead, and could not cry for some time. When he had me in his arms, he said, 'Here is a brave boy.' In a few weeks an inflammation was discovered on my buttock, which was at first, I think, taken for a burn; but soon appeared to be a natural disorder. It swelled, broke, and healed." Michael, proud to have a son and heir, magnanimously invited the whole town to celebrate with him.

Since genteel women did not suckle their own children, Sam was immediately handed over to a wet nurse, the wife of the local bricklayer. Her milk infected Sam (as well as her own son) with scrofula, or tuberculosis of the lymph nodes in the neck. The guilt-stricken Sarah believed that his disease was inherited from her family. She faithfully visited her firstborn son and took a different route every day so her solicitude would not appear ridiculous. Sam was brought home at ten weeks, "a poor, diseased infant, almost blind." His aunt Jane Ford, suggesting that many parents would have abandoned the hopelessly sick child, later told him, "she would not have picked such a poor creature up in the street." His namesake, godfather and family doctor, Samuel Swinfen, remarked that "he never knew any child reared with so much difficulty."[5]

Johnson suffered all the natural shocks that flesh is heir to. Like Shakespeare's Richard III, he was "unfinished, sent before [his] time / Into this breathing world scarce half made up." The tuberculosis affected both his optic and auditory nerves, impairing the vision in his right eye, blinding the left, and making him deaf in the left ear. A twentieth-century doctor has diagnosed "severe trauma and anoxia [lack of oxygen] at childbirth; early infections with bovine tuberculosis, invading the cervical [neck] glands and possibly the eye; loss of function of left ear, possibly due to birth trauma or smallpox [which also scarred him as a child]." These horrific diseases gave Johnson the sense that life was precarious, that he must struggle tenaciously in order to survive.

Sam was lucky to survive not only the diseases, but also the rigors of eighteenth-century medicine. To "cure" his blindness, an incision—without anesthesia and kept open with horsehair threads—was made in his left arm muscle to stimulate the discharge of noxious "humors" and withdraw the disease from the body. Fortunately, little Sam, his hand in a tempting custard, was unaware that the cut was being made. This incision became a repulsive oozing sore, deliberately kept open for six long years. But the assiduous doctors were not yet finished. They also surgically incised the child's neck glands, source of the scrofula, for drainage. The operation went badly, and his face was permanently disfigured by weltlike scars that ran down the left side of his face from ear to jaw. These scars were still visible, seventy-five years later, on his death mask.

The psychoanalyst Bernard Meyer vividly re-created the probable effects of this traumatic scene by emphasizing "the raw and brutal assault that surgery may signify to a helpless, terrified, screaming, and struggling child." In his life of the great Dutch physician Herman Boerhaave, with whom he closely identified, Johnson described Boerhaave's agonizing treatment for an ulcerating illness: "In the twelfth year of his age, a stubborn, painful, and malignant ulcer broke out upon his left thigh; which, for near five years, defeated all the art of surgeons and physicians, and not only afflicted him with the most excruciating pains, but exposed him to such sharp and tormenting applications, that the disease and remedies were equally insufferable."[6] Johnson's experience of pain, like Boerhaave's, taught him to feel compassion for the suffering of others.

In March 1712, when Sam was two years old, Sir John Floyer, a distinguished local physician and author of a best-selling tract on the therapeutic use of hot and cold baths, recommended that Sam be "touched" for scrofula, or "the King's Evil." The belief that the king had godlike powers and that when he touched a scrofulous victim God healed him began with Edward the Confessor in the eleventh century and continued into the age of Isaac Newton and John Locke. In *Macbeth* Shakespeare described the king's miraculous cure:

> strangely-visited people,
> All swoll'n and ulcerous, pitiful to the eye,
> The mere despair of surgery, he cures,
> Hanging a golden stamp about their necks.
> Put on with holy prayers.
> (4.3.150–54)

In the seventeenth century Charles II touched nearly 100,000 unfortunates. Queen Anne, the last Stuart monarch, touched for the King's Evil to demonstrate the divine right of kings and assert her hereditary claim to the crown. The order of service for this "touching" ritual was included in the Anglican *Book of Common Prayer* as late as 1728. In 1714 (the year of her death) Anne, who had a powerful belief in its efficacy, touched as many as 200 people in one ceremony. The historian T. B. Macaulay observed, "Theologians of eminent learning, ability, and virtue gave the sanction of their authority to this mummery; and what is stranger still, medical men of high note believed, or affected to believe in the balsamic virtues of the royal hand." In *The King's Evil,* Raymond Crawfurd wrote that Johnson, one of the last to experience this pointless treatment, "carried with him to the grave the abiding testimony of Anne's ineffectual handiwork."

Sarah felt guilty that Sam had contracted tuberculosis either from her family or from the wet nurse she had chosen. She therefore took great trouble, while pregnant with her second child, to take Sam on the long, difficult and expensive three-day journey to London. Following the traditional ruse of exiles and refugees, she sewed gold coins into her petticoat as a defense against highwaymen. Floyer provided a certificate confirming that Sam had the King's Evil, and a court surgeon verified the disease. Sarah and Sam took the stagecoach to London, in which he was sick and disgusted the other travelers. To save money, they returned by wagon, and he frightened the other passengers with his violent cough.

The solemn occasion in St. James' Palace began with a religious service that included a passage from Mark 16:18: "They shall lay their hands on the sick, and they shall recover." This was followed by the royal touch and the bestowal of a chained gold-piece that was placed around the victim's neck. The touch-piece was actually a gold angel, first coined in 1465, which showed St. Michael slaying a dragon on one side and a ship sailing before the wind on the other. Johnson wore the medal (now in the British Library) around his neck for the rest of his life. (Since he rarely bathed, it must have become incredibly filthy.) Too young to retain a clear impression, Johnson had "a confused but somehow sort of solemn recollection of a lady in diamonds, and a long black hood."

Sam's brother, Nathaniel, was born in October 1712. He was a healthy child, which may have made Sam envious, and soon became a rival for his mother's affections. After the christening, Sarah taught Sam to spell and pronounce the words "little Natty." Little is known about Nathaniel, who remains a shadowy and elusive figure. He seems to have been a failure, and died young. In his only surviving letter, written to Sarah shortly before his death in 1736, the young man referred to his mysterious "crimes," perhaps theft or embezzlement. He bitterly complained that Sam had never done anything to help and had even obstructed him: "as to my Brother's assisting me I had but little Reason to expect it when He would scarce ever use me with common civility and to whose advice was owing that unwillingness you showed to my going to Stourbridge" to set up a book business.[7] Twenty years later, Johnson had a memorable but unspecified dream about Nathaniel. At the end of his life he described his temperamentally opposite brother as a lively, noisy man who loved company, and tried to find out how he had lived and what had happened to him. Nathaniel, like all members of Johnson's family, gave him a gnawing sense of guilt.

III

Sam received an excellent, if severe, education in Lichfield. He attended Mrs. Oliver's dame school at the age of four, Thomas

Browne's school at six, the lower grammar school at seven, and the upper school from ten to sixteen. Sam's first violent episode took place at the age of four. Because of his poor eyesight, a servant usually escorted him home from school. One day, when she failed to arrive, the little boy set out on his own. Dame Oliver, worried about his safety in the dirty and sometimes dangerous streets, followed behind to keep an eye on him. As he turned the corner and caught sight of her, he maintained his manly independence by charging back and attacking her with punches and kicks.

The free grammar school had a single oak-paneled room and a small playground, and the boys were allowed to run around in a nearby field owned by the town clerk, Theophilus Levett. Johnson said that he excelled all the other young scholars, and was indulged and caressed by the under-master, Humphrey Hawkins. He remembered these kind townsmen later in life, when he became close friends with their namesakes, Robert Levet and Sir John Hawkins.

Caresses turned to cruelty when the lanky, lounging, gray-eyed Sam entered the upper school. The boys were completely immersed in studying Latin grammar, reading Latin authors from Cicero and Ovid to Horace and Virgil, and writing Latin exercises and themes. Their main text was the *Grammar* of William Lily, Renaissance humanist, headmaster of St. Paul's School and reviver of Greek studies in England. His book had been used in English schools, with some revisions, since the 1540s. The boys then advanced to Greek grammar and to reading the New Testament, Xenophon and Hesiod.

On the rare occasion when Sam failed an exam, his mother encouraged him to do better next time. "'We often,' said she, dear mother! 'come off best, when we are most afraid.'" (He was also deeply moved when Sarah gave him some of her coffee, an expensive luxury, to gratify his boyish appetite.) Returning to school after a vacation, leaving his homework till the very last minute and then writing very fast, he would "begin one of his exercises, in which he purposely left some faults, in order to gain time to finish the rest." This sluggish resolution, an odd combination of idleness and industry, became his permanent mode of composition. In school Sam learned that his brainpower could compensate for his ugly appearance. Tall and strong, he became popular with the other boys by correcting their work and dictating their themes. In tribute to his intellectual superiority, his classmates would come to his house in the morning and carry him to school, like a little prince, on their backs. In winter, when the pond was frozen, they tied a garter around his waist and pulled him along the ice.

Latin was drilled into the students' brains and beaten into their buttocks —a brutal curriculum and harsh punishment that went back to the Middle Ages. Exams took place on Thursdays and Saturdays, followed by the ritual beatings of the blockheads. Stephen Greenblatt writes that in Shakespeare's time (as in Johnson's) "the instruction was not gentle: rote memorization, relentless drills, endless repetition, daily analysis of texts, elaborate exercises in imitation and rhetorical variation, all backed up by the threat of violence. . . . Disciplinary whippings were routinely inflicted throughout society: parents frequently whipped children, teachers whipped students, masters whipped servants, beadles whipped whores, sheriffs whipped vagrants."[8] Painters even whipped children who posed for them if they failed to sit still.

The dreaded headmaster, John Hunter, who had a remarkably stern expression, kept back the town boys in the lower school for as long as possible in order to make room for the more profitable boarders. He flogged all the boys ruthlessly over a three-legged stool and justified his sadism by exclaiming, "This I do to save you from the gallows." Hunter fancied himself a sportsman as well as a scholar. The best way to earn his favor, the boys soon learned, was to tell him where to find the best covey of partridges.

Hunter whipped Sam severely for lounging about and for idleness. Even as an adult, Johnson trembled at the sight of Hunter's granddaughter, who looked just like the cruel headmaster. Johnson accepted these beatings and later whipped boys himself when he became a teacher. He defended corporal punishment and believed brutality was consistent with, indeed essential for, good pedagogy. He declared that Hunter, "abating his brutality, was a very good master," but criticized him for failing to discriminate among the boys he whipped: "He was very severe, and wrongheadedly severe. He used to beat us unmercifully; and he did not distinguish between ignorance and negligence; for he would beat a boy equally for not knowing a thing, as for neglecting to know it."[9] Though Sam seemed nonchalant about the whippings, they had a powerful impact on the unusually clever, sensitive boy with a gloomy temperament and unhappy home life. Bernard Shaw believed that Sam's schoolmaster "beat him savagely enough to force him to lame his mind—for Johnson's great mind *was* lamed—by learning his lessons."

There was a striking contrast between Johnson's physical disabilities and his formidable mind. When the eternally curious Boswell asked if he'd ever been taught by a dancing master, Johnson, who looked more like a dancing bear, replied: "Ay & a dancing mistress too says the Doctor. But I own to you I never took a lesson but one or two; my blind eyes shewed me I could never make a proficiency." Though blindness might have prevented him from seeing his partner, it would not necessarily impede his steps. He clearly found running, jumping and climbing in the countryside with his schoolmates Edmund Hector and John Taylor, as well as swimming in the local pond with his father, more congenial forms of exercise.

In a Latin poem (often more intimate than his English ones) he described a rare moment of happiness with Michael, a gentle instructor and protector, who taught him to swim at Stowe Mill near St. Chad's Church: "To this place, through green meadows, winds the clear stream where so often as a boy I bathed my young body. Here I was frustrated by the awkward movement of my arms playing me false when, with a kind voice, my father taught me to swim."[10]

But Sam's relations with his father were usually acrimonious. He was "an Old man's Child," he told Hester Thrale, "exhibited to every Company, through idle and empty Vanity." One day, just after Sam had learned to read, Sarah gave him the prayer book, showed him the collect for the day and told him to learn it by heart. She started climbing the stairs, and by the time she got to the second floor, Sam, following her, proudly announced, "I can say it." He then repeated the passage, which he'd only read twice. This intellectual feat encouraged Michael's embarrassing habit of showing him off.

Desperate to demonstrate that the ugly, awkward and half-blind Sam was an infant prodigy, Michael took every opportunity to parade his son before friends and relations. Sam came to hate Michael's seductive caresses, which always preceded a demand for precocious displays. Michael even made up a childish poem about accidentally stepping on a duck and attributed it to little Sam. "His own Parents had it seems teiz'd him so to exhibit his Knowledge," wrote Hester Thrale, "to the few Friends they had, that he used to run up a Tree when Company was expected, that he might escape the Plague of being show'd off to them."[11]

Despite his book learning, Michael provoked hostility rather than respect from Sam, who fought hard to break loose from his authority. Generalizing, as he usually did, from his own experience, Johnson told Boswell, "a father and a son should part at a certain time of life. I never believed what my father said. I always thought that he spoke *ex officio,* as a priest does. . . . There must always be a struggle between a father and son, while one aims at power and the other at independence."

Sam's relations with his nagging, querulous, intellectually limited and emotionally reserved mother were just as difficult. When he was three years old, after their trip to London to be touched by the queen, he was blissfully lying in bed with his mother. She told him about "the two places to which the inhabitants of this world were received after death; one a fine place filled with happiness, called Heaven; the other a *sad* place, called Hell." The idea of death and the threat of Hell destroyed his warm, safe, happy mood. These thoughts affected his childish imagination and eventually became the greatest fear of his life. Later, at the age of ten, he suffered another bout of acute anxiety. He was disturbed by religious doubts that preyed upon his mind and filled him with guilt. For the next decade, until he went up to Oxford, he stopped going to church and put all thoughts of religion out of his mind.

Narrow-minded and obsessed with trivial matters, Sarah also made him feel guilty about eating too much boiled leg of mutton while visiting his aunt Sally Ford in Birmingham. Sarah told him quite seriously that his gluttony would never be forgotten. As he grew older

Sam realized that Sarah, though long on criticism, was short on guidance for both his father and himself. His mother (he recalled) was
"always telling me that I did not *behave* myself properly; that I should
endeavour to learn *behaviour,* and such cant; but when I replied, that
she ought to tell me what to do, and what to avoid, her admonitions
were commonly, for that time at least, at an end."[12] He did not respect
his mother but loved her out of filial duty, just as, in later life, he du-
tifully idealized her.

IV

Sam was bred a bookseller and never forgot his trade. Later in life he
picked up a book in Lichfield and saw that he had bound it himself. But he disliked serving in the shop, and when people complained
that he remained absorbed in his books instead of serving them, he
loftily replied "that to supersede the pleasures of reading, by the attentions of traffic, was a task he never could master." He had no intention
of changing the habits of a lifetime to satisfy the whims of customers.

Though Sam occasionally used the cathedral lending library, he had
his own vast library at home. In addition to his usual stock, in 1706 and
with borrowed money, Michael had rather rashly purchased the 3,000-
volume library of the earl of Derby. Johnson, who used Turks to represent extreme fanaticism or sexual license, said that when sleepless in bed
he read like a Turk. He devoured books with deadly seriousness, in the
same way that he devoured food. He'd often keep a book on his lap
while dining, a habit that Boswell cheekily compared to a dog holding
a bone in its paws while chewing on scraps. Most of Sam's boyhood
reading was serendipitous rather than systematic, and he often made
interesting discoveries. One day, when he thought Natty had hidden
some apples behind a large folio on a high shelf, he climbed up to look
for them and instead found a volume of Petrarch's poems. Having heard
that Petrarch was a Renaissance restorer of classical learning, he immediately sat down and read the book. On another occasion he was quietly reading *Hamlet* in the basement kitchen when he came to the ghost
scene. Terrified by the spectral presence, he hurried upstairs to return to
reality and see people walking in the street. He had a lifelong interest in

the supernatural and rather paradoxically told Hester Thrale, "I am not afraid of Spirits *at all;* yet I think if I was to be afraid of anything it *would be* of Spirits." Acutely sensitive and imaginative, he found it unbearable to read about the all-too-vivid deaths of Shakespeare's innocent heroines, Ophelia, Desdemona and Cordelia.

He especially loved travel books and the English poets, and was mightily moved by a Spanish chivalric romance, *Félixmarte de Hircania.* Written by Melchior de Ortega in 1556, it was influenced by the fourteenth-century romance *Amadis of Gaul* and mentioned in chapter 32 of *Don Quixote.* Sam identified with the powerful hero, "who with one back-stroke cut asunder five giants through the middle," and was interested to discover that it was one of the books in Quixote's library that was condemned to be burned. These romances stimulated his imagination and cut him off from reality. He actually "attributed to these extravagant fictions that unsettled turn of mind which prevented his ever fixing in any profession."[13]

Like the eighteenth-century child prodigy, linguist and scholar Philip Barretier, whose life he would write, Johnson "had a quickness of apprehension, and firmness of memory, which enabled him to read with incredible rapidity, and at the same time to retain what he read, so as to be able to recollect and apply it." In 1763 he told Boswell that he'd read very hard in his youth and knew almost as much when he was eighteen as he did when he was fifty-four. He tore the heart out of books instead of reading every word to the end, and never wished any book longer except his three great favorites: *Don Quixote, The Pilgrim's Progress* and *Robinson Crusoe.* He identified with the three heroes of these books: a dreamy idealist, a spiritual seeker and a resourceful castaway.

Johnson absorbed most of what he read and years later could recite long passages in several languages by heart. His vast knowledge and almost total recall fueled the most powerful intellect in English literature and became a formidable weapon in his arsenal of argument. It's significant that his most intense period of study, from the age of twelve to eighteen, coincided with the time when religion dropped out of his mind. Books, the lifeblood of his family, gave him the comfort that religion failed to provide.

Sam's parents established a persistent pattern of escape that he followed throughout his life. Sarah believed that conditions could be improved by changing her routine. Michael, agreeing with her, would get on his horse and ride away for book orders when the domestic scene became intolerable. These long rides in the country sustained his mental as well as his physical health. For Sam, as for Michael, a change of scene always improved his mood.

In his adolescence Sam sought solace from friends as well as books. When things got rough he took off for rural retreats and protracted visits. He fled from the tedious progress of his class and Hunter's brutal beatings to the hospitality of his cousin Cornelius Ford in Stourbridge (a few miles west of Birmingham); from his depressing family and their stagnant bookshop to revitalizing conversations with Gilbert Walmesley in Lichfield or with his friend Edmund Hector in Birmingham. Later in life, he fled from poverty and struggles in London and his wife's whimsical demands to the prosperous John Taylor in Ashbourne (forty miles north of Lichfield). He repaired to Greenwich to finish his play *Irene*. Threatened by arrest for his political pamphlet, he went underground in Lambeth. During the last twenty years of his life he escaped from his deeply discontented household by living for part of each week with the Thrales and by leaving London every summer to spend a few months with friends in the Midlands. He changed his London residence (occasionally escaping his creditors) about twenty times. Though he had an insatiable longing for travel, he only managed to visit Scotland, Wales and Paris. Johnson believed, like that other uneasy wanderer D. H. Lawrence, "When in doubt, move."

In 1724 the teenage Sam went for a short visit to his mother's nephew, Cornelius Ford, and stayed for nine months. Fifteen years older than Sam, "Neely" was a reckless gambler and notoriously hard drinker. In William Hogarth's *Midnight Modern Conversation* (1732) a group of eleven drunken, stupefied rioters stand, sit, tilt, shout, vomit, collapse and pass out around a generous punchbowl on a tavern table. Amid this revelry the plump and placid Parson Ford, dressed in clerical gown and bands and puffing a long churchwarden pipe, decorously presides at the table and continues to ladle out the lethal potion.

A man of extensive knowledge and sharp wit, Ford had been a student at St. John's and then fellow of Peterhouse. At Cambridge he'd befriended the poet William Broome, who'd helped Pope translate Homer, and the Earl of Chesterfield, with whom Johnson would later quarrel about support for his *Dictionary*. Ford, who'd taken part in literary life before taking orders and becoming a typical absentee clergyman, had the worldly sophistication and sparkling conversation that Sam aspired to. He had retired to the country to escape his importunate creditors and married a wealthy old widow. He welcomed the half-blind, scarfaced provincial, put his extensive library at Sam's disposal and directed his reading. He advised him to "obtain some general principles of every science; he who can talk only on one subject, or act only in one department, is seldom wanted, and perhaps never wished for; while a man of general knowledge can often benefit and always please." In his life of Elijah Fenton, another of Pope's assistants, Johnson, ignoring his intellectual debt to Ford, expressed moral disapproval of his Hogarthian dissipation. He was "a clergyman, at that time too well known, whose abilities, instead of furnishing convivial merriment to the voluptuous and dissolute, might have enabled him to excel among the virtuous and the wise." But in Sam's youth the brilliant, warmhearted Ford was a refreshing change from his father's gloomy failure. Ford recognized the power of Sam's mind and ignited his ambition, and through him Sam glimpsed the possibilities of a literary life.

Sam had learned his lessons well. In 1726, when he was seventeen and again living with Ford, he did impressive translations of Addison's Latin poem "The Battle of the Pygmies and the Cranes," and of the Greek "Dialogue Between Hector and Andromache" in the sixth book of Homer's *Iliad*. Homer, Aristotle, Ovid and Pliny all believed that pygmies were supposed to have carried on warfare with cranes. Imitating Pope's heroic couplets and phrases like "the light militia of the sky" in "The Rape of the Lock," Sam wrote, "Breathless at length they leave the unfinish'd war / And hang aloft suspended in the air." Sam also made a notable blunder in this poem and pled guilty to an illogical couplet: "Down from the guardian boughs the nests they flung, / And kill'd the yet unanimated young." Since unborn chicks cannot be killed, he later changed that word to "crush'd."[14]

For his translation from Homer, Sam chose the deeply moving passage in which the Trojan hero Hector, departing to fight the Greeks and destined to be slain by Achilles, bids farewell to his devoted wife, Andromache, and his infant son, Astyanax. The baby, taken from his nurse's arms, is frightened by the flash of light reflected on his father's helmet. Pope's superbly compressed translation of these lines mentions a plumed crest on top of the helmet:

> Thus having spoke, th'illustrious Chief of Troy
> Stretch'd his fond Arms to clasp the lovely Boy.
> The Babe clung crying to his Nurse's Breast,
> Scar'd at the dazzling Helm, and nodding Crest.

Adding a fifth line and off-rhymed triplet, Sam offered a worthy rival to Pope:

> Hector, this speaking, with extended hands
> From the fair nurse Astyanax demands.
> The child starts back affrighted at the blaze
> Of light reflected from the polish'd brass.
> And in his nurse's bosom hides his face.

When Sam returned home after his nine-month unauthorized absence, Hunter (with an eye, perhaps, to greater profit from boarders) refused to readmit him. Accepting responsibility for his prolonged French leave, Ford arranged for him to finish his school days and board for six months with the headmaster of the Stourbridge school.

Johnson grew up in an England still recovering from the revolution and religious wars of the seventeenth century, and the memory of these fierce conflicts and fear of political instability still remained. The Civil War had ended with the beheading of the Stuart King Charles I in 1649 and the establishment of Cromwell's Puritan parliamentary rule. The monarchy had been restored with Charles II in 1660, but the question of who should succeed him remained a source of conflict into the next century. The English were opposed to having a Catholic on the throne.

James II, who ruled from 1685 to 1688, had tried to extend Catholic influence in British politics and foreign alliances, and was forced to flee the country in 1689. The Jacobites (from Jacobus, Latin for "James") remained loyal to his descendants, advocated the restoration of the Stuart dynasty and opposed the Hanoverian kings who ruled England from 1714. The Stuart pretender to the throne, "Bonnie Prince Charlie," a descendant of James II who'd spent his youth in France, was finally defeated in bitter fighting in Scotland during the second Jacobite Rebellion of 1745.

The country had two main parties, the Tories and the Whigs. The more conservative Tories, many of them country squires who owned small estates in the English provinces, "stood for the supremacy of the Church of England, desired a strong personal monarchy as the basis of constitutional stability, and reviled the moneyed classes who profited from wars through loans to the government, opportunities for graft, and lucrative contracts." The Whigs were bolstered by business interests in the cities and by the nobility who owned huge tracts of land in the countryside. They emphasized parliamentary rather than monarchical authority, tolerated Protestant dissenting sects, and supported Continental and colonial wars to expand markets and increase trade. Strongly pro-Hanoverian, they organized the accession of George I in 1714 and criticized the Tories for supporting the Catholic Stuarts. The Whigs exploited government patronage, gained firm political control and kept the Tories in the wilderness for the rest of the century. To Johnson's chagrin, they became the party of the established order.

Sam's second influential mentor, whom he came to know after he returned from Stourbridge and was working in Michael's bookshop, was Gilbert Walmesley, whose father had represented Lichfield in Parliament. Gilbert had been educated at Trinity College, Oxford, and trained as a lawyer at the Inner Temple. When Sam met him in 1727, the forty-seven-year-old bachelor was registrar (official keeper of records) of the Ecclesiastical Court at Lichfield and legal secretary to the bishop. The diocesan courts dealt with church facilities and tried clergymen below the rank of bishop who were accused of moral offenses. The courts also penalized people for failure to attend church, pay tithes and conform to the Church of England. The bishop chose to reside outside the town, and Walmesley lived splendidly in the bishop's palace, next to the cathedral. He later married Magdalen Aston, member of a prominent Whig family and younger sister of Molly Aston, whom Johnson adored.

Lichfield Cathedral had been heavily damaged by the Puritans during the English Civil War, and the town, loyal to the Stuart dynasty, was very High Church and High Tory. Walmesley, who could be both benevolent and suddenly irascible, aroused Sam's interest in the law and politics. Though Walmesley was a Whig and a lawyer skilled in argument, the young Sam confidently held his ground. He stuck to his Tory principles, inherited from Michael, and sharpened his wits in their political disputations. Alluding to Walmesley, he told Boswell, "there was a violent Whig, with whom I used to contend with great eagerness. After his death I felt my Toryism much abated."[15]

Johnson paid a handsome tribute to his mentor in his life of Walmesley's friend, the poet Edmund Smith:

> He was of an advanced age, and I was only not a boy; yet he never received my notions with contempt. He was a Whig, with all the virulence and malevolence of his party; yet difference of opinion did not keep us apart. I honoured him, and he endured me.
>
> He had mingled with the gay world, without exemption from its vices or follies, but had never neglected the cultivation of his mind; his belief of Revelation was unshaken; his learning preserved his principles; he grew first regular, and then pious.
>
> His studies had been so various, that I am not able to name a man with equal knowledge. His acquaintance with books was great; and what he did not immediately know, he could at least tell where to find. Such was his amplitude of learning, and such his copiousness of communication, that it is to be doubted whether a day now passes in which I have not some advantage from his friendship.

Walmesley respected Sam's arguments, and their political differences did not harm, perhaps even enhanced, their friendship. Later on, with Walmesley's example in mind, Johnson was also able to form close friendships with powerful Whigs like Edmund Burke. Walmesley, like Ford, was worldly and sophisticated, but he also had two qualities that Johnson revered: piety and knowledge. It's rather surprising that Johnson's description of his relative and benefactor Neely Ford was so severe. But Ford, though a clergyman, remained dissolute, while the older and more important Gilbert Walmesley (with no familiar nickname) had reformed and become devout. The extensive learning and stimulating conversation of his two mentors, educated at Cambridge and Oxford, successful in the church and the law, had a profound impact on Johnson. Ford and Walmesley rounded out his education during his local version of the Grand Tour.

Walmesley introduced Sam to another Lichfield luminary, Henry Hervey. The dissolute son of the 4th Earl of Bristol, Hervey was the younger brother of John, Lord Hervey, the notorious homosexual who'd been satirized as Sporus in Pope's *Epistle to Dr. Arbuthnot.* An officer in the dragoons, Henry had been stationed in the town garrison. After marrying Catherine, another of the irresistibly attractive Aston sisters, he added her name to his and became Walmesley's brother-in-law. Hervey, who later reformed and became a clergyman, was the first in a long line of rakes to whom Johnson was strongly attracted: Richard Savage, Topham Beauclerk, James Boswell and John Wilkes. Johnson later remarked that Hervey "was a vicious man, but very kind to me. If you call a dog Hervey, I shall love him."

In Johnson's time, when the average height of an Englishman was five feet, five inches, only three men in a thousand reached his impressive height of five feet, eleven. Johnson also had, and retained throughout his life, a distinct Staffordshire accent. He said "shuperior" and "shupreme," pronounced "there" like "fear," "once" like " woonse," and in a tavern loved to call for his favorite drink by asking, "who's for *poonsh?*" His strongest oaths were "dog" and "he deserves to be hanged." His characteristic traits, molded by his father and John Hunter, by Cornelius Ford and Gilbert Walmesley, were established in his youth: "his precocity, his curious oscillation between indolence and energy, his phenomenal powers of

memory, and his supremacy, alike physical and mental, over his school-
fellows."[16]

Just as one family legacy had allowed Michael and Sarah to build
their house and expand their business, so another one—£40 from
Sarah's rich widowed cousin Elizabeth Harriotts—paid for Sam's
tuition and lodging at Oxford, and enabled him to enter the university in 1728. Physically strange, lacking birth, property and rank,
wealth, office and status, Johnson would have to make his way in
the world solely by his intellectual abilities.

2

VILE MELANCHOLY
1728–1730

I

In late October 1728 the nineteen-year-old Sam Johnson and his father took the eighty-mile, two-day journey to Oxford on horseback. A wagon lumbered behind, carrying Sam's meager personal possessions and a substantial library of more than a hundred books in Latin and English. Despite the often strained relations of father and son, they both valued these books, which had depleted Michael's stock, and on this journey they were for once united. Michael had taught Sam to engage in learned conversation and to admire the great scholars of the past. While Sam aspired to join this brotherhood and win scholarly fame, his father longed for his son to fulfill his promise and redeem his own business failures. It was a great achievement for a poor bookseller's son to enter Oxford. As they rode into town, the young man was mightily impressed by the spires, domes and towers of the stately medieval and Renaissance buildings, their creamy yellow Cotswold stone shining in the soft golden sunlight.

Sam took up residence at Pembroke College, with eleven other new students, on October 31. Michael had declared himself a "gentleman"

Main gate and tower, Pembroke College, Oxford University—Valerie Meyers

on his son's baptismal certificate, and now signed in the annals of the college with the same title. In his *Dictionary*, Johnson would define "gentleman" as "a man raised above the vulgar by his character or post"—as Michael had been by his superior education and his election to high municipal office. Pembroke then had only one quad and was still building its own ornate chapel, completed in 1732. Forty men, both students and fellows (the latter all unmarried Anglican clergymen) lived and ate together in the college, and this intimate group knew each other very well. Sam's small, garretlike room was up a narrow winding staircase, on the second floor of the gatehouse tower.

Pembroke had been founded in 1624 and named after the Earl of Pembroke, then chancellor of the university. It was—with All Souls, Balliol, Magdalen and Oriel—one of the bastions of Toryism in Oxford. Pembroke was also said to be the stronghold of the Jacobites. In

later life Johnson took pride in Pembroke, whose alumni included the
playwright Sir Francis Beaumont and the sage Sir Thomas Browne
(both had attended Broadgates, the original college, before it was
refounded as Pembroke), as well as Johnson's namesake and godfather,
Dr. Samuel Swinfen, the Methodist leader George Whitefield, the eminent judge Sir William Blackstone and the poet William Shenstone,
born near Lichfield in the West Midlands. In his life of Shenstone,
Johnson wrote: "from school he was sent in 1732 to Pembroke College
in Oxford, a society which for half a century has been eminent for English poetry and elegant literature. Here it appears that he found delight
and advantage; for he continued his name in the [college] book for ten
years." Exaggerating its lyrical tradition, Johnson called Pembroke "a
nest of singing birds."

Michael started Sam's career at Oxford by showing him off. He
met Sam's tutor, the Reverend William Jorden, and bragged about
his homegrown, rough-hewn genius. With no convenient tree to
climb, Sam sulked silently in the corner. Then, seizing an opportune
moment to enter the conversation, he seemed to confirm Michael's
praise by quoting Macrobius, an obscure fifth-century Roman writer,
philosopher and author of *Saturnalia*. Johnson told Boswell that in
the two years before going up to Oxford, he'd read seriously and rav-
enously in the classics, and acquired a great store of uncommon
knowledge: "not voyages and travels, but all literature, all ancient
writers, all manly: though but little Greek, only some of Anacreon
and Hesiod; but in this irregular manner I had looked into a great
many books, which were not commonly known at the Universities,
where they seldom read any books but what are put into their hands
by their tutors."[1] Dr. William Adams, who became his tutor when
Jorden left Pembroke to take up a clerical living and who later became master of the college, recognized Sam's extraordinary ability and
called him the best qualified student he'd ever known at Oxford.

There was only a small number of students at the university in the early
part of the eighteenth century, and very few could equal Johnson's extensive reading and passion for learning. The historian George Trevelyan
noted that "in 1750 Oxford matriculated [only] 190 freshmen. Many of

these were noblemen and gentlemen, not intent on serious study; others were poor scholars, seeking to enter the Church." Johnson was confident of his intellectual abilities, but the social organization of the college soon put him in his place. Following the English habit of observing minute social gradations (with its attendant snobbery), the Oxford colleges divided students into four different ranks. The Gentlemen-Commoners and sons of noblemen, according to another social historian, "all stood on a different footing from ordinary undergraduates, wore handsomer dresses, paid higher fees, spent two or three times as much money, had servants as well as servitors to wait on them, were admitted to the Fellows' table, the Fellows' Common Room, even the Fellows' cellar." The Commoners—the largest group, to which Johnson belonged—ate at the common table. The Battelers paid lower fees and did their own chores. At the bottom of the social scale were "the Servitors or Sizars, eking out a scanty income by doing small menial services for the richer men. Oxford caricaturists drew descriptions of them, cleaning shoes and doing exercises [themes in Latin and Greek] for the more fortunate, calling them in the morning, carrying in their meals, inheriting perhaps their old clothes and books." In return for these light but humiliating duties, the Servitors received free room, board and tuition. The system thus permitted talented but penniless men to gain entry to the church and other learned professions.

The curriculum at Oxford in Johnson's time consisted entirely of classical history, literature and philosophy. Students were taught through lectures by professors and in individual meetings with their tutors, who assigned exercises that the students read aloud and discussed in their tutorials. Lynda Mugglestone writes that at Pembroke "work began straight after the [compulsory] six o'clock prayers; essays or themes were publicly presented in the Hall early every Saturday morning; classes on Logic preceded breakfast on Mondays, Wednesdays and Fridays; lectures took place on Saturdays and Sundays as well, beginning at 10 and continuing until 12." But there was a striking contrast between the work that was theoretically expected and that which was actually done. Many (perhaps most) of the students "filled their days with fox-hunting, riding, cock-fighting and drinking, rather than with reading and studying."[2]

The young Johnson began his first term with a highly idealized view of Oxford, soon dispelled by the appalling teaching and low intellectual standards. His disillusionment as a student was complete, yet in later life he frequently praised the university. Speaking of Oxford and Cambridge in *Idler* 33, he declared that "the number of learned persons in these celebrated seats, is still considerable, and more conveniences and opportunities for study still subsist in them, than in any other place. There is at least one very powerful incentive to learning; I mean the 'Genius of the place.'" The two universities were of course the best places to study because they were then the only universities in England.

In his life of the seventeenth-century Dutch classical scholar Peter Burman, Johnson asserted that students at English universities had a better knowledge of Latin than European students. "The English scheme of education trains students to hear lectures in Latin," he wrote. "It is more rigorous and sets literary honours at a higher price than that of any other country, extracts from the youth, who are initiated in our colleges, a degree of philological knowledge sufficient to qualify them for lectures in philosophy, which are read to them in Latin, and enable them to proceed in other studies without assistance." But once more Johnson gave Oxford credit for something it did not deserve. He glossed over the fact that most students had acquired their solid grasp of Latin long before they entered the university.

Sam, both idle and studious, resolved like most first-year students to work hard. Stimulated by the genius of the place, if not by the tutors and professors, he aspired to an ideal standard, and yearned to become famous for his learning and poetry. In *The Vanity of Human Wishes* he described his uneasy state of mind during his first term at Oxford by comparing the noble desire of the young Enthusiast ("one of elevated fancy, or exalted ideas") to a pathological fever and contagion:

When first the College Rolls receive his Name,
The young Enthusiast quits his Ease for Fame;
Through all his Veins the Fever of Renown
Burns from the strong Contagion of the Gown.

Christian clergymen taught the pagan classics. The author of a history of Oxford, describing Johnson's studies, wrote that at Pembroke he mastered "Homer and Euripides. He delighted in Horace's Odes. He dipped into metaphysics. He read [as always] desultorily and widely."[3] He also learned French at Oxford and while there read a book he later translated, Father Jerónimo Lobo's *Voyage to Abyssinia*.

Lacking funds, or perhaps unwilling to return to the discontented household in Lichfield, Sam remained at Oxford during the Christmas vacation. As an exercise his tutor asked him to translate into Latin verse Alexander Pope's 108-line *Messiah,* a poem based on passages in Isaiah foretelling the coming of Christ. Pope concluded with a traditional contrast between the ephemeral quality of the physical world and the eternal truth of the spiritual realm:

> The Seas shall waste; the Skies in Smoke decay;
> Rocks fall to Dust, and Mountains melt away;
> But fix'd His Word, His saving Pow'r remains;
> Thy Realm forever lasts! thy own Messiah reigns!

Charles Arbuthnot, son of Pope's friend Sir John and Johnson's fellow student, showed Pope a copy of Johnson's translation. Pope, the greatest poet of the century, praised the work and generously predicted that "the writer of this poem will leave it a question for posterity, whether his or mine be the original." When Sam heard this remark, he must have felt he'd become part of the "nest of singing birds" at Pembroke.

According to Sam's school and college friend John Taylor, his "translation of the *Messiah* was first printed by his Father, without his knowledge or consent. Johnson told Taylor he was very angry at this and in his violent manner said if it had not been his Father he would have cut his throat."[4] But Boswell discreetly deleted these murderous intentions from the *Life of Johnson.* Sam may have been angry about the publication, but Michael did not, in fact, print his translation, though he may well have stocked, advertised and sold it. Johnson's *Messiah,* his first published work, appeared in *A Miscellany by Several Hands,* published in 1731 by J. Husbands, a fellow of Pembroke, and printed in Oxford by "Leon: Lichfield." The printer's name was Leonard Lichfield, and Taylor mistakenly assumed that it had been published in the town of Lichfield. Johnson's violent response showed how deeply he resented his father's habit of promoting his achievements. Indeed, Michael's clumsy praise aroused unrealistic expectations in both Oxford and Lichfield, and increased the pressure on Sam to perform well in public.

II

Proudly showing Boswell around Oxford in 1775, Johnson declared, "here is a school where every thing may be learnt." But as a student he felt no strong calling for theology, medicine or the law, and soon lost his keen appetite for learning anything at all. Most professors held somnolent sinecures and, Trevelyan wrote, "seldom performed any of their supposed functions. . . . In their lazy, self-indulgent, celibate clericalism, the dons of the eighteenth century resembled the monks of the fifteenth, and were about as much use." To compensate for these hopeless cases, many wealthy students brought along their own private tutors. Though Johnson read *The Odyssey* and *The Iliad*, the Greek dramatists and Theocritus, Virgil, Horace and Juvenal, the curriculum merely continued the study of the classics he had learned in grammar school, and the abysmal teaching depressed and bored him. To overcome his inertia, he totaled up the number of lines in the most important texts in order to determine how long it would take to read them. Study had become a chore, and Oxford, the scene of his potential triumph, had proved to be an intellectual backwater.

Edward Gibbon went up to Magdalen College, Oxford, in 1752, at the age of sixteen. By that time conditions were no better, and he left after a year. In his *Autobiography* he later provided a devastating account of the stultifying place. Intellectual life was "narrow, lazy, and oppressive." Most professors had "given up altogether the pretense of teaching." His tutor offered neither guidance nor instruction: "No plan of study was recommended for my use; no exercises were prescribed for his inspection." Gibbon concluded by exclaiming, in characteristically sonorous sentences, that "the dons, steeped in port and privilege, spent their days in the chapel and the hall, the coffeehouse and the common room, till they retired, weary and well-satisfied, to a long slumber. From the toil of reading, or thinking, or writing, they had absolved their conscience. Their conversation stagnated in a round of college business, Tory politics, personal anecdotes, and private scandal. Their dull and deep potations excused the brisk intemperance of youth."[5] The greatest scholars of the age—Gibbon himself, the musicologist Charles Burney and the scientist Joseph Priestley—remained outside academic life.

Johnson always liked to take both sides of an argument. He could idealize Oxford, as he did with Boswell, but when his mood varied, he could also be critical and attack the hermetic indolence of the dons. In *Rambler* 180 he asserted that the scholarly life, cut off from the reality of the world, "has no other tendency than to vitiate the morals, and contract the understanding." In his life of Peter Burman he seemed to agree with Gibbon and contrasted Burman, an intellectual prodigy, with the majority of his complacent colleagues. Having "no higher object of ambition, [they] have relapsed into idleness and security, and spent the rest of their lives in a lazy enjoyment of their academical dignities."[6] When John Taylor wanted to come up to Pembroke in March 1729, Sam diverted him across the street to Christ Church, where the lectures were better and could be passed on to Johnson. But this plan did not work very well, as Taylor often had trouble remembering and gave Johnson a muddled account of what he had heard.

At Pembroke Sam expressed the utmost contempt for his instructors, didn't attend his lectures and neglected his exercises. He failed to compose the Latin poem that was required to mark the solemn anniversary of the Gunpowder Plot, a Catholic attempt to blow up Parliament in 1605. But he atoned for this lapse with some "truly Virgilian verses." In his lost poem "Somnium" (Sleep), he devised a modest but ingenious excuse by explaining "that the Muse had come to him in his sleep, and whispered that it did not become him to write on such subjects as politicks; he should confine himself to humbler themes." Johnson felt he had to obey the Muses.

Johnson told Hester Thrale that at Oxford he got into the habit of putting off work, doing the minimum and then scraping by. When his first public recital of Latin prose was due, he left it till the last moment, memorized some of it on the way to the hall and gave Jorden his only copy, but managed to give a creditable performance. "Trusting to his present powers for immediate supply," wrote Hester Thrale, "he finished by adding astonishment to the applause of all who knew how little was owing to study." When she observed that this was a risky experiment, he replied: "Not at all. No man I suppose leaps at once into deep water who does not know how to swim."

Always self-taught and continually struggling with his teachers, Sam preferred to read the books from which the lectures were obviously taken instead of listening to the tedious drone of the dons. When fined twopence for failure to attend a lecture on logic, he declared that it wasn't even worth a penny. When Jorden politely inquired about why he'd not been attending his tutorials, Sam replied that during that severe early winter he'd been amusing himself by sliding on the ice in Christ Church meadow. When Boswell heard this story, he remarked that it must have taken "great fortitude of mind" to cheek his tutor. But Johnson, who had no idea at the time that he was being disrespectful, called his youthful behavior "stark insensibility."

Though Sam despised Jorden's intellectual ability, he was touched by his kindness. Grateful that Jorden forgave his rudeness and invited him to his room for a glass of wine and a friendly talk, he said, "whenever a young man becomes Jorden's pupil, he becomes his son." Disdainful and rebellious, bitter and violent, conscious of his brilliance and miserably aware of his poverty, disregarding power and combating all authority, Sam was undoubtedly a difficult student. But the college treated him with exemplary understanding and restraint.

Sam's fellow students both feared his violent temper and admired his wit. Later on, when talking to his young scholarly friend Bennet Langton, Johnson distinguished between a facile ability to compose in Latin and the deeper knowledge that comes after long study: "when I was at Oxford I always felt an impulse to insult the Westminster [School] men who were come there; they appeared to arrogate so much to themselves upon their superficial talent of a readiness in making Latin verses."[7] With gifted students like John Meeke, his main rival, he felt extremely envious and competitive. Meeke had such a good grasp of Latin grammar and clear understanding of the poetry, and recited so well in tutorials, that Sam couldn't bear his superiority. He tried to sit as far from him as possible so he wouldn't have to hear him.

Sam not only neglected his own work, but also distracted his classmates. The Lichfield schoolmaster, John Hunter, had beaten him for "lounging" instead of working. At Pembroke he was often seen "lounging" in the college entrance and drinking at an alehouse near the gate. He entertained the students with his wit, kept them from their studies and roused them to rebellion. He took part in the ragging that was always a part of Oxford life, and especially disliked the officious discipline of the college servitor, whose job it was to check up on the students and make sure they were in their rooms by 10 PM. Sam got into trouble by pretending to be out and refusing to answer the intrusive knock on his door. But he took revenge by joining "the young men in the college in hunting, as they called it, the servitor. . . . This they did with the noise of pots and candlesticks, singing to the tune of 'Chevy Chase,' the words in that old ballad, 'To drive the deer with hound and horn.'"

A humiliating incident revealed Sam's poverty, bitterness and pride. He owned only one pair of shoes. When they became so worn that his large feet could be seen through them, he was too ashamed to visit Taylor at Christ Church. One morning a gentleman at Pembroke told his servitor to put a new pair of shoes outside Sam's door. But Sam, insulted and angered by the kindly gesture, threw them down the stairs.[8]

Sam stayed on at Oxford for the long summer vacation. Aware that he'd wasted time during his first year, he promised in his diary of October 1729, the beginning of his second, to "bid farewell to Sloth, being resolved henceforth not to listen to her syren strains." But he cast this resolution in mythological rather than personal terms and, like many a vow made throughout his life, was unable to keep it. He heard another "syren" call in the form of an unconscious desire to go home. One day at Oxford, as he was turning the key in his door, he thought he heard his mother distinctly call "Sam." He turned to see her, recalled that she was in Lichfield and thought no more of it. But he became restless and unhappy, just as he'd resolved to settle down to work at Oxford, and expressed a longing to travel, to expand his intellectual horizons and to escape the confines of the college. He declared, "I have a mind to see what is done in other places of learning. I'll go and visit the Universities abroad. I'll go to France and Italy. I'll go to Padua. . . . For an *Athenian* blockhead is the worst of all blockheads." Oxford students, he thought, were too arrogant and conceited to know their own limitations.[9]

The fall term was to be his last. In December 1729, Sam left Oxford as suddenly as he'd left school in Lichfield, and for the same reasons that cause students to drop out today. He had very little money, felt unable to work, loathed the discipline and despised his teachers. He was full of anguish and guilt about the time he'd wasted and the money he'd spent, and devastated with anxiety brought on by the contrast between his father's ambitions and his own sense of failure. All this coincided with his intense study of William Law's *Serious Call to a Holy Life* (1728), which precipitated a major crisis. In the grip of a religious obsession, he fell into a severe depression and suffered a nervous breakdown.

There are two oft-repeated misconceptions about Johnson: that he left Pembroke for lack of money and that later on he was unable to study law without a university degree. The Pembroke battels book, listing student expenses for 1729, shows that his weekly bill for board was usually eight shillings, which came to almost £24 for the fifty-eight weeks he was in residence. These charges, quite normal compared to the expenditures of other students and consistently higher than those of the poorest ones, showed that he'd made no attempt to economize during his first year. A. L. Reade pointed out that "there were also charges for chamber rent, for tutors' fees, for fuel and candles, for the servitors, and for the bedmaker," which came to another £24. Though a learned student, Sam was also fined, especially in his last term and more than any other Pembroke undergraduate, for failure to attend tutorials and lectures.

When he ran out of money he had two alternatives. He could have stayed on, with free room, board and tuition, if he'd been willing to become a Servitor. But he was too touchy, too proud and too aware of his intellectual superiority to become the servant of wealthy students. Even so, if Sam, whom Dr. Adams called the best-qualified student

he'd ever seen, "had remained in College in 1730 there were two schol-
arships for which he would have been eligible, and one of which Dr.
Hall [the master] did not doubt that he would have obtained."

When he decided to leave, Sam packed up his private papers and
the precious books his father had given him, and stored them with
John Taylor. Several scholars have argued that this meant Johnson
intended, or at least hoped, to return. But he may also have left
the books behind because he had no money to transport them and
thought that Taylor would bring them back to Lichfield. He might
also have been too depressed to care what happened to them. If he
had wished, he could have prolonged his stay by selling the 100
valuable books. If he got five shillings each for them, he would
have earned more than half the cost of a year as a Pembroke Com-
moner. Instead he abandoned them, as he abandoned his father's
hopes for his future. Though he left Oxford, "his name remained
on the college register until October 1731 and his bills in college remained unpaid until 1740."[10]

Just as it would have been possible for Johnson to remain at Oxford
when he ran out of money, so it would also have been possible for him
to study law without a university degree. About half the students at Pembroke did not complete their degree, and some of them went on to become barristers. Johnson always maintained that he had no money to
study law. But a great many lawyers were trained at the London Inns of
Court, rather than at the universities, before being called to the bar.
Oliver Edwards, Johnson's contemporary at Pembroke, left the college
early but practiced as a solicitor in Chancery. One of Edmund Burke's
contemporaries in the Inns of Court "maintained himself in the study of
the law by writing pamphlets in favour of the ministry"—something
Johnson could also have done. His dour friend and biographer Sir John
Hawkins did not have a university degree, but began as an articled clerk
to a solicitor, became an attorney in the City of London, rose to be chair-
man of the Middlesex justices and was knighted for services to the law.

In later life Johnson often maintained that he ought to have been a
lawyer. Boswell (himself an attorney) could not imagine anyone more
qualified for distinction in that profession. He had formidable knowledge,

penetrating intellect, sound judgment, quick wit, impressive command of language and tremendous powers of argument. In 1778 the chancellor of Oxford told him: "What a pity it is, Sir, that you did not follow the profession of the law. You might have been Lord Chancellor of Great Britain, and attained to the dignity of a peerage." But Johnson, infuriated by this compliment, exclaimed: "Why will you vex me by suggesting this, when it is too late?"[11] It was too late to follow the profession when he was nearly seventy, but it certainly would have been possible after he left Oxford at the age of twenty. Instead of leading to the church or the law, Oxford was a disaster that darkened his future and seemed to close off his prospects in life.

III

Johnson's sudden turn toward religion in the fall of 1729 contributed to his first mental collapse. He later told Boswell that he had had no religious belief until he was twenty years old:

> I myself was for some years totally regardless of religion. It had dropped out of my mind. It was at an early part of my life. Sickness brought it back, and I hope I have never lost it since. . . . When at Oxford, I took up Law's *Serious Call to a Holy Life,* expecting to find it a dull book (as such books generally are), and perhaps to laugh at it. But I found Law quite an overmatch for me; and this was the first occasion of my thinking in earnest of religion, after I became capable of rational inquiry.

Johnson believed religious faith could be, perhaps ought to be, based on rational thought. He first resisted and struggled with Law, as Jacob had wrestled with the angel of God, but was finally "overmatched" by him and wrenched into religion. His precarious mental state made his conversion far from joyful.

Johnson, who read extensively in religion, called William Law's recently published book "the finest piece of hortatory theology in any language." Gibbon commended the book's forceful teaching and effective literary qualities, and noted its dark threats of Hell:

"Law's masterwork, the *Serious Call,* is still read as a popular and powerful book of devotion. His precepts are rigid, but they are founded on the gospel. His satire is sharp, but it is drawn from the knowledge of human life, and many of his portraits are not unworthy of the pen of La Bruyère. . . . He expresses, with equal severity and truth, the strange contradiction between the faith and practice of the Christian world. Hellfire and eternal damnation are darted from every page of the book."[12]

Praising Law's work and emphasizing its powerful effect on Johnson, Hester Thrale said that it was "written with such force of Thinking, such purity of Style, & such penetration into human Nature; the Characters [used to exemplify moral precepts] too so neatly, nay so highly finished. . . . Johnson has studied it hard I am sure, & many of the *Ramblers* apparently took their rise from that little Volume." Walter Jackson Bate also showed how Law's ideas influenced the dominant theme of *The Vanity of Human Wishes,* the *Rambler* essays and *Rasselas*: "Following the prototype of [the vanity theme in] Ecclesiastes, Law turns on one after another of the desires, ambitions, or possessions at which the human imagination clutches. Time and again Law notes how empty these ultimately prove, how completely they fail to fill the heart, leaving the heart nowhere else to turn for stability and purpose except to religion." At Oxford Johnson's scholarly ambition had come to nought and his confidence was crushed. He clutched at the hope of salvation to give his wretched life some meaning and purpose.

Law stringently recommended careful study of the Bible and other devotional books. He also made a series of demands that Johnson found impossible to fulfill: early rising (for an insomniac who often went to bed at 3 AM), proper use of time (for a man who was constitutionally indolent), daily accounting of oneself (for a man who constantly felt he was wasting precious time), regular attendance in church (for a man who found the fatuous sermons intolerably boring), and an ethic of asceticism, renunciation and self-denial (for a man with a tremendous appetite for food and strong sexual passions).

Law's *Serious Call to a Holy Life* was Johnson's serious call to a nervous collapse. It kindled his spark of piety into a self-consuming flame, intensifying rather than alleviating his depression. Writing about his religion, one critic concluded that Law's book, ironically enough, "was actually a source of misery as Johnson tried, but failed, to live up to the high ideal of the Christian life that Law set before him."[13] Throughout his life Johnson suffered acute religious agonies and self-lacerating guilt for what he believed to be his devotional neglect, sinful behavior and sexual pollution. He did not see the Christian God as a kind and loving Father, but as a wrathful Old Testament Jehovah who, despite all his strenuous moral efforts, might well condemn him to eternal damnation. Like a shipwrecked man, he clung desperately to the stability of religious belief. Any expression of heterodox opinions or religious scepticism by writers like Hobbes and Voltaire, Hume and Gibbon, enraged him, undermined his perilous balance and even threatened his sanity.

Johnson had severe mental breakdowns in 1729 and again in 1764. He told Boswell, in a crucial revelation, "I inherited a vile melancholy from my father, which has made me mad all my life, at least not sober." In his *Dictionary* he defined "melancholy" as both a general malaise, "a gloomy, pensive, discontented temper," and a form of obsessive insanity: "a kind of madness, in which the mind is always fixed on one object." He defined "mad," "disordered in the mind; broken in the understanding, distracted," as his permanent condition ("all my life"). He then seemed to qualify this by adding that he was not "sober" (the opposite of "mad"), not "right in the understanding." Frances Reynolds, the artist Sir Joshua's sister and Johnson's friend, confirmed that she had "often heard him lament that he inherited from his Father a morbid disposition both of Body and Mind. . . . A terrifying melancholy, which he was sometimes apprehensive bordered on insanity," which made him perpetually gloomy and constantly fearful of another disastrous collapse.[14]

Sarah Johnson believed that Sam's physical illness came from her family; he believed that his mental illness came from his father. Half blind and half deaf, hideously scarred and physically repulsive, estranged from his middle-aged parents, ashamed of squandering their money and disappointing their hopes, either forced to leave or at least unable to continue at Oxford, apparently cut off from the learned professions, with no prospects but work in Michael's stagnant bookshop, he found religion an endless torment rather than a comfort. It's scarcely surprising that Sam's vile melancholy threatened to turn into actual insanity.

Boswell described the pathological symptoms that Johnson suffered after his return to Lichfield in December 1729: "he felt himself overwhelmed with an horrible hypochondria, with perpetual irritation, fretfulness, and impatience; and with a dejection, gloom, and despair, which made existence a misery. From this dismal malady he never afterwards was perfectly relieved; and all his labours, and all his enjoyments, were but temporary interruptions of its baleful influence." In this series of increasingly severe symptoms, irritation led to dejection, fretfulness to gloom, impatience to despair. He was so utterly disabled by languor and depression that when he stared at the town clock, he was unable to tell the time. He claimed that after 1729 his health, both mental and physical, seldom afforded him a single day of ease.

Johnson's frequent comments about madness illuminated his own condition. In a famous pronouncement in *Rasselas,* he declared, "of the uncertainties of our present state, the most dreadful and alarming is the uncertain continuance of reason." Johnson—renowned, ironically, for his common sense, sound judgment and rational thought—was terrified that his rational faculty would weaken and he would lapse into permanent darkness.

In his life of Addison, Johnson explained how madness could cripple reason without completely destroying it: "the variable weather of the mind, the flying vapours of incipient madness, from time to time cloud reason, without eclipsing it." His friend "poor [William] Collins" was a classic example of a poet who realized that he was losing his reason but was unable to do anything about it. Collins "languished some years under the depression of mind which enchains the faculties without destroying them, and leaves reason the knowledge of right without the power of pursuing it."[15] Like Collins, Johnson struggled with troubling thoughts and paralyzing inertia and suicidal impulses. In another self-reflective passage, Johnson, arguing against the absurdly naïve belief that madmen are happy and "disorders of mind increase felicity," forcefully insisted that "every madman is either arrogant and irascible, or gloomy and suspicious, or possessed by some passion or notion destructive to his quiet. He has always discontent in his look, and malignity in his bosom."

He also believed that sexual lust and sexual guilt often led to insanity and that "Melancholy & otherwise insane People are always Sensual; the misery of their Minds naturally enough forces them to recur for Comfort to their Bodies." When the mind loses control of the body, he thought, sensual desires become dominant and turn men into discontented and malicious beasts. In another startling revelation, he warned Hester Thrale to "'make your boy tell you his dreams: the first corruption that entered into my heart was communicated in a dream.' What was it, Sir, said I. '*Do* not ask me,' replied he with much violence, and walked away in apparent agitation."[16] Johnson hinted at a dreadful secret, but when his confidante boldly questioned him about it, he warned her off and withdrew into angry silence. It seems clear that his darkest dreams—which he would never have told his own mother—included sexual fantasies and perhaps caused nocturnal emissions that filled him with shame.

In December 1729, his mind in chaos and body convulsed, Sam returned, without money or prospects, to his miserable home in Lichfield. His depression was so severe that he desperately sought the advice of his two closest medical friends, Samuel Swinfen and Edmund Hector. Swinfen, his godfather, had been a student at Pembroke and had trained as a doctor. Close to Michael and Sarah, he'd lived with the Johnson family in Lichfield and had an intimate knowledge of Sam's pathological inheritance. No one was more suitable to receive his confidence, understand his condition and alleviate his suffering. In great distress, Sam wrote an account of his mental condition in Latin and gave it to Dr. Swinfen. Struck by its uncommon acuity, Swinfen showed it to several people and sought their opinions. When Sam learned of this betrayal of professional confidence, he was furious, broke with Swinfen and was never again fully reconciled to him. Their rupture may also have been caused by Swinfen's terrifyingly frank response to Sam's account. "From the symptoms therein described," he said, "he could think nothing better of his disorder, than that it had a tendency to insanity; and without great care might possibly terminate in the deprivation of his rational faculties." It's difficult to determine whether Swinfen was more tactless in revealing Sam's medical history to others or in shattering his confidence with the brutal truth.

Hector, also a doctor, hinted that Johnson might have been suicidal. He told Boswell that when the young man returned to Lichfield after fourteen months in Oxford, "I was apprehensive of something wrong in his constitution which might either impair his intellect or endanger his life." Boswell recorded in private notes: "Hector was afraid of Dr. Johnson's head. . . . Johnson had been conscious of [possible insanity] all along but had been afraid to ask Hector for fear of an answer in the affirmative. When at last in Birmingham he asked Hector if he had observed in him a tendency to be disordered in his mind. Hector said he had." When he renewed his friendship with Hector twenty-five years later, Johnson reminded him that his depression was permanent: "From that kind of melancholy indisposition which I had when we lived together in Birmingham, I have never been free, but have always had it operating against my health and my Life with more or less violence."[17]

Sam received no more consolation from the medical men than he had from Law's theological tract. Hector's all-too-honest response, like Swinfen's, confirmed his greatest fears. Their comments may have provoked the nervous tics that began after his breakdown and plagued him for the rest of his life. Before this mental collapse, his mind had always dominated his fractious body. Afterwards, as he struggled to control his violent emotions by turning them against himself, neither his mind nor his body was completely under control. He was always at war with himself.

Johnson attempted by every means in his power to fight off the continual threats to his reason. His tried to rivet his mind to reality by taking thirty-two-mile walks from Lichfield to Birmingham and back. Later on he occupied himself by tending his tiny garden, making elaborate mathematical calculations and conducting explosive chemical experiments. The direst danger was solitude, which made his mind stagnant and morbid. His great aim in life was to escape from himself, and he tried to prevent mental disease by constant company.

Throughout his life Johnson's physical eccentricities included a vo-racious appetite for food and drink, nervous hypochondria and a twitching body. Though Alexander Pope never actually met Johnson, he told the painter Jonathan Richardson, "he had an infirmity of the convulsive kind, that attacks him sometimes, so as to make him a sad Spectacle." Pope perceived that Johnson's condition, though chronic, could sometimes be controlled. But these traits inevitably shocked new acquaintances and even old friends, and constantly reminded Johnson that he was disgusting to others. He was often obliged to use his pow-erful intellect to overcome the revulsion he inspired.

Boswell, who observed his hero with microscopic intensity, recorded that "the scars of the scrophula were deeply visible. . . . He often had, seemingly, convulsive starts and odd gesticulations, which tended to excite at once surprize and ridicule. . . . So morbid was his temperament, that he never knew the natural joy of a free and vigor-ous use of his limbs: when he walked, it was like the struggling gait of one in fetters." Johnson was capable of covering great distances in the Midlands and (later on) in Scotland. But he usually walked like the monster in *Frankenstein,* with a heavy shuffling movement. Every step he took reminded him of his lifelong infirmity.

Several important encounters in Johnson's life—his first meeting with Boswell, as well as with the artists Thomas Gainsborough and William Hogarth, and with friends like Thomas Campbell and Fanny Burney—illustrate the contrast between the first horrified impressions of the phys-ical freak and the gradual perception of the real, inner man. After observing Johnson's comically convulsive heavings, habitual contortions and facial twitchings, Gainsborough felt he'd become infected by these movements. He wrote, "I became as full of the megrims [migraines] as the old literary leviathan himself and fancied that I was changed into a Chinese automaton and condemned incessantly to shake my head."

To Hogarth, Johnson seemed even more grotesque than his own satiric drawings. While talking to the novelist Samuel Richardson, Hogarth "perceived a person standing at a window in the room, shak-ing his head, and rolling himself about in a strange ridiculous manner. He concluded that he was an ideot, whom his relations had put under the care of Mr. Richardson. . . . To his great surprize, however, this figure stalked forwards and . . . displayed such a power of eloquence, that Hogarth looked at him with astonishment, and actually imagined that this ideot had been at the moment inspired."[18] Hogarth didn't know who he was and was not introduced to Johnson, who may even have enjoyed playing this startling game and astonishing the visitor.

The Irish clergyman Thomas Campbell emphasized Johnson's typically slovenly dress and the strange whistling sounds that sometimes impeded his speech, both of which intensified the negative impression: "He has the aspect of an Idiot—without the faintest ray of sense gleaming from any one feature. With the most awkward garb & unpowdered grey wig on one side only of his head, he is forever dancing the Devil's jig, & sometimes he makes the most driveling effort to whistle some thought in his absent paroxysms."

The young novelist Fanny Burney, who adored Johnson, gave the most perceptive and sympathetic accounts of his personal peculiarities. Though he was ugly and awkward, ill-mannered and constantly convulsed by his tics, which (as Boswell noted) excited ridicule in observers like Gainsborough and Hogarth, Fanny saw him as a pathetic example of human misfortune: "[He] has a Face the most ugly, a Person the most awkward, & manners the most singular, that ever were, or ever can be seen. . . . He has almost perpetual convulsive motions, either of his Hands, Lips, Feet, Knees, & sometimes all together. However, the sight of them can never excite ridicule, or, indeed, any other than melancholy reflections upon the imperfections of Human Nature."

In a later memoir of her musicologist father, Charles, a great friend and admirer of Johnson, Fanny softened, even idealized her portrayal, and ended with a hint of slapstick comedy: "He has naturally a noble figure; tall, stout, grand and authoritative; but he stoops horribly, his back is quite round: his mouth is continually opening and shutting, as if he were chewing something; he has a singular method of twirling his fingers, and twisting his hands: his vast body is in constant agitation, see-sawing backwards and forwards: his feet are never a moment quiet; and his whole great person looked often as if it were going to roll itself, quite voluntarily, from his chair to the floor." Modern doctors have diagnosed his condition as Tourette's syndrome—a series of facial and vocal tics, progressing to generalized jerking movements in any part of the body. This condition can now be treated with tranquilizers.

When he returned to Lichfield, Johnson was forced to confront his melancholy father and his censorious mother. He'd also disappointed his mentors Cornelius Ford and Gilbert Walmesley, who had high hopes for him. His mental breakdown lasted for exactly two years, until the death of his father in December 1731. But it took twenty-six years, until the publication of the *Dictionary* in 1755, for him to recover from his disaster at Oxford. Later in life he would feel overwhelming guilt for disobeying his sick father and for failing to visit his aged mother. But for now, he felt both antagonism for his parents and hatred of himself. For the next two years, as Donald Greene observed, "the rowdy, turbulent, quarrelsome, sometimes drunken, sometimes profane, sometimes almost mad young intellectual wandered about the Midlands."[19]

3

Preposterous Union
1730–1736

I

Michael Johnson—seventy-two years old, disappointed by Sam's retreat from Oxford and alarmed by the vile melancholy he'd passed on to his son—naturally expected Sam to take over the bookshop. But Sam, overcome by paralyzing depression, had no interest in commerce. He was clearly unable to revive the business, which had been weakened by the ill-fated attempt to manufacture parchment, and make it sufficiently profitable to support the family. His more amenable brother, Nathaniel, took up the slack. But after rejecting the bookshop, Sam would struggle for a long decade to gain a precarious toehold in the literary world.

After Sam returned to Lichfield, Michael was officially designated "a decayed tradesman" and granted a charitable donation of ten guineas from the town. In late 1731, sick in bed and perhaps dying, he asked Sam to look after his book stall on market day in Uttoxeter, about fifteen miles away. Sam refused to do this and would feel guilty about his disobedience for the rest of his life. In December Michael died of an inflammatory fever and was buried at St. Michael's Church on the seventh. His father's

death, which removed a source of anxiety and incidentally brought Sam
£20, ended the most severe phase of Sam's depression.

For the next five demoralizing years Sam tried to become a schoolmaster, a profession for which he was physically and temperamentally
unfit. Instead of fulfilling Michael's ambitions, he seemed to exhibit a
precocious disposition to failure. Though he'd been welcomed by Cornelius Ford and Gilbert Walmesley into polite and enlightened Midlands society, he could not, even with his brains and the influence of
local officials, secure the humble post of assistant teacher at a school.

Between 1731 and 1735 Johnson applied for four teaching jobs, all within
forty miles of Lichfield. He somehow managed to secure one position, but
soon left it. News traveled fast in that small area. He heard about the jobs
as soon as they became available, but the schools also learned about his
striking disabilities. In September 1731—toward the end of his severe depression and before his father's death—he heard of a position at the school
in Stourbridge. As a student there in 1725 he'd tangled with the head
master, Reverend John Wentworth, whom he called a lazy but severe man.
The Stourbridge usher (assistant master) was leaving after less than a year,
and the governors were considering the dismissal of Wentworth for prolonged absenteeism. Johnson was recommended by Gregory Hickman,
half-brother of Cornelius Ford, who'd died in August, but he was turned
down. His lack of a degree was a formidable obstacle, and he may also
have been blocked by the resentful Wentworth.

He was apparently more fortunate in March 1732. Sir Wolstan Dixie,
a local squire whose ancestor had been lord mayor of London in 1585,
controlled the school at Market Bosworth, twenty miles east of Lichfield.
Ignoring Johnson's lack of academic qualifications as well as his intellectual distinction, he offered an annual salary of £20 and a rent-free house.
Johnson eagerly accepted and walked from Lichfield to the school. A. L.
Reade portrayed Dixie, with unusual severity, as "a young bachelor of
about thirty, brutal, purseproud, domineering, boorish and with a very
violent temper. He was not only ignorant himself, but without any respect for learning in others." Dixie bragged about his absolute authority
in the school. Once, on a bet, he actually appointed his handsome butler as headmaster and kept him on the job for a month.

Johnson was bound to clash with this contentious and irascible tyrant, who subjected him to many petty humiliations. Once installed at the school, he found he had to live in Dixie's house (rather than in his own) as a kind of domestic chaplain and say grace at the table. Dixie may have reminded him of his humble position and forced him to perform menial tasks, mocked his manners and his convulsions, and criticized his teaching methods. Boswell reported that he "was treated with what he represented as intolerable harshness; and, after suffering for a few months such complicated misery, he relinquished a situation which all his life afterwards he recollected with the strongest aversion, and even a degree of horrour." Though Johnson had no money and no other prospects, he left, after only four months, in July 1732. When visiting his old friend John Taylor at Ashbourne, he always remembered the "horrour" and avoided the road that led to Market Bosworth. Still smarting from these wounds twenty years later, Johnson based Squire Bluster in *Rambler* 142 on Dixie. He portrayed him as spiteful and virulent, despotic and depraved, and caustically concluded, "he has birth without alliance, and influence without dignity. His neighbours scorn him as a brute; his dependents dread him as an oppressor, and he has only the gloomy comfort of reflecting, that if he is hated, he is likewise feared."[1]

In July 1732 Johnson heard that the usher at the Ashbourne school had suddenly died. He immediately sent off letters to the MP for Lichfield, a potentially influential backer, and to John Taylor, who was practicing law in the village. He asked Taylor "the means most proper to be used in this Matter" and said, "if there be any reason for my coming to Ashbourne, I shall readily do it." He added that leaving the humiliating drudgery at Sir Wolstan Dixie's, where every day was exactly the same, was "really *e Carcere exire*" (like coming out of prison). But when the governors met in August, another candidate, who also lacked a university degree, got the job. Taylor and other supporters may not have been sufficiently zealous on Johnson's behalf, and the school officials may also have heard about his unpleasant disputes with Dixie.

Despite these disheartening setbacks, Johnson kept trying, whenever he had the chance, to find a teaching job. In July 1735, after hearing that the headmaster of the Solihull school, near Birmingham, was leaving for Market Bosworth, Johnson tried to succeed him. Walmesley wrote to a friend there on Johnson's behalf. But Johnson clearly lacked the genteel charm and elegant manners necessary to overcome the surprise and mockery provoked by his appearance. The friend looked into Johnson's character and on August 30, well aware of the boys' natural tendency to mock their teachers, explained to Walmesley that Johnson had been rejected for his temperament as well as for his convulsions: "all agree that he is an Excellent Scholar, and upon that account deserves much better than to be schoolmaster of Solihull. But then, he has the Character of being a very haughty, ill natured Gent., and that he has such a way of distorting his Face (*which* though he can't help) the Gent. think it may affect some Young Ladds."[2]

A year later, in the fall of 1736, Johnson applied for the post of assistant master at Brewood, fifteen miles west of Lichfield. But the headmaster at Brewood, as with Solihull, had heard about and perhaps even seen him. The headmaster felt that Johnson would not be able to control his classroom and also feared his convulsions "might become the object of imitation or of ridicule among his pupils." All these rejections forced Johnson to realize that he would never secure a teaching position. In reality he was not fit to be a schoolmaster and didn't really want to become one. Though conscientious and intellectually well qualified for all these jobs, he was rejected for reasons he couldn't control. As less talented colleagues advanced in their careers, Johnson, overwhelmed by bitterness and despair, got nowhere.

In the fall of 1732 Johnson lived for six months with his school friend Edmund Hector, and in his convivial company drank freely of bishop, his favorite punch, a potent mixture of port, oranges and sugar. Hector, a surgeon, boarded in the house of a bookseller, Thomas Warren, who owned a newspaper, the *Birmingham Journal.* Johnson wrote some articles (now lost) for the paper, and Warren arranged for the printing of his first book, which they hoped would be both useful and profitable. This unlikely project was an English translation of *A Voyage to Abyssinia* by Father Jerónimo Lobo, a seventeenth-century Portuguese Jesuit missionary. The Portuguese had been exploring the coasts of Africa since the fifteenth century to gather scientific information, find a route to the rich spice trade of the Indies and spread the Christian faith. Abyssinia, a kingdom in the far east of Africa, was supposed to be fabulously rich. Its people were Christians who were threatened by pagans in the south and cut off from the west by the spread of Islam. Lobo's manuscript, hidden in a Lisbon monastery, remained unpublished until 1728, when a French priest, Joachim Le Grand, brought out the French version.

To help Johnson overcome his depression and wean him from indulging in bishop, Hector urged him to undertake a translation from the French edition. A printer was engaged and Johnson promised to supply him with copy, but his laziness soon prevailed and the work came to a sudden halt. Hector prodded Johnson to continue by appealing to his kindness and humanity. He told him that the printer couldn't take on any other jobs until the translation was completed and that the poor man's wife and children were suffering. Johnson did the absolute minimum. Boswell wrote that he "exerted the powers of his mind, though his body was relaxed. He lay in bed with the book, which was a quarto, before him, and dictated while Hector wrote. Mr. Hector carried the sheets to the press, and corrected all the proof sheets, very few of which were even seen by Johnson." The translation was published in 1735 in Birmingham, and following the common practice of provincial booksellers, the place of publication was listed as "London" on the title page. Johnson received the sum of five guineas.

Father Lobo's book described the history, religion and customs of the remote and exotic Abyssinians, as well as the geography, strange animals and tropical flowers of the Nile River and Red Sea coast. Johnson's brief, pungent preface praised Lobo for providing a truthful rather than fanciful account of this almost unknown country and for avoiding the incredible clichés of most voyagers: "The Portuguese traveler, contrary to the general vein of his countrymen, has amused his reader with no romantick absurdities or incredible fictions. . . . He appears by his modest and unaffected narration to have described things as he saw them, to have copied nature from the life, and to have consulted his senses not his imagination; he meets with no basilisks that destroy with their eyes, his crocodiles devour their prey without tears, and his cataracts fall from the rock without deafening the neighbouring inhabitants."

Johnson's version of Lobo was not a literal translation, but a condensation and adaptation. He actually introduced his own Protestant point of view and turned it into an anticolonial travel book. He toned down, and even attacked, Lobo's Catholic doctrine, and gave a negative portrayal of the Portuguese missionaries. In a noble passage that paraphrased John 15:17 and foreshadowed his political pamphlets, he condemned the Portuguese for their imperialistic invasion of Abyssinia and for trying to justify their savage massacres of Abyssinian Christians in the name of Christianity. These missionaries, he exclaimed, "preach the Gospel with swords in their hands, and propagate by desolation and slaughter the true worship of the God of Peace. . . . These men profess themselves the followers of Jesus, who left this great characteristick to his disciples, that they should be known 'by loving one another,' by universal and unbounded charity and benevolence." He condemned the Roman Catholic Church as cruel, insolent and oppressive, perpetrating "the most enormous villainies, and studying methods of destroying their fellow-creatures," engaging in religious massacres and conducting merciless courts of Inquisition.[3] His translation of Lobo first aroused his interest in travel and provided the Abyssinian background for *Rasselas*.

II

The passionate Johnson was probably a virgin when he married at the age of twenty-five. But both early and late in life he had firm views about sex and marriage. Sexual frustration made him idealize well-bred young women and place them on an unattainable pedestal, but he was well aware of the emotional undercurrents of ordinary social intercourse. He told Boswell (in a passage suppressed, like so many others, in the *Life of Johnson*) that "unless a woman has amorous heat she is a dull companion." He also believed, since his own sexual life was confined to his thoughts, that men could find the same physical satisfaction with any woman and that imaginative anticipation provided greater pleasure than actual experience. "Were it not for the imagination," he said, "a man would be as happy in the arms of a chambermaid as of a Duchess."

In another suppressed passage, Boswell asked why the standards of sexual behavior were different for men and for women. Johnson replied, in surprisingly frank language and without questioning this aspect of sexual morality, that women *had* to adhere to conventional standards if they wished to preserve their reputation: "I asked him if it was not hard that one deviation from chastity should so absolutely ruin a woman. Johnson. 'Why, no, Sir; the great principle which every woman is taught is to keep her legs together. When she has given up that principle, she has given up every notion of female honour and virtue, which are all included in chastity.'"[4]

Following the double standard of his time, Johnson condemned immorality in women and excused adultery in men (just as he later excused, or at least overlooked, the flagrant adultery of his patron Henry Thrale): "'Between a man and his wife, a husband's infidelity is nothing. They are connected by children, by fortune, by serious considerations of community. Wise married women don't trouble themselves about infidelity in their husbands.' Boswell. 'To be sure there is a great difference between the offence of infidelity in a man and that of his wife.' Johnson. 'The difference is boundless. The man imposes no bastards on his wife.'" In a society that emphasized social status, trade and wealth, he felt that a woman had to conform to strict morality in order to pass on her husband's name, property and money to his rightful heirs.

Johnson's tolerance of other men's failings did not extend to himself. When it came to his own behavior, he felt he was strictly accountable to God. Following Matthew 5:28—"whosoever looketh on a woman to lust after her hath committed adultery with her already in his heart"—he believed that the sinful thought or polluting dream was as evil as the sinful act itself. Marriage was an obvious answer to his dilemma. But he had little hope of finding a woman who would agree to marry him, and had serious doubts about whether he'd make a suitable husband. In a famous statement in *Rasselas,* he echoed St. Paul's pronouncement in I Corinthians 7:9, "it is better to marry than to burn," and conceded that though wedlock had numerous drawbacks, a single and solitary life was even worse: "marriage has many pains, but celibacy has no pleasures." Instead of enumerating the many pains, he noted the distinct disadvantages of celibates, who are prey to the dangers of the imagination and the vacuity of a meaningless existence: "they dream their time away without friendship, without fondness, and are driven to rid themselves of the day, for which they have no use, by childish amusements, and vicious delights." In *Rasselas* the astronomer idealizes the married state by explaining, "I have missed the endearing elegance of female friendship, and the happy commerce of domestick tenderness."[5]

In the first of twenty-seven sermons he wrote for John Taylor and other clergymen, Johnson, remembering his parents' unhappy union, emphasized the difference between the ideal hopes and the inevitable disillusions of marriage. Though marriage is supposedly "an institution designed only for the promotion of happiness, and for the relief of disappointments, anxieties, and distresses to which we are subject in our present state, [it] does not always produce the effects, for which it was appointed." He also saw marriage, however fortunate and fulfilling, as a kind of bondage that sapped the will and enslaved the husband. In his play *Irene,* which he worked on during the first years of his marriage, he proclaimed, "Know'st thou not yet, when Love invades the soul," that all men's faculties are bound by "chains." Continuing the metaphor of chains and whips that would later become a reality with Hester Thrale, he emphasized the power of women to subdue, humiliate and punish men: "a Woman has *such* power between the Ages of twenty-five and forty-five, that She may tye a Man to a Post and whip him if She will."[6] It's significant that when he did marry, his wife was nearly forty-six and just past the age when she could supposedly dominate him in this way.

In 1732, when Johnson was living in Birmingham, Edmund Hector introduced him to Henry Porter, a prosperous cloth merchant, and his wife, Elizabeth, known as Tetty (a Lichfield version of Betty).

Eighteenth-century Midlands society was closely knit, and he soon became part of their social circle. The second wife of John Hunter, the sadistic headmaster of Lichfield's school, was the sister of Henry Porter, sister-in-law of Tetty, and aunt of their two younger sons and daughter, Lucy, who was then seventeen. When Henry unexpectedly died in September 1734, Johnson began to court Tetty, with whom he'd established an intimate rapport, and the widow encouraged his overtures. In a revealing admission, he later told Hester Thrale that "he had never sought to please till past thirty years old, considering the matter as hopeless." But Tetty, whom he met soon after his humiliating experience with Sir Wolstan Dixie, gratified and even fulfilled Johnson's hopes when he was still in his early twenties. He was young enough to please her; she was too old to enslave him.

In contemporary drawings and literary sketches, Johnson appears eternally old and stout, but as a young man he was uncommonly thin and rawboned. Lucy Porter's description of Johnson, who didn't wear a fashionable wig and kept his hair in pigtails, shows that there was good reason to believe that he could never hope to please anyone:

> His appearance was very forbidding: he was then lean and lank, so that his immense structure of bones was hideously striking to the eye. . . . He also wore his [own] hair, which was straight and stiff, and separated behind: and he often had, seemingly, convulsive starts. . . . Mrs. Porter was so much engaged by his conversation that she overlooked all these external disadvantages, and said to her daughter, "this is the most sensible man that I ever saw in my life."

Johnson once described his old friend Robert Levet in terms that applied equally to himself and explained why Tetty was attracted to him: "Levet is a brutal ["rough, unpolished"] fellow, but I have a good regard for him; for his brutality is in his manners, not in his mind." As Birkbeck Hill astutely observed, "disadvantages of person and manner may be forgotten, where intellectual pleasure is communicated to a susceptible mind."[7] Just as Sarah Johnson knew her son's value, so Tetty also admired his moral character and quality of mind.

They were the only women who ever loved him, though Tetty, unlike Sarah, was able to express her love. Tetty is usually portrayed as a frivolous woman. But the well-off, middle-aged widow soon perceived (as few others did) the intellectual promise of the raw provincial youth and seized the chance to start a new life with him.

Though Johnson believed that "Marriage is more a League at last of Friendship than of Love," he said that his union with Tetty was "a love-marriage upon both sides." There is no reason to doubt his word. He loved Tetty for herself, was grateful for her love and loved her even more when she loved him. He thought her hair, as blond as a baby's, was extremely beautiful. In her bust-length portrait by an unknown artist at the time of her first marriage, she has fair hair parted in the middle, widely spaced eyes, a high forehead, strong nose and delicate lips. She shows a trace of a double chin above a long neck and sharply sloping shoulders, and wears a low-cut gown showing full breasts and a hint of cleavage. Her face is handsome, her expression alert.

Johnson's friends, influenced by their own attitudes toward Tetty, gave contrary accounts of her appearance and character. Elizabeth Desmoulins—daughter of Dr. Swinfen, close friend of Tetty and longtime member of Johnson's household—described the couple as beauty and the beast. She noted that Johnson (who liked the way Tetty read plays) valued her opinions and advice. She was "a lady of great sensibility ["quickness, perception, delicacy"] and worth; so shrewd and cultivated, that in the earlier part of their connection, he was fond of consulting her in all his literary pursuits; and so handsome, that his associates in letters and wit were often very pleasant with him on the strange disparity, which, in this respect, subsisted between husband and wife."[8]

By contrast, the Lichfield poet Anna Seward, who was implacably hostile to Johnson, thought the middle-aged widow was unattractive and strained to seem youthful with her young suitor. Her beauty "existed only in his imagination. She had a very red face, and very indifferent features; and her manners in advanced life, for her children were all grown up when Johnson first saw her, had an unbecoming excess of girlish levity, and disgusting affectation."

The actor David Garrick, once Johnson's pupil, agreed with Anna Seward about Tetty's appearance and affectations. But he thought Johnson's marriage was absurd, loved to make fun of him and, in his comically exaggerated account, conflated the middle-aged with the much older Tetty. Garrick described her as "very fat, with a bosom of more than ordinary protuberance, with swelled cheeks of florid red, produced by thick painting, and increased by the liberal use of cordials; flaring and fantastick in her dress, and affected both in her speech and her general behaviour."

The blind but perceptive Anna Williams, another future member of Johnson's household, agreed with Desmoulins that Tetty "had a good understanding and great sensibility," qualities that Tetty had praised in Johnson. Williams added that Tetty was (like Johnson himself) "inclined to be satirical"; and Johnson confirmed that Tetty could be tactless. She "had the Fault of shewing every one the bad Side of their own Profession—Situation & co. Would lament the Sorrows of Celibacy to an old Maid, & once told a Waterman he was no happier than a Galley Slave."[9] Though Tetty was long past the peak of her beauty, Johnson found her attractive, valued her intellect and admired her wit.

Speaking of his young scholarly friend Bennet Langton, Johnson told Boswell, "he has done a very foolish thing, Sir; he has married a widow, when he might have had a maid." Though Johnson himself could not have attracted a maid, there were in fact distinct advantages in marrying a widow. An experienced woman, rather than an innocent virgin, could more easily endure his eager but awkward passion and initiate him more gracefully into the rites of love. He didn't want to have children—fearing he would pass on his vile melancholy, subject them to infections or nervous diseases, and set up the inevitable conflict between father and son— and Tetty was well past the childbearing age. Like many widows, she also had a substantial dowry. Her £600 was enough to sustain a man, at a minimum subsistence level of £30 per annum, for twenty years.

When the twenty-five-year-old Johnson asked his mother's permission to marry the forty-five-year-old widow, she opposed the marriage (perhaps jealous of a rival) and refused her consent. Mocking the very idea, exaggerating Tetty's age and emphasizing her well-known extravagance, Sarah pointed out that her penniless, unemployed son was clearly unable to support a wife. "No, Sam," she said, "my willing consent you will never have to so preposterous a union. You are not yet twenty-five, and she is turned fifty. If she had any prudence, this request had never been made to me. Where are your means of subsistence? Porter has died poor, in consequence of his wife's expensive habits. You have great talents, but, as yet, have turned them into no profitable channel."

In contrast to Edward Gibbon, who, when his father refused to hear of his desire to marry a Swiss woman, "sighed as a lover and obeyed as a son," Johnson held his ground and followed his feelings, defended his decision and married Tetty against Sarah's sound but irrelevant opposition. He told her, "Mother, I have not deceived Mrs. Porter: I have told her the worst of me; that I am of mean extraction; that I have no money; and that I have had an uncle hanged." In a spirited and amusing response, Tetty, perhaps hiding her dowry from her suitor, sensibly replied "that she valued no one more or less for his descent; that she had no more money than myself; and that, though she had not had a relation hanged, she had fifty who deserved hanging."

Desmoulins told Boswell that Tetty had scant affection for Johnson and simply wanted someone to take care of her. But Tetty's family was even more passionately opposed than Sam's mother to their absurd union, and she must have had very strong feelings to overcome their hostility and wrath. Her late husband's brother, a successful businessman who was concerned about the reputation of the family, offered her a large annuity if she would agree to renounce her unworthy suitor. Her elder son, a naval officer, angrily rejected her and never saw her again. Her younger son, who spent most of his adult life in Italy, remained bitter and estranged for many years.

Only her daughter, Lucy, understood Tetty's feelings, supported her mother and remained close to Johnson, a devoted if distant stepfather, for the rest of his life. Anna Seward's description of Lucy suggests, if she resembled her mother, that Tetty was or had been attractive: "In her youth, [Lucy's] fair, clean complexion, bloom and rustic prettiness, pleased the men. More than once she might have married advantageously"—though she remained unmarried. After Sam and Tetty left Lichfield for London, Lucy moved into Sarah Johnson's house, helped her run the fading bookshop and on market days "took her place, standing behind the counter, nor thought it a disgrace."[10]

On July 9, 1735, ten months after the death of Henry Porter, Johnson married Tetty at St. Werburgh's Church in Derby, twenty-four miles northeast of Lichfield. Tetty, nearly forty-six, stated with poetic license that she was merely forty. According to one of Johnson's editors, the happy couple wished "to escape the angry notice of the widow's family and friends, [who'd] condemned him for cupidity and her for folly." The lovers traveled on horseback instead of taking the more comfortable coach and had their first quarrel on the way to the wedding. Fond, like Johnson, of reading chivalric romances, Tetty "had got into her head the fantastical notion that a woman of spirit should use her lover like a dog." When she first complained that he rode too fast, and then that he rode too slow, he rode briskly out of sight and left her far behind. He then waited for her to catch up and found the "pretty dear creature" in tears. Though sorry to have frightened her and hurt her feelings, he was pleased at the very beginning of their marriage to establish his domination over the older, wealthier and more experienced woman.

Tetty gave Johnson recognition and acceptance, and satisfied his hunger for love and sex. She provided comforting maternal affection, restored his battered self-esteem, pulled him out of his severe depression and helped overcome his chronic lethargy. He, in turn, gave up drink to set a good example for Tetty, who was overly fond of the bottle and addicted to the liberal use of cordials. Right after the wedding he sent to Oxford for his case of books, began to work on his tragedy *Irene* and with her money started his own school.

Tetty's few recorded remarks suggest that she was house proud, sharp-tongued about her husband's slovenly habits, astringent about his critical remarks, perceptive about his writing and, making a nice distinction between love and lust, surprisingly tolerant about his sexual behavior. Hester Thrale once asked him if "he ever disputed with his Wife (I knew he adored her). Oh, Yes, perpetually, my dear, says he; She was extremely neat in her disposition, & always fretful that I made the House so dirty—a clean Floor is *so* comfortable she would say by way of twitting."[11] Fed up with his complaints about the food, Tetty remarked, as he was about to say grace, "Nay hold says She, and do not make a Farce of thanking God for a Dinner which you will presently protest not eatable." He retaliated by chiding her for beating their cat in front of the maid, fearing that Tetty's bad example would encourage her to treat the cat with cruelty. But Tetty always thought well of his writing, and on this they were united. When the *Ramblers* appeared, she exclaimed that she'd never imagined he could have written anything so good.

In a sensitive passage suppressed in Boswell's *Life,* Johnson revealed that Tetty, assured of his deep affection and not threatened by younger women, told him, "I might lie with as many women as I pleased provided I loved her alone." He justified her attitude by explaining that it was indecent for a well-bred woman to reveal her sexual desires. Boswell, zeroing in on this fascinating question, inadvertently touched on an explosive issue—Tetty's unwillingness, toward the end of her life, to have sexual relations with Johnson: "Boswell. Suppose a woman to be of such a constitution that she does not like it. She has no right to complain that her husband goes elsewhere. Johnson. If she refuses it, she has no right to complain."[12]

III

Johnson could have used Tetty's money to prepare for a career in the church or the law. Instead, and despite his miserable experience at Market Bosworth, he started (as Donald Greene remarked) "perhaps the most unsuccessful private school in the history of education." Apart from the book trade, teaching was his only means of earning money. In June 1735, the month before his wedding, Johnson told a Lichfield school friend that he was going to furnish a house in the country and open a private boarding school for young gentlemen. He planned to imitate the mode of instruction at the most celebrated schools, and teach Latin and Greek with a more rational method than was usually practiced.

He rented, at twenty guineas a year, a building in Edial (two and a half miles west of Lichfield; pronounced *EE-jall*), where living expenses were much less than in town. He turned one of the ground-floor rooms into a spartan schoolroom and furnished the rest of the house with Tetty's belongings. Edial Hall, "a large brick box of a building with the roof in the shape of a sawn-off pyramid and a chimney resembling an Egyptian obelisk—had been put up seventy years previously."[13] From the start Johnson's school, which opened in the fall of 1735, was doomed. It was too close to Lichfield Grammar School, where most local people sent their sons.

Johnson's first and only pupils were the sixteen-year-old David Garrick; his younger brother, George, aged twelve; and one other sixteen-year-old. Garrick would become a lifelong friend and the most celebrated actor of the age. His grandparents were French Huguenots who had fled from Bordeaux to England in 1685, when the Edict of Nantes, which gave Protestants the same rights as Catholics, was revoked. His father, born in France, was a half-pay army officer, living in Lichfield. Only ten years younger than Johnson, David had traveled abroad and acquired a cosmopolitan air. When he was eleven years old, he'd lived for a year in Lisbon and worked for a relative in the wine trade. But he had little interest in commerce and preferred to show off his eloquent gifts by entertaining the English merchants and reciting dramatic passages at their banquets.

Edial Hall, a visible reminder of Johnson's poor judgment, was far too big for only Tetty, Lucy, the servants, his three pupils and himself. Like his father, he had great expectations from a venture that didn't work out. In July 1736, at the beginning of the second year, he placed an advertisement in the London *Gentleman's Magazine* that announced: "At Edial, near Lichfield, in Staffordshire, young gentlemen are boarded and taught the Latin and Greek languages by Samuel Johnson." Since he was then completely unknown, there were still no takers, and he plodded on with his minute constituency.

In his later writings Johnson always emphasized the negative aspects of teaching and the difficulty of persuading boys to learn their lessons. In his preface to the *Preceptor,* an educational manual in two volumes, he wearily stated the near impossibility of attracting and maintaining the pupils' attention: "Every man who has been engaged in teaching, knows with how much difficulty youthful minds are confined to close application, and how readily they deviate to any thing, rather than attend to that which is imposed as a task." In one of his sermons he mentioned the frustrations of having to degrade a brilliant adult mind to the level of children: "There is no employment in which men are more easily betrayed to indecency ["unbecoming, contrary to good manners"] and impatience, than that of teaching; in which they necessarily converse with those, who are their inferiours." He was even more critical in his life of Milton, where he stated that it was nearly impossible to coerce students into the three essential stages of learning—concentration, study and comprehension: "Every man, that has ever undertaken to instruct others, can tell what slow advances he has been able to make, and how much patience it requires to recall vagrant inattention, to stimulate sluggish indifference, and to rectify absurd misapprehension."[14]

Despite Johnson's declared intention to use a more rational method of instruction, his educational plan was not original. The historian A. S. Turberville pointed out that eighteenth-century teaching "probably had not altered substantially in 200 years. Booksellers could still sell fresh editions of the Latin grammar which, in its earliest form, [William] Lily had written with help from Erasmus" in 1509. Johnson, limited by defective eyesight, had been more inclined as a boy to study than to games. In his early preface to the *Preceptor*, he equated play with idleness and took the strictly traditional view that "children might be allowed, without injury to health, to spend many of those hours upon useful employments, which are generally lost in idleness and play." Later on, when advising Hester Thrale about how to bring up her numerous children, he softened his harsh views and argued that children should be allowed to have more freedom. "Our manner of teaching," he conceded, "cramps and warps many a mind, which if left more at liberty would have been respectable ["meriting respect"] in some way."[15]

Johnson was so tenderhearted that he couldn't bear to see Tetty beat their cat. But chiefly because of his own ineptitude as teacher and disciplinarian, he firmly advocated corporal punishment. Though he tended to be indulgent with his friends' children and realized that they always resented the infliction of pain, he agreed with contemporary parents and teachers that whipping was both necessary and unavoidable. He told Boswell, "the rod produces an effect which terminates in itself. The child is afraid of being whipped and gets his task, and there's an end on't." Though he intended this climactic phrase to terminate all discussion, it wasn't quite the end of this complex subject. Johnson distinguished, as his brutal master John Hunter had not, between boys who couldn't answer through ignorance and had to be taught, or through idleness and had to be whipped. But what of the boys who failed to learn their lessons *after* they were whipped? Would more punishment teach them what study had failed to do? Contrasting their heads and their bottoms, Johnson joked about this dilemma by noting, "what they *gain* at one end, they will *lose* at the other."

Johnson adhered to these harsh opinions throughout his life. He gave his most considered views in April 1772 when he helped Boswell defend a Scottish schoolmaster who'd been accused of brutally beating his pupils. He argued that if the teacher didn't do his duty and rule by fear rather than by reason, the school would soon descend into anarchy and chaos. Ignoring the psychological wounds and the dubious efficacy of the punishment, he harshly insisted that the master could beat the boys as long as he didn't blind or cripple them:

> Correction, in itself, is not cruel; children, being not reasonable, can be governed only by fear. To impress this fear, is therefore one of the first duties of those who have the care of children. . . . The discipline of a school is military. There must be either unbounded license or absolute authority. . . .
>
> Punishments, however severe, that produce no lasting evil, may be just and reasonable. . . . No scholar has gone from him either blind or lame, or with any of his limbs or powers injured or impaired.[16]

Later in life, Johnson seemed to discount the ferocious floggings he'd endured in his youth and maintained that the schoolboy was the happiest human being.

In his *Autobiography*, Edward Gibbon gave a far more realistic picture of eighteenth-century schoolboy life when he wrote, "at the expense of many tears and some blood, I purchased the knowledge of the Latin syntax." Recalling his miserable years at school, he compared the chronically unhappy student to a slave: "A school is the cavern of fear and sorrow; the mobility of the captive youths is chained to a book and a desk; an inflexible master commands their attention, which every moment is impatient to escape; they labour like the soldiers of Persia under the scourge, and their education is nearly finished before they can apprehend the sense or utility of the harsh lessons which they are forced to repeat." Traditional teaching methods, which Johnson followed, did not aim to develop young minds, but to drill children in mechanical responses by the threat or use of the whip.

While Johnson taught and beat the boys, Tetty, used to managing a household and bringing up three children, helped him by supervising the kitchen and servants, and acting as motherly matron to the boys. It must have been a strange experience for the lads to live in this half-empty, Poe-like house with the weirdly matched couple. Johnson's appetite for sex, they soon learned, was as strong as his appetite for food. Garrick later told Boswell (an expert on sex who boldly intruded on Johnson's "domestick privacies") that the young rogues took revenge for their beatings by listening "at the door of his bed-chamber, and peeping through the key-hole, that they might turn into ridicule his tumultuous and awkward fondness for Mrs. Johnson." The young voyeurs, curious about sex and ready to find it absurd, watched Johnson's gauche but violent performance, mocking Tetty's girlish affectations and his clumsy attempts at gallantry.

After Johnson became a famous London figure, Garrick would use these occasions to impersonate him for the amusement of their friends. In his little playlet, he portrayed Johnson sitting next to their bed after Tetty had retired, completely absorbed in the composition of *Irene*. As she impatiently summons him to his sexual duties, he ignores her call and reads out the ponderous verses of his play. He then absentmindedly seizes the bedclothes, which he mistakes for his shirttails and tries to tuck them into his breeches, while she shivers with cold and clutches at the covers. Finally, he runs around the room crying, "'I'm coming, my Tetsie. I'm coming, my Tetsie,' blowing and puffing all the time in his peculiar manner."[17] Using all of his comic talents (behind Johnson's back), Garrick made their friends ache with helpless laughter as tears streamed down their cheeks and they nearly rolled out of their chairs.

But there was little to laugh at in the classroom. Johnson hated teaching and, as his recourse to the rod suggests, wasn't terribly good at it. He told Edmund Hector that he didn't know if it were more disagreeable for him to teach the rules of grammar or for the boys to learn them. He agreed with his friend Oliver Goldsmith that the profession of schoolmaster was generally despised. In his life of Sir Richard Blackmore he wrote that the poet (like Johnson himself) was compelled by indigence to "teach a school; an humiliation with which . . . his enemies did not forget to reproach him, when he became conspicuous enough to excite malevolence." Boswell's father, who hated Johnson's political and religious principles and quarreled violently with him, mocked him by stating, in a strong Scots accent, "he keeped a schule and cau'd it an acaademy."

In January 1737, after fifteen months and still with only three students, Johnson was forced to close the school. He'd squandered most of Tetty's money and disappointed her hopes at Edial, just as he'd done with his parents' money and hopes at Oxford. A Lichfield historian mentioned "the wreck of her property." A modern scholar calculated, "if we allow Johnson and his wife the extravagance of spending £150 per year and another £100 for setting up the school, approximately £200 would still have remained from Tetty's fortune."[18] Leaving Tetty and Lucy to rattle around the deserted mansion, Johnson decided to use the remaining funds to support the family while he tried his luck in London. Tetty would remain at Edial till he could send for her.

Johnson had escaped from his oppressive parents and teachers when he stayed with Cornelius Ford in Stourbridge for nine months in 1725–26. In a similar fashion, he also left Tetty when he lived alone in London for eight months in 1737, and when, leaving her in London, he repaired to Lichfield and Ashbourne for nine months in

1739–40. In his life of Milton he seemed to reflect on his own situation by writing that the poet "expected all the advantages of a conjugal life," but his wife "seems not much to have delighted in the pleasures of spare diet and hard study." When she left to visit her friends, "Milton was too busy to much miss his wife; he pursued his studies." But Johnson's marriage was more problematical. Tetty had rejected a substantial offer to renounce him, and was alienated from her family and two sons. She had lost most of her fortune at the ill-fated school, and would lose her social standing when she moved to more constricted quarters in London.

Like the fictional heroes of Balzac and Flaubert, Johnson went to the capital to seek work, earn money and find excitement. He bid farewell to his mother, whom he would see only one more time before her death. But leaving his native town, where he knew nearly everyone, for a big city, where he knew no one at all, had corresponding dangers. As he later told John Taylor, "the transition from the protection of others to our own conduct is a very awful point of human existence."

He placed all his hopes in his tragedy, *Irene*. He'd completed three acts before he left for London, and occasionally read parts of it to Gilbert Walmesley. His friend asked, with the heroine already in dire circumstances, how he could possibly contrive to plunge her in deeper distress. Johnson, alluding to the notorious delays and abuses in Walmesley's jurisdiction, replied, "in the last act, I intend to put my heroine into the ecclesiastical court of Lichfield, which will fill up the utmost measure of human calamity." Amused by his wit and helpful as always, Walmesley mentioned Johnson's plan in a letter to a friend, saying he intended "to try his fate with a tragedy, and to see to get himself employed in some translation, either from the Latin or the French. Johnson is a very good scholar and poet, and I have great hopes will turn out a fine tragedy writer."[19]

Since Garrick would be passing through London on the way to his new school, which was supposed to prepare him for a career in the law, his family entrusted the boy to Johnson's care and master and pupil traveled south together. This strange pair—the large, awkward, shortsighted

Johnson and the small, agile, protean Garrick—set out for London, as in a fairy tale, to seek their fortune. With very little money and one horse between them, they left on March 2, 1737, took turns riding and walking, and spent several days on the 120-mile journey to the largest city in Europe.

As soon as they reached London, they learned that Garrick's father and Johnson's brother had suddenly died. Nathaniel Johnson, only twenty-four years old, had planned to emigrate to Georgia, in America, but got only as far as Frome, in Somerset, en route to the port of Bristol, before returning to Lichfield. He may have died in an epidemic or, if he inherited his father's melancholy, may even, as was rumored, have committed suicide.

Johnson was now twenty-seven, and his life thus far had been catastrophic. Permanently disfigured by a severe physical illness, he'd disobeyed his father and quarreled with his mother, dropped out of Oxford and ruined his prospects, had a nervous breakdown and come close to insanity. Stricken by a convulsive disease and mocked by his pupils, he'd failed as a schoolmaster, made an imprudent and even ludicrous marriage, wasted his wife's money and was unable to support her. He couldn't complete his play or find employment, and arrived in London penniless and completely unknown. Despite his disastrous career as a schoolmaster, he became a great teacher, educator and moral example. Sustained by physical strength, personal courage and intellectual power, he would eventually become the greatest writer of his time.

4

BENEVOLENT GIANT
1737

I

Though Johnson became stouter, more extreme in his habits, and more dogmatic as he grew older, his adult appearance and character were firmly in place when he set off for London in 1737. His coarse manners and Midlands accent impeded his progress, yet the force of his personality and the brilliance of his mind secured friends and admirers. Characterizing friends by comparing them to animals was a popular amusement, and in the course of his career Johnson was called a mastiff, a whale, an elephant, a bear and a bull. When ill humored, he was most like a shortsighted but dangerous rhinoceros, an animal he once observed in the royal menagerie of France. His slovenly dress, frantic convulsions, crude eating habits and notorious rudeness, as well as his formidable strength, courage and violence, were at one with his forbidding appearance.

Though people rarely bathed in the eighteenth century, they used scents and powders to try to disguise their earthy odors. Fine gentlemen of the period wore gold lace and raspberry-colored coats, silk stockings and satin breeches. A man of Johnson's class could not have afforded such elegant clothes, but he would have owned several sets of linen underwear, shirts and neckcloths, and at least one sober suit of dark wool cloth. His shoes had metal buckles, and in winter he wore a thick wool overcoat and a felt hat with a wide brim. It was fashionable for both sexes to wear powdered wigs, and considered low class to display one's own hair. Johnson, who refused to conform to the respectable norms of hygiene and dress, looked like a tramp or a beggar. The young Boswell, predisposed to admire, was shocked by his appearance when he first visited his rooms. In Boswell's comic description, Johnson, with no female supervision, could not seem to find any clothes to fit him. His wig was too small, his breeches too loose, his stockings too wrinkled, his shoes too slack: "His brown suit of cloaths looked very rusty; he had on a little old shrivelled unpowdered wig, which was too small for his head; his shirt-neck and knees of his breeches were loose; his black worsted stockings ill drawn up; and he had a pair of unbuckled shoes by way of slippers."

Ozias Humphry, who painted Johnson's portrait and scrutinized him with an artist's eye, at first thought (as Hogarth did) that he looked like a madman who'd escaped from a lunatic asylum. Humphry was astonished that he'd receive a guest while dressed "in a dirty brown coat and waistcoat, with breeches that were brown also (though they had been crimson), and an old black wig: his shirt collar and sleeves were unbuttoned; his stockings were down about his feet, which had on them, by way of slippers, an old pair of shoes." Johnson shuffled about his rooms in clothes more suitable for work than for display.

Another artist, James Northcote, described a comic incident in which Johnson was actually taken for a thief and forced to proclaim his innocence. Dirty and coarsely dressed for a social occasion at a fashionable establishment, Johnson was stopped at the entrance by an aggressive maid, who scornfully said, "You fellow, what is your business here? I suppose you intended to rob the house?" To which the mortified guest roared like a bull: "What have I done? What have I done?"[1] Despite his host's reassurance, he remained despondent during dinner, and could scarcely recover himself for the rest of the evening.

He was well aware of the horrific effect he had on gentlefolk as well as on servants. But when fine ladies gathered round to listen in the drawing room and contemplated him "as if he had been some monster from the deserts of Africa," Johnson, once again on the defensive, reassured them by saying, "Ladies, I am tame; you may stroke me." Sir Walter Scott shrewdly characterized him as "the benevolent giant of some fairy tale." A member of Lord Chesterfield's family, resolutely hostile to Johnson's satiric tongue and revolting appearance, said he was too "fond of Sarcasm, which has a double portion of Gall flowing from the most disgusting Voice & Person you almost ever beheld."[2]

Accustomed to being regarded with distaste and always bracing himself for rejection by a new acquaintance, Johnson employed an arsenal of weapons, most notably his wit, to combat adversaries who might be tempted to bait and mock him. In a suppressed passage, Boswell recorded that "after dinner Mr. Johnson rose and walked to the end of the room in a fit of meditation and threw himself into some of those attitudes which he does when deep in thought." Captain Brodie, a fellow guest, observing his solitary convulsions, caustically remarked, "Sir, if you be for dancing a minuet, had not you better go to the ladies?" Everyone expected an explosion. But "Johnson took no notice whatever of the speech for a good while. At last he came and sat down, and all at once turning to Mr. Beauclerk, said, 'Don't you think this Brodie a very coarse fellow?'" This Brodie, a one-armed naval hero, was married to Molly Aston, with whom Johnson had once fallen in love. So Johnson felt an uneasy and unequal sexual rivalry with him. Brodie had sensed the contrast between Johnson's quiet meditations and his comical convulsions, and ironically compared his uncontrollable tics to an elegant minuet. But the unrefined Johnson turned the tables on the mutilated Brodie by calling *him* a coarse fellow, and his delayed retribution was more effective than an immediate blast.

In a well-known epigram Johnson said that a man "who does not mind his belly will hardly mind anything else." He not only fed like an animal at a trough, but also devoured enormous quantities of food. Friends gradually became accustomed to his feral appetite, but strangers were always repelled. Boswell's veneration was balanced and brought down to earth by the shock of watching him eat:

When at table, he was totally absorbed in the business of the moment; his looks seemed rivetted to his plate; nor would he, unless when in very high company, say one word, or even pay the least attention to what was said by others, till he had satisfied his appetite, which was so fierce, and indulged with such intenseness, that while in the act of eating, the veins of his forehead swelled, and generally a strong perspiration was visible. To those whose sensations were delicate, this could not but be disgusting.

The wife of a scholarly friend, appalled by his feeding frenzy, exclaimed that he was "more beastly in his dress and person than anything I ever beheld. He feeds nastily and ferociously, and eats quantities most unthankfully."[3]

When traveling with Joshua Reynolds in his native Devon, Johnson consumed impressive amounts of food and drink. One hostess asked if he liked pancakes and was told, "Yes, Madam, but I never get enough." She provided a more than generous supply and he put away thirteen of them. He also ate large quantities of the local specialties, honey and clotted cream, besides drinking bountiful potations of new cider. Though his habits were crude, he could be quite fastidious about how food and drink were prepared and served. He was furious when a French footman picked up the lump of sugar with his fingers and popped it into the coffee. And at a disgraceful inn, where he stopped en route from London to Oxford, he roundly condemned the slab of mutton and traced the meat's flavor back to the sheep's origins. Summoning the terrified waiter, he announced, "It is as bad as bad can be: it is ill-fed, ill-killed, ill-kept, and ill-drest."

In his life of the deformed invalid Alexander Pope, Johnson excused Pope's overeating as a necessary palliative to the anguish of his life. Such a fault, he wrote, is "easily incident to those who, suffering much pain, think themselves entitled to whatever pleasures they can snatch." Johnson also loved drink, which alleviated the agonies of human existence, and was always tempted to alcoholic excess, for "he who makes a *beast* of himself, gets rid of the pain of being a *man*." He needed drink to raise his spirits and rouse him from depression, and confessed that he often drank in solitude. He felt better pleased with himself when drunk, but didn't want anyone to see him with his faculties impaired. Comparing the potency of various drinks, he famously remarked, "claret is the liquor for boys; port, for men; but he who aspires to be a hero (smiling) must drink brandy."[4]

Johnson could absorb great quantities of drink without feeling more than moderate exhilaration. One of his companions told Boswell that Johnson often drank two or even three bottles at a sitting, and kept drinking till he was unable to walk home. Though liquor impaired his limbs, it rarely affected his powers of thought. But in his youth, while living with Edmund Hector in Birmingham in 1732, he was overcome in a notorious drinking bout (suppressed by Boswell). Hector recalled that Johnson devised a plan to deal with a Ford cousin, one of his hard-drinking relatives. The young man

> engaged Johnson and Hector to spend the evening with him at the Swan Inn. Johnson said to Hector, "This fellow will make us both drunk. Let us take him by turns, and get rid of him." It was settled that Hector should go first. He and Ford had drunk three bottles of Port before Johnson came. When Johnson arrived, Hector found he had been drinking at Mr. [Henry] Porter's instead of saving himself. Hector went to bed at the Swan leaving Johnson to drink with Ford. Next morning he perceived that Johnson, who had been his bed-fellow, had been very drunk.

Johnson casuistically claimed that Hector, sound asleep when he came to bed, had never actually seen him drunk and merely assumed that he was. Hogarth's engraving of *Gin-Lane* portrayed gin-soaked laborers lying dead drunk in the streets, who were sometimes run over by coaches. Johnson was more concerned with maintaining the appearance and reputation of sobriety than with the risk of fatal accidents.

Johnson also feared the consequences of strong drink, and twice in his life felt obliged to become a total abstainer. He gave it up for Tetty's sake during their marriage (1736–52) and for five years afterwards. He resumed heavy drinking in 1757, when he began his monumental edition of Shakespeare. He gave it up again in 1764, after his second mental breakdown, and from that year until 1781 took only water, tea or lemonade. In his diary of April 21, 1764, he recorded that he would have to abandon alcohol, which undermined his rational faculties and his struggle to control sexual desires: "My thoughts have been clouded with sensuality, and, except that from the beginning of this year I have in some measure forborn excess of Strong Drink, my appetites have predominated over my reason."

He explained to the young author Hannah More that since he hadn't been able to control his drinking, he had to give it up completely or be overwhelmed by it: "I can't drink a *little,* child, therefore I never touch it. Abstinence is as easy to me, as *temperance* would be difficult." In *Adventurer* 102 he referred to the discomfort of remaining sober in the company of inebriated friends: "Their mirth grows more turbulent and obstreperous, and before their merriment is at an end, I am sick with disgust, and, perhaps, reproached with my sobriety." Johnson's criticism of his friends' drinking provoked an unusually sharp exchange with his close friend Joshua Reynolds, who remarked: "'You have sat by, quite sober, and felt an envy of the happiness of those who were drinking.' Johnson. 'Perhaps, contempt.–And, Sir, it is not necessary to be drunk one's self, to relish the wit of drunkenness.'"[5] In March 1781, when his sexual appetite had presumably abated, he returned for the last three years of his life to the pleasures of wine. In periods of abstinence Johnson compensated by drinking enormous amounts of tea, often downing as many as sixteen cups in one evening. "I don't count your wine," he told a hostess, who was weary of brewing and pouring endless pots, "don't count my tea."

In 1757, the year he resumed drinking after abstaining for more than two decades, he reviewed a crankish book by Jonas Hanway, prison reformer, champion of pauper children and chimney sweeps, a well-meaning bore and the first Englishman to use an umbrella. In his *Journal of Eight Days' Journey from Portsmouth to Kingston upon Thames,* Hanway appended an essay on tea, asserting that the pernicious leaf undermined health, obstructed industry and impoverished the nation. Rising to this provocation (and perhaps recalling the expensive tea his mother had spoiled him with as a child), the thoroughly addicted Johnson argued, "its proper use is to amuse the idle, and relax the studious, and dilute the full meals of those [like himself] who cannot use exercise, and will not use abstinence." Warming to the subject, Johnson confessed that tea had lubricated his social relations, soothed his troubled thoughts and (like prayers in a monastery and providing similar comfort) ceremoniously marked the hours of the day. Likening himself to a criminal, he admitted he was "a hardened and shameless tea-drinker, who has, for twenty years diluted his meals with only the infusion of this fascinating plant, whose kettle has scarcely time to cool, who with tea amuses the evening, with tea solaces the midnights, and, with tea, welcomes the morning."

A compulsive personality, Johnson had many obsessions besides food and drink. He was equally attentive to the precise manner in which he entered a room and the exact way in which he moved his body while speaking. With the most minute and vivid details, Boswell described his friend's strange superstitions and singularities. He had an

anxious care to go out or in at a door or passage by a certain number of steps from a certain point, or at least so that either his right or his left foot, (I am not certain which,) should constantly make the first actual movement when he came close to the door or passage. . . . I have, upon innumerable occasions, observed him suddenly stop, and then seem to count his steps with a deep earnestness; and when he had neglected or gone wrong in this sort of magical movement, I have seen him go back again, put himself in a proper posture to begin the ceremony, and, having gone through it, break from his abstraction, walk briskly on, and join his companion.

In *Rambler* 60 Johnson commended Sallust for describing Catiline's odd walk as "'now quick, and again slow,' as if an indication of a mind revealing something with violent commotion." Though deep thought may partly account for Johnson's strange gait, the arcane procedure seemed designed to impose a semblance of order on his chaotic life, protect him from evil and ensure the prosperity of his visit.

Equally strange and earnest were his simultaneous movements: rocking back and forth and sideways, with a *frottage* on his knee as if to balance the tremors. To these convulsions he added weird ululations that, while disconcerting his intellectual opponents, seemed to concentrate his attention and reinforce his arguments:

> While talking or even musing as he sat in his chair, he commonly held his head to one side towards his right shoulder, and shook it in a tremulous manner, moving his body backwards and forwards, and rubbing his left knee in the same direction, with the palm of his hand. In the intervals of articulating he made various sounds with his mouth, sometimes as if ruminating, or what is called chewing the cud, sometimes giving a half whistle, sometimes making his tongue play backwards from the roof of his mouth, as if clucking like a hen, and sometimes protruding it against his upper gums in front, as if pronouncing quickly under his breath, *too, too, too:* all this accompanied sometimes with a thoughtful look, but more frequently with a smile. When he has concluded a period, in the course of a dispute, by which time he was a good deal exhausted by violence and vociferation, he used to blow out his breath like a Whale.[6]

Johnson often seemed unable to control his body, but in middle and even old age performed some extraordinary athletic feats. This self-testing and urge to show off his skills astonished his friends. When a kangaroo (then little known in England) was mentioned in the course of a conversation, he rose from his chair, oblivious of his dignity, and offered to imitate the animal. "Nothing could be more ludicrous," an observer recalled, "than the appearance of a tall, heavy, grave-looking man, like Dr. Johnson, standing up to mimic the shape and motions of a kangaroo. He stood erect, put out his hands like feelers, and, gathering up the tails of his huge brown coat so as to resemble the pouch of the animal, made two or three vigorous bounds across the room!" His urge to teach was stronger than the need to preserve decorum.

One day, Johnson was suddenly overcome by an urge to roll down a steep hill. Though friends tried to dissuade him, he impulsively emptied his pockets of keys, penknife, pencil and purse. Then, "laying himself parallel with the edge of the hill, he actually descended, turning himself over and over till he came to the bottom." He always felt much better after behaving like a young man. In the countryside he was capable of even more impressive performances. After riding on horseback for more than fifty miles and still wearing his riding boots, he imitated Henry Thrale, who was twenty years younger, and leaped over a stool. On other occasions, after discarding his hat, wig and coat, he climbed a gate and jumped over a rail that he used to "fly over" as a schoolboy. To prove his youth and vigor, he also ran to a tree and, like a higher ape, climbed up the trunk and into the branches.

A tree figured significantly in another incident when the gigantic Johnson, in high spirits, challenged a tiny friend to a footrace: "The proposal was accepted; but, before they had proceeded more than half of the intended distance, Johnson caught his little adversary up in his arms, and without any ceremony placed him upon the arm of a tree which was near, and then continued running as if he had met with a hard match."[7] In this comical scene Johnson treated his rival like a baby—but at least he had the decency to go back and rescue the little fellow from his perch.

Though Johnson was no good at ball games, in which sharp vision was essential, he was a strong swimmer and intrepid rider. When he was in middle age but seemed much older, the professional "dipper," or bathing master, in Brighton, on the south coast, praised his strokes and proclaimed, "Why, Sir, you must have been a stout-hearted gentleman forty years ago." Though he got no pleasure from pursuing the fox, he also rode to the hounds in a manly fashion that combined both energy and his habitual sloth. Sir John Hawkins wrote, "he showed himself a bold rider, for he either leaped, or broke through, many of the hedges that obstructed him. This he did, not because he was eager in the pursuit, but, as he said, to save the trouble of alighting and remounting." Hester Thrale confirmed that "he certainly rode on Mr. Thrale's old hunter with a good firmness, and though he would follow the hounds fifty miles on end sometimes, would never own himself either tired or amused." He was greatly pleased when his horsemanship, like his swimming, was praised by an expert, who remarked that he had brawn as well as brains: "Why Johnson rides as well, for aught I see, as the most illiterate fellow in England."[8]

In a self-reflective passage in *Adventurer* 74, Johnson made the psychological connection between his physical disabilities, emotional struggles and sudden eruptions of violence: "the deformed were always insupportably vigilant, and apt to sink into sullenness, or burst into rage." Contemporaries admired Johnson for his roughness and ferocity, his physical prowess and considerable courage. He proved, again and again, that he was not afraid of anyone and that it was always unwise to mess around with him. Touchy and hot-tempered, he became pugnacious when anyone defied him. The actor and playwright Samuel Foote, also dangerous to provoke, was famous for comic mimicry and for savage caricatures of well-known people. When Foote threatened to mock on stage the "Caliban of literature," Johnson warned him that "the theatre being intended for the reformation of vice, he would step from the boxes on the stage, and correct him before the audience." Foote took the threat seriously and decided to focus on weaker targets.

Johnson once knocked down the bookseller Thomas Osborne with a folio volume (a duodecimo would not do), then put his foot on his neck and told him not to rise, threatening to compound the well-earned punishment by kicking him down the stairs. He forcefully recalled the event by explaining, "he was insolent, and I beat him." When Johnson heard that Osborne had told friends about the incident, he remarked, "I have beat many a fellow, but the rest had the wit to hold their tongues."[9]

Extremely touchy about his appearance and behavior, and with a notoriously short fuse, Johnson often found it difficult to live up to his own principles. In *Adventurer* 131 he stated that men who deviate from social norms have no right to object when their behavior is condemned: "he who differs from others without apparent advantage, ought not to be angry if his arrogance is punished with ridicule; if those, whose example he superciliously overlooks, point him out to derision, and hoot him back in again to the common road." James Northcote reported that Johnson, always the oddball, knocked down another man who'd insultingly imitated his uncouth gait and gestures: "Johnson said: 'you are a very weak fellow, and I will convince you of it.' And then immediately gave him a blow, which knocked the man out of the footpath and into the dirty street flat on his back, when the Doctor walked calmly on." By beating the impertinent stranger, Johnson (ever the teacher) showed him that a man with a weak physique and character should not make provocative insults.

When his arguments failed to persuade, violence did the trick. Boswell wrote that at the playhouse in Lichfield, "Johnson, having for a moment quitted a chair which was placed for him between the side-scenes, a gentleman took possession of it, and when Johnson on his return civilly demanded his seat, rudely refused to give it up; upon which Johnson laid hold of it, and tossed him and the chair into the pit."[10] In this marvelous account Johnson, *civilly* demanding, instead of politely requesting, the seat reserved for him on the stage (since he couldn't see well from far away), was greeted with a *rude* refusal. Since his adversary was clearly unreceptive to rational discourse, Johnson finally settled the dispute by taking possession of him and throwing the suddenly déclassé gentleman into the mob. It's not at all clear what happened to the unfortunates in the pit when, as they observed the heated argument, the chair and its occupant suddenly landed on top of them.

Johnson's athletic skill and bursts of violence were complemented by his reckless and stubborn courage. He was unafraid not only of men, but also—even when his life was in danger—of treacherous currents, explosive firearms, fierce dogs and criminal gangs. When told that a part of the river at Oxford was particularly perilous, he plunged into the very place where a man had recently drowned. Warned that an old gun might burst if overloaded, he charged it with six or seven bullets and fired it against a stone wall.

Hester Thrale was mightily frightened and impressed when two large dogs, brought into the parlor, began to attack each other. The owner found he couldn't control the dogs, and they "alarmed the People present not a little with their ferocity, till Johnson gravely laying hold on each Dog by the scruff of the Neck, held them asunder at Arm's length, and said, come, Gentlemen, where is your difficulty?'" After fearlessly subduing them, he boasted about how easy it was. Footpads were as menacing in the dark and narrow streets of London as fighting dogs were inside the house. Gangs usually preyed on older, weaker victims, but they met their match when they fixed on Johnson: "One night he was attacked in the streets by four men, to whom he would not yield, but kept them all at bay, till the watch came up, and carried both him and them to the round-house"—a constable's prison in which disorderly people were confined.

In one of his most deeply felt statements, Johnson said, "the cure for the greatest part of human miseries is not radical, but palliative."[11] His main palliatives, since religion gave him more anguish than comfort, were food and friendship. He often abstained from drink and sex, which could also have relieved his misery. During his marriage, he was sexually frustrated when separated from Tetty and (toward the end of her life) when she refused to sleep with him. Although he had strong sexual desires, he remained celibate from the time of her death (when he was forty-three) to the end of his life. Johnson's spontaneous athletic feats, outbursts of violence and displays of courage were all crucial outlets for his sexual feelings.

II

Always hard on himself, Johnson tended to exaggerate his humble origins and poverty (as he did when courting Tetty) as well as his hardships, laziness, poor health, mental problems and sinfulness. His weaknesses and faults—fear of loneliness, insomnia and sloth—fed on and intensified each other. Loneliness made him stay up late to prolong conversation, while late nights and insomnia kept him in bed all morning, and his inability to rise made it difficult to complete, or even begin, his work.

He believed that isolation left him prey to troubling thoughts and intensified his depression. As he wrote in his first sermon, "in solitude perplexity swells into distraction, and grief settles into melancholy." Social life and conversation with friends, especially late at night, allowed him to deploy his extensive knowledge and test the validity of his arguments.

Always unwilling to part from company, he was eager to prolong every social event and emphatically declared: "whoever thinks of going to bed before twelve o'clock is a scoundrel."[12]

Johnson loved sleep as much as anyone else and felt it relieved the miseries of life by providing welcome intervals of oblivion. But the diuretic effects of gallons of tea, as well as his voracious overeating, aggravated his chronic insomnia. His restless nights and late mornings made him vow to get up early, and he felt guilty when he could not keep his resolutions. Johnson associated night not with rest, but with nightmares and guilty conscience, with fits of mourning and lustful longings, with fears of death and damnation. Johnson found it so difficult to get up in the morning that he thought of using a mechanical pulley, turned by a wide-awake servant, who would place a chain under his arms and gradually raise him from his bed. He identified with (and perhaps envied) the idle yet somehow industrious poet Elijah Fenton. Like Johnson himself, Fenton "was tall and bulky, inclined to corpulence, which he did not lessen by much exercise; for he was very sluggish and sedentary . . . would lie a-bed and be fed with a spoon . . . rose late, and when he had risen, sat down to his book or papers."

Once Johnson had bestirred himself and breakfasted, he made sure to stay fully occupied throughout the day and night. During both his marriage and his celibate years he dealt capably with practical details and tried (though he had servants) to be self-sufficient. A friend told Boswell that "the Dr. valued himself a good deal on being able to do everything for himself. . . . He knew how to mend his own stockings, to darn his linen or to sew a button on his cloaths. 'I am not (he would often say) an helpless man.'"[13]

Johnson had an endlessly inquiring mind. A contemporary of the distinguished chemists Joseph Priestley and Antoine Lavoisier, he loved to occupy himself with chemical experiments, and suggested both the delightful and magical aspects of chemistry by calling it "enchanting." Hawkins recalled that in his early years in the Middle Temple, Johnson (like Sherlock Holmes) furnished his chambers with alembics, retorts and other vessels suitable for practical inquiries.

Later on, when he moved in with the Thrales at Streatham, he infected Hester with his passion. They rigged up a laboratory and amused themselves by distilling herbs, extracting essences, coloring liquids and observing that some of their bubbles were hexagonal. The playwright Arthur Murphy, an old friend, once discovered Johnson, "all covered with soot like a chimney-sweeper, in a little room, with an intolerable heat and strange smell, as if he had been acting Lungs in [Ben Jonson's play] *The Alchymist,* making *aether.*" Henry Thrale, fearful that Johnson might ignite himself or blow up the house, was forced to intervene. Hester, also alluding to alchemy, wrote that Henry was "persuaded, that [Johnson's] short sight would have been his destruction in a moment, by bringing him close to a fierce and violent flame. . . . Future experiments in chemistry were too dangerous, and Mr. Thrale insisted that we should do no more towards finding the philosopher's stone," which, if it could ever be found, would magically transform base metals into gold.

Johnson was sufficiently objective to satirize his own experiments as both perilous and pointless. In his critical self-portrait in *Idler* 31, he noted that Mr. Sober "draws oils and waters, and essences and spirits, which he knows to be of no use; sits and counts the drops as they come from his retort, and forgets that, while a drop is falling, a moment flies away." In *Rambler* 199 he also wrote, with comic exaggeration, about the terrible effects of up-to-date scientific inquiries—shock treatments, human flight and blood transfusions—when scientists attempted to experiment on themselves: "I have fallen eleven times speechless under the shock of electricity; I have twice dislocated my limbs, and once fractured my skull, in essaying to fly; and four times endangered my life by submitting to the transfusion of blood."[14]

As his behavior and experiments suggest, Johnson was a man of extremes. He told Hester, when analyzing his swings of mood, that "in all our conversation my *genius* ["nature, disposition"] is always in extremes; I am very noisy, or very silent; very gloomy, or very merry; very sour, or very kind." Throughout his life he struggled hard to find a proper balance. Boswell confirmed that his mirth was as violent and extreme as his habitual gloom. On one notable occasion, and with very slight provocation, he "burst into such a fit of laughter, that he appeared to be almost in a convulsion; and, in order to support himself, laid hold of one of the posts at the side of the foot pavement, and sent forth peals so loud, that in the silence of the night his voice seemed to resound from Temple-bar to Fleet-ditch," that is, from one end of Fleet Street to the other.[15]

By contrast, and very frequently, the tenderhearted and confidently masculine man of feeling, intensely aware of the sadness of life, would unashamedly collapse into a puddle of tears. He was deeply moved when reading from his *Vanity of Human Wishes* about the terrible obstructions the poor scholar had to suffer; and he burst into tears when he read the *Dies Irae* (Days of Wrath), a Latin hymn on the Day of Judgment, often sung in a requiem mass. He parted with tears of tenderness from his close friend Richard Savage in London and from a Benedictine prior he met in Paris, knowing, or at least fearing, that he would never see them again. After his habitual rudeness, he would tearfully apologize; after his last quarrel with Hester, he wrote her that tears stood in his eyes.

Thoughts of dead friends always moved him deeply. He wept when he spoke about his friend's son, the late Dr. Richard Bathurst, when he told Hester about the death of his old family servant Kitty Chambers and when standing at David Garrick's grave. Frances Reynolds saw him break into tears when she mentioned a monument that a widowed mother had erected on the grave of her dead child. He again burst into tears when Boswell told him that friends had tried to secure a government grant to finance his longed-for trip to Italy. Another friend saw him weep copiously when, burning his mother's letters, he realized how much he still missed her. On all these occasions Johnson, sensitive, intense and overwhelmed by emotion, wisely allowed himself to express his feelings and release them with his tears.

Though Johnson was emotional, he was equally intellectual. Everyone was impressed by his universal knowledge. The great economist Adam Smith once observed that Johnson "knew more books than any man alive." His hero was the seventeenth-century Dutch jurist and theologian Hugo Grotius, who annotated the Bible and used his sharp legal mind to demonstrate the truth of the Christian religion. Johnson's mind, as he wrote in *Rambler* 122 of the learned seventeenth-century historian Edward Hyde, earl of Clarendon, was "crouded with ideas, and desirous of imparting them," and he praised the intellectual qualities that he shared with Clarendon: "knowledge of nature and of policy; the wisdom of his maxims, the justness of his reasonings."

Johnson believed that even his greatest strength carried grave liabilities. The most richly endowed men had the greatest responsibility, he wrote in *Rambler* 77, to use their God-given talents to the fullest and were seriously remiss if they failed to do so: "Those, whom God has favoured with superiour faculties, and made eminent for quickness of intuition, and accuracy of distinctions, will certainly be regarded as culpable in His eye, for defects and deviations which, in souls less enlightened, may be guiltless."[16]

Johnson was deeply troubled by the agonizing disparity between his mental and physical faculties. As he observed in a poignant passage in *Adventurer* 120, a man's "mind, however elevated, inhabits a body subject to innumerable casualties, of which he must always share the dangers and the pains . . . at one time groaning with insufferable anguish, at another dissolved in listlessness and languor." He struggled not only to overcome his physical disabilities, but also to maintain rational control during his deep depressions and nervous breakdowns.

When Johnson's friends tried to define his essential character, which combined rudeness and cruelty with gentleness and kindness (especially toward the weak and the unfortunate), they came up with a series of contradictions. Murphy variously mentioned "his lassitude, his morbid melancholy, his love of fame, his dejection, his tavern-parties, and his wandering reveries." Boswell insisted that his harsh qualities were more than balanced by his profound goodness and purity of spirit. He was "hard to please and easily offended, impetuous and irritable in his temper, but of a most humane and benevolent heart."[17]

Johnson's character, conversation and writing had a great deal in common with another great Englishman, Winston Churchill, equally courageous and eager for experience. Both were plagued by the "Black Dog" of depression, which they inherited from their fathers, first experienced when young and struggled with throughout their lives. Both ate and drank to excess, and cried frequently and abundantly. They tried to keep themselves feverishly busy, exhausted their friends and did not go to bed till the early hours of the morning. They were brilliant talkers, especially adept at cruel but witty insults, and came up with memorable lines in almost every conversation.

Both had idiosyncratic writing habits, employed a team of researchers and aides, and were extremely productive. They left crucial work until the very last moment, then dictated as fast as they could to earn much-needed money. Both invented speeches about political events in Parliament, wrote in the grand rhetorical style and signed their letters (in Churchill's case anachronistically) "Your obedient servant." Both were intensely chauvinistic about England. Johnson exclaimed, "for any thing I see, foreigners are fools." Churchill agreed with him, asserting: "Why be apologetic about Anglo-Saxon superiority? We are superior."[18] Both men embodied the spirit of their age.

GRUB STREET
1737

I

J ohnson had set out for London, accompanied by Garrick, in
March 1737. After three days on the road, he reached the hills on
the northern side of London. He saw the city extended below him,
partly shrouded in the smoke from coal fires, and the Thames curving
around the southern edge, filled with the bobbing masts of trading
ships. In those days "the built-up area was about three miles across,
from Hyde Park in the west to Stepney in the east. Nowhere had
development extended farther than a mile north of the Thames, so that
open fields were still everywhere within walking distance." What sort
of life did Johnson find there, and how did he manage to make his way
in that huge, unfamiliar city of more than half a million people?

He loved the coffeehouses and taverns, the teeming crowds and
spectacle of humanity that swirled around him. He thought that Fleet
Street (his usual residence) had "a very animated appearance," but that
"the full tide of human existence [was] at Charing Cross."[1] Yet the
volatile crowds, excited by brutal entertainments—bloody cockfights
and bull-baiting, boxing matches and female combatants—could

quickly become cruel, ferocious and violent. Women in bodices and short petticoats fought till their blood flowed, and had their wounds stitched up right in front of the spectators. A man who'd starved his idiot wife to death and was condemned to hang was eager to choose a less horrible end for himself: "Apprehensive of being torn in pieces [by the mob], he hastened the executioner to perform his office." When people got completely out of control, a magistrate would publicly read the Riot Act of 1715, and the mob had to disperse or risk being fired on by the soldiers called out to keep order.

Coming from a provincial town, Johnson would have been shocked by the surging traffic, ear-shattering noise and splattering filth. A. R. Humphreys wrote that London had an "unruly populace, sewage and offal in the roads, cobbles slippery with mud, iron-sheathed posts to guard jostling pedestrians from the wheels of carriages, shop-signs hiding the sky and creaking in the wind." The heads of traitors, especially those who'd been drawn and quartered after the Jacobite Rebellions of 1715 (and later, in 1745), were mounted on pikes and displayed until 1777 on Temple Bar (the elegant stone gate designed by Sir Christopher Wren, between Fleet Street and the Strand).

The large shop signs darkened the narrow streets at midday, and when Johnson first arrived there was scarcely any illumination at night. His mother told him there were two kinds of people in London: the peaceful folk who gave way at the wall when someone approached them and moved toward the dangerous center of the street, and the aggressive types who "took the wall" and kept safely to it. Johnson no doubt kept the wall, and people gave way when they saw the approach of his huge bulk. Ladies and gentlemen protected themselves from the mob by riding in coaches or traveling in sedan chairs, carried on long poles by burly porters. In *Idler* 28 Johnson has one of the carriers complain about the inequities of his job: "It is common for men of the most unwieldy corpulence to croud themselves into a chair, and demand to be carried for a shilling as far as an airy young lady whom we scarcely feel upon our poles."[2]

The coal smoke destroyed most plants and flowers and wrecked many human lungs. It so enveloped the sky that Johnson, after living in London for some time, no longer noticed the change of seasons. The historian

Liza Picard emphasized the cacophonous noise: "The screech of iron tyres on cobbles and granite streets, crashing and bumping over the potholes and drains, horses' metal-shod hooves clattering, wooden axles squeaking, coachmen and carters shouting, dogs barking." Since most of London's trade in commodities like coal, salt, milk and oatcakes was carried on outside the shops, the street vendors and ballad singers had to pitch their cries above the competing din. All this must have distracted poor Johnson, who liked to sleep late and found it hard to begin his work.

The filth and smells of eighteenth-century London were noxious and all-pervasive. People rarely bathed in the household basins or pumps in the yard—Johnson himself hated total immersion—and everybody smelled powerfully of sweat, tobacco, bad breath, dirty clothes and dirtier bodies. Glittering rooms contained chamber pots, which were brought out and used by the men after the dinner had been consumed and the ladies had left the table. Giacomo Casanova, visiting from Italy, was surprised to see in fashionable St. James' Park "the hinder parts of persons relieving nature in the bushes." Johnson exclaimed that London "abounds with such heaps of filth, as a savage would look on with amazement."[3] The rubbish that was supposed to be thrown in the great ditch outside the city walls was more conveniently flung out of the window and (quite often) onto the heads of pedestrians. Animal and human excrement, dead cats and dogs, and every other kind of refuse ran down open drains in the middle of the streets, a system that remained until the nineteenth century.

Though bricks began to replace wood after the Great Fire of London had destroyed vast areas of the city in 1666, most buildings were still made of timber and thatch. Fire—used for cooking, heating and light—was a constant hazard. Since there were almost no street numbers, houses were identified by their proximity to local landmarks. Most houses, except the meanest, had piped water by 1737. The poorest inhabitants lived in damp underground dwellings, where several people of different sexes and ages might share the same bed.

Like most people, Johnson ate his main meal in the late afternoon. "Most cooking," wrote Hogarth's biographer, "was done on an open range or taken to the bakers' ovens, and the common diet was starchy and substantial—bread, beef, beer and cheese, and broths of peas and beans." Though Johnson loved to talk, he focused intently on his food and declared, "a man is in general better pleased when he has a good dinner upon his table, than when his wife talks Greek."

Johnson paid scant attention to clothing, which in the eighteenth century could be quite elaborate—like the costumes worn in Mozart's elegant operas. Women wore voluminous skirts and petticoats, but went without knickers; they wore stays (or corsets) to enhance their figures and fortified deficient eyebrows with strips of mouse's skin. Men wore breeches that had a front flap instead of a fly. They shaved their heads and wore nightcaps to keep warm in bed. Liza Picard wrote that their fancy "wigs were powdered white with wheat starch for formal occasions. If the wearer had a powdering closet he could sit masked and caped while the powder was blown on to his wig with bellows." A contemporary wrote, "in hot weather, fat unwieldy men who are obliged to walk the street are doubling up their wigs to go in their pockets and putting their handkerchiefs between their hats and their foreheads."[4] Thieves, melting into the crowd, carried little boys on their shoulders to pluck expensive wigs from the heads of unwary pedestrians. Wigs were all the rage until the 1770s, when they suddenly went out of fashion. Beards, popular in the seventeenth and nineteenth centuries, were not worn in the eighteenth.

II

Johnson soon saw that in London distinctions of rank—based on birth, title, wealth, residence and occupation—were more clear-cut, and more extreme, than in Lichfield. There was an inhuman disparity between the rich and the poor. In the eighteenth century legal rights, moral standards and social behavior matched the interests of the wealthy, landowning class. The historian Roy Porter noted that England's "political institutions and its distributions of wealth and power were unashamedly inegalitarian, hierarchical, hereditary and privileged." Johnson accepted this social system, despite its economic inequities, and justified it (with rather shaky logic) by telling Boswell: "Mankind are happier in a state of inequality and subordination. Were they to be in a pretty state of equality, they would soon degenerate into brutes. . . . They would have no intellectual improvement. All intellectual improvement arises from leisure; all leisure arises from one working for another." Laborers toiled in the fields and towns so that gentlemen would be free to think and write.

People constantly flocked into London from the countryside, only to live there in degrading poverty. During the unusually cold winter of 1739, two years after Johnson arrived, the temperature stayed below freezing for three whole months. When the price of coal shot up, the poor could no longer afford to buy it, and thousands froze to death or died of starvation. Beggars swarmed in the streets, and each week about twenty of them died there. Johnson was acutely aware of their suffering. He always felt compassion and pity for these unfortunates, and did everything in his power to help them. He believed that "there is scarcely, among the evils of human life, any so generally dreaded as poverty," that "the miseries of the poor are such as cannot easily be borne" and that "a decent provision for the poor is the true test of civilization."[5]

Instead of condemning beggars, Johnson sympathized with their plight. He blamed their inability to survive, in a world that afforded no protection for the poor, on "impotence, idleness, ignorance of the arts of life, or misfortune." He believed that most beggars were willing to work, but were forced to be idle. When an elaborate display of fireworks was put on in Green Park to celebrate a (temporary) suspension of hostilities in the war with France, he criticized the wasteful spectacle and sensibly argued that "many widows and orphans, whom the war has ruined, might be relieved, by the expence which is now about to evaporate in smoke, and to be scattered in rockets."

Johnson identified with the poor from a kindhearted, Christian sense of charity, as well as from the raw wounds of his own early poverty and failures. When he was still poor, he frequently gave all his small coins to beggars, who watched for him when he left his house to dine at the tavern. He also pressed pennies into the hands of children, bundled in rags and sleeping in the street, so they could have a crust of bread for breakfast. He took pleasure in thinking how happy the starvelings would be when they woke up in the morning and found the unexpected bounty. When asked why he constantly wasted money on beggars, he sweetly replied that it enabled them to beg on. Hester Thrale observed, "he loved the poor as I never yet saw any one else do, with an earnest desire to make them happy.—What signifies, says some one, giving halfpence to common beggars? They only lay it out in gin or tobacco. 'And why should they be denied such sweeteners of their existence (says Johnson)?'"[6]

The children of the poor suffered even more than the adults. They were habitually whipped by their parents, teachers and masters; and many, with no chance of education, were sent out to work at an early age. There were about 500 little chimney sweeps in London who were also used to extinguish fires. They enriched their employers, but were often burned in the process. Hundreds of wretched boys who couldn't find work, wrote the distinguished blind judge Sir John Fielding (half-brother of the novelist Henry), were abandoned by their families: "Strangers to Beds, they lay about under Bulks [overhangs projecting from shopfronts] and in ruinous empty Houses." Children taken into the poorhouse, maintained by the parish for indigent residents, endured even harsher conditions. In the early 1750s, infant mortality in these institutions was as high as 90 to 100 percent. Many children, driven to crime, were severely punished. Roy Porter reported that "when a seven-year-old girl was hanged in Norwich for stealing a petticoat, no one protested." In contrast to the prevailing attitude, Johnson sympathized with these children.

Poverty forced many desperate adults into crime, and stealing was the most common offense. The dark streets were patrolled by incompetent watchmen, whom Henry Fielding described as "poor old decrepit people who are from want of bodily strength incapable of getting a living by work." Since there was no police force and it was very difficult to catch criminals, those unfortunate enough to be apprehended were cruelly punished. Criminal penalties included standing in the pillory while being pelted with rotten vegetables, as well as flogging, branding and transportation to the American colonies. Crime and punishment were still medieval. Witchcraft remained an offense until 1736, and the legal authorities authorized barbaric methods of torture. In the reign of George II (1727–60) a man was "pressed to death by . . . *peine forte et dure* for refusing to plead on a charge of felony."[7]

Prisons were so unhealthy and crowded—and the inmates so ravaged by hunger, brutal conditions and contagious diseases—that confinement often amounted to a sentence of death. Bridewell, a house of correction, had a stern regime of hard work to punish petty offenders. But prisons were mainly used as places of detention. They were not intended to punish or reform, but to prevent the debtor from absconding or to hold the suspected criminal until the trial, which might lead to freedom or to hanging. The Marshalsea and the Fleet were debtors' prisons. The forbidding and infamous Newgate, the main criminal prison for metropolitan London, housed serious offenders and was run by notoriously corrupt warders. It provided nothing but chains, bread and water (inmates had to buy their own food and drink), and was synonymous with misery, despair and death.

A historian noted that "in 1716 as many as 60,000 debtors, some for the smallest sums, were imprisoned in England and Wales: the Marshalsea alone had 700–800, of whom . . . [in 1719] 300 had died in less than three months." In 1759 Johnson estimated that there were still 20,000 debtors in prison, which amounted to three percent of England's population of six million. There were so many imprisoned debtors, in fact, that the authorities, instead of building another place to house them, allowed some to be given a ticket of leave in the liberties of the Fleet, where they could live outside the prison and not be subject to arrest.

In his farsighted *Idler* 38, Johnson attacked debtors' prisons as inhumane, corrupt and economically absurd. If the debtors could not pay their creditors when they were outside prison and still able to work, they certainly could not redeem themselves when closely confined. Johnson condemned "the corrosion of resentment, the heaviness of sorrow, the corruption of confined air, the want of exercise, and sometimes of food, the contagion of diseases from which there is no retreat, and the severity of tyrants against whom there can be no resistance." Aware that male prisoners, by paying the warder one shilling, could have sex for a night with a female inmate, Johnson crusaded against the way in which "the lewd inflame the lewd, the audacious harden the audacious." Estimating that a quarter of the debtors died each year, he emphasized the futility of the system: "Thus perish yearly five thousand men, overborne with sorrow, consumed with famine, or putrefied by filth; many of them in the most vigorous and useful part of life; for the thoughtless and imprudent are commonly young, and the active and busy are seldom old." Appealing for sympathy and pity for those trapped by debt, he argued for the abolition of these prisons. The system caused endless suffering, "the wife bewailing her husband, or the children begging the bread which their father would have earned."

Worse by far than the prisons were the laws that demanded hanging for minor offenses. In an age when property was considered far more valuable than human life, crimes like theft and poaching, coining and forging, which threatened ownership, business and trade, were punished with unrivaled savagery. It was certainly easier to execute than to imprison or try to reform a criminal. There were ninety-seven executions in 1785, of which seventy-four were for robbery and only one for murder. Roy Porter wrote, "there had been fifty capital offenses in 1689; by 1800 there were four times that number. Many specified death for small-scale theft such as pickpocketing goods valued more than 1 shilling, or shoplifting items worth more than 5 shillings." Ian Gilmour's more detailed discussion added, "the death penalty was applicable . . . not only to murder and robbery, but to such bizarre crimes as being disguised within the Mint, maliciously cutting hop-binds growing on poles, being a soldier or a seaman wandering about without a pass . . . consorting with gypsies, cutting down growing trees, stealing fish out of any river or pond, or impersonating the out-pensioners of Greenwich Hospital."[8]

The extreme severity of the law actually served to mitigate the punishments. Juries, reluctant to convict for capital crimes, usually valued the stolen items at less than five shillings, and only about half the people convicted were actually hanged. Those who reached the gallows were usually hardened offenders, people without influential patrons, perpetrators of particularly horrible crimes and criminals convicted when the authorities wanted to frighten the mob with exemplary punishments. The criminologist Leon Radzinowicz recorded the grim statistics: "During the twenty years from 1750 to 1769, 909 offenders were capitally convicted, of whom 551 were executed, for crimes committed in London and Middlesex only. In the year 1770 alone, 91 capital verdicts were given and 49 offenders were put to death."

In the eighteenth century 1,200 people were hanged in London. Except for three religious feasts—Easter, Whitsuntide (the seventh Sunday after Easter) and Christmas—the principal holidays were the eight public hanging days at Tyburn. Hanging was not merely a deterrent to crime, but a source of entertainment. The ritual that began with the morbid procession of the condemned, and ended with the spectacle on the gallows, was as formal as a play:

> The condemned, each wearing a halter around his neck and accompanied by his coffin, were taken in carts the three miles from Newgate to Tyburn [across the city from east to west and down what is now Oxford Street to Marble Arch]. . . .
>
> The crowd regarded victims as heroes, especially when they exited with a swagger. The procession from prison to gallows . . . would last about two hours, the carts stopped at taverns, and many condemned men were drunk by the time they reached their end—they would promise to pay for their drink "when they came back." . . .
>
> The execution carts were driven up to the triangular gallows, and when all the preliminaries had been completed, the noose adjusted around the neck and a cap pulled down over the face, the carts were driven away and the condemned left dangling. . . .
>
> Death by hanging was in fact slow strangulation because the drop was not sufficient to break the victim's neck, and to pull down the feet was an act of mercy frequently performed. . . .
>
> The hangman [a contemporary wrote] does not give himself the trouble to put them out of their Pain; but some of their Friends or Relations do it for them. They pull the dying Person by the Legs, and beat his Breast, to dispatch him as soon as possible.[9]

Johnson was passionately opposed to this indiscriminate use of capital punishment. Two members of his household, Robert Levet's wife and Bet Flint, were acquitted of hanging crimes—theft and pickpocketing—that they had actually committed. He also defended (as we shall see) four people accused or convicted of capital offenses: the poet Richard Savage and Admiral John Byng, in print, after their deaths; the lexicographer Giuseppe Baretti and the clergyman William Dodd, in person, while they were still alive. Savage was pardoned for, and Baretti acquitted of, murder (both were Johnson's close friends); Byng was unjustly executed for cowardice, Dodd for forgery.

Johnson believed that criminal law, however harsh, was ineffective. Emphasizing men's sinfulness and indifference to damnation, he told Boswell that they "are evidently and confessedly so corrupt, that all the laws of heaven and earth are insufficient to restrain them from crimes." Drawing on works like Thomas More's *Utopia* (1516), Charles Montesquieu's *The Spirit of the Laws* (1748) and Henry Fielding's *An Enquiry into the Late Increase of Robbers* (1751), he argued that the punishment must fit the crime and that robbery, unlike murder, should not be a capital offense. His close friends agreed with him. Oliver Goldsmith believed that Parliament should reform rather than increase the severity of the law. Edmund Burke consistently opposed the multiplication of penal laws, thought the whole system was "radically defective" and agreed that the criminal law was abominable.

Rambler 114, one of Johnson's greatest essays, passionately advocated a "more rational and equitable adaptation of penalties to offences." Basing his argument on the biblical injunction in John 8:7—"He that is without sin among you, let him first cast a stone"—he insisted that everyone watching a criminal dragged to execution must ask in his own heart, "who knows whether this man is not less culpable than me?" If people could truly grasp their own essential sinfulness, he argued, "few among those that croud in thousands to the legal massacre, and look with carelessness, perhaps with triumph, on the utmost exacerbations of human misery, would then be able to return without horror and dejection." He then condemned the current state of the law in which "capital infractions are multiplied, and crimes very different in their degrees of enormity are equally subjected to the severest punishment."

After demonstrating the moral and legal flaws of indiscriminate capital punishment, Johnson showed that the system simply did not work: "the experience of past times gives us little reason to hope that any reformation will be effected by a periodical havoc of our fellow beings." He concluded by stating his characteristically humane belief that "the heart of a good man cannot but recoil at the thought of punishing a slight injury with death." In his *Thoughts on . . . Falkland's Islands* he continued his crusade in a digression that condemned the "mischievous cunning . . . held by [Sir Matthew] Hale that children may be hanged."[10] Boswell, who had a morbid streak and obsessively attended public hangings (sometimes of his own unfortunate clients), experienced both horror and dejection, but Johnson strongly disapproved and never went. Far ahead of his time, his writings paved the way for legal reforms that would not be made until the mid-nineteenth century.

III

Many eighteenth-century writers enjoyed a professional income and did not have to live entirely on their writings. Samuel Richardson was a printer, Henry Fielding a magistrate, Laurence Sterne a clergyman, Tobias Smollett a doctor. But Johnson had no private income or salary, no university degree, no influential relations or friends, no aristocratic patrons. After his failure as a teacher, he abandoned the quest for a modest but secure salary, and looked for work that would not be compromised by his appearance. In London, where poverty could quickly lead to starvation or prison, he committed himself to the uncertain and exiguous income of a hack writer on Grub Street, now called Milton Street. Johnson defined it as "a street near Moorfields in London, much inhabited by writers of small histories, dictionaries, and temporary poems." Living day to day and hand to mouth, he was condemned to toil in the service of demanding editors.

Johnson was particularly fond of Richard Savage, Oliver Goldsmith and Christopher Smart, all of whom had experienced the hardships of Grub Street. And he always had before him the fearful example of Samuel Boyse, one of the starving writers on the *Gentleman's Magazine,* who was forced to pawn his shirt, then his breeches and waistcoat, and finally the rest of his clothes and his bedsheets. Though stripped of all essentials, Boyse continued to turn out the words to fend off starvation: "He sat up in bed with a blanket wrapped about him, through which he had cut a hole large enough to admit his arm, and placing the paper upon his knee, scribbled, in the best manner he could, the verses he was obliged to make." Hester Thrale added some vivid details about this wildly improvident hack: "when he was almost perishing with hunger, and some money was produced [by Johnson] to purchase him a dinner, he got a bit of roast beef, but could not eat it without ketchup, and laid out the last half guinea he possessed in truffles and mushrooms, eating them in bed too, for want of clothes or even a shirt to sit up in."

When Johnson first arrived in London, the bookseller John Wilcox loaned him five guineas and then asked, "how do you mean to earn your livelihood in this town?" Johnson innocently replied, "by my literary labours." Wilcox, staring at his scarred face and broad shoulders, shook his head and declared: "By your literary labours!—You had better buy a porter's knot." This double shoulder pad, with a loop passing around the forehead, would have turned him into a beast of burden.

A poor Irish painter soon gave Johnson useful advice on how to disguise his poverty while surviving on the dignity of deprivation:

[He said that] thirty pounds a year was enough to enable a man to live there without being contemptible. He allowed ten pounds for clothes and linen. He said that a man might live in a garret at eighteen-pence a week; few people would inquire where he lodged; and if they did, it was easy to say, "Sir, I am to be found at such a place." By spending three-pence in a coffee-house, he might be for some hours every day in very good company; he might dine for six-pence, breakfast on bread and milk for a penny, and do without supper. On *clean-shirt day* he went abroad, and paid visits.

But Johnson, indifferent to personal hygiene and attire, rarely had a clean shirt.

He first took lodgings in the house of a Mr. Norris, a stay maker on Exeter Street near the Strand, who had Staffordshire connections. He also found, in the big city, cosmopolitan conversation with anonymous friends. He told Boswell:

> I dined very well for eight-pence, with very good company, at the Pine Apple in New-street, just by. Several of them had travelled. They expected to meet every day; but did not know one another's names. It used to cost the rest a shilling, for they drank wine; but I had a cut of meat for six-pence, and bread for a penny, and gave the waiter a penny; so that I was quite well served, nay, better than the rest, for they gave the waiter nothing.

Johnson, who had wanted to be served at Oxford and refused to become a Servitor, tipped the poor waiter, though very poor himself.

When still living in Lichfield, in November 1734, Johnson had sent a letter to Edward Cave, owner of the *Gentleman's Magazine,* the leading periodical of the time. He offered "on reasonable terms" (any terms, really) to fill a column with "short literary Dissertations in Latin or English, Critical remarks on Authors Ancient or Modern, forgotten Poems that deserve Revival."[11] He signed the letter "S. Smith," in case his offer was, as he feared, rejected. Cave, though hungry for copy, was unimpressed by this offer and did not respond (though he saved the letter). Johnson later placed an equally hopeless advertisement in the magazine for his Edial school.

Johnson's grossly flattering Latin poem "Ad Urbanum," an allusion to Cave's pseudonym "Sylvanus Urban" (a man of the country and the city), was far more effective. This poem, his first known contribution to the *Gentleman's Magazine,* appeared in March 1738, a year after he reached London. Later translated into English, it gallantly defended Cave against the rude treatment of his jealous rivals:

> Hail Urban! indefatigable man,
> Unwearied yet by all thy useful toil!
> Whose num'rous slanderers assault in vain;

Whom no base calumny can put to foil.
But still the laurel on thy learned brow
Flourishes fair, and shall for ever grow.

The poem got him the job and launched his career, and he became a
faithful, hardworking editor of the magazine from 1738 to 1745. He
worked above St. John's Gate in Clerkenwell (the only surviving part
of a medieval priory, which had two square towers above a wide arch)
just as he had in his room above the gateway of Pembroke College.

In his brief "Life of Edward Cave" (1754), Johnson wrote that his
boss, patron and "kind benefactor" was born in 1691 in Warwickshire
(the neighboring county to Johnson's Staffordshire), and had worked as
a collector of excise taxes, on a weekly newspaper in Norwich and in a
printing house. He married a young widow and saved enough money
to buy the *Gentleman's Magazine* in 1731. He was, like Johnson, "a man
of large stature, not only tall but bulky, and was, when young, of remarkable strength and activity." When Cave's wife died in 1751 (the year
before Tetty's death), "he seemed not at first much affected by her death,
but in a few days lost his sleep and his appetite, which he never recovered." The eighteenth-century historian John Nichols recorded that
Cave "had no great relish for mirth. . . . His temper was phlegmatic. . . .
[He was] a man of saturnine disposition."

Cave usually began a conversation with visitors by asking their
opinion of his magazine. He never looked out the window, Johnson
said, without thinking how he could improve the contents of the periodical. Obsessed with sales and subscriptions, he'd urge on his writers by exclaiming, "Let us have something good next month." Johnson
praised his energy and persistence, a useful complement to his own
sluggish mode of operation: "his resolution and perseverance were very
uncommon; in whatever he undertook, neither expense nor fatigue
were able to repress him; but his constancy was calm, and to those
who did not know him appeared faint and languid; but he always went
forward, though he moved slowly. . . . His mental faculties were slow.
He saw little at a time, but that little he saw with great exactness."[12]
Johnson liked and admired Cave, and had a lot in common with him.

Both tall, strong, hardworking, self-made men came from the West Midlands and had gloomy temperaments. They both married widows who predeceased them, and both were deeply affected by their wives' deaths.

The early issues of the *Gentleman's Magazine,* before Johnson joined the staff, published grossly indecent verse and advertised indecent books in gross language. But it was soon cleaned up and began to bring out a miscellany of poetry, essays, book reviews, financial notes and articles on foreign affairs, as well as personal notices and useful information on tides, births and deaths, and bankruptcies. Over the years Johnson, writing as much as he could as fast as he could, published verse, reviews, short biographies, translations and abridgements of foreign works, and the highly successful *Debates in Parliament.* With learning and sarcasm he blasted the disorderly squadron of enemies who had dared to attack the magazine. Seizing the moral high ground and assuming a haughty tone, he declared: "Of the clamours, rage and calumnies of our competitors, we have seldom taken any notice; not only because it is cruelty to insult the depressed, and folly to engage with desperation, but because we consider all their outcries, menaces, and boasts, as nothing more than advertisements in our favour, being evidently drawn up with the bitterness of baffled malice and disappointed hope."

Though he helped bring the circulation up to 10,000 copies a month in the late 1730s, the ragged Johnson was poorly rewarded by his "kindly benefactor." He signed one of his letters to Cave (whose name is the Latin word for "Beware") with the Latin word *impransus,* "without dinner." When Cave was entertaining a guest at dinner, "a plate of victuals was sent behind a screen, which was to Johnson, dressed so shabbily, that he did not choose to appear." He ate, as he wrote, anonymously, but was delighted to overhear the visitor praise his work. Johnson felt no resentment about his humble status, and after his patron's death exclaimed, "Poor dear Cave. I owed him much."[13]

While working for Cave, Johnson met three extraordinary writers, his first friends in literary London. Elizabeth Carter, eight years younger than Johnson, and the daughter of a Kentish clergyman, had been educated by her father and was a brilliant linguist. In addition to French, Italian, Spanish, Portuguese and German, she knew Latin and Greek, Hebrew and Arabic. She translated Jean Pierre de Crousaz' *Examen* while Johnson translated his *Commentary,* both of which attacked Pope's *Essay on Man.* She was honored when Johnson asked her to contribute to the *Rambler,* and she wrote numbers 44 and 100.

Generously praising both her feminine and scholarly accomplishments, Johnson said, "my old friend, Mrs. Carter, could make a pudding, as well as translate Epictetus from the Greek, and work a handkerchief as well as compose a poem." Her standard translation of the Stoic philosopher, who believed that to live a peaceful life a man must learn how to endure and abstain, would have appealed to Johnson. Tetty, who didn't know Greek and prepared meals that Johnson criticized, was not well pleased when he praised Mrs. Carter. Despite her customary form of address, she remained unmarried. Referring to Louis XIV (the great enemy of England in the seventeenth century), and assuming the role of French courtier, Johnson told Cave that Elizabeth "ought to be celebrated in as many different Languages as Lewis le Grand." Fanny Burney mentioned Mrs. Carter's appealing innocence and described her "as being as ignorant of life as any nun."[14] Johnson sometimes dined with Mrs. Carter, and they became lifelong friends.

Johnson had an unaccountably soft spot for the second writer he met, the attorney and musicologist Sir John Hawkins, who became his first biographer. Hawkins seems to have been despised by most people, especially by his fierce rival James Boswell. Using Johnson's familiar name for his friend, Boswell bluntly asserted, "Hawky is no doubt very malevolent." Bishop Percy called him "a most detestable fellow"; and Samuel Dyer—linguist, scholar and respected member of Johnson's Club— agreed that he was "a man of the most mischievous, uncharitable, and malignant disposition." Even the kindly Joshua Reynolds felt that Hawkins compounded ill nature with hypocrisy: "though he assumed great outward sanctity, he was not only mean and groveling, but absolutely dishonest."

Fanny Burney, always alert and vivid, recorded Johnson's considered view of Hawkins. He began by praising Hawkins' fundamental honesty and concluded with a devastating assassination of his character:

"I believe him to be an honest man at the *bottom,*—but to be sure he is penurious; & he is mean;—& it must be owned he has a degree of brutality, & a tendency to savageness, that cannot easily be defended." . . . He said that Sir John & he once belonged to the same Club—but that, as he *Eat no supper,* after the first night of his admission, he desired to be excused *paying his share!*" "And *was* he excused?" "O yes—for no man is angry at another for being inferior to himself! . . . Sir John was a most *unclubable* man!"[15]

Hawkins, though grateful for his admission to the elite Club and intent on making a favorable impression at his debut dinner, could not help revealing his meanness with money. Johnson characteristically used his perverse individual behavior to establish a general principle of human nature.

The weirdest of the three authors he met while working for Cave was the pious rogue George Psalmanazar, whose real name is unknown. He took his pseudonym from Shalmaneser, the obscure despotic Assyrian king in 2 Kings 17:3 who suppressed a rebellion of the Israelites, but then softened it, with a nod to the biblical King David, to suggest the Psalms. Born in southern France in 1689/90, this cosmopolitan hybrid posed as an Irish pilgrim, studied theology, served in a German regiment, pretended he was Japanese and then, after coming to London in 1703, passed himself off as a native of Formosa. He roundly abused the Jesuits and claimed to be a convert to the Church of England.

In 1704 Psalmanazar published a *Historical and Geographical Description of Formosa,* an imaginary embellishment of a Dutch description of Japan, which invented a fake language, history and mythology, religion, customs and manners. In those days, when no one was able to check or confirm his account, the gross fraud was generally accepted as a faithful narrative. His book was a perfect example of the "romantick absurdities and incredible fictions" that Johnson had condemned in his preface to

Lobo's *Voyage to Abyssinia,* in which he had also attacked the Jesuits. Psalmanazar was even sent to Oxford by the bishop of London to teach Formosan to young gentlemen who were training to become missionaries and convert the heathen Chinese. If these zealots ever reached Formosa, they must have had some difficulty when trying to speak to the natives in a language that didn't exist.

The narrator in Jonathan Swift's "A Modest Proposal" (1729) justified his ironic plan to cannibalize Irish infants by alluding to Psalmanazar, who'd claimed that 18,000 boys were sacrificed annually on the Chinese island: "he confessed that this Expedient was put into his Head by the famous Salmanaazor, a Native of the Island of Formosa, who came from thence to London, above twenty Years ago, and in Conversation told my Friend, that in his Country, when any young Person happened to be put to Death, the Executioner sold the Carcase to *Persons of Quality,* as a prime Dainty." In *The Expedition of Humphry Clinker* (1771), Smollett described Psalmanazar's typically Grub Street descent from penury to charity to the threat of the poorhouse: "Psalmanazar, after having drudged half a century in the literary mill, in all the simplicity and abstinence of an Asiatic, subsists on the charity of a few booksellers, just sufficient to keep him from the parish."

In 1728, at almost the same time as Johnson, Psalmanazar had been suddenly converted by Law's recently published *Serious Call.* In 1747, after a long delay (for he had to earn a living), he publicly admitted his fraud; and he gave a full recantation in his *Memoirs,* published the year after his death, in 1764. A great lover of penitents, Johnson reverenced Psalmanazar, who'd confessed his sins, reformed his character and become pious, endured prolonged hardships and—though an opium addict—died an exemplary Christian. Though Johnson rarely made the first social overture (even with King George III), he told Boswell that he frequently sought out Psalmanazar and used to join him at an alehouse in the city. When someone asked Johnson if he'd ever mentioned Formosa, he said "he was afraid to mention even China." When asked if he ever contradicted him, Johnson replied, "I should as soon have thought of contradicting a bishop." Johnson called him "the *best* Man he had ever known." He told Hester Thrale, in a rare tribute, that his "piety, penitence, and virtue exceeded almost what we read as wonderful even in the lives of saints."[16]

Johnson, used to hardships and thrilled by his first publications, soon adjusted to Cave's slave-driving patronage and to the oppressions of Grub Street. His disabilities did not interfere with his writing, in which he could use his God-given talents. He'd finally found his true métier at the very heart of London journalism and began to acquire a circle of learned friends. During the next few years he turned out an impressive amount of work and helped make the *Gentleman's Magazine* a great success. In 1738 the publication of his poem *London* would show the literary world that he was the coming man.

6

LONDON OBSERVED
1737–1739

I

After Johnson had settled down to work with Cave, he'd echo the lament in Ecclesiastes 12:12, "of making many books there is no end," and complain about the "epidemical conspiracy for the destruction of paper." Yet, desperate to be recognized in the mass of print, he had to write unceasingly, both under his own name and anonymously. He tried his hand at every genre: translations, poetry, book reviews, parliamentary debates, periodical essays, literary criticism, Oriental fables, political pamphlets, biographies, letters, a verse tragedy, a travel book, even medical prescriptions. Despite his enormous output, Johnson actually suffered from writer's block. He had an inner compulsion to write and at the same time a disabling anxiety about writing itself.

When he finally got down to writing, his anxiety about the specific task was compounded with a sense of guilt about not writing enough, not practicing his craft. "He that has already trifled away those months and years, in which he should have laboured," he wrote in *Rambler* 71, "must remember that he has now only a part of that of which the whole is little; and that since the few moments remaining are to be considered as the last trust of heaven, not one is to be lost."[1] He felt his God-given talent, "the trust of heaven," was (in Milton's words) "death to hide." He experienced the deathlike inertia of depression and tortured himself with the fear that he was betraying his high purpose in life.

Johnson never completely dispelled his block, but learned how to deal with it. Once aroused from his characteristic indolence, he wrote with astonishing speed and insight, and from the beginning to the end of his career he was continually in demand. The process of writing is the subject of his greatest work, *The Lives of the Poets*; the sorrows of literary life appear in his two major poems, *London* and *The Vanity of Human Wishes*. Johnson's work constantly addresses the paradox of writer's block: the inability to work and the absolute necessity to do so. A great teacher, Johnson described the techniques he used to overcome procrastination and spur himself to work; he gave practical tips on how to get ideas, edit and revise; and with moral exhortation he urged writers to persevere to the end.

One source of his anxiety was his acute sense of the disparity between intention and execution, between what he'd hoped to achieve and the disappointing result. Infallibly pessimistic, Johnson was never satisfied with his work. His perennial sluggishness originated in this striving for perfection. As he explained to Hester Thrale, "he had never worked willingly in his Life *Man or Boy* nor ever did fairly make an Effort to do his best except three Times whilst he was at School." The fear of failure prevented him from completing or even starting a book. He had inscribed in Greek on his pocket watch the admonition from John 9:4: "the night cometh" when no man can work. In his life of Pope he mentioned "indolence, interruption, business, and pleasure" as impediments to literary work.[2] He discussed this issue, which preyed on his mind, in several of the essays in the *Idler* and the *Rambler*. He observed that when writers attempt to complete a piece of work, they are often paralyzed by fear. The mind is so often filled "with anxiety, that an habitual dislike steals upon us, and we shrink involuntarily from the remembrance of our task." Even if they summon up the energy to complete it, they are often overcome by a period of exhaustion that prevents further effort: "any uncommon exertion of strength, or perseverance in labour, is succeeded by a long interval of languor and weariness." Johnson's inability to complete a piece of writing made him feel that time was running out and often led to thoughts of futility and death: "procrastination is accumulated on procrastination, and one impediment succeeds another, till age shatters our resolution, or death intercepts the project of amendment."[3]

Johnson made writing sound so wretched, so full of mental anguish, that it's surprising he ever wanted to be an author. But he took satisfaction in the life of the mind and pride in his growing reputation. Early on, he discovered how to engage in literary work by accepting commissions from publishers rather than trying to generate ideas of his own. His early writing, completed in his twenties, was slow and laborious. He could scarcely face the task of translating Jerónimo Lobo's *Voyage to Abyssinia* and did the absolute minimum. His play *Irene,* his most elaborately planned and extensively revised work, took two years to write and was his most notable failure.

Johnson always required external stimuli to write—the stick of a deadline or the carrot of money. His arrest on two occasions for debt and the imminent threat of prison were, he found, a great spur to composition. He proceeded with habitual delay and characteristically sluggish resolution, dragging his feet but pressing forward. Since writing was painful and difficult, he considered financial rewards (however modest) an essential motivation. In one of his most famous pronouncements, Johnson, exaggerating for rhetorical effect, exclaimed, "No man but a blockhead ever wrote, except for money." Though he never dedicated his own work to anyone, the "blockhead" himself often wrote, free of charge, many prefaces and dedications—as well as advertisements, lines of poetry, chapters of novels, election speeches, legal briefs, law lectures, sermons, pleas for mercy and epitaphs—for close friends and deserving acquaintances who needed help or money. Loyalty to friends and appeals to his charity would immediately set him to work.

Despite his own mental struggles with writing, Johnson believed that it was above all a craft and maintained that a man could write "at any time, if he will set himself doggedly to do it." He criticized the poet Thomas Gray for his peculiar belief that he could compose only "at certain times, or at happy moments; a fantastic foppery" to which a man of learning and virtue should have been superior. Yet Johnson conceded that magical spurts of poetic inspiration could sometimes occur spontaneously—an unexpected benefit from getting down to the job. He noted "the lucky moments of animated imagination . . . those felicities which cannot be reproduced at will by wit and labour, but must arise unexpectedly in some hour propitious to poetry," and the influence exerted "by the causes wholly out of the performer's power, by hints of which he perceives not the origin, by sudden elevations of mind which he cannot produce in himself, and which sometimes rise when he expects them least."[4]

Johnson believed that intellectual preparation was the most effective way to break through his intermittent writer's block. He had grown up with books, and had spent years cataloguing Sir Robert Harley's 13,000-volume library. He took notes on books he read and enjoyed intense discussions with learned and lively friends. Once he got started, Johnson, whose head was stocked with books and mind full of ideas, could compose quickly. "When a man writes from his own mind," Johnson said, "he writes very rapidly. The greatest part of a writer's time is spent in reading, in order to write: a man will turn over half a library to make one book." Just as the writer may be struck by a happy inspiration during the process of writing, so he may get ideas from saturating himself in books. Using a botanical metaphor in *Rambler* 184, Johnson explained how reading could inspire a thought, which he would turn around in his mind and eventually put down on paper: "A careless glance upon a favorite author . . . is sufficient to supply the first hint or seminal idea, which enlarged by the gradual accretion of matter stored in the mind, is by the warmth of fancy easily expanded into flowers, and sometimes ripened into fruit."[5] Though getting started could be torture, he clearly enjoyed the preparatory process of reading and thinking.

Focusing directly on the problem of composition, he drew on his own experience when advising a young clergyman how to write and edit. First, Johnson said, when faced with a blank page, he should concentrate on getting his ideas down on paper without worrying about the precise order or exact expression. Then, with concrete words to work on, he should revise until he achieves the desired form. The miraculous creation of something out of nothing would give him the necessary confidence to continue: "in the labour of composition do not burden your mind with too much at once, do not exact from yourself at one effort of excogitation, propriety of thought and elegance of expression. Invent first and then embellish. The production of something where nothing was before, is an act of greater energy, than the expansion or decoration of the thing produced." Johnson told another young divine to compose in haste and revise at leisure: "I would say . . . 'Here is your [biblical] text; let me see how soon you can make a sermon.' Then I'd say, 'Let me see how much better you can make it.'" Johnson also warned against being seduced by the cant phrase and the fashionable word. Writers should be critical of their own work and strive for precision: "Read over your compositions, and where ever you meet with a passage which you think is particularly fine, strike it out."[6]

Johnson knew he had a limited impulse to work. More a sprinter than a long-distance runner, he broke down his major works into brief, manageable sections. As he said of the Earl of Rochester, "his pieces are commonly short, such as one fit of resolution would produce." He was able to take on potentially overwhelming projects like the *Dictionary,* the *Rambler,* the edition of Shakespeare and *The Lives of the Poets,* which took many years to complete, by building them up from individual words, short essays, separate plays and brief biographies.

In practice, Johnson did not follow his own excellent recommendations. He not only wrote with extraordinary speed, but seldom revised, or even reread, his apparently polished prose. He became so expert that he often produced his articles and essays under pressure and at the last minute, as the printer's boy stood ready for copy. During his sudden shifts from paralytic indolence to frenzied bouts of creativity, he followed the examples of both John Milton and Alexander Pope. Like Milton, he "composed as many lines as his memory would conveniently retain" before actually writing them down. Like Pope, he wrote in the first white heat of concentrated activity. Pope recalled, "the things that I have written fastest have always pleased me most. I wrote the *Essay on*

Criticism fast. . . . *The Rape of the Lock* was written fast. . . . I wrote most of the [translation of] *The Iliad* fast." Johnson's friend Thomas Percy, the collector of traditional ballads, explained Johnson's method: "[He] used to revolve the subject in his mind, and turn and form every period, till he had brought the whole to the highest correctness and the most perfect arrangement. Then his uncommonly retentive memory enabled him to deliver a whole essay, properly finished, whenever it was called for."[7]

Ironically, in view of his obsession with idleness and procrastination, Johnson wrote faster than any other major writer in English and sometimes produced as many as 12,000 words, or about 30 printed pages, in one sitting. At Oxford, in 1729, he translated into Latin the 108 lines of Pope's *Messiah* in one afternoon and the next morning. From 1740 to 1743 he invented the elaborate arguments and extended rejoinders of the *Debates in Parliament*—based solely on another man's brief notes on what the speakers had said—and wrote them down even faster than most men could transcribe the words. His heroic feats were legendary. John Nichols reported that Johnson, like a racehorse shooting out of the starting gate, often turned out "three columns of the [*Gentleman's*] *Magazine* within the hour. He once wrote ten small-print, double-columned pages in one day, and that not a long one, beginning perhaps at noon, and ending early in the evening." Since a column had about 600 words, this amounted to about 1,800 words an hour, 30 words a minute or one elegant word every two seconds.

Johnson translated from French six sheets, or 48 quarto pages, of Jean Pierre de Crousaz's *Commentary* on Pope's *Essay on Man* in one day. Since he rarely got up before noon, he often wrote by candlelight at night. He also composed in one sitting 48 octavo, or 24 quarto, pages of his great *Life of Richard Savage* (1744), staying up all night to do it, and prided himself on completing the 180 pages in a total of thirty-six hours. In one night he turned out his 5,000-word fable, *The Vision of Theodore, the Hermit of Teneriffe* (1748)—which he, but no one else, thought the best thing he ever wrote—after a convivial evening with friends in Holborn. He composed the first 70 lines (or even the first 100, according to another source) of his finest poem, *The Vanity of Human Wishes* (1749), in one morning, and had thought out the entire poem before putting a single couplet on paper. This titanic achievement seemed to belie his firm conviction that all human wishes were vain.

Between 1750 and 1752 he turned out regular copy on a journalistic treadmill. Twice a week and single-handedly he wrote the essays that made up the *Rambler*. In the final number he mournfully listed the difficulties he'd struggled to overcome. "He that condemns himself to compose on a stated day," he observed, "will often bring to his task an attention dissipated, a memory embarrassed, an imagination overwhelmed, a mind distracted with anxieties, a body languishing with disease." Despite these impediments, Johnson faithfully produced nearly all the 208 *Ramblers* "in haste, as the moment pressed, without even being read over by him before they were printed." He often wrote the 1,000 words (or 2 1/2 printed pages) of the *Idler*, a lighter sequel to the *Rambler*, with equal velocity. Told that the post would leave in half an hour, he exclaimed, "then we shall do very well," and instantly sat down and dashed it off.[8]

Johnson didn't seem to be troubled by anxiety when he wrote for someone else. He wrote twenty-seven sermons—most of them for his schoolboy friend the worldly lawyer and cleric John Taylor—tossing one off after a hearty dinner and posting it that night. He famously composed his Oriental fable *Rasselas* (1759) in the evenings of one week to pay for his mother's funeral. The political pamphlets of the 1770s, published toward the end of his life, were written with the same polish and panache. Proudly, even boastfully noting the exact day and time, he said *The False Alarm* (1770; 27 printed pages), an attack on the radical MP John Wilkes, was started at the Thrales' house at 8 PM on Wednesday and finished, 16 hours later, at noon on Thursday. He wrote *The Patriot* (1774; 11 pages), another attack on Wilkes, in a similarly expeditious fashion. His friends called for the pamphlet on a Friday and he completed it the following day. *Taxation No Tyranny* (1775; 44 pages), his attack on the American rebels, was, in a more leisurely fashion, knocked off within a week. The book-length, 165-page *Journey to the Western Islands of Scotland* (1775), based on letters sent to Hester Thrale, he wrote up as a diary in only 20 days.

Even when he was turning out enormous amounts of work and had become a respected man of letters, Johnson still felt he had not done enough. Despite his phenomenal output, he reproached himself for idleness. In his diary of April 1775 he revealed his anxiety and guilt: "When I look back upon resolutions of improvement and amendments, which year after year have been made and broken, either by negligence, forgetfulness, vicious idleness, casual interruption, or morbid infirmity, I find that so much of my life has stolen unprofitably away, and that I can descry by retrospection scarcely a few single days properly and vigorously employed."[9] Success could never assuage these feelings, because he was caught in a vicious circle: writing was hard work, and his efforts might come to nothing. This was bad enough, but success could also tempt him to laziness and complacency, and make him lose all he had gained: "labour and care are rewarded with success, success produces confidence, confidence relaxes industry, and negligence ruins that reputation which accuracy had raised."[10] Just as he always feared for his spiritual salvation, so he doubted that anything he wrote would fulfill his own high standards. Being a writer meant being in a state of constant vigilance and constant striving. For Johnson, writing well was a moral imperative and a lifelong struggle.

II

Johnson began his literary career with a weight of learning, and he brought an authoritative intellectual power to all his assertions and arguments. He believed that a man of letters could write about anything— poetry, history, science, travel—and that "heroes in literature" were obliged to "enlarge the boundaries of knowledge by discovering and conquering new regions of the intellectual world." They must use this new knowledge to build on and enhance the literary achievements of the past: "He that wishes to be counted among the benefactors of posterity, must add by his own toil to the acquisitions of his ancestors and secure his memory from neglect by some valuable improvement."

Johnson followed a traditional path when he began as a writer. He translated several works from French, and in his first major poem imitated Juvenal's Latin verse. But he believed that poets, who developed and sustained the language, were supreme. He confessed that translators had a much lower status, that "no man ever grew immortal by a translation" and that "no man was ever great by imitation."[11] Though he enthusiastically praised John Dryden's *Virgil* and Pope's *Homer,* he was, paradoxically, sceptical about translating poetry and told Boswell: "You may translate books of science exactly. You may also translate history, in so far as it is not embellished with oratory, which is poetical. Poetry, indeed, cannot be translated; and, therefore, it is the poets that preserve languages; for we would not be at the trouble to learn a language, if we could have all that is written in it just as well in a translation."

In the spring of 1734, while still idling in Lichfield and thrashing around for a subject, Johnson had planned to edit the Latin poems of Angelo Poliziano (1454–94), known as Politian. Always interested in learned Renaissance humanists, he was attracted to the man who wrote poems in Greek, Latin and Italian, and was closely associated with the Medici dynasty in Florence. On June 15, 1734, a friend borrowed from Pembroke College library, "for the use of Mr. Johnson," *Angeli Politiani Opera.* Johnson never returned this book to the college, and it was found in his library after his death. On August 5 he issued a proposal and solicited advance subscriptions for his edition, to guarantee a number of buyers and defray the costs of publication. He planned to include a life of the author, notes on the poems and a history of Latin poetry from Petrarch (whose work he'd discovered in his father's bookshop) to Politian. But the response was tepid, and he was forced to abandon the project.

Johnson was able to persuade publishers to commission translations of what then appeared to be promising, salable books by Lobo (1735), Paolo Sarpi (1738) and Crousaz (1739), but which now seem extremely obscure (even for a university press). In a letter to Cave of July 1737, Johnson suggested a translation from two languages of the text and notes of Father Paolo Sarpi's *History of the Council of Trent* (1619), which has been called "the last great monument of Italian Renaissance historiography." The book, Johnson wrote, had in 1736 "been translated into French, and published with large Notes by Dr. [Pierre-François] Le Courayer. The Reputation of that Book is so much revived in England, that it is presumed, a new translation of it from the Italian, together with Le Courayer's Notes from the French, could not fail of a favourable Reception."

The Council of Trent (1545–63) took place after the Lutheran Reformation and attempted to reform the Catholic Church under Jesuit guidance. Since Sarpi was a highly respected scientist and priest, his opposition to papal authority, especially to the pope's political encroachment on the independence of Italian city-states, was then of considerable interest to English Protestants. Cave was responsive to Johnson's proposal. In August 1738, a year after Johnson's letter, Cave printed 6,000 copies of the proposal and began paying him for chapters of the slow-moving translation. That month, Johnson, adopting an unusually deferential tone, tried to reassure his employer, who had not been receiving copy for cash: "As to Father Paul, I have not yet been just to my proposal, but have met with impediments which, I hope, are now at an end, and if you find the Progress hereafter not such as You have a right to expect, You can easily stimulate a negligent Translator." A rival translator (and there always seems to be a rival for any project a writer undertakes) objected to his proposal. Faced with considerable opposition, Johnson gave it up, and the rival (as so often happens) never completed his own translation.

Johnson never published his projected life of Politian, but he did rescue part of his aborted project by bringing out a brief life of Sarpi. Like all his brief lives, his "Sarpi" was a translation, paraphrase and synopsis of a previous biography—in this case, by Le Courayer. In many of his early lives he identified with his distinguished subject. Johnson—who had prodigious powers of recollection and, as a small child, had astonished his mother by instantly memorizing a passage from the prayer book—wrote that Sarpi "was born for study, having . . . a memory so tenacious, that he could repeat thirty verses upon once hearing them." Praising both Sarpi and his *History*, he stated that the priest was "hated by the Romans as their most formidable enemy, and honoured by all the learned for his abilities, and by the good for his integrity," that his book was "unequalled for the judicious disposition of the matter, and artful texture of the narration, commended by Dr. [Gilbert] Burnet as the completest model of historical writing."[12]

In his life of Pope, Johnson expressed admiration for the learning of Crousaz, a professor at the University of Lausanne, and respect for his orthodox religious beliefs: "Crousaz was a professor of Switzerland, eminent for his treatise of Logick, and his *Examen de Pyrrhonisme* [Extreme Scepticism], and, however little known or regarded here, was no mean antagonist. . . . His incessant vigilance for the promotion of piety disposed him to look with distrust upon all metaphysical systems of Theology, and all schemes of virtue and happiness purely rational."

Crousaz, a mathematician and philosopher, wrote a *Commentary on Mr. Pope's Principles of Morality* (1738), which Johnson translated. But Crousaz did not know English, and had based his ill-informed book on French translations, in verse and prose, of Pope's popular poem *An Essay on Man* (1734). Pope believed in the basic goodness of the universe and the rightness of man's place in it, and expressed his doctrine of cosmic optimism in the line: "Whatever is, is right." Crousaz attacked Pope for "all the newer secular speculations that seemed to him to impugn traditional orthodoxies about God's and man's free will." Johnson did not try to justify Pope's naïvely optimistic philosophy, but in the footnotes to the text he defended him from Crousaz's attacks on passages that were not in the poem itself: "If he had no Way of distinguishing between Mr. Pope and his Translator, to throw the Odium of Impiety, and the Ridicule of Nonsense entirely on the former, is at least *stabbing in the Dark,* and wounding, for ought he knows, an innocent Character." Pope's biographer observed that Crousaz "devoted much of his attention to criticizing expressions nowhere to be found in Pope's English and assailing propositions that his victim would have found as unacceptable as he." As Pope, satirizing such misguided commentators, wrote in his *Essay on Criticism* (1711): "These leave the Sense, their Learning to display, / And those explain the Meaning quite away."

Though Johnson earned very little from his translations, he always remained interested in such projects. In the last year of his life, he considered translating Jacques-Auguste Thuanus (1553–1617), the French statesman, historian and author of *Historia sui Temporis* (History of His Own Time). When John Nichols said this would be a tough job, Johnson insouciantly replied, "I should have no trouble but that of dictation, which would be performed as speedily as an amanuensis could write."[13]

After translating Crousaz, Johnson concentrated on biography. Beginning with the life of Sarpi, he published eight brief lives in Cave's *Gentleman's Magazine* between 1738 and 1742: on the English privateer Sir Francis Drake and the English admiral Robert Blake, the Dutch physician Herman Boerhaave, the German scholar John Philip Barretier, the French botanist Louis Morin, the Dutch classicist Peter Burman and the English doctor Thomas Sydenham. These rather random and derivative lives have little historical value, but Johnson's personal comments reflect his interest in war, philology, medicine and science, and his attempt to interpret the military and cultural history of the previous centuries.

The life of Drake is a vivid narrative of his voyage in 1572–73 to Panama and the edge of the Pacific Ocean, and of his circumnavigation of the world in 1580. Admiral Blake had defeated Maarten Tromp in the First Dutch War (1652–54) and shattered Holland's supremacy at sea. The patriotic motive for publishing these two lives in 1740 "was to compare the glorious past naval history of England with the disastrous efforts of Admiral [Edward] Vernon." In 1740, during the War of Jenkins' Ear—provoked by Spanish abuse of British sailors in the West Indies—Vernon had failed miserably against the Spanish in the assault on Cartagena. The first paragraph in "Blake" connects his life to contemporary events by condemning "the insults, ravages, and barbarities" of the Spanish and by angrily calling for vengeance against them.

The life of "the learned, the judicious, the pious Boerhaave"[14] (as Johnson wrote in *Rambler* 114) was by far the most interesting of the early biographies. Johnson saw him as a heroic model, identified with many aspects of his life—especially his agonizing illnesses, which taught him to feel compassion for others. Boerhaave became a professor of medicine at the University of Leyden in 1701, a time when the

Dutch were admired for their tolerance and enlightenment, and when many Scots, including Boswell, went abroad to study Roman law at Utrecht.

Johnson often seemed to be writing about himself (or foreshadowing his own future) when discussing his subject. He described Boerhaave as "tall and strong, and remarkable for extraordinary strength . . . formed by nature for great designs, and guided by religion in the exertion of his abilities." Keith Crook has pointed out that when translating from his Latin source, Johnson—deeply interested, like Boerhaave, in scientific experiments—heated up the prose: "*Chemiam dies noctesque exercuit* [he practiced chemistry day and night] became 'His insatiable curiosity after knowledge engaged him now in the practice of chemistry, which he prosecuted with all the ardour of a philosopher.'" Just as Boerhaave "was one of those mighty capacities to whom scarce anything seems impossible," so Johnson would also be capable of undertaking, almost single-handedly, monumental projects like the *Dictionary of the English Language*. In a magnificent conclusion, Johnson observed, "he was an admirable example of temperance, fortitude, humility, and devotion. His piety, and a religious sense of his dependence on God, was the basis of all his virtues, and the principle of his whole conduct."[15] In this passage Johnson revealed his own character and aspirations, and projected his own future ambitions.

III

All Johnson's apprentice efforts were based on well-known sources. He translated and adapted lives from previous biographies, and took the story of *Irene* from a history of the Turks. His first major poem was an imitation of the Third Satire of the Latin poet Juvenal, a xenophobic attack on the pernicious influence of Greeks and Jews in ancient Rome. Lobo's book took place in Abyssinia, *Irene* in Turkey; Johnson's *London* (1738) described the danger, violence and corruption that took place in the English capital as well as in these Eastern despotisms.

Juvenal's major themes were the vileness of the city, the contrast between rich and poor, and the corrupt foreigners who were ruining the honest Romans. His narrator exclaims that it's impossible for a decent man to remain in Rome, that it's no longer worth living in a city where the jerrybuilt houses are dangerous and the traffic intolerable. Finally, he bids farewell to Rome and to the friend who's come to say good-bye, and leaves to enjoy a quiet existence in the country. According to Moses Hadas, Juvenal "incidentally provides a lively picture of the teeming life of the capital—its sights and sounds, dangers and annoyances, luxury and meanness, and empty social observances."

The classicist Gilbert Highet noted that such attacks on the vileness of the city went back to the biblical Sodom and Gomorrah and to Babylon. Since ancient times writers have believed that people in the country are exceptionally virtuous and commonsensical, while those in the city are immoral and corrupt. English authors in the first half of the eighteenth century—the self-consciously Augustan Age, named after the great Roman emperor and patron of Virgil, Horace and Ovid—saw many parallels between Rome and London.

Johnson knew Juvenal through his close study of the poet, through previous translations and imitations, and through scholarly explications in the main editions. Viewing him as both a moralist and a wit, Johnson said, "the peculiarity of Juvenal is a mixture of gaiety and stateliness, of pointed sentences [i.e., sharp epigrams] and declamatory grandeur." Boswell mentioned that Johnson found some of the satires "too gross for imitation," but he was drawn to the Third Satire, which afforded striking comparisons between the ancient and modern cities. Niall Rudd, comparing Juvenal and Johnson, observed, "Johnson has expanded the opening scene, the first part of the speaker's diatribe, and the later picture of the countryside, whereas he has shortened the woes of poverty and the dangers of city life."[16]

Johnson was of course familiar with the fine translation of Juvenal's Third Satire—also in closed couplets—that Dryden had made as a schoolboy, but there were no exact parallels between his work and Johnson's. In a charming passage on the advantages of country life, Juvenal wrote:

Est aliquid, quocunque loco, quocunque recessu,
Unius sese dominum fecisse lacertae.

In Dryden's version this becomes:

'Tis somewhat to be lord of some small ground,
In which a lizard may, at least, turn round.

Johnson's version omits the lizard and is far more satiric. He emphasizes
the venal politician, caught red-handed and forced to give up his rural
retreat, and the squalid urban cellars in which poor writers are condemned to live:

There might'st thou find some elegant Retreat,
Some hireling Senator's deserted Seat,
And stretch thy Prospects o'er the smiling Land,
For less than rent the Dungeons of the Strand.

Describing the dangers of collapsing and burning houses, Dryden
wrote, in a triplet prolonged by an elegant alexandrine:

What scene so desart, or so full of fright,
As tow'ring houses tumbling in the night,
And Rome on fire beheld by its own blazing light?

Johnson is again more savage and severe, introducing other perils and
an apparently incongruous female atheist, who pointedly connects
physical with spiritual death:

Here Malice, Rapine, Accident, conspire,
And now a Rabble rages, now a Fire;
Their Ambush here relentless Ruffians lay,
And here the fell Attorney prowls for Prey;
Here falling Houses thunder on your Head,
And here a female Atheist talks you dead.[17]

Johnson emphasizes the constant danger of being attacked in the street, and condemns the breed of rapacious lawyers who trap innocent and unsuspecting clients.

Unlike Dryden, Johnson chose to imitate rather than translate Juvenal. He called this "a kind of middle composition between translation and original design, which pleases when the thoughts are unexpectedly applicable, and the parallels lucky." He told Cave that "part of the beauty of the performance (if any beauty be allow'd it) consisted in adapting Juvenal's Sentiments to modern facts and Persons," and printed the corresponding passages from Juvenal at the bottom of the page so that the careful reader could note these parallels.

A modern historian, writing about Hanoverian England and puzzled by Johnson's attitude toward the city, remarked that it is strange "to find Johnson, whose love of London itself was matched only by his contempt for the barrenness of Scotland, writing: 'For who would leave, unbrib'd, Hibernia's Land, / Or change the rocks of Scotland for the Strand?'"[18] But if Johnson had been angry first in Oxford and then when he returned to Lichfield, he was ten times angrier in London. In the city he was an outsider, hungry for sustenance and fame, poor, isolated and constantly tempted by volatile companions like Richard Savage. Johnson was undoubtedly sincere, and not just imitating Juvenal, in his attack on the vices of London. There was a great difference between his harsh view of London during the lonely, obscure and impoverished years of his youth and his enthusiastic attitude during the later years of friendship, fame and comfort. His hero Thales—named after one of the seven wise men of ancient Greece—speaks for Johnson just as Umbricius speaks for Juvenal. It's worth noting that though Thales leaves London for Wales, Johnson's narrator, like Juvenal's, remains behind.

The themes of Johnson's *London* are political, personal and social. He condemns the voracious greed and violent crime, the excise tax and political pensions, as well as the Italian *castrati,* French fashions and Spanish insolence, and he particularly attacks the Whigs' craven policy toward Spain. His reference to Queen Elizabeth's birthplace in Greenwich, like his patriotic lives of Drake and Blake, contrasts the military triumphs of the past with the degrading appeasement of the present:

> Struck with the Seat that gave Eliza birth,
> We kneel, and kiss the consecrated Earth;
> In pleasing Dreams the blissful Age renew,
> And call Britannia's Glories back to view.

He took up the same themes in his essay "Thoughts on Agriculture," written sixteen years later in 1754. He again contrasted the morals of country and city, and raged against the "luxury, avarice, injustice, violence, and ambition, that take up their ordinary residence in populous cities; while the hard and laborious life of the husbandman will not admit of these vices."

In *Rambler* 166 Johnson returned to the most personal theme in *London,* his work as a Grub Street galley slave, and asserted, "no complaint has been more frequently repeated in all ages than that of the neglect of merit associated with poverty." He draws attention to this idea in the most personal couplet of the poem: "This mournful Truth is ev'ry where confest, / *Slow rises Worth, by Poverty deprest.*"[19]

Johnson's poem substantiates a social historian's assertion that "the dominating impression of life in eighteenth-century London, from the standpoint of the individual, is one of uncertainty and insecurity." Another modern historian notes that danger prevailed in the city from the 1720s, through the time that *London* was published, to the late 1740s: "[Daniel] Defoe claimed in the late 1720s that in London a man was not safe going about his business even in the daytime. A peace always produced a crime wave because of the return of many discharged soldiers and sailors without employment, and after the War of Austrian Succession [1740–48] Henry Fielding likewise thought that the streets of London would shortly be impassable 'without the utmost hazard.'" Echoing "man that is born of a woman is of few days, and full of trouble" (Job 14:1), Johnson, in Sermon 23, emphasized this sense of danger while trying to turn the minds of men from the hazards of daily existence to the eternal truths of religion:

"That the life of man is unhappy, that his days are not only few, but evil, that he is surrounded by dangers, distracted by uncertainties, and oppressed by calamities, requires no proof."[20]

Johnson published his journalistic hack writing anonymously, and didn't even sign *London,* lest his first major effort be condemned. He called authors a *"genus irritabile,* 'a generation very easily put out of temper'"; but thought critics—weak and idle, ignorant and vain— were even worse. Eighteenth-century critics, unconstrained by libel laws, could be savage in their ad hominem attacks. They rejoiced in mocking Pope's hunchbacked deformity and his pitiful attempts to have sex with prostitutes. But Johnson said he'd rather be attacked than unnoticed and felt it was worse to ignore an author than to condemn him. In a magniloquent passage in *Rambler* 144, he explained how "the first appearance of excellence unites multitudes against it" and provokes "the envious, the idle, the peevish, and the thoughtless, to [attack vulnerable authors] and obstruct that worth which they cannot equal":

> What caution is sufficient to ward off the blows of invisible assailants, or what force can stand against unintermitted attacks? . . . No sooner can any man emerge from the crowd and fix the eyes of the publick upon him, than he stands as a mark to the arrows of lurking calumny, and receives, in the tumult of hostility, from distant and from nameless hands, wounds not always easy to be cured.[21]

London was, in fact, well received by Johnson's fellow poets. Thomas Gray called it "one of those few imitations, that have all the ease and all the spirit of an original." Later on, in the Victorian Age, Lord Tennyson claimed, "the 'high moral tone' of some of its couplets had never been surpassed in English satire." The most precious praise came from Pope, whose couplets Johnson had imitated in *London* ("And now a Rabble rages, now a Fire"). More severely handicapped than Johnson, Pope as a Catholic could not earn a university degree or practice a profession. Pope had admired Johnson's Latin translation of his *Messiah,* and probably knew about Johnson's defense of his *Essay on Man*. He now recognized new talent and generously predicted that "the author [of *London*], whoever he is, will not long be concealed."[22]

IV

In the fall of 1737, about six months before the publication of his poem, Johnson returned to Lichfield and, leaving the twenty-two-year-old Lucy Porter with relatives in the country, brought Tetty to London. They found lodgings, superior to his bachelor digs, in Castle Street, near Cavendish Square, in the more fashionable western part of town. By now Tetty's fortune was nearly exhausted. Johnson had earned a respectable ten guineas for *London,* but he couldn't produce a major poem every week and still hadn't found a producer for his play, *Irene.* After the initial excitement of seeing his work, if not his name, in print and enjoying the succès d'estime of *London,* the thrill wore off. He feared that he wouldn't be able to support his wife, who was used to luxury and inclined to extravagance, and would be condemned to penurious drudgery for the rest of his life.

Johnson soldiered on at the *Gentleman's Magazine* for another year. But in the summer of 1739—after publishing his translation of Crousaz, his lives of Sarpi and Boerhaave, and *London*—he made one last effort to find a teaching job in the Midlands. Boswell wrote that "he felt the hardship of writing for bread; he was, therefore willing to resume the office of a schoolmaster, so as to have a sure, though moderate income for his life. An offer was made to him of the mastership of a school [at £60 a year], provided he could obtain the degree of Master of Arts."

The trustees of Appleby Grammar School in Market Bosworth, thirteen miles east of Lichfield, thought Johnson was a strong candidate and wanted to hire him as headmaster. But they stuck rigidly to the rules and were not, like Sir Wolston Dixie, willing to ignore that old obstacle, his lack of a university degree. Initiating a tangled trail of influence, the trustees asked Pope to recommend him to Lord Gower, a local landowner and powerful politician. Gower wrote to an unnamed friend of Jonathan Swift, the dean of St. Patrick's Cathedral in Dublin. Gower asked the friend to ask Swift to recommend the anonymously published Johnson—personally unknown to the trustees, Pope, Gower, Swift's friend and Swift himself—for an unearned and purely cosmetic mail-order degree from the University of Dublin.

Though this was the way influence worked in the eighteenth century, there was little likelihood of success. Gower doubted whether the college authorities would be inclined to debase their degree by posting it on demand to an unknown person. But on August 1, 1739, he faithfully wrote to Swift's friend, emphasizing Johnson's desperation and his willingness to appear for a *viva* in distant Dublin. He stated that the school trustees

> do me the honour to think that I have interest enough in you, to prevail upon you to write to Dean Swift, to persuade the University of Dublin to send a diploma to me, constituting this poor man Master of Arts in their University. They highly extol the man's learning and probity; and will not be persuaded, that the University will make any difficulty of conferring such a favour upon a stranger, if he is recommended by the Dean. They say he is not afraid of the strictest examination, though he is of so long a journey; and will venture it, if the Dean thinks it necessary; choosing rather to die upon the road, *than be starved to death in translating for booksellers.*

Gower, mentioning yet another difficulty, said the M.A. degree from across the sea had to be granted within six weeks, by September 11, when the trustees would meet to choose the new headmaster. He then pessimistically added: "if you see this matter in the same light as it appears to me, I hope you will burn this, and pardon me for giving you so much trouble about an impracticable thing."[23]

Even if Gower's letter was not burned and eventually reached Swift, and there is no proof that it did, he was in no position to help Johnson. Johnson later wrote in his life of Swift that as a student at Trinity College, Dublin, Swift himself had been found "conspicuously deficient" by the examiners and had obtained his bachelor's degree "at last by *special favour,* a term used in that university to denote want of merit. . . . It is easy to imagine that the mode in which his first degree was conferred left him no great fondness for the University." A modern authority on Irish universities noted that Trinity College reciprocated Swift's animosity: "Trinity College was one of the few public institutions in Ireland which made no effort to honour itself by honouring Dean Swift. There is no indication that he was ever popular within its walls until after his death."

Moreover, as the editor of Swift's letters wrote, he had no power or influence in the university at that time. In May 1730, when the Duke of Dorset had succeeded Swift's friend Lord Carteret as lord lieutenant, Swift wrote frankly to Pope that he could "anticipate the loss of the little influence remaining" to him. In any case, the editor added, "it would have been impossible for Swift, in the time at his disposal, to obtain what was requested."[24] The final irony was that since the Appleby school required a master of arts degree from Oxford or Cambridge, the Dublin degree, even if obtained, would not have qualified Johnson for the position he sought. Since he believed that Swift had refused to act on his behalf, Johnson remained hostile to the dean throughout his life and roundly condemned him in *The Lives of the Poets.*

A. L. Reade, attempting to account for Johnson's intense dislike, concluded, "even if Swift really was approached, and declined to help, and his refusal became known to Johnson (a rather long chain of assumptions), it is hard to believe that lasting enmity would have resulted." Boswell seemed to confirm this by recording, "I once took the liberty to ask him if Swift had personally offended him, and he told me he had not." Despite this testimony, Johnson remained virulently hostile to both Gower and Swift. Unaware of Gower's letter and embittered by his failure to get the job at Appleby, he took revenge when writing the *Dictionary.* He told Boswell, "when I came to the word *Renegado,* after telling that it meant 'one who deserts to the enemy, a revolter,' I added, *Sometimes we say a GOWER.* Thus it went to press;

but the printer had more wit than I, and struck it out."[25] If Johnson was angry with Gower, he must also have been angry with Swift. Like the school trustees, he mistakenly believed that Swift had the power to get him the Dublin M.A. and that the university would surely have conferred the degree if Swift had recommended him.

From the beginning of his adult life Johnson had struggled against a series of humiliating failures. Now, despite all his hard work for Cave and the success of *London,* he seemed destined for a life of starvation, slaving away for the booksellers.

7

POLITICS AND PASSION
1739–1744

I

In August 1739, while trying to secure the teaching position at Appleby Grammar School, Johnson went to the Midlands. In no hurry to return to the querulous Tetty, he prolonged their second separation for eight months, until April 1740. His visits to country houses, complete with servants and comforts, provided a pleasant contrast to his tedious drudgery and exiguous existence in London. He stayed with his old school friend John Taylor, now married and a prosperous lawyer in Ashbourne, and with his mother in Lichfield. Sarah's bookshop still limped along, with help from Lucy Porter, who'd moved into her house, and from her faithful servant Kitty Chambers. To raise some urgently needed cash, Johnson took out a mortgage on the Lichfield house with the town clerk, Theophilus Levett, and received £80 at 4 1/2 percent interest.

Taylor introduced Johnson to three neighboring women whom the young ogre found extremely attractive. Johnson once attacked the poet Matthew Prior by saying, "he wrote of love like a man who had never felt it." The poet William Cowper, in his letters, later made the same charge against Johnson: "I admire Johnson as a man of great Erudition, and

Sense, but when he sets himself up for Judge of Writers upon the Subject of Love, a passion which I suppose he never felt in his life, he might as well think himself qualified to pronounce upon a treatise of Horsemanship or the Art of Fortification." Cowper was quite mistaken about Johnson's passions. He loved Tetty and was about to fall in love with another woman—and he knew a great deal about horses and fortification.

Johnson described the appearance of the rather grand seventeen-year-old Mary Meynell with fine discrimination: "She would have been handsome for a queen . . . her beauty had more in it of majesty than of attraction, more of the dignity of virtue than the vivacity of wit." A few years later, Mary married the amiable but feckless William Fitzherbert, and devoted the rest of her life to saving his soul from corruption and preserving his estate for their children. "She stood at the door of her Paradise in Derbyshire," Johnson declared, with exalted diction, "like the angel with the flaming sword, to keep the devil at a distance."[1]

Mary's close friend Miss Hill Boothby, born in 1708, became important to Johnson after Tetty's death, when he was searching for a second wife and was seriously interested in marrying her. The sharp-tongued Anna Seward called her "the sublimated Methodistic Hill Boothby, who read her Bible in Hebrew." She appeared in Richard Graves' novel *The Spiritual Quixote* (1773) as the pious Miss Sainthill, "pleasantly argumentative and strictly virtuous." When Johnson first met her in 1739 he competed for her favors with George Lyttleton, a future lord. Johnson later disparaged his rival in *The Lives of the Poets* as "poor Lyttleton," who, like Johnson himself, had an awkward body and an ugly face. In contrast to the obscure, unemployed Johnson, Lyttleton was born to privilege and achieved high office. Educated at Eton and Christ Church, Oxford, he was MP for Okehampton, Devon, from 1735 to 1756, and in the mid-1750s became a privy councillor and chancellor of the exchequer. He was also a minor poet and liberal patron of the arts, a friend of Pope and of Fielding, who dedicated *Tom Jones* to him. Unimpressed himself by Lyttleton's rank and influence, Johnson was outraged by Hill Boothby's unaccountable attention to the unprepossessing poet and her failure to recognize his own obvious merit. "She *would* delight in that fellow Lyttleton's company," he told Hester Thrale, despite "all that I could do; and I cannot forgive even his memory the preference given by a mind like hers."

Johnson sometimes fell in love with attractive young women, but shy and fearful of rejection, dared not declare his feelings. On this visit he also met Molly Aston, three years older than himself, who had for him the fatal combination of intellect and piety. She had a graceful figure, fine complexion, golden-brown hair and charming manners, but her brains and wit made her unpopular with the ladies. Anna Seward, who called her "a wit, a beauty, and a toast" of drinking men, thought her handsome but haughty.[2] Johnson, however, was ecstatic. He told Hester Thrale: "I wonder when any body ever experiences measureless delight. *I* never did I'm sure except the first Evening I spent Tete à Tete with Molly Aston. . . . That indeed was not happiness, it was rapture; but thoughts of it sweetened the whole year. . . . Molly was a beauty and a scholar, and a wit and a Whig; and she talked all in praise of liberty." Molly's cries for liberty inspired his Latin epigram, which slyly suggested she had enslaved him. Translated, it read: "Persuasions to freedom fall oddly from you: / If freedom we seek—fair Maria, adieu!" Johnson also respected Molly's literary judgment and alluded to her in his life of Pope: "I once heard a Lady of great beauty and excellence object" to a line in one of Pope's epitaphs. She said that his tribute, "No arts essay'd, but not to be admir'd," contained "an unnatural and incredible panegyrick."

The contrast between the blooming Molly and the aging Tetty was obvious, and Johnson aroused his wife's jealousy when he described the young beauty he'd been dallying with in her absence. He later recalled that one day a passing gypsy looked at his hand and said: "Your heart is divided, Sir, between a Betty and a Molly: Betty loves you best, but you take most delight in Molly's company: when I turned about to laugh, I saw my wife was crying. Pretty charmer! She had no reason!" The prophecy sounds more like Johnson than the gypsy and revealed the inevitable tensions in his shaky marriage.

On January 31, 1740, Johnson wrote to console Tetty for a recent injury, which she may have exaggerated to attract his attention and sympathy. His emotional response to her letter expressed regret that he couldn't relieve her misery, and reaffirmed his esteem and affection for her: "After hearing that You are in so much danger, as I apprehend from a hurt on a tendon, I shall be very uneasy till I know that You are recovered, and beg that You will omit nothing that can contribute to it, nor deny Yourself any thing that might make confinement less melancholy. You have already suffered more than I can bear to reflect upon."[3] He sweetened her pain by promising to send £20 of the mortgage money.

Molly Aston was at the center of a circle of closely connected Midlands friends. Lawrence Offley, who had been one of his three students at Edial, was related to the Aston family. Molly was first cousin to the mother of Topham Beauclerk, whom Johnson later befriended in London. One of her sisters, Magdalen, married Gilbert Walmesley, his Lichfield mentor; another sister, Catherine, married Henry Hervey; and his two close Lichfield friends then became brothers-in-law. Molly remained an unattainable goddess in Johnson's eyes. His friends' marriages to her sisters (like George Lyttleton's friendship with Hill Boothby) made him acutely aware that his family, social status and fortune were distinctly inferior.

Johnson's tightly knit Midlands society knew all about one another, and remained important to him throughout his life. George Hector, the "man-midwife" who'd delivered Johnson, was the uncle of his childhood friend Edmund Hector. Elizabeth Desmoulins, a friend of Tetty's who later became a member of Johnson's household, was the daughter of his godfather, Dr. Swinfen. Johnson's brutal teacher, John Hunter, married Henry Porter's sister and was Anna Seward's grandfather. Cornelius Ford was a college friend of Lord Chesterfield, putative patron of Johnson's *Dictionary,* who made Ford his chaplain. Johnson later tried to save William Dodd, who was sentenced to death for forging the name of Chesterfield's son on a document.

Johnson habitually described his family and friends in the most glowing terms. Sometimes his superlatives were formulaic reassurances, suited to the occasion, as when he wrote to his injured wife or dying mother. Tetty was "the most amiable woman in the world"; Sarah was "the best mother, and I believe the best woman in the world." But his other encomiums were entirely sincere. George Psalmanazar was "the *best* man he had ever known." Two minor figures in Cave's circle also received high praise. The writer Tom Birch "knew more small particulars [of literary gossip] than anybody." Jack Ellis, a moneylender behind the Royal Exchange, provided, Johnson said, "the most literary conversation that I ever enjoyed."

Johnson surpassed himself when describing the ladies. Mary Meynell "had the best understanding he had ever met with in any human being." Molly Aston was "the loveliest creature I ever saw!!!" After naming several outstanding women, he declared that Charlotte Lennox "was superior to them all." He loved his *"dear, dear"* Dr. Richard Bathurst "better than ever [he] loved any human creature." Creating a new superlative, Johnson exclaimed that David Garrick was "the cheerfullest man of his age." The earth, he declared, "does not bear a worthier man than Bennet Langton." After the death of Langton's rakish friend Topham Beauclerk, Johnson wrote, "such another will not often be found among mankind."

Johnson reserved the highest praise for his three most distinguished friends. Oliver Goldsmith was "the best writer he ever knew upon every subject he wrote about." He declared that he knew "no man who has passed through life with more observation than Reynolds." Edmund Burke was simply "the greatest man [he] had ever yet seen." The Corsican patriot General Pasquale Paoli had "the loftiest port of any man he had ever seen." In a similar fashion, King George III, having graciously granted Johnson an interview, was (almost pro forma) "the finest gentleman I have ever seen." Johnson gave the devoted Hester Thrale a double superlative. He told her that she had *"more* wit than any woman I know," and added: "I do certainly love you better than any human Being I ever saw—better I think than even poor dear Bathurst."[4] Some of Johnson's heartfelt praise piously memorialized dead friends, but he was always careful to define their distinctive qualities. Since he had few family ties, making and keeping friends whom he adored and exalted was exceptionally important to him.

II

Johnson's political writings, both before and after his trip to the Midlands, can best be understood by examining the political situation of the time. The most important issues were the succession to the monarchy, maintenance of the Protestant Church of England and relations with Holland, France and Spain. Until 1832 voting was limited to freeholders worth forty shillings a year; women, common laborers and the poor had no political power. The leading ministers, who determined the government's policy in Parliament, represented the interests of the great landowners and country gentlemen, leading lawyers, prosperous merchants, directors of the East India Company and rich colonial planters. The small number of voters were easily bought with free drinks. The historian Basil Williams wrote that in the provinces "candidates for election were generally fixed upon by small cliques of local magnates and country gentlemen. . . . Their prime interests were local, their estates, their dependents, their duties as country justices, not least their dogs and horses, their hunting and shooting." Members of Parliament from the boroughs, or city districts, included landed gentry, "merchants and lawyers, shipowners, contractors, officers of the army and navy, government officials, representatives of the big corporations." The king had the power to appoint and dismiss his ministers.

Johnson adhered to what Donald Greene called the "traditional 'old Tory' isolationist principles—the theory that Britain, secured by her fleet and her insularity, should remain clear of 'entangling alliances' on the continent." He wished to support and preserve the traditional order, and felt "the change of old establishments is always an evil." Though he approved the deposition of James II, and his lingering belief in the divine right of kings was undermined by Queen Anne's failure to cure him (when he was an infant) of the King's Evil, he remained a monarchist. He declared in *Adventurer* 45 that "all the forms of government instituted among mankind, perpetually tend towards monarchy." Johnson supported the Hanoverian succession of 1714, which ensured that England would remain Protestant, but found it hard to become enthusiastic about the philistine George I, who could scarcely speak English, or the equally undistinguished George II.

Despite his momentary enthusiasm for George III, Johnson ultimately condemned the whole dynasty by declaring: "George the First was a robber, George the Second a Fool, and George the Third is an idiot."[5]

In 1730 Johnson wrote a satirical quatrain that contrasted the poetical glory of Virgil in the reign of Augustus Caesar and Edmund Spenser in the time of Queen Elizabeth with the lamentably untalented Colley Cibber, who'd recently been appointed poet laureate by George II:

> Augustus still survives in Maro's strain,
> And Spenser's verse prolongs Eliza's reign;
> Great George's acts let tuneful Cibber sing;
> For Nature form'd the Poet for the King.

In *London* (1738) he took another satiric swipe at Parliament and George II, who frequently visited his native Hanover, at the expense of the British public, to consort with his German mistresses:

> Propose your Schemes, ye Senatorian Band,
> Whose Ways and Means support the sinking Land;
> Lest Ropes be wanting in the tempting Spring,
> To rig another Convoy for the King.

He also shared the pervasive fear that the King's German political interests would have a malign influence on British foreign policy.

The only alternatives to the boorish German kings were the descendants of James II: his son, the Old Pretender to the throne, James Stuart; and his grandson, the Young Pretender, the romantic but ineffectual Bonnie Prince Charlie. Their supporters, the Jacobites, advocated the restoration of the exiled house of Stuart, whose forces threatened Britain in the rebellions of 1715 and, more seriously, of 1745. The first Scottish rising failed when the Duke of Argyll blocked the road south at Stirling and the Jacobites were decisively defeated at Preston, Northumberland. In the second rebellion, after invading England from the north and penetrating as far south as Derby in the Midlands, only 140 miles from London, the Jacobites retreated to

Scotland. They were irrevocably defeated and slaughtered in the Battle of Culloden, near Inverness, in April 1746: "Outnumbered and outgunned, Charles's Highland army had been shot to bits at close range by [the Duke of] Cumberland's artillery; many of those who survived were bayoneted as they tried to escape, and the wounded were left unattended on the battlefield. . . . An eye-witness reported that for nearly four miles the ground was 'covered with dead bodies.'"[6]

Johnson has been mistakenly called a Jacobite. His father had sympathized with their cause, and there was a traditional association between the Jacobites and the High-Church Tories. But Johnson certainly did not want a foreign-backed invasion and bloody civil war, a Catholic king of England and an occupation by France and Spain. Boswell heard him declare, in a definitive statement, "that if holding up his right hand would have secured victory at Culloden to Prince Charles's army, he was not sure he would have held it up; so little confidence had he in the right claimed by the house of Stuart, and so fearful was he of the consequences of another revolution on the throne of Great-Britain." As Donald Greene concluded, he frequently attacked Stuart activity, condemned "the 1745 insurrection and expressed thanks to Providence for its defeat. . . . If the word 'Jacobite' means one who seriously desired the restoration of the Stuarts to the throne, there is not the slightest evidence that it could ever have been applied to Johnson at any time of his life."[7]

The Tories lost power after the death of Queen Anne and the arrival of King George I in 1714, and they remained in the political wilderness throughout Johnson's lifetime. The parliamentary opposition to the dominant Whigs came not from the impotent Tories, but from the Whig factions that had split from the main party. A modern historian wrote that Johnson, who believed in firm government and respect for authority, felt Whiggism—represented by the aristocratic owners of vast estates and the business interests in the City of London—"fed on discontent and encouraged sedition. . . . 'Whig' conjured up images of death and destruction: he saw rebels, king-killers, surly malcontents, men who would brook no authority." His notorious definitions in the *Dictionary* suggested that he was rabidly partisan: "*Tory:* One who

adheres to the ancient constitution of the state, and apostolical hierarchy of the church of England"; "*Whig:* The name of a faction."

But in reality he thought the two parties had a great deal in common
and that it didn't greatly matter which one of them controlled the government. He told Boswell that "a wise Tory and a wise Whig, I believe,
will agree. Their principles are the same, though their modes of thinking are different. . . . I would not give half a guinea to live under one
form of government rather than another. It is of no moment to the
happiness of an individual. Sir, the danger of the abuse of power is
nothing to a private man." As he explained in the lines he wrote for
Goldsmith's *The Traveller,* most people are far more concerned with
personal matters than with forms of government:

How small, of all that human hearts endure,
That part which laws or kings can cause or cure.

The trouble was that most Tories as well as most Whigs were foolish rather than wise. In a magnificent peroration, which still resonates
today, Johnson blasted the political zealots who blindly followed the
party line and rejected reality: "men, being numbered, they know not
how nor why, in any of the parties that divide a state, resign the use
of their own eyes and ears, and resolve to believe nothing that does not
favour those whom they profess to follow. . . . [They] deny the most
notorious facts, contradict the most cogent truths, and persist in
asserting to-day what they asserted yesterday, in defiance of evidence,
and contempt of confutation."[8] Despite all his ranting against "vile
Whigs" (one of his star turns), who he felt lacked respect for the
church and the king, many of Johnson's friends, from Walmesley and
Boothby to Gibbon and Burke, were Whigs.

Johnson's first political satires, *Marmor Norfolciense* (Norfolk Marble) and *A Compleat Vindication of the Licensers of the Stage* (both 1739),
develop the themes of *London. Marmor* attacked the corruption of the
Whig government, whose ministers (and even George II) openly
bought votes by bribing members of Parliament, while the MPs
bought elections by bribing the voters. As Burke's biographer wrote,

"The cement which held a Party together consisted for the most part of places, pensions, contracts, honours, promotions and open and secret favours of all kinds, the whole sweetened by a small allowance of money from the Secret Service fund." *Vindication* condemned the government's censorship of the stage, which was legislated to suppress political attacks.

Sir Robert Walpole, the first minister from 1721 to 1742, was the principal target of both Swift's *Gulliver's Travels* (1726) and Johnson's *Marmor.* Swift dedicated *A Tale of a Tub* (1704) "To Prince Posterity"; Johnson's inscription on his Norfolk stone was addressed "To Posterity." In Johnson's pamphlet a buried slab of marble is discovered in Norfolk, Walpole's home county, inscribed with an ancient political commentary that applies to the contemporary political scene. The narrator is a pedantic scholar, struggling to interpret the inscription, written in "monkish rhyme." Johnson clearly based his pamphlet on Swift's *Famous Prediction of Merlin* (1709), which also describes a mock prophecy, but he also had a more important source. Johnson admired the Christian themes and high style, rich diction and rhythmical power of the seventeenth-century doctor and author Sir Thomas Browne. In his life of Browne he wrote, "in 1658, the discovery of some ancient urns in Norfolk gave him occasion to write '*Hydriotaphia, Urn-burial, or a Discourse of Sepulchral Urns,*' in which he treats, with his usual learning, on the funeral rites of ancient nations." Browne's account of the buried urns in Norfolk gave Johnson the idea for his pamphlet.

In his satire Johnson attacked the exploitation of farmers, the perils of a standing army and, despite their marauding privateers that preyed on British shipping in the West Indies, the government's cowardly appeasement of Spain. In the conclusion, he drops his irony, condemns zealots and assumes the role of a disinterested patriot: "I intreat all sects, factions, and distinctions of men among us, to lay aside for a time their party-feuds and petty animosities, and by a warm concurrence on this urgent occasion, teach posterity to sacrifice every private interest to the advantage of their country."

The prophetic inscription, warning of dire calamities, contained a bold couplet that treasonably hinted at the restoration of the Jacobite monarchy: "Then o'er the world shall Discord stretch her wings, /

Kings change their laws, and kingdoms change their kings."[9] After Johnson's identity as the author was discovered, the government issued a warrant for his arrest and he went into hiding in Lambeth, south of the Thames, till the danger subsided.

In 1737 Walpole, infuriated by being lampooned on the stage, forced the Licensing Act through Parliament, which required plays to be approved by the government before they could be presented in public—a law that remained in force until 1968. In *London* Johnson had protested against this infringement of British liberty by comparing the newly censored playwrights to *castrati* and writing: "With warbling Eunuchs fill a licens'd Stage, / And lull to Servitude a thoughtless Age." Henry Brooke's tragedy *Gustavus Vasa* was the first play to be suppressed under the new law. Though ostensibly about the patriotic warrior king of Sweden, it was actually a "pointed allegory of the downfall of a corrupt Prime Minister (and the expulsion of the foreign king who supported him)."

In the *Vindication*, Johnson's narrator, like a Swiftian persona, is ironic, fatuously supporting the censorship that Johnson strongly opposes. He vindicates the present ministry, defends the licenser's authority and condemns the seditious playwright who "looks upon freedom as the only source of publick happiness and national security." He complacently concludes that the authority of the licenser will allow the nation to "rest at length in ignorance and peace."[10]

III

Edmund Burke's biographer described the physical setting and membership of the eighteenth-century Parliament, which sat in St. Stephen's Chapel in Westminster Palace. (The present Houses of Parliament were not built until 1840–50.) "The House of Commons was a small chamber, converted from a monastic chapel, about 58 foot by 33. . . . The Speaker sat in a chair of state on a dais at one end. The benches could not comfortably accommodate all 558 members. . . . A gallery around three sides of the chamber provided additional seating. . . . No more than forty members were regular speakers. Many debates were concluded with a dozen or so speeches."

Members wanted to be protected against the Crown and remain independent of the public; they feared that their speeches, if reported, would distort their meaning and compromise their freedom of argument. In a 1738 debate William Pulteney, MP, arrogantly declared that "to print or publish the speeches of gentlemen in the House looks very like making them accountable without doors for what they say within." Since the debates remained secret, a conflict arose between parliamentary privilege and liberty of the press. In 1728 Cave himself had been fined and imprisoned for supplying a journal in Gloucester with material about parliamentary affairs.

The enterprising Cave was determined to find a way around this dilemma. The educated, middle-class, increasingly literate public in London and provincial towns were curious about politics and keenly interested in what went on in Parliament. In 1738, taking another risk, he and Johnson came up with a bold plan to satisfy this curiosity. Inventing a fifth voyage of *Gulliver's Travels*, for Captain Gulliver's grandson, Cave published monthly accounts of the proceedings, transparently disguised as "debates in the senate of Lilliput." He used obvious distortions of the politicians' names: "Walelop" for Walpole, "Ptit" for William Pitt. In 1741, the year before Walpole fell from power, Johnson took over the job of reporting, and his work was posthumously published as the *Debates in Parliament*. During the next three years, while still living from hand to mouth, he secretly wrote 54 monthly installments, totaling nearly half a million words in 910 printed pages, in the *Gentleman's Magazine*. To reduce the risk of arrest, no debates were published while Parliament was in session.

Johnson almost never attended Parliament in person, and created rather than reported the speeches. As Boswell wrote, "they were frequently written from very slender materials, and often from none at all,—the mere coinage of his own imagination." Johnson explained that Cave's covert informants could take only the most sketchy and surreptitious notes:

I never had been in the gallery of the House of Commons but once. Cave had interest with the door-keepers. He, and the persons employed under him, gained admittance: they brought away the subject of discussion, the names of the speakers, the side they took, and the order in which they rose, together with notes of the arguments advanced in the course of the debate. The whole was afterwards communicated to me, and I composed the speeches in the form which they now have in the Parliamentary debates.[11]

Johnson had heard ministers deliver sermons in church and actors recite words on stage. In *Irene* he wrote lines for the actors to speak; in the *Debates* he wrote the speeches after the politicians had spoken. Composing with his usual dispatch, as if this were the easiest task in the world, dealing with complex issues and creating dramatic effects, he wrote imaginary speeches and published them as true records of what had actually been said. It was an amazing literary tour de force.

When writing what they might have said, Johnson often included phrases like "spoke to this effect," "spoke in substance," "spoke as follows" and "spoke to the following purpose." His speeches were notable for their elaborate sentence structure, dramatic expression and intellectual acuity. Among many varied subjects, he invented speeches about the cleaning of Westminster, insurance of ships, exports of corn, seditious papers, the numbers of seamen, officers on half pay, standing regiments, the state of the army, removal of Walpole and petitions to the king.

Johnson sounded his characteristic criticism of Walpole's regime in the debate of March 9, 1742, when he wrote that for the last twenty years, since Walpole had assumed power, both "foreign and domestic affairs have been managed with equal ignorance, negligence or wickedness." Two other, more personal speeches on spirituous liquors and on cider expressed his own style and mood. In the first speech, in February 1743, Lord Hervey (Henry Hervey's older brother) advocated imposing a duty to curb the harmful effects of alcoholic drinks. Rising to the occasion, Johnson, in a fine rhetorical flourish, described the perilous progression that began by heating the body and ended in total collapse: "these liquors, my Lords, liquors of which the strength is heightened by distillation, have a natural tendency to inflame the blood, to consume the vital juices, destroy the force of the vessels, contract the nerves, and weaken the sinews . . . they not only disorder the mind for a time, but by a frequent use precipitate old age, exasperate diseases, and multiply and increase all the infirmities to which the body of man is liable."

The second, complementary speech defended cider as forcefully as Hervey had attacked liquor, and anticipated Johnson's spirited defense of tea. In this speech a Tory backbencher maintained that the stimulating Herefordshire cider conferred great social as well as physical benefits: "The Cyder, Sir, which I am now rescuing from contemptuous Comparisons, has often exhilarated my social Hours, enlivened the Freedom of Conversation, and improved the Tenderness of Friendship, and shall not therefore now want a Panegyrist. It is one of those few Subjects on which an Encomiast may expatiate without deviating from the Truth."[12]

The *Gentleman's Magazine* was politically neutral. When praised by friends for his impartiality, Johnson—striking a familiar pose— famously declared: "I saved appearances tolerably well; but I took care that the WHIG DOGS should not have the best of it." Though the Whigs who opposed Walpole frequently seemed more successful in his debates, Johnson did not distort the views of the speakers and, since he made them sound so much better than they were, the MPs did not complain about the speeches attributed to them. Like an alchemist in his laboratory, Johnson effectively transformed leaden talk into golden rhetoric. One of his learned friends, who'd spent years translating the ancient orations of Demosthenes, declared that the style and language of a dazzling speech by Pitt surpassed anything he had ever read. As the encomium subsided, Johnson quietly remarked, "that speech I wrote in a garret in Exeter-street." (Though he'd left that address in the spring of 1737 and was not living there when he wrote the speech, his point was essentially valid.) He portrayed the speakers with impressive skill while managing to express his own ideas on liberty, morality, and the virtues and limitations of representative government.

But Johnson, as so frequently happened, suffered a crisis of conscience. When his invented speeches were translated into French, Spanish and German and accepted as genuine, he regretted his hoax and dropped out of the morally dubious project. In his preface to the *Literary Magazine* (1756), without disclosing that he himself had written the speeches, he made a tacit recantation:

> The chief political object of an Englishman's attention must be the great council of the nation, and we shall therefore register all public proceedings with particular care. We shall not attempt to give any regular series of debates, or to amuse our readers with senatorial rhetoric. The speeches inserted in other papers have long been known to be fictitious, and produced sometimes by men who never heard the debate, nor had any authentic information.

Despite Johnson's efforts to clarify the matter, his speeches were reprinted, beginning in 1803, in William Cobbett's *Parliamentary Debates* and became part of the official record.

Cave had no such qualms. The debates were so successful that the circulation of the *Gentleman's Magazine* sharply increased from 10,000 to 15,000 copies a week. To celebrate his newfound fortune and show the world his wealth, Cave bought a coach and horses; and instead of a coat of arms put a picture of St. John's Gate on its door. Johnson, of course, remained as poor as ever.

In September 1742 the bookseller Thomas Osborne embarked on another lucrative project. He bought for the enormous sum of £13,000 a vast library of 7,000 manuscripts, 50,000 books and 350,000 pamphlets. The library had belonged to Robert Harley, 1st Earl of Oxford, the leading Tory politician in the reign of Queen Anne, and was sold after the death of his son. In the fall of 1743, when Johnson was at work on the *Debates in Parliament,* Osborne offered him the congenial task of compiling a catalogue for the great Harleian library. Besides being immensely well read himself, Johnson had learned about this kind of work from his father. In 1706 (three years before Johnson was born) Michael Johnson had bought the 3,000-volume library of the Earl of

Derby, with large holdings on the church fathers and French history, and had catalogued those books himself. The Harley library included books by every important writer since the invention of printing in the mid-fifteenth century. Johnson's main job was to organize the thousands of books into general categories and provide annotations to individual works. His familiarity with this material later proved to be of inestimable value when he compiled the *Dictionary* and edited the plays of Shakespeare.

Besides organizing and annotating the books, Johnson wrote a brief "Account of the Harleian Library" (1743), which was meant to solicit subscriptions for the catalogue and to stir up interest in the forthcoming sale of its contents. He also wrote an "Introduction to the *Harleian Miscellany:* An Essay on the Origin and Importance of Small Tracts and Fugitive Pieces" (1744), some of which had been collected in this *Miscellany*. In the "Account," he simply stated, "by this catalogue, we may inform posterity of the excellence and value of this great collection, and promote the knowledge of scarce books, and elegant editions." In the "Introduction," he emphasized the historical value of these elusive political pamphlets: "they preserve a multitude of particular incidents, which are forgotten in a short time, or omitted in formal relations, and which are yet to be considered as sparks of truth, which, when united, may afford light in some of the darkest scenes of state."[13]

Osborne had a reputation for being a vulgar slave-driver. Pope had depicted him in the *Dunciad*, engaged in a pissing contest with another mercenary bookseller, Edmund Curll. Having paid a fortune for the Harleian library, Osborne was eager to recoup his investment as quickly as possible. When he saw Johnson absorbed in reading one of the books, a necessary part of his task, he reproached him in coarse language for inattention and delay. Justly offended, Johnson flew into a rage, knocked him down and then put his foot on his neck. Johnson recalled the incident by exclaiming, "he was insolent and I beat him, and he was a blockhead and told of it." After the dust-up, the adversaries found that they still needed each other. Osborne was eventually permitted to get up, and Johnson, always pressed for money, somehow made peace with his employer. He successfully completed the work, and the catalogue was published in five volumes in 1743–45. Parliament bought the precious manuscripts in 1753 and placed them in the library of the British Museum. In his life of Pope, Johnson, still nursing a grudge, called the boorish bookseller "a man intirely destitute of shame, without sense of any disgrace, but that of poverty."[14].

IV

J ohnson's finest biography, inspired by his attachment to the subject, was his life of Richard Savage (?1697–1743). Based on intimate friendship with a man he admired, and written from the heart, it was an important transition from his early derivative lives to the full-bodied *Lives of the Poets*. First published in 1744, it was included thirty-five years later in that book. Johnson was fascinated by Savage's amazing life. Touchy and aggressive, a dozen years older than Johnson, he was a publicly confessed bastard and a poet, spendthrift and sponger, street bum and jailbird. Savage, who quarreled with everyone, especially his benefactors, got along famously with the temperamental Johnson. They had in common extreme poverty, literary aspirations, hatred of the corrupt government, and deep-rooted resentment of those less talented but more successful than themselves. Johnson structured the *Life* by a series of contrasts: high birth and illegitimacy, nobility and degradation, wealth and penury, fame and obscurity, sobriety and drunkenness, calm and violence, freedom and bondage.

Savage had a mysterious aristocratic birth, was nearly kidnapped as an infant and had been apprenticed to a humble shoemaker. He became a poet, playwright and actor, and was a friend of the leading writers of his time—Pope and Richard Steele, James Thomson and Edward Young. A forger and blackmailer, he was always in trouble with the law. Arrested during the Jacobite Rebellion, he was acquitted of treason. Imprisoned and condemned to death for murder, he was pardoned by King George II. In 1728 he published his poem *The Bastard*, a virulent attack on his cruel mother, which described a fatuous aristocrat as the "tenth transmitter of a foolish face." He failed to become poet laureate, an honor awarded to Pope's great enemy Colley Cibber, but was granted a pension from Queen Caroline—and lost it after her death in 1737. Always impoverished and out of control, he was rusticated like a wild Oxford student, sent down from London to Wales and pensioned off by his friends. Arrested again for debt en route to Swansea, he died in a Bristol prison. Savage's recent biographer noted his "fine manner and bearing, though a little lofty, vivacious hilarity, and extraordinary conversational powers."

Johnson had met Savage through Cave and the *Gentleman's Magazine* in 1738–39, was close to him during their years of bitter poverty and knew him better than any other poet. Savage had contemptuously rejected a bundle of clothing that had been left for him at a coffeehouse, just as Johnson had angrily thrown out the pair of boots left outside his room at Oxford. Each man hated solitude, was unwilling to separate from friends and would prolong "his visits to unseasonable hours, and disconcert all the families into which he was admitted" (3.178). Savage, like Johnson, "could neither be persuaded to go to bed in the night, nor to rise in the day" (3.179). Both men, having no profession, became authors by necessity. Both constantly formed illusory schemes to publish their work—Johnson's projects included a history of parliament, a life of Oliver Cromwell and a play about Charles XII of Sweden—and designs to bring their tragedies upon the stage. Savage, like Johnson, exemplified the italicized theme of *London*: "*Slow rises Worth, by Poverty deprest.*"

Johnson, who always had great difficulty in getting himself to write, was intensely interested in the various ways that authors composed their works. (The exact mode of writing is still a favorite question during authors' interviews today.) The blind Milton, "when he had composed as many lines as his memory would conveniently retain," would call for an amanuensis (1.265). Pope roused his weary servant four times during a fierce winter night "to supply him with paper, lest he should lose a thought" (4.59). But Savage's mode of composition was unique. Deprived not only of room and fuel but also of writing implements, "he used to walk and form his speeches, and afterwards step into a shop, beg for a few moments the use of the pen and ink, and write down what he had composed upon paper he had picked up by accident" (3.130).

Johnson described Savage's life with great sympathy, for he had endured many of the same hardships. After the struggles described in *London,* he'd still not climbed out of poverty, and in 1739 had to sell the precious silver cup, engraved with his name, that his mother had given him when he was touched for the King's Evil in 1712. When Savage lacked the few pence to pay for the meanest lodging among the most profligate "riot and filth," he "walked about the streets till he was weary, and lay down in the summer upon a bulk, or in winter, with his associates in poverty, among the ashes of a glass-house" (3.165). As Pope wrote in *The Dunciad*: "Thus the soft gifts of Sleep conclude the day, / And stretch'd on bulks, as usual, Poets lay." The frozen poet's bed of hot ashes is both dreadful and ingenious.

Boswell related that Johnson and Savage, "for want of a lodging," spent many nights walking through the darkened streets of London. In the daytime Savage could go to a publisher's office, a coffeehouse or a public place. But at night, having alienated all the friends who might give him a bed or a pallet on the floor, he was forced to roam the city and sleep outdoors. Johnson, unlike Savage, never actually starved and had respectable lodgings with Tetty in Castle Street. It would seem that Tetty, like most people who got involved with the predatory Savage, thought him a bad influence on her husband, would have nothing to do with him and wouldn't allow him in her house. Johnson—who loved to walk, talk and stay up late—willingly strolled the streets with Savage for the pleasure of his company and conversation.

Savage may even have tempted him to take a few drinks to lubricate their talks. As Johnson wrote in the life of Addison: "he that feels oppression from the presence of those to whom he knows himself superior, will desire to set loose his powers of conversation; and who, that ever asked succour from Bacchus, was able to preserve himself from being enslaved by his auxiliary?" (3.21). Boswell added that the two friends "were not at all depressed by their situation; but in high spirits and brimful of patriotism, traversed the square for several hours, inveighed against the minister [Robert Walpole], and 'resolved they would *stand by their country*'" in the face of a corrupt regime.[15]

Johnson admired both the virtuous Boerhaave and the vicious Savage, for as he wrote in *Rambler* 70, "the purest virtue is consistent with some vice." Savage, like Psalmanazar, may also have been a fraud—the case remains open. Johnson never demanded from Savage—as he did from James Macpherson during their violent dispute about the authenticity of the Ossian poems—the documentary evidence to support his dubious claim that he was the illegitimate son of the 4th Earl Rivers by the Countess of Macclesfield. Twice in the *Life* Johnson wondered, but did not explain, why the vengeful countess tried to starve her son, transport him to the American plantations, bury him as a shoemaker's apprentice and cut him off from a legacy. She even tried to hasten the hand of the public executioner after Savage had been convicted of murder in a tavern brawl, similar to the one in which Christopher Marlowe was murdered. Johnson was so obsessed with Savage that he never considered the most convincing explanation for her persistent cruelty: that the fraudulent Savage was *not* her real son and that she therefore did everything possible to get rid of him.

Johnson not only uncritically accepted Savage's provocative satire on the clergy, but also condoned the murder for which Savage, against the wishes of the countess, was pardoned. "The hurry of the dispute was such," he wrote, "that it was not easy to discover the truth" (3.134). Johnson believed that Savage's life, like his own at that time, "afforded no other comforts than barren praises, and the consciousness of deserving them" and must therefore rather "excite pity than provoke censure" (3.188, 130). In the *Rambler* he'd implored his readers to look into their hearts and ask if they were any better than the criminals who were about to be hanged. Now he concluded that no "wise man will presume to say, 'Had I been in Savage's condition, I should have lived or written better than Savage'" (3.188). But Savage could certainly have been more restrained in his vituperative self-pity, more careful with the money he extracted from his benefactors and more grateful for the bounty they conferred upon him.

Johnson wrote that in Bristol, starving as usual and forced to turn on the charm, Savage "was reduced to roaming the streets . . . clothed in rags, hunting hungrily from house to house for an invitation to dinner." He gave a moving account of Savage's death, at the age of forty-six, in the grim precincts of a Bristol prison. Seeing the keeper at his bedside, Savage "said, with uncommon earnestness, 'I have something to say to you, Sir,' but, after a pause, moved his hand in a melancholy manner; and finding himself unable to recollect what he was going to communicate, said, "'Tis gone!'" (3.185). Leaving his very last idea unexpressed, Savage announced the loss of money, freedom, reputation and life itself with "'Tis gone!" In the fluttering gesture of his hand, Johnson subtly suggested both the attempt to grasp his elusive thought and the departure of his soul at the moment of death.

Johnson concluded with a noble apologia for his recently deceased companion, which both recognized and justified his faults: "The insolence and resentment of which he is accused were not easily to be avoided by a great mind, irritated by perpetual hardships, and constrained hourly to return the spurns of contempt, and repress the insolence of prosperity" (3.188). The *Life of Savage* is not only a biography, but also a memorial and an elegy. The biographer Richard Holmes perceptively observed that Johnson "takes scandalous materials—an adultery case among the aristocracy, a birthright claim, a blackmail campaign, a murder trial, an obscenity charge, a backstreet night-life existence, and a prison death—and turns them into a meditation on virtue."[16]

Savage had a powerful influence on Johnson. In *London* (May 1738) the narrator bids farewell to Thales, who departs for Wales. A year later, in July 1739, Johnson bade farewell to Savage, who, with tears in his eyes, also left for Wales. Wimsatt said that in this "peculiarly poignant instance, life had been the realization of poetic vision." But Johnson may well have heard, in advance, of plans to rescue Savage by sending him to Wales. The *Rambler* was probably named after Savage's poem *The Wanderer* (1729). His humiliating death in a debtors' prison inspired Johnson's attempts to abolish these inhuman institutions. Johnson's compassion for the poor and the homeless, his belief that poverty—not evil—provoked crime, also grew out of his personal experience with Savage. In Sermon 19 he sympathized with the "wretches wandering without an habitation, exposed to the contempt of the proud, and the insults of the cruel, goaded forward, by the stings of poverty, to dishonest acts, which perhaps relieve their present misery, only to draw some more dreadful distress upon them.".

<h1 style="text-align:center">V</h1>

In a crucial passage that discreetly but unmistakably hinted at the possibility of Johnson's early drinking and whoring, Boswell alluded to the conflict between sensuality and intellect in Romans 7:23: "Johnson was not free from propensities which were ever 'warring against the law of his mind'—and in his combats with them, he was sometimes overcome. . . . It was well known, that his amorous inclinations were uncommonly strong and impetuous. . . . His conduct, after he came to London, and had associated with Savage and others, was not so strictly virtuous, in one respect, as when he was a younger man."[17]

Boswell's suggestions that Johnson was sometimes overcome by his strong passions and was not always virtuous invite speculation about his sexual life when he was separated from Tetty and consorting with Savage. Prices for whores in London ranged from fifty guineas for a beautiful woman in a splendid setting to a shilling and a glass of wine for a slut on the Strand. Giacomo Casanova, a connoisseur in these matters, found a bargain in a London bathhouse, where he was "initiated into the select bagnios, where a rich man goes to bathe, sup, and sleep with a choice prostitute. It is a magnificent festival, which costs six guineas in all." As Johnson and Savage roamed the streets at night, they saw many wretched prostitutes.

Bishop Percy and Sir John Hawkins both wrote that Johnson often took such women to taverns and heard them recite their sordid histories: "he was very inquisitive as to their course of life, the history of their seduction, and the chances of reclaiming them." His firsthand experience and titillating interrogations inspired his sympathetic defense of whores—the "band of miserable females, covered with rags, shivering with cold, and pining with hunger"—in two of his finest periodical essays. Just as he did for the starvelings, beggars and poor folk driven to crime, he felt compassion rather than disgust for these unfortunates.

Like later investigators of the urban poor—Henry Mayhew, Friedrich Engels, Beatrice and Sidney Webb, and George Orwell— Johnson blamed social conditions rather than personal immorality for their downfall. In *Rambler* 170 he taught complacent readers to understand how defenseless women were forced onto the streets by financial coercion and sexual degradation: "Many of the beings which are now rioting in taverns, or shivering in the streets, have been corrupted not by arts of gallantry which stole upon the affections and laid prudence asleep, but by fear of losing benefits which were never intended, or of incurring resentment which they could not escape; some have been frighted by masters, and some awed by guardians into ruin."

In *Rambler* 171 he mentioned women as concubines in whorehouses or on the streets. While neither accusing nor excusing them, he emphasized the cruelties and miseries of their lives, and urged men to rescue rather than exploit them:

> [They are] sometimes the property of one man, and sometimes the common prey of accidental lewdness; at one time tricked up for sale by the mistress of a brothel, at another begging in the streets to be relieved from hunger by wickedness. . . . See the wretches that lie crowded together, mad with intemperance, ghastly with famine, nauseous with filth, and noisome with disease. . . . [One must not] harden against compassion, or repress the desire . . . to rescue such numbers of human beings from a state so dreadful.[18]

Later on, Johnson even invited whores to join his household.

Exploring the lives of streetwalkers and hearing their intimate revelations—like hearing about the sexual exploits of his rakish friends, Savage, Beauclerk and Boswell—may have provided vicarious erotic pleasure or occasional amusement. He once asked a whore why "her Maker had bestowed on her so much beauty? Her answer was—'To please the gentlemen, to be sure; for what other use could it be given me?'" Yet when his young friends boldly asked if his pernicious association with Savage ever seduced him from the tavern to the brothel, Johnson, ascending to a Latin euphemism, said he was more repelled rather than excited by their sordid confessions: "we never proceeded to the *Opus Magnum.* On the contrary, I have rather been disconcerted and shocked by the replies of these giddy wenches, than flattered or diverted by their tricks."[19]

Sometimes separated from Tetty or rejected by her (for her desires rarely matched the intensity of his own), Johnson had to find other outlets, apart from prostitutes, for his passions. On one occasion, in a garden in Lichfield, he saw an enticing statue of Venus and exclaimed, "throw her into the pond to hide her nakedness, and to cool her lasciviousness." He wasn't troubled by the public display of nudity, but felt the statue—like the "white bubbies" of Garrick's actresses—heated up his *own* lascivious feelings.

His fantasies and "polluting thoughts" also made him feel lecherous. In a passage deleted from the *Tour,* Johnson, who *often* thought about the possibilities of sexual license, insisted that if he had Oriental concubines, they would have to be protected against filth and kept clean: "I have often thought that if I kept a seraglio, the ladies should all wear linen gowns. . . . I would have no silk; you cannot tell when it is clean. It would be very nasty before it is perceived to be so." Asked if he would admit Boswell to his private harem, Johnson warmed to the subject and brightened at the prospect of castrating his lusty young friend while he remained virile: "Yes, if he were properly prepared; and he'd make a very good eunuch."

Another of Johnson's fantasies combined emotional and physical pleasure, the feeling of flirtation and speed in a closed space. "If I had no duties," he confided, "and no reference to futurity, I would spend my life in driving briskly in a post-chaise with a pretty woman." Though this desire for perpetual propulsion seems fantastic, George Trevelyan noted that "to drive a lady in a phaeton built for two, with its high wheels and smart pair of horses, was a fashionable diversion in the last part of the [eighteenth] century." Edmund Burke's treatise on the sublime and the beautiful provided a philosophical basis for this joyride: "being swiftly drawn in an easy coach, on a smooth turf, with gradual ascents and declivities . . . will give a better idea of the beautiful . . . than almost any thing else."[20]

Johnson was sometimes able to turn his fantasies into reality. More like the Frog Prince than Prince Charming and sexually hors de combat in polite society, he felt licensed to take certain liberties with young ladies. When he first met the author Charlotte Lennox, he gave her cakes, held her on his knee like a child and carried her in his arms to see his library. Boswell recorded another pleasing incident that took place when they were touring Scotland: "a neat, pretty girl sat down upon Mr. Johnson's knee, and upon being bid by some of the company, put her hands round his neck and kissed him. 'Do it again,' said he, 'and let us see who will tire first.'" The disparity in age, the girl's bold move and Johnson's wish to prolong the pleasure—expressed to her in the simplest language—made this one of the most delightful moments in his life.

Bolder still was his intensely emotional but carefully choreographed parting from the attractive actress and playwright Frances Brooke:

> At a farewell party on the evening before she sailed for Canada, where her husband was chaplain to the garrison at Quebec, Johnson contrived to see Mrs. Brooke alone in the parlour and told her . . . that as she was setting off on a long journey and he might never see her again, therefore, "My dear . . . I wanted to have a kiss of you before you went, & being conscious of my own awkward figure I called you aside that I might do it with more convenience than before all the company."[21]

In this sly incident, Johnson, well aware of his repellent appearance, managed with a far-fetched explanation to steal a kiss. In all these dramatic scenarios, Johnson, under the guise of playful innocence, contrived to play the privileged gallant (or court jester) and express his powerful feelings.

Confessional chats with prostitutes and a few furtive kisses could not slake Johnson's passions. It was natural for a young man (and later on, a middle-aged widower) to seek other outlets for his impulses. The letter "M" appeared mysteriously in his *Diaries,* which, as Dr. Bernard Meyer observed, provide "telling evidence that he was entangled in a painful and unceasing struggle with masturbation." In the eighteenth century and beyond, masturbation (specifically condemned in Genesis 38:9) was considered a shameful and dangerous practice that ruined the complexion and left dark patches under the eyes, telltale signs of depravity. Works like James Graham's *Onania, or the Heinous Sin of Self-Pollution* (c.1724) also "proved" that masturbation "led to physical and psychological damage": frigidity, sterility, even madness. In view of Johnson's poor health, fear of insanity, and sense of sin and guilt, the compulsion to relieve himself, despite the sensational warnings in tracts like *Onania,* must have been overwhelming.

Hawkins—who knew Johnson for most of his adult life, from the days of the *Gentleman's Magazine* to his deathbed—suggested that his fear of death was based on guilt about his sexual irregularities. He stole Johnson's private papers to "protect" them and, adopting a grave and earnest demeanor, told Boswell (in a passage omitted from the *Life*): "'I have read his diary. I wish I had not read so much. He had strong amorous passions.' Boswell. 'But he did not indulge them?' Hawkins. 'I have said enough.'"[22]

8

DOOM OF MAN
1745–1749

I

J ohnson's previous work, however humble and ill paid, was excellent preparation for his monumental *Dictionary of the English Language,* which he began in 1746, completed almost single-handedly in 1754 and published the following year. He'd written lives of several scholars, scientists and naval heroes; re-created the *Debates in Parliament;* catalogued the massive Harleian Library; and written the proposals and some of the articles for Dr. Robert James' three-volume *Medical Dictionary* (1743–45). In Johnson's time there was no work in English comparable to the dictionaries compiled in 1612 by many scholars in the Accademia della Crusca (the Academy of the Chaff, founded in Florence in 1582 to maintain the purity of the Italian language) and in 1694 by the Académie Française. His *Dictionary* was modeled on and competed with these works; and in his "Plan of an English Dictionary" (1746) he spoke of his "contest with united academies and long successions of learned compilers."

The bookseller Robert Dodsley—who'd started out as a footman and would publish *The Vanity of Human Wishes*—thought up the idea of an English dictionary and led a consortium that agreed to finance the venture. Among them was the Scotsman William Strahan, who also printed the *Dictionary*, became the king's printer and on his death left a vast fortune of £95,000. In June 1746 Johnson signed the contract, for a fee of £1,575, and rather optimistically agreed to complete the project in three years. When his friend William Adams of Pembroke College cautioned him that "the French Academy, which consists of forty members, took forty years to compile their Dictionary," Johnson assumed a patriotic stance, did some quick calculations and explained how he could do it: "Let me see; forty times forty is sixteen hundred. As three [years is] to sixteen hundred, so is the proportion of an Englishman to a Frenchman." Though he actually took eight years to complete the project, an Englishman was by his reckoning still worth considerably more than a Frenchman.

His "Plan," addressed to a potential patron, Lord Chesterfield, and written before he started the work, should not be confused with the "Preface to the *Dictionary*" (1755), which was written after he had completed the work. In the "Plan" he ironically described the lexicographer as a weary donkey, "bearing burthens with dull patience, and beating the track of the alphabet with sluggish resolution." In fact, he worked not slowly and surely, but in spurts of energetic effort. He planned to include material on the proper orthography, pronunciation, etymology, syntax and interpretation of words. Following the precedent of the European academies, he declared that his *Dictionary* would be one "in which the pronunciation of our language may be fixed, and its attainment facilitated; by which its purity may be preserved, its use [and meaning] ascertained, and its duration lengthened."[1] Later on, when he was more experienced, he changed his mind on these points. In the "Preface" he confessed that the attempt to stabilize and "fix" the language was both pointless and impossible. The *Dictionary* was descriptive, not prescriptive. It showed how the language was actually used, instead of how Johnson thought it should be used.

Most of the funds for the *Dictionary* came in piecemeal as he produced copy for the printer. But the initial payment, which gave him a lot of money for the first time in his life, enabled him to rent a substantial house, for £30 a year, in which to do the work. Seventeen Gough Square—the only one of his eighteen London residences still standing—is a four-story house, built in 1700, on the corner of a

Johnson's House, 17 Gough Square, off Fleet
Street, London—Valerie Meyers

small square just north of Fleet Street. An iron railing runs along the
sides of the front steps and around the basement windows; another
railing, with an arched gate, separates the side door and tiny garden
from the street. The front door was secured with a heavy chain. The
kitchen and pantry are in the basement, the parlor and dining room
on the main floor, and a narrow staircase leads up to four rooms on
the first and second floors. Johnson worked in the garret, which was
fitted out like a countinghouse and filled with rickety furniture and
piles of bought, borrowed and often battered books. The house did
not have running water; but there was an ample supply of chamber
pots and an outdoor privy in the garden. Johnson lived in Gough
Square longer than anywhere else in London, from late 1746 to the
spring of 1759.

To help with the mechanical aspects of his labor, Johnson hired six
amanuenses, the humblest of starving hacks. Five of them, despite his

supposed and oft-repeated dislike of their country, were Scots. Alexander Macbean, who'd helped Ephraim Chambers with his *Cyclopaedia* (5th edition, 1746), brought in his younger brother William. Robert Shiels began as a printer; he was the ghostwriter of Theophilus Cibber's *Lives of the Poets* and later composed a blank verse poem, "The Power of Beauty," praising *Irene*. (To paraphrase Johnson, if Shiels says so, Shiels lies.) He died of consumption in 1753. Francis Stewart was the son of an Edinburgh bookseller. Mr. Maitland remains obscure. Johnson's irascible Italian friend Giuseppe Baretti called V. J. Peyton, who'd taught French and was the only English scribe, "a fool and a drunkard. I never saw so nauseous a fellow." Peyton was later reduced to penury, and when he died in 1776, Johnson had to bury both him and his wife.

Johnson usually had only three or four assistants working for him at one time, and some of them may have lived and dined in his house. He had four workers in August 1748 and at least two the following spring. The garret seemed like a schoolroom, with the unruly lads toiling fitfully at their tables, and the master and turnkey dictating to them. The severe yet kindhearted Johnson also assumed the paternal role and had to deal with many of their personal problems: laziness, carelessness, inefficiency, poverty, dishonesty, petty disputes, occasional violence, marital discord, alcoholism, depression, sickness, even death.

Johnson paid all his assistants just over £2 a week. Assuming they worked fifty weeks a year for about four years, by which time most of their transcriptions would be finished, their combined wages came to £400. This sum and the £240 rent for eight years ate up more than a third of Johnson's fee. He had to buy tables and benches, stacks of books and reams of paper, quill pens and knives to sharpen them, ink and inkhorns, scissors and glue, candles for the many dark days and early nights, coal for the fire, food to stoke the workers. And he had to maintain a commanding presence to keep the cadre of scribblers in efficient order. Johnson also had to fork out for costly mistakes when he was still searching for the best way to work. When, to save money, he wrote copy on both sides of the paper and the printer refused to accept the illegible text, he had to pay an additional £20 in labor and paper to have it recopied on only one side. (Eighteenth-century sums of money should be multiplied by about seventy to find the rough modern equivalent.)

The *Dictionary* might have been profitable if Johnson had completed it in three superhuman years, but since it took eight years he actually lost money on it. In March 1750, halfway through the project, he was forced to begin simultaneous work on the *Rambler* and turn out two substantial essays every week for the next two years. In November 1751 Strahan threatened to cut off payments until Johnson's little army produced more copy. But Johnson, as the unfortunate Osborne had learned during their work on the Harleian catalogue, would not be bullied. In contrast to the humbly apologetic letter written to Cave in April 1738 about the slow progress of his translation of Sarpi's *History,* he now adopted a combative stance. He fortified himself for the impending siege and, like an experienced commander, prepared to repel the assault. Employing a military metaphor, he told Strahan, "my citadel shall not be taken by storm while I can defend it, and if a blockade is intended, the country is still under the command of my batteries."[2]

Johnson far surpassed his immediate English predecessor, Nathan Bailey's *Dictionarium Britannicum* (1730; 2nd edition 1736), by making two significant innovations. Following the traditional practice of Greek and Latin lexicographers, he included, for his 42,000 words, 116,000 illustrative quotations, from the greatest English writers of the past. He also divided his words into carefully shaded definitions. The word "set," for example, as verb and noun, had ninety-nine different meanings. His method was also innovative. Though he was half blind, Johnson began by reading books and searching for the appropriate words instead of starting with a list of words that had to be defined. He occasionally used Chaucer, but extracted most of his words from books published in the two centuries between the birth of Sir Philip Sidney (1554–1586) and the death of Alexander Pope (1688–1744), who was Johnson's contemporary for thirty-five years.

The main sources of Johnson's quotations (in the revised edition of 1773) ranged from John Milton (with 200 citations), George Chapman, his favorite William Law, and Edward Young (the last two still living when the *Dictionary* was first published) to Abraham Cowley, Michael Drayton, Alexander Pope and the Bible (with 71 citations). He had to include Milton, whose politics he abhorred, but took care to exclude anyone who'd supported Oliver Cromwell and the English Interregnum between the execution of Charles I in 1649 and the accession of Charles II in 1660. To protect his readers from atheists and freethinkers, he also blackballed notorious infidels like Thomas Hobbes and Lord Boling-broke. He cunningly co-opted the latter, however, to illustrate "irony": "A mode of speech in which the meaning is contrary to the words: as, *Bolingbroke was a holy man.*"

Johnson bent the rules to slip in a few worthy contemporaries and friends: James Beattie under "weak," Charlotte Lennox under "talent," David Garrick under "giggle," Oliver Goldsmith under "venerate," and Samuel Richardson, whose epistolary novel *Clarissa* (1748–49) provided both belligerent and moralistic entries: "A man who is gross in a woman's company, ought to be *knocked down* with a club" and "A good clergyman must love and *venerate* the gospel that he teaches, and prefer it to all other learning." Johnson also quoted himself (why not?), both by name and under "anonymous," no fewer than forty-eight times. He cited nine illus-trations from *Irene* for the words "disjoint," "from," "idler," "important," "imposture," "intimidate," "obscurely," "stagnant" and "sultaness"; eight from *The Vanity of Human Wishes,* including "lacerate" and "relax"; and from both *London* and the *Life of Savage,* "dissipate." He began with a disproportionate number of illustrations for the letter "A" but, realizing he was getting hopelessly bogged down, cut the examples on subsequent let-ters in order to forge ahead.

After some initial experimentation, Johnson fixed on a fairly effi-cient method. Whenever, in the course of his reading, he found a word that was well illustrated by its context, he penciled the first letter of the word in the margin of the book and made two slanted strokes to in-dicate the end of the quotation. After finishing the book, he gave it to his assistants, who copied the passages down on slips of paper and crossed out the marginal letter to show that the quotation had been recorded. They then pasted these thousands and thousands of slips, under the key word, into eighty large folio notebooks (which resembled the heavy, blue, partly handwritten volumes of the old British Museum catalogue). Many of these slips must have been lost along the way. When the assistants had compiled and compared all the passages illustrating a single word, Johnson wrote the definitions, put them into a logical sequence and added the illustrations to buttress the meaning. A formidable task!

The words in the *Dictionary* ran from "abacke" to "zootomy." Johnson enlivened his scholarly work with many playful, idiosyncratic and revealing definitions, which expressed his social and political views as well as his personal prejudices:

Dedication: A servile address to a patron.

Dull: Not exhilarating; not delightful; as, *to make dictionaries is* dull *work*.

Enthusiasm: A vain belief of private revelation; a vain confidence of divine favour or communication.

Excise: A hateful tax levied upon commodities, and adjudged, not by the common judges of property, but wretches hired by those to whom excise is paid.

Favourite: One chosen as a companion by his superiour; a mean wretch whose whole business is by any means to please.

Lexicographer: A writer of dictionaries; a harmless drudge, that busies himself in tracing the original, and detailing the signification of words.

Lich: *Lichfield*, the field of the dead, a city in Staffordshire, so named from martyred Christians. *Salve magna parens* [from Virgil: "Hail, great parent"].

Oats: A grain, which in England is generally given to horses, but in Scotland supports the people.

Patriot: One whose ruling passion is love of his country. It is sometimes used for a factious disturber of the government.

Patron: One who countenances, supports, or protects. Commonly a wretch who supports with insolence, and is paid with flattery.

Pension: An allowance made to any one without an equivalent. In England it is generally understood to mean pay given to a state hireling for treason to his country.

Stammel: Of this word I know not the meaning.

Stockjobber: A low wretch who gets money by buying and selling shares in the funds.

Johnson made a few notable errors. When a lady asked why he defined "pastern" as the knee rather than the foot of a horse, he nonchalantly replied, "Ignorance, Madam, pure ignorance." Though "leeward" and "windward" are antonyms, he defined both as "Towards the wind." "Cricket," which he probably never watched, he confusingly described as "A sport, at which the contenders drive a ball with sticks in opposition to each other." "Network" was hopelessly obfuscating: "Any thing reticulated or decussated, at equal distances, with interstices between the intersections." A modern *History of the English Language* notes that "words like *budge, coax, nonplus, shabby, squabble, stingy, tiff, touchy, wobbly,* which were recorded with proper disparagement by Dr. Johnson, have since passed into standard speech."[3]

In the "Preface" Johnson remarked, "as politeness increases, some expressions will be considered as too gross and vulgar for the delicate." When some respectable ladies "very much commended the omission of all *naughty* words," he exposed their hypocrisy by asking, "What, my dears! Then you have been looking for them?" It's rather surprising, therefore, to discover that he included many coarse and obscene words that would have shocked the ladies: "arse," "bitch," "clap" ("A venereal infection"), "fart" ("To break wind from behind"), "pimp" ("One who provides gratifications for the lust of others"), "piss," "puke," "snot," "trollope" ("A slatternly loose woman"), "turd" and "whore." But he had to draw the line somewhere and prudently excluded "prick," "cunt," "fuck" and "shit."

The *Dictionary* was a map of Johnson's mind and summa of his intellectual interests, a tribute to the range of his reading and the depth of his erudition. Matthew Arnold's ideal, expressed in "The Function of Criticism at the Present Time" (1864), described it perfectly: "a disinterested endeavour to learn and propagate the best that is known and thought in the world."[4]

II

In 1749 Johnson published his best poem, *The Vanity of Human Wishes*, and had his tragedy *Irene*, which had been languishing since completion in 1737, produced at the Drury Lane Theater. He imitated Juvenal's Tenth Satire in *Vanity*, as he'd imitated the Third Satire in *London*. In the earlier poem he'd stayed close to the original, updating Juvenal with an angry, satiric catalogue of London life, but his new poem broke fresh ground. With a stately style and gloomy philosophical argument, it went beyond imitation and was more like an original poem. The grave dignity and Christian stoicism of *Vanity*, which recur in the *Rambler* and in *Rasselas*, are central to Johnson's style and thought.

Dryden had translated Juvenal's Tenth Satire in 1693 and summarized his main themes: "The poet's design, in this divine satire, is to represent the various wishes and desires of mankind, and to set out the folly of 'em. He runs thro' all the several heads of riches, honors, eloquence, fame for martial achievements, long life, and beauty; and gives instances, in each, how frequently they have prov'd the ruin of those that own'd them." Johnson had a temperamental affinity with Juvenal's gravity and moral sense, his remorseless pessimism and Roman stoicism. *Vanity* looks back on centuries of human struggle, on illusory hopes and inevitable fate, on sudden shifts in political power and the cruel indignity of death. It portrays disillusion, from the disgraced Cardinal Wolsey and the murdered Thomas Wentworth, to the young student burning for renown and the poor scholar crushed by "Toil, Envy, Want, the Garret and the Jail." It expresses Johnson's tragic sense of life, his belief that the pain and misery of human existence far outweigh its pleasure and happiness. Warning against self-delusion and the foolish conceit that human wishes could be fulfilled, he insisted:

Yet hope not Life from Grief or Danger free,
Nor think the Doom of Man revers'd for thee.

Lord Byron, constitutionally opposed to Juvenal's gravity and Johnson's gloom, ironically commented, "the 10th Satire has always been my favourite, as I suppose indeed of every body's. It is the finest recipe for making one miserable with his life, & content to walk out of it, in any language."

Johnson's title originates in the dire motto of Ecclesiastes 1:2: "Vanity of vanities; all is vanity," a word he defined in the *Dictionary* as "uncertainty," "fruitless desire" and "falsehood." Believing with George Herbert that "A verse may finde him who a sermon flies,"[5] Johnson uses the poem to preach from a deeply pessimistic text. His title implies that certainty and truth can be found, despite the temptations of the world, only by adhering to a spiritual path and following God's will, a message John Bunyan had powerfully delivered in *Pilgrim's Progress* (1678). Instead of emphasizing the joy and consolation of Christian belief, and the hope of redemption it offers, Johnson distilled into the poem twenty years of bitterness, failure and struggle for faith. His poem is not simply pessimistic, but strains against optimism, against the possibility that human life could actually get better.

In *Rasselas* Johnson expressed the neoclassical preference for the general over the particular by observing, "the business of the poet is to examine, not the individual, but the species; to remark general properties and large appearances: he does not number the streaks of the tulip, or describe the different shades in the verdure of the forest. He is to exhibit in his portraits of nature such prominent and striking features, as recall the original to every mind." In his poem Johnson followed his own precepts. He examines the vanity of human wishes for political power, intellectual achievement, military glory, long life and physical beauty.

Juvenal began his Tenth Satire with "*Omnibus in terris, quae sunt a Gadibus usque / Auroram et Gangem*" ("In every land from Cadiz to the Ganges and the dawn"). In his "Essay on Epitaphs" (1740) Johnson had quoted a variant of these lines—from Spain to India—in the epitaph on the Renaissance philosopher Pico della Mirandola: "*cetera norunt / Et Tagus et Ganges*" ("the rest of his story is known by the Tagus and the Ganges"). Dryden had compressed Juvenal's theme into his first lines:

Look round the habitable world: how few
Know their own good; or knowing it, pursue.[6]

In the opening of *Vanity*, Johnson brilliantly reaches far out and in deep. He adopts Dryden's rhyme, yet disdains Dryden's narrower scope and condensed wit in favor of Juvenal's vast geography and magisterial tone:

> Let Observation with extensive View,
> Survey Mankind from China to Peru.

In his *Lectures on Shakespeare*, Coleridge, who disliked personification, called these lines tautological bombast and mockingly paraphrased them as "Let observation with extensive observation observe mankind extensively." Though "observe," "survey" and "view" have similar meanings, Coleridge ignored Johnson's majestic movement from the personified "Observation" to the concrete "China to Peru." In this way, Johnson defined the poem's geographical range and the scope of its human activities. A poet traveling westward and observing mankind from China to Peru would cover (except for the Pacific Ocean) the entire world.

Peru, in the western hemisphere, was associated with the gold of the Incas and symbolized infinite wealth. China, in the eastern hemisphere, represented the wisdom of an ancient civilization. Johnson's review of Jean Baptiste du Halde's *History of China* (1738) described the Chinese as a "celebrated people, whose antiquity, magnificence, power, wisdom, peculiar customs, and excellent constitution, undoubtedly deserve the attention of the public." He praised the country where brainpower was respected and intellectual ability led to high office, "where nobility and knowledge are the same, where men advance in rank as they advance in learning, and promotion is the effect of virtuous industry."[7] Johnson may have thought that if he lived in China, his knowledge and virtue, instead of confining him to Grub Street, would propel him into the ruling class.

The deep emotions that surge through *Vanity* are controlled by the form of Juvenal's satire and by the masterly style: its confident abstractions and stately balance, its magisterial rhythm and forceful rhymes, its moral grandeur and epigrammatic wisdom. In a superb line that with four verbs—the polysyllabic one prolonging the process—encapsulates the huge arc of ambition and disappointment, he writes of suppliants: "They mount, they shine, evaporate, and fall." Johnson's echoes from Milton and Pope, as well as from Juvenal and Dryden, add poignant dignity to the poem. The meter and rhyme, the elevated mood and ascendant sensation in Milton's "And, O ye Dolphins, waft the hapless youth" recur in Johnson's line, "And Virtue guard thee to the Throne of Truth." The sense of impending death in Pope's

> Years foll'wing Years, steal something ev'ry day,
> At last they steal us from ourselves away

inspired Johnson's thematic couplet:

> Year chases Year, Decay pursues Decay,
> Still drops some Joy from with'ring Life away.[8]

Johnson insisted on decorum in writing, and his elevated diction and moral urgency unify his style and strengthen his verse. Aiming for a smooth and serious tone, he eliminated Juvenal's obscenities and his description of sexual impotence. Dryden had compressed these lines into "The limber nerve, in vain provok'd to rise, / Inglorious from the field of battle flies." A modern translator, Niall Rudd, renders them more graphically as: "if you try to stimulate him, his thin tool with its enlarged vein lies limp and will remain so although it be caressed all night." In his life of Dryden, Johnson criticized the poet for lack of taste and defined the qualities he'd hoped to capture in his own poem: "The general character of [Dryden's] translation . . . preserves the wit, but wants the dignity of the original. The peculiarity of Juvenal is a mixture of gaiety and stateliness, of pointed sentences and declamatory grandeur." Johnson achieved such acuity and splendor, and his memorable lines, like those of Shakespeare and Kipling, form part of our cultural heritage. His expression of danger and *angst*:

> Now Fears in dire Vicissitude invade,
> The rustling Brake alarms, and quiv'ring Shade,

and the sense of being helplessly swept away by forces beyond his control:

> Must helpless Man, in Ignorance sedate,
> Roll darkling down the Torrent of his Fate?[9]

describe his inner torments.

Just as the vast geographical scope of *Vanity* strengthens its general thesis, so Johnson's contemporary equivalents of Juvenal's characters emphasize the folly of worldly success. Juvenal had used the warriors Hannibal and Alexander the Great to exemplify the mutability of fortune and the inevitability of decay. Johnson's examples from more recent history—Charles XII and the Duke of Marlborough, who illustrate the delusive attempts to conquer Europe and the misery of an inglorious death—were familiar to his readers. Johnson's view of history always tended to be biographical. He had once planned to write a play about Charles XII (1682–1718), the warrior king of Sweden. Victorious in battle during the Great Northern War in Russia, the Baltic, Poland, Germany and Denmark, he was defeated in 1709 by Czar Peter the Great at Poltava in the Ukraine. After five years of exile in Turkey, Charles returned to battle and, while looking over a parapet during an assault on an obscure fortress in Norway, was shot through the head by a Danish sniper.

In an extended 32-line sketch of Charles' character and career, Johnson first portrays him as a world-vanquishing Tamerlane: "A Frame of Adamant, a Soul of Fire, / No Dangers fright him, and no Labours tire." Then, after a series of triumphs, he comes to an ignominious end. During an insignificant conflict in a remote wasteland, not worth fighting or dying for, he's slain by an unknown soldier. The lines shift from the geographical setting and small fort to the single enemy who fired the fatal shot:

> His Fall was destin'd to a barren Strand,
> A petty Fortress, and a dubious Hand.
> He left the Name, at which the World grew pale,
> To point a Moral, or adorn a Tale.

John Churchill, Duke of Marlborough (1650–1722)—after stunning victories against the French at Blenheim, Ramillies and Malplaquet (1704–09)—became the leading European general and statesman during the reign of Queen Anne. He was also a bitter enemy of Jonathan Swift, who repeatedly attacked him in his political pamphlets and in his "Satirical Elegy on the Death of a Late Famous General" (1722). Alluding to the families of the tens of thousands of soldiers who died so that Marlborough could achieve military glory and accumulate great wealth, Swift wrote: "True to his profit and his pride, / He made them weep before he dy'd." Four years after Swift's death, Johnson takes up the motif of tears and links the two adversaries in a savage couplet. Showing the evils of old age and alluding to the rumor that the mad Swift was exhibited for money by his servants, he wrote: "From Marlb'rough's Eyes the Streams of Dotage flow, / And Swift expires a Driv'ler and a Show."

Johnson's examples of vanity among the great are not entirely convincing. Many eighteenth-century men who lived into their seventies expired as dotards or droolers. But none attained Marlborough's military triumphs or Swift's literary achievements, which suggest the glorious realization of ambition rather than the vanity of human wishes. Johnson himself was in poor physical condition at the end of his life, but that does not detract from his own impressive work. In "Blood and the Moon" W. B. Yeats more acutely related Swift's prophetic madness to his portrayal of the Yahoos in *Gulliver's Travels* and to his bleak vision of the human condition: "Swift beating on his breast in sibylline frenzy blind / Because the heart in his blood-sodden breast had dragged him down into mankind."[10]

The belief that "all is vanity" may encourage the passivity and inaction, the indolence and procrastination that Johnson struggled against throughout his life. If all human endeavor is vain and destined to disappointment, then it would seem that all effort is useless and that it would be wise to do nothing at all. If the only answer lies in religious salvation, then it would be best to renounce the tempting but worthless world and retire to the seclusion of a monastery. But Johnson, brought up in the Protestant tradition, rejected this unworldly choice of life.

Despite its historical apparatus, the poem essentially centers on Johnson's personal dilemma: how can I conquer my desire for love and fame? How can I love God, when all that awaits me is disillusionment and death? He does not answer these questions, but in the concluding lines offers several ways of escape. One can tame sexual desire: "Pour fourth thy Fervours for a healthful Mind, / Obedient Passions, and a Will resign'd"; adhere to the virtues of love, patience and faith; stoically accept the onset of death: "Count Death kind Nature's Signal of Retreat"; and trust in Christian belief, despite imperfect faith: "With these celestial Wisdom calms the Mind, / And makes the Happiness she does not find." In his own life, Johnson, terrified of death and fearful of damnation, fought desperately against nature's signal. Though he practiced the Christian virtues, he found in religion not peace and happiness, but profound misery and devastating despair. His own attempt to discover joy in religion was the vainest wish of all. The tension between his beliefs and his feelings makes *Vanity* a classic English poem.

Recognizing *Vanity* as one of his major works, Johnson published the poem—as he later did only with *Irene,* the *Dictionary,* the edition of Shakespeare and *The Lives of the Poets*—under his own name. Major poets of the nineteenth and twentieth centuries enthusiastically praised his work. Sir Walter Scott said, "he had more pleasure in reading *London,* and *The Vanity of Human Wishes,* than any other poetical composition he could mention." Ezra Pound remarked that *Vanity* "is the most typical of its mode, and it most brilliantly illustrates and attains the apogee and top notch of that mode . . . its triumph is of the perfectly weighed and placed word." T. S. Eliot—echoing Johnson's rhetorical question, "If Pope be not a poet, where is poetry to be found?"—said of the portrait of Charles XII, "if lines 189–220 of *The Vanity of Human Wishes* are not poetry, I do not know what is." He concluded by asserting that Johnson's two major poems "seem to me to be among the greatest verse Satires of the English or any other language; and, so far as comparison is justifiable, I do not think that Juvenal, his model, is any better."[11]

III

Johnson's relations with David Garrick, his oldest friend, were more complex and troubled than with any other man. Ten years younger than Johnson, and his former pupil at Edial, Garrick not only had been subject to his physical punishment, but was also the intimate witness to his strange and sometimes comical marriage to Tetty. Garrick had spent an adventurous year in Lisbon while Johnson was still stuck in Lichfield. They had traveled to London together and competed for distinction. Garrick's astonishing success, fame and wealth had been achieved far earlier and was far greater than Johnson's. He became a celebrity at twenty-four and dominated the English stage for the next thirty-five years.

Garrick's parents wanted him to study law, but his interest in the subject was short lived. After a brief stint in the London wine trade with his older brother, he had his first burlesque put on at the Drury Lane Theatre in 1740. The following year (when Johnson was still toiling obscurely on Grub Street), he made his stunning debut as Shakespeare's deformed and villainous Richard III. He wrote many prologues and epilogues, several lively farces and, with George Colman, his best comedy, *The Clandestine Marriage* (1766). In 1747 he became manager of Drury Lane, where, with great acclaim, he produced and acted in many of Shakespeare's plays. He took the spectators off the stage, improved the scenery and lighting, and developed a natural rather than histrionic style of acting. In 1749 he married the Catholic Eva Veigel, a dancer from Vienna. He last appeared onstage in 1776, when he sold his share of the theater for the enormous sum of £35,000.

Johnson befriended many actors—Garrick, Savage, Arthur Murphy, Tom Davies (who moved from bookselling to the stage) and the playwright and MP Richard Brinsley Sheridan—and had tangled with the cruel mimic Samuel Foote. But partly because of his impaired sight and hearing, he had a low opinion of actors, whose notorious immorality incited the Puritans to close the theaters in Cromwell's time. Johnson thought success on the stage brought disproportionate rewards and felt obliged to cut vain actors down to size. Boswell's editor remarked,

"Johnson's jealousy of Garrick's success made him belittle acting as a profession, and Garrick's merit in particular; Garrick, in turn, was hurt that his old teacher and friend, whom he admired so greatly, refused to give him the praise which he had earned, and which the rest of the world offered in abundance."

The author Hannah More added, "Johnson with all his genius had no taste for Garrick's acting; and with all his virtues was envious of his riches." Johnson didn't want riches himself, but felt that Garrick didn't deserve such wealth merely for strutting on the stage. Boswell noted Johnson's quasi-protective and proprietary attitude toward Garrick, whom he treated as if he were still his underling: "Johnson considered Garrick to be as it were his *property*. He would allow no man either to blame or to praise Garrick in his presence, without contradicting him."[12]

Most of Johnson's comments about Garrick were comic put-downs. He mocked his facial contortions, equated him with the buffoon in the Italian *commedia dell'arte* and denigrated his greatest tragic role. He maintained that Garrick "*looks* much older than he *is;* for his Face has had double the Business of any other man's,—it is never at rest." The painter Thomas Gainsborough confirmed Johnson's statement by observing, "so flexible and universal was the countenance of this great player that it was as impossible to catch his likeness as it is to catch the form of a passing cloud." When Garrick reasonably yet pretentiously complained that Johnson spoke loudly behind the scenes when he was acting on stage, Johnson would have none of it. Hester Thrale recorded Garrick saying, "do have done with all this Rattle—it spoyls my Thoughts, it destroys my *Feelings*—No No Sir returns the other—(loud enough for all the players to hear him)—I know better things—*Punch* has no *feelings*." Johnson offered a deflating definition of an actor as a person with no art or talent: "a fellow who claps a hump on his back, and a lump on his leg, and cries, '*I am Richard the Third.*'" Using another superlative, equating reading aloud with acting and making it all seem as if it were the easiest thing in the world, Johnson told Hester Thrale that "his Wife read Comedy better than ever he heard anybody— in Tragedy he said I did better. She always mouthed ["uttered with a voice affectedly big"] too much."[13]

Johnson faulted Garrick for his defects of character as well as for his *louche* profession, in which the actresses were notoriously free with their favors. Johnson remembered taking tea with Garrick when his friend, living with the actress Peg Woffington, complained that she wasted it and made it too strong. Though rich, Garrick was still tight with money. Johnson also declared that "David, thro' the false censure he underwent of stinginess, escaped the real censure which he deserv'd for his luxury." In *Rambler* 200, recalling Pope's satiric portrait of the Duke of Chandos in the "Epistle to Burlington" as a man of great wealth and poor taste, Johnson created the character of Prospero, a vulgar nouveau riche, to satirize Garrick's crass display of fine furniture and Dresden china.

In one of the best and most autobiographical *Ramblers,* Johnson wrote that the narrator and Prospero had once "set out in the world together; and for a long time mutually assisted each other in our exigencies." Both, from ironically different points of view, "still remembered with pleasure the days in which he and I were upon the level." The essay describes "the miseries which I endured in a morning visit to Prospero, a man lately raised to wealth by a lucky project, and too much intoxicated by sudden elevation, or too little polished by thought and conversation, to enjoy his present fortune with elegance and decency." The narrator is permitted to approach but not to enter the best apartments, which are ostentatiously open, and says that his "old friend, receiving me with all the insolence of condescension at the top of the stairs, conducted me to a back room, where he told me he always breakfasted when he had not great company."

Prospero rudely emphasizes the difference in their status, constantly puts the narrator in his place and makes it perfectly clear that he is inferior to the other guests. Moving to the sensitive subject of tea, the narrator says, "Prospero then told me, that another time I should taste his finest sort, but that he had only a very small quantity remaining, and reserved it for those whom he thought himself obliged to treat with particular respect." Though Johnson's tone seems nonchalant, he expresses real pain and anger about Garrick's intolerably pretentious and patronizing attitude.

Joshua Reynolds' pen portrait of Garrick, noting his tendency to act both on and off the stage and never take tea without a stratagem, confirmed his pompous and egoistic character:

[He] made himself a slave to his reputation. Amongst the variety of arts observed by his friends to preserve that reputation, one of them was to make himself rare. It was difficult to get him and when you had him, as difficult to keep him. He never came into company but with a plot how to get out of it. He was for ever receiving messages of his being wanted in another place. It was a rule with him never to leave any company saturated. Being used to exhibit himself at a theatre or a large table, he did not consider an individual as worth powder and shot.[14]

Since Johnson's ego was as great as Garrick's and he tended to overwhelm Garrick even more than other friends, their relations were cool and prickly. He withheld from Garrick the ultimate benediction of membership in the illustrious Club, founded in 1764, maintaining that "he will disturb us by his buffoonery" and did not admit him to the promised land until 1773. Johnson may well have heard about Garrick's hilarious impersonations of his tumultuous and awkward intimacy with Tetty, which would certainly have amused rather than disturbed the members. And he must have known about the convincing imitations in which Garrick, while mocking both himself and his old master, would exclaim in an imperious, bow-wow voice, "'Davy has some convivial pleasantry about him, but 'tis a futile fellow,' which he uttered perfectly with the tone and air of Johnson." Yet Garrick could also be engagingly modest about himself and tolerant of Johnson's occasional unkindness. "It is very natural," he admitted, "is it not to be expected he should be angry, that I, who have so much less merit than he, should have so much greater success."[15]

When in the right mood, Johnson was sometimes inclined to praise Garrick. He said Garrick had written more good prologues, essential to the success of a play, than Dryden. And he generously helped him, as he helped all his friends, with his literary work.

When Garrick had trouble composing an epitaph for the painter William Hogarth ("Farewell, great Painter of Mankind"), he humbly sought Johnson's assistance and agreed beforehand to all his corrections: "I shall certainly tire you, for I am tired myself—the following alterations are submitted to you—shall I beg yr opinion once more? If it is tolerable, you may run yr Pen thro' the lines you like the least, & avoid giving yrself the trouble of writing, unless you chuse to alter anything, which will be a greater Favour."

When touring Scotland with Boswell, Johnson praised Garrick's talent while alluding to his upstart status. He said that "Garrick's great distinction is his universality. He can represent all modes of life but that of an easy, fine-bred gentleman." Acclaimed as the finest actor of his age, Garrick was buried in Westminster Abbey. Two years later, in 1781, Johnson recognized his merits, paid his final tribute and declared, in his life of Edmund Smith, that Garrick's death had "eclipsed the gaiety of nations, and impoverished the publick stock of harmless pleasures."[16]

IV

In 1746, three years before the publication of *Vanity* and the production of *Irene,* Johnson's old mentor Gilbert Walmesley wrote to David Garrick expressing his faith in Johnson's talent and lamenting his disappearance into the obscurity of Grub Street: "When you see Mr. Johnson, pray give my compliments, and tell him I esteem him as a great genius—quite lost both to himself and the world." The following year Johnson emerged from obscurity to write, at Garrick's request, the "Prologue Spoken by Mr. Garrick at the Opening of the Theatre in Drury-Lane, 1747." It attempted, among other things, to soothe and seduce the potentially violent audience that had wrecked the theater in 1743 and would do so five more times in the next thirty-three years.

The "Prologue," a brief history of the theater in verse, moved from the glories of Shakespeare's richly imagined characters and plots, which had impressed audiences by their passion and their truth, through Ben Jonson and the licentious poets of the Restoration, to the recent Augustan Age.

Johnson's strategy was to flatter the play-goers, praise their judgment and forestall their hostility. He wrote that contemporary authors, subject to vagrant fortune and "the wild Vicissitudes of Taste," had to amuse and delight their audience in order to survive:

> Ah! let not Censure term our Fate our Choice,
> The Stage but echoes back the publick Voice.
> The Drama's Laws the Drama's Patrons give,
> For we that live to please, must please to live.

In the closing lines he asked the audience to encourage playwrights and inaugurate a new age of theater by being kind rather than severe in their judgment: "Bid scenic Virtue form the rising Age, / And Truth diffuse her Radiance from the Stage." In contrast to most playwrights, Johnson felt the purpose of the theater, like that of the pulpit, was to provide moral lessons and encourage virtue.

Johnson was better at writing prologues than plays. Garrick had no illusions about the dramatic quality of *Irene* when he agreed to advance Johnson's career and fortunes by putting it on at Drury Lane. The action of the play takes place a few days after one of the most cataclysmic events in world history: the conquest of Constantinople in May 1453 by the Turkish sultan Mahomet II, which led to the collapse of the Byzantine Empire. After the fall of the city, Irene, a beautiful Greek maiden (whose name means "peace"), is handed over to the sultan, who falls passionately in love with her and offers her a crown if she will embrace his religion. Mahomet's followers are horrified by his love-inspired weakness and, led by Cali, they plot to overthrow him. Irene's good friend Aspasia tries to dissuade her from giving in to temptation, but Irene succumbs to the lure of worldly power and agrees to convert. She then falls victim to slander and is executed by Mahomet. The renunciation of her Orthodox faith occurred at a time when militant Islam was expanding westward and eclipsing Greek Christianity.

The background and composition of the play are far more interesting than the play itself. The source was Richard Knolles' *Generall*

Historie of the Turks (1603), which Johnson extolled in *Rambler* 122: "none of our writers can . . . justly contest the superiority of Knolles, who in his history of the Turks, has displayed all the excellencies that narration can admit." A. L. Reade pointed out that Irene's "story was at least a century old in print when Knolles wrote, and had appeared in Italian, French and Latin works, as well as in English. And after Knolles there were at least three plays on the subject before Johnson began a fourth, so that the tale was rather hackneyed." Voltaire's last play, *Irène* (1778), was yet another version. Knolles' book also had a powerful effect on Lord Byron, who remembered it, a few weeks before his death in Greece, as "one of the first books that gave me pleasure when a child; and I believe it had much influence on my subsequent wishes to visit the Levant, and gave, perhaps, the oriental colouring which is observed in my poetry."[17]

In 1480 Gentile Bellini traveled from Venice to Constantinople and painted a superb portrait of the infamous Mahomet II. In *The Decline and Fall of the Roman Empire* Johnson's friend Edward Gibbon described the sultan's cruelty and sexual perversions. Mahomet's "passions were at once furious and inexorable; in the palace, as in the field, a torrent of blood was spilt on the slightest provocation; and the noblest of captive youth were often dishonoured by his unnatural lust." Gibbon also argued that the Greeks were responsible for their own destruction and that their selfish greed had paved the way for the Turkish invasion of their city: "the avarice of the rich denied the emperor, and reserved for the Turks, the secret treasures which might have raised in their defence whole armies of mercenaries." In a footnote to this sentence, Gibbon—conflating seven of Johnson's lines into four and misquoting them—added, "Dr. Johnson, in the tragedy of *Irene,* has happily seized this characteristic circumstance:

> The groaning Greeks dig up the golden caverns,
> The accumulated wealth of hoarding ages;
> That wealth which, granted to their weeping prince,
> Had rang'd embattled nations at their gates."

A modern historian, Sir Steven Runciman, based his physical description of the sultan on Bellini's portrait and recognized some positive aspects of his character:

> He was handsome, of middle height but strongly built. His face was dominated by a pair of piercing eyes, under arched eyebrows, and a thin hooked nose that curved over a mouth with full red lips. . . . His manner was dignified and rather distant. . . . He would never make himself beloved; he had no desire for popularity. But his intelligence, his energy and his determination commanded respect. . . . His generosity was always curtailed by suspicion.

After the fall of Constantinople, the sultan treated the civilians harshly. The Greek women were sent into captivity and the godchildren of the Emperor Constantine "were taken into the Sultan's seraglio. The girl, Thamar, died there while still a child; the boy was slain by the Sultan for refusing to yield to his lusts."

Shakespeare's *Othello* also influenced *Irene*. Johnson described Othello in terms that suggest Mahomet: "boundless in his confidence, ardent in his affection, inflexible in his resolution, and obdurate in his revenge."[18] Like Othello, Mahomet is a Moslem conqueror who, submitting to intense pressure from his comrades, kills a Christian woman whom he loves. Othello smothers Desdemona. When Irene is falsely accused of plotting to assassinate Mahomet, he sentences her to death and—like Othello—discovers too late that she is innocent.

Irene gave Johnson more trouble, and was a greater artistic failure, than anything he ever wrote. His first draft, in prose, outlined the characters and plot in considerable detail. He started it while teaching at his Edial school in 1736, continued writing it in lodgings in Greenwich in 1737, completed it in Lichfield that summer and revised it in the 1740s. But Johnson had no dramatic skill. *Irene*—a static, declamatory tragedy, suffocated by its own rhetoric —imitated Addison's *Cato* (1713), which was already outmoded by the time Johnson began his play. He later defended Shakespeare's rejection of neoclassical dramatic theory, but his own tragedy was strangled by his adherence to the Aristotelian unities of time, place and action: one day, one place and a single plot. As Johnson said of *Cato, Irene* was "rather a poem in dialogue than a drama. . . . Its hopes and fears communicate no vibration to the heart."

Garrick, well aware of the defects of *Irene,* paraphrased the "Prologue Spoken at Drury-Lane" by declaring, "when Johnson writes tragedy, *declamation roars, and passion sleeps:* When Shakespeare wrote, he dipped his pen in his own heart." Infinitely more experienced than Johnson in the theater, Garrick tried to inject some life into the dead lines. But Johnson, rejecting what he saw as an egoistic stunt, complained, "the fellow wants me to make Mahomet run mad, that he may have an opportunity of tossing his hands and kicking his heels." He was surely thinking of Garrick's antics when he described Bottom's ludicrous acting in Shakespeare's *A Midsummer Night's Dream:* "he declares his intention to be for a tyrant, for a part of fury, tumult, and noise, such as every young man pants to perform when he first steps upon the stage."[19]

Johnson's blank-verse tragedy in three acts portrays a series of moral disputations in an exotic setting. It features Mahomet, the despotic sultan, and Irene, the Greek slave girl; the rivalry between Demetrius and Abdalla, who contend for the love of Aspasia, the Greek woman captured during the sack of the city; and Cali's foiled plot against the sultan that leads to his execution. The central conflict focuses on whether Irene will repel the sultan's passion and remain faithful to her religion or become queen of Turkey and lose the hope of heaven. Aspasia, a moral guide who refuses to convert to Islam and is saved at the end of the play, sententiously tells Irene, who's finally condemned for her self-serving apostasy: "Thus life, with loss of wealth, is well preserv'd. / And virtue cheaply sav'd with loss of life. . . . None are great, or happy, but the virtuous."

Johnson ignored the dramatic potential of this material, larding the tragedy with sinking lines like "In Sophia's Temple!—What alarm!—Proceed." He delineated generic Turkish characters with a mechanical adjective-noun formula: "Th' unpractis'd dervise, or sequester'd faquir." Demetrius, with no time to explain what has happened, solemnly says (as no real person or vivid character could ever say): "The pressing exigence forbids relation." The finest couplet, describing Irene's submission to the sultan, echoes Eve's succumbing to Satan's temptation in Milton's *Paradise Lost*: "With soften'd voice she dropp'd the faint refusal, / Smiling consent she sat, and blushing Love." But as Martin Booth observed in his "Introduction" to *Irene,* Johnson fatally failed to take advantage of all the promising aspects of the plot:

> Johnson is not interested in the love element, the conspiracy, or the possibility of a fight. What really concerns him is the moral and religious issue, and Irene herself becomes an inert figure, a battleground between the forces of moral right and human corruption. . . . Those who stand up for virtue escape unharmed to a better life, while Irene, who succumbs to heathen luxury, pays with her neck.[20]

Johnson's play is autobiographical as well as historical, and concerns an important personal event: his marriage to Tetty. Many of her family and friends believed that Tetty, like Irene, was a noble character who'd been alienated from her own people and sacrificed to a rude barbarian. But Johnson, who started work on the play soon after he married Tetty, saw himself, not his wife, in the sacrificial role. He feared the power of women, who could (he said) tie up and whip submissive men. The play portrays Irene's preternatural power over the sultan and his need to free himself from bondage by killing her.

Johnson naturally took an active interest in the rehearsals of his long-awaited play. Boswell reported, "he used at one time to go occasionally to the green room of Drury-lane Theatre, where he was much regarded by the players, and was very easy and facetious with them." Johnson recalled that all the wenches knew him and curtsied deferentially as he walked onto the stage. But when their white bubbies made his genitals quiver, he was terrified by temptation and came no more behind the scenes.

On opening night, February 6, 1749, Johnson made a startling appearance in a gold-laced scarlet waistcoat and hat, the only time in his life that he ever displayed such finery. To liven things up, Garrick planned to have Irene strangled on stage with a traditional Turkish bow-string, but when the actors tried to do this at the first performance, the audience, fully absorbed in the tragedy, protested with shouts of "Murder! Murder!" Following tradition, Irene was then dispatched offstage. The unusually long run of nine nights was due less to the merits of the play than to Garrick's well-placed puffs in print, the effective acting (with Garrick as Demetrius), the lavish costumes, the splendid scenery of the Turkish seraglio and gardens, and the addition of light entertainment after the first few nights. Johnson, well paid for his efforts, received nearly £200 for the play and £100 for the copyright when it appeared in print.

The play was never revived, and Johnson was naturally disappointed by its reception. When a friend later read *Irene* aloud at a country house, Johnson suddenly left the room. He judged the play severely and later explained, "I thought it had been better." Told that Mr. Pot, an admirer, thought the play was "the finest tragedy of modern times," he firmly replied: "If Pot says so, Pot lies!" Asked how he felt about the failure of his tragedy, he referred to the high column designed by Christopher Wren that commemorated the Great Fire of London in 1666 and replied: "Like the Monument." Boswell took this to mean that "he continued firm and unmoved as that column."[21] Putting a positive spin on this defensive comment, he failed to see that Johnson meant that he'd turned himself to stone to protect his wounded feelings. Like Viola in *Twelfth Night*, he "sat like Patience on a monument, / Smiling at Grief."[22]

9

GREATEST GENIUS
1750–1752

I

Though immensely learned and industrious, Johnson was no wunderkind and did not produce his major works until middle age. By 1750 he had turned forty and had been at work on the *Dictionary* for four years. He'd spent most of the payments on expenses, found it difficult to maintain his household, let alone make a profit, and saw no end in sight. Edward Cave suggested that he could earn extra money by writing a biweekly essay, and in this way the *Rambler* was born. Two other publishers joined Cave in sponsoring the periodical, and Johnson was paid a flat fee of two guineas for each issue. The money kept him going, but the extra work inevitably delayed the completion of the *Dictionary.* Though the *Rambler* was never a financial success—each edition sold no more than 500 copies, at tuppence each—the venture was profitable for the publishers. The essays were widely reprinted in London and in the provinces, Scotland and America, but since there were no copyright laws, there was no further payment to Johnson. They were collected in book form in 1752 and reached the seventeenth edition in 1816.

Johnson told Joshua Reynolds that "when I was to begin publishing that paper, I was at a loss how to name it. I sat down at night upon my bedside, and resolved that I would not go to sleep till I had fixed its title. The *Rambler* seemed the best that occurred, and I took it." Following his usual practice, he had to impose a deadline to come up with an answer. He may also have been thinking of Richard Savage's poem *The Wanderer*, for both titles suggest roaming freely from subject to subject and mood to mood, from jovial to grave. The *Rambler* was later translated into Italian and published in book form as the slightly comical *Il Vagabondo* (a tramp rather than a rambler).

The work on the periodical added to his drudgery. On every Tuesday and Saturday between March 20, 1750, and March 15, 1752, Johnson published—again, almost single-handedly—208 essays of about 1,200 to 1,700 words. Most of them were dashed off at the last minute on Monday and Friday nights. In times of overwhelming sloth, emotional crises or physical illness, Johnson summoned literary friends and acquaintances, probably at short notice, to fill in for him. Catherine Talbot, Elizabeth Carter and Samuel Richardson wrote four of the essays; Hester Mulso, Joseph Simpson and David Garrick contributed fictitious letters in three others. Despite the rigors of the treadmill, the *Rambler* presented Johnson with a great opportunity. Forced to come up with ideas that he could expound on in a few pages, and free to write on anything that interested him, he developed a distinctive prose style and authoritative voice. His sales were poor, but there were many more readers than buyers. The quality of the essays varied, but he hit his stride as a writer, and began to establish his reputation and to attract a respectful audience.

His publishers hoped Johnson would achieve the popular success of his more lighthearted predecessors, Addison and Steele's *Tatler* (1709–11) and *Spectator* (1711–12). But Johnson, who had no talent for that sort of essay, wanted the *Rambler* to be serious and to improve the moral and intellectual qualities of his readers. He published it anonymously and tried to keep the authorship secret. As Walter Jackson Bate wrote, "he deeply wished the purity and soundness of the work to be free from the prejudices the reader might bring to it if he knew the author." But Garrick and others recognized his somber, didactic tone and Latinate diction, his pious thought and display of learning, and the identity of the grave and learned Mr. Rambler soon became well known.

Johnson's essays spanned a number of genres. The literary essays covered pastoral and Metaphysical poetry, Milton, the novel, biography and history, as well as the problems of a writer's life, the scourge of "Criticks," the fickleness of patrons and the public. He was fond of transparent allegories, and included both Arctic and Oriental fables. His essays considered, as one critic noted, "his love of London, the differences between personal and political liberty, his contempt for parental authority, his interest in realistic writing, his distrust of literary 'rules.'" The political essays attacked contemporary social evils, the moral essays offered practical and pious advice.

The essays sometimes took the form of letters written by Johnson and attributed to his characters, and some of them even criticized the Rambler himself. Like a modern columnist, Johnson offered advice about how to solve his correspondents' problems and improve their lives. He satirized modern society and created generic characters to illustrate common pitfalls and ruling passions. He discussed marriage and portrayed arrogant, stubborn or foolish men and insipid, coquettish or house-obsessed women. Many of his typical characters were descended from an ancient family in the country, with a comfortable inheritance left by a careful and generous father. One of them, contrasting urban and provincial life, complacently described himself as "the son of a gentleman, whose ancestors, for many ages, held the first rank in the country."[1]

Johnson took his moral and religious themes, his dogmatic language and pious teaching from the wisdom literature of the Old Testament, especially the book of Ecclesiastes, which emphasizes man's righteous conduct in daily life. He was also influenced by the epigrams of the *Greek Anthology*; Renaissance humanists like Politian, Erasmus and Grotius; Michel de Montaigne and Francis Bacon; seventeenth-century religious writers like Richard Hooker and Jeremy Taylor; and William Law's *Serious Call*. At the head of each essay, as in the biblical text of a sermon, Greek and Latin quotations suggested the major themes, which were recapitulated in the final paragraph. Johnson fortified his arguments by classical quotations, from Homer and Aristotle to Virgil and Horace, and

gave his characters Latin names, like Ferocula, Florentulus and Fortu-
nio, to suggest their dominant traits.

To this apparatus of classical learning and humanistic reading, Johnson added the weight of experience, a comprehensive vision of life and
an encyclopedic knowledge. He reinforced his lofty views with a
solemn Latinate style, studded with obscure and polysyllabic diction.
His lengthy sentences were composed of tripartite elements, antithe-
ses and alliteration, parallel words and phrases, often drawn from science and medicine. His balanced clauses resounded through carefully
controlled rhythms. At best, it is an impressive, dignified and noble
style, but it can be also be difficult to read. One sentence of *Rambler*
20, on "the folly and inconvenience of affectation" (which should be
read aloud to convey its full effect), is a typical example of Johnsonese:

> If we therefore compare the value of the praise obtained by ficti-
> tious excellence, even while the cheat is yet undiscovered, with that
> kindness which every man may suit by his virtue, and that esteem
> to which most men may rise by common understanding steadily
> and honestly applied, we shall find that when from the adscititious
> happiness all the deductions are made by fear and casualty, there
> will remain nothing equiponderant to the security of truth.

In other words, it's better to be honest than to lie about yourself.

This style, fine as it could be, did not appeal to all of Johnson's contemporaries. In several essays Johnson took note of his critics and, seeking to educate his audience and demanding an effort on their part,
asserted the dignity and value of his grand style. In *Idler* 70 Johnson
seemed to recognize that moral authors could be more effective if they
used more colloquial language. But he defended his diction by stating
that "words are only hard to those who do not understand them, and the
critick ought always to enquire, whether he is incommoded by the fault
of the writer, or his own." Since, as Johnson argued in *Rambler* 175, trea-
tises of morality are "persuasives to the practice of duties," the writer
"may therefore be justly numbered among the benefactors of mankind,
who contracts the great rules of life into short sentences, that may be easily impressed on the memory, and taught by frequent recollection to

recur habitually to the mind." But Johnson himself rarely felt the urge to contract his ideas into brief sentences. Putting his Christian beliefs in the simplest terms, as if there were no moral ambiguities in the choice of good and evil, he stated, "virtue is the highest proof of understanding, and the only solid basis of greatness; vice is the natural consequence of narrow thoughts; it begins in mistake, and ends in ignominy."[2]

Johnson admired the didactic epistolary novels of Richardson, with their spiritual crises and struggles between virtue and vice, and condemned the coarse language and immoral characters of Henry Fielding and Laurence Sterne. Whatever the subject of the essay, even in the mildly humorous ones, Johnson managed to evoke a moral or religious theme. In *Rambler* 2, for example, he wrote about the human tendency to hope for a better future and neglect the problems of the present, and turned out a prose version of *The Vanity of Human Wishes.* Hope itself did not sustain the sufferer and help him survive, but infected him with "the writer's malady," the habit of glorying in imaginary success instead of getting down to work immediately. The dreamer's crime was putting off "the choice of life" and wasting precious time. Johnson's recurrent themes were the quest for contentment in an inevitably disappointing life and the primacy of spiritual over worldly values. He advised readers to dread guilt as much as they dread pain, to examine their own lives and detect lurking dangers, to perform their duties and suppress unruly passions. As he declared in his poem "Festina Lente" (Make Haste Slowly): "Let Reason with superior force controul, / The floods of rage, and calm thy ruffled soul."

Johnson had expressed the essence of his Christian pessimism in his early "Essay on Epitaphs" (1740): one must "bear the evils of life with constancy, and support the dignity of human nature under the most pressing afflictions." Edmund Wilson observed that his characteristic tone, "dolorous, steadfast and somber, gives emotional depth to his work,"[3] and this dark view of human existence resonated through the *Ramblers* like a mournful dirge. In *Rambler* 165 Johnson insisted that "he that indulges hope will always be disappointed. . . . The utmost felicity which we can ever attain, will be little better than alleviation of misery, and we shall always feel more pain from our wants than pleasure from our enjoyments." In *Rambler* 143 he suggested there might be some slight mitigation for the wretchedness of life. Poets, writing about the theme of mutability, "lament the deceitfulness of hope, the fugacity of pleasure, the fragility of beauty, and the frequency of calamity; and for palliatives of these incurable miseries they would concur in recommending kindness, temperance, caution and fortitude." In *Rambler* 52 he echoed François La Rochefoucauld's sardonic maxim, "In the adversity even of our best friends we always find something not wholly displeasing," but gave it a different emphasis. Such news can provide only a respite from our own misery: "the relation of other men's infelicity may give a lasting and continual relief. . . . It can lull the memory of misfortune, or appease the throbbings of anguish, to hear that others are more miserable."[4]

Johnson also used the *Ramblers* to survey the important social and political issues of his time. Despite his religious pessimism, he expressed compassionate and surprisingly modern views. In his greatest essays (as we've seen), he urged charity toward prostitutes, favored mitigating the criminal code, especially concerning the imprisonment of debtors, and opposed capital punishment for minor offenses. In other essays he pitied the animals whose peaceful life was sacrificed to sport and attacked the experimental torture of helpless beasts by vivisection. He advocated the abolition of slavery and condemned the barbarity of war, the savagery of colonial ventures and the slaughter of indigenous peoples.

Johnson's most personal *Ramblers,* like his satire of Garrick as Prospero (200), are filled with autobiographical revelations. Among the best are those on biography (60), crime and punishment (114), prostitution (107, 170 and 171) and the Rambler's farewell to his readers (208). Recalling his editorial role at the *Gentleman's Magazine,* he described his kindhearted reluctance to reject or even to read the manuscripts of starving authors who anxiously awaited his decision: "I, who know the passions of an author, cannot remember how long they have lain in my boxes unregarded, without imagining to myself the various changes of sorrow, impatience, and resentment, which the writers must have felt in this tedious interval."[5] He knew that his procrastination, which raised hopes in the Grub Street garrets, delayed rather than softened the blow.

Johnson took pains to persuade his readers to accept the persona of the wise and solemn Rambler, and not expect to find the lighter material of the earlier periodicals. He confronted the disappointed expectations of his readers and quoted criticism from imaginary correspondents. One dissatisfied customer found the essays unreadable: "I am no great admirer of grave writings, and therefore very frequently lay your papers aside before I have read them through." Some readers "were angry that the Rambler did not, like the Spectator, introduce himself to the acquaintance of the publick, by an account of his own birth and studies, and enumeration of his adventures, and a description of his physiognomy. Others soon began to remark that he was a solemn, serious, dictatorial writer, without sprightliness or gaiety, and called out with vehemence for mirth and humour."

In *Rambler* 109 he portrayed himself as a sobersides and paraphrased one of his readers, who complained about his vast stock of mournful subjects. The reader imagined Mr. Rambler in his cozy den, preparing to relish human misery: "at this instant I see the Rambler snuffing his candle, rubbing his spectacles, stirring his fire, locking out interruption, and settling himself into his easy chair, that he may enjoy a new calamity without disturbance." The correspondent continued his complaint by insisting, "it is certain, that whatever be your subject, melancholy for the most part bursts in upon your speculation, your gaiety is quickly overcast, and though your readers may be flattered with hopes of pleasantry, they are seldom dismissed but with heavy hearts."[6]

But Johnson refused to appease such critics or court popular taste by providing a description of his background and appearance. He could not give an accurate account of his repulsive features and slovenly dress, nor create the pleasant image of a handsome man, neatly dressed and working in an orderly study. He felt obliged to convey his sober message for the benefit of his readers, and continued to prescribe heavy-hearted cures for the wicked world. The crucial difficulty was that he retailed his bleak pessimism, based on bitter personal experience, as if it were the universal condition of mankind. Most of his readers thought Christianity relieved sorrows rather than exacerbated them, and rejected his gloomy jeremiads. They wanted to relish life and enjoy what they read. In the robust optimism of the eighteenth century, Johnson's voice seemed too serious and too sad.

As early as *Rambler* 2 Johnson mentioned the difficulty of attracting and retaining an audience with moral essays, but confessed that he preferred hostility to neglect: "He that endeavours after fame by writing, solicits the regard of a multitude fluctuating in pleasures, or immersed in business, without time for intellectual amusements. . . . There is nothing more dreadful to an author than neglect, compared with which reproach, hatred, and opposition, are names of happiness." In this way, authors since Johnson's time have consoled themselves for harsh reviews.

Rambler 208, his poignant valediction, summed up Johnson's achievement and acknowledged his failures and successes. He noted that though his work had been professedly serious—and too serious to be popular—he had also written three lighter kinds of essays: "harmless merriment," "disquisitions of criticism" and "pictures of life." Elegantly and elegiacally, he stated that "time, which puts an end to all human pleasures and sorrows, has likewise concluded the labours of the Rambler," and regretfully admitted that "I have never been much a favourite of the publick." He confessed that his mind had been contracted by perpetual application to his task and described, with stylistic grandeur, the formidable difficulties he'd had to overcome, twice a week, for the last two years:

> He that condemns himself to compose on a stated day, will often bring to his task an attention dissipated, a memory embarrassed, an imagination overwhelmed, a mind distracted with anxieties, a body languishing with disease: He will labour on a barren topick, till it is too late to change it; or in the ardour of invention, diffuse his thoughts into wild exuberance, which the pressing hour of publication cannot suffer judgment to examine or reduce.

In the end, confident that he'd maintained his literary standards, he formed a high opinion of the *Rambler.* In beautifully balanced parallels (something . . . something, to the elegance . . . to the harmony, of its construction . . . of its cadence) he wrote of his own magnificent contribution to the English language: "something perhaps, I have added to the elegance of its construction, and something to the harmony of its cadence." The author Samuel Rogers recorded him declaring, "my other works are wine and water; but my *Rambler* is pure wine."[7]

Exactly a year after he'd completed the *Ramblers,* and while still toiling on the *Dictionary,* he embarked on another periodical voyage. Counting on Johnson's growing reputation and intellectual weight, John Hawkesworth invited him to write for his *Adventurer,* a periodical with the same format as the *Rambler.* It sold at the same tuppence a copy, and came out on the same Tuesday and Saturday each week. Between March 1753 and March 1754, Johnson wrote twenty-nine issues. He announced his intention to teach (or preach) "the everlasting and unvariable principles of moral and religious truth." Censorious and saturnine, he argued that "virtue is uncommon in all the classes of humanity," which displeased the ladies and offended the upper class, that "misery is the lot of man, [and that] our present state is a state of danger and infelicity." He concluded with recourse to his favorite Ecclesiastes and predictably insisted, "the wisest of men terminated all his experiments in search of happiness, by the mournful confession, that 'all is vanity.'"[8]

While at work on the *Ramblers,* Johnson had met Charlotte Lennox, a sophisticated literary woman with an unusual background. One of the select group who was cited in the *Dictionary* and contributed to the *Rambler,* she became one of his closest and most admired female friends. She was born in 1729, the daughter of a Scottish officer who'd served in Gibraltar. Ten years later she accompanied her father to Albany, New York, where he commanded troops on the colonial frontier. When he died in 1742, she was sent back to England, at the age of thirteen, to be educated. She was pretty enough to try her luck on the London stage, and when she failed to establish herself as an actress, she became a writer. She met the publisher William Strahan and married his employee Alexander Lennox. When she needed a teacher to help her translate the Italian sources of the plays for her pioneering book *Shakespear Illustrated,* her husband found Giuseppe Baretti in a coffeehouse. She introduced Baretti to Johnson, who became his friend and benefactor.

Though Johnson was generous with all his friends, he helped Charlotte more than anyone else, writing six of her dedications, the proposals for publishing her original *Works,* two sections of her translation of Pierre Brumoy's *Greek Theatre* and a chapter of her picaresque deflation of romantic expectations, *The Female Quixote* (1752). In the penultimate chapter of this novel, she gratefully declared that "the Author of the *Rambler*" was "the greatest Genius in the present Age." His contribution (book 9, chapter 11) was a rather pedantic and leaden dialogue, between a Johnsonian clergyman and the heroine, Arabella, about the effects of dangerous books on morals and virtue. As in *Vanity* and the *Rambler,* he stressed "the imperfection of all human Happiness" and offered his "Reflections upon human Misery." In the heading, Charlotte wrote that it was "in the author's opinion the best chapter in this history."

When Charlotte published her first novel, *The Life of Harriot Stuart,* in the spring of 1751, Johnson organized a jolly dinner to celebrate the event and pay gallant homage to the young author. The party, which began at 8 PM at the Devil Tavern near Temple Bar and included about twenty people, lasted till well past dawn. Even the dour John Hawkins was overcome by merriment and described how Johnson, at his most charming, played the genial host and imaginative master of ceremonies:

> Our supper was elegant, and Johnson had directed that a magnificent hot apple pie should make a part of it, and this he would have stuck with bay leaves, because, forsooth, Mrs. Lennox was an authoress, and had written verses; and further, he had prepared for her a crown of laurel, with which, but not till he had invoked the muses by some ceremonies of his own invention, he encircled her brows. . . . About five, Johnson's face shone with meridian splendour, though his drink had been only lemonade; but the far greater part of us had deserted to the

colours of Bacchus. . . . The waiters were so overcome with sleep, that it was two hours before we could get a bill, and it was not till near eight that the creaking of the street door gave the signal for our departure.[9]

II

Religion in England had for two centuries been inseparably linked to political power, and in Johnson's time it was still a contentious issue. Within a period of only twenty-five years, England changed its religion three times. It had been Catholic till 1533, and Protestant till 1553, under Henry VIII and Edward VI; Catholic till 1558 under Mary; Protestant afterwards under Elizabeth. The Catholic James II had ruled from 1685 to 1688, but the established church remained Protestant. There was a danger of Catholic succession to the throne when Queen Anne, the last of the Stuart monarchs, died without living children in 1714, and again during the Jacobite Rebellions of 1715 and 1745. To Johnson and most Englishmen, Anglicanism was the moderate middle way between Puritanism and Popery. He adhered to the established church, but his own religious beliefs and practices were far from moderate.

Most parish priests had negligible duties: they offered communion thrice a year and gave an occasional sermon. But their livings were controlled by the local aristocracy; their preferment depended on how well they got on with those in power, so most of them trimmed their political views to fit the prevailing winds. Johnson's close friend John Taylor, whom he frequently visited, was distinctly unclerical, more concerned with increasing his ecclesiastical income, living a comfortable life and raising his prize bulls than in fulfilling his pastoral duties and caring for his congregation. Johnson expected the clergy to conform to traditional views and seemly behavior, but accepted Taylor's lack of spirituality and pursuit of worldly goods. Assuming that a bishop must be an authority on doctrinal matters, he had respectfully said of George Psalmanazar, "I would as soon think of contradicting a bishop." But no eighteenth-century bishop was elevated for his piety. They were all political appointees, promoted by the supposedly despicable Whigs. Rewarded for services rendered to learning, patrons or

John Taylor by John Opie, c.1780—Samuel Johnson
Birthplace Museum

the party, the twenty-six bishops were obliged to support the government and vote obediently in the House of Lords.

In fact, the Church of England accommodated many schools of philosophical and religious thought and many strange and eccentric divines. In
one famous incident, Johnson violently contradicted a bishop, George
Berkeley, whose idealist philosophy attacked the materialism of John
Locke and Isaac Newton. Boswell noted that he rejected Berkeley's "ingenious sophistry to prove the non-existence of matter, and that every thing
in the universe is merely ideal . . . by striking his foot with mighty force
against a large stone, till he rebounded from it, 'I refute it *thus.*'" Keith
Crook has shown that Johnson's physical rejection of Berkeley was based
on an empirical argument by Locke, who wrote: "If any one asks me, *what
this solidity is,* I send him to his senses to inform him. Let him put a flint
or a football between his hands, and then endeavour to join them, and he

will know." Johnson also indignantly condemned an oddball clergyman and celebrated author for his bawdy behavior: "I was but once in Sterne's company, and then his only attempt at merriment consisted in his display of a drawing too indecently gross to have delighted even in a brothel"— though it would be hard to imagine a brothel as prudish as the one he had in mind.[10]

Though deeply and earnestly religious, Johnson rarely went to church, and preferred to pray and meditate at home and in private. He often criticized his own failure to attend divine services, but there were many reasons why he didn't go. He couldn't rouse himself to get there on time; his deafness prevented him from hearing the service; he distracted the congregation and called unwelcome attention to himself with his nervous gesticulations; and he was terribly bored by the banality of the sermons, which usually provided an unhappy contrast to the beauty of the liturgy and to the sublime cadences of the King James Bible and *The Book of Common Prayer.*

Pope had confidently exclaimed, "Whatever is, is right," a sanguine view of life that Johnson could not share. He turned this assertion upside down, declaring in *Rambler* 175: "The depravity of mankind is so easily discoverable, that nothing but the desert or the cell can exclude it from notice. . . . What are all the records of history, but narratives of successive villainies, of treasons and usurpations, massacres and wars?" His dire prognostications in the *Ramblers* went against the grain of the religious optimism that prevailed in the eighteenth century. George Trevelyan pointed out that "the best of the upper class aimed at the full and rational enjoyment of this life, rather than at preparation for the next, of which they spoke seldom and then with a cheerful scepticism." J. H. Plumb added that "evil and guilt, sin and redemption—the whole personal drama and appeal of religion— was forgotten or rationalized away and eupeptic optimism . . . pervaded the teaching of the Church."[11] The dissenting John Wesley and his Methodist revival offered followers a hopeful future and the promise of salvation. Johnson, by contrast, experienced religion as a personal drama and could smell the fire and brimstone in his own nostrils. The concept of Hell, which was distant, vague and abstract to most believers, was for Johnson horrific and all too real.

Johnson could be coolly sceptical about any sort of dogma. He brought his formidable intelligence and penetrating logic to bear on questions concerning oaths to the monarch and the Calvinistic belief in predestination. In "Remarks on the Militia Bill" he forcefully argued that "every man who takes these oaths is or is not already faithful to his king. If he be faithful, how is his fidelity increased? If he be not, how is his loyalty improved, by diminishing his honesty?" When an acquaintance who believed in preordained fate offered to take his message to Hester Thrale in Bath, he ironically and amusingly instructed him to "tell her in what state of health you find me in—But, naw, Sir, I have told her all that in a letter myself—& so tell her—tell her—what it is predestined you are to tell her."

But Johnson refused to question his own religious belief. As Birkbeck Hill observed, "Johnson, with his horror of annihilation, caught at everything which strengthened his belief in the immortality of the soul." In his view, doubts about the afterlife would undermine and even shatter the only conviction that redeemed the pain of living. He vehemently declared, "every man who attacks my belief, diminishes in some degree my confidence in it, and therefore makes me uneasy: and I am angry with him who makes me uneasy."[12] But Johnson's protestations of faith could not assuage his doubts. He could exclude quotations by Hobbes and Bolingbroke from his *Dictionary*, but not from his mind; and he fought what turned out to be a losing battle against the sceptics and freethinkers of his time.

In the *Rambler*, Johnson unremittingly exposed the uneasy and precarious foundations of his religious beliefs:

—The only happiness ordained for our present state, [is] the confidence of divine favour, and the hope of future rewards. (No. 120)
—We are happy or miserable, according as we are affected by the survey of our life, or our prospect of future existence. (No. 41)
—The utmost excellence at which humanity can arrive, is a constant and determinate pursuit of virtue, without regard to present dangers or advantage; a continual reference of every action to the divine will; an habitual appeal to everlasting justice. (No. 185)

—He that grows old without religious hopes . . . falls into a gulph
of bottomless misery, in which every reflexion must plunge him
deeper, and where he finds only new gradations of anguish, and
precipices of horrour. (No. 69)

The most striking aspect of these passages is the violent conflict between good and evil, salvation and damnation; the constant whistling
in the dark while struggling against the overwhelming danger, misery,
anguish and horror. Johnson had religious fears, but not religious
hopes. He was, contrary to these brave passages, far from certain about
his own fate, consumed by gulfs of darkness and overwhelmed by
precipices of doubt.

Religion for Johnson was not only a terrifying system of belief, but
also a way (maybe the only way) to control dangerous impulses like
violence, drink and sex.[13] If he'd never answered Law's serious call to
become a fervent Christian, he could have drunk, fought and fornicated without constantly worrying about eternal damnation. Yet
religion was the polestar that kept his life on its unsteady course and
may even have prevented him from going mad. In a valuable article,
the historian of religion Owen Chadwick concluded that Johnson
"developed a Calvinistic sense of the load of original sin without any
Calvinistic sensation of the omnipotence of God in lifting the load
from a person's back." Johnson told Boswell, "the Christian religion
is a most beneficial system, as it gives us light and certainty where we
were before in darkness and doubt." Though he well understood the
futility of worldly ambition and tried hard to prepare himself for the
afterlife, he himself failed to find the happiness he promised to those
who embraced Christianity.

Johnson had used *The Vanity of Human Wishes* and the *Ramblers* to
teach his religious message. He also composed twenty-seven theological
sermons, most of them for John Taylor, who was too idle or indifferent
to write them himself. Neither Johnson nor Taylor felt the clergyman
was obliged to compose his own homilies or that Johnson should get
credit for his anonymous work. So Johnson sometimes had the strange
but pleasurable sensation of sitting in a pew—as if he were in a theater

watching his own play—and listening to Taylor (his vicarious vicar) preach familiar yet inspiring sermons.

James Gray observed that Johnson expressed his theological beliefs in "tightly organized, brilliantly phrased, ringingly eloquent, and sometimes solemnly poetic" sermons, "whose urgent rhetoric of unworldliness aims at wooing man away from the domination of the senses and of wealth and power to a contemplation of future destiny." His now familiar themes, which he never tired of repeating and which reappear in *Rasselas,* are "the fear of death, the mystery of the future state, the search for happiness. . . . [The sermons] survey the pleasures, the wisdom, the folly, the inequity of this life, the illusory nature of earthly happiness, the human preoccupation with the things of this world, the mystery of God's purposes and the certainty of worldly disappointment."[14]

Three passages from Johnson's sermons suggest the essence of his pulpit oratory. In Sermon 5, on the meaning of evil, he confidently states his dominant beliefs while teaching the congregation to reject the world—"the uncertainty of prosperity, the vanity of pleasure, and the inquietudes of power, the difficult attainment of most earthly blessings, and the short duration of them all"—and turn to God. In Sermon 10, on the future state of the soul, he assumes a threatening tone and warns sinners "living under the divine displeasure, in a state, in which it would be very dangerous to die . . . cut off before the season of repentance, and exposed to the vengeance of an angry God."

He had developed this theme in Sermon 2, and was certainly thinking of himself when he described the sorrowful condition of those who have offended God and are destined to suffer the punishment of a wrathful Jehovah: "[It is] a state of gloomy melancholy, or outrageous desperation; a dismal weariness of life, and inexpressible agonies at the thought of death; for what affright or affliction could equal the horrours of that mind, which expected every moment to fall into the hands of implacable omnipotence?"

The sermons expressed Johnson's public, hortatory and dogmatic view of religion. His *Prayers and Meditations* (1785)—one of the saddest books of the century—reveals his private doubts, fears and agonies. The ruthlessly self-scrutinizing and self-tormenting diaries that accompany the prayers list the personal faults that he constantly struggled to overcome: "idleness, intemperate sleep, dilatoriness, immethodical life, Lust, Neglect of Worship and Vain scruples" [religious "doubts" and "perplexities"]. His resolutions to correct and improve his conduct—repeatedly made, impossible to keep and constantly broken—were "to rise early, to study religion, to go to Church, to drink less strong liquors, to keep a journal, to oppose laziness." Instead of cheerfully adhering to these resolutions, he was horribly depressed by his inability to follow them. "Every Man," he recorded, while stressing the futility of his vows, "naturally persuades himself that he can keep his resolutions, nor is he convinced of his imbecility but by length of time, and frequency of experiment."[15] To remind himself that time was running out, he bought, for the considerable sum of seventeen guineas, a metal watch with a tortoise-shell case and engraved upon it the minatory inscription "the night cometh."

Johnson often recorded his personal prayers on New Year's Day, the anniversary of Tetty's death, Easter, his birthday or when undertaking an arduous new project. The prayers were strongly influenced by the sixteenth-century Anglican *Book of Common Prayer;* by the 9th of the 39 Articles of the Church of England, which emphasizes man's inherent evil: "Original sin . . . is the fault and corruption of the Nature of Every man . . . so that the flesh lusteth always contrary to the spirit"; and by the *Dies Irae* (Day of Wrath, Day of Judgment), a hymn addressed to Christ and sung in Latin at solemn requiems: "You wearied yourself in finding me. / You have redeemed me through the cross. / Let not such great efforts be in vain." Hester Thrale wrote that when Johnson recited these verses "he could never pass the stanza ending [with the original Latin of the last line] *Tantus labor non sit cassus* without bursting into a flood of tears."

Johnson's most moving prayers were confessions of his faults, pleas for guidance and supplications for mercy: "Enable me to break the chain of my sins, to reject sensuality in thought, and to overcome and suppress vain scruples. . . . Deliver and preserve me from vain terrors. . . . What shall I do to be saved?"[16] His life-shattering fears made him unwilling to go to bed at night and caused insomnia when he did so. If he slept, he feared he might die; and feared that if he died, he might be condemned. When he told William Adams, "'I am afraid I may be one of those who shall be damned' (looking dismally)," Adams asked, "'What do you mean by damned?' Johnson. (passionately and loudly) 'Sent to Hell, Sir, and punished everlastingly!'" Adams, politely disagreeing, took a more hopeful view and suggested that God was infinitely good: "I don't believe that doctrine. . . . Being excluded from Heaven will be a punishment; yet there may be no great positive suffering."

Johnson's fear of damnation inspired his spontaneous exhibitions of public prayer. The Scottish economist Adam Smith was quite startled by and contemptuous of his enthusiastic performance: "I have seen that creature bolt up in the midst of a mixed company; and, without any previous notice, fall upon his knees behind a chair, repeat the Lord's Prayer and resume his seat at table. He has played this freak over and over, perhaps five or six times in the course of an evening. It is not hypocrisy, but madness." No wonder Johnson sympathized with the poet Christopher Smart's unhappy vacillation of mind. He compassionately told Boswell, while expressing fears that he might also lose his reason, that poor Smart should not have been confined in a lunatic asylum: "I did not think he ought to be shut up. His infirmities were not noxious to society. He insisted on people praying with him; and I'd as lief pray with Kit Smart as any one else."[17]

Unlike Adams and so many other hopeful believers, Johnson did not expect to be greeted after death by the full chorus of saints and angels. Instead, he felt the fright and panic—the sense of being cast from divine favor and destined for damnation—that were powerfully expressed by his younger contemporary William Cowper in "The Castaway" (1799):

Nor soon he felt his strength decline,
    Or courage die away;
But wag'd with death a lasting strife,
    Supported by despair of life. . . .
No voice divine the storm allay'd,
    No light propitious shone;

When, snatch'd from all effectual aid,
We perish'd, each alone.

Johnson was, as Auden wrote of Søren Kierkegaard, "a man who sits in the anguish of death, in fear and trembling and much tribulation."[18]

III

Johnson's wife, Tetty, died on March 17, 1752, three days after he published the last *Rambler*. Their marriage had been difficult, and he needed all his inner strength and all the resources of religion to deal with the emotional crisis that followed her death. Tetty had been forced to live in inferior lodgings, though he'd tried to do everything possible for her, and after her money ran out she'd suffered humiliating poverty. She had endured Johnson's squalid habits and his often unwelcome lovemaking. They were forced into hiding after the publication of his inflammatory attack on Walpole, *Marmor Norfolciense*. According to the dark hints of John Hawkins, he may have consorted with prostitutes when Tetty was in Lichfield and he walked the streets by night with Richard Savage. Tetty was repeatedly mocked and condemned, as Johnson may have suspected, by many of his closest friends. She disliked his louche companions and the grubby scribes in the garret who worked on the *Dictionary*. Except for a few female friends, she had very little social life.

Johnson lived apart from Tetty both at the beginning and at the end of their marriage, when they realized their incompatibility and seemed happier on their own. At the start, she pleaded with him to come to bed; at the end, she excluded him from her room. When she had no desire for sexual relations, he forced himself upon her; when she refused to sleep with him, he dallied with her friend. No wonder she took refuge in drink and drugs, and that he felt guilty about her difficult life and failing health.

In the mid-eighteenth century the hilltop village of Hampstead was separated from London by open fields. Tetty took lodgings there to enjoy the benefits of a healthier climate, and Johnson visited her whenever he could. Her companion Elizabeth Desmoulins, who after her own marriage was over had lived with Tetty in Hampstead, resented her airs, her extravagance and her indifference to her husband's needs. She told Boswell that Tetty "indulged herself in country air and nice living, at an unsuitable expense, while her husband was drudging in the smoke of London, and that she by no means treated him with that complacency ["pleasure, satisfaction, gratification"] which is the most engaging quality in a wife."

While temporarily residing in Johnson's house in Gough Square and lying ill in bed, Tetty had an unexpected visitor. Her son, Jervis, a naval captain, had opposed her unsuitable marriage and severed all contact with her. But on one of his rare visits to port, Jervis apparently had a sudden impulse, after ten or fifteen years (the date is uncertain), to call on his mother and show her how well he'd got on in the world. The long-lost son, handsome and impressive in his naval uniform,

> knocked at the door and asked the maid if her mistress was at home? She answered, "Yes, Sir, but she is sick in bed." "O!" says he, "if it is so, tell her that her son Jervis called to know how she did"; and was going away. The maid begged she might run up to tell her mistress, and, without attending his answer, left him. Mrs. Johnson, enraptured to hear her son was below, desired the maid to tell him she longed to embrace him. When the maid descended, the gentleman was gone, and poor Mrs. Johnson was much agitated by the adventure: it was the only time he ever made an effort to see her.

Jervis seems to have suddenly changed his mind about seeing and perhaps disturbing the sick old lady, becoming emotionally entangled with her and with the even more difficult Johnson. His kind impulse had a cruel outcome. It excited her maternal emotions and rekindled her sense of loss and regret.

There was a great difference between the middle-aged Tetty who married Johnson in 1735 and the aged invalid of the 1750s. Most of what we know about her (apart from Garrick's mockery) comes from friends of Johnson who knew her at the end of her life. She grew corpulent, heightened her florid complexion with liberal potations of alcohol and still cultivated an absurdly girlish manner. Hester Thrale recorded, "Garrick says the Woman was a little painted Poppet; full of Affectation and rural Airs of Elegance; old [Dr. Robert] Levet says She was always drunk & reading Romances in her Bed, where She killed herself by taking Opium."[19] Opium dissolved in alcohol, called laudanum, was a common remedy for many ills until well into the twentieth century. Excessive doses of the drug would have diminished, if not extinguished, Tetty's sexual desires.

John Taylor was even harsher about poor Tetty. He said she "was the plague of Johnson's life, was abominably drunken and despicable in every way, and Johnson had frequently complained to him of the wretchedness of his situation with such a wife." The clergyman and Celtic scholar William Shaw, who published a memoir of Johnson in 1785, confirmed the negative view of Tetty and added that many friends knew about their unhappy marriage. Tetty "had, especially in the latter part of her life, addicted herself to drinking, some say, opium," and "a suspicion of [Johnson's] conjugal infelicity on this account certainly went abroad and procured him much commiseration among his friends." Emotionally unfulfilled with his mother, Johnson was sexually unfulfilled with his wife.

Boswell was riveted by the intimate details of Johnson's life. An inquisitive and insistent detective, he managed to extract from Elizabeth Desmoulins some fascinating revelations about Johnson's flying visits to Hampstead. Donald and Mary Hyde, providing useful background, wrote that Desmoulins, seven years younger than Johnson,

was the daughter of Johnson's godfather, Dr. Swinfen, a gentleman of very ancient family, an excellent physician, but a poor manager, who died leaving a large family in indigence. While very young, Elizabeth Swinfen married Mr. Desmoulins, a Huguenot refugee and writing master in Birmingham. Her married life was of short duration, for within a few years she was in London, a widow, maintaining herself and her children, working first at a machine for stamping crepe and subsequently keeping a boarding school.[20]

Boswell suppressed and kept secret his lengthy and penetrating interview with Desmoulins, as the painter Mauritius Lowe listened in, on April 20,

1783, while Johnson was still alive. Desmoulins emphasized that Johnson, when denied sexual relations by his wife, struggled to control his lustful impulses. She insisted, "there never was a man who had stronger amorous inclinations than Dr. Johnson. But he conquered them."

Desmoulins may have been treated more like a servant than a paid companion (though she was better off than when forced to stamp crepe) and seemed jealous of Tetty's superior status. As critical of Tetty as were Garrick and Levet, Taylor and Shaw, she blamed Tetty for the marriage problems and described how she deceived Johnson to keep him from her bed:

> I believe she never had any love for him but only to get money from him. They did not sleep together for many years. But that was her fault. She drank shockingly and said she was not well and could not bear a bedfellow. I remember once when at Hampstead a young woman came on a visit. I lay in the room with Mrs. Johnson in a small bed. She said, "It will not hold you both. So if you will promise not to tell Mr. Johnson, you shall sleep with me. But if he should know this, he'd say, 'If you can bear a bedfellow, why not me as well as another?'"

Boswell was never shy when pressing people for information. Taking advantage of his social status, he proceeded with a lawyer-like cross-examination. Nailing down precise details to satisfy his prurient interest, he persuaded Desmoulins to confess that she actually got into bed with Johnson while Tetty was sleeping in the next room. She told him that Johnson

> commanded his passion. But when I was a young woman and lived with Mrs. Johnson at Hampstead, he used to come out two or three days in a week, and when Dr. [Richard] Bathurst lived there, he'd go and stay with him till two or three in the morning. The maid went to bed, as she could not be kept up, and I used to sit up for him; and I have warmed his bed with a pan of coals and sat with him in his room many an hour in the night and had my

head upon his pillow. . . . He'd desire me to go out of the room, and he'd go to bed; but to come back in a little while and talk to him—and I have come and sat on his bedside and laid my head on his pillow.

In one of the most vivid and revealing moments in Boswell's journals, the amateur detective managed to discover, by coaxing and probing the reluctant yet compliant Desmoulins, exactly what happened in Johnson's bed. By dramatizing the reactions of the three actors—for she refused to be deflected by Lowe's ill-informed comments about Johnson's supposed sexual incapacity—Boswell created a brilliant seduction scene, complete with stage directions, modeled on Restoration comedy. After establishing that Johnson "showed strong signs of his passion" with an erection, Boswell (excited himself) asked a series of staccato questions:

Boswell. "What would he do? Come now." (Lowe like to jump out of his skin), "would he fondle you? Would he kiss you?" Mrs. Desmoulins. "Yes, Sir." . . . Boswell. "But would he, eh?" Mrs. Desmoulins. "He never did anything that went beyond the limits of decency." . . . Lowe. "You were certain he was capable?" "Y-yes, Sir." Boswell. "But he conquered his violent inclination?" "Yes, Sir. He'd push me from him and cry, 'Get you gone.'" . . . Boswell. "So you saw the struggle and the conquest?" "I did. . . .

I have many times considered how I should behave, suppos-ing he should proceed to extremities. . . . [Though Johnson was] so terribly disgusting . . . such was my high respect for him, such the awe I felt of him, that I could not have had resolution to have resisted him."[21]

Tempted, like St. Anthony, by the demons of sexuality, Johnson wanted to see how far he could go toward "extremities" before he re-gained control of himself and thrust the temptress from his pres-ence. Though he dallied with the widowed Elizabeth, he kept within the bounds of permissible behavior by stopping short of consum-mation. Tetty and Desmoulins, his two Elizabeths, were the closest he ever came to realizing his fantasies about having a Turkish seraglio.

Ill in Hampstead, Tetty did not attend the opening night of *Irene*. She returned briefly to Gough Square and was there when Jervis Porter called. But when her health grew worse, she returned to the salubrious air and to different rooms in Hampstead. Johnson later told Fanny Burney:

> I remember that my wife, when she was near her end, poor woman, was advised to sleep out of town; and when she was carried to the lodgings that had been prepared for her, she complained that the staircase was in very bad condition, for the plaster was beaten off the walls in many places. "Oh," said the man of the house, "that's nothing but by the knocks against it of the coffins of the poor souls that have died in the lodgings!" He laughed, though not without apparent secret anguish, in telling me this.

Tetty's fears were well founded. On March 12, five days before she died, Johnson wrote Charlotte Lennox, "poor Tetty Johnson's Illness will not suffer me to think of going any whither out of her call. She is very ill, and I am much dejected."

Immediately after Tetty's death at the age of sixty-two or sixty-three, Johnson sent a letter to his clergyman friend John Taylor, absentee prebendary at Westminster Cathedral but residing there at the time, which "expressed grief in the strongest manner he had ever read." The letter (now lost) reached Taylor at 3 AM. He immediately dressed and went to Johnson, and "found him in tears and in extreme agitation." The next morning Johnson wrote again to Taylor, the man closest to him in London, begging him to "let me have your Company and your Instruction.—Do not live away from me. My Distress is great." Hawkins agreed that his melancholy "was of the blackest and deepest kind."[22] They wrapped Tetty in a wool shawl, took off her wedding ring and placed her in a coffin. Her funeral and burial in Bromley, Kent, was arranged by the author John Hawkesworth, who was living there. Johnson was too distraught to attend.

Tetty had lived long enough to see Johnson publish the *Ramblers* and fulfill the promise she'd perceived when they first met. But she suffered with Johnson during his long years of obscurity and poverty, and died shortly before he achieved literary fame with the *Dictionary* and finally gained financial independence. Johnson lamented his unhappy marriage when Tetty was alive, yet glorified her after her death. In Sermon 25, written for Taylor to deliver, he memorialized her by declaring that no one could know her "without esteem, or tenderness. To praise the extent of her knowledge, the acuteness of her wit, the accuracy of her judgment, the force of her sentiments, or the elegance of her expression, would ill suit with the occasion." Taylor normally had no scruples about passing off Johnson's sermons as his own, but he disliked Tetty and thought her despicable. Believing the praise of her virtues was excessive, he risked offending Johnson, who was still in deep mourning, and refused to preach it.

Johnson took a philosophical attitude toward other people's bereavement. In letters to friends he stated that "the business of life summons us away from useless grief. . . . There is no wisdom in useless and hopeless sorrow." He knew that Tetty, much older than he and in poor health, would probably die first, yet his frequently professed stoicism broke down when she died. Just as marriage to Tetty had pulled him out of his depression, so her death plunged him into it. When Jonathan Swift's beloved Stella died, he wrote, "a servant brought me a note, with an account of the death of the truest, most virtuous, and valuable friend, that I, or perhaps any other person ever was blessed with." When John Donne's wife died, Isaak Walton recalled, "his very soul was elemented of nothing but sadness; now, grief took so full a possession of his heart, as to leave no place for joy."[23] Like Swift and Donne, Johnson was overwhelmed by useless grief and hopeless sorrow. As he told Boswell, "(in a solemn, tender, faltering tone) I have known what it was to *lose a wife.*—It had almost broke my heart."

He told another friend, "when my dear Mrs. Johnson expired I sought relief in my studies, and strove to lose the recollection of her in the toils of literature." At first even literature could not console him, and he sought relief in solitude and in physical exertion. In a crucial account of Johnson's reaction, William Shaw reported that he did not want to reveal himself in the depths of despair to companions who'd shared his past life and who may have disliked his Tetty:

Johnson often said he never knew how dear she was to him, till he lost her. Her death affected him so deeply, that he grew almost insensible to the common concerns of life. He then stayed little within, where her image was always recalled by whatever he heard or saw. Study disgusted him, and books of all kinds were equally insipid. He carefully avoided his friends, and associated most with such company as he never saw before. And when he thought himself a burden, and felt the pressure of time becoming insupportable, the only expedient he had was to walk the streets of London,

as he'd once walked, when depressed, between Lichfield and Birmingham.

Two and a half years after Tetty's death, Johnson, who was intensely social and usually hated to be alone, told a scholarly friend that he was still suffering from a feeling of alienation from the world: "I have ever since seemed to myself broken off from mankind, a kind of solitary wanderer in the wild of life, without any certain direction or fixed point of view. A gloomy gazer on a World to which I have little relation."[24] Tetty was not an ideal wife, but they had an intensely emotional bond and she had kept him (in Donne's words) "involved in mankind." Johnson felt sorrow and remorse, grief and guilt. He regretted that he'd neglected Tetty and been unkind to her, that he had made her unhappy and could not make amends. Now that she was no longer a disturbing presence—with all her extravagances, illnesses and addictions—he was free to remember the time when he idealized her and first fell in love.

Johnson continued to record his grief-stricken, guilt-ridden memories of Tetty, who remained a vivid presence in his heart and mind until the end of his life. In 1770, nearly twenty years after her death, he wrote, "when I recollect the time in which we lived together, my grief for her departure is not abated, and I have less pleasure in any good that befalls me, because she does not partake it." Eight years later, he stated that they were both responsible for the breakdown of their marriage but insisted, as he'd once told Boswell, that it was "a love-marriage on both sides": "Poor Tetty, whatever were our faults and failings, we loved each other." In 1782 he was still tormented by remorse: "on what we did amiss, and our faults were great, I have thought of late with more regret than at any former time."

He described the experience of her loss most clearly in a letter of condolence to his personal physician, Dr. Thomas Lawrence. He said that after a wife's death the course of life is torn and a man hangs in meaningless uncertainty. If you outlive a wife you have loved, Johnson wrote, "the continuity of being is lacerated. The settled course of sentiment and action is stopped, and life stands suspended and motionless till it is driven by external causes into a new channel. But the time of suspense is dreadful."[25]

IV

Johnson's attitude toward women was respectful and sentimental. He was physically repulsive and tended to be rude, yet these qualities were balanced by his intellect and wit. He liked the company and conversation of women; he respected their piety, intellect and talent; and though he could not attract the ladies, he could charm them. His relations with his mother were strained, and he felt guilty about neglecting her in later life. But he formed important friendships with his stepdaughter, Lucy Porter; with the genteel provincial ladies Mary Meynell, Hill Boothby and Molly Aston; with the young authors Elizabeth Carter and Charlotte Lennox; with the poor women he took into his household, Anna Williams, Elizabeth Desmoulins, Bet Flint and Poll Carmichael; with the congenial and amusing Frances Reynolds, Hester Thrale, Fanny Burney and Hannah More. A demanding and slovenly guest, he sometimes had strained relations with friends' wives, like Margaret Boswell.

He felt more at ease with women, like Tetty Porter, older than himself; he idealized women of his own age; and he took flirtatious liberties with young women, carrying them in his arms, sitting them on his lap, even kissing them when he got the chance. He was fond of little girls, especially Queeney and the other Thrale children, took an active interest in their education and questioned them about their studies. He was fascinated—and tempted—by loose-living actresses and desperate whores.

In April 1753, thirteen months after Tetty's death, Johnson proposed "to seek a new wife, without any derogation from dear Tetty's memory." He wanted, like any widower, to assuage his grief, relieve his anxious solitude and satisfy his "vain longings of affection." He famously believed that a second marriage, after an unhappy first one, was "the triumph of hope over experience." Eventually he fixed on Hill Boothby, a learned, pious and self-sacrificial woman, a year older than he, whom he'd met through John Taylor at Ashbourne in 1739. She had impressed and even surpassed Johnson by reading the Old Testament in Hebrew.

But Boothby, though unmarried, was not free. Her best friend, Mary Fitzherbert, had died in 1753, leaving six children. Boothby had then moved in with the Fitzherbert family, devoted herself to taking care of the children and tried to protect them from what she considered their father's malign influence. The unworldly, almost nunlike Boothby said she disliked "plays (except for *Irene!*) . . . fox hunting, Bath society, the 'great,' most novels . . . and London."26 Johnson, by contrast, liked plays (except for *Irene*), later enjoyed the pleasures of Bath, occasionally mingled with the great, eagerly read novels and lived in London.

He was an awkward suitor. In the six letters to Boothby that have survived (December 1755–January 1756), he portrayed himself as a wretched man, desperately in need of a woman's companionship and sustenance: "If I turn my thoughts upon myself what do I perceive but a poor helpless being reduced by a blast of wind to weakness and misery." But, he suggested, Miss Boothby could save him from himself. Paraphrasing René Descartes, he boldly exclaimed, "I write therefore I am alive. . . . I am alive, therefore I love Miss Boothby."

Proceeding on this romantic path the following day, he addressed her as "My Sweet Angel" and using the high-flown diction of conventional courtship, begged, "Dear Angel, do not forget me. My heart is full of tenderness. . . . I love you and honour you, and am very unwilling to lose you." Then, fatally descending from the declarations of a chivalric lover, Johnson offered homely advice about constipation: "Give me leave, who have thought much on Medicine, to propose to you an easy and I think very probable remedy for indigestion and lubricity of the bowels."[27]

Boothby portrayed herself in letters to Johnson as a feeble invalid who believed she would not live very long. A valetudinarian, like her suitor, she liked describing her illnesses to a sympathetic listener. But he seemed far too rough and physical for this delicate virgin, who confessed, "I have a very tender, weak body, and it is next to a miracle that it has stood up so long. . . . But on last Friday sevennight, a violent fit of colic seized me, and till yesterday disabled me."

She was very deferential to the great man and flattering about his work on the *Dictionary.* "Nobody," she said, "can more value your correspondence, or be with greater esteem than I am." Johnson kept pressing her for a meeting, and she insisted that she wanted to see him. But when she finally visited London, she was constantly preoccupied by family business and never fixed a time to meet him. She was clearly more at ease in letters than in person. When she resumed their correspondence, she encouraged him by writing about her feelings and her prayers: "I love your letters, and always rejoice to find myself in your thoughts. You are very frequently in mine, and [I'm] seldom without a petition to Heaven for you."

Blinded by his own feelings, Johnson might have mistaken her declarations of esteem for expressions of love. Though Boothby certainly respected and admired him, there's no evidence that she ever thought of him as a potential husband, and her poor health and moral obligations to the children would have prevented marriage even if she had wished it. Hill Boothby died in January 1756, at the age of forty-seven. Disappointed by his failure to find a wife, Johnson later criticized her religiose character: "She pushed her piety to bigotry, her devotion to enthusiasm; she somewhat disqualified herself for the duties of *this* life, by her perpetual aspirations after the next."[28]

10

INTELLECTUAL
ENTERTAINMENTS
1752–1754

I

Lonely and afraid of solitude, sociable by nature and with no close family ties, Johnson believed "life has no pleasure higher or nobler than that of friendship." He was curious about people's lives and loyal to his friends, and in conversation frequently emphasized the importance of personal relations. "I look upon every day to be lost, in which I do not make a new acquaintance," he told Boswell. "If a man does not make new acquaintance as he advances through life, he will soon find himself alone. A man, Sir, should keep his friendship *in constant repair.*" Johnson's friends, his audience and his emotional support, were central to his life. His social circle was wide, including many people whose nationality, religion and politics were very different from his own.

He felt that "to a man whose pleasure is intellectual, London is the place," and enjoyed everything it had to offer.[1] In London the tavern was not only for eating and drinking, but also the heart of social life and conversation. Roy Porter explained that "more dignified taverns like the Mitre in Fleet Street housed concerts, dinners, canvassing and clubs.

In a town of lodging dwellers, they were used to entertain friends, to hear the news or to settle business." Here Johnson exercised his virtuoso talent for talking.

John Nichols, noting Johnson's intellectual superiority, observed that "had he determined to make only those his friends whose endowments were equal to his own, his life would have been that of a Carthusian." But he was not cut out for a monastery. In his zealous pursuit of new people, who ranged from common prostitutes to the king himself, he met some of the most distinguished men and brilliant minds of his age—Giuseppe Baretti, Bennet Langton, Topham Beauclerk, Charles Burney, Thomas Percy, Edward Gibbon, Joshua Reynolds, Oliver Goldsmith—and at least one intellectual equal, Edmund Burke. He knew aristocrats and actors, bishops and artists, professors and scholars, doctors and attorneys, landed gentry and city merchants, well-off publishers and penniless writers. Langton, Beauclerk and Gibbon inherited money; Garrick and Reynolds were artistic stars who earned great fortunes. Burney and Percy had large families to support; Burke was prosperous but extravagant and overreached himself; Johnson, Baretti and Goldsmith lived on their writing and were comparatively poor. This lively and congenial group were drawn together by Johnson and became friends with one another. They not only met in taverns, but also had dinner parties, went to theaters and exhibitions, were guests at country houses, and constantly encouraged and helped each other.

Johnson could be censorious in print, yet in social life his sympathetic tolerance enabled him to form close friendships with men whose moral standards were dubious, whose professions he deprecated and even disdained, and whose politics he hated. Hervey, Savage, Beauclerk and Boswell were dissipated; Burney was a musician, Reynolds a painter, Garrick an actor; Burke was a vile Whig. Yet Johnson managed to find common ground with all these disparate characters. Langton, Beauclerk, Percy and Gibbon had all been educated at Oxford. Savage, Baretti, Paoli, Gibbon, Reynolds and Goldsmith were congenial bachelors. (Most of Johnson's women friends—Lucy Porter, Elizabeth Carter, Hill Boothby, Anna Williams, Frances Reynolds, Fanny Burney and Hannah More—were also unmarried.)

Johnson dominated his friends not only by the force of his personality and power of his mind, but also by his unusual height and strength. He was nearly six feet tall, while Gibbon was less than five feet; Garrick only five feet, four inches; Reynolds five feet, five; Goldsmith and Boswell five feet, six. Johnson was also considerably older than his friends—old enough, in many cases, to be their father. The patriarch of his circle, he was ten years older than Garrick and Baretti; about fifteen years older than Reynolds and Burney; twenty years older than Burke, Percy and Goldsmith; thirty years older than Gibbon, Langton, Beauclerk, Boswell and Hester Thrale; forty years older than Fanny Burney. Despite his physical defects, illnesses and obesity, Johnson had an iron constitution and outlived younger men like Goldsmith, Garrick and Beauclerk.

Johnson's paternal role permitted him to address his chums with familiar nicknames. He called Mrs. Thrale's eldest daughter, Hester Maria, "Queeney" (after the biblical Queen Esther); the writer Arthur Murphy was "Mur"; Garrick, "Davy"; Hawkins, "Hawky"; Langton, "Lanky"; Beauclerk, "Beau"; Frances Reynolds, "Renny"; Edmund Burke, "Mund"; Boswell, "Bozzy"; Goldsmith, "Goldy." The names of Burney and Percy came ready-made. Yet no one dared call Johnson "Sammy" or "Johnny." Goldsmith (in vain) stood on his dignity and complained to Boswell, "I have often desired him not to call me *Goldy.*"[2]

Johnson did everything he could to encourage and help his friends, bonding with them and silently strengthening their work by mingling his own words with theirs. Like a master painter touching up the work of his apprentices, he wrote lines of poetry for Goldsmith, Hawkesworth and George Crabbe, for Anna Williams, Frances Reynolds and Hannah More; prologues for Garrick and Goldsmith as well as for Milton's granddaughter and the Irish playwright Hugh Kelly; sermons for John Taylor, political speeches for Henry Thrale and law lectures for Robert Chambers. He also wrote six pieces for the work of the accomplished linguist, traveler and scholar Giuseppe Baretti, who translated *Rasselas* into French. Writing for others kept him occupied when he was not engaged with his own work.

II

B ritain was frequently at war with France and Spain during the eighteenth century, and in between times relations were strained and
hostile. Johnson had no French or Spanish friends but formed close re-
lationships with Italians, first Baretti and later the teacher and translator
Francesco Sastres and the Corsican general Pasquale Paoli. Voltaire called
the volatile, fiery-tempered and sometimes explosive Baretti the Italian
Zoilus, after the proverbial carping critic who'd launched an attack on
Homer. Born in Turin in 1719, Baretti got into trouble for his satirical attack on an eminent classical scholar and university professor. He immi-
grated to London in 1751, and met Johnson through Charlotte Lennox.

Johnson and Baretti were both hypersensitive, shortsighted and
short-tempered. A translator and lexicographer, Baretti modeled his
Italian and Spanish dictionaries on Johnson's. Baretti's biographer
wrote, "they were both men of learning, rather than original writers, yet
both were as interested in their fellow-men as in their books, delight-
ing in society and well calculated to shine in conversation. Both were
warm-hearted and charitable, with plenty of sound common sense, but
both were overbearing and rough in manner." Baretti once declared,
"had I Johnson's Genius, or he my Spirit of Application & Drudgery,
we might have [prospered and] driven our Coaches and Six long ago."

Baretti hurt his career and ruined his prospects by quarreling with
almost everyone he ever met—including (as we shall see) Hester Thrale
and Johnson himself. A characteristic incident took place in the summer
of 1754 when William Huggins invited Baretti to his estate in Surrey to
examine and improve his long-pondered translation of Ariosto's *Orlando
Furioso*. According to Baretti, Huggins gave him as partial payment for
his literary labors a gold watch worth forty guineas, which he took with
him when he left. Huggins claimed that he'd merely lent the watch and
that Baretti had stolen it. To protect himself from Huggins' energetic attempts to recover his property, Baretti placed himself under the protection of the Sardinian ambassador. He first refused to return the watch,
and then pawned it. Huggins, infuriated, took the matter to the highest levels. Through the intercession of one of the secretaries of state, he
forced the ambassador to withdraw his protection and finally secured his

watch from the pawnbroker. In the midst of the quarrel Johnson was called in as a mediator and, as he told Huggins, "endeavoured honestly and, what is more, kindly, to moderate the violence of this dispute." But since Huggins was "more affected by the provocation than the loss, and more intent on resentment than the disputed property," Johnson suffered "the common fate of intermeddlers, and received no thanks on either side."[3]

Despite Baretti's erratic behavior, Johnson retained respect for his work, if not for his character. Referring to Baretti's *Account of the Manners and Customs of Italy* (1768), he told Boswell, using an appropriately aggressive metaphor, "his account of Italy is a very entertaining book; and, Sir, I know no man who carried his head higher in conversation than Baretti. There are strong powers in his mind. He has not, indeed, many hooks; but what hooks he has, he grapples very forcibly."

In a letter of January 1776 to his brothers in Italy, Baretti expressed his ambivalent attitude toward Johnson, a fearsome but learned *brutta bestia*. He frankly described his physical defects and crude behavior while praising the range of his knowledge and intellectual powers:

> [He is] a nasty old man, a giant both in body and mind, always absent-minded, fierce, touchy, dirty, full of unpleasant habits, always shifting his body when he is seated, and always moving his jaw like an ox chewing the cud; but as he is rightly believed to possess more learning than any other man in this kingdom, he is feared and respected by all, perhaps more than he is loved. Although he is a great critic in French, and knows almost as much Italian as I do, he can speak neither language; but he speaks Latin as vehemently as Cicero.[4]

Johnson had known Bennet Langton's father, who belonged to an old Lincolnshire family and had once offered him a valuable church living if were willing to take holy orders. But Johnson didn't want to leave London and felt unfit for parochial duties. The young Langton was an extraordinary six feet, six inches tall, a "meager, long-visaged man, much resembling . . . a stork standing on one leg." In 1752, when he was still an undergraduate at Oxford, he wrote to Johnson and was invited to Gough Square. He was, like so many others, shocked by Johnson's shabby *déshabille*:

> Mr. Langton was exceedingly surprised when the sage first appeared. He had not received the smallest intimation of his figure, dress, or manner. From perusing his writings, he fancied he should see a decent, well-drest, in short, a remarkably decorous philosopher. Instead of which, down from his bed-chamber, about noon, came, as newly risen, a huge uncouth figure, with a little dark wig which scarcely covered his head, and his clothes hanging loose about him.

One night soon after they met, when Langton had been drinking with his college friend Topham Beauclerk till 3 AM,

> it came into their heads to go and knock up Johnson, and see if they could prevail on him to join them in a ramble. They rapped violently at the door of his chambers . . . till at last he appeared in his shirt, with his little black wig on top of his head, instead of a nightcap, and a poker in his hand, imagining, probably, that some ruffians were coming to attack him. When he discovered who they were, and was told their errand, he smiled, and with great good humour agreed to their proposal: "What, is it you, you dogs! I'll have a frisk with you." He was soon drest, and they sallied forth together into Covent-Garden.

They went to another tavern and drank a bowl of Johnson's favorite bishop. They then strolled down to the Thames, took a boat and rowed across to Billingsgate. "Pleased with their amusement, they resolved to persevere in dissipation for the rest of the day," but Langton had agreed to breakfast with some ladies. Johnson scolded him for "leaving his social friends, to go and sit with a set of wretched *unidea'd* girls." With his love of serious talk and boisterous humor, he was well pleased that the two young bucks could drop all pretension to formality and consider the forbidding sage a worthy companion on their frolics. He failed to see how pretty young girls could compete with the pleasure of his own company.

Langton, like Johnson, was a Tory and High Churchman. He later married the widowed Countess of Rothes and had ten children with her. Johnson admired his friend's piety, knowledge of the classics and enjoyment of life, but criticized his failure to manage his money and take proper care of his enormous family. He subtly judged Langton "a worthy fellow, without malice, though not without resentment," and affectionately concluded: "the earth does not bear a worthier man than Bennet Langton."5

Langton's great friend Topham Beauclerk had been his companion on the Grand Tour, when as young men they traveled through Europe to complete their education and polish their manners. Beauclerk was, like Richard Savage (if Savage's story were true), an illegitimate descendant of an illustrious line. He was the grandson of the Duke of St. Albans; and the great-grandson of Nell Gwynn, who began life as an orange seller in Covent Garden and became a popular actress, and of her lover Charles II, whom Johnson admiringly called "the last King of England who was a man of parts." Beau "had inherited the brooding, dark good looks . . . of the Stuart king and the wit, charm and powers of seduction of the most famous of royal mistresses." A contemporary wrote, "he possessed an exquisite taste, various accomplishments, and the most perfect good breeding"—which more than offset his slovenly person and abundant body lice.

Topham Beauclerk, jaunty by name and by nature, energetic, dissipated and profane, was very different from the phlegmatic, moral and pious Johnson, though they shared a taste for explosive experiments in chemistry. Beau's scandalous relations with his future wife provoked one of Johnson's severest and most memorable comments. Lady Diana Spencer, daughter of the 3rd Duke of Marlborough, had been unhappily married to Viscount Bolingbroke. She left her husband and had a secret affair and illegitimate child with Beauclerk, followed by an equally unhappy marriage with him. While Boswell tried to justify her behavior and defend her romantic passion, Johnson viewed this episode purely in terms of black and white. He simply denounced the aristocratic adulteress, exclaiming: "never accustom your mind to mingle virtue and vice. The woman's a whore, and there's an end on't."[6]

Beauclerk, as if by royal right, took more liberties with Johnson than anyone else and was not afraid to challenge him. Johnson criticized Beau's acid remarks and retorted, "you never open your mouth but with intention to give pain." On one occasion a fairly trivial discussion about the use of pistols in suicide attempts suddenly flared into a heated argument. When it came to the point of contention, Beauclerk exclaimed:

"This is what you don't know, and I do."

Johnson. "Mr. Beauclerk, how came you to talk so petulantly to me? . . . One thing *I* know, which *you* don't seem to know, is that you are very uncivil." Beauclerk. "Because *you* began by being uncivil (which you always are)." . . .

Johnson. "My friend, Mr. Beauclerk, should have [commanded his temper] some time ago." Beauclerk. "I should learn of *you*, Sir." Johnson. "Sir, you have given *me* opportunities enough of learning, when I have been in *your* company. No man loves to be treated with contempt." Beauclerk. (with a polite inclination towards Johnson) "Sir, you have known me twenty years, and however I may have treated others, you may be sure I could never treat you with contempt." Johnson. "Sir, you have said more than was necessary."

Beau stood up to Johnson, but both men drew back before things got out of control and feelings were irreparably hurt. Though combative in argument, Johnson was always eager for reconciliation and never broke off a close friendship.

Yet a certain resentment lingered in Beauclerk. When talking to Boswell about "Johnson's way of saying rough and severe things to people in company, Beauclerk said he wondered it had never happened that some violent man [gave him a beating.] He wished to see it, to teach Johnson how to behave. 'To be sure, a man would be a brute who did it. But it would do good.'" Stout men, however, were reluctant to challenge Johnson in a fight or in an argument. Despite Beau's taunts, Johnson retained the deepest affection for him. As Beau lay dying in April 1780, Johnson said, "I would walk to the extent of the diameter of the earth to save Beauclerk." When he died, Johnson paid heartfelt tribute to his impressively contradictory qualities. "His wit and his folly," he said, "his acuteness and maliciousness, his merriment and reasoning, are now over. Such another will not often be found among mankind."[7]

Responsive to the overtures of strangers, Johnson met Charles Burney after Burney had written him an admiring letter about the *Dictionary*. Born in Shrewsbury in 1726, he was a church organist and music teacher in King's Lynn, Norfolk. They first met in the spring of 1758, two years before Burney finally settled in London. A minor composer, amateur astronomer and connoisseur of painting, Burney was a learned and genial companion. Though Johnson confessed, "all Animated Nature loves Music—Except myself," he wrote the dedication for Burney's *General History of Music* (1776–89) and sided with him during his intense rivalry with Sir John Hawkins, who also published a *General History of Music* in 1776.

Burney idolized Johnson. He indulged his taste for late-night conversation, and they talked as long as the candles, fires and servants lasted. Burney emphasized that Johnson behaved quite politely in personal conversations, when he wasn't trying to display his powers in public, overwhelm his adversaries and retain his preeminence in disputation. Comparing Johnson, as was so often done, to an animal, Burney said: "he is in private often pleasant, candid, charitable, to a degree of weakness, & as good-natured as a family mastiff, whom you may safely pat & stroke at the fire-side without the least fear of his biting you. The utmost he will do if you are rough with him is to growl."

Johnson's charming exchange with Charles' daughter, the novelist Fanny Burney, revealed the depth of feeling between Johnson and Burney as well as Johnson's intense need for affection and fear that his friends might not love him:

"I love Burney,—my heart *goes out* to meet him!"

"He is not ungrateful, Sir," cried I,—"for most heartily does he love *you*."

"Does he, Madam? —I am surprised at that."[8]

Thomas Percy, like Johnson, came from humble origins and had a spectacular career. A scholar, antiquarian and cleric, he became chaplain to the Duke of Northumberland and then to King George III, and was appointed dean of Carlisle and finally bishop of Dromore, near Belfast, in northern Ireland. In 1765 he published the *Reliques of Ancient English Poetry*, a pioneering collection of medieval ballads, with a dedication written by Johnson.

Like Beauclerk, Percy got into a fierce dispute with Johnson about a trivial issue—the supposed merits of the Welshman Thomas Pennant's *A Tour in Scotland* (1769), which Johnson had praised. Percy, having the same name as and warmly attached to the House of Northumberland,

could not sit quietly and hear a man praised, who had spoken disrespectfully of Alnwick-Castle and the Duke's pleasure grounds. . . .

Percy. "But, my good friend, you are short-sighted, and do not see so well as I do." [Boswell] wondered at Dr. Percy's venturing thus. Dr. Johnson said nothing at the time; but inflammable particles were collecting for a cloud to burst. . . . Johnson. "Hold, Sir! Don't talk of rudeness; remember, Sir, you told me (puffing hard with passion struggling for a vent), I was short-sighted. We have done with civility. We are to be as rude as we please." Percy. "Upon my honour, Sir, I did not mean to be uncivil." Johnson. "I cannot say so, Sir; for I *did* mean to be uncivil, thinking *you* had been uncivil." Dr. Percy rose, ran up to him, and taking him by the hand, assured him affectionately that his meaning had been misunderstood; upon which a reconciliation instantly took place. Johnson. "My dear Sir, I am willing you shall *hang* Pennant."

Though Percy had gone too far and descended to ad hominem remarks in the heat of argument, Johnson eagerly accepted his apology.

Paying handsome (if convoluted) tribute to Percy's intellect, Johnson described him as "a man out of whose company I never go without having learned something. . . . So much extension of mind, and so much minute accuracy of enquiry, if you survey your whole circle of acquaintance, you will find so scarce, if you find it at all, that you will value Percy by comparison."[9]

Though not a close friend of Johnson, Edward Gibbon was an illustrious member of his social circle. Born in 1737 of a good family in Putney, outside London, he was a sickly child and a voracious reader. After Westminster School, he spent a wasted year, at the age of fifteen, at Magdalen College, Oxford. He then studied for five years at Lausanne and was briefly engaged to a Swiss woman. He traveled widely in Europe, flirted (like Boswell) with Catholicism and (like Boswell and Goldsmith) had met Voltaire. The pampered, chubby Gibbon served improbably as captain in the Hampshire militia, and in 1774 became a notably silent Whig MP.

Bizarre in appearance, Gibbon was very short and fat, with "a big head, bulging forehead, round eyes and a small squat nose between bulging cheeks." A French woman said he "was so ugly that she refrained with difficulty from bursting into laughter at the sight of him." Boswell, also repelled by his ugliness, called him an "affected, disgusting fellow, who poisons our literary club," and was unwilling to record Johnson's praise of his historical work. Johnson's touchy relations with Gibbon were complicated in two ways, one intellectual and one social: by Gibbon's criticism of Christianity in his *Decline and Fall* and by the awkward fact that Johnson's cousin Phoebe Ford was Gibbon's housekeeper in Bentinck Street from 1773 to 1783. Gibbon voiced his own uneasiness in their most notorious exchange. Johnson remarked, "'we are told, that the black bear is innocent; but I should not like to trust myself with him.' Mr. Gibbon muttered, in a low tone of voice, 'I should not like to trust myself with *you*.'"[10]

In a description that imitated Johnson's famous comparisons of Homer and Virgil, Dryden and Pope in the *Lives of the Poets,* the playwright George Colman the younger likened the magisterial prose styles of Johnson and Gibbon: "Johnson's style was grand, and Gibbon's elegant; the stateliness of the former was sometimes pedantick, and the polish of the latter was occasionally finical. Johnson marched to kettle-drums and trumpets; Gibbon moved to flutes and haut-boys;—Johnson hewed passages through the Alps, while Gibbon leveled walks through parks and gardens."

Johnson influenced Gibbon in two notable passages. At the end of his life, when revising the last volume of *Decline and Fall,* Gibbon echoed "from China to Peru" in the second line of *Vanity* by asking, "have Asia and Africa, from Japan to Morocco, any feeling or memory of the Roman Empire?" And a reflective moment in Johnson's *Journey to the Western Islands of Scotland* (1775)—"I sat down on a bank, such as a writer of romance might have delighted to feign. . . . Here I first conceived the thought of this narration"—inspired the most famous moment in Gibbon's *Autobiography* (1796): "It was at Rome, on the 15th of October 1764, as I sat musing amid the ruins of the Capitol . . . that the idea of writing the decline and fall of the city first started to my mind."[11]

II

Johnson's most intimate and important friendships were with the immensely talented Joshua Reynolds, Edmund Burke and Oliver Goldsmith. Reynolds, whose clergyman father was named Samuel, was (like Johnson) hard of hearing and also spoke with a pronounced provincial accent. Born in Devon in 1723, he was of medium height, with a stocky figure verging on plumpness, a face marked with smallpox and a deformed upper lip, swollen like that of a trumpet player. His friend and editor Edmond Malone wrote that he had "a florid complexion, and a lively and pleasing aspect; well made, and extremely active. His appearance at first sight impressed the spectator with the idea of a well-born and well-bred English gentleman." Reynolds and Garrick—as opposed to privileged aristocrats and political favorites—earned great wealth through their own talent and genius.

Reynolds' moderate, tolerant and easy-going personality was the opposite of Johnson's abrasive, confrontational and violent character. He lacked passion and zeal, was inhumanly cool and calm, and, as Goldsmith wrote in "Retaliation," "His manners were gentle, complying and bland." Hester Thrale, who preferred a more fiery figure, criticized this aspect of Reynolds' character by noting that though "he is a Man very generally beloved . . . he is however not much a Man to my natural Taste: he seems to have no Affections." Her friend Fanny Burney found him more appealing: "I like his Countenance, & I like his manners: the former I think expressive, soft, & sensible; the latter gentle, unassuming, & engaging."

Reynolds' lack of passion prevented him from marrying, though he was attracted to and tempted by the Swiss painter Angelica Kauffmann. He told Edmond Malone, with somewhat specious reasoning, that ladies lost interest in him as rapidly as he became disaffected with them, and that his erotic passion evaporated with consummation: "He said the reason why he would never marry was that every woman whom he had liked had grown indifferent to him, and he had been glad that he did not marry her. He had no reason therefore to suppose that it would not be the same as to any other woman." Women at first excite our desire, he said, but "after fruition . . . in the act of enjoyment [we find] the ardours of our desires abate and after a few repetitions change into disgust."[12]

Reynolds had spent two years studying in Rome, shortly before meeting Johnson in 1756, and soon became the most successful painter in England. Contrasting Reynolds' modesty to Prospero/Garrick's vulgar display of wealth, Johnson remarked, "there goes a Man not to be spoiled by Prosperity." Admiring the painter's eye, he added, "I know no man who has passed through life with more observation than Reynolds." He too commented on Reynolds' astonishing tolerance, even when provoked, and censured his apparent virtue by telling him, "Reynolds, you hate no person living. But I like a good hater." In saying this, he was thinking of his passionate friend "dear Bathurst," "a man to my very heart's content: he hated a fool, and he hated a rogue, and he hated a *whig;* he was a very good *hater*."[13]

Johnson could be aggressive and provocative while Reynolds remained calm and unassuming. Offended one evening when they were neglected by their host and treated as if they were "low company,"

Johnson pretended to be a common laborer, disrupted the proceedings and called attention to himself by loudly asking Reynolds: "how much do you think you and I could get in a week, if we were *to work as hard as we could?*" The ironic subtext was that Reynolds could make in a day what Johnson earned in a month. In 1769, as a tribute to Reynolds and after long years of abstinence, Johnson drank wine to celebrate his friend's knighthood. Johnson's finest tribute was a solicitous and characteristically elaborate letter offering to comfort Reynolds during his illness: "If the amusement of my company can exhilarate the languor of a slow recovery, I will not delay a day to come to you, for I know not how I can effectively promote my own pleasure as by pleasing you, or my own interest as by preserving you, in whom if I should lose you, I should lose almost the only Man whom I call a friend." When Reynolds received the letter, he summoned Johnson to his bedside.

Perceptive about his combative character, Reynolds said that Johnson would use any rough means to conquer his opponents: "he fought upon every occasion as if his whole reputation depended upon the victory of the minute. . . . He opposed, directly and abruptly, his antagonist. He fought with all sorts of weapons; with ludicrous comparisons and similes; and if all failed, with rudeness and overbearing. He thought it necessary never to be worsted in argument."[14] Like Charles Burney, Reynolds also mentioned that he did not strive for victory during intimate conversations with his friends.

Reynolds, willing to put up with Johnson's rudeness, treasured his talk and learned a great deal from him. He freely "acknowledged the highest obligations to him" and admitted that Johnson "may be said to have formed my mind and to have brushed off from it a deal of rubbish." By this he meant that Johnson, by challenging his ideas, forced him to avoid the common faults of conversation—cant, falsehood, hypocrisy, received ideas and trivial repartee—and made him think for himself.

In Reynolds' *Discourses on Art* (1797), written in the Johnsonian style and probably polished by the master, he paid tribute to Johnson by noting that "the conversation of learned and ingenious men, is the best

of all substitutes for those [like himself] who have not the means or opportunities of deep study." A friend described how much Reynolds had
learned from Johnson, whose original ideas he often passed off as his
own:

> His mind was active, perpetually at work. He aimed at origi-
> nality, and threw out observations and sentiments as new,
> which had often been discussed by various authors; for his
> knowledge was principally acquired by conversation, and
> thereby superficial. However, he was a most pleasing, amiable
> companion; his manners easy, conciliating, and unaffected. He
> had great good sense, and an exquisite correct taste; and if his
> ideas were not always new, they were often set off by liveliness
> of imagination; and his conversation abounded in pleasing and
> interesting anecdotes.[15]

Reynolds not only tolerated Johnson's rudeness, but also paid another penalty for his learned and stimulating talk. Johnson's nocturnal visits to Reynolds' house were frequent, long and inconvenient.
Always unwilling to retire, he extended his stay until the early hours
of the morning, "deranging, by his immobility, the domestic oeconomy of the house." Let us commence talking, Johnson might have
said, and see who shall tire first. Reynolds well understood the reasons
for Johnson's eccentric behavior—his dislike of being alone and fear of
insanity—and in a perceptive passage observed: "solitude to him was
horror; nor would he ever trust himself alone in writing or reading. He
has often begged me to accompany him home to prevent his being
alone in the coach. Any company to him was better than none; by
which he connected himself with many mean persons whose presence
he could command."[16]

Johnson maintained close relations with both Joshua and his younger
sister, Frances, just as he did with both Charles and Fanny Burney.
Frances, also an artist, was mistress of Joshua's grand house and gallery
in Leicester Square; but when they quarreled late in life, Reynolds replaced her with his favorite younger niece. Though Johnson mentioned

her tendency toward introspection, perplexities and irresolution, which matched his own, he sympathized with her in difficult times, corrected her poems and posed for her. Near the end of his life he wrote, "I sat to Mrs. Reynolds yesterday for my picture, perhaps the tenth time, and I sat near three hours, with the patience of *Mortal born to bear.* At last She declared it quite finished and seems to think it fine."

Frances was as perceptive as her brother, relating—in painterly terms—Johnson's faults to his defects, his intellect to his moral standards:

For being totally devoid of all deceit, free from every tinge of affectation or ostentation, and unwarped by any vice, his singularities, those strong lights and shades that so peculiarly distinguished his character, may the more easily be traced to their primary and natural causes.

The luminous parts of his character, his soft affections, and I should suppose his strong intellectual powers, at least the dignified charm or radiancy of them, must be allowed to owe their origin to his strict, his rigid principles of religion and virtue.

According to Reynolds' biographer, the family believed that Johnson "had actually proposed to her" and that she "might have married the great Dr. Johnson if she had chosen to."[17] In fact, Frances, who lived until 1807, never married. Like Hill Boothby, she revered Johnson but didn't love him.

The great artists of seventeenth-century England—Sir Peter Lely, Grinling Gibbons and Sir Godfrey Kneller—were born in Holland and Germany. The real English school began in the 1730s with William Hogarth, followed in the 1750s by Thomas Gainsborough and Reynolds. Joshua painted four major portraits of Johnson between 1756 and 1775. In the first, full-face portrait (1756–57, National Portrait Gallery), Johnson is seated on a green-and-white-checked easy chair. He wears a cloudlike, grayish wig that frames his fleshy face and touches his shoulders; a long open brown coat and buttoned brown waistcoat, tightened by his protruding belly; a white collar and ruffled cuffs. He holds a short quill pen in his right hand, and presses down hard with the bent fingers of his left hand (showing the whites of the knuckles) on a sheet of writing paper that rests on an olive-green tablecloth. Pale-faced and ruddy-cheeked, with full lips and broad nose, he tilts his head to the right. Poised between thought and words, he seems to be searching reflectively, even dreamily, for literary inspiration.

The second, and greatest, painting (1769, Harvard University) portrays Johnson half-length and in profile. His own hair (without a wig) and his heroic posture convey a sense of personal immediacy. He wears an open white collar and a tan monkish robe with draped hood; and his bold features and meditative eyes, under heavy brows, stand out against the dusky background. His powerful hands, held in front of his massive chest, have nervously bent, twisted, convulsive fingers. They seem to be playing a difficult piece on the violin, and curl back in the same way as the scroll of paper in the right background. The scroll rests on a stack of three books, the thickest one a volume of the *Dictionary.* In this portrait he's a tormented figure, struggling with anguished thoughts.

Both Frances and Joshua analyzed the peculiar movements that were so poignantly captured in this portrait. Frances wrote, using two vivid similes, "as for his gestures with his hands, they were equally strange; sometimes he would hold them up with some of his fingers bent, as if he had been seized with the cramp, and sometimes at his Breast in motion like those of a jockey on full speed; and often would lift them up as high as he could stretch over his head, for some minutes." Joshua connected these gestures to Johnson's sense of guilt. Observing that Johnson's odd tricks and movements occurred only when he was not engaged in conversation, he conjectured that they "proceeded from a habit he had indulged himself in of accompanying his thoughts with certain untoward actions, and that those actions always appeared to him as if they were meant to reprobate some part of his past conduct. . . . His mind appeared to be preying on itself; he fell into a reverie accompanied with strange antic gesticulations."

The third, a half-length, full-face portrait (c.1772–78, Tate Gallery), portrays Johnson with a grayish-white wig, tight white collar, and the brown buttoned suit and waistcoat he usually wore. He has a furrowed brow, thick wavy eyebrows and deep-set eyes; a wide nose and double chin; and half-opened lips that suggest the force of his conversation and the dangerous stream of his invective. His anxious expression and nervous fingering of his waistcoat suggest a man deeply immersed in troubled thoughts.

In the fourth, a half-length, three-quarter-view picture (1775, Huntington Library), Johnson wears a familiar wig and velvety burgundy coat, edged with white collar and cuffs. Absorbed in his reading, he tightly grips a book—bending it backward, crushing it and almost breaking the spine. He holds it close to his eyes as if he were devouring the print and physically squeezing out the words. Blind in one eye and myopic in the other, Johnson did not believe spectacles would help him and tried to improve his vision by squinting. Though his sight was defective, his gaze was intense. Hester Thrale wrote that "his Eyes, though of a light blue [or light gray] Colour, were so wild, so piercing, and at Times so fierce, that Fear was I believe the first Emotion in the hearts of all his Beholders."

Reynolds had portrayed Giuseppe Baretti—even more nearsighted than Johnson—reading a duodecimo volume that was almost pressed against his nose. In one self-portrait the artist is shown cupping his hands to his deaf ear, in another wearing spectacles, and these personal details make the pictures more striking and memorable. But Johnson—sensitive, as in his argument with Percy, about being shortsighted—was extremely displeased with Reynolds' final portrait. He told Hester Thrale that "he would not be known by posterity for his *defects* only, let Sir Joshua do his worst. . . . He may paint himself as deaf if he chuses; but I will not be *blinking Sam*."[18]

Johnson looks quite different in the four Reynolds portraits, painted at various stages of his life. He's a meditative figure, set back from the frame, in the first; a tormented classical hero in the second; and a bewigged sage, seen close up and filling the frame, in the third and fourth. He stares at the viewer in the first and third portraits, at his book (ignoring the viewer) in the fourth, and inwardly in the third. He seems more troubled, after his severe mental breakdown in 1765, in the heroic portrait. In all four paintings Reynolds used these intense gestures and expressions to reveal Johnson's anguished intelligence.

IV

Burke and Goldsmith were both Irish Protestants (though Burke's mother and wife were Catholics), and contemporaries at Trinity College, Dublin. Burke, a spellbinding orator, was the son of an attorney who named him after the poet Edmund Spenser, a distant ancestor. He had traveled in France and studied law in London, though he never qualified for the bar. Happily married, he had one son, Richard, who predeceased him. He published his elegantly written and influential treatise, *A Philosophical Inquiry into the Sublime and the Beautiful* in 1759, and was elected to Parliament in 1766. He became political secretary to Lord Rockingham, who was prime minister in 1765–66 and then opposed the government until he again became prime minister in 1782, the year of his death. Burke was an influential figure among the Rockingham Whigs. Diametrically opposed to Johnson on almost every political issue, he supported the American colonists and the political radical John Wilkes.

Considered by some to be a wild Irishman, Burke drank too much and got into financial difficulties after buying a lavish estate at Beaconsfield and trying to provide for many feckless members of his family. Eloquent and persuasive in public life, he was charming and endearing in private. Fanny Burney praised his character: "Such spirit, such intelligence, so much energy when serious, so much pleasantry when sportive,—so manly in his address, so animated in his conversation,—so eloquent in argument, so exhilarating in trifling."

Unlike Reynolds, who was cautiously temperate, and Goldsmith, always willing to expose his ignorance and play the buffoon, Burke was as obstinate and opinionated, as irascible and inflexible, as competitive and overbearing as Johnson. The two met for the first time at Garrick's Christmas dinner in 1758. Burke's biographer described "his modest social origins; his difficult personality, ill adapted to compromise or to working in a team; his temper and lack of self-control." Insecure and ambitious, "Burke was driven by a need to show off his knowledge and his eloquence, habitually turning the most casual social encounter . . . into an opportunity for ostentation." Not noted for his tact, Burke loved to dominate the conversation and rarely gave way in argument. A famous and brilliant contender, he was well aware of his faults. "It is but too well known [he confessed] that I debate with great Vehemence and asperity and with little management either of the opinions of persons or many of my adversaries."

Edmond Malone, a friend of both Johnson and Burke, noted how similar they were in habit and temperament, and in their need to dominate every discussion. Burke, "by his eloquence and habitual assertions in company . . . would keep his guests too much under. . . . His manner of conversation, were it not for the great superiority of his talents and knowledge, would be disagreeable. He seldom appears to pay any attention to what is said by the person or persons with whom he is conversing but, disregarding their remarks, urges on whatever rises in his mind."[19] Johnson and Burke's almost miraculous friendship, which transcended politics and potential conflicts, was based on profound mutual respect.

Johnson was torn between personal esteem for Burke and hatred of his Whiggism. Donald Greene wrote that though they were close friends, "they had only the harshest things to say about each other's politics; each accused the other of essential dishonesty in his political activities." Johnson once angrily described Burke as "a lion, who lashes himself into Fury with his own Tail." When Boswell asked if men who disagreed on fundamental principles could be friends, Johnson said they might: "why, Sir, you must shun the subject as to which you disagree. For instance, I can live very well with Burke: I love his knowledge, his genius, his diffusion and affluence of conversation; but I would not talk to him of the Rockingham party."[20]

Well aware of the perils of clashing with Johnson, Burke adhered to their tacit agreement and avoided contentious subjects. After dining with Johnson at Reynolds' house, he told Boswell, "we had a very good day, as we had not a sentence, word, syllable, Letter, comma, or tittle, of any of the Elements that make politics." Burke's fierce Whig principles must have reminded Johnson of Gilbert Walmesley's; and he was probably thinking of both men when he wrote of his old mentor in *The Lives of the Poets*: "he was a Whig, with all the virulence and malevolence of his party; yet difference of opinion did not keep us apart. I honored him, and he endured me."

Johnson admired Burke's personal distinction and vast knowledge, his command of language and intellectual force. When Burke was elected to Parliament, Johnson predicted he would have an outstanding career: "Burke is a great man by Nature, and is expected soon to attain civil greatness."[21] Johnson noted that Burke in private was as impressive as he was in public. "Burke is the only man," he said, "whose common conversation corresponds with the general fame which he has in the world. Take up whatever topick you please, he is ready to meet you." His exceptional qualities were immediately apparent: "You could not stand five minutes with that man beneath a shed while it rained, but you must be convinced you had been standing with the greatest man you had ever yet seen." Contending with this intellectual gladiator, he felt, required all the strength he could muster. He told Boswell, "'His stream of mind is perpetual.' . . . Once, when Johnson was ill, and unable to exert himself as much as usual without fatigue, Mr. Burke having been mentioned, he said, 'That fellow calls forth all my powers. Were I to see Burke now, it would kill me.'"[22]

Burke, like Johnson, was a social being. Though brought up as an Anglican, his religious credentials were suspect in both Ireland and England. Always an Irish outsider in London, he sought "to be accepted . . . and elevated friendship and connection to a social principle." The Irish political writer Conor Cruise O'Brien explained, "Burke's acceptance by Johnson and his circle was of great psychological importance to Burke. In the London of the mid-eighteenth century an Irish person was automatically suspect in a certain degree, and it was quite a high degree if he had Catholic connections: the anti-Catholic Penal Laws were still in full force."

Boswell described an emotional scene when Burke and several other friends attended Johnson's sickbed: "Burke said to him, 'I am afraid, Sir, such a number of us may be oppressive to you.' 'No, Sir, (said Johnson), it is not so; and I must be in a wretched state, indeed, when your company would not be a delight to me.' Mr. Burke, in a tremulous voice, expressive of being very tenderly affected, replied, 'My dear Sir, you have always been too good to me.'" In a moving parliamentary speech, Burke declared that his friendship with Johnson had been "the greatest consolation and happiness in his life."[23]

V

Oliver Goldsmith, another Irishman of genius, was (unlike Burke) a worldly failure. Thomas Percy introduced him to Johnson at a literary supper given by Goldsmith at his new lodgings on May 31, 1761. Goldsmith had praised Johnson in his periodical *The Bee* (1759); and Johnson had been greatly impressed by Goldsmith's "Chinese Letters" (1760–61), supposedly written by a philosophical Chinaman living in London, and later collected as *The Citizen of the World.* Johnson appeared at the supper dressed quite out of character, in a new suit of clothes and nicely powdered wig. When Percy asked the reason for his transformation, he replied: "I hear that Goldsmith, who is a very great sloven, justifies his disregard of cleanliness and decency, by quoting my practice, and I am desirous this night to show a better example."

Goldsmith was solidly but not heavily built, with a fair complexion; brown hair; a balding, bulbous forehead and features badly disfigured by smallpox. Boswell wrote, "his person was short, his countenance coarse and vulgar, his deportment that of a scholar awkwardly affecting the easy gentleman." The son of an Irish clergyman, he had briefly studied medicine at the universities of Edinburgh and Leiden. He'd traveled in France, Switzerland and Italy, living mainly by his wits, and returned to England, at the age of twenty-six, in 1756. Malone wrote, "he applied to several apothecaries in hopes of being received in the capacity of a journeyman, but his broad Irish accent, and the uncouthness of his appearance, occasioned him to meet with insult from most of the medicinal tribe."[24] Though he never earned a medical degree, Goldsmith was called "Dr." In his *Life*, Boswell formalized Johnson's speech and called him "Dr." to dignify his subject, but Johnson never used that honorific title and was usually addressed as "Mister."

If Garrick was the true comedian and wit of Johnson's social circle, Goldsmith was the inspired idiot and court jester. Despite his considerable literary talent, he did not inspire admiration and respect. The bookseller Tom Davies (who would introduce Boswell to Johnson) noted Goldsmith's strange mixture of good and bad qualities—the bad tending to swamp the good. His character was "a compound of absurdity, envy, and malice, contrasted with the opposite virtues of kindness, generosity, and benevolence." The actor and playwright Arthur Murphy mentioned his greatest fault and ruling passion: "the leaven of envy which corroded the mind of that elegant writer, and made him impatient, without disguise, of the praises bestowed on any person whatever."

Goldsmith, who also seized the chance to arouse envy in others, strutted before Boswell when he'd been invited to tea with Johnson and Anna Williams, and Boswell was left out. Ignoring Lord Chesterfield's belief that an eighteenth-century gentleman should maintain a *volto sciolto e pensieri stretti* (open countenance and hidden thoughts), Goldsmith freely displayed his childish emotions and provoked disdain for his foolishness. A friend observed:

> He was awkward, had no dignity of bearing, no power of concealing his thoughts or feelings, either by facial expression or by silence. Added to these superficial defects, there were his poverty and his extreme good-nature. He had not much power to favour, and too much generous sensibility to wound. As he inspired no fear, and did no harm to any one, he was regarded with a certain tolerant liking—as being a butt for practical jokes, and an amusing piece of absurdity—but certainly not with deference. In such a one it was found hard to acknowledge the presence of genius.[25]

There was no consistency and harmony between Goldsmith's speech and writing. As Garrick exclaimed in an impromptu epitaph: "Here lies Nolly Goldsmith, for shortness call'd Noll, / Who wrote like an angel but talk'd like poor Poll." Though Goldsmith composed a *History of the Earth and Animated Nature,* a book of natural history adapted from the French writer Georges-Louis Buffon, he could scarcely tell a turkey from a goose, a donkey from a mule. Reynolds said his "mind was entirely unfurnished," and Johnson agreed, "it's amazing how little Goldsmith knows. He seldom comes where he is not more ignorant than any one else." Having been told that Goldsmith said, "as I take my shoes from the shoemaker, and my coat from the taylor, so I take my religion from the priest," Johnson declared, "Sir, he knows nothing; he has made up his mind about nothing."[26]

Goldsmith was completely unaware of the impression he made on other people. After uttering "a laboured sentence, so tumid as to be scarce intelligible, [he] would ask if that was not truly Johnsonian." His speech and antics were both comic and pathetic. At an exhibition in London, "when those who sat next to him observed with what dexterity a puppet was made to toss a pike, he could not bear that it should have such praise, and exclaimed with some warmth, 'Pshaw! I can do it better myself.'" On the way home to dinner with Burke, he "broke his shin by attempting to exhibit to the company how much better he could jump over a stick than the puppets."

Goldsmith was occasionally capable of making some memorably witty remarks. Like Reynolds and Burke, he was struck by how Johnson would use any fair or foul means to win a dispute. "There's no arguing with Johnson," he said, "for if his pistol misses fire, he knocks you down with the butt-end of it." When Goldsmith commented that the skill in writing an animal fable consisted in making the little fishes speak in character, and Johnson burst out laughing, he smartly added: "why, Dr. Johnson, this is not so easy as you seem to think; for if you were to make little fishes talk, they would talk like WHALES."[27] Goldsmith made an amusing riposte when visiting Westminster Abbey with Johnson. As they surveyed the Poets' Corner, Johnson quoted Ovid in Latin, translated as "Perhaps our names will also mingle with these." When they got to Temple Bar, Goldsmith pointed to the traitors' heads on spikes and, alluding to their Tory principles, reversed the meaning and slyly whispered in Latin, "Perhaps our names will also mingle with THESE."

After a Scottish nobleman "regretted that Johnson had not been educated with more refinement, and lived more in polished society,"
Baretti replied, "'no, no, my Lord, do with him what you would, he
would always have been a bear.' 'True (answered the Earl, with a smile),
but he would have been a *dancing* bear.'" Goldsmith then defended
him by affectionately remarking, "Johnson, to be sure, has a roughness
in his manner; but no man alive has a more tender heart. *He has nothing of the bear but his skin.*"

The characters and careers of Johnson and Goldsmith were strikingly similar. Like Johnson, Goldsmith was ugly, socially awkward and
scarred by smallpox. He was slovenly but tried to compensate for his
defects with lavish dress, which he could ill afford; Johnson dressed like
a mendicant. Goldsmith also had strained relations with his mother;
suffered from hereditary indolence; and seemed to disappear for several
"obscure years," when little was known about his life.

Goldsmith came to London penniless and unknown, and made his
way by merit alone, "without friends, recommendations, money or
impudence." A Tory in politics, he was tolerant of Catholics and benevolent to the poor. Goldsmith often gave away everything he had and
became indigent; Johnson also gave generously, but prudently kept back
what was needed to support his wife and dependent household. Goldsmith, too, had no interest in architecture or painting, no feeling for
rugged mountains or wild landscapes. He disliked Scotland and was not
impressed by France. Both men were quite capable of violence. When a
man behaved impudently, Johnson beat him. When John Evans, editor of
the *Universal Magazine,* published an article that ridiculed not only Goldsmith, but also some respectable ladies, Goldsmith hastily set off for Pa-
ternoster Row and caned Evans in his own shop.

After several unsuccessful attempts to teach school, Goldsmith
began his literary career as a translator from French. Chronically
short of money, he spent long years in Grub Street, writing many
articles for the *Monthly Review* (as Johnson did for the *Gentleman's
Magazine*) and periodical essays for *The Bee* (as Johnson did for the
Rambler). An expert in synthesizing material from standard histories, Goldsmith turned out copy with remarkable rapidity. Like

Johnson with Lord Chesterfield, Goldsmith rejected patronage and said, "I have no dependence on the promises of great men: I look to the booksellers for support." Both Goldsmith and Johnson lived on advances from publishers for literary projects. Goldsmith never started work on some of them, failed to finish many others and died deeply in debt. Johnson scrupulously fulfilled his contracts and left a substantial sum to his heirs.

Goldsmith's poverty, a strong bond between them, was even greater and lasted longer than Johnson's. Johnson's comment on Richard Steele fit Goldsmith perfectly: "imprudence of generosity, or vanity of profusion, kept him always incurably necessitous." In October 1762 Goldsmith desperately called for Johnson's help, just as Johnson, right after Tetty's death, had sent a middle-of-the-night letter to John Taylor. Johnson told Boswell:

I received one morning a message from poor Goldsmith that he was in great distress, and, as it was not in his power to come to me, begging that I would come to him as soon as possible. I sent him a guinea, and promised to come to him directly. I accordingly went as soon as I was drest, and found that his landlady had arrested him for his rent, at which he was in a violent passion. I perceived that he had already changed my guinea, and had got a bottle of Madeira and a glass before him. I put the cork into the bottle, desired he would be calm, and began to talk to him of the means by which he might be extricated. He then told me he had a novel ready for the press, which he produced to me. I looked into it, and saw its merit; told the landlady I should soon return, and having gone to a bookseller, sold it for sixty pounds. I brought Goldsmith the money, and he discharged his rent, not without rating his landlady in a high tone for having used him so ill.[28]

Though Goldsmith had not paid the rent, he felt aggrieved, became indignant and took refuge in drink, and though he'd completed the novel and was desperate for money, he had not taken the trouble to sell it. He was ineffectual, hopeless and violent, while Johnson was calm, practical and in command of the situation. Johnson knew that writers living on the edge of destitution had to help each other survive. He saw the value of *The Vicar of Wakefield* (which became a great and lasting success) and quickly resolved the problem.

Johnson always defended Goldsmith, as he defended Garrick, against his detractors. He was extremely generous to Goldsmith, his chief literary competitor, while Goldsmith was intensely jealous of Johnson's domination of the literary scene. Johnson called Goldsmith's poem *The Traveller* (1765), which, like *Rasselas,* portrayed a wide-ranging search for happiness, "a production to which, since the death of Pope, it will not be easy to find anything equal." And he asserted, without qualification, that "Goldsmith was the best writer he ever knew upon every subject he wrote upon."

As always, Johnson fortified his praise with practical assistance. He wrote nine lines of *The Traveller,* the prologue to Goldsmith's play *The Good-Natur'd Man* (1768), the epitaph for his tombstone (1774), and the concluding and best lines of *The Deserted Village* (1770). In the preface to his edition of Shakespeare's plays, Johnson said that the playwright stood out like an indestructible rock against the forces of decay: "the stream of time, which is continually washing the dissoluble fabricks of other poets, passes without injury by the adamant of Shakespeare." He returned to this theme in the last lines of Goldsmith's poem:

> That trade's proud empire hastes to swift decay,
> As ocean sweeps the labour'd mole away;
> While self dependent power can time defy,
> As rocks resist the billows and the sky.[29]

It's ironic that Goldsmith was dependent on Johnson for the splendid lines exalting independence.

Boswell pointed out that Goldsmith based the character of Croaker in *The Good-Natur'd Man* on Johnson's Suspirius, the screech owl in *Rambler* 59, a satiric self-portrait and ironic critique of the gloomy lamentations in *Vanity*. Johnson wrote of the harsh-crying bird: "these screech-owls seemed to be settled in an opinion that the great business of life is to complain, and that they were born for no other purpose than to disturb the happiness of others, to lessen the little comforts, and shorten the short pleasures of our condition, by painful remembrances of the past, or melancholy prognosticks of the future." In Goldsmith's play, Croaker, a wealthy tradesman married to a cheerful wife, is a discontented man who laments misfortunes he never experienced, a professional pessimist who ruins his own happiness by worrying about hypothetical evils. Speaking of the appropriation of his character, Johnson contrasted Goldsmith's faults with his potential and told Fanny Burney that Goldsmith "was not *scrupulous;*—but he would have been a great man, had he known the real value of his internal resources." Nevertheless, he praised the play by saying that "it was the best comedy that has appeared since [Sir John Vanbrugh's 1728 play] *The Provoked Husband,* and that there had not been of late any such character exhibited on the stage as that of Croaker."[30]

Five years later, when Goldsmith begged for help on his next play, as well as for money for his immediate needs, Johnson readily provided both. Appealing to Johnson's critical expertise, as Garrick had done, Goldsmith pleaded:

My Dear Mr. Johnson,
Could you come round here this evening? I have at length concluded the Play, and shall entitle it *She Stoops to Conquer* subject to your better judgement. I should also be glad if you could advance me Ten guineas until I close with Mr. Tonson [the publisher], when amount shall be punctually repaid.

I saw Sir Joshua last Sunday. Had an attack of gout and melancholia, but smiled when he saw me and questioned me [as a doctor] about that little difficulty.

In gratitude, Goldsmith dedicated the play to Johnson. On opening night, March 15, 1773, both Johnson and Benjamin Franklin were in the audience. One spectator reported that the literary arbiter set the tone of the evening: "all eyes were fixed upon Dr. Johnson, who sat in a side-box, and when [like a king or dictator] he laughed, everyone felt themselves at liberty to roar." Johnson loved the play and declared, "I know of no comedy for many years that has so much exhilarated an audience" and made them merry.[31]

Despite the success of his novel, poems and plays, Goldsmith died impoverished and depressed, a victim of his own medical treatment. His death from a kidney infection was hastened by excessive and self-prescribed doses of Dr. James' popular Fever Powders, an antimony-based febrifuge that brought on fits of violent vomiting. In response to the query of a doctor who tried to restrain him, "is your mind at ease?" his last recorded words were: "no, it is not."

Johnson believed that "Goldy," adept at extracting money from booksellers but feckless to the end, was an impressive writer and told mutual friends:

> He died of a fever, made, I am afraid, more violent by uneasiness of mind. His debts began to be heavy, and all his resources were exhausted. Sir Joshua is of the opinion that he owed not less than two thousand pounds. Was ever poet so trusted before? . . . He had raised money and squandered it, by every artifice of acquisition and folly of expence. But let not his frailties be remembered. He was a very great Man.

He expanded this judgment, through an elaborate series of parallels, in his life of the Irish poet Thomas Parnell, whose biography Goldsmith had written. Goldsmith was "a man of such variety of powers, and such felicity of performance, that he always seemed to do best that which he was doing; a man who had the art of being minute without tediousness, and general without confusion; whose language was copious without exuberance, exact without constraint, and easy without weakness."[32]

In addition to forming spontaneous affinities with all these closely connected men, Johnson maintained different bonds with each of them. He admired Baretti for his linguistic ability and scholarship; Langton for his classical learning and Tory politics; Beauclerk for his royal blood and dazzling personality; Percy for his devotion to poetry and to religion; Reynolds for his artistic ability and sweet temper; Burke for his range of knowledge and intellectual prowess; Goldsmith for his prodigal generosity and literary talent.

11

SLUGGISH RESOLUTION
1755–1758

I

On April 15, 1755, after nine years of difficult and often tedious work, Johnson finally published his *Dictionary of the English Language* in two large, double-columned folio volumes of more than 2,500 pages. The first edition of 2,000 copies cost £4.50—an expensive set—but the book was later issued in weekly sections and in many cheaper versions. Johnson had received an honorary master of arts degree from Oxford in February, just in time for the title to be put after his name on the title page. Recalling Johnson's "Plan" of 1747, in which he declared himself in one-man competition with the many learned members of the French Academy, Garrick composed a chauvinistic couplet to celebrate his achievement: "And Johnson, well arm'd like a hero of yore, / Has beat forty French, and will beat forty more." Johnson's fame was now secure, and he was known ever after as "Dictionary Johnson."

As Johnson's work on the *Dictionary* came to an end, he wrote a remarkable "Preface." Like all prefaces, it informed the reader about the scope of work, but it also did much more. A concise, analytic masterpiece, it defined the art and limitations of the lexicographer, defended his principles of selection, and justified his methods of gathering and organizing the material. Johnson also used the occasion for a serious discussion of language and meaning, and for a moving personal reflection on the humble aspects of the task and the years of hard labor it had cost him. Sad and pessimistic as always, Johnson was unable to celebrate his achievement. He felt his work had ended but could never be completed, that in a fundamental way it had been a doomed and impossible endeavor.

He stressed "the lowly reputation of lexicographers, the pains of their work . . . their inevitable failures, the heroism of their struggles." The maker of dictionaries belonged to a lower class of writers, one who cleared the path for literary genius to press forward to conquest and glory. He noted the gap between his design and execution, ambition and achievement. When he'd first started, he said, "I pleased myself with the prospect of the hours I should revel away in the feasts of literature . . . and the triumph by which I should display my acquisitions to mankind. . . . But these were the dreams of a poet doomed at last to wake a lexicographer."

Johnson apologized for omitting technical words: "I could not visit caverns to learn the miner's language, nor take a voyage to perfect my skill in the dialect of navigation, nor visit the warehouses of merchants, and shops of artificers." But he could at least have learned about these words by talking to miners, sailors and merchants without descending into the depths of the earth or braving the waves of the sea. He did, in fact, include many such words, which "favourable accident, or easy enquiry brought within my reach." Like all his works, however, the *Dictionary* had a moral and didactic purpose, and he'd ranged widely in his reading. "I was desirous," he declared, "that every quotation should be useful to some other end than the illustration of a word; I therefore extracted from philosophers principles of science; from historians remarkable facts; from chymists complete processes; from divines striking exhortations; and from poets beautiful descriptions."[1]

Johnson claimed a certain level of success. He had brought some order to chaotic spelling, pronunciation and meaning, and had gathered more words than anyone had ever done before. But his chief goal proved illusory. He had set out to write a prescriptive dictionary, but now realized that he'd made a record, not a reformation of the language. In the "Plan" of 1747 he had aimed to fix the meaning of words, but in the "Preface" he notes that he could not "embalm his language, and secure it from corruption and decay." No one could prevent words from becoming obsolete, and no one could stop the development of new words and expressions. By alluding to the union of angels and humans, of spirit and flesh in Genesis 6:2: "the sons of God saw the daughters of men that they were fair," he suggested that *words are the daughters of earth, and things are the sons of heaven.*" To Johnson, language was a man-made instrument, words were constantly changing signs, yet the concepts that words described were divine and transcendent. He'd once believed that his *Dictionary* could help purify and stabilize the language, but now he was wiser. "I wish," he wrote, "that signs might be permanent, like the things which they denote." In yet another variation on the vanity of human wishes, Johnson reminded his readers of mortal transience and human imperfection.

Johnson described the difficulty of defining the most basic words in English, and his labor in distinguishing various shades of meaning. In a poetic analogy, he compared the shifting layers of significance in a living tongue to the effects of stormy weather. Precise meaning, he wrote, "can no more be ascertained in a dictionary, than a grove, in the agitation of a storm, can be accurately delineated from its picture in the water." Johnson had taken pains to register the progress of meaning, but felt he had not always arrived at exact definitions. Responding in advance to critics "that have never considered words beyond their popular use," he magisterially noted, "every art is obscure to those that have not learned it" and "it must be remembered that I am speaking of that which words are insufficient to explain."

Despite his assurances that he anticipated criticism and did not expect praise, Johnson expressed a sense of achievement in the "Preface." As always, he reminded us that work itself has dignity. But his relief at the work's conclusion was mixed with regret at the personal cost, in money, health and bereavement. Most poignantly, Johnson revealed that he'd worked almost alone, without benefit of a country estate or a college fellowship, writing the *Rambler* at the same time, yet constantly pressed for money: "the *English Dictionary* was written with little assistance of the learned, and without any patronage of the great; not in the soft obscurities of retirement, or under the shelter of academick bowers, but amidst inconvenience and distraction, in sickness and in sorrow."[2] In a letter of 1755, which suggested the onset of the emphysema that would plague him later in life, he described his recurrent "sickness" and the perilous medical treatment he himself had encouraged: "I had a cough so violent that I once fainted under its convulsions. I was afraid of my Lungs. My Physician bled me yesterday and the day before, first almost against his will, but the next day without any contest. I had been bled once before, so that I have lost in all 54 ounces."

His sorrow was occasioned by the deaths of Gilbert Walmesley in August 1751 and of Tetty in March 1752. In the "Preface" he paid tribute to his wife's importance in both his emotional and literary life by declaring: "I have protracted my work till most of those whom I wished to please, have sunk into the grave, and success and miscarriage are empty sounds; I therefore dismiss it with frigid tranquility, having little to fear or hope from censure or from praise." Johnson returned to this theme and recalled his own despondent mood in his life of the Renaissance humanist Roger Ascham (1761). Writing about *The Scholemaster,* an influential treatise on education, he noted, "this work, though begun with alacrity, in hope of a considerable reward, was interrupted by the death of the patron, and afterwards sorrowfully and slowly finished, in the gloom of disappointment, under the pressure of distress."[3]

II

The run-up to the publication of the *Dictionary* led to a dramatic confrontation with a formidable adversary. Johnson had addressed the "Plan" of the *Dictionary* to Lord Chesterfield in 1747; Chesterfield eulogized the forthcoming work in two articles published in the *World* in November and December 1754; and Johnson wrote a bitter rebuke to Chesterfield in February 1755. Though Johnson's reputation today is far greater than Chesterfield's, who's now mainly remembered as the target of Johnson's devastating attack, it's essential to recall that before the *Dictionary* appeared, Johnson was still an obscure and impoverished author, and Chesterfield, one of the most powerful and influential men in England. Chesterfield, as Johnson wrote of Addison, "not only stood long in the highest rank of wit and literature, but filled one of the most important offices of state."

Philip Stanhope, 4th Earl of Chesterfield (1694–1773), was an outstanding example of the hereditary nobility that ruled England in the eighteenth century. He was ambassador to Holland, lord lieutenant of Ireland, and one of the two secretaries of state, in charge of all domestic and foreign affairs as well as of Scotland, Ireland, the colonies, the army and the navy. A brilliant conversationalist, he was famous for his eloquent speeches in the House of Lords. He drafted the bill to synchronize the English and continental calendars, and opposed (as Johnson did) Walpole's Licensing Act of 1739. Johnson rewrote Chesterfield's speech against stage censorship in the *Debates in Parliament,* where he nobly declared that the oppressive act would tend "towards a Restraint on the Liberty of the Press, which will be a long Stride towards the Destruction of Liberty itself." Some of the speeches written by Johnson were later included in an edition of Chesterfield's *Works.*

Distinguished by his noble lineage, great wealth and arrogant hauteur, Chesterfield, author of *Letters to His Son,* was also considered an arbiter of correct manners and language. A friend of Montesquieu and Voltaire, he was a notable patron of letters and had supported Pope, Fielding and Smollett. Johnson's publishers naturally felt that Chesterfield's backing would lend prestige and authority to the *Dictionary,* and encouraged Johnson to address the "Plan" to him. In the "Plan" Johnson had recognized Chesterfield's stature and, bending the knee, graciously written, "since you, whose authority in our language is so generally acknowledged, have commissioned me to declare my own opinion, I shall be considered as exercising a kind of vicarious jurisdiction."

When puffing the *Dictionary* in the *World,* Chesterfield responded to Johnson's papal metaphor by wittily declaring, "I will implicitly believe in him as my pope, and hold him to be infallible while in the chair." In conclusion, Chesterfield suggested in all seriousness that

Johnson (who'd had quite enough of lexicography) should also bring out a small supplemental dictionary of polite words for the use of the beau monde: "we shall frequently meet with it in ladies dressing-rooms, lying upon the harpsichord, together with the knitting bag, and [the violinist] signor Di-Giardino's incomparable concertos; and even sometimes in the powder-rooms of our young nobility, upon the same shelf with their German-flute, their powder mask, and their four-horse whip."[4]

Chesterfield's notice, instead of inspiring Johnson's gratitude, provoked his fury. He'd long since rejected the idea in the "Plan" of fixing the language, which Chesterfield implicitly ascribed to him; and he hated the intolerably precious, condescending conclusion that removed his book from the study and consigned it to a frivolous boudoir worthy of "The Rape of the Lock." Chesterfield's essays suggested that he'd taken a serious interest in Johnson's project since 1747. In fact, though he enjoyed an annual income of £30,000, he had given Johnson the grand total of £10. After promising to help, he had—under pressure of official business and with no sign of progress on the *Dictionary*—casually dropped him. There was also a persistent rumor (denied by Johnson, who argued from principle rather than from personal affront) that his lordship had kept Johnson waiting at length in an antechamber while he entertained the despicable hack Colley Cibber. When the great work was finally completed and about to come out, Chesterfield suddenly reappeared to take credit for supporting him and (Johnson said) "fell a-scribbling in the *World* about it." Though Chesterfield's essays did not solicit a dedication, he may well have expected one.

In a spirited defense of Johnson's well-intentioned patron, written in the early nineteenth century but not published until 1945, Thomas De Quincey asked, "How was Lord C. to praise a book before it was finished? That was impossible for *him*. And to Dr. J. it would have been useless." Then, descending to an irrelevant condemnation of Johnson's grotesque appearance, De Quincey placed the blame on the rude author: "Dr. J's behaviour was that of a sturdy beggar, who refuses to ask for money, but expects to have it delivered to him instanter on looking

through the window with the face like that of Frankenstein's monster."
Chesterfield, of course, could have waited until the book was published,
but it would have been too late to secure the dedication. Johnson never
directly asked for money any more than Chesterfield did for a dedication, but these requests were implied in their literary minuet.

Though he wrote numerous dedications to help other writers,
Johnson never dedicated his own books to anyone. In the *Rambler*
he attacked both dedications and patrons as essentially immoral,
arguing that "nothing has so much degraded literature from its natural rank, as the practice of indecent and promiscuous dedication,"
and that the fatuously flattered dedicatee "can receive only a short
gratification, with which nothing but stupidity could dispose him to
be pleased." He condemned patronage by emphasizing the disparity
between rich benefactors and poor scribblers, and the inevitable disappointment that results from their degrading relations: "none of the
cruelties exercised by wealth and power upon indigence and dependence, is more mischievous in its consequences" than patronage. The
author inevitably finds "the favours [for] which he had long been
encouraged to hope, and had long endeavoured to deserve, squandered at last on nameless ignorance."[5] In the "Preface" to the *Dictionary* he emphasized that he had written it "without any patronage
of the great."

Despite his belief in "subordination," or natural social hierarchy,
and their vast differences in birth, rank, wealth, office and power,
Johnson felt bound to assert his moral and intellectual superiority.
Insulted and outraged, he was determined to punish Chesterfield for
his insolence, and was stunningly rude to the principal exponent of
good manners. Instead of a flattering dedication, Chesterfield received
a stinging letter—first published by Boswell in 1790 and one of the
best things Johnson ever wrote:

> Seven years, My Lord, have now past since I waited in your out-
> ward Rooms or was repulsed from your Door, during which time
> I have been pushing on my work through difficulties of which it
> is useless to complain, and have brought it at last to the verge of

Publication without one Act of assistance, one word of encouragement, or one smile of favour. Such treatment I did not expect, for
I never had a Patron before. . . .

Is not a Patron, My Lord, one who looks with unconcern on a
Man struggling for Life in the water and when he has reached
ground encumbers him with help. The notice which you have
been pleased to take of my Labours, had it been early, had been
kind; but it has been delayed till I am indifferent and cannot enjoy
it, till I am solitary and cannot impart it, till I am known and do
not want it.

The grand style and tone of personal sadness, the cutting irony
and controlled invective, are magnificent. Johnson's triplets—"one
act," "one word," "one smile"—and his balanced parallels—"early-
kind," "indifferent-enjoy," "solitary-impart," "known-want"—are
gravely effective. His allusion to Tetty—"delayed till I am solitary"—
is deeply moving. He'd struggled for life in the water—not waving,
but drowning—and managed to swim to safety without being
weighed down (perhaps even sunk) by Chesterfield's assistance. Even
De Quincey, sympathetic to Chesterfield but taking up Johnson's
idea of "natural rank," believed that Johnson's letter narrowed the
gap between patron and client and "elevated the social rank of literary men in England." Johnson lost Chesterfield's patronage, but retained his self-respect.

According to Boswell, Chesterfield disclaimed responsibility for
repulsing Johnson from his door and insisted that "he would have
turned off the best servant he ever had, if he had known that he denied
him to a man who would have been always more than welcome." Instead of ignoring or concealing Johnson's letter, Chesterfield, faithful to
the principle of *volto sciolto e pensieri stretti,* feigned indifference to
Johnson's abuse and suggested that he could not possibly be hurt by
such a rude underling. He left the letter on a table where visitors could
see it and even called attention to it by remarking, "'this man has great
powers,' pointing out the severest passages, and observing how well
they were expressed."[6]

Chesterfield's *Letters* of advice to his illegitimate son, published twenty years later in 1774 as a guide to personal conduct, were as influential in eighteenth-century England as Castiglione's *The Courtier* (1528) had been in Renaissance Italy. His guiding principle was always to behave in a discreet and expedient fashion. In a typical letter, of July 1, 1748, Chesterfield wrote, "I never mention to you . . . Religion and Morality." Middle-class readers, who disapproved of this advice, accused him of pardoning, even promoting, adultery and deceit. His irreverent attitude naturally infuriated Johnson, who memorably declared that the much admired *Letters* "teach the morals of a whore, and the manners of a dancing master."

Chesterfield, the antithesis of Johnson, was always polite, charming and reserved; Johnson could be rude, offensive and outrageous. The self-possessed Chesterfield claimed that in adult life he had never laughed out loud, while the earthy Johnson's loud laughter (according to Boswell) "seemed to resound from Temple-bar to Fleet-ditch." Chesterfield mocked Johnson's grotesque appearance and disgusting eating habits (though he never dined with him), and in a letter to his son condemned him as a half-tamed savage: "His figure (without being deformed) seems made to disgrace or ridicule the common structure of the human body. . . . He throws any where, but down his throat, whatever he means to drink, and only mangles what he means to carve. . . . The utmost I can do for him, is to consider him as a respectable Hottentot—the opposite of a gentleman." Johnson slyly retaliated by changing "Garret" to "Patron" in his revision of *Vanity*: "There mark what Ills the Scholar's Life assail, / Toil, Envy, Want, the Patron, and the Jail."

Johnson had been an effective translator, journalist, critic, biographer and poet, but he did not become famous until the age of forty-six, when the *Dictionary* finally made his name.[7] But he was not entirely pleased by his long-awaited success. Though he later told Boswell, "I knew very well what I was undertaking,—and very well how to do it,—and have done it very well," he had grave doubts (some of which he expressed in the "Preface") about its limitations. He informed other friends that "a perfect performance of any kind is not to be expected, and certainly not a perfect dictionary." Echoing his belief that he had "little to fear or hope from censure or from praise," he told Charles Burney that whatever he said about the *Dictionary* would make Johnson unhappy: "if you find faults, I shall endeavour to mend them; if you find none, I shall think you blinded by kind partiality." He felt the need to revise after hearing from friends and readers, and in his advertisement to the 4th folio edition of 1773 modestly stated: "I have endeavoured, by a revisal, to make it less reprehensible. . . . Many faults I have corrected, some superfluities I have taken away, some deficiencies I have supplied. I have methodised some parts that were disordered, and illuminated some that were obscure."[8]

Johnson's *Dictionary of the English Language* remained the standard work, beloved and widely used, for at least a hundred years, and its influence was felt until the twentieth century. The economist Adam Smith, reviewing it in the *Edinburgh Review* just after it came out, recognized its originality and wrote: "when we compare this book with other dictionaries, the merit of its author appears very extraordinary." Samuel Taylor Coleridge, a student of German scholarship and a Romantic poet in revolt against the style of the previous age, disagreed. Coleridge knew that the etymologies were poor, the prefatory material on the history and grammar of English weak, the style sometimes awkward. Writing in *Biographia Literaria* (1817), in convoluted language, he acknowledged the *Dictionary's* merits but emphasized its limitations: "I should suspect the man of a morose disposition who should speak of it without respect and gratitude as a most instructive and entertaining *book*; but I confess, that I should be surprized at hearing from a philosophic and thorough scholar any but very qualified praises of it, as a *dictionary*."

In Thackeray's *Vanity Fair* (1847) the *Dictionary* symbolizes the amoral Becky Sharp's rejection of conventional education and middle-class aspirations, and Johnson himself becomes a satiric figure. Miss Pinkerton, the snobbish and ignorant proprietor of a ladies' academy, revered the Great Lexicographer, whose visit to her establishment had enhanced her reputation and her fortune. Miss Pinkerton's sister secretly gives Becky a cheap copy of the *Dictionary* as a going-away present, but as her coach drives off, the defiant Becky flings the book out of the window. The Victorian poet Robert Browning, by contrast, read the *Dictionary* from cover to cover to prepare himself for the profession of poetry. H. L. Mencken, in *The American Language* (1919), testified to its potent influence in American education. The great *Oxford English Dictionary*, finally completed, after seventy years, in 1928, adopted many of Johnson's methods, also used quotations to define the meaning of the words and reproduced about seventeen hundred of his definitions.

James Sledd and Gwin Kolb, in their bicentennial volume on the *Dictionary*, perceptively summarized Johnson's struggle to overcome formidable obstacles with characteristically sluggish resolution: "the ill-kempt and melancholy genius, assiduously cultivating in words the elegance which his person and surroundings lacked; an association of booksellers, one of them [Robert Dodsley] a footman who had abandoned livery for literature, promoting an enterprise which royal and noble patronage had not supported; the author struggling with debt, disease, and grief for his wife's death while printer and publisher were thriving; the book itself embodying the triumph of desperate industry over admitted laziness."

Liberated at last from his years as a literary galley-slave, Johnson felt more depressed than joyous. Like Lord Byron's prisoner of Chillon, he missed the familiar security of his chains. In "Know Thyself," a poem in Latin, the language he used to express his most personal thoughts, he feared that he would be overwhelmed by idleness and depression, and that without daily employment might fall victim to mental breakdown and even insanity: "though now freed from my task, I am become my own master, the harsh lot of slothful idleness awaits me, and black and gloomy leisure, more burdensome than any labour, and the tedium of sluggish living. Worries beget worries, and a pestering company of troubles harass me, and the bad dreams of an empty mind."[9]

III

Johnson's combative encounter with Chesterfield took place amid the almost continuous series of wars, mostly against France, which Britain fought throughout the eighteenth century. In addition to the turbulent Jacobite Rebellions of 1715 and 1745, the only battles that took place on British soil, the British fought in the War of Spanish Succession (1701–13), the War of the Quadruple Alliance (1718–20), the War with Spain (1727–29), the War of Jenkins' Ear (1739–41), the War of Austrian Succession (1740–48), the Seven Years' War (1756–63) and the War of the American Revolution (1775–83).

Johnson wrote many essays about the Seven Years' War, the most important historical event in his lifetime, which broke out the year after the *Dictionary* was published. This global war pitched Britain, Hanover, Prussia and Denmark against France, Austria, Saxony, Sweden, Russia and Spain. Like the previous war, it concerned a struggle for territory in Silesia and other parts of Europe, and for colonial supremacy in India, the West Indies and North America. War, the historian Linda Colley wryly observed, gave British aristocrats "an opportunity to carry out what they had been trained to do since childhood: ride horses, fire guns, exercise their undoubted physical courage and tell other people what to do." After her glorious triumph in the war, confirmed by the Peace of Paris in 1763, Britain secured a lucrative overseas empire that included India, Canada, islands in the Caribbean, Senegal in West Africa and Florida in North America.

In 1739–40, in his chauvinistic *London, Marmor Norfolciense* and life of Admiral Blake, the young Johnson had attacked the Whigs' appeasement of Spain in the West Indies and rabidly supported war against the marauding privateers. In his poem, for example, he condemned with bitter irony the corrupt followers of a cowardly policy:

Here let those reign, whom Pensions can incite
To vote a Patriot black, a Courtier white;
Explain their Country's dear-bought Rights away,
And plead for Pirates in the Face of Day.

Though Johnson remained personally belligerent, even violent, he was now politically older and wiser. In his political pamphlets he strongly opposed a large standing army, entangling alliances on the Continent and colonial acquisitions in remote parts of the world, and roundly condemned war as both unjust and dehumanizing. Since overseas wars were waged with small professional armies, fortified by foreign mercenaries from Hanover and other territories in Europe, they caused relatively little disturbance in insular England. But Johnson tried to make his compatriots aware of the harsh realities of war.

He bluntly portrayed the conflict between Britain and France in North America as a dispute between two highwaymen, as "only a quarrel of two robbers for the spoils of a passenger." Despite the rich profits from the colonies, he opposed the prevailing jubilation about Britain's victory, and exclaimed, "war is one of the heaviest of national evils, a calamity, in which every species of misery is involved." In a magnificent peroration, he contrasted the heroic image of war with the horrid actuality, the glorious sacrifice in battle with death by agonizing disease, the honor of a military funeral with the degradation of an unmarked abyss. Moving from battle to disease, from dying to death "without notice"—a death both sudden and ignored—he declared:

War has means of destruction more formidable than the cannon and the sword. Of the thousands and ten thousands that perished in our late contests with France and Spain, a very small part ever felt the stroke of an enemy; the rest languished in tents and ships, amidst damps and putrefaction; pale, torpid, spiritless, and helpless; gasping and groaning, unpitied among men made obdurate by long continuance of hopeless misery; and were at last whelmed in pits, or heaved into the ocean, without notice, and without remembrance.[10]

Johnson opposed the acquisition of colonies as vehemently as he opposed the wars that won them, and again resisted the prevailing tide of public opinion. Unlike most of his contemporaries, he thought that the welfare of indigenous people was more important than the prosperity of British merchants, that European expansion into America, Africa and Asia was a disgraceful episode in modern history. Instead of glorifying the Roman Empire, as all Englishmen were taught to do, he emphasized its oppression and slaughter, declaring that "the commonwealth of Rome grew great only by the misery of the rest of mankind." Instead of extolling the fame of military heroes, he strongly condemned them: "I would wish Caesar and Catiline, Xerxes and Alexander, Charles [XII] and Peter [the Great], huddled together in obscurity or detestation." And he told the translator of Camoes' epic *The Lusiad* (1572), which celebrated the exploits of Portuguese explorers: "It had been happy for the world, Sir, if your Hero [Vasco da] Gama, Prince Henry of Portugal, and Columbus had never been born, or that their schemes had never gone farther than their own imaginations."[11] Like Burke and Goldsmith, he also felt compassion for the miseries of the Irish Catholics and detested their barbarous treatment by the English.

George Trevelyan wrote that eighteenth-century soldiers were "unpopular because they acted as the only efficient police force against rioting and smuggling," and that discipline in the army was brutal: "one soldier of George II had received 30,000 lashes in sixteen years— 'yet the man is hearty and well and in no ways concerned.'" But Johnson had grown up in a garrison town and sympathized with soldiers. Two superb but little-known essays—"The Bravery of the English Common Soldiers" and "Cloathing French Prisoners of War" (both 1760)—celebrated the brutalized lower ranks and (a century before the enactment of the Geneva Convention) advocated humane treatment for foreign prisoners. The first essay makes clear that though he accepted the social hierarchy in principle, he did not love a lord. Still angry about his recent dispute with Lord Chesterfield, he claimed that the Englishman, born without a master, "looks not on any man, however dignified by lace or titles, as deriving from Nature any claims to his respect, or inheriting any qualities superior to his own." Brains and talent were worth more than birth and rank, which he disdainfully reduced to decorative lace.

In his essay on heroism and self-sacrifice, qualities usually attributed only to officers, Johnson argued that "our nation may boast, beyond any other people in the world, of a kind of epidemick bravery, diffused equally throughout all its ranks." He accounted for this courage by the essentially democratic basis of English society and strengthened his argument by paraphrasing Milton's great essay

"Areopagitica," on freedom of the press. Though officers might complain about the lack of respect or proper distinction between ranks, Johnson believed such insubordination was actually beneficial: "good and evil will grow up in this world together; and they that complain, in peace, of the insolence of the populace, must remember, that their insolence in peace is bravery in war."[12]

British victories brought a few thousand French prisoners of war to England. John Wesley saw these poor wretches closely confined "without any thing to lie on but a little dirty straw, or any thing to cover them but a few foul, thin rags, either by day or night, so that they died like rotten sheep." Johnson was asked by the committee that raised money for the prisoners to provide written justification for giving charity to enemies in time of war. Using an epigraph from the Roman playwright Terence, "I am a man; nothing human is alien to me," and stressing as always the principles of Christian humanism and sympathy for the oppressed, he said: "we know that for the prisoners of war there is no legal provision; we see their distress, and are certain of its cause; we know they are poor and naked, and poor and naked without a crime. . . . [Charity] alleviates captivity, and takes away something from the miseries of war. The rage of war, however mitigated, will always fill the world with calamity and horror." Donald Greene pointed out that Johnson's exemplary essay was reprinted in the official journal of the International Red Cross, published in Geneva in December 1951.

A dramatic incident in the Seven Years' War inspired Johnson's noble defense of another victim, at the opposite end of the social scale: Admiral John Byng. When the war broke out, this well-intentioned but undistinguished officer was sent to the Mediterranean with a squadron of ships. His mission was to protect the British naval base on the island of Minorca, captured from Spain in 1708. On May 20 he encountered a superior French fleet near the island. He fought the enemy, sustained serious damage and retired south to Gibraltar. When the British garrison on Minorca surrendered to the French on May 28, there was a public outcry against Byng, who was forced to take the blame for the loss of Minorca. To cover up the mistakes made by the prime minister, the Duke of Newcastle; and the First Lord of the Admiralty, George Anson; the government censored official reports, suppressed evidence, and ignored the protests of the admiral's fellow officers, friends and family. Dudley Pope, a modern authority on these events, concluded that "the trial and execution of Admiral the Honourable John Byng was one of the most cold-blooded and cynical acts of judicial murder in the whole of British history."[13]

In October 1756, between Byng's recall to England and his court-martial, Johnson reviewed two pamphlets that defended him against the attacks by Newcastle and Anson. Johnson first exposed the spurious charges and pointed to those who were really responsible for the disaster: "Mr. Byng is stigmatised with infamy, and pursued with clamours artfully excited to divert the public attention from the crimes and blunders of other men, and while he is thus vehemently pursued for imaginary guilt, the real criminals are hoping to escape." Then, like a lawyer addressing a jury, he demolished these charges in a magisterial summation:

It appears to us that Byng has suffered without sufficient cause.

That he was sent to the relief of Minorca, when relief was known to be no longer possible.

That he was sent without land forces, the only forces that could raise the siege.

That his fleet was inferior, and long before the battle was known at home to be inferior to that of the French.

That he fought them, and retreated only when he could fight no longer.

That a second engagement would only have increased the loss suffered in the first.

That a victory at sea would not have saved Minorca.

That there was no provision for the chances of a battle.

That the nation has been industriously deceived by false and treacherous representations.

That Minorca if not betrayed has been neglected.

That Byng's letter [explaining his actions] has been mutilated injuriously, fraudulently mutilated.

That every act of defamation has been practised against him.

That unless other evidence can be produced, Byng will be found innocent.

Despite the daunting force of this argument, the government was determined to sacrifice the admiral. In January 1757 Byng was court-martialed for cowardice and for failure to actively engage the enemy. In March, on the quarterdeck of the warship *Monarque* in Portsmouth harbor, he was executed by firing squad. The unjust death of Admiral Byng confirmed Johnson's belief that colonies like Minorca were not worth the human and material cost.

Voltaire, who witnessed the execution, also defended Byng in a famous ironic passage in *Candide* (1759), which exposed the weakness of the charges against him and the savagery that incited his murder:

—And why kill this admiral?

—The reason, they told him, is that he didn't kill enough people; he gave battle to the French admiral, and it was found that he didn't get close enough to him.

—But, said Candide, the French admiral was just as far from the English admiral as the English admiral was from the French admiral.

—That's perfectly true, came the answer; but in this country it is useful from time to time to kill one admiral to encourage the others [*pour encourager les autres*].[14]

IV

Johnson's review of Soame Jenyns' *A Free Inquiry into the Nature and Origin of Evil* (1757), which also appeared during the Seven Years' War, emphasized once again the human misery he'd described in his essays on French prisoners and on Admiral Byng. The dim-witted *Inquiry*, heavily buttressed by the cosmic optimism of Pope's *Essay on*

Man, has been immortalized by Johnson's masterly demolition job. Jenyns argued that "pain is necessary to happiness, that our pleasure depends on the sufferings of other creatures, that poverty is necessary to balance the economic order of the universe . . . and that there are 'Superior Beings' who may enjoy life by the miseries of others." Johnson resented this absurd justification for suffering and license for callous indifference. He violently opposed Jenyns' casual, even fatuous treatment of evil, so radically different from his own deep-rooted sense of sin and troubled view of the all-pervasive wickedness in the world.

Human suffering, always real to Johnson, could not be trivialized or explained away. He discussed Jenyns' abstract theories in the context of the harsh realities he'd personally experienced. Jenyns euphemistically described poverty as "want of riches"; Johnson insisted that many people must struggle to survive and that "there is yet another poverty which is *want of necessaries,* a species of poverty which no care of the public, no charity of particulars, can preserve many from feeling openly, and many secretly." Jenyns claimed that human suffering produces beneficial effects, although he'd never experienced the miseries he thought inferior beings could so easily endure. Infuriated by Jenyns' indifference, Johnson likened the intense suffering of the poor to "that of a malefactor who ceases to feel the cords that bind him when the pincers are tearing his flesh."

In a bitterly ironic passage worthy of Swift, Johnson destroyed Jenyns' notion of "some beings above us" who benignly control the world and replaced it with his own dark view of the human condition: "these *hunters, whose game is man* have many sports analogous to our own. As we drown whelps and kittens, they amuse themselves now and then with sinking a ship, and stand around the fields of Blenheim, or the walls of Prague [where 20,000 men were killed in battle in 1757], as we encircle a cockpit. As we shoot a bird flying, they take a man in the midst of his business or pleasure, and knock him down with an apoplexy."

After Johnson's death, Jenyns retaliated with a mock epitaph that, like Chesterfield and De Quincey, resorted to animal imagery. Jenyns mentioned his admirable qualities, but stressed his barbaric behavior:

Here lies poor Johnson. Reader, have a care,
Tread lightly, lest you rouse a sleeping bear;
Religious, moral, generous, and humane
He was—but self-sufficient, rude, and vain;
Ill-bred and overbearing in dispute,
A scholar and a Christian—yet a brute.[15]

Poverty, a pleasant abstraction for Jenyns, was still a threat to Johnson in the 1750s, just as it had been for the previous two decades. The scholar J. D. Fleeman has calculated the earnings for his major works: £10.50 for *London* in 1738, £15.75 for *Vanity* and £196 for *Irene* in 1749, £437 for 208 *Ramblers*, from 1750 to 1752, £1,575 for the *Dictionary* from 1746 to 1755 and £100 for *Rasselas* in 1759. Fleeman concluded that Johnson earned more than £2 a week in the 1740s; averaged £3.35 a week for nine years' work on the *Dictionary*, but had to pay his amanuenses and had many other expenses; and earned £4.20 a week for writing the *Ramblers*. He gave away a great deal of money to the poor, and was often disturbed by creditors coming to his house and demanding money he could not pay.

In March 1756, after twenty years on Grub Street, the most distinguished author in England was practically penniless. Arrested in front of his neighbors and led through the streets by a bailiff, he was brought to a sponging house (a holding place where debtors could be "squeezed") and confined at his own expense till the debt could be paid. Just as Goldsmith would beg for Johnson's help when arrested for debt in 1762, so Johnson —unable to reach his publishers—sought help from the prosperous printer and author of *Clarissa*, Samuel Richardson. "I am obliged to entreat your assistance," he wrote. "I am now under an arrest for five pounds eighteen shillings. Mr. Strahan from whom I should have received the necessary help in this case is not at home, and I am afraid of not finding Mr. Millar. If you will be so good as to send me this sum, I will very gratefully repay You, and add it to all former obligations." Richardson immediately sent the money, and Johnson, after being forced to drink with his keeper and pay for the adulterated wine, was released.

Two years later, while Johnson was working on his edition of Shakespeare, another creditor pursued him, and he was arrested for a much larger debt. This time he sought help from his current publisher, Jacob Tonson, and apologized for troubling him: "An accident has happened to me which Mr. Strahan will tell you, and from which I must beg to be extracted by your assistance. The affair is about forty pounds. I think it necessary to assure you that no other vexation can happen to me, for I have no other [debt] of any consequence but to my friends."[16] Johnson received the money and was again set free.

Johnson had hoped that the *Dictionary* would release him from Grub Street, but now realized that his payment had been far below the value of his work. Publishers were always far more prosperous than writers, and he was still completely dependent upon them. He believed that "the chief glory of every people arises from its authours," but his glory was sadly diminished by bitter poverty and public degradation. His financial straits continually reminded him of the painful truth: "*Slow rises Worth, by Poverty deprest.*"

12

DANGEROUS IMAGINATION
1759–1762

I

In July 1749 Johnson wrote his stepdaughter, Lucy Porter, that the black seal on her letter (signifying the death of her uncle) had given him a terrible scare: "You frighted me, you little Gipsy ["a name of slight reproach to a woman"], with your black wafer, for I had forgot you were in mourning and was afraid your letter had brought me ill news of my mother, whose death is one of the few calamities on which I think with horrour." Ten years later he learned that the aged Sarah was indeed dying. When writing to her, Johnson emphasized the depth of his feelings and the effect her death would have on *him*: "Your weakness afflicts me beyond what I am willing to communicate to you. I do not think you ought to fear death, but I know not how to bear the thought of losing you." He hadn't visited his mother since his last trip to the Midlands in 1740. He now told Lucy that he fervently wanted to see her before she died, but he did not set out for Lichfield. He respected but found it difficult to love his mother, whose nagging, querulous, critical character had made his father's life so miserable. He may now have felt that they had grown apart and he had nothing to say to her.

Ashamed of his long neglect, he was too guilt-ridden to face her. Death, and the question of life after death, filled him with dread.

Sarah's death on January 20 or 21 (the date is uncertain) at the age of eighty-nine precipitated a psychological crisis. The prodigal son had not wanted to confront the formidable matron, or return home till he'd finally achieved success and a measure of fame with the *Rambler* and the *Dictionary.* He seemed to have forgotten her, yet when she died, all the pent-up misery of his childhood, his grief and guilt, suddenly surged up. He again contrasted his own mental state with Sarah's and wrote Lucy: "You will conceive my sorrow for the loss of my mother, of the best mother. If she were to live again, surely I should behave better to her. But she is happy, and what is past is nothing to her; and for me, since I cannot repair my faults to her, I hope repentance will efface them."[1]

Johnson frequently advised bereaved friends to respond to the death of their loved ones with stoical detachment. But when Tetty had died, at age sixty-two or sixty-three, in March 1752, he'd suffered a nervous breakdown. When Sarah died he was again plunged into profound grief. His difficult and sometimes contentious relations with both women increased his suffering, and their loss intensified his sense of isolation. Sarah had been his last blood tie in the world and the last generational barrier between him and death itself. He desperately told the rather chilly, remote and self-sufficient Lucy that she was "the only person now left in the world with whom I think myself connected."

Johnson wrote *Rasselas, Prince of Abyssinia* (1759), a philosophical and moral fable, in one week to pay for his mother's funeral. Writing it was therapeutic and provided him with an excellent excuse for not going to Lichfield, but his failure to attend the ceremony exacerbated his guilt and need to repent. He could not face the real death of anyone who was close to him; and though in London at the time, he did not attend the funeral of his friend Oliver Goldsmith in 1774. Just as he'd distinctly heard, or thought he heard, his mother call "Sam" when he was entering his room at Pembroke, so (he told Hester Thrale) long after Sarah's death he again heard her voice call, from the next world,

"Sam." As with the dead Tetty, he idealized the "best mother" for the rest of his life to atone for neglecting his filial duties.

When his father died, Johnson simply wrote in his diary: "*Patre orbatus est*" (I have lost my father). But he publicly expressed his grief for his mother in *Idler* 41, published a week after her death, and in chapter 18 of *Rasselas*, published in April. In the *Idler* he wrote, "the life which made my own life pleasant is at an end, and the gates of death are shut upon my prospects." The phrase "made my own life" suggested that she'd both created and influenced his life. Her death left him in "a state of dreary desolation in which the mind looks abroad impatient of itself, and finds nothing but emptiness and horror." By using the words "desolation" and "horror," he emphasized how his dangerously wandering mind, confronted with nothingness, could prey upon itself and succumb to depression and to madness.

Though in the grip of existential dread, Johnson was able to reflect on his own wretched state of mind while he wrote to earn some urgently needed money. In *Rasselas* a philosophical sage teaches his pupils how to lead a happy life, to govern the passions and to conquer sadness by stoical indifference to human suffering. But when his own child dies, his stoicism collapses and he's overwhelmed by human grief. As he confesses to Rasselas: "My daughter, my only daughter, from whose tenderness I expected all the comforts of my age, died last night of a fever. My views, my purposes, my hopes are at an end: I am now a lonely being disunited from society. . . . 'What comfort,' said the mourner, 'can truth and reason afford me? of what effect are they now, but to tell me, that my daughter will not be restored?'"

The sage's sense of being "disunited from society" echoes Johnson's own fear, expressed after Tetty's death, of being "broken off from mankind." Later on in *Rasselas*, another wise man alludes to Johnson's two great losses by lamenting, "I have neither mother to be delighted with the reputation of her son, nor wife to partake the honours of her husband."[2] These two so-called sages are an ironic comment on his own inability to deal rationally with the loss of his wife and his mother.

II

Rasselas, once a popular classic, has gone into innumerable editions and translations, and has remained continuously in print for more than 250 years. Its quaint and charming characters, leisurely style, gentle humor and wise morality attracted an audience well into the Victorian era. Johnson's magisterial opening sentence, combining sonorous effects with portentous content, sets the tone: "Ye who listen with credulity to the whispers of fancy, and pursue with eagerness the phantoms of hope; who expect that age will perform the promises of youth, and that the deficiencies of the present day will be supplied by the morrow; attend to the history of Rasselas, prince of Abissinia."[3] "Listen with credulity" and "whispers of fancy" are finely balanced by "pursue with eagerness" and "phantoms of hope"; "age" is contrasted with "youth"; "deficiencies of the present day" with "supplied by the morrow." The short, sententious chapters in *Rasselas* are like a series of *Ramblers*. The reader is reminded to "attend" as well as to "listen" to this solemn yet occasionally amusing story.

Meditating on how he could write a short fable, Johnson drew on his earlier work. He used Father Lobo's *Voyage to Abyssinia* as the source for the eponymous hero and Oriental setting of *Rasselas,* just as he'd based the story of *Irene* on Knolles' *Generall Historie of the Turks*. Prince Rasselas, his Johnsonian tutor Imlac, his sister Princess Nekayah and her favorite companion Pekuah live safely enclosed in the remote paradise of the Happy Valley.[4] Imlac's name, which means "plenitude" and "repletion" in Hebrew, comes from I Kings 22:8: "And the king of Israel said unto Jehoshaphat, There is yet one man, Micaiah, son of Imlah, by whom we may enquire of the Lord." Imlac's three disciples, subjected for years to his lordly tuition, yearn for a year of study abroad.

Many fictional characters start in misery and search for happiness; Rasselas starts with happiness in a kind of El Dorado, searches for new experience in his travels and finds misery wherever he looks. In this allegory or pilgrim's progress, Rasselas is like John Bunyan's truth-seeking character Christian, with Imlac as his worldly wise guide. Johnson must also have been thinking of the time when he'd left home, eager to discover a wider world, and found failure and disillusionment in London. Rasselas is twenty-six years old, the same age as Johnson at that major turning point in his life. In 1735, just after translating Lobo, he'd worked on *Irene,* married Tetty and opened the school at Edial, which was doomed to failure. In the tale, Imlac mentions that in the past he too had "opened a school, and was prohibited to teach."

In the Happy Valley every desire is immediately gratified. Restless, confined and curious, as bored there as he might be in Heaven itself, Rasselas searches with jaunty despair for a way to escape. He naïvely asks: How is it possible to be happy? What is the purpose of living? He wants a real "choice of life" instead of being forced to accept this uneasy contentment. Imlac, the voice of experience, teaches him that men in the outside world are wicked and cruel.

When a local inventor, hoping to surpass the soaring eagles, plans to help Rasselas escape over the mountains and tries to fly on manufactured wings, the dénouement is charming and witty: "he waved his pinions a while to gather air, then leaped from his stand, and in an instant dropped into the lake." But he's not injured in the crash. "His wings, which were of no use in the air, sustained him in the water, and the prince drew him to land, half dead with terrour and vexation." After the persistent Rasselas discovers a terrestrial means of escape, the gang of four set out on a journey of discovery.

Every disillusioning experience is designed to help the young prince make the necessary choice of life, yet every encounter confirms Imlac's pessimistic conclusions. The pyramids they visit outside Cairo, for example, are not impressive examples of human genius, but sermons in stone, "monuments of the insufficiency of human enjoyments." Rasselas finally learns, from his own experience, Imlac's great lesson: "Human life is every where a state in which much is to be endured, and little to be enjoyed."[5] In the final chapter, "in which nothing is concluded," he plans to return to the Happy Valley and devote himself to governing his little kingdom. His traveling companions hope to become religious and academic administrators: Pekuah as the prioress of a convent, Nekayah as the headmistress of a school. The joys of romance, family and sexual life (God forbid), the very stuff of fiction, are conspicuously missing.

Though chaste and innocent, his hero is confined in a landscape that's teeming with sexual imagery and unintentionally suggests Johnson's repressed desires. The valley can be entered only by a secret passage through a cavern: "the outlet of the cavern was concealed by a thick wood, and the mouth which opened into the valley was closed with gates of iron." Rivulets descend from the mountains and form a lake that's suggestively orgasmic: "this lake discharged its superfluities by a stream which entered a dark cleft." The sexual imagery recurs later on when Rasselas, discussing marriage with his sister, employs a simile of *frottage* to suggest that husbands and wives "might wear away their dissimilitudes by long cohabitation, as soft bodies, by continual attrition, conform their surfaces to each other."

Johnson's plot is static and unexciting, his characters fixed and flat. In his few attempts at fiction, he disregarded the realistic characters and contemporary speech in the innovative novels published by Richardson, Fielding and Smollett in the 1740s. His comment on Richardson's long and slow-paced epistolary novel *Clarissa* also applies to his own much shorter tale: "if you were to read Richardson for the story, your impatience would be so much fretted that you would hang yourself." Both books must be read for their moral insights and truth about human nature. The fanciful framework of *Rasselas* is ultimately overwhelmed by Johnson's dire pessimism, intensified by the mournful circumstances in which he wrote it. Though he states that nothing "is more common than to call our own condition, the condition of life," he generalizes (as usual) from his own experience and suggests that his dark outlook applies to the whole of mankind.[6]

Rasselas, a detached observer, is not deeply involved in the events he experiences. He never has an emotional crisis or has to make a moral decision. Johnson misses a great chance for dramatic action when, in the course of their journeys, the Christian Pekuah is abducted by the Moslem Arabs of the Egyptian desert. Johnson had fantasized about what captive women would wear if he had his own seraglio and said that Boswell, if castrated, would make a fine eunuch. In *Irene,* the good Aspasia warns the Greek heroine about succumbing to the temptations of the Turkish sultan:

Soon shall the dire seraglio's horrid gates
Close like th'eternal bars of death upon thee. . . .

Beneath each curse of unrelenting Heav'n,
Despair, and slav'ry, solitude, and guilt.

The captured Pekuah fears the Arabs might attempt to use her body to satisfy their ardent desires and cruel urges. But her unaccountably pure-minded and gentlemanly abductors never touch her. As safe with them as in a convent, she's ransomed and returned inviolate. By contrast, in Voltaire's *Candide* (another tale of a naïve hero and his journey to enlightenment), Cunegonde is traumatized, tortured and raped.

Instead of speaking distinctively, all the characters orate in the same unnatural and homiletic manner:

> [Imlac:] If you had seen the miseries of the world, you would know how to value your present state.
>
> [Rasselas:] Now you have given me something to desire; I shall long to see the miseries of the world, since the sight of them is necessary to happiness.
>
> [Nekayah:] I am equally weary of confinement with yourself, and not less desirous of knowing what is done or suffered in the world.
>
> [Pekuah:] I had no reason to suppose . . . that [the Arabs] would forbear the gratification of any ardour of desire, or caprice of cruelty.

Even when Rasselas speaks familiarly to his sister, he employs self-parodic Latinate diction: "you fall into the common errours of exaggeratory declamation, by producing, in a familiar disquisition, examples of national calamities."[7] In other words, you overstate disasters.

The most personal passage, in chapter 44, describes one of Johnson's greatest fears: "the dangerous prevalence of imagination." Ever since the Romantic period, our culture has valued imagination and associated it with creativity and innovation. But Johnson saw it as a perilous path to insanity, and his unwillingness to release his imaginative powers in *Rasselas* explains his inability to write convincing fiction. In *Rambler* 8, as if anticipating Francisco Goya's belief that "the sleep of reason produces monsters," he warned that it was essential to keep "reason a constant guard over imagination." In *Rasselas* he repeated that "all power of fancy over reason is a degree of insanity."[8] Johnson equated freeing the imagination with indulging in pure fantasy. He felt the total absence of reason was a state of madness.

The hermit whom Rasselas encounters on his travels is particularly troubled by these dangers. He illuminates the state of Johnson's mind by complaining, "I have been for some time unsettled and distracted: my mind is disturbed with a thousand perplexities of doubt, and vanities of imagination, which hourly prevail upon me, because I have no opportunities for relaxation, or diversion." This obsessive anchorite— who could quell his imaginative perplexities by conversation and charity, by study and travel—desperately needs to escape from his prayerful cave and divert himself with rest and recreation.

In an anonymous review in the *Annual Register* of 1759, which Johnson must have treasured, Edmund Burke praised his moral insights and poetic style: "no book ever inculcated a purer or sounder morality; no book ever made a more just estimate of human life, its pursuits, and its enjoyments. The descriptions are rich and luxuriant, and shew a poetic imagination not inferior to our best writers in verse. The style, which is peculiar and characteristical of the author, is lively, correct, and harmonious."

Johnson's description of the Happy Valley in the kingdom of Amhara influenced Coleridge, who assimilated its words and ideas into his most famous poem. The valley, as we've seen, could be approached only by a concealed cavern and was watered "by a stream which entered a dark cleft of the mountain . . . and fell with dreadful noise from precipice to precipice." In that fertile valley "the sides of the mountains were covered with trees, the banks of the brooks were diversified with flowers." Coleridge recalled this exotic passage when composing "Kubla Khan" (1816) and re-created the Romantic aspects of an imaginative journey to an exotic place. In the poem—as Coleridge intensifies Johnson's sexual imagery— the Abyssinian maid sings of her native mountains and of a river, enriching fertile ground, that gushes through a deep throbbing chasm:

In Xanadu did Kubla Khan
A stately pleasure-dome decree:
Where Alph, the sacred river, ran
Through caverns measureless to man
  Down to a sunless sea. . . .
And there were gardens bright with sinuous rills,
Where blossomed many an incense-bearing tree. . . .
And from this chasm, with ceaseless turmoil seething,
As if this earth in fast thick pants were breathing,
A mighty fountain momently was forced.[9]

Though influenced by *Rasselas,* "Kubla Khan" was actually inspired by an opium vision. Its poetic power contradicts Johnson's belief in reason and argues for the value of unleashing a wild imagination.

III

Johnson hadn't visited Lichfield for the last nineteen years of Sarah's life. Liberated after her death, he returned there almost every year for the rest of his life. Travelers in eighteenth-century England had to endure close confinement in a backbreaking coach, with noisy, dirty and often smelly passengers. They faced the ever-present danger of highwaymen and suffered the exiguous comfort of the inns. The cumbersome stagecoaches, moving slowly over rough roads, averaged fifty to sixty miles a day. A contemporary said the mid-century stagecoach was "covered with dull black leather, studded by way of ornament with broad-headed nails, with oval windows in the quarters, the frames painted red. . . . The roof rose in a high curve with an iron rail around it. The coachman and guard sat in front upon a high narrow boot. . . . Behind was an immense basket supported by iron bars. . . . The machine groaned and creaked as it went along." In his first return visit to the Midlands, in the winter of 1761, Johnson left London at 9 AM on a Thursday and reached Lichfield, thirty-eight hours later, at 11 PM on Friday. By 1772, improvements in roads and coaches had cut the time of the journey to only fourteen hours.

The coaching inns, where travelers ate and slept, are familiar settings in English literature from Chaucer to Dickens and figure prominently in Fielding's *Tom Jones*. A typical inn had an arched entry into a cobble-stoned courtyard, a reception hall, dining parlor and coffee room. Travelers often had to share the flea-infested bedrooms with strangers. Johnson described the inconveniences of summer travel in *Idler* 58: "The road is dusty, the air is sultry, the horses are sluggish, and the postilion brutal. [The traveler] longs for the time of dinner that he may eat and rest. The inn is crouded, his orders are neglected, and nothing remains but that he devour in haste what the cook has spoiled, and drive on in quest of better entertainment." Despite the discomforts, which never much bothered him, Johnson liked riding in a coach. He found it an adventurous escape from routine life and loved the captive audience. Hester Thrale explained: "in the first place, the company was shut in with him *there;* and could not escape, as out of a room: in the next place, he heard all that was said in a carriage, where it was my turn to be deaf." While driving rapidly along in a post-chaise with Boswell, he joyfully exclaimed, "life has not many things better than this."[10]

Idler 58 celebrates the joy of arriving, after an arduous journey, when the traveler "at last enters his native province, and resolves to feast his mind with the conversation of his old friends, and the recollection of juvenile frolicks." In a letter of July 1762 Johnson described his first return as if he were Robinson Crusoe or Lemuel Gulliver coming back from a long sea voyage to a once familiar and now strange place: "Last winter I went down to my native town, where I found the streets much narrower and shorter than I thought I had left them, inhabited by a new race of people, to whom I was very little known." One witness recorded Johnson's eccentric habit of signaling his arrival, which combined energetic eagerness to see old friends with restless impatience to await their appearance. Returning to Lichfield, he would knock on a series of doors and then rush on without stopping for an answer, pursued by frantic servants all trying to persuade him to enter *their* house.[11]

He was most eager to see his stepdaughter, Lucy Porter, and his old school friend, John Taylor of Ashbourne. Lucy, now forty-six years old (six years younger than Johnson) and still living in his house in the market square, had lost her youthful bloom and given up all hope of marriage. Miss Porter, he rather sharply told Baretti, "from whom I expected most, and whom I met with sincere benevolence, has lost the beauty and gaiety of youth, without having gained much of the wisdom of age." Though more kind and civil than he expected, she was, as he finely phrased it, "a little discoloured by hoary virginity." Lucy eventually inherited a considerable fortune from her brother, Captain Jervis, and in 1766 built a grand house in town, where Johnson often stayed. One of her lady friends suggested that Lucy's relations with Johnson could be tense, despite his unusual deference; that she seemed, on her own turf, to have the upper hand; and that Johnson apparently realized his strange habits could make him a trying guest: "Poor Doctor Johnson was always in fears of *Incommoding his Dear Lucy*—I have heard him often say no Person ever kept him in so much order as Lucy—I am sure he was *ever* attentive and kind to her, and she has frequently behaved most ungraciously to him, but she was a strange woman."

Johnson made similar allowances for John Taylor, with whom he could recall juvenile frolics and remember the days of his youth. Taylor had also inherited money, become richer by acquiring ecclesiastical sinecures and eventually accumulated an enormous income of £7,000 a year. A modern scholar rather acidly wrote that Taylor embodied "many of the characteristics Johnson openly detested: . . . a blatant disregard for his sacred calling, a consuming greed which placed him in constant pursuit of wealthy and influential patrons, and an overriding vanity that expressed itself in ostentatious display and sumptuous living."

Nevertheless, Johnson's loyalty to their long-standing friendship and fondness for their treasured memories allowed him to overlook Taylor's egregious faults. He wrote many sermons for the worldly and materialistic clergyman, cried out for Taylor's help when he was in extremis just after Tetty's death and continued to visit his comfortable estate. Speaking of Taylor's failings and of his beloved prize cattle, and subjecting him to his moral scrutiny, he told Boswell, "I love him; but I do not love him more; my regard for him does not increase. As it is said in the *Apochrypha*, 'his talk is of bullocks.' I do not suppose he is very fond of my company.

Michael Johnson, engraving by Edward Francis Finden,
c.1830 – Samuel Johnson Birthplace Museum

Samuel Johnson by Sir Joshua Reynolds, 1756–57
– National Portrait Gallery, London

David Garrick by Thomas Gainsborough, 1770
– National Portrait Gallery

Elizabeth Johnson, artist unknown – Houghton Library,
Harvard University

Bennet Langton, artist unknown – Samuel Johnson
Birthplace Museum

Giuseppe Baretti, after Sir Joshua Reynolds, 1773
– National Portrait Gallery

Samuel Johnson by Sir Joshua Reynolds, 1769
– Houghton Library, Harvard University

Self-Portrait by Sir Joshua Reynolds, 1747–48 – National Portrait Gallery

Edmund Burke, studio of Sir Joshua Reynolds
– National Portrait Gallery

Oliver Goldsmith, studio of Sir Joshua Reynolds,
1769–70 – National Gallery of Ireland

Anna Williams by Frances Reynolds
– Dr. Johnson House, Gough Square, London

Francis Barber, attributed to Sir Joshua
Reynolds – Dr. Johnson House, Gough Square

Blinking Sam by Sir Joshua Reynolds, 1775 – Huntington Library,
Art Collections, and Botanical Gardens, San Marino, California

James Boswell by Sir Joshua Reynolds, 1785
– National Portrait Gallery

Hester Thrale Piozzi, drawing by George Dance, 1793 –
National Portrait Gallery

Fanny Burney by Edward Burney – National Portrait
Gallery

His habits are by no means sufficiently clerical: this he knows that I see; and no man likes to live under the eye of perpetual disapprobation."[12]

IV

Johnson wrote his third and last series of periodical essays, the 104 *Idlers,* every Saturday between April 1758 and April 1760 for a new weekly newspaper, the *Universal Chronicle.* Once more, he persuaded several friends to write for him. Bennet Langton and the Oxford professor Thomas Warton contributed, and Joshua Reynolds also wrote three essays on painting. The *Ramblers* and *Adventurers* were distractions from Johnson's work on the *Dictionary*; the *Idlers,* a diversion from his edition of Shakespeare's plays. Usually shorter in length, simpler in style, gentler in tone and less analytical than their predecessors, the *Idlers* focused on contemporary events and were more widely read. The essays ranged from a revealing self-portrait, a satiric sketch of an acquisitive wife, and a lively piece on the practical and moral benefits of biography, to savage attacks on vivisection and on war.

The autobiographical Mr. Sober in *Idler* 31 built on Johnson's public image after the appearance of the *Ramblers* and the *Dictionary,* when his personality and conversation had become widely known in London literary circles. His portrait was instantly recognizable: "Sober is a man of strong desires and quick imagination, so exactly ballanced by the love of ease, that they can seldom stimulate him to any difficult undertaking. . . . [His] chief pleasure is conversation: there is no end to his talk or his attention; to speak or to hear is equally pleasing." But he fears being left alone when his friends are occupied early in the morning or sleeping late at night. To counter his dangerous imagination, Sober tries to occupy himself with all kinds of practical activity: carpentry, shoemaking, tin-beating, plumbing, pottery and especially passionate dabbling in "chemical distillation."

A husband in *Idler* 35 amusingly complains about his wife (with hints at Tetty's self-indulgence), who buys obsessively at auctions until "by hourly encroachments my habitation is made narrower and narrower" and "my house has the appearance of a ship stored for a voyage to the colonies." This was the kind of light, entertaining journalism that Johnson, if he wished, could do very well.

Idler 84 on biography, or more specifically on autobiography, complements Johnson's views on the dignity and usefulness of this genre in *Rambler* 60. He begins by frankly acknowledging that people read about other men's lives to help them live their own: "biography is, of the various kinds of narrative writing, that which is most eagerly read, and most easily applied to the purposes of life." He particularly values those narratives in which the writer tells his own story. Though tempted to self-aggrandizement and even falsehood, "the writer of his own life has at least the first qualification of an historian, the knowledge of the truth."[13]

Not all of these essays were lighthearted or informally instructive. *Idler* 17 is a fierce polemic on vivisection, which—like Hogarth in his *Four Stages of Cruelty* (1751)—Johnson considered as bad as the torture of human beings. Ignoring or rejecting the medical discoveries and benefits that came from experiments on animals, he condemns the "race of wretches, whose lives are only varied by varieties of cruelty; whose favorite amusement is to nail dogs to tables and open them alive; to try how long life may be continued in various degrees of mutilation, or with excision or laceration of the vital parts."

Johnson's grimmest *Idler,* number 22, also concerns man's inherent savagery. Written, like number 17, during the Seven Years' War, it was so misanthropic, so insistent on the depravity of human nature, that it was excluded from the first collected edition of the *Idlers.* Taking up his familiar theme, "the general condition of life is full of misery," Johnson created a dialogue between two vultures: a mother and child, an Imlac instructing a Rasselas. The mother raptor's answers to the naïve fledgling's questions suggest that men who engage in mutual slaughter are more morally debased than scavengers of carrion and expose the heart of darkness in modern Europe. "'But when men have killed their prey,' said the pupil, 'why do they not eat it? When the wolf has killed a sheep he suffers not the vulture to touch it till he has satisfied himself. Is not man another kind of wolf?' 'Man,' said the mother, 'is the only beast who kills that which he does not devour, and this quality makes him so much a benefactor to our species. . . . [He seems] eminently delighted with a wide carnage.'"[14]

In January 1762 Johnson was asked to join a local committee to investigate another vexing issue: the existence of the Cock Lane ghost. A man named William Parsons, who lived in Cock Lane (near Smithfield Market in the East End of London) maintained that his house was haunted by a ghost who made strange sounds and scratchings. His twelve-year-old daughter, lying in bed in a trancelike state, interpreted the noises. She said they were made by a woman who claimed she'd been poisoned by her brother-in-law and could not rest until her murderer was hanged.

Johnson naturally wished to find out "whether departed spirits are ever permitted to appear in this world, or in any way to operate upon human life." He'd twice thought he heard his mother call "Sam"—once from distant Lichfield, and again from the still more distant realm of the dead—and believed, or wanted to believe, that he'd actually heard her real voice. Ghost hunters hoped that verifying such spirits would prove the existence of a spirit world and the possibility of communicating with the dead. Inclined to credulity and fascinated by ghosts, Johnson declared: "this is a question which, after five thousand years, is yet undecided; a question whether in theology or philosophy, one of the most important that can come before the human understanding. . . . [It is still] undecided whether or not there has ever been an instance of the spirit of any person appearing after death. All argument is against it; but all belief is for it." In the *True Relation of the Apparition of Mrs. Veal* (1705) (a story he may have invented to help sell books), Daniel Defoe had declared his belief in the existence of ghosts.

When Parsons' daughter was removed from the scene and kept under close observation, the mysterious sounds suddenly ceased. After a Sherlock Holmesian inquiry, Johnson hardheadedly concluded, in the *Gentleman's Magazine,* that "the child has some art of making or counterfeiting, a particular noise, and that there is no agency of any higher cause."[15] It turned out that the sister-in-law had actually died of smallpox and that Parsons had concocted the drama to get revenge on a man who'd sued him for debt. Though forced to stand in the pillory at the end of Cock Lane, Parsons managed to ingratiate himself with the crowd, who gave him money instead of pelting him with garbage.

V

In 1760 George III had succeeded to the throne. The first of his line to be born in England, he did not speak with a German accent and never visited his domain in Hanover. He ruled as a constitutional monarch, made some Whiggish accommodation with the Tories, and distributed patronage to deserving artists and writers. In 1762 the Scottish-born prime minister, Lord Bute, proposed that Johnson be granted a pension of £300 a year. Such pensions came from the Secret Service fund, which the king used for minor grants as well as for spies.

The pension, which Johnson saw as a mark of royal favor, represented an enormous advance in income. To put it into economic perspective: workmen then earned about £40 a year; clergy, and army and navy officers, £50 to £100; successful lawyers £200 (which placed them in the richest 5 percent of the population); prosperous merchants and tradesmen £350. Boswell's annual allowance from his father, which enabled him to live like a gentleman in London, was £200 a year; the annual rent of a fashionable house in Grosvenor Square was £300. The bountiful pension would finally free Johnson from long years of debt and journalistic hackwork, enable him to maintain his household of poor dependents, to increase his charitable gifts and to travel whenever he wished.

But Johnson feared that accepting the pension would compromise his independence. In the *Dictionary* he'd notoriously defined "pension" (and left the definition unaltered in later editions), as "pay given to a state hireling for treason to his country." By "treason" he meant obediently following the orders of those who paid him instead of voting on principle for the good of the country. The usually self-confident Johnson, concerned that his definition would be held against him, consulted Joshua Reynolds about whether he ought to accept the royal grant. Aware of Johnson's poverty and convinced of his worth, Reynolds reassured him that "there could be no objection to his receiving from the King a reward for literary merit; and that certainly the definitions in his *Dictionary* were not applicable to him." Lord Bute himself confirmed that the Whig government was neither trying to silence Johnson nor bribe him to support their policies. The pension, he said, "is not given for anything you are to do, but for what you have done."

In a courtly letter of acceptance to Lord Bute, the antithesis of his angry letter to Lord Chesterfield, Johnson emphasized that he did not belong to a political faction or hold political office, that he had not sought the award and had won it solely on literary merit: "Bounty always receives part of its value from the manner in which it is bestowed: your Lordship's kindness includes every circumstance that can gratify delicacy or enforce obligation. You have conferred your favours on a Man who had neither alliance nor interest, who has not merited them by services, nor courted them by officiousness; you have spared him the shame of solicitation, and the anxiety of suspense."

Always passionately honest when expressing his opinions, Johnson had made many literary and political enemies. As anticipated, he was virulently attacked on two vulnerable points. Despite his notorious dislike of Scots and Scotland, he had accepted patronage from a prominent Scot, Lord Bute. He was strongly opposed to the restoration of a Catholic Stuart king in England, yet was rumored to be a Jacobite supporter and accused of betraying his principles. As he wrote of the poet Sir Richard Blackmore, "his enemies did not forget to reproach him, when he became conspicuous enough to excite malevolence." The satirist Charles Churchill, a political enemy, condemned his apparent apostasy in *The Ghost* (1762): "He damns the *Pension* which he takes, / And loves the STUART he forsakes."[16] When the surgeon and political pamphleteer John Shebbeare, who'd been sentenced to stand in the pillory for his libels, was also awarded a pension in 1762, the wits could not resist ludicrously linking "the *He*-bear and the *She*-bear."

In his *Memoirs,* written in 1771 but not published until 1822, the author, aesthete and dilettante Horace Walpole, recorded his venomous hatred of Johnson. He condemned Johnson's Tory politics, marauding opposition to his father, Sir Robert, and criticism of his intimate friend Thomas Gray in *The Lives of the Poets.* Walpole damned the satanic Demogorgon for his tasteless pedantry and jaw-breaking diction, his absurd pretensions and monkish prejudice, his ignorance and rudeness. He exclaimed: "Johnson was an odious and mean character. By principle a Jacobite, arrogant, self-sufficient, and over-bearing by nature, ungrateful through pride and of *feminine bigotry*, he had prostituted his pen to party even in a diction-ary, and had afterwards for a pension, contradicted his own definitions. His manners were sordid, supercilious, and brutal; his style ridiculously bombast and vicious."

For Johnson the government pension remained a rather touchy sub-ject, and he became angry when unworthy men received it. He lashed out at the author, actor and teacher of elocution Thomas Sheridan (a friend of Swift and father of the playwright Richard Brinsley Sheridan), whom he called "Sherry" and whose writing and self-inflated oratory he heartily disliked. In a passage suppressed by Boswell, Johnson said: "if they have given him a pension, it is time for me to give up mine." Sheridan, he thought, was even worse than Shebbeare. In one of his most devastating remarks, he declared, "Sherry is dull, naturally dull; but it must have taken him a great deal of pains to become what we now see him. Such an excess of stupidity, Sir, is not in Nature."

In the end, however, Johnson thought financial security was well worth a few waspish sneers. Echoing Reynolds' words, he stuck to his beliefs and justified his behavior, telling Boswell:

> I have accepted a pension as a reward which has been thought due to my literary merit; and now that I have this pension, I am the same man in every respect that I have ever been; I retain the same principles. It is true, that I cannot now curse (smiling) the House of Hanover; nor would it be decent for me to drink King James's health in the wine that King George gives me money to pay for. But, Sir, I think that the pleasure of cursing the House of Hanover, and drinking King James's health, are amply over-balanced by three hundred pounds a year.[17]

_13_

SOCIETY OF THE AFFLICTED
1762–1763

I

Beginning in Gough Square, where he lived until 1759, and then in his houses off Fleet Street in Johnson's Court (1765–76) and Bolt Court (1776–84), Johnson gathered around him a group of poor dependents, a substitute family whose dynamics of distress re-created the gloomy atmosphere of his childhood home. (When he lived in rented rooms between 1759 and 1765, his companions took lodgings elsewhere.) Johnson's Court was in a short crooked alley, a few yards from Gough Square. Anna Williams lived on the ground floor, Robert Levet in the garret, and Francis Barber (usually known as Frank) in the servant's room. Bolt Court was also close by. In this three-story house Johnson had his study and books (many of them torn and dusty) on the top floor, which had good light and air, and he watered the plants in the small garden at the back. Elizabeth Desmoulins and Poll Carmichael joined the household in Bolt Court and lived on the second floor.

Johnson nourished and cared for a number of life's casualties who found with him a sure but sorrowful retreat from the evils of the world. Impoverished and miserable, huddled uncomfortably together, the proud and quarrelsome band of unfortunates vied for his favor. Yet this contentious and gloomy hairshirt household satisfied some deeply felt needs: his sense of social obligation, sympathy for the poor, nursing instinct and desire for a family. They often made his life miserable by their petty disputes and nagging complaints, but any company was better than none. Putting up with them answered his longing for penance and helped relieve his sense of sin and guilt.

With his generous pension and literary earnings, Johnson could have lived in a manner more suited to a famous literary figure, with more pleasant accommodations and more efficient domestic help. But he preferred to live in narrow houses with bare wooden floors, rickety staircases and cramped, steerage-class surroundings, which matched the exiguous circumstances of his guests. Indifferent to comfort (not to mention the handsome furniture made in the age of Chippendale and Sheraton), he alarmed visitors by balancing his bulk on a crippled chair, missing one leg, while precariously resting one corner against the wall. The cooking facilities were equally makeshift. Johnson had no jack or spit to turn his joint in the fireplace, and hung the smaller cuts over the fire with pieces of string, which the flames sometimes burnt along with the roast. On Sundays he used the local baker's oven to cook his meat pie.

Johnson's household included Anna Williams, a shrewish blind woman; Francis Barber, a freed black slave; Poll Carmichael and Bet Flint, two prostitutes who occasionally reverted to their trade; Elizabeth Desmoulins, a perpetually discontented widow; Robert Levet, a medical quack; and some of their dependents. This curious group had gravitated to London from Wales, Jamaica, Scotland, the Midlands and Yorkshire. The genteel Hester Thrale, appalled by the lot of them, summed them up as "a Blind woman & her Maid, a Blackamoor and his Wife, a Scotch Wench who has her Case as a Pauper depending in some of the Law Courts; a Woman whose Father once lived at Lichfield & whose Son is a strolling Player,— and a superannuated Surgeon to have Care of the whole *Ship's Company*, such is the present State of Johnson's Family resident in Bolt Court—an Alley in Fleet Street, which he gravely asserts to be the best Situation in London." As if this ragged crowd weren't enough, Johnson also opened his doors and emptied his pockets for a whole mob of Grub Street hacks. "When he is at home," Hester added, "he keeps a sort of odd Levee for distress'd Authors, breaking [bankrupt] Booksellers, & in short every body that has even the lowest Pretensions to Literature in Distress."

All these insulted and injured had a function in Johnson's life and a place in his heart, and over the years he formed strong emotional bonds with them. He discussed his illnesses with Levet, who provided medical attention, and shared his visual disability with Williams, who offered polite conversation. He had a sexual dalliance with Desmoulins, who managed the household, tried to rescue Carmichael and Flint from alcoholism and prostitution, and helped liberate Barber from slavery. Desmoulins and Carmichael were troublesome, but Levet and Williams gave him companionship. Johnson anchored his waking hours between breakfast with Levet at noon and tea with Williams at 2 AM. Through Williams and Desmoulins he kept alive the cherished memories and idealized image of Tetty, who had been their close friend, without having to bear the tedious burden of her actual existence.

Explaining Johnson's pity and compassion—his most impressive traits, apart from intellectual power—John Hawkins observed that Johnson felt personally responsible for all of them: "poverty and distressed circumstances seemed to be the strongest of all recommendations to his favour. When asked by one of his most intimate friends how he could bear to be surrounded by such necessitous and undeserving people as he had about him, his answer was, 'If I did not assist them no one else would, and they must be lost for want.'"[1] Despite their wretched condition, several members of his household lived to a grand old age. Desmoulins reached seventy, Levet and Williams (a few years older than Johnson) reached seventy-seven. The last two died shortly before Johnson, abandoning him to desolation and solitude.

Robert Levet, no great favorite with Johnson's friends, was born into a poor family near Hull, in Yorkshire. He'd worked for a woolen-draper in that town and as a servant to Lord Cadogan in London, had traveled in Europe and been a waiter in a Paris café frequented by surgeons. He met the ever-curious Johnson in a London coffeehouse in 1746. The jovial, garrulous Boswell said Levet "was of a strange grotesque appearance, stiff and formal in his manner, and seldom said a word while any company was present."

Hawkins was more satiric about the forbidding creature, whose behavior and appearance disgusted the rich and terrified the poor. His account of Levet (taken from the *Gentleman's Magazine*) recalls Arthur Murphy's description of Johnson as Lungs in *The Alchemist*. Hawkins wrote that Levet's "person was middle-sized and thin; his visage swarthy, adust and corrugated. His conversation, except on professional subjects, barren. When in deshabille, he might have been mistaken for an alchemist, whose complexion had been hurt by the fumes of the crucible, and whose clothes had suffered from the sparks of the furnace." Hawkins would have been horrified to learn that Johnson thought he was as coarse as Levet. Defending Levet's behavior—and his own—to Hester Thrale, he said, "Levet, madam, is a brutal [rough, unpolished] fellow, but I have a good regard for him; for his brutality is in his manners, not in his mind." He also said of Hawkins, without the redemptive qualification, "he has a degree of brutality, & a tendency to savageness, that cannot easily be defended."[2]

The career of Levet, *un médecin malgré lui*, was even stranger than Goldsmith's. He had no medical training apart from what he'd picked up from casual contacts and odd lectures. He'd passed no examinations, belonged to no professional organization, had no license to practice and took whatever fees he could extract from his impoverished clientele. His single failing, according to Johnson, was a rather frequent departure from sobriety. He was a unique case of a man who became intoxicated through prudence. Since he could not afford to refuse the gin and brandy offered by his patients in lieu of a fee, he took whatever liquors he could get and became, more or less, unwillingly drunk.

But Levet had certain qualities that earned Johnson's "good regard." As Johnson wrote, thinking of Levet, in *Rambler* 19, he suffered, like most practitioners, the "melancholy attendance upon misery, mean submission to peevishness, and continual interruption of rest and pleasure." He may have killed more people than he cured, but he followed the Christian path—"I was sick, and ye visited me"—and his very willingness to walk all over London to help the poorest of the poor, whom no one else would help, surely alleviated their suffering.

In 1762, when he was fifty-seven, the silent and forbidding bachelor entered a disastrous four-month marriage to a prostitute and street thief. They'd successfully conned each other: he posed as a physician with a considerable practice; she convinced him that she was about to inherit a considerable fortune. As soon as they were married, he was sued for his wife's debts and went into hiding, while she was tried at the Old Bailey for picking pockets. Levet had to be dissuaded from attending the trial and urging the judge to hang her; she pleaded her own case and was acquitted. This episode left Levet destitute, thus assuring him Johnson's protection, and in 1762 he became a permanent member of his household. Noontide visitors invariably found them at breakfast. Johnson, just risen from bed, was still not dressed. Levet, silently pouring endless cups of tea for himself and his patron, let Johnson do most of the drinking and all of the talking. Though disagreeable to everyone, Levet acted as the house physician, bleeding and blistering Johnson as well as all the others.

II

The Welsh woman Anna Williams, blinded by cataracts in both eyes since 1740, was the daughter of Zachariah Williams, another untrained medical practitioner. The British government had offered a prize of £20,000 to anyone who could determine longitude at sea; Zachariah thought he had discovered a way to do this and hoped to win the prize. In about 1750 he wrote to Johnson, by now almost a charitable institution, for help. In 1755 Johnson composed an account of Zachariah's scheme for longitude, but someone else finally won the prize in 1765. When Zachariah became sick and impoverished, he entered the Charterhouse, a charitable home for old men. Anna moved in to nurse him, which was strictly against the rules, and after much wrangling they were forcibly ejected. When her father died, Anna was left destitute. Johnson recommended an eye operation, and when it failed he felt responsible for her. He encouraged Anna's visits to his ailing wife, and she became friendly with Tetty. Shortly after Tetty's death in March 1752, first Anna, and then Frank Barber, moved into Johnson's house in Gough Square.

Though plain in appearance, cold in temperament and easily provoked to anger, Williams was an educated, intelligent and interesting woman. She knew French and Italian, and had some literary talent. In 1750 Johnson wrote a "Proposal for *Essays* by Anna Williams," soliciting subscriptions and optimistically stating that she hoped to live as a writer, though "now cut off by a total privation of sight."[3] After a long, unexplained delay, he wrote the advertisement for her *Miscellanies in Verse and Prose* (1766) and filled out the volume with his rather heavy-handed fairy tale "The Fountains."

Though Williams sometimes had a servant to assist her with the ruder domestic chores, she was—despite Johnson's frequent moves and the difficulty of adjusting to new places—an active and industrious member of the household. Boswell noticed that she put her finger inside the cup and poured till she felt the tea touch it, and that "from her manner of eating, in consequence of her blindness, she could not but offend the delicacy of persons of nice sensations." Her habit of splattering bits of her meals, however, was far less offensive than Johnson's gross method of shoveling food into his mouth. The blind Williams, unable to see Johnson's physical defects, could retain an ideal image in her mind.

Blindness, sickness and pain, old age, poverty and wounded pride made Williams so sour and exacting that Johnson had to bribe the maids to stay with her. She and Levet made Johnson's life miserable because he could not make their lives happy. Hawkins reported that "Levet would sometimes insult Johnson, and Miss Williams, in her paroxysms of rage, has been known to drive [Johnson] from her presence." When Beauclerk asked Johnson why he kept Williams in his house, he replied with his usual mixture of loyalty and compassion: "why, sir, she was a friend to my poor wife, and was in the house with her when she died. And so, sir, as I could not find it in my heart to desire her to quit my house, poor thing!, she has remained in it ever since."

Hawkins' daughter Laetitia remembered seeing the aged but elaborately dressed Williams shortly before her death. She was "a pale shrunken old lady, dressed in scarlet made in the handsome French fashion of the time, with a lace cap, with two stiffened projecting wings on the temples, and a black lace hood over it; her grey or powdered hair appearing. Her temper has been recorded as marked with the

Welsh fire, and this might be excited by some of the meaner inmates of the upper floors." When she died in September 1783, Johnson, excusing her bad temper, praised her mind, her virtue and her stoicism. She was, he wrote, "a Woman of great merit both intellectual and moral. Her curiosity was universal, her knowledge very extensive, and she sustained forty years of misery with steady fortitude. Thirty years and more she had been my companion, and her death has left me very desolate."[4]

Elizabeth Desmoulins, like Anna Williams, was the daughter of a doctor. Her father was Johnson's godfather, Samuel Swinfen of Lichfield, for whom he'd written a Latin description of his first mental breakdown. She was the widow of a writing master in Birmingham; had lived with Tetty in Hampstead in the early 1750s; and by 1778 had become a permanent resident of Bolt Court. She'd waited up in Hampstead to warm Johnson's bed (and submit to some fondling), as Williams stayed up late to take tea with him in London. The more efficient Desmoulins eventually replaced Williams as mistress of the kitchen. But Williams, who'd ruled supreme for a quarter of a century, fought bitterly with the hated interloper, criticized the inadequacy of her management and bravely, if hopelessly, tried to regain her former command.

Johnson told Fanny Burney of the perpetual animosity and uneasy truce of the two rivals. Williams disliked the other residents, he said, "but their fondness for her is not greater. She and Desmoulins quarrel incessantly; but as they can both be occasionally of service to each other, and as neither of them have any other place to go, their animosity does not force them to separate." In a style that disguised his affection for them, he complained to the ever-sympathetic Hester Thrale that anarchy prevailed in his kingdom and that he was forced to serve as mediator and peacekeeper: "discord and discontent reign in my humble habitation as in the palaces of Monarchs. Mr. Levet and Mrs. Desmoulins have vowed eternal hate. Levet is the more insidious, and wants me to turn her out." In 1783, when their quarrels became intolerable, Desmoulins moved out; but she triumphantly returned a few months later, after Williams had died.

Williams and Desmoulins were respectable women with pretensions to gentility. Poll Carmichael and Bet Flint were whores, thieves and alcoholics, plucked right off the swarming streets and (in Poll's case) closely quartered in the room that Desmoulins already shared with her daughter. Normally, as a London traveler reported in 1772, women like Poll and Bet repaired to a quite different kind of chamber. The prostitutes "range themselves in a file in the foot-paths of all the great streets, in companies of five or six, most of them dressed very genteelly. The low taverns serve them as a retreat to receive their gallants in: in those houses there is always a room set apart for that purpose."[5] Johnson rather naïvely hoped to reform them.

Poll was probably the prostitute Johnson found lying sick in the street late one night and carried home on his back. He nursed her back to health, cared for her at considerable expense and tried to lead her on the path to virtue. He asked Hawkins to help Poll recover her little patrimony in the law courts, but it's not clear if he succeeded. Johnson himself, who found it very difficult to get a straight answer out of the endlessly vacillating woman, frankly said: "Poll is a stupid slut; I had some hopes of her, at first; but when I talked to her tightly & closely, I could make nothing of her—she was wiggle-waggle, & I could never persuade her to be categorical."

Bet Flint, who visited the house and sometimes lived there, was a more colorful character than Poll. Boswell reported, with a touch of petulance, that Bet, "with some eccentrick talents and much effrontery, forced herself upon [Johnson's] acquaintance" by writing her life in verse and asking him—who better?—to furnish a preface. She'd either accumulated some money or had a wealthy patron. With considerable pretensions, she rented respectable lodgings, played on a spinet and hired a boy to walk in front of the sedan chair that carried her through the streets she had previously strolled. Bet was once arrested for stealing a quilt and tried at the Old Bailey. She played up to the judge, who loved a wench, and when acquitted, complacently said, "now that the counterpane is *my own,* I shall make a petticoat of it." Johnson, playfully using adverbs and exhibiting a certain roguish fondness for the whore, said that Bet "was *habitually* a slut & a Drunkard, & *occasionally* a

Whore & a Thief." He added that Williams, forced to consort with lowlife, "did not love Bet Flint,—but Bet Flint made herself very easy about that!"[6]

III

Struggling against contemporary opinion in his pamphlets and essays, Johnson was as adamantly opposed to slavery as he was to mistreatment of prostitutes, vivisection, debtors' prisons, capital punishment for minor offenses, cruelty to foreign prisoners, colonial conquests and war. Yet slavery prevailed, indeed thrived, in Britain throughout the eighteenth century. During that period, British ships transported 2.5 million slaves from West Africa: 1.4 million were sent to their colonies in the Caribbean, 348,000 to North America. Slaves were considered essential for the production of sugar, tobacco and rice on plantations, and for commercial expansion and financial profit throughout the world. In one year, 1771, twenty-three ships sailed from Bristol, fifty-eight from London and one hundred and seven from Liverpool, carrying 50,000 slaves across the ocean.

Johnson frequently attacked this barbaric practice. In *Idler* 87 he wrote, "of black men the numbers are too great who are now repining under English cruelty." In his "Essay on Epitaphs" (1740), he maintained that slavery is "the most calamitous estate in human life," a condition "which has always been found so destructive to virtue, that in many languages a slave and a thief are expressed by the same word." At a dinner in Oxford in the 1770s, he shocked a group of learned men by raising his glass and proposing a subversive toast: "Here's to the next insurrection of the negroes in the West Indies."[7] Johnson particularly fulminated against Jamaica as "a place of great wealth and dreadful wickedness, a den of tyrants and a dungeon of slaves." When told that a Jamaican planter had died, Johnson, certain that he'd been sent to Hell for his sins, exclaimed: "he will not, whither he is now gone, find much difference, I believe, either in the climate or in the company."

In 1764 there were as many as 20,000 Africans in London, and many newspaper ads sought to sell or recapture slaves. Blacks often served as seamen on the North Atlantic passage and as personal servants on land.

Reynolds and other contemporary artists portrayed aristocrats and fashionable ladies attended by their faithful and ornamental black pages.

Johnson's black servant, Francis Barber, the son of a house slave called Grace, was originally given the common African name of Quashey. He was born in about 1742 on the Orange River Plantation in North Jamaica, owned by Colonel Richard Bathurst. The colonel was the father of Johnson's dear friend Dr. Richard Bathurst (whom he praised as a "very good hater"). Frank Barber might have become a stable groom, footman, valet or even a barber in the great house if the colonel had not sold the plantation.[8] From his portrait he looks more like a mulatto than a full-blooded African, and could conceivably have been the son of Bathurst himself or a member of his family. Frank's paternity might explain why Bathurst took such special care of the boy.

In 1750 the colonel brought the eight-year-old orphan to England, gave him an English name and sent him to a school in Yorkshire. Two years later, soon after Tetty's death, Dr. Richard Bathurst, who assumed responsibility for Frank, gave him to Johnson. The self-sufficient Johnson, Hawkins noted, required a servant even less than Diogenes (a classical philosopher with few material needs, famous for living in an earthenware tub). But Frank gave Johnson the opportunity to compensate at least one man for the injustice of slavery. He loved the boy for himself as well as for his connection to Dr. Bathurst, instructed him in religion and sent him to study in Birmingham. In about 1755 the colonel died, and in his will freed Frank from slavery and left him a bequest of £12. When Frank reached the age of fourteen, he returned to work for Johnson in Gough Square, but after quarreling with Williams he ran away to serve as an apothecary's assistant with a Mr. Farren in Cheapside.

Though short, slight and scarred by smallpox, Frank was considered attractive. Hester Thrale thought "he was very well-looking for a Black a Moor." With a touch of paternal pride, Johnson proudly told her and her friends about Frank's romantic adventure during their journey in 1764: "Frank had been eminent for his success among the girls. . . . I must have you know, ladies, that Frank has carried the empire of Cupid further than most men. When I was in Lincolnshire so many years ago, he attended me thither; and when we returned home together, I found that a female haymaker had followed him to London for love."

Frank served as Johnson's valet, waited at his table, answered the door, ran errands and bought supplies for the house. He also accompanied Johnson on his weekly visits to the Thrales' house in Streatham, outside London, as well as on more distant journeys to the country houses of friends like Langton, Percy and Reynolds. He supplied Boswell with information, letters and memorabilia; and when asked if he ever heard his master swear, replied: "No; the worst word he ever uttered when in a passion was, *you dunghill dog.*" An acquaintance who called at the house when Johnson was absent provided a glimpse of Frank's social life with other black servants. When Frank opened the door, he recalled, "a group of his African countrymen were sitting round a fire in the gloomy anteroom; and on their all turning their sooty faces at once to stare at me they presented a curious spectacle."⁹

In July 1758, at the age of sixteen, the always impulsive and volatile Frank ran away for the second time and joined the navy. He may have been bored by his domestic duties and tired of Johnson's cloistered tuition (as Rasselas tired of Imlac's). He yearned for adventure and wanted to escape from what Hawkins called the "unwarrantable severity" of Anna Williams, who took out her frustration and rage on the nearest and most vulnerable victim. There was always a need for sailors to supply British ships, especially during the Seven Years' War when naval battles decimated the ranks, and men were often press-ganged and forced into service. Frank remembered sailing from Jamaica to England as a young child, thought he knew about life aboard ships and wanted to join other blacks who served at sea.

More in touch with reality, Johnson knew about the navy's generous grog ration and gross immorality, its inhuman conditions and brutal floggings, and was shocked by Frank's sudden departure. Thinking, perhaps, of Frank, and the dangers that could befall a young boy in the navy, he declared, "no man will be a sailor who has contrivance to get himself into a gaol. . . . There is, in a gaol, better air, better company, better conveniency of every kind; and a ship has the additional disadvantage of being in danger. . . . Being in a ship is being in a gaol with the chance of being drowned."

In March 1759, prompted either by Frank's pleas or by his own affection for him, Johnson asked the novelist Tobias Smollett to intercede with the influential MP John Wilkes to secure Frank's release from the navy. Smollett obliged by writing that month to Wilkes, but couldn't resist mocking Johnson's role as literary dictator and referring to him as a khan, a despotic lord or prince: "I am again your petitioner, in behalf of that great CHAM of literature, Samuel Johnson. His black servant, whose name is Francis Barber, has been pressed on board the *Stag* frigate, Captain Angel, and our lexicographer is in great distress." Eight months later, in November 1759, Johnson himself wrote to one of the Lords of the Admiralty:

> I had a Negro Boy named Francis Barber, given me by a Friend whom I much respect, and treated by me for some years with great tenderness. Being disgusted ["offended"] in the house he ran away to Sea, and was in the Summer on board the Ship stationed at Yarmouth to protect the fishery. It would be a great pleasure, and some convenience to me, if the Lords of the Admiralty would be pleased to discharge him, which as he is no seaman, may be done with little injury to the King's Service.[10]

The officials eventually obliged, and Frank, deemed expendable, was discharged after two years of service in August 1760. Two years later, "*dear, dear* Bathurst," the naval doctor whom Johnson loved better than any human creature, died of a fever in Havana after the British had captured the town from the Spanish.

In the late 1760s Johnson encouraged Frank to resume his studies and sent him to a grammar school in Hertfordshire. In all he paid £300 in fees for his five years there. A black man and naval veteran in his late twenties must have seemed wildly out of place among rural English schoolboys. But Frank improved his ability to read and write English, and even picked up some Latin and Greek. In 1773 he married a white woman, Elizabeth Ball, and during their contentious marriage they had three children. His first son, named Samuel, died at the age of fourteen months, in 1775. A second son, born in 1783, also called Samuel, later became a successful Methodist preacher in the Midlands.

Hester Thrale, describing an incident that took place during the annual two-day party for her servants at Streatham, illuminated Frank's fiery temper and Johnson's paternal solicitude. Jealous of the attention paid to his pretty wife, Frank angrily left the house and set off on foot for London. Mrs. Thrale and Johnson, taking a drive in her carriage, overtook him on the road and stopped to question him:

> "What is the matter, child (says Dr. Johnson), that you leave Streatham to-day? *Art sick?*" He is jealous (whispered I). "Are you jealous of your wife, you stupid blockhead (cries out his master in another tone)?" The fellow hesitated; and, *To be sure, Sir* I *don't quite approve Sir,* was the stammering reply. "Why, what do they *do* to her, man? Do the footmen kiss her?" No Sir, no!—Kiss my *wife Sir!*—*I hope not Sir.* "Why, what *do* they do to her, my lad?" Why nothing Sir, I'm sure Sir. "Why then go back directly and dance you dog, do; and let's hear no more of such empty lamentations."

Using very different forms of address—"child," "stupid blockhead," "my lad," "you dog"—and suddenly alternating his tone from affectionate to critical and back again, with a different emphasis on *do,* Johnson wisely persuaded Frank to get over his pique, be more tolerant of his wife's innocent flirtations and return to enjoy the festivities.

There was one more pampered inhabitant of Johnson's menagerie—the cat Hodge, named to suggest a medley or hodge-podge. Johnson spoiled him with oysters, which he bought himself at the fishmonger's, not only to spare Frank's feelings but also to prevent him from taking out his resentment on the cat. Johnson told Bennet Langton of a mad gentleman who'd been "running about town shooting cats. And then in a sort of kindly reverie, he bethought himself of his own favourite cat, and said [with subtle variations], 'But Hodge shan't be shot; no, no, Hodge shall not be shot.'"

Johnson liked to talk while Hodge scrambled up his chest and had his back rubbed and tail gently pulled. When Boswell, who disliked cats, flattered Hodge by remarking that he was a fine cat, Johnson said, "'Why yes, Sir, but I have had cats whom I liked better than this'; and then as if perceiving Hodge to be out of countenance, adding, 'but he is a very fine cat, a very fine cat indeed.'" Boswell's finely observed "out of countenance" (was Hodge's mouth turned down?) is nicely balanced by Johnson's elegant repetition. With Christopher Smart's cat, Jeoffrey ("the servant of the Living God"), and Thomas Gray's Selina ("Her coat, that with the tortoise vies, / Her ears of jet, and emerald eyes"), Hodge is one of the most famous cats of the eighteenth century.[11]

Johnson enjoyed a lively intellectual and social life in coffeehouses, taverns and the comfortable country houses of his friends. His home life was a different world. His circle of social outcasts showed him no gratitude, often made him miserable and even insulted him, as no one else was ever allowed to do. Referring to the hostility seething in his "seraglio," where the bored inmates preyed upon one another, Johnson told Hester Thrale: "Williams hates every body. Levet hates Desmoulins and does not love Williams. Desmoulins hates them both. Poll loves none of them." After a stay at the Thrales', he wrote Hester that he'd come back "to two sick and discontented women, who can hardly talk, if they had anything to say, and whose hatred of each other makes one great exercise of their faculties."[12] If he went visiting, he was sure to return for the weekend to take up his penitential duties. He broke up fights, soothed injured feelings and treated everyone to a few good dinners. Johnson was devoted to his discontented family, who were a constant source of interest and friendship. He understood that maintaining their dignity was just as important as providing them with food and shelter.

14

CONTAGION OF DESIRE
1763–1764

I

Johnson had experienced several major turning points in his life: leaving Oxford, getting married, completing the *Dictionary* and receiving his government pension. The events that took place in the twenty months between May 1763 and January 1765—befriending James Boswell and founding the Literary Club, as well as meeting the Thrales—would also transform his life in fundamental ways. Johnson's literary reputation and financial security were now firmly established, but he was still struggling with severe depression and would soon suffer a second mental breakdown.

The fateful encounter between the twenty-two-year old Boswell and the literary lion he'd been stalking took place on May 16, 1763, in the back room of Tom Davies' bookshop at 8 Great Russell Street, near what is now the British Museum. Boswell became not only an intimate friend and surrogate son, but also the devoted recorder of Johnson's life. With his usual dramatic flair, Boswell described one of the great hostile-turned-friendly meetings in literature. He already had a clear idea of Johnson's appearance from engravings of Reynolds' first portrait of him, pen in hand and deep in meditation, and first saw him through a glass door, portentously approaching like the ghost of Hamlet's father. Boswell's tracking shot of a ghost seen through glass then became a sharp close-up of Johnson's rocky face and mountainous belly.

Boswell knew that Johnson was notoriously hostile to the Scots. He particularly disliked the Presbyterian Church, the Jacobite threat of a civil war and the restoration of a Catholic Stuart king. He disapproved of the inordinate Scottish influence in England, symbolized by Lord Bute, George III's close friend and prime minister, who (ironically enough) had given him his comfortable pension. In *The False Alarm* Johnson maintained that "every one knows the malice, the subtilty, the industry, the vigilance, and the greediness of the Scots." Boswell, ecstatic with anticipation, begged Davies not to mention that he was a Scot, though his accent would immediately betray him. Davies provocatively announced that Boswell came from Scotland, and Boswell defensively pleaded, "I do indeed come from Scotland, but I cannot help it." Johnson, seizing the opening and twisting it to mean that Boswell had been forced to leave his impoverished home, crushed him with "that, Sir, I find, is what a very great many of your countrymen cannot help." He thus implied that the English had not been able to staunch the invasion of immigrants from the north.

Johnson told Davies that Garrick had refused to give him a free theater ticket for Anna Williams (he rarely asked favors for himself, but often solicited them for friends). Eager to edge into the conversation, Boswell committed a second humiliating gaffe. " 'O, Sir,' Boswell said, 'I cannot think Mr. Garrick would grudge such a trifle to you.' 'Sir, (said he, with a stern look), I have known David Garrick longer than you have done: and I know no right you have to talk to me on the subject.' " Boswell's comment made Johnson, always possessive about Garrick, even angrier by emphasizing the rudeness of his refusal.

Much mortified but not entirely defeated by his rough reception, the irrepressible Boswell struggled to maintain his precarious foothold and was rewarded with more talk. Johnson mentioned John Wilkes, the radical MP whose political views he loathed, but who'd helped secure Frank Barber's release from the navy. He spoke of Wilkes' criticism of the royal family and insisted that he had behaved outrageously.

Though Wilkes was protected by parliamentary privilege, he deserved to be chastised: "I think he is safe from the law, but he is an abusive scoundrel; and instead of applying to my Lord Chief Justice to punish him, I would send a half a dozen footmen and have him well ducked." After Johnson left, Boswell, though battered by his blows, felt that he was an essentially good-natured man. Davies consoled him by saying, "don't be uneasy. I can see he likes you very well."[1]

Boswell's relationship with his father had taught him to endure harsh treatment. Born in Edinburgh in 1740, he was five feet, six inches tall, robust and plump, with dark skin, wavy hair and the hint of a double chin. Cursed with a feckless character and a morbid Calvinistic streak, he was constantly criticized by his severe and disapproving father, the High Court judge Lord Auchinleck, whom he compared to a cold surgical instrument. Boswell's father (who was two years older than Johnson) first forced him to study English and Scottish law, and then told him that he was not qualified to practice because "it would cost him more trouble to hide his ignorance in these professions than to show his knowledge." In Johnson, Boswell found a stern but forgiving father figure, with the warmth, encouragement, humor and affection that his own father lacked.

When Boswell called on him a few days after the bookshop encounter, Johnson was characteristically shabby and disheveled. But Boswell found that Davies had been right. They immediately hit it off, and launched into an engrossing conversation. They discussed the authenticity of Macpherson's *Ossian* poems, the madness of the poet Christopher Smart, the motives for truly moral behavior and the evidences of the Christian religion. Though Boswell twice offered to leave, Johnson pressed him to stay and keep the talk on the boil. As they parted after Boswell's second visit, Johnson urged him to come as often as he could and said he'd always be glad to see his new friend. During their third meeting, at Johnson's favorite tavern, the High-Church-sounding Mitre, they conversed about the poetry of Colley Cibber and Thomas Gray, and the new plays at Drury Lane. Johnson encouraged Boswell to pursue his studies, to travel in little-known Spain and to write a book about it. Johnson told him, "give me your hand; I have taken a liking to you." By the time he'd been introduced to Goldsmith and Anna Williams, Boswell said his mind had become *"strongly impregnated with the Johnsonian aether."*[2]

Though pushy and self-promoting, an anxious and ambitious outsider, Boswell nevertheless managed to charm. Childishly egoistic, he had a zest for life and curiosity about other people, an acute perception and lively imagination. Insecure yet cocky, melancholy yet high-spirited, he won people over with his great good humor. Boswell and Johnson had a spontaneous and intuitive affinity. By August 1763, when Boswell left England to study Roman law (closely connected to Scottish law) at Utrecht, they'd become good friends. Protestant Holland, the home of Erasmus and Spinoza, was famous for its religious toleration and freedom of speech, and the Dutch King William III had replaced James II and ruled England from 1689 to 1702. In the 1660s, when Germany was still a weak collection of princely states, Holland had a great empire. Britons went there to study in the eighteenth century just as they would go to Germany in the nineteenth.

Johnson loved a leisurely ramble in a coach with plenty of time to talk. As a mark of his affectionate regard, he offered to accompany Boswell on the two-day stagecoach journey to Harwich, on the North Sea coast, and see him out of England. At dinner the first night he repaid Boswell's adoration by teasing him in front of strangers. He said "that gentleman there (pointing at me), has been idle. He was idle at Edinburgh. His father sent him to Glasgow, where he continued to be idle. He then came to London, where he has been very idle; and now he is going to Utrecht, where he will be as idle as ever." Johnson may well have reflected that he too had been idle at Oxford and had not, like Boswell, earned a university degree. His theme and variations on Boswell's idleness—past, present and future—were based on Boswell's confessions about his studies in Scotland, Johnson's own observations about Boswell's wasteful life in London and his shrewd prediction about what was bound to happen in Holland. Boswell protested about this public ridicule, but Johnson, ignoring his complaint, said the people didn't know him and would think no more about it.

When it was time for him to leave, Boswell, idealizing Johnson as "majestick, " recorded their farewell:

My revered friend walked down with me to the beach, where we embraced and parted with tenderness, and engaged to correspond by letters. I said, "I hope, Sir, you will not forget me in my absence." Johnson. "Nay, Sir, it is more likely you should forget me, than that I should forget you." As the vessel put out to sea, I kept my eyes upon him for a considerable time, while he remained rolling his majestick frame in his usual manner: and at last I perceived him walk back into the town.

He then faded out of Boswell's view as slowly as he'd first appeared in Davies' bookshop.

Johnson's parting from Boswell, en route to study in Holland, inevitably reminded him of his equally emotional farewell to Savage, en route to exile in Wales, in July 1739. Savage left London, Johnson recalled, "having taken leave with great tenderness of his friends, and parted from the author of this narrative with tears in his eyes." Savage had drifted out of his life, and Johnson may well have wondered if he'd ever see Boswell again. But they corresponded as promised, and resumed their warm friendship when Boswell returned to England—after two and a half years in Holland, Germany, Switzerland, Italy and France—in February 1766.

Buoyed by his meetings with Johnson, Boswell sailed to Holland, where his studies came a distant second to wenching and drinking. He then set off on a Grand Tour of the continent and successfully courted two more literary celebrities, the notorious Voltaire and Jean-Jacques Rousseau, whose lives and thought were antithetical to Johnson's. He took an adventurous trip to the wilds of bandit-ridden Corsica, then ruled by the Republic of Genoa, where he met the revolutionary hero Pasquale Paoli. He passionately admired Paoli and supported his effort to free his country. Boswell's *Account of Corsica* (1768), dedicated to Paoli, established the patriot's reputation in Europe, made him welcome in England when he was forced into exile, and influenced British and

French policy toward the island. On his way home, Boswell, a fox in charge of a hen, escorted Rousseau's mistress, Thérèse Le Vasseur, from Paris to England, and seduced her on the way. Both commented tartly on the experience. She allowed he was a "hardy and vigorous lover, but [had] no art." He ungallantly described her performance as "agitated, like a bad rider galloping downhill."[3]

In later years Boswell, escaping from his dour father and tedious law practice—he lost several clients to the gallows and morbidly witnessed their executions—was always delighted to be with Johnson in London. They usually saw each other in the spring, when both were at their best. Having survived the illnesses and gloom of an English winter, Johnson was cheered by Boswell's high spirits and gossipy talk. Boswell felt that being with Johnson was the high point of his life. Finding himself in the exalted company of Johnson and Goldsmith, he alluded to Swift's poem ("They hug themselves, and reason thus: / 'It is not yet so bad with us'") and ecstatically recorded, "I felt a completion of happiness. I just sat and hugged myself in my own mind."

Boswell also had a dark side. His mental instability, though not as extreme as Johnson's, was evident in his periods of intense boredom and depression, reckless gambling and alcoholism, sexual debauchery and venereal disease. Though he solemnly insisted "there cannot be higher felicity on earth enjoyed by man than the participation of genuine reciprocal amorous affection with an amiable woman," his relations with women were often more commercial than congenial.[4] He was consistently unfaithful to his attractive and tolerant wife. Over a ten-year period in the 1760s, the charming but not particularly attractive Boswell slept with three married women, had liaisons with four actresses, kept three lower-class mistresses and paid for quick, sometimes stand-up sex in dark alleys with more than sixty whores. He fathered and neglected two bastards.

Johnson remained chaste after his wife's death, while Boswell, acting out the passions that Johnson forced himself to suppress, fornicated insatiably. Johnson disapproved of Boswell's immorality and (after his marriage to a cousin in 1769) of his adultery, which Boswell unsuccessfully tried to conceal from his moral guide. Yet he also envied his sexual freedom, and observed the vices of rakish friends with surprising tolerance. He too had been guilty of heavy drinking and sexual adventures when consorting with Savage, and still longed for drink and sex after he'd become rigorously abstinent and celibate. His athletic feats and occasional violence were a physical release from oppressive desires, and he got vicarious pleasure from Boswell's exploits.

A drunkard and sometimes a buffoon, Boswell played Falstaff to Johnson's Prince Hal. Johnson's "Notes" on Falstaff in *Henry IV, Part 2* suggest they were written with Boswell in mind and that Johnson saw the parallels: "Yet the man thus corrupt, thus despicable, makes himself necessary to the prince that despises him, by the most pleasing of all qualities, perpetual gaiety, by an unfailing power of exciting laughter, which is the more freely indulged, as his wit is not of the splendid or ambitious kind, but consists in easy escapes and sallies of levity, which make sport but raise no envy."

Johnson and Boswell complemented each other's personalities and shared significant traits. Johnson had hoped to be a lawyer; Boswell, the son he never had, became one. Johnson found it difficult to start writing; Boswell was a compulsive writer for whom nothing was real till he'd recorded it. Johnson was the first literary celebrity; Boswell the first modern biographer. Obsessed with literary fame, Boswell was perhaps the first writer to review his own work. He even dedicated an anonymous ode to himself, thanking "James Boswell, Esq. . . . for your particular kindness to me, and chiefly for the profound respect with which you have always treated me."

Both men frequently made and broke vows, and felt corrosive guilt after the deaths of their wives. Both suffered from crippling indolence and profound dejection. Boswell's melancholy frightened Johnson and threatened to undermine his own precarious sanity. He strongly warned Boswell not to discuss "the exaltations and depressions of your mind [of which] you delight to talk, and I hate to hear. . . . Make it an invariable and obligatory law to yourself, never to mention your own mental diseases."[5]

Boswell was drawn to Johnson's mind and character by a contagion of desire, like a lover eager to know everything about the beloved. Except when too drunk to record the conversation, he never stopped inquiring and observing. In his *Life* Boswell devoted himself to delineating minute particulars of Johnson's behavior, to painting a realistic Flemish picture, to making him as vivid as possible. Boswell was with Johnson for about 425 days during the last twenty-two years of Johnson's life, a quarter of them during their tour of Scotland in 1773. But the amount of time they spent together was not as important as the depth of intimacy that developed between them. The emotional power of Boswell's feeling for Johnson drove the dramatic narrative of the *Life*.

Fanny Burney, a more discreet diarist, satirically observed the observer observing. She noted that Boswell's senses were fully alert and his body responsive to Johnson's speech, that his mouth hung open like a fish cruising for bait: "the moment that voice burst forth, the attention which it excited in Mr. Boswell amounted almost to pain. His eyes goggled with eagerness; he leant his ear almost on the shoulder of the Doctor; and his mouth dropt open to catch every syllable that might be uttered: nay, he seemed not only to dread losing a word, but to be anxious not to miss a breathing; as if hoping from it, latently, mystically, some information."

Anyone who's tried to write the lives of living authors knows how keen they are to elude the biographer's net. Johnson also felt pursued by Boswell and was sometimes greatly vexed by his unremitting inquiries. Undeterred by occasional outbursts and setbacks, Boswell asked provocative questions, assiduously (sometimes tactlessly) collected material, took indiscreet notes immediately after conversations and deliberately incited Johnson's wrath in order to create memorable scenes.

Edmund Burke, for one, disapproved of Boswell's pernicious pursuit of his quarry, which interfered with the free and open talk between close friends. As Edmond Malone explained to Boswell, "The true cause I perceive, of Burke's coldness, is that he thinks your habit of recording throws a restraint on convivial ease and negligence." Johnson complained to Hester Thrale, "one would think the Man had been hired to be a spy upon me," and was more directly confrontational with Boswell himself. Irritated by Boswell's obsessive interrogations, he exploded with "I will not be put to the *question*. Don't you consider, Sir, that these are not the manners of a gentleman? I will not be baited with *what,* and *why;* what is this? what is that? why is a cow's tail long? why is a fox's tail bushy? . . . You have but two topicks, yourself and me. I am sick of both."[6]

Yet Johnson could not help joining in Boswell's biographical game. Their relationship had begun with Boswell paying court to Johnson and Johnson slapping him down, and this pattern continued until the end. Johnson retaliated by ridiculing and teasing. He loved to arouse Boswell's curiosity, even about the most trivial details, and then withhold the precious information. Boswell noticed that Johnson saved the peel of squeezed oranges, scraped them neatly and let them dry. When Johnson adamantly refused to explain what he did with this treasure, Boswell said, with mock solemnity: "'then the world must be left in the dark. It must be said . . . he never could be prevailed upon to tell.' Johnson. 'Nay, Sir, you should say it more emphatically:—he could not be prevailed upon, even by his dearest friends, to tell.'" In fact, Johnson used the dried peel as tinder to start fires and, when ground into a powder and taken with liquid, as a laxative and remedy for indigestion.

Johnson's criticism of Boswell's Scottish origins was a recurring tease. Boswell quoted, among Johnson's other pronouncements, "the noblest prospect which a Scotchman ever sees, is the high road that leads him to England!" Johnson always mocked Boswell's idleness and dissipation. In front of the rakish John Wilkes he declared, with some truth, that Boswell lived "among savages in Scotland, and among rakes in England."[7] Boswell hardened his carapace, but sometimes, when Johnson was genuinely angry, his painful barbs struck home. After Boswell claimed to be vexed by public affairs, Johnson insisted that neither Boswell's food nor sleep were ever disturbed by events in Parliament. He then ordered Boswell to "clear your *mind* of cant," which he defined as "a whining pretension to goodness, in formal and affected terms." When Boswell wished he'd lived in the Augustan Age, Johnson told him that if he'd been alive in Pope's time he would have been immortalized by being put into the *Dunciad.*

A sharp exchange that reversed their roles (and was too strong to be included in the *Life*) took place when Boswell told the deaf Johnson, whose hearing improved in a closed coach, that the rattling of the chaise made it impossible to hear him. Annoyed that Boswell couldn't bear to miss a minute of his conversation, Johnson shocked him by retorting: "then you may go hang yourself." Johnson, who had a realistic idea of hanging and often mentioned it, replied in a similar fashion to a particularly foolish but well-intentioned question. When Johnson was seriously ill, Boswell asked if he'd gone outside that day. Aware of the gravity of his own condition, Johnson shot back, "Don't talk so childishly. You may as well ask if I hanged myself to-day."[8] But Boswell, fortunately for posterity, was impervious to insult. Like a large rubber doll, he always bounced back when Johnson knocked him down.

II

The eighteenth century was the great age of men's clubs. In *Spectator* 9 (March 10, 1711) Joseph Addison wrote, "man is a sociable animal and we take all occasions and pretences of forming ourselves into those little nocturnal assemblies which are commonly known as *clubs.*" In the spring of 1714 Swift, Pope, Dr. John Arbuthnot, the poet Thomas Parnell and the Tory prime minister Robert Harley, Earl of Oxford, formed the illustrious Scriblerus Club. In Johnson's time there were Tall Clubs, Ugly Clubs, Surly Clubs, Farters' Clubs and even Mollies' Clubs, which catered to those with a taste for cross-dressing.

Johnson, with no wife or children and a misery-making household, oppressed by melancholy and fearful of solitude, enlivened his life with conversation and cheered himself up in company. He craved intellectual entertainment and constantly searched for "some kindred mind with which he could unite in confidence and friendship." In the winter of 1748–49, while working on the *Dictionary,* he founded the Ivy Lane Club, which gathered at the King's Head beefsteak house and tavern, near St. Paul's Cathedral, for good food and lively conversation. The club—including Dr. Richard Bathurst, John Hawkins and John Hawkesworth—had arranged the all-night celebration for Charlotte Lenox in 1751, and lasted until about 1756.

Five months after Boswell's departure for Holland, Johnson helped to found the famous Literary Club, which met for the first time in

January 1764. The Club's aim was to elect the leading man in every profession. In contrast to the contentious losers in his dysfunctional household, the brilliant members, from the artistic and intellectual elite of England, liked and admired one another. The nine founding members included many of Johnson's closest friends: Reynolds, Burke, Goldsmith, Hawkins, Langton and Beauclerk, as well as Dr. Richard Nugent, Burke's father-in-law, and Anthony Chamier, secretary of the war office. The Club gradually elected other illuminati: Percy, Garrick, Boswell, Gibbon, Adam Smith, Richard Brinsley Sheridan, Charles Burney and the naturalist Joseph Banks, and became the most brilliant concentration of genius in English literary history. By the time of Johnson's death in 1784, it had thirty-five members, including four lords and an earl.

The Club met informally and under Johnson's benign gaze, once a week at 7 PM at the convivial Turk's Head Tavern on Garrard Street in Soho, and continued to eat and drink till late at night. Boswell was predictably bumptious, Gibbon was silent and Burke was unconstrained and fooled around. Johnson, more formal and guarded, was always ready for aggressive argument. The unclubbable Hawkins was frozen out after his intolerable rudeness to Burke. Beauclerk defected to more fashionable clubs, but later regained admission.

Many distinguished men keenly sought to join. There was a good deal of discussion about who should be let in and kept out, and members tended to defer to Johnson's wishes. Garrick brazenly declared he would join; Johnson said they might not want a mere player; and Garrick had to cool his heels offstage till 1773. The Irish MP and friend of Burke, Agmondesham Vesey (who should have been admitted on the strength of his first name alone), was so anxious about his fate that he hired couriers to race with the news of his vote. No women were allowed; and friends like Hawkesworth, Henry Thrale and Baretti were either not proposed or blackballed.

The leading Club members not only had extensive knowledge and experience, but also came from diverse social origins and geographical backgrounds. Beauclerk had royal blood; Percy was the son of a grocer. Most of them were born outside of London. Burke, Goldsmith and

Nugent came from Ireland; Boswell and Adam Smith from Scotland. Others were from the English provinces: Johnson and Garrick from the Midlands; Reynolds from Devon; Percy and Burney from Shropshire in the west; Langton from Lincolnshire in the east. Burke, Gibbon and Sheridan (like the brewer Henry Thrale and bookseller William Strahan) were Members of Parliament. Joseph Banks had traveled around the world on the *Endeavour* with Captain James Cook.

On their tour of Scotland in 1773, Johnson and Boswell fantasized about creating their own university in St. Andrews, a kind of Institute for Advanced Study staffed by the luminaries of the Club. Boswell wrote:

> I was to teach Civil and Scotch Law; Burke, Politics and Eloquence; Garrick, the Art of Public Speaking; Langton was to be our Grecian, [George] Colman our Humanist; Nugent to teach Physic. . . . Goldsmith, Poetry and Ancient History; Chamier, Commercial Politics; Reynolds, Painting and the arts which have beauty for their object; [Robert] Chambers, the Law of England. Mr. Johnson at first said, "I'll trust Theology to nobody but myself." But upon due consideration that Percy is a clergyman, it was agreed that Percy should teach Practical Divinity and British Antiquities, and Mr. Johnson himself, Logic, Metaphysics, and Scholastic Divinity.

It was a fascinating idea. Boswell might have enrolled Hawkins and Burney to teach music. Garrick could have also taught acting. Goldsmith would have disappointed students by his hapless ignorance, lack of preparation and lost lecture notes. Reynolds could have tried out his *Discourses* on art. Chambers, as in real life, would have had his law lectures ghostwritten by Johnson. The polymath Johnson graciously ceded theology to a divine, but kept three subjects—more than anyone else had—for himself. (It's not clear if he meant to use a whip on his pupils.) He could have said, as a wag said of the nineteenth-century Oxford don Benjamin Jowett: "I am the Master of this college: / What I don't know isn't knowledge."

The members of the exclusive, close-knit Club shared an unusual mixture of rivalry, competition and magnanimity. Aware of their mutual foibles and faults, they indulged in high-minded discourse and repeated juicy gossip, jockeyed for position and tried to shine in the bright swordplay of wit. At the meeting on April 3, 1778, the shifting conversation ranged from intellectual topics like ancient art, the Irish language and travel writing, to political questions like emigration, speeches in parliament and suppliants for office, to practical matters like replenishing their nearly exhausted hogshead of claret. In the outside world they pulled strings and granted favors for friends, and were pleased by individual achievements and collective success. Like a kindly schoolmaster, Johnson addressed his friends by their nicknames (though "Goldy" objected) and kept the unruly class in order.

Pasquale Paoli—the Garibaldi of his time—was not elected to the Club, probably because he was a foreigner, had an imperfect command of English and always planned, when circumstances permitted, to return to rule Corsica. A contemporary wrote, "Paoli is of a fair and florid complexion with dark and piercing eyes, and about five feet nine inches tall (as I guess); strongly made, but not in the least clumsy. He uses many gestures in his conversation as other Italians do. . . . He looks and speaks like one who had been accustomed to command, yet there is nothing rough or assuming about him, but on the contrary the utmost politeness."[9] The kindly and dignified old soldier, well read in the classics, had been made wealthy by his British government pension of £1,200 a year, granted for his patriotic struggles against Genoa and then France. He charmed Fanny Burney, who described him as "a very pleasing man, tall and genteel in his person, remarkably well bred and very mild and soft in his manners."

Boswell introduced his two heroes in London in October 1769, when Paoli first arrived in England, and interpreted as they spoke in French. Johnson, impressed by Paoli, said "he had very much the air of a man who had been at the head of a nation."[10] Both men had huge appetites and liked to dine and drink together. They discussed languages, marriage and melancholy; visited Rochester together, and met in Wales.

Paoli, later accorded the rare honor of a bust in Westminster Abbey, was among the distinguished mourners at Johnson's funeral.

III

Johnson almost never went to the theater after the production of *Irene* in 1749, had no appreciation of music or opera, couldn't dance, rarely drank, and was bored by cards and games. Without these diversions, he concentrated on the stimulus of learned conversation. He craved, above all, the *"animated reciprocation of Ideas,"* which enabled him to display before an appreciative audience his intellect and his wit.

Like Dryden in *The Lives of the Poets*, Johnson "did not offer his conversation, because he expected it to be solicited." He was, as Fielding said of a character in *Tom Jones*, "like a ghost, [who] only wanted to be spoke to" and then "readily answered."[11] Once jump-started, however, he shot out amusing and sometimes devastating salvoes. He said of a bothersome acquaintance, "I never did the man an injury; yet he would read his tragedy to me." Asked to join friends on a visit to Westminster Abbey and thinking it might be his final resting place, he replied, "No . . . not while I can keep out." Sometimes Johnson's own verbal faux pas enraged him. Defending a certain woman, he insisted she "had a bottom of good sense." Boswell said "the word *bottom* thus introduced, was so ludicrous when contrasted with his gravity, that most of us could not forbear tittering and laughing." Furious that he'd provoked ridicule and determined to exercise despotic power, Johnson dug himself into a deeper hole by suggesting the word "anus." "Where's the merriment?" he asked, then slowly pronounced, "I say the *woman* was *fundamentally* sensible."[12]

Johnson could talk brilliantly on any subject that came up and could argue, with the perverse virtuosity of a lawyer, on either side of an issue. He often began a statement contrary-wise, with "No, Sir," and his opponent's rejoinder, no matter how reasonable, sounded rather feeble after his thunderous argument. Boswell recorded that Johnson even defended the horrors of the Spanish Inquisition, maintaining that "false doctrine should be checked on its first appearance; that the civil power should unite with the church in punishing those who dared to attack the established religion." As he wrote of Dryden in *The Lives of the Poets*, "when once he had engaged himself in disputation, thoughts flowed in on either side: he was no longer at a loss; he had always objections and solutions at command."

Johnson liked to think of himself as good-humored and polite, but he had a talent for invective and with astonishing rapidity thought up humiliating rebukes and crushing put-downs. He could, if irritated (and it was all too easy to irritate him), be as cruel as Swift and as caustic as Voltaire. He had an instinctive need to provoke and to shock, and his personal insults were the verbal equivalent of his physical violence. He observed in the *Ramblers* that every man, like "every animal, revenges his pain on those who happen to be near," and that passionate men (like himself) are "provoked on every slight occasion, to vent their rage in vehement and fierce vociferations, in furious menaces and licentious reproaches."[13]

Arthur Murphy, appalled by his frightening outbursts, called Johnson "a stranger to the arts of polite conversation; uncouth, vehement, and vociferous." Boswell, more forgiving and more perceptive, explained that Johnson was not only deeply disturbed by his own inner struggles, but also vented his rage at the intolerable foolishness and heartbreaking injustice in the world: "Johnson's harsh attacks on his friends arise from uneasiness within. There is an insurrection aboard. His loud explosions are guns of distress."

He was not above lowlife exchanges. When a Thames boatman attacked him with coarse raillery, Johnson retaliated by piling up insults. He shouted, "your wife, *under pretence of keeping a bawdy-house,* is a receiver of stolen goods"—and let the boatman determine whether it was worse to be a whore or a thief. But most of his cutting remarks were more subtle. Dr. Bernard maintained that no man could improve after the age of forty-five. Johnson riposted that "there was great room for improvement in him, and he wished that he would set about it."[14] A pompous gentleman coming out of a service in Lichfield Cathedral said, "'Dr. Johnson, we have had a most excellent discourse to-day!' 'That may be,' said Johnson, 'but it is impossible you should know it.'" A cheeky young gentleman, slightly drunk, resolved to bait him (as people often did) by asking: "'what would you give, old gentleman, to be as young and sprightly as I am?' 'Why, Sir,' said he, 'I think I would almost be content to be as foolish.'"

Women, as well as complacent and presumptuous men, could also be the victims of his sudden blasts. Pressed to read and comment on the work of a tedious female, who said she had no time to correct it herself because she had so many irons in the fire, he shot out: "then, Madam, I would advise you to put this where your *Irons* are." Women who'd been trying to be kind were especially shocked and frightened by his outbursts. Frances Reynolds, though sympathetic to Johnson, recalled an occasion when he made free with the name of the Lord. When the lady in a country house "was pressing him to eat something, he rose up with his knife in hand, and loudly exclaim'd, 'I vow to God I cannot eat a bit more,' to the great terror of all the company."[15] After another woman said she'd been deeply affected by the tender sentiments in a novel by Laurence Sterne, Johnson, who thought Sterne an irreverent clergyman, crushed her with, "that is, because, dearest, you're a dunce." When she complained (as few people ever did) that he'd been rude, he disingenuously replied: "Madam, if I had thought so, I certainly should not have said it." No wonder, then, when a puzzled woman asked him why he was not courted by the great and invited to dine at their tables, he bluntly explained, without the slightest admission that his behavior was improper, "because, madam, great lords and ladies do not like to have their mouths stopped."

One of Johnson's most devastating rejoinders, which annihilated a balding, high-voiced, timorous young clergyman and supposedly ended his promising career, was described in Max Beerbohm's amusing fantasia "A Clergyman" (1918). Beerbohm first quoted Boswell's anecdote: "Boswell. 'What sermons afford the best specimens of English pulpit eloquence?' Johnson. 'We have no sermons addressed to the passions that are good for any thing; if you mean that kind of eloquence.' A Clergyman (whose name I do not recollect). 'Were not [William] Dodd's sermons addressed to the passions?' Johnson. 'They were nothing, Sir, be they addressed to what they may.'" Beerbohm then added his own gloss: "The suddenness of it! Bang!—and the rabbit that had popped from its burrow was no more. I know not which is the more startling—the début of the unfortunate clergyman, or the instanta-neousness of his end."[16] Beerbohm's vignette was doubly ironic. Johnson contradicted the mild query of a clergyman, a profession he usually respected; and though the clergyman could not know it, Johnson himself had written Dodd's last prison sermon before he was executed for forgery.

Many victims who lacked Boswell's resiliency limped away from Johnson's attacks, licking their wounds and believing he'd been a bully and a boor. His cutting comments, however, were not made merely to vent his spleen, but to teach a moral lesson. They were usually incited, as he wrote in *Rambler* 40, not to gratify his pride "by the mortification of another," but to improve mankind "by the hopes of reforming faults." As we saw in his disputes with Beauclerk and Percy, Johnson usually felt sorry when he drew blood and made conciliatory gestures to the injured party. As Boswell learned from painful experience, "when he did say a severe thing, it was generally extorted by ignorance pretending to knowledge, or by extreme vanity or affectation."[17]

15

BANDYING CIVILITIES
1765–1772

I

I t's surprising, in view of Johnson's statement that biography "enchains the heart by irresistible interest," that he neither wrote about Shakespeare's life and character nor saw any parallels between the playwright's life and his own. Yet the two authors had a great deal in common. Both were born in the Midlands; and Shakespeare's Stratford, in Warwickshire, was only about thirty-five miles south of Johnson's Lichfield, in the adjacent county of Staffordshire. Their fathers' families were socially inferior to those of their mothers. Shakespeare's father used leather for glove making; Johnson's father used it for bookbinding. Shakespeare's father was fined for engaging in illegal wool trade; Johnson's father was fined for illegal tanning. Both fathers owned substantial houses in town; and both fathers, liked and trusted by their townsmen, held a series of municipal offices before becoming bailiff (or mayor).

Both fathers lost their social standing, through business failures and financial difficulties, just at the time their sons were becoming adults. Shakespeare was unable to attend Oxford; Johnson dropped out after a year. Both authors married older, wealthier wives, left their wives behind when they went to London, and were separated from them for long periods of time. Johnson's statement that Shakespeare "came to London a needy adventurer, and lived for a time by very mean employments," and Stephen Greenblatt's account of Shakespeare, "a young man from a small provincial town—a man without independent wealth, without powerful family connections, and without a university education—moves to London in the late 1580s," describes the countrified background and early careers of both authors.

In April 1745 Johnson had published his *Miscellaneous Observations on the Tragedy of Macbeth,* including his proposal for a new edition of the plays to be brought out by his old publisher Edmund Cave. This sixty-four-page pamphlet gave a sample of his editorial method, with notes on specific passages and general comments on *Macbeth,* that was intended to entice subscribers. But the project was blocked by the influential bookseller Jacob Tonson, who claimed that he owned the copyright of all of Shakespeare's works and threatened to defend his valuable property with an expensive lawsuit in Chancery.

Johnson later reprinted his original notes on *Macbeth,* with a few changes, in his 1765 edition of the plays. He was drawn to the speech in which Lady Macbeth says, "Yet do I fear thy nature; / It is too full o' the milk of human kindness / To catch the nearest way" (1.5.17–19), and echoed the last phrase in two of his best-known works. In *Rasselas,* Imlac warns the hero not to "consult only our own policy, and attempt to find a nearer way." And in one of his best poems, "On the Death of Dr. Robert Levet," Johnson concludes more positively: "Death broke at once the vital chain, / And free'd his soul the nearest way."[1]

Ten years after his first proposal for an edition, Johnson returned to this project and in June 1756 published his "Proposals for Printing, by Subscription, the Dramatick Works of William Shakespeare" (the poems were not included). This time Tonson, along with Longman and other publishers, sponsored the work of the now famous lexicographer. Johnson promised to finish his edition in eighteen months, but (as with the *Dictionary*) he actually took nine years. While working on the *Dictionary,* he was writing the *Rambler* and Tetty died; while working on his *Works of Shakespeare,* he was writing the *Idler* and his mother died.

As with the early "Plan" and late "Preface" for the *Dictionary*, Johnson wrote early "Proposals" for Shakespeare and, many years later, a more substantial "Preface" to Shakespeare in October 1765. In his "Proposals" he sensibly stated that the business of the textual editor was twofold: to "correct what is corrupt, and to explain what is obscure." Johnson's primary task was to establish a correct text. During Shakespeare's lifetime eighteen of his plays were published in Quartos, often with extremely corrupt texts based on the faulty memories of members of the cast. The First Folio of 1622–23 published thirty-six plays, eighteen for the first time, and arranged them into comedies, histories and tragedies. Three other Folios appeared, in 1632, 1663 and 1685. In the eighteenth century, editions of Shakespeare had been produced by Nicholas Rowe (1709), Alexander Pope (1725), Lewis Theobold (1733), Thomas Hanmer (1744) and William Warburton (1747). Johnson was the first editor to recognize the authority of the First Folio, and restored many passages from that superior text. But he did not compare all the earlier texts to determine which was closest to what Shakespeare actually wrote. A modern scholar noted that "although he had undertaken, in 1756, to make a completely fresh collation of the texts, Johnson did no such thing, but, like other eighteenth-century editors, printed from his predecessors' texts, notably Warburton's 1747 edition and the 1757 reissue of Theobold."

Johnson succeeded very well, however, in completing the secondary task of explaining obscure words, expressions and allusions. The method announced in the "Proposals" was also clear and straightforward: "when any obscurity arises from an allusion to some other book, the passage will be quoted. When the diction is entangled, it will be cleared by a paraphrase or interpretation." Of the 116,000 quotations in the *Dictionary*, about a third of the poetical ones came from Shakespeare. So the *Dictionary* was an essential source for his editing and supplied definitions for many of Shakespeare's words. Previous editors had ignorantly and recklessly changed Shakespeare's lines; Johnson's unrivaled understanding of Elizabethan English enabled him to respect and preserve the text.

Later on, in the "Preface," Johnson explained why the texts of the plays were so unreliable. Shakespeare, indifferent to fame, had published no collection of his works in his lifetime. Since it was always easier to alter than to explain, Johnson's predecessors had corrupted many passages in the plays. Johnson himself, reluctant to make emendations and remaining faithful to the original texts, hoped to get closer to Shakespeare's real words and true intentions. The "Preface" also set forth Johnson's ideal standards: "In perusing a corrupted piece, [the editor] must have before him all possibilities of meaning, with all possibilities of expression. Such must be his comprehension of thought, and such his copiousness of language. Out of many readings possible, he must be able to select that which best suits with the state, opinions, and modes of language prevailing in every age, and with his authour's particular cast of thought, and turn of expression." In 1910 Walter Raleigh praised Johnson's editorial principles: "the whole duty of a Shakespearean commentator and critic is here. The complete collation of early editions; the tracing of Shakespeare's knowledge to its sources; the elucidation of obscurities by a careful study of the language and customs of Shakespeare's time; the comparison of Shakespeare's work with that of other great poets, ancient and modern."[2]

Johnson realized the difficulty of his task, and in a noble passage, which compared the progress of knowledge to a contest between light and darkness, observed that "the tide of seeming knowledge which is poured over one generation, retires and leaves another naked and barren; the sudden meteors of intelligence which for a while appear to shoot their beams into the regions of obscurity, on a sudden withdraw their lustre, and leave mortals again to grope their way." He concluded by justly summarizing his achievement: "not a single passage in the whole work has appeared to me corrupt, which I have not attempted to restore; or obscure, which I have not endeavoured to illustrate." But, with a characteristic metaphor of struggle, he modestly admitted his limitations: "in many [places] I have failed like others; and from many, after all my efforts, I have retreated, and confessed the repulse." Though Johnson was not always able to fulfill his editorial ideals, he came closer than any of his predecessors to achieving his ambitions.

Johnson's edition of Shakespeare drew him back into Garrick's world, and their relations, as always, were rather strained. They had diametrically opposed ideas about Shakespeare. Johnson wanted to preserve the

most accurate text; Garrick changed the plays at will. As the leading
producer and actor of his time, Garrick was instrumental in reviving, in-
terpreting and popularizing Shakespeare. At Drury Lane, between 1747
and 1776, "Garrick averaged forty-four performances of Shakespeare annually . . . produced twenty-eight different Shakespearean plays, and he
himself assumed eighteen Shakespearean roles." Garrick constantly
avowed his admiration for Shakespeare's genius, yet cut and chopped
the plays to suit himself.

A modern critic wrote, "Garrick's attitude towards Shakespeare was
as inconsistent as it was reprehensible. When, in 1756, he compressed
The Winter's Tale into the limits of an afterpiece (styled *Florizel and
Perdita*), he mendaciously avowed in his prologue: ''Tis my chief
wish, my joy, my only plan, / To lose no drop of that immortal man.'
. . . His abbreviation of *The Taming of the Shrew* held the stage to the
utter exclusion of the original for a century."[3] Garrick thought his
own versions of the plays were superior to Shakespeare's. He cut out
the Fool and wrote a happy ending to *King Lear,* in which Edgar marries Cordelia. He also boasted, when he put on *Hamlet,* "I rescued
that noble play from all the rubbish of the 5th act. I have brought it
forth without the grave Diggers, Ostrick, & the Fencing Match." As
the great classical scholar Richard Bentley said of Pope's translation of
the *Iliad,* though "it is a pretty poem, Mr. Pope, you must not call it
Homer."

Johnson also quarreled with his old friend about using Garrick's
valuable collection of Shakespeare's plays. The bookseller's son was
notorious for his rough treatment of books. He wrote in them, bent
back their spines, threw them face down on the dusty floor, stained
them with food and failed to return them to their owners. Garrick did
let Johnson use his library while working on his edition and also
helped by reading the proof sheets. But Johnson nevertheless resented
Garrick's prudent unwillingness to lend his precious rare books. When
Boswell asked why Johnson didn't thank Garrick in his "Preface,"
Johnson, touchy as ever, bombarded him with many reasons for his refusal: "I would not disgrace my page with a player. Garrick has been

liberally paid for mouthing Shakespeare. . . . He has not made Shakespeare better known. He cannot illustrate ["explain"] Shakespeare. He does not understand him. Besides, Garrick got me no subscriptions. He did not furnish me with his old plays. I asked to have them, and I think he sent me one. It was not worth while to ask again."

In September 1769, four years after the publication of Johnson's *Plays of William Shakespeare*, Garrick staged an extravagant, vulgar and rather dismal Shakespeare Jubilee in Stratford. (Boswell drew attention to himself and added to the absurdity by appearing in the outlandish regalia of a Corsican chieftain.) Brian Vickers pointed out that the Jubilee "was not a serious cultural event—there was no theatre in Stratford, and no Shakespeare play was or could be performed. With a firework display, an oratorio, a public breakfast, a ball, an elaborate procession of 217 people, 170 of them dressed as Shakespeare's characters, it was more like a popular pageant or annual festival."[4] Several of the events were ruined by fierce thunderstorms and heavy floods. Johnson, the greatest living authority on Shakespeare, foresaw the foolishness and was notably absent from the festivities.

II

In the "Preface" to his edition of Shakespeare, completed in the summer of 1765, Johnson magnificently rose to the occasion, defining the art and spirit of Shakespeare more fully and sympathetically than anyone had done before. He began by asking why, despite all Shakespeare's imperfections (according to contemporary notions of drama and taste), his work had had such enduring appeal. Johnson's Shakespeare is a dramatic realist who mingles tragic and comic styles, a master of character and of the English language, whose poetry was written by a man who "sees with his own eyes." Yet Johnson does not hero-worship his subject. The essay works so well because he engages so completely with Shakespeare, applying his own cultural and moral biases, finding plenty to criticize, and developing fruitful and fascinating contradictions. Many of his ideas—innovative and original in his own time—have been so completely assimilated into our thinking about the plays that they now seem familiar, even obvious.

For Johnson, Shakespeare is the creator of living characters with real feelings. He is "above all writers . . . the poet of nature; the poet that holds up to his readers a faithful mirrour of manners and of life." Contrasting Shakespeare with contemporary dramatists, who focus on love alone, Johnson praises his realization that all human passions can inspire great drama. His characters endure because they are a species, while in other authors they are merely individuals. His characters are so credible and his stories so representative that his plays guide us in the conduct of our lives. No matter what the setting or story, "Shakespeare approximates [brings closer] the remote, and familiarizes the wonderful."

Confronting the vexed question of genre, Johnson defends Shakespeare against critics like Voltaire, who accused him of violating the Aristotelian unities of time, place and plot. The mixture of comic and tragic scenes, he argues, is intrinsic to Shakespeare's realism, and his comprehensive genius allows him to violate every rule and get away with it. Johnson learned from his own experience with the disastrous *Irene,* and realized the limitations of severely constricted plays like Addison's *Cato.* Appealing to common sense, he writes that since the theater is a real, not illusory, place, it was dramatically acceptable to break the stranglehold of the unities: "the truth is, that the spectators are always in their senses, and know, from the first act to the last, that the stage is only a stage, and that the players are only players. . . . The different actions that compleat a story may be in places very remote from each other; and where is the absurdity of allowing that space to represent first Athens, and then Sicily, which was always known to be neither Sicily nor Athens, but a modern theatre." Johnson acknowledged that the play existed not only for readers of the page, but also for spectators in the theater.

Johnson believed the comedies were more intuitive than learned and superior to the tragedies. "In tragedy," Johnson wrote, "Shakespeare is always struggling after some occasion to be comick, but in comedy he seems to repose, or to luxuriate, as in a mode of thinking congenial to his nature. In his tragick scenes there is always something wanting, but his comedy often surpasses expectation or desire.

His comedy pleases by the thoughts and the language, and his tragedy for the greater part by incident and action. His tragedy seems to be skill, his comedy to be instinct." In a perceptive comment that illuminates Johnson's humane preference, W. H. Auden noted, "the difference between Shakespeare's tragedies and comedies is not that the characters suffer in the one and not in the other, but that in comedy the suffering leads to self-knowledge, repentance, forgiveness, love, and in tragedy it leads in the opposite direction into self-blindness, defiance, hatred."[5]

Living in what he believed to be a more refined society than Shakespeare's, Johnson maintained that "the English nation, in the time of Shakespeare, was yet struggling to emerge from barbarity." His cultural bias explains his criticism of what he took to be Shakespeare's faults: his gross jests and licentious repartee, particularly between men and women; his pompous and overelaborate diction, and tendency to let puns and wordplay run away with him; his loosely designed and frequently improbable plots; and, most important, his lack of explicit moral instruction. "He makes no just distribution of good and evil," Johnson remarked. "He sacrifices virtue to convenience, and is so much more careful to please than to instruct, that he seems to write without any moral purpose."[6] Yet Shakespeare must be given credit, he argued, for arousing the interest of both illiterate and learned audiences. In a sense Johnson admires the teeming characters and meandering plots, the "hustle" on stage that makes the plays successful.

The "Preface," though shrewd and illuminating, is full of unintentional contradictions. The Elizabethan age was barbaric, yet Shakespeare represents the very pinnacle of English literature. He did not offer moral instruction, but his plays guide the conduct of our lives. The comedies were superior, yet Johnson was more deeply affected by the tragedies. The tragedies were forced and wanting, yet were unendurably moving. He knew the stage and actors were not real, yet could scarcely bear to see the most tragic scenes.

In addition to the "Preface," Johnson's major contribution to Shakespeare studies was his elucidation of difficult passages (many of them now incorporated into the explanatory notes of modern editions) and his concluding comments on each of the plays. Some of his remarks were surprisingly personal. His comment on the tailor in *King John,* who hastily puts his shoes on the wrong feet, said more about Johnson's slovenly dress than about his critical insight: "he that is frighted or hurried may put his hand into the wrong glove, but either shoe will equally admit either foot." He said the lines in *Cymbeline*—"Your Highness / Shall from this practice but make hard your heart," spoken by the herbalist to the queen, who intends to test poisons on animals—required no explanation. But Johnson could not resist elaborating his comment and reaffirming his angry protest, in *Idler* 17, against cruelty to animals. Shakespeare's "thought would probably have been more amplified, had our authour lived to be shocked with such experiments as have been published . . . by a race of men that have practised tortures without pity, and related them without shame, and yet suffered to erect their heads among human beings."

Johnson concluded his remarks on the far-fetched plot of *Cymbeline* —which includes a secret marriage, improbable wager, attempted murder, sexual disguise, revival after death, a headless corpse and prophetic documents—with his most exasperated and extreme condemnation of any play: "to remark the folly of the fiction, the absurdity of the conduct, the confusion of the names and manners of different times, and the impossibility of the events in any system of life, were to waste criticism upon irresisting imbecility, upon faults too evident for detection, and too gross for aggravation."[7]

It's fascinating to see Johnson's adventurous intellect grappling with the complex and often elusive meaning of the major tragedies. He found scenes that were unbearable to read even more unbearable when acted on stage. The greater the performance, the more excruciating the effect on him. As a boy, he'd been terrified by reading the ghost scene in *Hamlet* that "chills the blood with horror," and had rushed outside to calm his fears. As a man, he was still frightened and overwhelmed by the power of his own vivid and hypersensitive imagination. He wrote that in the description of night in *Macbeth*—with its dead nature, wicked dreams and rampant witchcraft—"nothing but sorcery, lust, and murder, is awake. . . . He that peruses Shakespeare, looks round alarmed, and starts to find himself alone."

In his discussion of the scene in *King Lear* when Edgar and the blind Gloucester are supposedly on the cliffs of Dover, Johnson vividly reveals how Shakespeare achieves his effects by placing the tragic characters in the context of men and nature: "he that looks from a precipice finds himself assailed by one great and dreadful image of irresistible destruction. But . . . the enumeration of the choughs and crows, the samphire-man and the fishers, counteracts the great effect of the prospect, as it peoples the desert of intermediate vacuity, and stops the mind in the rapidity of its descent through emptiness and horrour."

Johnson repeatedly asserted that the most horrific scenes in Shakespeare were so shocking that one could hardly bear to read or see them. He noted that extreme horror risked alienating the audience, who might reject the scene as unrealistic, even absurd. The tearing out of Gloucester's eyes in *King Lear* "seems an act too horrid to be *endured* in dramatick exhibition, and such as must always compel the mind to relieve its distress by incredulity." He was deeply disturbed by the hanging of the virtuous Cordelia at the end of *King Lear*, which was "contrary to the natural idea of justice," and added a personal note: "I was many years ago so shocked by Cordelia's death, that I know not whether I ever *endured* to read again the last scenes of the play till I undertook to revise ["re-examine"] them as an editor." In a similar way, he wrote of Othello's murder of the innocent Desdemona, "I am glad I have ended my revisal of this dreadful scene. It is not to be *endured*."[8]

Johnson's characterization of Polonius in *Hamlet*—the rather pompous windbag, father of Ophelia and Laertes—first elevated him with praise and then deflated him with a final alliterative description: "Polonius is a man bred in courts, exercised in business, stored with observation, confident of his knowledge, proud of his eloquence, and declining into dotage." His analysis of the tragic characters in *Othello* is valuable for both its sublime style and its critical penetration, which suggests the depth of meaning in the play. Othello and Desdemona were fatally entwined, and contrasted with Iago by the word "artless"; and Johnson himself shared the hero's boundless confidence, ardent affection for his friends and inflexible resolution:

The beauties of this play impress themselves so strongly upon the attention of the reader, that they can draw no aid from critical illustration. The fiery openness of Othello, magnanimous, artless, and credulous, boundless in his confidence, ardent in his affection, inflexible in his resolution, and obdurate in his revenge; the cool malignity of Iago, silent in his resentment, subtle in his designs, and studious at once of his interest and his vengeance; the soft simplicity of Desdemona, confident of merit, and conscious of innocence, her artless perseverance in her suit, and her slowness to suspect that she can be suspected, are such proofs of Shakespeare's skill in human nature, as, I suppose, it is vain to seek in any modern writer.

Johnson had been awarded an honorary M.A. degree from Oxford just before the publication of the *Dictionary*; in July 1765 he received an honorary LL.D. degree from Trinity College, Dublin (which had refused to grant him a degree in 1739) just before the publication of his *Plays of William Shakespeare*. The edition, eight volumes in octavo, had a first printing of 1,000 copies. The unconscionably long delay in publication left Johnson vulnerable and provoked his enemies. Portraying Johnson as the unscrupulous Pomposo, the satiric poet Charles Churchill penned some wicked couplets in *The Ghost* (1762):

He for *Subscribers* baits his hook,
And takes their cash—but where's the Book?
No matter where—*Wise* fear, we know,
Forbids the robbing of a Foe,
But what, to serve our private ends,
Forbids the cheating of our Friends?[9]

This attack seemed to have had a positive effect, rousing Johnson from his sloth and encouraging him (three years later) to fulfill his contractual obligations.

When the edition finally appeared, Johnson amusingly but disingenuously—since the publisher must have known who the subscribers were—told Boswell why he hadn't followed the common practice of the time: "I have two very cogent reasons for not printing any list of subscribers [in the book];—one, that I have lost all the names,—the other, that I have spent all the money." For his arduous editorial work, he received the modest sum of £375 for the first edition, and an additional £100 for the second edition in 1768. He revised both the 4th edition of the *Dictionary* and the 3rd edition of the *Plays of William Shakespeare* in 1773.

Though Johnson's editing surpassed his eighteenth-century predecessors, he did not add much to our knowledge of Shakespeare's life, contemporaries or theater. Yet the "Preface" remains an influential landmark in Shakespeare studies. Johnson's majestic abstractions and formal criticism fell out of favor in the next century, and in 1817 the Romantic critic William Hazlitt wrote condescendingly, "we have a high respect for Dr. Johnson's character and understanding, mixed with something like personal attachment: but he was neither a poet nor a judge of poetry." By contrast, the French novelist Stendhal paid silent tribute to Johnson by incorporating a considerable portion of his "Preface" into his romantic manifesto, *Racine et Shakespeare* (1822). In a balanced judgment, the modern scholar Jacob Isaacs has justly concluded, "the faults of his edition are atoned for by his magnificent critical preface and comments on individual plays, [and] by his pioneer recognition that only the first of the folios has textual authority."[10]

III

Johnson's edition of Shakespeare solidified the reputation that he'd built with the *Rambler,* the *Dictionary* and *Rasselas,* and he was in great demand in the fashionable world. No man in the highly stratified society of eighteenth-century England moved more easily than Johnson from his own humble household to the exalted sphere of bishops, lords and kings. The literary lion and weird eccentric dined out as frequently as Henry James did in Edwardian England. During the week of January 11, 1771, between bouts of copious bleeding by his doctors, he was engaged seven times—with his personal physician, Dr. Thomas Lawrence, and with Reynolds, Langton, the poet Thomas Warton, the bishop of Chester and two ladies, wives of an MP and of a prosperous tallow-chandler.

In *Rambler* 21 Johnson wrote, "acquaintance with the great is generally considered as one of the chief privileges of literature and genius." In February 1767, five years after receiving his government pension, he was accorded this supreme privilege. He was a friend of Frederick Barnard, natural son of the Prince of Wales and royal librarian, and had often used the library, which was open to scholars, for his work on Shakespeare. King George III had expressed a desire to converse with him on his next visit. At that time, before he contracted porphyria, went mad and lost the American colonies, the king was personable, well educated and quite rational. A modern historian described him as "tall, well made, with a fair fresh coloring, blue eyes, good teeth, and light-auburn hair"—though his eyes were protuberant and his jowls fleshy. Unlike his Hanoverian predecessors, he spoke good English and had excellent manners.

After informing the twenty-nine-year-old king of Johnson's presence and finding the monarch at leisure, Barnard led the way by candlelight through a suite of rooms and entered the library by a private door, to which the king had the key. The magnificent library of 65,000 volumes, each one finely bound and stamped with the royal coat of arms, was located in the queen's house, on the present site of Buckingham Palace. It had a high vaulted ceiling decorated with rosettes, towering twelve-foot-tall stacks, expansive reading tables, a huge map case and a high white marble fireplace.

Johnson was deep in study when Barnard bent over to whisper, "'Sir, here is the King.' Johnson started up, and stood still. His Majesty approached him, and at once was courteously easy." The king, in fact, was more nervous than Johnson himself, and had approached the interview, like a schoolboy to his task, with a mixture

of eagerness and reluctance. Their wide-ranging talk concerned Johnson's recent visit to Oxford, the state of the university libraries, his
extensive reading, the learned bishop William Warburton, Lord Lyttleton's recently published *History*, the fashionable quack Dr. John
Hill, literary journals, and learned publications like the *Journal des
Savans* and the *Philosophical Transactions*.

The most important part of the conversation, Boswell reported,
focused on Johnson's work. The king asked if he were writing anything,
and Johnson replied he was not. He had told the world what he knew
and now had to stock his head with more books to acquire more knowledge. He thought he had already "done his part as a writer. 'I should
have thought so too, (said the King), if you had not written so well.'"
When asked if he replied to this compliment, Johnson answered, "No,
Sir. When the King had said it, it was to be so. It was not for me to
bandy civilities with my Sovereign." Knowing Johnson's greatest strength
and wanting to encourage him, "His Majesty expressed a desire to have
the literary biography of this country ably executed, and proposed to Dr.
Johnson to undertake it. Johnson signified his readiness to comply with
his Majesty's wishes."[11] Thus were planted, in the royal palace and a
decade before he actually began work, the seeds that eventually grew
into *The Lives of the Poets*.

Two years later Johnson moved from polite conversation in a palace
to desperate maneuvers in a prison. He had known Giuseppe Baretti,
the distinguished author of the standard *Italian-English Dictionary*,
since Baretti had first arrived in London in the early 1750s. On the
night of October 6, 1769, while walking in the Haymarket, Baretti was
accosted by a prostitute who, as he said in court, "clapped her hands
with such violence about my private parts, that it gave me great pain."
Frightened and hurt by her aggressive way of soliciting business, the
nearsighted Baretti struck out at her. The woman screamed for help
and he was attacked by three ruffians. Baretti tried to run away, but
was pursued and caught by the men who were (he said) "continually
beating and pushing me." Surrounded and threatened, he pulled out
his knife, "gave a quick blow to one who beat off my hat with his fist"
and stabbed him in the chest.

After the brawl, Baretti rushed into a shop, called for help and was arrested. Accused of assaulting and wounding one of his attackers, Evan Morgan, he was committed to prison to await trial. Two days later, Morgan died of his stab wound and Baretti was charged with murder. An Italian scholar, one of his visitors in prison, subjected him to a bit of gallows humor. He asked him for a letter of recommendation, which he planned to present to Baretti's former pupils after he was hanged. "You rascal," replied the furious prisoner, ready to commit another murder, "if I were not *in my own apartment,* I would kick you down stairs directly."

The situation looked grim for Baretti, who seemed to be the classic example of a treacherous Italian armed with a hidden stiletto. In his address to the court, possibly written by Johnson, the fifty-year-old scholar argued that despite his concealed weapon, he was merely defending himself and certainly had no murderous intent: "I hope your Lordship . . . will think that a man of my age, character, and way of life, would not spontaneously quit my pen to engage in an outrageous tumult. I hope it will easily be conceived, that a man almost blind could not but be seized with terror on such a sudden attack as this. I hope it will be seen, that my knife was neither a weapon of offence or defence: I wear it to carve fruit and sweetmeats, and not to kill my fellow-creatures."[12]

All the leading members of the Club—Johnson, Burke, Reynolds, Goldsmith, Garrick and Beauclerk—loyally rallied round and turned the prison cell into their meeting room. Hester Thrale noted the emotional scene: "when Johnson & Burke went to see Baretti in Newgate, they had small Comfort to give him, & bid him not hope too strongly:—*Why what can he fear* says Baretti, placing himself between 'em—*that holds two such hands as I do.*"

Well known for his short fuse, Baretti had previously characterized himself as "something of a savage and fearless wild beast . . . a fiery fellow who turns savage in a moment and whose hand flies to his sword." So the witnesses testifying for Baretti were forced to stretch the truth to free their friend. At the murder trial of Richard Savage in 1727, the witnesses (according to Johnson) had portrayed him as "a modest, inoffensive man, not inclined to broils, or to insolence, who had, to that time, been only known for his misfortunes and his wit." At the Old Bailey trial Johnson, an impressive witness, described the self-styled "savage beast" as a sober, tranquil and terribly shy scholar: "I began to be acquainted with Mr. Baretti about the year '53 or '54. I have been intimate with him. He is a man of literature and a very studious man, a man of great diligence. He gets his living by study. I have no reason to think he was ever disordered with liquor in his life. A man that I never knew to be otherwise than peaceable, and a man that I take to be rather timorous."[13] Recalling, no doubt, the line about the dangers of the city in his poem *London*—"Their Ambush here relentless Ruffians lay"—Johnson added in his cross-examination:

Question: Was he addicted to pick up women in the street?
Dr. Johnson: I never knew that he was.
Question: How is he as to his eye-sight?
Dr. Johnson: He does not see me now [from this distance], nor do
    I see him. I do not believe he could be capable of assaulting
    any body in the street, without great provocation.[14]

Johnson's testimony that Baretti was a mild, inoffensive character and carried a knife merely to cut fruit at dinner was not true. No Englishman carried a knife for that purpose. A naturally violent man, sorely provoked by a whore, Baretti probably overreacted and tried to kill his assailant. (We don't have the story of the two surviving ruffians, which would not, in any case, have carried much weight in court.) But after the judge heard the character references of his eminent friends, who justly argued that when trapped and beaten by a gang of criminals he was forced to defend himself as best he could, Baretti was acquitted.

While Baretti was being tried, Johnson was in the process of composing a series of law lectures for his friend Robert Chambers. In the eighteenth century most attorneys were considered rogues and cheats; and Johnson himself had inaugurated several centuries of lawyer jokes when he wittily said of a gentleman he'd met in an eating-house, "I do not like to traduce any Man—but I suspect he is an Attorney." Yet he'd once aspired to become an attorney and—hoping to improve social conditions for slaves, debtors, prostitutes and petty criminals threatened with capital punishment—took a keen interest in the law. He'd first met Robert Chambers when the shy, learned scholar was still an undergraduate at Oxford. In 1766 the insecure twenty-nine-year-old Chambers had succeeded the great jurist Sir William Blackstone as the second Vinerian professor of law at Oxford. To paraphrase the satiric couplet on Sir John Pringle, who succeeded Isaac Newton at Cambridge, "Chambers sat in Blackstone's chair / And wondered how the devil he got there." Overwhelmed and paralyzed by Blackstone's writings and reputation, and unable to fulfill his academic responsibilities, Chambers secretly sought Johnson's help in preparing the sixty lectures he was required to give each year.

Like many academics, then and now, Chambers wanted the prestige and benefits of the job without actually doing much work. Always willing to help a friend, Johnson agreed that Chambers, having assumed the Vinerian chair, was not morally or professionally obliged to write his own law lectures, any more than John Taylor had been obliged to compose the sermons that he preached. (Similarly, Americans today, though obsessed by plagiarism, don't believe that politicians or corporate executives are obliged to write the words they speak.)

Johnson had great difficulty beginning his own work, but was able to jump-start the law lectures for Chambers. Between 1766 and 1770, in London and in Oxford, he discussed, supervised and dictated many passages of the Vinerian lectures, an encyclopedic survey of British constitutional law, amounting to two stout volumes of more than 350,000 words. Though Hester Thrale was made privy to the pact, the ever-inquisitive Boswell was not told of Johnson's work. In fact, the secret was kept for two centuries, until E. L. McAdam brought out *Dr. Johnson and English Law* (1951), which tried to define Johnson's contribution on stylistic grounds. Johnson's work was not published until Thomas Curley's edition of the Johnson-Chambers *Course of Lectures in English Law, 1767–1773* (1986).

Curley wrote that "in all likelihood Johnson lacked the detailed technical learning to play the leading role in drafting the Vinerian course," and that "Chambers adapted any Johnsonian dictation to suit the style and sentiments of his discourses." In a useful summary, Curley noted that the ambitious lectures covered

in four parts the basic concepts, traditions, and statutes making up the British constitution. An eloquent Introduction of four lectures sets forth the metaphysical and quasi-utilitarian foundations of all law as well as the Saxon and Norman roots of the common law. Then follows Part I on the public law tracing the ancient and modern structure of the British government in sixteen lectures, which, like the preceding Introduction, contain legal assumptions found in Johnson's later political writings. Part II catalogues the criminal law in fourteen lectures, which, except for the underlying thesis of human malignity, seems generally contrary to Johnson's humane views on the subject. Finally Part III reviews the private law of property and equity.

A lecture on the nature of punishment in criminal law seems to express Johnson's views. He listed three objects of punishment: benefit to the offender through rehabilitation, benefit to the suffering party through reparation and benefit to the general public through increased security. He specifically condemned the right of private vengeance as "a principle so opposite to quiet, order, and security that every nation may be considered as more civilized and every government as nearer to perfection in proportion as it is more effectually repressed and extinguished."[15] After delivering these partially ghostwritten lectures, Chambers went on to a distinguished career in India. He was appointed to the Bengal supreme court in 1774, was knighted in 1778 and served as chief justice from 1789 to 1799.

IV

While Johnson was helping Chambers with his law lectures, he became involved in a sensational political controversy that concerned a vital question of constitutional law. His opponent was

John Wilkes, whom he'd called "an abusive scoundrel" during his
first meeting with Boswell in 1763. The son of a wealthy distiller,
Wilkes was born in 1727 and educated at Leiden University in Holland. He bought the parliamentary seat for Aylesbury in 1757 and became a colonel in the Buckinghamshire militia. Edward Gibbon said
Wilkes had "infinite wit and humour, and a great deal of knowledge;
but [was] a thorough profligate in principle as in practice." Well
known for his geniality, charm, flamboyance, irreverence and bravery (he'd fought in a duel), he became the most popular politician of
his time.

Wilkes' troubles started when he was arrested in April 1763 for seditious libel of King George III in number 45 of the *North Briton*. He
edited this journal with the poet Charles Churchill, who'd satirized
Johnson as Pomposo. In February 1764 Wilkes fled to France to avoid
trial for sedition and for publishing (but not writing) a parody of Pope's
Essay on Man, the pornographic *Essay on Women.* The thirteen copies
of this pamphlet, privately printed for the rakish and dissolute members of his Hellfire Club, featured a title page with an erect penis, an address of a "Dying Lover to His Prick" and a blasphemous skit on *Veni
creator spiritus* ("Come, Holy Spirit, Creator Blest"), one of the most
widely used hymns in the church. The House of Lords condemned this
pamphlet, which seemed to imitate the most outrageous poems of the
Earl of Rochester, as a "scandalous, obscene and impious libel."

Pressed for money and still an outlaw, Wilkes risked returning to
England in March 1768. He remained a popular hero and was elected
to Parliament for the county of Middlesex. But in April he was arrested and convicted of the old charge of seditious libel and obscenity, fined £1,000 and sentenced to twenty-two months in prison. His
imprisonment provoked cries of "Wilkes and Liberty" and considerable mob violence in London. Believing he'd lose his political influence if he were deprived of his seat in Parliament, the House of
Commons expelled him in February 1769, annulled each of his three
reelections and seated the opponent he had defeated.

Edmund Burke supported Wilkes in this controversy, in which the
power of the people to elect Members of Parliament opposed the power

of Parliament to determine its membership. As Burke's biographer wrote, "he was on the side of the people, who needed to be protected from a corrupt Court which was dead to all decency and shame. Burke took an active part in organizing petitions and protest meetings against the action of the House of Commons in the Middlesex Election dispute." Burke's *Thoughts on the Present Discontents* (April 1770) "defended the popular discontent, declaring that 'in all disputes between the people and their rulers the presumption was at least upon a par in favour of the people.'"[16]

The Whig prime minister Lord Bute called on Johnson to support the government's campaign against Wilkes, a task for which he was temperamentally and intellectually well suited. As the historian John Cannon wrote, "he was unsentimental about the past, disturbed by the present, and apprehensive for the future."[17] To Johnson, religious freethinkers, sexual libertines and political anarchists were the external manifestations of the dangerous chaos within him. "When sedition and uproar have once silenced law, and confounded property," he'd thundered in Sermon 23, "then is the hour when chance [rather than reason and order] begins to predominate in the world." His four major political pamphlets of the early 1770s, Roger Lonsdale observed, passionately defended his political ideals: "defence of government, obedience to lawful authority, subordination, and custom against Satanic forces of disorder, violence, irrationality, and rabble-rousing faction in the name of 'liberty' and 'patriotism.'" Johnson was surely thinking of Wilkes, whom he also attacked in *The Patriot* (1774), when in 1775 he called patriotism "the last refuge of a scoundrel."[18]

Johnson's *The False Alarm* (January 1770) was an attack on the mob's cry for liberty, which he thought an essentially mistaken concept. He argued that despite Wilkes' victory in the Middlesex election of April 1769, the House of Commons was the only judge of its own rights and had unlimited power to expel undesirable members. He asked, in a loaded question, "whether Middlesex shall be represented or not by a criminal from a jail," and violently condemned Wilkes' character and politics: "lampoon itself would disdain to speak ill of him of whom no man speaks well. It is sufficient that he is expelled [from] the House of Commons, and confined in jail as being legally convicted of sedition and impiety. . . . The expelled member cannot be admitted. He that cannot be admitted, cannot be elected, and the votes given to a man ineligible being given in vain, the highest number for an eligible candidate becomes a majority."[19]

In *A Letter to Samuel Johnson* (February 1770), his bitter response to *The False Alarm,* Wilkes attacked him for recanting his early denunciations of the Whig government, and wrote that in the *Life of Savage* he was "contented—*in the open air*—to growl at the *moon,* and Whigs, and [Sir Robert] Walpole, and the [German] House of Brunswick." Mocking Johnson's elephantine style and groveling to the present government, Wilkes called him "the spitter forth . . . of servility and bombast . . . [in] sesquipedalian documents," and condemned his "ignorance and absurdity," his "wicked, or ridiculous" principles. In a final twist of the knife, he accused Johnson of betraying his beliefs for a bribe: "the wages of prostitution, once tasted, are too delicious to be relinquished. . . . By a well-placed pension of *three hundred pounds a year* he has expiated his own sins and those of his country."[20] Despite physical ugliness, religious nonconformity, considerable debt (paid off by wealthy friends), criminal conviction and time in jail, Wilkes, acting as spokesman for the radical elements in the City, was elected alderman of London in 1769 and lord mayor in 1774. That year he was again elected to Parliament and finally regained his seat for Middlesex.

Johnson disliked Wilkes more intensely than any man he knew. But as a depraved and charming scoundrel, he must have reminded Johnson of similarly rakish friends who boldly acted out the impulses he forced himself to repress. Boswell loved to orchestrate volatile situations that set off Johnson's sparks and ignited his explosions. When Boswell wanted him to meet the controversial Whig historian Catherine Macaulay, Johnson—clouds gathering on his brow—saw through the ruse and replied: "No, Sir; you would not see us quarrel, to make you sport. Don't you know that it is very uncivil to *pit* two people against one another?"

Nevertheless, Johnson had dined with the cheeky actor Samuel Foote, whom he later threatened to thrash if Foote dared to mimic him on stage. He told Boswell how Foote's irresistible humor gradually melted his defensive sulkiness: "having no good opinion of the fellow, I was resolved not to be pleased; and it is very difficult to please a man against his will. I went on eating my dinner pretty sullenly, affecting not to mind him. But the dog was so very comical, that I was obliged to lay down my knife and fork, throw myself back upon my chair, and fairly laugh it out. No, Sir, he was irresistible."

Using his consummate diplomatic skills, Boswell arranged the potentially traumatic meeting between Johnson and Wilkes. He dared not make the proposal directly, for if he'd asked Johnson to dine with his adversary, he would have said, "Dine with Jack Wilkes, Sir! I'd as soon dine with [the hangman] Jack Ketch." But he persuaded Johnson to accept any company at dinner and overcame the obstacle of Johnson's previous engagement with Anna Williams. "When I had him fairly seated in a hackney-coach with me," Boswell wrote of his captive, "I exulted as much as a fortune-hunter who has got an heiress into a post-chaise with him to set out for Gretna-Green" (just over the border in Scotland, where legal marriages—without license, banns or priest—could be quickly arranged).

At the publisher Charles Dilly's house and using Johnson's gargantuan appetite as a lure, Wilkes, determined to charm and please him "against his will," played the attentive and obsequious servant. Boswell described the dinner, on May 15, 1776, as if it were a seduction scene in a witty Restoration comedy by William Wycherley or William Congreve:

Mr. Wilkes placed himself next to Dr. Johnson, and behaved to him with so much attention and politeness, that he gained upon him insensibly. No man eat more heartily than Johnson, or loved better what was nice and delicate. Mr. Wilkes was very assiduous in helping him to some fine veal. "Pray give me leave, Sir:—It is better here—A little of the brown—Some fat, Sir—A little of the stuffing—Some gravy—Let me have the pleasure of giving you some butter—Allow me to recommend a squeeze of this orange; —or the lemon, perhaps, may have more zest." "Sir, Sir, I am obliged to you, Sir," cried Johnson, bowing and turning his head to him with a look for some time of "surly virtue," but, in a short while, of complacency.[21]

Boswell brought this comic scene to life by describing Wilkes cunningly creeping up on his prey and playing on the great man's weakness; by the delicious details and ingratiating tone; by transforming Johnson, fattened by food and flattery, from surly to sociable and even pleasant. Johnson, of course, saw through Wilkes' deception, but *enjoyed* being seduced by the villain. By meeting Wilkes man to man, he was able to overcome their personal and political differences.

In March 1771, fourteen months after the controversy with Wilkes, Johnson published another major political pamphlet, *Thoughts on the Late Transactions Respecting Falkland's Islands.* The dispute was a complicated residue of the Seven Years' War. After a quarrel over these remote and barren islands in the South Atlantic Ocean, 300 miles east of the Strait of Magellan, Spain had agreed to give up Port Egmont in the Falklands, which she'd recently captured from the English settlers, but did not grant sovereignty of the islands to Britain. Some chauvinistic British politicians, who felt Spain had insulted the navy, wanted to declare war on Spain to preserve "national honour." Johnson, always opposed to colonial adventures and foreign wars, argued that the government wanted to start a pointless war and gain useless land for no other reason than commercial profit: "the whole system of European empire can be in danger of a new concussion, by a contention for a few spots of earth, which, in the deserts of the ocean, had almost escaped human notice."

Warming to his subject, he majestically described the Falklands as "a bleak and gloomy solitude, an island thrown aside from human use, stormy in winter, and barren in summer; an island which not the southern savages have dignified with habitation; where a garrison must be kept in a state that contemplates with envy the exiles of Siberia." Emphasizing the human cost of war, which politicians habitually ignored,

Johnson described the fate of soldiers and sailors in recent wars with France and Spain. After a horrible death, they were denied a proper burial and a lasting memorial, and "were at last whelmed in pits, or heaved into the ocean, and without notice and without remembrance."[22] In the end, Johnson's views prevailed, though not on rational or humanitarian grounds. Spain backed down after France refused to support her; Madrid renounced the actions of Spanish officials in the Falklands, and the useless, unprofitable islands reverted to wasteland.[23]

16

DOMESTICK PLEASURES
1765–1772

I

Johnson's two monumental projects, the *Dictionary of the English Language* and his eight-volume edition of Shakespeare's plays, had occupied him for twenty years. After the *Dictionary*, Shakespeare had absorbed him; but after Shakespeare there was no comparable undertaking to engage his attention. By the spring of 1765, when his edition was nearly ready for the press, Johnson faced a great void in his life. While at work on the *Dictionary*, he had foreseen the inevitable depression that would overwhelm him. As he wrote in *Idler* 59, "any uncommon execution of strength, or perseverance in labour, is succeeded by a long interval of languor and weariness." After his *Plays of William Shakespeare* was published, Johnson could not enjoy his new liberty. With a comfortable pension, he no longer had to write for money, but he missed his familiar routine and worried when he had no project to work on. He was oppressed by what he called slothful idleness, gloomy leisure, vacant mind, endless worries and bad dreams, and realized that he had to stay occupied to keep his sanity. He was haunted by his two ever-present terrors: fear of madness in this world and of damnation in the next.

"From that kind of melancholy indisposition," he'd told Edmund Hector in 1756, "which I had when we lived together in Birmingham, I have never been free, but have always had it operating against my health and my Life with more or less violence." Johnson's melancholy, with its continuous series of paroxysms and remissions, could recur at any moment. At Easter he usually analyzed and recorded his mental and moral state. He anticipated the onset of another mental breakdown as early as Easter 1761, when he wrote in his *Diaries*: "I have led a life so dissipated [distracted] and useless, and my terrours and perplexities have so much encreased, that I am under great depression and discouragement." Four years later he seemed to be living in a miasma of self-reproach: "I have reformed no evil habit, my time has been unprofitably spent, and seems as a dream that has left nothing behind. My memory grows confused, and I know not how the days pass over me."[1]

In *Rasselas* Johnson had pronounced, as if it were a generally accepted truth, "of the uncertainties of our present state, the most dreadful and alarming is the uncertain continuance of reason." Surveying his past life as one of his Easter duties, he found nothing but anguish, "a barren waste of time with some disorders of body, and disturbances of the mind very near to madness." His pathologically negative account of his life, in a letter to Hester Thrale, sounded like the lamentations of Jeremiah— or of Franz Kafka. "Little has been done," he wrote, "and little has been enjoyed, in a life diversified by misery, spent part in the sluggishness of penury, and part under the violence of pain, in gloomy discontent, or importunate distress."[2]

Johnson's friend William Adams, his tutor at Pembroke and later master of the college, described in the spring of 1765 the classic stages of Johnson's nervous condition—recurrence of his melancholy; withdrawal, like a wounded animal, from society; extreme mental anguish; and obsession with himself:

At about this time he was afflicted with a very severe return of the hypochondriack [upset "in the imagination"] disorder, which was ever lurking about him. He was so ill, as, notwithstanding his remarkable love of company, to be entirely averse to society, the most fatal symptom of that malady. Dr. Adams told [Boswell] that, as an old friend, he was admitted to visit him, and that he found him in a deplorable state, sighing, groaning, talking to himself, and restlessly walking from room to room. He then used this emphatical expression of the misery which he felt: "I would consent to have a limb amputated to recover my spirits."

Making a sort of bargain with God, Johnson was quite serious about preferring an amputation to depression. He could endure any amount of physical suffering, but psychological pain he found intolerable.

Johnson had personally known poets who'd suffered incurable mental breakdowns and had visited asylums for the insane. In March 1754 he wrote to the clergyman and critic Joseph Warton, sympathizing—and identifying—with the recent mental deterioration of William Collins: "I knew him a few years ago full of hopes and full of projects, versed in many languages, high in fancy, and strong in retention. . . . Are there hopes of his recovery? Or is he to pass the remainder of his life in misery and degradation? Perhaps with complete consciousness of his calamity." Nine months later he added, "I have often been near his state, and therefore have it in great commiseration."

Christopher Smart was another fearful example. After a brilliant beginning at Cambridge, where he was elected a fellow of Pembroke College, Smart destroyed his career by binge drinking and reckless spending, drifted into religious mania and was sent to a madhouse. After his release he was arrested for debt, and in 1771 he died (like Richard Savage) in prison. In his major poem *Jubilate Agno: Rejoice in the Lamb: A Song from Bedlam* (composed in 1759–63, but not published until 1939), Smart prayed, "God be gracious to Samuel Johnson." Johnson thought Smart should not have been confined merely for asking strangers to pray with him. Four years after Smart's death, Johnson told Boswell that he'd once charitably contributed to a journal owned by the poet, and wittily distanced himself from the madman: "I wrote for some months in *The Universal Visitor*, for poor Smart, while he was mad . . . thinking I was doing him good. I hoped his wits would soon return to him. Mine returned to me, and I wrote in *The Universal Visitor* no longer."[3] Collins and Smart confirmed the truth of Dryden's aphorism, "Great wits are sure to madness near allied," and made Johnson fear for his own sanity.

In the eighteenth century the insane were punished rather than treated, and often kept in barbaric squalor. Johnson was afraid that if his melancholy turned into permanent madness, he'd be confined— like Tom Rakewell in Hogarth's *A Rake's Progress* (1735)—with the crowd of incurable madmen in Bedlam, the Bethlehem Hospital for the Insane, conveniently located near Grub Street. A social historian described the cruel practices, forbidden today in zoos, that took place in Bedlam: "The [inmates] were chained, whipped, starved, and otherwise ill treated by the keepers, who were men of the lowest class. Any person on the payment of twopence was allowed to wander through the wards unattended, to tease the patients, to stimulate their ravings, and make them a public exhibition." Sightseers could divert themselves by prodding and stabbing the victims with sharp sticks.

Johnson's cousin Elizabeth Herne had lost her reason and was committed to Bedlam in 1766, and he left money in his will to maintain that "lunatick." Drawn by morbid fascination and horror, Johnson first visited Bedlam early in 1746. On that occasion he saw a lunatic taking out his fury on a man he imagined to be the son of George II, who'd murdered many wounded men and prisoners after defeating the Jacobites at Culloden in April 1746. Johnson's attention was "arrested by a man who was very furious, and who, while beating his straw, supposed it to be William Duke of Cumberland, whom he was punishing for his cruelties in Scotland."[4] He went once more in 1775 with Boswell, who was also deeply disturbed by the spectacle of mental anguish. Most visitors thought the afflicted were completely different from themselves. Johnson felt he was one of them.

II

Johnson was in a precarious mental state when he first met Hester and Henry Thrale, a wealthy and attractive young couple who befriended him and transformed his life. Arthur Murphy—the Irish lawyer, actor, dramatist and translator of Tacitus —introduced Johnson to the Thrales at their country house in Streatham on January 9, 1765, two weeks before Hester's twenty-fourth birthday. The first visit was a success, and they agreed to meet the following week. Hester replaced Boswell, who was then traveling on the Continent, as friend, confidant and supporter.

Murphy wrote that shortly after these meetings, in the spring of 1765, Johnson's "constitution seemed to be in a rapid decline, and that morbid melancholy, which often clouded his understanding, came upon him with a deeper gloom than ever." He withdrew from society, Murphy added, but the Thrales tracked him down to Johnson's Court. They found the despairing recluse on his knees, "beseeching God to continue to him the use of his understanding."

In her memoir Hester also described this shocking episode, in which Johnson expressed his greatest fear—that he was going mad—and swore them to secrecy:

His health, which he had always complained of, grew so exceedingly bad, that he could not stir out of his room in the court he inhabited for many *weeks* together, I think *months*.

Mr. Thrale's attentions and my own now became so acceptable to him, that he often lamented to us the horrible condition of his mind, which he said was nearly distracted; and though he charged *us* to make him odd solemn promises of secrecy on so strange a subject, yet when we waited on him one morning, and heard him, in the most pathetic terms, beg the prayers of [Reverend Dr. John] Delap, who had left him as we came in, I felt excessively affected with grief, and well remember my husband involuntarily lifted up one hand to shut his mouth, from provocation at hearing a man so wildly proclaim what he could at last persuade no one to believe; and what, if true, would have been so very unfit to reveal.

Instead of retreating in confusion and alarm, as most people would have done, the Thrales felt instinctive pity and sympathy for Johnson and resolved to do everything in their power to help him recover.

Hester believed that Johnson's morbid obsession exacerbated his condition, that his very fear of madness almost drove him mad. He "had given particular attention to the diseases of the imagination," she wrote, echoing *Rasselas,* "which he watched in himself with a solicitude destructive of his own peace, and intolerable to those he trusted." She warned him about this unremitting analysis by asking, "will *any* body's mind bear this eternal microscope that you place upon your own?"[5] He seemed to agree with her in *Rambler* 74, when he observed, "too close an attention to minute exactness, or too rigorous a habit of examining every thing by the standard of perfection, vitiates the temper, rather than improves the understanding." But he could not stop his own compulsive introspection.

Johnson sometimes quoted Shakespeare to illuminate his condition. Tortured by his guilty conscience and "troubled with thick-coming fancies," he identified with Macbeth's appeal for help:

Canst thou not minister to a mind diseased,
Pluck from the memory a rooted sorrow,
Raze out the written troubles of the brain,
And with some sweet oblivious antidote,
Cleanse the stuffed bosom of that perilous stuff
Which weighs upon the heart?

(5.3.40–45)

It was a tall order. But the sensitive, warmhearted Hester was the only one who knew how to deal with his sorrows and troubles. She encouraged him to give up drinking once again, offered generous hospitality, provided maternal care, alleviated his terrors, eased him out of his nervous breakdown and brought him back to a precarious sanity—just as the sensible Tetty had done when they first married, thirty years before, in 1735.

Hester was the most important woman in Johnson's life. Like most of his female friends, she was well educated and well read, intelligent and skilled in foreign languages. Johnson took a serious interest in her daughters' education and made sure they had the same advantages as their mother. Like Boswell, she was more than thirty years younger than Johnson. Born Hester Lynch Salusbury, in Wales in January 1741, she was the daughter of a capricious but appealing father, who'd tried and failed to make his fortune in Nova Scotia. She was a precocious child, and at the age of seventeen had modeled for the young woman in *The Lady's Last Stake* (1758–59) by William Hogarth, her father's friend. Only four feet, eleven inches tall—the same size as Gibbon and a whole foot shorter than Johnson—she was plump and bosomy, with large hands and nose, chestnut hair and gray eyes, a firm chin and clear complexion. Though not beautiful, she was attractively animated. Her close friend and household intimate, Fanny Burney, captured her charm by calling her "extremely lively and chatty; has no supercilious or pedantic airs, and is really all gay and agreeable."

Hester's character was full of complexities and contradictions, perceptively noted by the editor of her journals:

> She was at the same time brilliantly shrewd in her estimates of people, and largely unaware of the deeper well-springs of character; she was schooled in the worldly wisdom of her age, and yet offended her world's code at its most vulnerable spot, by her second marriage; she was both rational and sentimental; she knew herself and her own limitations . . . yet saucily declared that she was in love with herself; . . . she was unusually candid, but often dissimulated; she was a lover of solid knowledge, and a collector of trivia; she was naturally witty, and yet could be . . . downright tedious; . . . she was self-controlled and yet impetuous, docile yet self-assertive; she was a staunch and active friend, and yet could break off her most intimate friendships without a qualm at a suspicion of treachery.

Boswell, more obviously in love with himself, was her great rival for Johnson's attention and favor, but since he traveled abroad and lived mainly in Scotland she had a distinct advantage. She saw Johnson more often and knew him more intimately. She would later infuriate her rival by publishing her vivid *Anecdotes* in 1786 and luring away his potential readers five years before his biography appeared. Just after her book was published, Boswell unjustly called her "a little artful impudent malignant Devil."[6] But Hester, having scooped Boswell, made herself very easy about that.

Henry Thrale, a hardheaded and self-indulgent businessman and politician, was very different from his wife. Born in about 1729 and eleven years older than Hester, he was educated at University College, Oxford, and then traveled through Europe on the Grand Tour. In 1729 his father, Ralph, had bought the Anchor Brewery in Southwark (now owned by Courage) for £30,000, and became an MP for that borough in 1741. Henry took over his father's business, married Hester in 1762 and three years later was elected to his seat in Parliament.

The Anchor Brewery was built just south of the Thames, on the site of Shakespeare's Globe Theatre, where a modern version of the Globe now stands. There was an almost insatiable demand for beer in Johnson's England and Anchor was an extremely profitable business. In the early part of the eighteenth century London had more than 200 inns, 450 taverns and—to alleviate the harsh life of the poor—nearly 6,000 beer houses and 8,700 brandy shops. A historian noted that "in 1722 no less than 33,000,000 bushels of malt were used for brewing, representing a 36-gallon barrel of beer for every man, woman, and child of the population." The brewers' spent mash was used to fatten hogs.

Henry had "an assured market, a single staple product, great technical efficiency, vast capital and large profits. . . . Production had leapt from the level of 32,000 barrels at which Henry had found it at his father's death [in 1758] to 75,000 in 1776 and 87,000 in 1778." Despite his success, he never fulfilled his ambition to surpass the production of his leading rivals, Whitbread and Felix Calvert. In the summer of 1771 his desire to outdo his competitors nearly drove him into bankruptcy. Gulled by an inventor who claimed to have found a way to brew beer without malt and hops, he recklessly invested a whole year's output in this untested process and lost a fortune when it failed. Henry then fell into a deep depression. But Hester, with no previous business experience, resourcefully borrowed money from family and friends, and managed to save the brewery.

The Thrales had two homes: a townhouse next door to the brewery in unfashionable Southwark, which Hester hated; and a grand establishment in Streatham (on what is now Tooting Bec Common), about six miles south of Southwark. Henry continued to make fine improvements, and by 1771 "the estate, covering 89 acres, had new wings, walled gardens, sloping lawns, a lake, stables, coachhouses, farm buildings, an icehouse, even a summerhouse for Johnson, in which to meditate and write. Thirteen pictures by Reynolds of the Thrales and their friends were commissioned," and the new library was enhanced by superb portraits of Hester, their daughter Queeney, Johnson, Burke, Goldsmith, Garrick, Murphy, Baretti, Charles Burney, Robert Chambers and Reynolds himself.[7] Eventually, Streatham became a splendid new venue for Johnson's Club.

The providential Streatham house was a welcome contrast to the austere rooms he'd rented with Tetty and the household of malcontents in Johnson's Court. He liked to escape from their anger and squalor—as well as from the crowds, noise and pollution of London—to a luxurious and orderly home, with well-trained servants and bountiful food. Johnson's comfortably furnished room, according to the Streatham auction catalogue, had a bedstead, wash-hand table, swing glass, commode, walnut bureau, mahogany bidet, painted wardrobe, Kidderminster carpet and large easy chair. Reluctant to leave these comforts, he compromised by spending the weekdays at Streatham, where he had no responsibilities, and weekends in London, where he sorted out the quarrels and restocked the larder. The Thrales' hospitality enabled him to cut down his own expenses and be even more generous to his dependents and charities.

The glassed-in conservatories at Streatham produced a prodigious quantity of grapes, nectarines, peaches and pineapples, which Johnson relished. As Hester recorded, "he loves *Fruit* exceedingly, & though I have seen him eat of it immensely, he says he never had his Bellyful of Fruit but twice." The Thrales' dinners, regularly served at 4 PM, more than satisfied Johnson's gargantuan appetite. He ate to repletion—and well beyond. Hester, describing his tastes, wrote, "he loves a good Dinner dearly—eats it voraciously, & his notions of a good Dinner are nothing less than delicate—a Leg of Pork boyl'd till it drops from the bone almost, a Veal Pye with Plumbs & Sugar, & the outside Cut of a Buttock of Beef are his favourite Dainties." By insisting on ordering the food and managing the kitchen himself, Henry spoiled some of Hester's pleasure in feeding her grateful guest.

Johnson's Lucullan dinners, wolfed down with sweating face and bulging veins, were nothing compared to Henry's outsized consumption. A female visitor, greatly impressed by the quantity of food on the table, reported that the genial host loved feasting and provided meals that surpassed the most aristocratic houses of England: "everything was most splendid and magnificent—two courses of 21 Dishes each, besides Removes ["dishes to be changed while the rest of the course remains"]; and after that a dessert of a piece with the Dinner—Pines [Pineapples] and Fruits of all Sorts, Ices, Creams, &c., &c., &c., without end—everything in [silver] plate, of which such a profusion, and such a Side Board: I never saw such at any Nobleman's."

Hester and Henry, who greatly admired Johnson, were willing and able to entertain their frequent and demanding houseguest. Normally domineering and tyrannical, he repaid Henry's lavish hospitality with excessive deference and respect, and meekly submitted to the rule of the man he called his "Master." Henry, the only one allowed to cut him off in mid-sentence, would become bored by his long disquisitions. Unwilling to spoil his meal, he would coldly tell him: "there, there, now we have had enough for one lecture, Dr. Johnson; we will not be upon education any more till after dinner, if you please."[8]

Hester found Henry more difficult to manage than Johnson, who was a constant witness to their marital discord and became involved in all their family problems. Discussing conjugal vexations in *Rambler* 39, Johnson had emphasized a common cause of unhappy marriages, and wrote, "husbands are often not taken by [women] as objects of affection, but forced upon them by authority and violence." Hester, married at twenty-one, had accepted Henry to please her mother. She explained that she had almost never been alone with Henry during their strictly chaperoned courtship: "except for *one* five minutes only by mere Accident, I never had a Tete à Tete with my Husband in my whole Life till quite the Evening of the Wedding Day."

Though Hester never loved her husband, she was a dutiful wife. She tried to make the best of an awkward mismatch—cushioned by stupendous wealth, luxury and the brilliant circle of friends she attracted through Johnson. In her diary she recorded the positive aspects of Henry's appearance and character: "[his] Person is manly, his Countenance agreeable, his Eyes steady and of the deepest Blue: his Look . . . thoughtful and Intelligent: his Address ["manner"] is neither caressive nor repulsive, but unaffectedly civil and decorous." Though sober and "decent," even tempered and not given to oaths, Henry was intolerably selfish and egoistic. He was, Hester added, "a Man exceedingly comfortable to live with, while the easiness of his Temper and slowness to take Offence add greatly to his Value as a domestic Man. . . . With regard to his Wife, tho' little tender of her Person, he is very partial to her Understanding—but he is obliging to *nobody.*"

Hester wrote that when she casually mentioned his lack of affection, Henry shocked her with a cruel and quite unjustified response. Claiming (in Horatian terms) that she was neither *utile* nor *dulce,* he said that she knew nothing about brewing—though she'd rescued him from bankruptcy; that she lacked wit—though she'd drawn to Streatham the most distinguished men in England; and that she was preoccupied with babies—though he kept her almost continually pregnant:

> One Day that I mentioned Mr. Thrale's cold Carriage to me, tho' with no Resentment, for it had occasioned in me no Dislike; He said in Reply—Why how for Heaven's Sake Dearest Madam should any Man delight in a Wife that is to him neither Use nor Ornament? He cannot talk to you about his Business, which you do not understand; nor about his Pleasures, which you do not partake; if you have Wit or Beauty you shew them nowhere, so he has none of the Reputation ["credit, honour"]; if you have Economy or Understanding you employ neither in Attention to his Property. You divide your Time between your Mama and your Babies, & wonder you do not by that means become agreeable to your Husband.

Hester's biographer, emphasizing their radical differences, concluded:

It would have been difficult to find a bride and groom who were temperamentally more unsuited to each other. Henry Thrale was essentially a business man, matter-of-fact and unemotional, with the cynicism of his rakish companions in London. Hester Lynch, on the contrary, had been a precocious child, petted and admired by an adoring family who had led her to believe that she was an unusual person with remarkable gifts as a poet. Sentimental, intensely introspective, artistic, she was the antithesis of her husband.[9]

Their marriage problems were more serious than these passages suggest. Henry was a reckless gambler and, like Boswell, consistently unfaithful to his wife. Eighteenth-century women, who had no money of their own and could not get divorced (except by an act of Parliament, scandalous and difficult to obtain), had no choice but to tolerate their husbands' adultery. Hester even had to treat Henry's venereal disease, and he may well have infected her with gonorrhea. In the spring of 1773 the widely read *Westminster Gazette,* like a modern tabloid, unearthed details of his early love affairs and described them in a manner that made him look ridiculous. Henry's bastard son, the sickly Jeremiah Crutchley, became an embarrassing intimate of the family and even paid incestuous attention to his half-sister Queeney Thrale.

Hester was also forced to entertain the young, ivory-necked, extremely beautiful and learned Greek scholar Sophia Streatfeild, who charmed the men and irritated the women. She and Hester had had the same tutor; they met in Brighton and Hester invited her to Streatham. Feminine, seductive, yet somehow cold and aloof, Sophia had the uncanny ability to shed tears at a moment's notice without losing her smile or compromising her rosy complexion. Prompted to begin her lachrymose performance, she would force two tears of sensibility to well up in her eyes and roll down her soft cheeks. Henry found Sophia ravishing and Hester acknowledged that she was a formidable rival: "she had a power of captivation that was irresistible; her beauty joined to her softness, her caressing manners, her Tearful Eyes, & alluring looks, would insinuate her into the Heart of *any* man she thought worth attacking."

Like an infatuated adolescent, Henry lavished the affection on Sophia that he'd never felt for his wife. Cataloguing her dramatic charms and wiles, Hester lamented to her diary: "Mr. Thrale is fallen in Love *really* & *seriously* with Sophia Streatfeild—but there is no wonder in that: She is very pretty, very gentle, soft & insinuating; hangs about him, dances round him, cries when She parts from him, squeezes his Hand slyly, & with her sweet Eyes full of Tears looks so fondly in his Face." When Henry became seriously ill, his physical decline intensified his emotional longings. Imitating Sophia's operatic gestures, he "pressed her Hand to his Heart (as She told me herself) & said Sophia we shall not enjoy this long, & tonight I will not be cheated of my *Only Comfort*." Johnson, impervious to her Circean enchantments, thought Sophia, apart from her Greek, as flighty and ignorant as a butterfly.

One evening Sophia provoked a public crisis that revealed the troubled emotional undercurrents at Streatham. When they were all seated at the table, Henry asked Hester to change places with Sophia, who was developing a sore throat and might be harmed (he felt) by a draft from the door. Hester, bursting into tears, said "perhaps ere long the lady might be at the head of Mr. Thrale's table" and rushed out of the room. After dinner Hester asked Johnson and Burke if she were to blame for what had happened. Johnson replied: "'Why, possibly not; your feelings were outraged.' I said, 'Yes, greatly so; and I cannot help remarking with what blandness and composure you witnessed the outrage. Had this transaction been told of others, your anger would have known no bounds; but, towards a man who gives good dinners, you were meekness itself.' Johnson coloured, and Burke, I thought, looked foolish; but I had not a word of answer from either."[10]

Henry's romantic attachment to Sophia humiliated Hester. She did not confront Henry at the time or tell him that she was quite comfortable in her usual place and had no desire to move. Though Johnson, to maintain his privileged position, had to ignore Henry's infidelities, she insisted that he and Burke take sides on this moral issue. She criticized them for their craven silence, emphasized their subservience to

Henry (which matched her own) and, for once, reduced the two great speakers to silence. Hester's account of her triumph and of Johnson's meekness seems rather unconvincing, for she never challenged him any more than she did her husband. But there's no doubt that she was deeply wounded after Henry had made his attachment so public and appeared to displace her. Henry's flirtation, though serious, was chaste. He loved Sophia, but never managed to bed her. The seductress, everybody's admiration and nobody's choice, died a spinster, at the age of eighty-one, in 1835.

III

Georgian couples, unlike the Victorians, did not have enormous families. In the eighteenth century the average number was only 2.5 children. There were, of course, famous exceptions. In the previous century John Donne's wife had twelve children in fifteen years; six of them died, and she too died with her last stillbirth. The unremitting infant mortality of Queen Anne's numerous issue led to the extinction of the Stuart dynasty in England. She had twelve miscarriages and gave birth to six royal heirs, all of whom perished. Johann Sebastian Bach's two wives had a grand total of twenty children, of whom half died in infancy; Bennet Langton's wife had ten. A fifth of English babies died in their first year, a third of them before the age of five; and in 1700 the average life expectancy was only thirty-seven years.

Hester Thrale's loveless marriage was scarred by laborious pregnancies and depressing miscarriages that wore down her body and spirit, difficult childbirths without anesthetics that constantly put her life in danger, and the heartbreaking deaths of most of her children. In the fourteen years between 1764 and 1778 she had two boys and ten girls, of whom eight, including both sons, died in infancy or childhood.[11] In August 1779 Hester had been confined to the house, and even to her bed, by the threat of miscarriage. Henry, well aware of the danger, insisted she go to the brewery and conduct some business. After completing her task, she begged him to take her home immediately. But he would not be hurried, and neither entreaties nor pain "could make him set out one *Moment* before the appointed hour." She suffered terribly in the jolting "Coach all the way from

London to Streatham in a State not to be described, nor endured;—*but by me:*—& being carried to my Chamber the Instant I got home, miscarried in the utmost Agony before they could get me into Bed, after fainting five Times." On this occasion Henry, selfish as always, didn't seem to care whether his wife and child died.

Hester's four surviving daughters—Hester Maria (called Queeney), Susanna, Sophia and Cecilia—all disliked her. In 1770 Hester exclaimed that the cold, reserved, six-year-old Queeney, clearly her father's daughter and a complete contrast to her mother, had "a Heart void of all Affection for any Person in the World." But Hester was responsible for alienating the affections of her daughters, who lined up against her in a phalanx of disapproval and maintained that *she* was the one with no heart. She put her social life before everything else, showed them little affection and often beat them for the slightest infraction. Hester tried to protect herself from suffering after the deaths of her children—many of them, no doubt, unwanted—by refusing to become attached to any of them.

With the Thrales, Johnson had his most extensive experience with English children. His own childhood had been unhappy, and Tetty was too old to have more children by the time they married. He was devoted to his servant Frank Barber, who came to him as a boy and repaid his kindness by running away. Though Johnson was theoretically fond of children (and pressed pennies into the hands of boy beggars who slept in the streets), he tended to see them as either unwelcome intruders or dangerous threats. In *Rasselas* he wrote, with deep scepticism, "an unpractised observer expects the love of parents and children to be constant and equal; but this kindness seldom continues beyond the years of infancy: in a short time the children become rivals to their parents."[12]

Johnson told Boswell that he never wanted to have a child of his own. When Hester asked him how he would have educated his children, if he had any, he suggested that children cause suffering, and that he would have been even more distant with them than she'd been with her daughters: "I would have lived on Bread & Water that they might learn, but I would not have had them about me: Boarding Schools are made to relieve Parents from that anxiety which only torments them." On another occasion, he shocked Hester by generalizing from his own experience and declaring, though none of her children seemed about to kill themselves, "get your Children into Habits of loving a Book by every possible means; . . . it might one Day save them from Suicide." No wonder, though Johnson could not stop giving advice, that his admonitions were often ignored. As he wrote in *Rambler* 87, "few things are so liberally bestowed, or squandered with so little effect, as good advice. . . . Advice, as it always gives a temporary appearance of superiority, can never be very grateful, even when it is most necessary or most judicious."[13]

Johnson could be tender and affectionate with children, and told the young Thrales (implying that they were often driven to tears), "after dinner we shall have good sport playing all together, and we will none of us cry." But he often terrified children, and even precocious youngsters must have felt the urge to run screaming from the room when the ogre subjected them to his intimidating doctoral examinations. Things went unusually well when he asked an unschooled boy, rowing him across the Thames, "what would you give, my lad, to know about the Argonauts?" and the little Argonaut pleased him by replying, "Sir, I would give what I have"—which was precious little, but precious enough.

Johnson expected children to be well read and impossibly learned, and could be unduly stern when he was disappointed. Questioning Thomas Percy's little daughter while holding her on his knee, and hearing that she hadn't read one of his favorite books, *The Pilgrim's Progress,* he dismissed her with "'No! then I would not give a farthing for you,' and he set her down and took no further notice of her."[14] After a father had unwisely bragged about his son's great abilities, "Johnson, as a test of the young scholar's attainments, put this question to him:—'At what time did the heathen oracles cease?' The boy, not in the least daunted, answered:—'At the dissolution of the religious houses.'" Though his answer was wildly off the mark and concerned Tudor England rather than ancient Rome, he deserved some credit for his cheeky self-assurance. In fact, as a modern classicist explains, "the heathen oracles ceased (in the sense of being suppressed) during the reign of Theodosius. He forbade all public pagan sacrifices and closed down the temples in a decree of February 24, 391."[15]

Johnson recommended Giuseppe Baretti, who'd killed a man but was desperately in need of a job, to the Thrales. In October 1773 he was hired to live at Streatham as language tutor to the nine-year-old Queeney. The introduction of another volatile personality into the unhappy family made Hester's relations with her daughter even more difficult. Though well mannered and superficially polite, Baretti completely lacked the typical English reserve. His gestures were operatic, his voice loud, his expressions extreme. He called Voltaire's work on Shakespeare "infamous *shitt*." Instead of behaving deferentially and acknowledging Hester as mistress of the house, he constantly defied and undermined her authority. Baretti, twenty-two years older than Hester, admitted that Henry "is urbane and affable, and I live with him like a brother and scold his wife in front of him when I think fit, for I regard her more as a daughter than anything else." Hester and Baretti cordially detested each other, but she kept him in the house because he was an excellent teacher.

Baretti, like Reynolds and Goldsmith, was a bachelor who loved children. He adored Queeney, gave her the affection that Hester withheld and wrote, with pardonable exaggeration, "she resembles the angels in every way and I am seven thousand times fonder of her than I have ever been of anyone." Since Baretti and Hester had very different ideas about how to bring up children, they quarreled fiercely about whether the girls should be expected to behave like adults or left free to play as they wished, be beaten when they were naughty or corrected by gentler means, be medicated by their mother or treated by qualified physicians. More kindly and tolerant than Hester, Baretti exploded on their trip to Bath and confessed, "my bile suddenly rose to such a degree, that I am sure I uttered my indignation in the most severe terms, and swore she would soon send the daughter to keep company with the [dead] son, if she gave her any more of her damn'd pills."

Baretti was right about how to regulate, discipline and medicate the children. Hester agreed that he took excellent care of them when she was away, and regretted that she was so peevish with him. But she felt obliged to reject his advice, which seemed to usurp her authority with the servants and alienate the loyalty of her children. Hester felt that Baretti, by teaching Queeney independence, encouraged her to disobey her mother, and that by siding with Henry, he encouraged him to deny her quite reasonable requests.

If Johnson had not been a tactful mediator, offering advice and calming the situation, Hester would not have put up with the touchy and temperamental Italian. In a letter to her, Johnson counseled tolerance and shrewdly explained why Baretti found it difficult to accept his subservient position: "Poor Baretti! do not quarrel with him, to neglect him a little will be sufficient. He means only to be frank, and manly, and independent, and perhaps, as you say, a little wise. To be frank he thinks is to be cynical, and to be independent, is to be rude. Forgive him, dearest Lady."[16]

17

MIND DISEASED
1765–1772

I

Johnson spent so much time with the Thrales and became so dependent on Hester that Reynolds and other close friends complained they'd seen very little of him in London. Hester found him an instructive companion who enlivened her life and relieved the tedium of polite society. Though she liked to exhibit her caged lion, Johnson proved easier to display than to live with. To escape being shown off by the Thrales as he'd been by his parents, he would sometimes remain conspicuously silent and draw aside from the company to study the books on the shelves. Often delighted by the stimulating talk and the abundant tea and sympathy, he could also show his disdain and impatience with foolish or vexatious remarks. He was used to setting the tone and expounding the subject, and had little tolerance for small talk.

Johnson was equally intolerant of the ordinary upsets of family life. Once comfortably and routinely ensconced at Streatham, he became difficult and demanding: selfish, censorious and severe. His temper was easily ignited, his explosions offensive. He was furious when the Thrales' spoiled dog, Belle, ate his buttered toast while he was sounding off to

Hester. He was equally awkward on expeditions to London, and she noted that going to Covent Garden with an eccentric celebrity had its drawbacks. He was "an exceedingly bad playhouse companion, as his person drew people's eyes upon the box, and the loudness of his voice made it difficult for me to hear any body but himself." Lamentably deaf, he rarely whispered or spoke quietly. Despite all the differences in age, experience and income, the young Hester willingly became Johnson's friend, hostess, benefactor, nourisher, companion, correspondent, confidante, admirer, disciple, biographer, nurse, mother confessor—and chastiser. No wonder he told Hester, when totally absorbed by her, "I do certainly love you better than any human Being I ever saw."

Johnson sometimes took up the role of court poet, and Hester and her family inspired some of his most charming and impromptu light verse. His poems, like those the older Jonathan Swift wrote to his adored friend Esther Johnson (known as "Stella"), express admiration, tenderness and fearful dependence. Eager to see the ailing Stella, while delayed by rough seas in Wales, yet reluctant to return to Ireland, the sixty-year-old Swift wrote to her:

Before, I always found the wind
To me was most malicious kind,
But now the danger of a friend,
On whom my fears and hopes depend,
Absent from whom all Climes are curst,
With whom I'm happy in the worst,
With rage impatient makes me wait
A passage to the Land I hate.

In his poem on Stella's forty-sixth and final birthday, Swift urged her to feel sympathy for *him,* who suffered because he loved her and she was ill:

O then, whatever Heav'n intends,
Take Pity on your pitying Friends;
Nor let your Ills affect your Mind,
To fancy they can be unkind.

Me, surely Me, you ought to spare,
Who gladly would your Suff'rings share.[1]

Johnson resembled Swift in both his playful and his serious moods.
When Hester reached her thirty-fifth birthday, in 1776 (halfway through
the biblical span of three score and ten), she felt worn down by domestic
cares, numerous children and the constant perils of childbirth. But Johnson wrote a poem to celebrate the day. Pointing out that his rhyming
words ("alive," "arrive" . . . "thrive," "wive") were in alphabetical order, he
cheered her up by maintaining that her best years lay ahead:

Oft in Danger yet alive
We are come to Thirty-five.
Long may better Years arrive,
Better Years than Thirty-five. . . .
He that ever hopes to thrive
Must begin by Thirty-five:
And those who wisely wish to wive,
Must look on Thrale at Thirty-five.

One evening, Queeney was deliberating about whether to wear her
fine new hat to a dinner party. Johnson, taking up the classical theme
of carpe diem and its undertone of sadness, urged her to seize the day
and adorn herself while she was still young and pretty:

Wear the Gown, and wear the Hat,
Snatch your pleasures while they last;
Hadst thou nine Lives like a Cat,
Soon those nine Lives would be past.

Johnson's "Short Song of Congratulation," written to celebrate the
twenty-first birthday of Henry Thrale's nephew Sir John Lade, is a
lighthearted warning to a rich young man heading for almost certain
disaster. Johnson's ironic tone and witty octosyllabic quatrains influenced the later poetry of A. E. Housman and John Betjeman:

Long-expected one and twenty
Ling'ring year, at last is flown,
Pomp and Pleasure, Pride and Plenty
Great Sir John, are all your own.

Loosen'd from the Minor's tether,
Free to mortgage or to sell,
Wild as wind, and light as feather
Bid the slaves of thrift farewell.

Call the Bettys, Kates, and Jennys
Ev'ry name that laughs at Care,
Lavish of your Grandsire's guineas,
Show the Spirit of an heir.[2]

Sir John fulfilled Johnson's predictions by marrying the mistress of a highwayman and wasting his inheritance.

Grateful for his poetic tributes, Hester tried to please Johnson as much as possible. At Streatham his every taste was gratified, every whim indulged, every outburst forgiven. Hester recorded that despite his gruff manner and rough tongue, Johnson, with a comical lack of insight, solemnly praised his own good manners: "I am well-bred to a degree of needless scrupulosity. . . . No man is so cautious not to interrupt another; no man thinks it so necessary to appear attentive when others are speaking; no man so steadily refuses preference to himself, or so willingly bestows it on another, as I do; no body holds so strongly as I do the necessity of ceremony, and the ill effects which follow the breach of it: yet people think me rude." Hester found it difficult to agree with him. Comparing her friends to animals in her diary, she called Sophia Streatfeild a dove, Fanny Burney an antelope, Baretti an ill-tempered bear and Johnson a trampling elephant.[3] On her chart rating the qualities of her friends, Johnson received the maximum of 20 for religion, morality and general knowledge, and a disgraceful 0 for person and voice, general manner and good humor.

The "well-bred" Johnson often violated the rules of social decorum and embarrassed Hester by demolishing guests he thought cheeky or conceited. Sir John Lade, the subject of his poem, once felt his lash. Hester recorded, "a young Fellow of great Fortune . . . called to him rather abruptly—& he fancied disrespectfully . . . —would you advise me to marry? I would advise *no Man* to marry answered he, bouncing from his Chair & leaving the Room in a fret—that is not likely to propagate Understanding. The young Fellow looked confounded"—as many others would be by his retorts. When a pretentious young coxcomb seated at her table lamented, "I have lost all my Greek," Johnson trounced him with, "Ay Sir and I on the same day lost all my Estate in Yorkshire."

Ladies, including friends' wives and even Hester herself, were also fair game. Fanny Burney, pen at the ready, noted that Johnson, disgusted by the effusions of the Bluestocking Hannah More, shot her down with "Madam, before you flatter a man so grossly to his Face, you should consider whether or not your flattery is worth his having!" Mrs. Bennet Langton, showing off her grotto (made fashionable by Alexander Pope's damp cave in his garden at Twickenham) and asking "if he did not think it a pretty convenient habitation?" received a rude put-down: "Yes Madam—for a Toad."[4] All his remarks had a moral force, enlivened by wit, and must have seemed extremely amusing to anyone but the embarrassed hostess and wounded victims. But after correcting human folly, he soon forgave it.

Considering Hester's kindness and Johnson's love for her, it's surprising that he also attacked her. He thought that Hester, pampered by luxury and immune to real suffering, had no right to complain about her exhaustion and illness. In her diary she remarked that if she said she felt ill, "Johnson, who thinks no body poor till they want a Dinner, or sick till they want breath, would only suppose I was calling for Attention; & shewing Consequence by bringing Physicians about me." Henry, even worse, "will neither see the danger, nor care about it if he saw it." In their different ways, both Johnson and Henry depended on Hester and didn't want to know when she was in pain.

Perceiving a paradox in Johnson's normally kind character, Hester noted that he applied different standards of behavior to himself and to others. He felt great tenderness for poor people, but felt no compassion when she experienced the devastating loss of a parent, child or friend.

Thinking of his grief for Tetty, Hill Boothby, his mother and Richard Bathurst, she wrote, "nobody suffered more from pungent sorrow at a friend's death than Johnson, though he would suffer no one else to complain of their losses in the same way." Withholding the sympathy she expected him to express, he called her grief mere "Distresses of Sentiment" and "Wounds given only to Vanity or Softness." The real sufferers, he believed, were the ragged and starving London poor.

Johnson's criticism of Hester went far beyond the question of which degree of suffering deserved the most sympathy. Close friends like Fanny Burney and Frances Reynolds were astonished by his occasional ferocity with Hester and by her meek acceptance of his attacks. The rather timid Fanny wrote: "the freedom with which Dr. Johnson condemns whatever he disapproves, is astonishing! & the strength of Words he uses would, to most people, be intolerable; but Mrs. Thrale seems to have a sweetness of Disposition that equals All her other excellencies, & far from making a point of vindicating herself, she generally receives his admonitions with the most respectful silence."[5]

Frances Reynolds gave a specific example of Johnson's rude behavior. Though none of the ladies dared to criticize him directly, they questioned Hester and wondered at her response: "one Day at her own Table, before a large company, he spoke so very roughly to her, that every person present was surprised how she could bear it so placidly; and on the Ladies withdrawing, one of them express'd great astonishment how Dr. Johnson could speak in such harsh terms to her! But to this she said no more than 'Oh! Dear good man!'" Hester, who admired his essential goodness and knew how much he loved her, was also aware of his terrible fears and constant struggles to control himself. She believed in the principle that *tout comprendre c'est tout pardonner.*

When Johnson's rudeness hurt her friends and went beyond what even Hester could bear, she would occasionally try to restrain him. But it was a tricky maneuver. Fanny Burney (not Hester herself) recorded a dramatic dialogue that revealed his jesuitical arguments:

Mrs. T. When you are *angry,* who *dares* make speeches so bitter & so cruel?

Dr. J. Madam, I am always *sorry* when I make bitter speeches, & I never do it, but when I am insufferably vexed.

Mrs. T. Yes, Sir,—but you do suffer things to vex *you*, that Nobody *else* would vex at. I am sure *I* have had my share of scolding from you!

Dr. J. It is true, you have;—but you have borne it like an Angel—& you have been the *better* for it. . . .

To F. B. Mrs. Thrale is a sweet Creature, & *never* angry; she has a Temper ["calmness of mind"] the most delightful of *any* woman I ever knew.

Johnson, who rarely admitted his faults, claimed to be sorry, but instead of apologizing, he justified his rudeness. He first said he was bitter only when "insufferably vexed," as he so often was, and then outrageously claimed that his bitter condemnations actually improved her character. Finally, he retreated with a flattering concession: "I don't mean Mrs. Thrale & Miss Burney, when I talk of *women!*—they are Goddesses!—& therefore I except them."

Johnson never attacked his other goddess, Fanny Burney, who was as fragile and delicate as a piece of porcelain. She was the daughter of his musician-friend Charles Burney, and he loved her as her father's child as well as for her own admirable qualities: vivacity, charm, perception and talent. Born in King's Lynn, Norfolk, in 1752 and young enough to be Johnson's granddaughter, she was nearsighted, sharp-witted and quick to blush. He described her affectionately as "Lilliputian"; her biographer portrayed her as "slightly built, with very thick brown hair, lively, intelligent eyes and [a] large nose. She had an inward-sloping upper lip . . . small hands and narrow shoulders."

Johnson met Fanny in 1777, when she was twenty-five, the year before she published her first novel, *Evelina.* Cast in the form of letters to and from its naïve but lively heroine, the witty and satiric novel portrays an obscure young woman making her way in society. Evelina, a beautiful and intelligent girl, abandoned by her father, turns out to be an heiress and, after many complications, marries the handsome Lord Orville. The book appeared anonymously, but the author was soon discovered and enthusiastically admired by Johnson, Burke, Reynolds, Goldsmith and Sheridan. Overcoming false modesty, Fanny felt obliged to record Johnson's extravagant praise: "I admire her for her observations,—for her good sense,—for her humour,—for her Discernment,—for her manner of expressing them,—& for *all* her *Writing* Talents." He told Charles Burney (faithfully recorded by Fanny) that "no writer so young and inexperienced ever analyzed character so penetratingly or observed contemporary manners so accurately."[6]

In her journal Fanny revealed both Johnson's playful and his combative character. Recalling his dog-eat-dog days on Grub Street, he urged the shy maiden to follow his fierce example. He told her to struggle against Elizabeth Montagu, the leading woman writer of the time, to attack her, topple her from the throne and seize her place in the literary hierarchy:

> Dr. Johnson began to see-saw with a Countenance strongly expressive of *inward fun,*—&, after enjoying it some Time in silence, he suddenly, & with great animation, turned to me, & cried "*Down* with her Burney!—*down* with her!—spare her not! attack her, fight her, & *down* with her at once!—*You* are a *rising* Wit,—*she* is at the *Top,*—& when *I* was beginning [in] the World, & was nothing & nobody, the Joy of my Life was to fire at all the established Wits!—& then, every body loved to hallow [shout] me on;—but there is no Game *now,* & *now,* every body would be glad to see me *conquered:* but *then,* when I was *new,*—to vanquish the Great ones was all the delight of my poor little dear soul!—So at her, Burney!—at her, & *down* with her!"

Johnson's dubious assumption that the gentle Fanny would adopt his aggressive tactics and eagerly rush into battle showed both the comic and ferocious aspects of his character. She explained that he could be court jester as well as court poet and disciplinarian: "Dr. Johnson has more *fun,* & comical humour, & Laughable nonsense about him, than almost any body I ever saw: I mean, when with those he likes; for otherwise, he can be as severe & as bitter as Report relates of him." Having seen the worst of his faults, Fanny overlooked them and confirmed Hester's judgment of the "Dear good man": "he is as great a *souled* man, as a *Bodyed* one, & were he less furious in his passions, he would be demi-divine."[7]

II

In a brief but suggestive entry in her diary of August 1782, Hester wrote "we have now lived together above 18 Years, & I have so fondled and waited on him in Sickness & in Health." Two years later Johnson, deeply grateful for her care, told her, "I am very ready to repay for that kindness which soothed twenty years of a life radically wretched." Though widely admired as the leading man of letters of his time, Johnson felt, with some justification, that his life from birth to old age had been essentially miserable. He resorted to desperate measures when struggling to restrain his passions and assuage his fears. An unusual item, with Hester's handwritten note attached, appeared in the sale of her personal effects after her death: "Johnson's Padlock committed to my care in the year 1768." A Latin entry in his diary of March 31, 1771, throws light on this padlock: "*De pedicis et manicis insana cogitatio*" ("mad thoughts of fetters and handcuffs").[8]

Musing in her diary about her "Strange Connections" with Johnson, Hester wrote that there was "a dreadful & little suspected Reason for *ours* God knows—but the Fetters & Padlocks will tell Posterity the Truth." Hester's editor explained that Johnson actually bought and kept these articles "to help enforce the discipline of 'confinement and severity,' which he resorted to when his delusion [that he was insane] became strongest." He did not keep such shackles in his own much smaller and more crowded home, where he had no one to confide in and could more easily be discovered. Johnson submitted to chains and handcuffs, and had his door padlocked, when he felt the onset of madness. But it would have been quite impossible for the tiny Hester, even with the help of several manservants, to restrain and shackle a crazed, rampaging and uncommonly strong Johnson. He had bought these implements to restrain himself during periods of madness, but he was depressive, not manic, and never had to employ them. But he did actually use them in the closet drama of his ritualistic whippings.

From the eighteenth century onward, flagellation has been associated with perverse forms of sexual passion. In 1764 the French police reported that "many people are being reduced to this extremity, and today there is no brothel without a number of birch-rods." Among Johnson's contemporaries, Rousseau (1712–78) confessed that he took pleasure in being spanked by Mlle. Lambercier; the Marquis de Sade (1740–1814) turned flagellation into a fine art; and John Cleland's *Memoirs of a Woman of Pleasure* (known as *Fanny Hill*, 1748–49) also portrayed this practice.

Medieval flagellants hoped to achieve redemption by subduing the flesh. In the twentieth-century Italian novel, *The Leopard*, Giuseppe Tomasi di Lampedusa described the expiatory discipline of the hero's ancestor, the Saint-Duke, who followed this ascetic tradition. He "had scourged himself alone, in the sight of his God and his estates, and it must have seemed to him that the drops of his own blood were about to rain down on the land and redeem it."[9] Sadomasochistic whipping figured prominently in nautical novels and prison memoirs of the nineteenth and twentieth centuries: Dana's *Two Years before the Mast*, Melville's *White Jacket*, Dostoyevsky's *The House of the Dead*—even Kafka's *The Trial*. While serving in the Tank Corps in the 1920s, T. E. Lawrence persuaded a young friend to whip him at regular intervals for more than ten years, usually on the anniversary of his torture and rape in the Arabian campaign. This assuaged his guilt and gave him sexual pleasure. Swinburne's *The Whippingham Papers* and Proust's *Time Regained* portray an all-too-eager submission to the perverse aspects of flagellation.

Johnson's practice, rather different from these savage punishments, combined voluntary humiliation, masochism (rather than sadism), displaced sexuality and religious penance. In 1779 he told the thirty-eight-year-old Hester—who called him "my Slave"—"a Woman has *such* power between the Ages of twenty five and forty five, that She may tye a Man to a post and whip him if She will." She explained his comment in a categorical and undeniable annotation: "this he knew of him self was *literally* and *strictly* true I am sure." He also told Boswell, while thinking of his own masochistic impulses, "Madmen are all sensual in the lower stages of the distemper. They are eager for gratifications to soothe their minds, and divert their attention from the misery which they suffer: but when they grow very ill, pleasure is too weak for them, and they seek pain."

In early June 1773 Johnson and Hester exchanged two letters, probably meant to be delivered by hand inside the house, which referred to the strangest and most poignant events in his life. At that time, conditions at Streatham were particularly tense. The house was being extensively renovated, Hester's children were threatened by an epidemic of measles and her mother was dying of breast cancer. Instead of trying to alleviate the situation, Johnson became even more demanding.

He wrote her a pathological letter (translated here into English) in formal and stilted French, which the servants could not read. Uncharacteristically passive, submissive and weak, Johnson began by placing himself completely in Hester's power and begging her to lock him in his room whenever she saw fit:

> [Kindly tell me] what is allowed and what is forbidden. . . . I beg you to spare me the need to constrain myself, by taking away the power to leave the room when you want me to stay. [You would] only have to turn the key in the door twice a day. You must be the absolute mistress, so that your judgment and vigilance will help my weakness. . . .
>
> That won't be difficult for you; you will be able to devise a regime that is practical without trouble and effective without risk.

He then criticized her for neglecting her duties and reminded her of her promise to help him, which suggests that Hester was a reluctant secret sharer in Johnson's ritual:

> Is it too much to ask a soul like yours that, as mistress of others, you might also become mistress of yourself and overcome your inconstancy?
>
> [You've failed] to impose your own laws, forgotten so many promises, and condemned me to so many recurrent pleas, that I'm horrified by the very thought of it. . . .

He concluded by encouraging her to participate and by stressing the pleasure he found in his self-imposed slavery:

> It's essential to remember our agreement. I wish, my protector, that your authority will always be clear to me, and that you will keep me in that form of slavery which you know so well how to make blissful.[10]

Impressively patient and tolerant, under great pressure, Hester gently tried to ease Johnson out of his self-destructive yet somehow necessary obsessions, which bound them together in a connection more intimate than sex. Responding to Johnson's unreasonable demands for attention and complaints that she was neglecting him, she tried to release herself from the obligation he'd imposed upon her. She had been forced to transform what was a hateful idea to her—punishing the fettered Johnson as he groveled before her—into a pleasurable experience for him:

> You were saying but on Sunday that of all the unhappy you were the happiest, in consequence of my Attention to your Complaint; and to day I have been reproached by you for neglect, and by myself for exciting that generous Confidence which prompts you to repose all Care on me, and tempts you to neglect yourself, and brood in secret upon an Idea hateful in itself, but which your kind partiality to me has unhappily rendered pleasing.

She urged him to get rid of his obsessions, which were even worse than the manacles she used to bind him, and free himself of his fixation with bondage and punishment:

> If it be possible shake off these uneasy Weights, heavier to the Mind by far than Fetters to the body. Let not your fancy dwell thus upon Confinement and Severity. I am sorry you are obliged to be so much alone; I foresaw some ill Consequences of your being here while my Mother was dying thus; yet could not resist the temptation of having you near me, but if you find this irksome

and dangerous Idea fasten upon your fancy, leave me to struggle with the loss of one Friend [her mother], and let me not put to hazard [our friendship] what I esteem beyond Kingdoms, and value beyond the possession of them.

If we go on together your Confinement shall be as strict as possible except when Company comes in, which I shall more willingly endure on your Account.

She encouraged him to distract and amuse himself in Boswell's company. Calling herself his governess, both a protective nanny and severe disciplinarian, she begged him not to demand the whippings she found increasingly difficult to provide:

Dissipation is to you a glorious Medicine, and I believe Mr. Boswell will be at last your best Physician. For the rest you really are well enough now if you will keep so; and not suffer the noblest of human Minds to be tortured with fantastic notions which rob it of all its Quiet. I will detain you no longer, so farewell and be good; and do not quarrel with your Governess for not using the Rod enough.

Hester also noted that after confessing his fears of insanity soon after they met, "our stern Philosopher Johnson trusted me about the Years 1767 or 1768," when she first used the chains and whips, with this second secret. Struck by the difference between Johnson's solemn public persona and his private self-abasement, and finding it difficult to reconcile his two roles, she added: "how many Times has this great, this formidable Doctor Johnson kissed my hand, ay & my foot too upon his knees!"[11]

Katharine Balderston (the editor of Hester's diaries) was the first to discover the significance of Johnson's chains and whips. The most controversial essay ever written on Johnson boldly yet convincingly concluded:

It seems inescapably evident that his compulsive fantasy assumed a masochistic form, in which the impulse to self-abasement and pain predominated. The fetters, the padlocks, and the whippings, which must be inflicted by the beloved object, are phenomena fairly commonplace in the records of sex pathology. . . .

Her ministrations were only those of a person who could help to distract and allay his morbid fears of insanity—and whose efforts to do so for eighteen years at last wore out her patience.

Hester frequently beat her children; Johnson had been savagely whipped in school and had whipped his own pupils. It's not surprising, therefore, that a man tormented by lifelong sin and guilt would seek penance and want to be gently whipped—not severely beaten, which would have been beyond her strength and her desire—by the woman he adored. In *Psychopathia Sexualis,* Richard von Krafft-Ebing wrote that whoever submits to whipping wants to be "unconditionally subject to the will of a person of the opposite sex; [to be] treated by this person as by a master, humiliated and abused" for sexual pleasure. Chained up and on his knees, kissing her feet and becoming her "slave," Johnson was totally at her mercy. He felt masochistic pleasure in pain and humiliation, which both satisfied and punished his sexual urges.

Describing the beloved inspirer of Edmund Waller's love poetry, Johnson mentioned the three crucial aspects of his relationship with Hester: dominance, manacles and insanity. Waller's love was "a sublime predominating beauty, of lofty charms and imperious influence, on whom he looks with amazement rather than fondness, whose [metaphorical] chains he wishes, though in vain, to break, and whose presence is *wine* that *inflames to madness.*"[12] By reversing their roles and becoming the dominant figure, Hester allowed Johnson to act out his sexual fantasies. But the chains and whips, however perverse, had a positive effect on his psychosexual life. This poignant and tragic discipline enabled him to alleviate his guilt, prevent an outbreak of insanity, and satisfy his sexual urges by displacing his love for the forbidden and unobtainable Hester.

18

SAVAGE CLANS
1772–1777

I

Johnson's assertion that "when a man is tired of London, he is tired of life; for there is in London all that life can afford" is one of his most famous and most frequently misinterpreted remarks. Though always eager for life, Johnson in his sixties and seventies sometimes became weary of the dirt, noise, crowds and bustle of the city, and longed for the quiet and tranquility, the silence and solitude of rural retreats. In 1776 he moved to Bolt Court, off Fleet Street, where he remained for the rest of his life. There he took delight in growing and watering plants in the little garden behind the house.

Johnson combined intense chauvinism with keen curiosity about foreigners and a restless desire to travel to distant places. Baretti, with some exaggeration and tactfully omitting any mention of Italians, quoted Shakespeare's *Richard II* and called Johnson "a real *true-born Englishman*. He hated the Scotch, the French, the Dutch, the Hanoverians, and had contempt for all other European Nations." He shared the views of his countrymen and thought every foreigner a fool till he proved otherwise. As George Trevelyan observed, the British, unlike subjects of the *anciens régimes* on the Continent, enjoyed "Parliamentary control, and freedom of speech, press and person. . . . They looked with contempt on French, Italians and Germans as people enslaved to priests, Kings and nobles, unlike your freeborn Englishmen."[1]

Compared to his friends, Johnson's travel experience was limited. Garrick had been apprenticed to the wine trade in Portugal, traveled to Italy and lived for a year in France. Reynolds had studied for two years in Italy. Goldsmith had attended three universities and seen six countries in Europe. Burke had toured northern France; Burney had ranged widely on the Continent. Boswell had studied in Holland and ventured as far as Corsica. Henry Thrale had done the Grand Tour. Psalmanazar was born in France; Baretti, born in Italy, had visited Spain. Charlotte Lennox had been to America; Robert Chambers became a judge in Bengal, India; Joseph Banks had sailed round the world. Even the humble members of his household were more cosmopolitan than Johnson. Levet had worked in France, where he'd picked up medical tidbits. Frank Barber, born in Jamaica, had gone to sea.

With Boswell, who was always urging him to travel, Johnson dreamed about journeys to remote and exotic destinations. Over the years, he talked of traveling to Iceland, Sweden, Poland and the Baltic countries. He vaguely hoped to turn up in some part of Europe, Asia and Africa; and oddly thought of going to Constantinople (where Turkish was spoken) to learn Arabic. Inspired by travel books and thinking of the wanderings of his own Rasselas, he told Hester of his fantastic plans, were he not bound to Streatham, to "go to Cairo, and down the Red Sea to Bengal, and take a ramble in India." He felt particularly enthusiastic about seeing the Great Wall of China, and in 1772 expressed a wish to join the *Resolution* and sail around Antarctica with Captain Cook. Writers, free to wander, long for the farthest corners of the earth. Johnson could say, with D. H. Lawrence, "I wish I were going to Thibet—or Kamschatka—or Tahiti—to the Ultima, ultima, ultima Thule."

These imaginary voyages were more a quest for knowledge than for pleasure. "The use of traveling," he wrote Hester, "is to regulate imagination by reality, and instead of thinking how things may be, to see them as they are." He fervently believed that "a man who has not seen

Italy, is always conscious of an inferiority, from his not having seen what is expected a man should see. The grand object of travelling is to see the shores of the Mediterranean." It's rather surprising, therefore, that in October 1764 Johnson had given up his one great opportunity for a long-sought visit to the Mediterranean. George Collier, captain of the HMS *Edgar* and a friend of Frances Reynolds, was taking his wife on a voyage to the Mediterranean and invited Frances and Johnson to join them. Instead of seizing what turned out to be his only chance, Johnson—who thought ships were even more unpleasant and danger-ous than jails—made all sorts of excuses to Frances: "I cannot go now. I must finish my [edition of Shakespeare]. I do not know Mr. Collier. I have not money before hand sufficient. . . . I do not much like obli-gations, nor think the grossness of a Ship very suitable to a Lady"—though the captain thought it was quite suitable for his wife.

In the eighteenth century, travel in the remoter parts of Europe could be very rough. Sea crossings, particularly in the Hebrides Islands, were dangerous. The towns were small, the countryside sparsely populated, the roads poor; travelers were often threatened by thieves and highwaymen. Accommodations were bug-infested, rations crude. Nevertheless, at an age when most men would have preferred to stay at home, Johnson was on the move, eager to make up for lost time and to see what he could of the world. He reached the peak of his travels in the early 1770s, when he went to Scotland with Boswell, and to Wales and France with Henry and Hester Thrale. Just after returning from Paris, he compared himself to a wandering vessel and told John Taylor, "fixed to a spot when I was young, and roving the world when others are contriving to sit still, I am wholly unsettled. I am a kind of ship with a wide sail, and without an anchor."[2]

II

In the summer of 1773 Boswell finally persuaded Johnson to visit the Highlands and Hebrides. He first had to overcome Johnson's deep-rooted prejudice against Scotland. The Act of Union in 1707 (two years before Johnson was born) had united the governments of Eng-land and Scotland in the London Parliament and combined their two flags in the Union Jack. After the Jacobite Rebellions of 1715 and 1745,

Johnson regarded Scotland as a persistent threat to England's peace and security. He loathed the Presbyterianism that opposed the sacred doctrines of the Church of England and "did not think that Calvin and John Knox were proper founders of a national religion"; he detested the freethinking, even atheistic views of Scottish philosophers such as David Hume; the prevailing Whiggism north of the border; and the disproportionate influence in the English government, exceeding their real merit, of Scots like the royal favorite Lord Bute.

Inspired as always by travel books, Johnson was both excited and alarmed when he read Martin Martin's description in 1703 of the Corryvreckan whirlpool that threatened to overwhelm small craft in the Hebrides: "the sea begins to boil and ferment with the tide at flood, and resembles the boiling of a pot; and then increases gradually, until it appears in many whirlpools, which form themselves in sort of pyramids, and immediately after sprout up as high as the mast of a little vessel, and at the same time make a loud report." Johnson was also familiar with the vertiginous passage about the beating billows and howling storms in the "Autumn" section of James Thomson's *The Seasons* (1730), which described the islands as wild and savage wastelands:

Or where the *Northern* Ocean, in vast Whirls,
Boils round the naked melancholy Isles
Of farthest *Thulè*, and th' *Atlantic* Surge
Pours in among the stormy *Hebrides*.

Two major themes of Johnson's travel book, *A Journey to the Western Islands of Scotland* (1775), are the effects of the '45 rebellion on Highland life and the extreme poverty of that barren land. After the defeat at Culloden the Highlanders were forbidden to bear arms and to wear their traditional tartan dress. The old clan system was breaking down, the lairds had lost their feudal power over tenants and there was massive emigration to America. A historian explained how the economic consequences of the peace had strangled a once vital society: "the chiefs, no longer reckoning their wealth in fighting men, began to demand rents from their principal tenants, the 'tacksmen' [leaseholders], whose main obligation hitherto had been to maintain the military strength of the clan and act as officers. Many tacksmen emigrated; those who remained demanded rent from their sub-tenants."[3]

Johnson granted that "every government must be allowed the power of taking away the weapon that is lifted against it." But when he saw the results with his own eyes, he believed the English repression had been too severe. In his book he echoed the famous passage in Tacitus in which a British chieftain surveyed the destruction of his country by the Romans and said "they make a wilderness and call it peace":

To hinder insurrection, by driving away the people, and to govern peaceably, by having no subjects, is an expedient that argues no great profundity of politicks. To soften the obdurate, to convince the mistaken, to mollify the resentful, are worthy of a statesman; but it affords a legislator little self-applause to consider, that where there was formerly an insurrection, there is now a wilderness. . . .

The clans retain little now of their original character, their feroc-ity of temper is softened, their military ardour is extinguished, their dignity of independence is depressed, their contempt of govern-ment subdued, and their reverence for chiefs abated.

Johnson disapproved of the rebellion, but felt sympathy for the repressed, hungry and dispirited people.

John Brewer pointed out that Johnson experienced a common par-adox of travel. After the rebellions were crushed: "the improvements that enabled travelers like Johnson . . . to visit the Highlands—coaches and improved communications with Scotland; roads into the Highlands built by General Wade after the Jacobite rebellion of 1715; the pacification after the rising of 1745 that ensured law and order and safe travel—were already intruding on the 'natural' primitiveness which travellers had come to observe."[4]

Johnson's itinerary—by coach, horseback, foot and boat—took him to Edinburgh, where he met Boswell; up the east coast; along the north coast; down the west coast; across the sea to seven islands in the Inner He-brides: Skye, Rassay, Coll, Mull, Ulva, Inch Kenneth and Iona; back to the mainland at Oban; southeast to Glasgow; and then south to Boswell's family estate at Auchinleck, in Ayrshire. During the Scottish trip, which lasted from August 14 to November 21, 1773, Johnson wrote Hester fourteen long, diary-like letters, which formed the basis of his book.

In Johnson's time the Highlands were considered violent, treacherous, impoverished and backward. Writing to Hester on September 30, he described contemporary Scotland in the same way that he'd portrayed Shakespeare's England: the Scots "are a Nation just rising from barbarity, long contented with necessaries, now somewhat studious of convenience, but not arrived at delicate discriminations." In the *Journey* he amplified this judgment and enraged many readers by insisting on the superiority of the English and comparing the Scots to the world's allegedly most primitive people: "till the Union made them acquainted with English manners, the culture of their lands was unskillful, and their domestick life unformed; their tables were coarse as the feasts of Esquimeaux, and their houses filthy as the cottages of Hottentots."

He found a perfect example of this kind of rude cottage on the isle of Skye, where his bedroom combined a promising appearance with a nasty surprise: "I found an elegant bed of Indian cotton, spread with fine sheets. The accommodation was flattering; I undressed myself, and felt my feet in the mire. The bed stood upon the bare earth, which the long course of rain had softened to a puddle." Johnson was still tough enough, at the age of sixty-four, to adapt to these spartan conditions. But, accustomed to the luxury of Streatham, he felt justified in emphasizing the hardships he endured.

Johnson seems to have been an excellent traveler, invigorated by the challenge of deprivation and stimulated by new sights and new acquaintances. As in London, he ranged from low to high society, from the mean turf cabins of the poor to the castles of the noblemen and chieftains. At the end of his journey he gloomily concluded: "of these islands it must be confessed, that they have not many allurements, but to the mere lover of naked nature. The inhabitants are thin, provisions are scarce, and desolation and penury give little pleasure." Yet he found the bleak surroundings were constantly redeemed by the abundant generosity of the natives, who often welcomed strangers as guests when there was no other place to stay. "The hospitality of this remote region," he wrote Hester, "is like that of the golden age [of plenty, innocence and happiness]. We have found ourselves treated at every house as if we came to confer a benefit."[5]

Johnson reached the spiritual pinnacle of his journey on the island of Iona. The monastery, founded there in 563 by the Irish saint Columba, had once been the center for Celtic Christianity and for missionaries who spread the Gospel to the heathens in Scotland and Northumbria. Johnson was saddened by the ruins of the illustrious churches and chapels, the monasteries and convents, where "savage clans and roving barbarians [had once] derived the benefits of knowledge, and the blessings of religion." Iona inspired the noblest passage in the book, when he pitted the body against the mind, the delusive senses against the strength of thought, which could summon up the glories of the past: "whatever withdraws us from the powers of our senses; whatever makes the past, the distant, or the future predominate over the present, advances us in the dignity of thinking beings."

The ruined churches of Iona also inspired a furious passage that was suppressed in the printed book. Johnson connected the stripping of lead roofs from Scottish churches in time of war with an urge to commit similar depredations to a sacred building, Lichfield Cathedral, which had always been close to his heart. With characteristic violence, he imagined the would-be predators suffering a medieval torture that would burn out their guts: "let us not however make too much haste to despise our neighbours. There is now, as I have heard, a body of men, not less decent or virtuous than the Scottish council, longing to melt the lead of an English cathedral. What they shall melt, it were just that they should swallow."

Johnson ended the *Journey* in a mood of elegiac tenderness. The "sixty-year-old smiling public man" investigated conditions at an Edinburgh school for the deaf. Partly deaf from birth himself, he identified with the handicapped children, who were taught to speak, write, and read both books and lips, a rare educational feat. "After having seen the deaf taught arithmetick," he optimistically asked, "who would be afraid to cultivate the Hebrides?" The first edition of his *Journey*, which appeared in January 1775, was 4,000 copies and cost five shillings. Johnson was paid £210 plus an additional £70 for a one-third share of his copyright.

Just after publication, Johnson's attack on James Macpherson's Ossian poems, the most contentious part of the book, boiled over into a fierce controversy. In the early 1760s Macpherson, a Scottish schoolmaster, had translated and published three volumes of prose poems that he attributed to Ossian, a third-century Gaelic bard. The poems soon became famous throughout Europe and were quoted extensively in Goethe's *Sorrows of Young Werther* (1774). Since Macpherson, when challenged, could never produce a genuine Gaelic manuscript, the poems could not be authenticated. Struggling against the contemporary tide of enthusiasm, Johnson took a forceful, even belligerent stance. In the *Journey* he declared: "I believe the [poems] never existed in any other form than that which we have seen. The editor, or author, could never shew the original; nor can it be shewn by any other; to revenge reasonable incredulity, by refusing evidence, is a degree of insolence, with which the world is not yet acquainted; and stubborn audacity is the last refuge of guilt."[6]

Thinking of the bitter battles on Grub Street, in his life of Sir Thomas Browne Johnson noted, "the reciprocal civility of authors is one of the most risible scenes in the farce of life." In January 1775 Macpherson, greatly affronted, sent Johnson a threatening letter. Relishing a fight, Johnson sent back a magnificent denunciation that equaled his fierce letter to Lord Chesterfield:

I received your foolish and impudent note. Whatever insult is offered me I will do my best to repel, and what I cannot do for myself the law will do for me. I will not desist from detecting what I think a cheat, from my fear of the menaces of a Ruffian.

You want me to retract. What shall I retract? I thought your book an imposture from the beginning. I think it upon yet surer reasons an imposture still. For this opinion I give the publick my reasons which I here dare you to refute.

But however I may despise you, I reverence truth and if you can prove the genuineness of the work I will confess it. Your rage I defy. . . .
You may print this if you will.

Johnson replaced the stout walking stick that was stolen from him in the Highlands with one even stouter to deal with Macpherson. He also sent a categorical letter to Boswell, who desperately wanted to believe his countryman and to preserve the honor of Scotland, carefully weighing the evidence: "Every thing is against him. No visible manuscript; no inscription in the language: no correspondence among friends: no transaction of business, of which a single scrap remains in the ancient families." Gibbon agreed with him, and in October 1775 wrote, "the dogmatic language of Johnson . . . seems to have given the bard a dangerous, if not a mortal wound."[7] Later on, Scott and Wordsworth also called the Ossian poems fakes, but Johnson's literary instinct and sceptical attitude had struck the first blow.

III

B oswell shaped Johnson's life by luring him to Scotland, even as he was preparing to write it. Johnson published his *Journey* fourteen months after completing the trip. He gave Boswell himself only a minor role, and focused on the historical, social and economic issues inherent in the barren landscape and rocky islands. He left out descriptions of his challenging intellectual discourse in Edinburgh and Glasgow, then at the height of the Scottish Enlightenment, as well as his heated dispute with Boswell's father at Auchinleck. Boswell published his *Tour to the Hebrides* in October 1785, a decade later and ten months after Johnson's death. Following Johnson's advice in *Rambler* 60 (which Johnson had ignored) and foreshadowing the method he would use in his *Life of Johnson* (1791), Boswell chose to lead "the thoughts into domestick privacies, and display the minute details of daily life." Johnson's book is about Scotland; Boswell's book is about Johnson.

Boswell's physical proximity to Johnson during their three-month tour, when they sometimes slept side by side on the bare floor, encouraged intimate revelations. He began his book with an intensely realistic portrait of Johnson's appearance and dress, which emphasized his vast size, scarred face, defects of hearing and vision, and jerky tremors. Overcoming these disabilities and completing the arduous journey, Boswell suggested, was a heroic feat:

His person was large, robust, I may say approaching to the gigantic, and grown unwieldy from corpulency. His countenance was naturally of the cast of an ancient statue, but somewhat disfigured by the scars of that *evil* which it was formerly imagined the *royal touch* could cure. He was now in his sixty-fourth year, and was become a little dull of hearing. His sight had always been somewhat weak . . . [but] his perceptions were uncommonly quick and accurate. His head and sometimes also his body shook with a kind of motion like the effect of a palsy; he appeared to be frequently disturbed by cramps or convulsive contractions, of the nature of that distemper called St. Vitus's dance. He wore a full suit of plain brown clothes with twisted-hair buttons of the same colour, a large bushy greyish wig, a plain shirt, black worsted stockings, and silver buckles. Upon this tour, when journeying, he wore boots and a very wide brown cloth greatcoat with pockets which might almost have held the two volumes of his folio dictionary, and carried in his hand a large English oak stick.

Boswell mentioned that Johnson was well aware of his forbidding, even ogreish appearance. "'Would you not, sir,' Boswell asked, 'start as Mr. Garrick does if you saw a ghost?' 'I hope not. If I did, I should frighten the ghost.'" Assuming a deep voice and Polyphemus persona, he told a little girl that "he lived in a cave and had a bed in the rock, and she should have a little bed cut opposite to it." Johnson's convulsive motions seemed to amuse Boswell's four-month-old daughter, Veronica, who allowed him to hold her and gave proof that his figure was not horrid. Paradoxically, though he looked like a monster and wolfed his food in the crudest way, he could be unusually delicate. When a waiter picked up a lump of sugar with his greasy fingers and dropped it into Johnson's cup, he indignantly flung the tea out the window and seemed ready to knock the servant down.

On two occasions Boswell's display of domestic privacies led, rather surprisingly, to down-to-earth discussions of domestic privies. Noting the lack of "that very essential particular," the "little-house," in one grand house, Johnson said, "if ever a man thinks at all, it is there. He generally thinks then with great intenseness. He sets himself down as quite alone." Noting on another occasion how rare the convenient "temple of Cloacina" was on the Hebridean islands, Johnson remarked, "you take very good care of one end of a man, but not of the other."[8] This was a somewhat cruder variant of his comment about whipping boys' bottoms at school.

At Loch Ness they asked an ancient crone where she slept in her cottage and, fearing they had designs upon her person, she seemed perturbed by the question. Her reaction inspired some good-natured banter. Playing on Boswell's sexual propensities and Johnson's frightening demeanor, they exchanged the roles of villainous and virtuous men.

> [Johnson]: She'll say, "There came a wicked young fellow, a wild young dog, who I believe would have ravished me had there had not been with him a grave old gentleman who repressed him. But when he gets out of the sight of his tutor, I'll warrant you he'll spare no woman he meets, young or old." "No," said I, "She'll say, 'There was a terrible ruffian who would have forced me, had it not been for a gentle, mild-looking youth, who, I take it, was an angel.'"

Another apparently minor incident provoked a furious reaction from Johnson. As Boswell started to ride ahead in the Highlands to warn the innkeeper of their imminent arrival, "Mr. Johnson called me back with a tremendous shout, and was really in a passion with me for leaving him. . . . He said doing such a thing made one lose confidence in him who did it." In the evening "Johnson was still violent upon that subject, and said, 'Sir, had you gone on, I was thinking that I should have returned with you to Edinburgh and then parted, and never spoke to you more.'" The critic Michael Joyce wrote that Boswell's apparent desertion and betrayal made "the whole universe seem hostile" to Johnson, but didn't explain why he felt that way. It may have reminded the always guilt-ridden Johnson of his ride to Derby on his wedding day, when he too rode out of sight, left Tetty behind and found her in tears as she caught up with him. His primordial fear of being abandoned by his guide in a barren and desolate region may also have recalled, deep within him, the sense of being abandoned by his mother to the wet nurse—the very source of his unhappiness.

Johnson was far less frightened when his life actually was in danger. His courage was tested as they crossed the open sea from Skye to Coll, ran into a fierce storm and were hit by "a prodigious sea with immense billows coming upon a vessel, so as that it seemed hardly possible to escape." Boswell was terrified and feared for his life. But "Johnson had all this time been quiet and unconcerned. He had lain down on one of the beds, and having got free of sickness, was quite satisfied. . . . He was lying in philosophic tranquillity, with a greyhound at his back keeping him warm."⁹

Though Boswell's chief concern was to describe daily life with his fascinating traveling companion, he suppressed many passages in the first edition that showed Johnson in a negative light. They were not restored until the text of the original manuscript was published in 1936. He did not include Johnson's piquant remarks about privies, nor describe how Johnson, enraged by the Reverend Kenneth Macaulay's disrespect for the English clergy, called him, in uncharacteristically vulgar language, "the most ignorant booby and the grossest bastard."

Most significant were the passages Boswell omitted at the end of the *Tour*, when Johnson met Boswell's wife and forbidding father in Auchinleck. Margaret, Boswell's first cousin and devoted wife, was thirty-five in 1773, two years older than her husband. Veronica, their first child, was born that year, and they later had four other children. Margaret served Johnson tea until two in the morning and gave up her own bedroom for him to sleep in. But she was unimpressed by his genius and disliked his irregular hours and eccentric behavior, which the Thrales so obligingly tolerated. Writing to Hester from Auchinleck, Johnson described Margaret as a suitable companion for his friend, in a way that suggested Tetty at her best: "Mrs. Boswell has the mien and manners of a Gentlewoman, and such a person and mind, as would not be in any place either admired or contemned. She is in a proper degree inferiour to her husband; and she cannot rival him, nor can he ever be ashamed of her."

Both Margaret and Lord Auchinleck resented Johnson's overwhelming influence on Boswell and compared his mentor to a bad-tempered beast. His father was the first to pun on the name of a starry constellation and call him "Ursa Major," the Great Bear. Margaret acerbically remarked, "I have seen many a bear led by a man: but I never before saw a man led by a bear." When Johnson was especially rude on his trip to Edinburgh, a departing guest gave the host a shilling and said, as if visiting a zoo, "have I not seen your *bear?*"[10] Boswell carefully cut out these sharp remarks.

Though Johnson had managed to avoid personal confrontations with political adversaries like Walmesley, Burke and Wilkes, he got into an explosive argument—despite several warnings—with Boswell's father, Lord Auchinleck, a year older than himself. "He was," Boswell nervously wrote, "as sanguine a Whig and Presbyterian as Dr. Johnson was a Tory and Church of England man." Boswell had tried to provoke a fight with Wilkes and now tried to prevent one with his father, but was foiled both times. Anxious that all should be well, he begged Johnson "to avoid three topics, as to which they differed very widely: Whiggism, Presbyterianism, and—Sir John Pringle," who had liberal religious views. "The contest began," Boswell wrote, "while my father was showing him his collection of medals; and Oliver Cromwell's coin unfortunately introduced Charles the First, and Toryism. They became exceedingly warm and violent, and I was very much distressed by being present at such an altercation between two men, both of whom I reverenced."[11] Submitting, for once, to discretion, he was unwilling to entertain the public with the dispute between two intellectual gladiators. But Boswell's *Tour* still contained a lively portrait of Johnson, who read and approved the book in manuscript, endorsing Boswell's method and general veracity. Despite the dangers and discomforts it described, the popular book also encouraged travelers to explore the most remote and wild regions of Britain.

IV

Eight months after returning from Scotland, Johnson was ready once again to hoist his sail and start roving the world. On July 5, 1774, he set out for Wales with the Thrales. The main point of the three-month trip with Henry, Hester and Queeney was to inspect the property that Hester had inherited in her native land. Their own coach and four fast horses first carried them to Lichfield and Ashbourne to see Johnson's old friends, including his step-daughter Lucy Porter, David Garrick's brother Peter and his old school chum John Taylor, who put them up for eleven days. In North Wales they stayed with Hester's uncle Sir Lynch Cotton, near Denbigh, for three weeks. They then traveled along the north coast to Anglesey, had a chance meeting with General Paoli in Caernarvon and visited Hester's birthplace at Bodvel, in the Lleyn Peninsula. They returned along the north coast through Bangor and Conway; saw Edmund Hector in Birmingham; and spent the last days at Burke's country estate in Beaconsfield, about twenty miles northwest of London.

In the eighteenth century the pristine rural landscape—with no factories, highways or mechanical transport—had pure air, glistening streams, clear birdsong and night skies filled with bright stars. Because of his poor vision, Johnson did not respond to the spectacular scenery, but he was intensely curious about everything else, especially the Welsh language, churches and religious services. He also seemed determined to dislike everything he saw, in both the west of England and the north of Wales. His diary, repeating the word "mean," recorded an endless series of disappointments while visiting the great houses and cathedrals. He noted that Chatsworth, the grand estate of the Duke of Devonshire, "fell below my ideas of the furniture." Dovedale "did not answer my expectation." Kedleston was "very costly but ill contrived," with bedchambers "fitter for a prison than a house of splendour." Lord Kilmurrey's house in Shropshire "was not splendid. . . . He has no park, and little water." The disturbing precipices at Hawkstone had "the horrour of solitude, a kind of turbulent pleasure between fright and admiration." Chester Cathedral was "not of the first rank." The house at Bachycraig "was less than I seemed to expect." The bishop's palace at St. Asaph was "but mean." Cotton's summerhouse was "meanly built and unskilfully disposed." John Middleton's home at Gwaynynog was "below the second rate." Lord Bulkeley's house was "very mean." In Hugh Griffiths' garden "fruit trees did not thrive, but . . . reached some barren stratum and wither." In Bangor Cathedral "the Quire was mean, the service was not well read." At Bodvel the churches were "mean and neglected to a degree scarcely imaginable."[12]

When Hester finally reached her childhood home, she wandered through the rooms and summoned up remembrance of things past. Johnson, taking a characteristically self-centered view, recorded, "this species of pleasure is always melancholy"—for him, perhaps, though not for her. Their hostess Mrs. Cotton (another relative), already intimidated by Johnson, was not used to being treated rudely by him or anyone else. At her home, he wrote with a certain schadenfreude, "we then went to see a cascade, I trudged unwillingly, and was not sorry to find it dry." Though the water eventually flowed and produced a striking cataract, he teased Mrs. Cotton about her dry cascade till she was ready to water it with her own tears. Trudging unwillingly through Wales, Johnson felt obliged to criticize everything in order to balance Hester's forced enthusiasm. "Why is it," he asked her, "that whatever you see, and whoever you see, you are to be so indiscriminately lavish of praise?" Rather saucily, she replied, "Why I'll tell you, Sir, when I am with you . . . I am obliged to be civil for *two*."[13]

Back in London and contrasting Scotland to Wales (perhaps to please Hester), Johnson wrote that the former "seems to me little more than one continued rock, covered from space to space with a thin layer of earth," while the latter was "a very beautiful and rich country, all enclosed, and planted." But in a letter to John Taylor he also reduced Wales to a nullity, declaring, "I am glad that I have seen it, though I have seen nothing, because I now know there is nothing to be seen." He paradoxically found value in nothing and seemed to think almost any place was worth seeing—if only to prove that there was, in fact, nothing at all to see. Mentioning a fashionable resort on the Dorset coast, he wrote Hester, "I think You will do well in going to Weymouth for though it be nothing, it is, at least to the young ones, a new nothing, and they will always be able to tell that they have seen Weymouth."[14]

The following year, from mid-September to mid-November, the itinerant Thrales, accompanied by Johnson and the indispensable Baretti as their majordomo and dragoman, took Johnson on his first trip to the Continent. The Thrales must have been extremely tolerant and optimistic to embark on a long journey with two such contentious personalities. Johnson's hostility toward France was even greater than his dislike of Scotland. To most Englishmen of his time, Catholic France seemed superstitious, decadent, militaristic and repressive. France was England's most formidable enemy, and in 1700 its population was three times larger. The British fought several major wars with the French throughout the eighteenth century: the War of Spanish Succession (1702–13), the War of Austrian Succession (1743–48) and the Seven Years' War (1756–63). In 1775 they were gearing up for another series of battles in the War of American Independence (1778–83). Visiting France that year would have been like visiting hostile Germany in the 1930s, soon after one war and just before the next. Since the British had defeated the French in the first three wars, Johnson felt justified in asserting, "we had drubbed those fellows into a proper reverence for us, and their national petulance required periodical chastisement."

In his youth, Johnson had taught himself to read and write French. A modern critic has concluded that his French was undoubtedly that "of a well educated Englishman, but it also shows a strong vocabulary and a reasonable grasp of idiom, together with a courtliness of expression that would be considered rare at the present time." But Johnson's accent was atrocious and the wretched French found his speech incomprehensible. He used language as part of his struggle against the French, and as he told Frances Reynolds, "I spoke only Latin, and I could not have much conversation: There is no good in letting the French have a superiority over every word you speak."[15]

En route to Paris the travelers passed through the cathedral towns of northern France and came back by a slightly different route. Between Rouen and Paris, as they were descending a steep hill, the postilion fell off the lead left horse, the straps broke and one of the horses was run over. Henry Thrale leaped out of the carriage and sustained a minor injury. Everyone was astonished and indignant about Johnson's behavior.

He remained as calm and apparently unconcerned about the accident as he'd been during the perilous storm at sea in Scotland.

Led by the multilingual Baretti and spurred on by Johnson's eagerness to see everything in Paris, they visited monuments, palaces and collections of art, as well as places where goods were manufactured: the École Militaire, Observatory, Courts of Justice, Bastille and orphanage; the Palais Royal, Palais Bourbon and Luxembourg Gardens; the king's cabinet of curiosities, king's library and paintings in the Tuileries; the king's watchmaker, the Gobelins carpet factory, the Sèvres porcelain factory, a looking-glass factory and, of course, a brewery. Johnson especially enjoyed his visit to the monastery at St. Cloud, just west of Paris, and his day with the English Benedictine monks, who spoke Latin well and said they'd always keep a cell ready for his use.

They also traveled to notable sites outside the capital. At Versailles, another "mean town," ten miles southwest of Paris, Johnson saw in the royal menagerie some of the wild animals with whom he'd been compared: a bear and an elephant, as well as a lion and tiger. The rhinoceros had his long horn broken and pared away, and his "skin folds like loose cloth doubled over his body, and cross his hips." At the Prince of Condé's magnificent mansion in the lace-making town of Chantilly, twenty-five miles north of Paris, he was struck by "a young hippopotamus preserved, which, however, is so small, that I doubt its reality. It seems too hairy for an abortion, and too small for a mature birth. Nothing was in spirits; all was dry."

Johnson had been touched by Queen Anne in 1712 and had conversed with King George III in 1767. He encountered his third monarch, Louis XVI, at Fontainebleau, thirty-five miles southeast of Paris, "a large mean town, crouded with people." After being admitted to the king's bedchamber, he was allowed, like courtiers and other spectators, to watch the king and queen eat dinner. He also saw the queen, Marie Antoinette, daughter of the Empress Maria Theresa of Austria, riding through the forest. Both king and queen were destined to be overthrown in the Revolution and to die on the guillotine. Dining in Paris with Madame Bocage, a literary lady of rank, was a less fortunate occasion. As in Scotland, Johnson had a run-in with an indelicate servant, whom he honored with an English nickname. After noting that the French would spit anywhere, he said that "the footman took the sugar in his fingers, and threw it into my coffee. I was going to put it aside; but hearing it was made on purpose for me, I e'en tasted Tom's fingers."[16]

Johnson's judgment of France was even harsher than his criticism of Scotland and of Wales. He was distressed to find that the country towns were filled with beggars and disturbed by the extreme contrast between rich and poor. He also disliked the food: "the great in France live very magnificently, but the rest very miserably. There is no happy middle state as in England. The shops of Paris are mean; the meat in the market is such as would be sent to a gaol in England . . . the cookery of the French was forced upon them by necessity; for they could not eat their meat, unless they added some taste to it." After returning to London, Johnson assumed a chauvinistic John Bull stance in letters to Edmund Hector and John Taylor: "I have seen nothing that much delighted or surprised me. Their palaces are splendid, and their Churches magnificent in their structure, and gorgeous in their ornaments, but the city in general makes a very mean appearance. . . . The French have a clear air and a fruitful soil, but their mode of common life is gross, and incommodious, and disgusting."[17] His *tour de France,* like his previous journeys to Scotland and Wales, confirmed his belief in the superiority of the English.

After France, the Thrales planned a long-awaited trip to Italy, but in March 1776 their hopes were cruelly disappointed. Their last surviving son and heir, the promising nine-year-old Harry, fell sick one morning. After a violent illness that lasted only a few hours, he died mysteriously, possibly of convulsions, a ruptured appendix or a cerebral aneurysm. Since he'd nearly reached adolescence, his death was very difficult to bear, and Henry Thrale was absolutely devastated. Knowing that now he had no son to take over the prosperous brewery, he began to lose interest in both beer making and Parliament. Lapsing into gloomy inertia and consoling himself with food, he outdid Johnson in devouring gargantuan meals, suffered a series of strokes and hastened toward death.

Attempting to console Hester but unable to do so, Johnson wrote, "I know that such a loss is a laceration of the mind. I know that the whole system of hopes, and designs, and expectations is swept away at once, and nothing left but bottomless vacuity." Though not especially religious or prone to guilt, Hester blamed herself for the death of her favorite child and felt she'd reached the very limits of her endurance. "I was too proud of him, and provoked God's Judgments by my Folly. . . . Suffer me no more to follow my Offspring to the Grave." Harry's death forced the Thrales to cancel "the grand object of all travelling," the trip to Italy and the shores of the Mediterranean.

Harry's death also led to the final break with Baretti, nearly three years after his arrival at Streatham. He suddenly erupted, like a little Vesuvius, and took off after another quarrel. "On this day I quitted Streatham without taking leave," he indignantly wrote in June 1776, "perfectly tired of the impertinence of the Lady, who took every oppor-tunity to disgust me, unable to pardon the violent efforts I made at Bath to hinder her from giving tin-pills to Queeney." Johnson thought Baretti, who had no other prospects, had acted foolishly and would re-gret his impulsive decision. He told Boswell that "Baretti went away from Thrale's in some whimsical fit of disgust, or ill-nature, without taking any leave. It is well if he finds in any other place as good an habi-tation, and as many conveniences."[18] Without Baretti's provocations and tantrums, the household settled down to deal with their grief, and Johnson and Hester became increasingly intimate.

Baretti later vented his spleen against Hester with vindictive annota-tions in his copy of her *Letters to and from the Late Samuel Johnson* (1788). Little Ralph Thrale had died at the age of twenty months from a con-genital softening of the brain, which (the autopsy revealed) was almost dissolved in water. But Baretti, with savage irony, blamed Hester for his death: "he died within the year of the innoculated small-pox, during which the mother used to wash him in cold water in consequence of her great skill in physic." He also unjustly blamed her for the death of young Henry and for trying to conceal the evidence that she had killed him. Annotating Johnson's letter of March 25, 1776 (two days after Henry's death), but without suggesting the motives for her alleged behavior, Baretti wrote: "here our Madam has sunk the letter to which this is an answer. Did she own in it that she herself poisoned little Harry, or did she not?" Hester was deeply wounded when Baretti published some of his malignant accusations in the *European Magazine* of May 1788. She expressed her grief by recording that "Baretti alone tried to irritate a wound so very deeply inflicted, and he will find few to approve his cruelty." She condemned him as "the man in the World I think whom I most abhor, & who hates, & professes to hate *me* the most."[19]

Unusually tolerant and forbearing with Baretti, Johnson also quarreled with him at the end. A high point of the French trip, he told Levet, was when he raced Baretti (who was ten years younger) and beat him. When Baretti played several games of chess with Omai—a handsome "Noble Savage," brought home by Captain Cook from Tahiti and enthusiastically taken up by London society—Omai also beat him. As Hester remarked, "you would have thought Omai the Christian, and Baretti the Savage." Greatly amused by the result of this unequal contest, Johnson—who could be a cruel tease—enraged Baretti, on his last visit to Bolt Court in 1782, by constantly referring to his humiliating defeat. After the quarrel, according to Baretti, he exploded and took off exactly as he'd done at the Thrales: "[Johnson] recollected that Omai had often conquered me at chess; a subject on which, whenever chance brought it about, he never failed to rally me most unmercifully, and made himself mighty merry with. This time, more than he had ever done before, he pushed his banter on at such a rate, that at last he chafed me, and made me so angry, that, not being able to put a stop to it, I snatched up my hat and stick, and quitted him in a most choleric mood."[20]

V

Between his return from Wales and departure for Paris Johnson wrote his last political pamphlet of the 1770s, *Taxation No Tyranny* (March 1775). Commissioned by the British government, it defended Parliament's right to tax the American colonies. In May, Garrick wrote Boswell in Scotland about how eagerly this work was received: "our friend has this day produc'd another political pamphlet call'd, *Taxation No Tyranny*, a very Strong attack upon Americans & Patriots—it is said to be well & masterly done—I shall devour it the Moment I have finished this letter."

Johnson's pamphlet, written in a fury of chauvinism and loathing of rebellion, combined bitter vituperation with false reasoning. He angrily complained that the Americans "multiply with the fecundity of their own rattle-snakes," and famously asked: "how is it that we hear the loudest yelps for liberty among the drivers of negroes?"[21] But Johnson, as an Englishman, was in no position to attack the American treatment of slaves. Despite the loud yelps of evangelicals in England, slavery was not abolished in the British Empire until 1833.

The essential issues raised by the American Congress in September–October 1774 were, according to Donald Greene, "first, did the central government at Westminster, the Parliament of Great Britain, have the constitutional right to enforce fiscal legislation in the outlying parts of the British dominions, and, second, is 'taxation without representation' legal and equitable? To both questions the Congress answers no and Johnson yes." Johnson believed that the principle "no taxation without representation" was false because millions of Britons, who were not qualified by land or income to vote for members of Parliament, had to pay taxes. But this argument could not convince American landowners and farmers, who produced great wealth for the empire and got precious little in return. Johnson's argument was doubly fallacious because even British citizens without the vote were represented by a Member of Parliament for their district. The Americans had neither a vote nor members to protect their interests. Johnson's statement "as all are born the subjects of some state or other, we may be said to have been all born consenting to some system of government" was (as the subjunctive "may be said" suggested) also specious. There could be no such tacit consent by infants at birth, and American adults strongly contested this so-called acquiescence.

In the end, Johnson advocated the use of force to maintain the power of the central government and the unity of the empire: "government is necessary to man, and where obedience is not compelled, there is no government. If the subject refuses to obey, it is the duty of authority to use compulsion. Society cannot subsist but by the power, first of making laws, and then of enforcing them." This was clearly an argument for war. He concluded with a completely unrealistic plan to threaten the Americans with a huge army, which would make them submit to British authority without loss of blood: "I cannot forbear to wish, that this commotion may end without bloodshed, and that the rebels may be subdued by terrour rather than by violence; and therefore recommend such a force as may take away, not only the power, but the hope of resistance, and by conquering without a battle, save many from the sword."[22]

Once the War of Independence began, Johnson abandoned this notion and seemed to thirst for American blood. In April 1778 he forcefully told Boswell, "I am willing to love all mankind, *except an American. . . .* Rascals—Robbers—Pirates . . . [I'd] burn and destroy them." Three years later he wanted, like the Roman generals in ancient Britain, to make a wilderness and call it peace: "had we treated the Americans as we ought, and as they deserved, we should have at once razed all their towns,—and let them enjoy their forests."

Johnson's Tory blast in *Taxation* provoked many replies. Burke made his great speech on reconciliation with America on March 22, 1775, just after the appearance of Johnson's pamphlet. He forcefully argued that the Americans "were fighting for the same liberties, including the principle of no taxation without representation and consent, as those which Englishmen had given their lives to defend during previous centuries." John Wesley plagiarized the essence of Johnson's tract in his *Calm Address to Our American Colonies* (1775). The Americans avidly responded to Johnson's pronouncement. Benjamin Franklin, in his *Retort Courteous* (c.1776), replied to Johnson's remark about slavery and ironically declared: "an order arrives from England, advised by one of their most celebrated *moralists*, Dr. Johnson, in his *Taxation No Tyranny,* to excite these slaves to rise, cut the throats of their purchasers, and resort to the British army, where they would be rewarded with freedom."[23]

Franklin's counterattack was especially significant for, as James Basler observed, American political leaders particularly valued Johnson's work:

In 1750 Benjamin Franklin was quoting *The Vanity of Human Wishes* in *Poor Richard's Almanac,* in 1757 twenty-year-old John

Hancock acquired his own copy of *The Rambler.* . . . Harvard
College listed *The Rambler* and *Idler* in a catalog of the most frequently used books in its library in 1773, and the next year Alexander Hamilton . . . cited Johnson's *Dictionary* in his first political
essays. John Adams quoted *London* and *The Vanity of Human
Wishes* in some of his earliest writings, and periodically sniped at
Johnson in his private letters. George Washington himself had in
his library both Johnson's *Dictionary* (the 1786 folio edition) and,
more surprisingly, *The World Displayed* [1759], with Johnson's vehemently anti-imperialist, anti-slavetrade introduction. Johnson
was part of the consciousness of every literate American during the
Founding Era.

The politically conservative Coleridge, usually hostile to Johnson, took
his side against the Americans and in August 1833 recorded: "I like Dr.
Johnson's political pamphlets better than any other parts of his works—
particularly his *Taxation No Tyranny* is very clever and spirited." Johnson's views on America were reactionary because he hated revolutionary
chaos on principle, and he resorted to any kind of argument against it.
But he was progressive on most other questions, and during the next
thirty years his ideas influenced the vital social issues of that time: the
abolition of slavery, prison reform, rehabilitation of prostitutes and
treatment of the poor.

Johnson had been awarded honorary degrees every ten years. He had
received a master of arts degree from Oxford in 1755; a doctor of laws
degree from Trinity College, Dublin, in 1765 (which made him Dr.
Johnson); and a doctor of civil laws degree from Oxford in 1775. Since
the prime minister, Lord North, was also chancellor of Oxford and
Johnson's last degree was awarded three months after *Taxation*
appeared, it was generally considered the reward for his political pam-
phleteering. When some politicians suggested that Johnson—equaled
only by Burke as an intellectual, writer and speaker—stand for a pocket
borough in Parliament, Lord North refused. Fearing that Johnson
could not be controlled, North compared him to a rogue elephant in
battle, "quite as likely to trample down his friends as his foes."[24] In the

1780s Johnson's government pension was listed in the category "Writers Political," but in June 1784 he complained to Hester that he hadn't been paid for nearly a year and was very poor.

VI

In 1727 Johnson's friend Richard Savage was tried and convicted of murder, and given a royal pardon. In 1769 Giuseppe Baretti was also tried for murder, but was acquitted. In May 1777 (two years after *Taxation*), Johnson—who'd defended Savage in print and testified for Baretti in court—became involved in another murder case, but this time the defendant was convicted and hanged. Johnson's sceptical mind had exposed three frauds and forgeries: William Lauder's claim that John Milton had plagiarized Renaissance Latin poets in 1750, the Cock Lane ghost in 1762 and Macpherson's Ossian poems in 1775. He did not believe in the authenticity of Thomas Chatterton's pseudo-medieval Rowley poems, supposedly the work of a fifteenth-century Bristol poet. Yet when William Dodd, a popular and successful clergyman, was charged with forgery, Johnson was called in to assist with the defense.

Dodd, the son of a clergyman, was born in Lincolnshire in 1729 and educated at Cambridge. Extremely good-looking and charming, he soon became famous for his theatrical preaching and charitable work. A historian characterized him as "an adroit and ambitious divine who founded his career on the fashion for sentimental sermonizing. His performances in the pulpit were highly regarded, not least by philanthropic ladies disposed to pity the plight of fallen women and distressed debtors."

In *Reflections on Death* (1763) Dodd described how some of his contemporaries had met their end. He'd preached a sermon against the excessive use of capital punishment, but in 1772, after being shot at by a highwayman, he gave evidence that led to the criminal's execution. Dodd had been chaplain to George III, but lost that position when his wife attempted to bribe the lord chancellor in order to secure a lucrative living for her husband. William Cowper, who considered Dodd histrionic, hypocritical and self-serving, portrayed him in *The Task* (1785) as "a stranger to the poor; / Ambitious of preferment for its gold." Handsome and polished, worldly and fashionable, materialistic and greedy, Dodd was the antithesis of Johnson. After their first and only meeting, in 1751, Dodd condescendingly described him as "the oddest and most peculiar fellow I ever saw. He is six feet high, has a violent convulsion in his head, and his eyes are distorted. He speaks roughly and loud."[25]

The 4th Earl of Chesterfield, to whom Johnson had written his angry letter about the *Dictionary*, had hired Dodd to tutor his cousin and heir, who succeeded him in 1773. But Dodd's substantial income could not match his luxurious way of life. On February 1, 1777, he forged papers to procure a loan of £4,200, ostensibly for the 5th Earl, and pocketed the money. The truth came out when the earl was asked about the loan. Dodd immediately repaid £3,600 and gave promissory notes for the remaining £600, but he was arrested anyway and charged with forgery. Leon Radzinowicz, the historian of criminal law, wrote, "owing to Dodd's social standing, his fashionable life, his great popularity and the circumstances of his offence, the case at once became the sensation of the day." Dodd's case was "the first to stir the public conscience, and to force it to question whether the absolute capital punishment was socially and morally justifiable."

Johnson's principal motives for helping Dodd were compassion for the criminal, desire to have Dodd publicly confess his crime, and belief that it was wrong to execute a clergyman. As he wrote to the Reverend John Taylor: "it is a thing almost without example for a Clergyman of his rank to stand at the bar for a capital breach of morality. I am afraid he will suffer [the penalty]. The Clergy seem not to be his friends. The populace that was extremely clamorous against him, begin to pity him." Most important, he thought such a penalty for forgery was unjust and in Dodd's case amounted to judicial murder.

Johnson took up Dodd's case with tremendous energy. He wrote an eloquent speech, which Dodd delivered at his Old Bailey trial, but which carried scant legal weight. After Dodd's conviction on February 22, Johnson wrote petitions of clemency to the lord chancellor and the chief justice, to the secretary of state for war and to the king himself. When asked why he took up Dodd's cause, he recalled his own fear of death and replied: "I thought with myself, when Dr. Dodd comes to the place of execution, he may say, Had Dr. Johnson written in my behalf, I had not been here, and (*with great emphasis*) I could not bear the thought."[26]

All Johnson's efforts failed to secure a royal pardon, despite a public petition of 23,000 signatures and the fact that Dodd was personally known to the king. He then composed Dodd's last solemn declaration in the form of a convict's sermon addressed to his "Unhappy Brethren." The sermon stressed the need for Dodd's personal contrition and for his recognition that the verdict was, according to the law, both inevitable and just. Delivering the ghostwritten sermon in Newgate prison on June 6, 1777, Dodd declared: "of him, whose life is shortened by his crimes, the last duties are humility and self-abasement. . . . For my own part, I confess, with deepest compunction, the crime which has brought me to this place; and admit the justice of my sentence, while I am sinking under its severity." Paul Alkon explained Johnson's subtle and effective rhetorical technique in this sermon: "the speaker includes himself among the condemned, thus collapsing ordinary distinctions between preacher and audience. . . . [Johnson] places one simultaneously in the position of a condemned man and his chaplain, who in this case is the voice of that man's conscience."

Dodd's impending execution inspired one of Johnson's most famous declarations: "Depend upon it, Sir, when a man knows he is to be hanged in a fortnight, it concentrates his mind wonderfully." But, ironically enough, the irrepressible Dodd still didn't believe he was about to be hanged. He had £500 in his pocket and hoped to bribe the turnkeys to let him escape, but they were watched too closely to be suborned. Ever optimistic, Dodd thought to the very end that he would be reprieved or even pardoned. And he was still trying, until a few days before his death, to get his comedy produced on the London stage. Dodd was executed, four months after his trial, on June 27. A modern critic noted that Garrick's Drury Lane production that year of John Gay's *The Beggar's Opera* commented on this case. By substituting "a specific royal pardon for the poetic reprieve" in Gay's play, Garrick alluded "to the king's refusal to pardon the celebrated clergyman forger, Dr. Dodd."[27]

Johnson disliked the disorder and violence that accompanied public executions, but he himself was capable, on occasion, of inciting discord and civil unrest. In 1749 he'd attacked the absurdity of a government-sponsored fireworks display to celebrate the Peace of Aix-le-Chapelle in the Seven Years' War: "nothing more is projected, than a crowd, a shout and a blaze; the mighty work of artifice and contrivance, is to be set on fire, for no other purpose, that I can see, than to shew how idle pyrotechnical virtuosos have been busy. . . . How many widows and orphans, whom the war has ruined, might be relieved, by the expence which is now about to evaporate in smoke, and to be scattered in rockets."

Twenty-five years later, in about 1774, Johnson and the Shakespearean editor George Steevens went to see Signor Torré's display of pyrotechnics at Marylebone Gardens. It had been raining, and the management told the sparse crowd that the fireworks were thoroughly water-soaked and had to be cancelled. Johnson, like a spoiled child, demanded an impossible treat:

"This is a mere excuse," says the Doctor, "to save their crackers for a more profitable company. Let us but hold up our sticks, and threaten to break those coloured Lamps that surround the Orchestra, and we shall soon have our wishes gratified. The core of the fireworks cannot be injured. . . .

Some young men who overheard him, immediately began the violence he had recommended, and an attempt was speedily made to fire some of the wheels which appeared to have received the smallest damage; but to little purpose were they lighted, for most of them completely failed.[28]

Even Johnson could be irrational and violent, yet he was properly horrified when attacks on public order and property rights broke out during the first week of June 1780. Lord George Gordon, leading the Protestant Association and demanding the "repeal of more liberal legislation for Roman Catholics," "taught to ignorant men most violent ways, / And hurled the little streets upon the great." Pat Rogers described the chaos of the Gordon Riots:

The crowd attacked the homes and coaches of prominent figures believed to be responsible for the measure, including [the
chief justice] Lord Mansfield, as well as targeting the houses
and businesses of Catholics. Mass-houses were burnt and jails
opened to release the prisoners. The Bank of England was
seized for a time and the outlook for the authorities appeared
bleak. On 7 June thirty-six fires were in progress. Among the
civic authorities attempting to quell the riot was John Wilkes,
as City Chamberlain. The soldiers, militia and citizen bands
gradually gained the upper hand.

During that week, the most disastrous civil disturbance in modern
British history, crowds shouting "No Popery" destroyed more than a
hundred houses and did more than £100,000 worth of damage. Burke's
home near St. James' Square was threatened by the mob and saved only
by the timely appearance of a detachment of soldiers.

On the scene and ignoring the danger, like a modern war correspondent, Johnson wrote Hester (who was safely taking the waters in Bath)
a vivid eyewitness report of the riots:

At night they set fire to the fleet [district], and to the kingsbench,
I know not how many other places; you might see the glare of the
conflagration fill the sky from many parts. The sight was dreadful.
Some people were threatened. [The publisher] Mr. Strahan moved
what he could, and advised me to take care of my self. Such a time
of terrour you have been happy in not seeing.

The King said in Council that the Magistrates had not done
their duty, but that he would do his own, and a proclamation was
published directing us to keep our servants within doors, as the
peace was now to be preserved by force. The Soldiers were sent out
to different parts, and the town is now quiet.

Two months later, Johnson told Boswell how Thrale's brewery, a
prime target for the drunken crowd, had been saved by a cunning and

comparatively cheap stratagem: "in the late disturbances, Mr. Thrale's house and stock were in great danger; the mob was pacified at their first invasion, with about fifty pounds in drink and meat; and at their second, were driven away by the soldiers."[29] The "time of terrour" showed the English how easily a mob could be roused to destruction, and helped inoculate them against the revolutionary violence that would erupt in France in 1789.

19

ENCHAIN THE HEART
1778–1781

I

On March 29, 1777—a month after Dodd's conviction—a delegation representing forty London publishers approached Johnson during his Good Friday devotions, knowing full well that he would not be inclined to bargain on that sacred day. He quickly agreed to an extremely low fee of £200 (later topped up with a lagniappe of another £100) for a series of biographical and critical prefaces to an elegantly printed, pocket-sized, 52-volume edition of the English poets. The publishers wanted to protect their copyright, fight off Scottish competitors who were poaching on their territory and reprint the most saleable poets.

In his *Dictionary of the English Language* (1755) Johnson chose words sanctioned by writers who'd lived mainly between 1550 and 1750. In his *Lives of the Poets* (1779–81) the publishers chose poets from 1625 to 1773, excluding those still living, like Cowper and George Crabbe. They therefore excluded not only Geoffrey Chaucer, Edmund Spenser, Sir Philip Sidney and Shakespeare, but also John Donne and George Herbert (who'd appeared in Isaak Walton's *Lives*), Ben Jonson and Robert Herrick, Andrew Marvell and Sir John Suckling, Richard Lovelace and

Henry Vaughan—though all but the last two were at least mentioned by Johnson. They also unfortunately excluded the recently deceased Charles Churchill, who'd satirized Johnson in *The Ghost*; Thomas Chatterton, whose faux-medieval Rowley poems Johnson disliked; Christopher Smart, in and out of Bedlam, whose *Song to David* was considered bizarre; and Johnson's greatly admired friend Oliver Goldsmith, whose works (including Johnson's impressive lines in "The Traveller" and "The Deserted Village") were still in copyright. Accomplished women poets, like the Countess of Winchelsea and Lady Mary Wortley Montagu, did not make the cut.

The poets Johnson wrote about fall into four categories: those who are still considered major authors: Milton, Dryden, Pope and Swift; those read by scholars: Prior, Congreve, Gay, Thomson, Collins and Gray; dilettante Restoration aristocrats: Rochester (whose poems Johnson had "castrated"), Roscommon, Dorset, Halifax and Buckingham; and the mass of obscure poetasters who've been saved from complete oblivion only by a page or two in the *Lives*. After 225 years, the reputations of Rochester, Congreve, Gay and Gray are bullish, while those of the once-admired Cowley, Butler, Waller and Addison are distinctly bearish. Johnson, with thrifty husbandry, recycled his previously published life of Savage (1744), his characters of Roscommon (1748) and Collins (1763), and his essay on epitaphs (1756), which was awkwardly tacked on to the end of the life of Pope. Johnson's biographies covered 150 years of turbulent British history. The poets had lived through the reign of Charles I, the Civil War, the Puritan Commonwealth, the Restoration of Charles II, the brief years of Catholic James II, the Protestant Revolution of 1688, the years of Dutch William and Queen Anne, and the Hanoverian accession that brought in the German Georges.

Johnson wrote *The Lives of the Poets* con amore. Noting the fascination of gossip, the "delight the mind feels in the investigation of secrets," he declared, "the biographical part of literature is what I love most." He believed that biography, more than any other kind of writing, is the most personal and the most useful, the "most eagerly read, and most easily applied to the purposes of life." The judicious and faithful life-writer should not be general or abstract, but must "lead the thoughts into domestick privacies, and display the minute details of daily life."[1]

In a noble passage in the life of Addison, Johnson contrasted the apparent permanence of history to the evanescence of biography, which depended on fallible memory: "History may be formed from permanent monuments and records; but Lives can only be written from personal knowledge, which is growing every day less, and in a short time is lost for ever" (3.18). He was deeply concerned, as early as in his life of Sir Thomas Browne (1756), that these precious details, if not immediately captured, would quickly disappear: "silent excellencies are soon forgotten; and those minute peculiarities which discriminate every man from all others, if they are not recorded by those whom personal knowledge enables to observe them, are irrevocably lost." In some cases, when Orwellian revolutionaries tried to destroy the past, the need for preservation was urgent. In Cromwell's time, Johnson gravely noted, "it was seriously proposed, that all the records in the Tower should be burnt, that all memory of things past should be effaced, and that the whole system of life should commence anew" (2.8).

Though many of the fifty-two poets in Johnson's Lives are now forgotten (if indeed modern readers have ever heard of them), they all had significant reputations in their lifetime. Johnson's research for most of the poets was extremely cursory and slapdash, and he was not always conscientious about assembling and checking the accuracy of his information. "To adjust the minute events of literary history, is tedious and troublesome," he confessed in "Dryden," and "often depends upon enquiries which there is no opportunity of making, or is to be fetched from books and pamphlets not always at hand" (2.98). He complained to Hester that the monumental scope of the Lives compelled him to have "something to say about Men of whom I know nothing but their verses, and sometimes very little of them."

Many of Johnson's dates were wrong; and he needed (but didn't have) an officious Boswell to root out the necessary facts. There was a striking contrast between Bozzy's willingness "to run half over London, in order to fix a date correctly" and Johnson's perverse unwillingness to meet the accommodating Lord Marchmont, an intimate of Pope. "If it rained knowledge," Johnson exclaimed in his most imperious manner, "I'd hold out my hand; but I would not give my-self the trouble to go in quest of it."[2]

Several of the poets—Hammond, Shenstone, Gray, Collins and Akenside—were younger contemporaries of Johnson; and he was acquainted with many besides Marchmont who had known the poets he considered. Richard Savage, a friend of Pope and Steele, had been an especially good source. Johnson's father, a careful observer of his times, had told young Sam that the reception of Dryden's *Absalom and Achitophel* was extremely eager and the sale large; and he'd described the fervent preaching of Thomas Sprat. But the oral tradition became increasingly embroidered and unreliable as it moved further and further away from the original source. As Johnson wrote in "Milton": "A very particular story of his escape [after the Restoration] is told by Richardson in his Memoirs, which he received from Pope, as delivered by Betterton, who might have heard it from Davenant" (1.263).

Despite the need to preserve information, Johnson's all too frequent confessions of ignorance now seem shocking and would be inexcusable in a modern biography:

—I have sought intelligence among [Fenton's] relations . . . but have not obtained it. (3.89)
—Of Mr. Somervile's life I am not able to say anything that can satisfy curiosity. (3.118)
—Of the next years of [Denham's] life there is no account. (1.236)
—How [Philips] was employed, or in what station he passed his life, is not yet discovered. (4.111)
—The account [of Prior] therefore must now be destitute of his private character and familiar practices. (3.56)

Even more shameful was his throwing in the towel before he began, his brazen refusal to reach over to the bookshelf and take a cursory glance at the poets he was writing about:

—Of [Congreve's] plays I cannot speak distinctly; for since I inspected them many years have passed. (3.71)

—Of [Blackmore's] books, if I had read them, it could not be expected that I should be able to give a critical account. (3.83)

When he did read major poems like Dryden's *Absalom and Achitophel,* he considered the "work so well known, that particular criticism is superfluous" (2.135). In one case his indifference was so great that he subcontracted someone else to write the life of Edward Young. Johnson's extreme condensation and haste to finish the work was sometimes quite ludicrous. In the life of Waller he squeezed perhaps a quarter century of sexual activity and domestic fecundity into a single sentence by declaring: "Of this wife, his biographers have recorded that she gave him five sons and eight daughters" (2.30). The booksellers should have told him, as Gertrude Stein told Hemingway, "begin over again and concentrate." But they seemed to have been intimidated by Johnson, whom they'd secured at a bargain price. He complacently told one of them, John Nichols, that "the criticism was tolerably well done, considering that he had not read one of Rowe's plays for thirty years."

Johnson stated, with considerable exaggeration—since he was personally acquainted only with Richard Savage, William Collins and Lord Lyttleton—that "nobody can write the life of a man, but those who have eat and drunk and lived in social intercourse with him." He meant by this, and proved in his life of Savage, that the best lives are based on intimate knowledge. But this knowledge is often compromised by the need to spare the feelings of family and friends, and by pressure (which Boswell felt) to suppress the truth. He recognized that telling all was risky and in "Addison" said, "the necessity of complying with times, and of sparing persons, is the great impediment of biography. . . . What is known can seldom be immediately told; and when it might be told, it is no longer known. The delicate features of the mind, the nice discriminations of character, and the minute peculiarities of conduct, are soon obliterated" (3.18). When considering the heavy drinking of Addison and Parnell, Johnson insisted that truth must prevail: "If a man is to write *A Panegyrick,* he may keep vices out of sight; but if he professes to write *A Life,* he must represent it as it was."[3] Johnson began his life of Cowley (the first in the book) with a plea for a detailed, rather than indistinct, life; for history, not funeral oration; for truth, not praise. Though he scrupulously adhered to the veracity of available evidence, he followed the ideal of judicious restraint and sensitively refrained from publishing controversial material that might give pain to living people.

II

While balancing biography and criticism, Johnson took care to delineate each poet's character and express authoritative judgments on his poetry. He used a logical tripartite structure in both his sermons ("firstly," "secondly," "thirdly") and in the *Lives* (life, character, works). He often contrasted "vigour" (a favorite word) with elegance and refinement. Though his approach was serious, he brightened the *Lives* by flashes of wit and by telling anecdotes—not moralistic, but often with a moral. Blackmore's heroic poem *Eliza* fell "*dead-born from the press*" (3.78). Steele's failure to complete a portrait of Addison showed that "the promises of authors [meant to seduce publishers] are like the vows of lovers" (3.22). Voicing his prejudice against rebellious America, he noted that Waller's eldest son "was disinherited, and sent to New Jersey, as wanting common understanding" (2.43). Though Johnson didn't invent the phrase, he gave wide currency to the clever mot about the successful author and producer of the first English musical, *The Beggar's Opera*, which made Gay rich and Rich gay.

Johnson's aphoristic critical judgments were, like Dryden's, handed down from on high, and he too could "without usurpation, examine and decide" (2.112). Of *Paradise Lost* he observed, "None ever wished it longer than it is" (1.290); of Congreve's romance *Incognita*, he admitted, "I would rather praise it than read it" (3.66). Thomson's equally impenetrable poem *Liberty* was consigned to the darkest corners of the library and "condemned to harbour spiders" (4.99). He could not conceive how in Addison's projected tragedy on the death of Socrates (who was forced to commit suicide for corrupting the youth of Athens), "love [interest] could have been appended" (3.16). Though Johnson had an exalted view of the power of judicious criticism, he also dismissed Dennis' and Dryden's censure of Addison's *Cato* by exclaiming: "as we love better to be pleased than to be taught, *Cato* is read, and the critick is neglected" (3.36).

The biographer, Johnson observed in *Rambler* 60, "enchains the heart by irresistible interest" in personal details. He mentioned that Milton traveled from Rome to Naples "in company of a hermit; a companion from whom little could be expected" (1.247). He described how the dreamy and solipsistic young John Philips, like a modern stoned hippie, "retired to his chamber; where his sovereign pleasure was to sit, hour after hour, while his hair was combed by somebody, whose service he found means to procure" (2.66). More exciting and more telling was his vivid account of the near-fatal accident of the crippled and helpless Alexander Pope, saved from drowning by the providential intervention of a brave and loyal servant. In one long sentence composed of a series of short, rapid phrases, Johnson described the crisis and the rescue: "Pope was returning home from a visit in a friend's coach, which, in passing a bridge, was overturned into the water; the windows were closed, and being unable to force them open, he was in danger of immediate death, when the postilion snatched him out by breaking the glass, of which the fragments cut two of his fingers in such a manner, that he lost their use" (4.31).

Johnson's weightier anecdotes revealed the aristocrat's careless indifference to the lives—indeed, the very existence—of the poets (well illustrated by Johnson's relations with his would-be patron Lord Chesterfield). When the pointlessly industrious Nicholas Rowe applied to the Earl of Oxford for a public position, "Oxford enjoined him to study Spanish; and when, some time afterwards, he came again, and said that he had mastered it, dismissed him with this consolation, 'Then, Sir, I envy you the pleasure of reading *Don Quixote* in the original'" (2.202). John Gay's audience with the Princess of Wales was pure slapstick: "When the hour came, he saw the princess and her ladies all in expectation, and advancing with reverence, too great for any other attention, stumbled at a stool, and falling forwards, threw down a weighty Japan screen. The princess started, the ladies screamed" (3.98). The brutal rejection by a favorite, even beloved, friend, was even more cruel and wounding. When the ill and aged Pope wished to summon Martha Blount to his bedside, Lord Marchmont "waited on the Lady; who, when he came to her, asked, '*What, is he not dead yet?*' She is said to have neglected him, with shameful unkindness, in the latter time of his decay" (4.52).

If Johnson's lives were often limited by lack of serious research, his criticism was sometimes compromised by dogmatic prejudice and notable blindness. He disliked mythology and condemned "Lycidas" by exclaiming, "the diction is harsh, the rhymes uncertain, and the numbers unpleasing" (1.278). (Johnson's poem "On the Death of Dr. Robert Levet," though not nearly as great an elegy as Milton's, is certainly more heartfelt and more moving.) Johnson had no appreciation of sonnets, which went out of fashion between Milton and Wordsworth. He dismissed Milton's finest sonnets as "not bad" and denounced the magnificent "Methought I saw my late espoused saint" as "poor." He insisted that closed couplets were superior to blank verse, which he'd used in his disastrous tragedy *Irene,* and said if it "be not tumid and gorgeous, it is crippled prose" (3.119). He hated the vogue for the medieval in Chatterton and in Macpherson's *Ossian.* Disgusted with pastorals, he insisted that in Shenstone "an intelligent reader, acquainted with the scenes of real life, sickens at the mention of the *crook,* the *pipe,* the *sheep,* and the *kids*" (4.129). Johnson's strictures, though severe, did lead to a salutary cleansing of exhausted mythological and pastoral baggage.

Johnson's greatest gaffe was oddly combined with unusual perspicacity. He was the first to recognize the significance of the Metaphysical poets, but failed to perceive their merit. His definition of Metaphysical poetry went back to his description of Sir Thomas Browne's style in 1756: "a mixture of heterogeneous words . . . drawn by violence into the service of another." He repeated and refined this definition in "Cowley" and famously wrote that their wit is "a kind of *discordia concors* [harmonious discord]; a combination of dissimilar images, or discovery of occult resemblances in things apparently unlike. . . . The most heterogeneous ideas are yoked by violence together" (1.200).

Instead of recognizing the genius of Donne's "A Valediction: of Weeping," in which the lovers' tears form a globe, a world—"Till thy tears mixt with mine do overflow / This world, by waters sent from thee my heaven dissolved so"—Johnson quotes it to condemn the learned conceit. In his review of Herbert Grierson's edition of *The Metaphysical Poets,* which revived Donne's reputation in 1921, T. S. Eliot—who conceded that Johnson was "a dangerous person to disagree with"—convincingly argued that "the force of [Johnson's] impeachment lies in the failure of the conjunction, the fact that often the ideas are yoked but not united. . . . But a degree of heterogeneity of material compelled into unity by the operation of the poet's mind is omnipresent in poetry."[4]

Johnson's two great strengths as a biographer and critic were intellect and imagination. He had, as he said of Dryden, "a mind very comprehensive by nature, and much enriched with acquired knowledge. His compositions are the effects of a vigorous genius operating upon large materials" (2.148). Johnson himself had an astonishing poetic range. He wrote amusing extemporaneous verse and tributes to pretty ladies, witty epigrams and parodies of ballads, translations of Horace and Virgil into English and of the *Greek Anthology* into Latin, intensely personal Latin poems, ingratiating prologues to plays and the poignant elegy on Dr. Levet, the embittered satire of *London* and majestic melancholy of *The Vanity of Human Wishes. Vanity's* famous couplet foreshadows the theme of the *Lives*: "Yet hope not Life from Grief or Danger free, / Nor think the Doom of Man revers'd for thee."

The theme of failure, the heartbreaking difference between "great promises and small performance," pervades Johnson's book. As Robert Burns shrewdly observed a decade after it appeared, "there is not among all the Martyrologies that ever were penned, so rueful a narrative as Johnson's *Lives of the Poets.*" In his "Project for the Employment of Authors" (1756), published after eight years of work on the *Dictionary,* the "harmless drudge" asserted: "If I were to form an adage of misery, or fix the lowest point to which humanity could fall, I should be tempted to name the life of an author . . . worried by critics, tormented by his bookseller, and hunted by his creditors."[5] The recurrent theme of the *Lives*—as of *Vanity,* the *Rambler* and *Rasselas*—is that "the general lot of mankind is misery." As he wrote in "Savage," "The heroes of literary as well as civil history have been very often no less remarkable for what they have suffered than for what they have achieved" (3.120).

Johnson was especially good on four subjects of riveting interest: love, sex, insanity and death. His description of love, whether passionate or tranquil, emphasized its ephemeral nature. In a nicely balanced adverbial sentence that suggested the hopeless incompatibility of emotions, he wrote that James Hammond's "love of a lady, whose name was Dashwood, for a time disordered his understanding. He was unextinguishably amorous, and his mistress inexorably cruel" (3.116). Lord Lyttleton, by contrast, "lived in the highest degree of connubial felicity: but human pleasures are short; she died in childbed . . . and he solaced his grief by writing a long poem to her memory" (4.186).

Johnson's discussion of sexual life, especially during the immoral Restoration, was witty, racy, even sensational. Yet he drew a discreet veil over Lord Rochester, the most notorious and self-destructive of the rakes, and didn't mention that he had once hired ruffians to beat up Dryden in a London alley. Johnson merely recorded that he was "remarkable for many wild pranks and sallies of extravagance. . . . He unhappily addicted himself to dissolute and vitious company, by which his principles were corrupted, and his manners depraved" (2.11–12). The modern reader longs for the juicy details and amusing obscenities in the opening lines of "A Ramble in St. James's Park," which refer to fornication and sodomy: "Much wine has passed with grave discourse, / Of who fucks who, and Who does worse." Rochester's play *Sodom,* performed at court, contained startling stage directions and a live performance of the sexual act. But Johnson, conscious of his moral responsibility to his audience, kept his narrative deliberately vague.

He was more forthcoming about Davenant's syphilitically ravaged nose, which "had suffered such diminution by mishaps among the women" that it had to be concealed by a telltale patch (2.99). The Duke of Buckingham, one of Rochester's corrupt companions, was about to be introduced to Samuel Butler, whom he'd agreed to recommend for royal favor. But "observing a pimp of his acquaintance . . . trip by with a brace of ladies, immediately quitted his engagement, to follow another kind of business" (2.3). Johnson, offering a royal anecdote, imitated King James' Scottish pronunciation of the word "lie": "a certain lord coming in soon after, his Majesty cried out, 'Oh, my lord, they say you lig with

my Lady.' 'No, Sir,' says his Lordship, in confusion; 'but I like her company, because she has so much wit.' 'Why then,' says the King, 'do you
not lig with my Lord of Winchester?'" (2.27). All these anecdotes,
despite their sexual content, had a moral undertone: the terrible consequences of immorality, the crass indifference of the great, a dissolute
court and cuckolded king.

Madness in others always elicited Johnson's sympathy. He wrote that
Denham's second marriage "disordered his understanding" and that he
was "lampooned for his lunacy." But "his frenzy lasted not long; and he
seems to have regained his full force of mind" (1.237). Johnson knew
"poor Collins" and was deeply concerned with his melancholy depression and tragic fate. Like Johnson, Collins "designed many works; but
. . . the frequent calls of immediate necessity broke his schemes, and
suffered him to pursue no settled purpose" (4.120). Johnson did not
quote Collins' "Ode to Fear," which ends, "Who, *Fear*, this ghastly
Train can see, / And look not madly wild, like Thee?"[6] But in one of
the most poignant and personal passages in the *Lives*, he described how
the poet (like Johnson himself) was assailed by the dreadful calamities
of disease and overwhelmed by the terrors of madness. Collins

languished some years under that depression of mind which
enchains the faculties without destroying them, and leaves reason
the knowledge of right without the power of pursuing it. These
clouds which he perceived gathering on his intellects, he endeavoured to disperse by travel, and passed into France; but found
himself constrained to yield to his malady, and returned. He was
for some time confined in a house of lunatics [until death finally
came to his relief]. (4.122)

Johnson always wrote poignantly about the way his subject died. He
observed that Pope's death was ludicrously hastened, if not caused, by his
overfondness for rich and exotic dishes, and by "a silver saucepan, in which
it was his delight to heat potted lampreys" (4.56). Milton was blessed with
a peaceful end. His "gout, with which he had been long tormented, prevailed over the enfeebled powers of nature. He died by a quiet and silent

expiration" (1.273). Otway's bizarre suffocation—incited by "indigence, and its concomitants, sorrow and despondency"—was so dreadful that Johnson was at first unwilling to mention it:

> Having been compelled by his necessities to contract debts, and hunted, as is supposed, by the terriers of the law, he retired to a publick-house on Tower-hill, where he is said to have died of want; or, as it is related by one of his biographers, by swallowing, after a long fast, a piece of bread which charity had supplied. He went out, as is reported, almost naked in the rage of hunger, and, finding a gentleman in a neighbouring coffee-house, asked him for a shilling. The gentleman gave him a guinea; and Otway going away bought a roll, and was choaked with the first mouthful. (2.226)

The vivid details—"hunted by the terriers of the law . . . almost naked in the rage of hunger," the desperate wandering in search of succor, the unexpected generosity, the supposed extinction of gnawing hunger and the sudden, ironic death—all make this scene one of the most moving and memorable in the *Lives*.

III

Biography, which explores the self as well as the subject, often turns into a kind of self-portrait. More interesting, even, than Johnson's characters and criticism is the strong current of autobiography that surges through the *Lives*. The most intriguing autobiographical passages appear in "Savage" and in "Swift." But his discussion of Milton's mode of teaching and Addison's rapid writing reveals Johnson's own experience in the classroom and the study. Fascinating portraits of his friends also appear unexpectedly in the minor lives. His literary cousin Cornelius Ford pops up in "Fenton"; Gilbert Walmsley and David Garrick make cameo appearances in "Edmund Smith"; and Goldsmith receives a handsome tribute in "Parnell."

Recalling his own traumatic birth and hasty christening, Johnson wrote of Addison, whose father was dean of the cathedral in Lichfield, "appearing weak and unlikely to live, he was christened the same day" (3.1). Like Dryden, Johnson himself "appears never to have . . . much pleased himself with his own dramas" (2.81). Like Addison with *Cato*, Johnson, on the opening night of *Irene*, wandered "behind the scenes with restless and unappeasable solicitude" (3.11).

Johnson's own life and beliefs influenced his portrayal of the poets. He was personally sympathetic to Pope, Collins and Savage; hostile to Milton, Gray and Swift. Pope, the greatest poet of the eighteenth century, had played a significant role in his life. He had generously praised Johnson's undergraduate translation of his *Messiah* into Latin; admired the Popean couplets of the anonymously published *London*; supported his application for a Dublin University master of arts degree; and encouraged him to undertake the monumental *Dictionary*. As Johnson wrote in his "Plan" of the *Dictionary*, three years after Pope's death, "were he still alive, solicitous as he was for the success of this work, he would not be displeased that I have undertaken it."

Though Pope was an extreme physical contrast to Johnson, one dwarfish, the other gigantic, both were physically grotesque. Johnson mentions that Pope—a tubercular hunchback, bent double and less than five feet tall—was too weak to dress himself and had to expand the bulk of his slender legs with three pairs of stockings. Never entirely free from pain himself, Johnson identified with Pope's chronic illness. In a revealing passage in his edition of Shakespeare, he explained how Pope overcame his defects with intellectual and artistic brilliance: "Whoever is stigmatised with deformity has a constant source of envy in his mind, and would counterbalance by some other superiority these advantages which he feels himself to want."

The life of Pope, the longest and best in the book, is filled with vivid anecdotes. When they dined with the waspish Voltaire, the Frenchman's gross language drove Pope's pious mother from the room. On the day the *Dunciad* was published, a crowd of hacks, fearful they would be pilloried and smarting in advance from the satire, attempted to suppress the poem. Pope could state, with some justice, "Yes, I am proud; I must be proud to see / Men not afraid of God, afraid of me."[7] But when reading Colley Cibber's retaliatory attacks and insouciantly claiming "*these things are my diversion*," Pope's features were "writhen with anguish" (4.51).

Johnson treated Pope's youthful pastorals with uncommon tenderness and called his translation of the *Iliad* "certainly the noblest version of poetry which the world has ever seen" (4.17). In a grand rhetorical flourish, inspired by the comparison of Homer and Virgil in "Dryden," he concluded his famous comparison of the two poets by stating: "If the flights of Dryden therefore are higher, Pope continues longer on the wing. If of Dryden's fire the blaze is brighter, of Pope's the heat is more regular and constant. Dryden often surpasses expectation, and Pope never falls below it. Dryden is read with frequent astonishment, and Pope with perpetual delight" (4.66).

IV

Johnson had repeated a crucial idea in Milton's *Areopagitica,* " I cannot praise a fugitive and cloistered virtue," when in *Adventurer* 126 he wished that "virtue would not withdraw the influence of her presence, or forbear to assert her natural dignity by open and undaunted perseverance in the right." But Milton's sour character and puritan politics affected Johnson's negative portrayal of him in the *Lives.* We have seen Johnson's irreverent dismissal of "Lycidas" and the sonnets, and his put-down of *Paradise Lost.* He devoted only two sentences to the superb *Samson Agonistes,* which he felt had "been too much admired" (1.292). He mentioned the odd fact that Milton was one of the last Oxbridge students to suffer "the publick indignity of corporal correction," which may have helped turn him into "an acrimonious and surly republican" (1.243, 276). Johnson, who made Milton's politics seem close to Satan's, insisted that they were "founded in an envious hatred of greatness, and a sullen desire of independence; in petulance impatient of controul, and pride disdainful of superiority" (1.276).

Johnson's domestic companion Anna Williams must have provided a vivid and immediate example of the frailties of the blind. But in a crucial passage about Milton's precarious fate after the Restoration, Johnson exhibited a notable lack of imaginative understanding: "no sooner is he safe, than he finds himself in danger, *fallen on evil days and evil tongues, and with darkness and with danger compass'd round* [*Paradise Lost,* 7.25–27]. . . . But the charge itself seems to be false; for it would be hard to recollect any reproach cast upon him . . . through the whole remaining part of his life" (1.268–269). Though Milton—blind and in his third difficult marriage—was protected by Marvell and Davenant, he was closely connected to the defeated Puritans, was at the mercy of his political enemies and naturally feared for his safety, if not for his life.

Gray (who died in 1771) found Johnson, as Johnson found Milton, "surly, morose, Dogmatical and imperious." According to a clergyman friend, Gray "disliked Johnson and declined his acquaintance; he disapproved his style, and thought it turgid, and vicious."[8] Johnson, in turn, disliked Gray's cloistered life among the Whigs at Cambridge, his "troublesome and punctilious jealousy" and his "affectation in delicacy, or rather effeminacy," which hinted at homosexuality and all-too-ardent friendships (4.176, 179). This "fantastick foppery" Johnson related to Gray's precious notion that he could write only at inspired moments. Johnson, of course, could write at high speed under the most arduous conditions and the most persistent pressure. He also disdained the puerilities of Gray's "obsolete mythology." In a famous denigration, he stated that Gray assumed in his Pindaric odes "a kind of strutting dignity, and is tall by walking on tiptoe" (4.183).

His dislike of the odes inspired a perverse rejection of two of Gray's finest works. His petulant literalism prevented him from appreciating one of the most charming and amusing poems in our language, "Ode on the Death of a Favourite Cat." He noted sourly that Selima "is called a nymph, with some violence both to language and sense" (4.181). And he reduces Gray's "Ode on a Distant Prospect of Eton College" to absurdity by exclaiming: "His supplication to father *Thames,* to tell him who drives the hoop or tosses the ball, is useless and puerile. Father *Thames* has no better means of knowing than himself" (4.181).

Johnson both identified with and attacked Swift. He saw Swift as an extreme version of himself: more savage about the frailties of mankind, more sceptical about religion, more mentally unbalanced. In contrast to Savage—a liar, parasite and murderer—Swift (like Johnson) was a High Tory and Church of England man who "desired the prosperity, and maintained the honour of the Clergy" (3.209). He was dedicated to his duties as dean of St. Patrick's Cathedral in Dublin and "performed all the offices of his profession with great decency and exactness" (3.192).

He was generous to the poor and defended the rights of the oppressed Irish, with whom Johnson also sympathized. Johnson, who frequently quoted Swift in the *Dictionary*, had been strongly influenced by him when writing the *Debates in Parliament* as if they'd taken place in the senate of Magna Lilliputia, and when ironically using an obtuse narrator in his early satire on Sir Robert Walpole, *Marmor Norfolciense*. Despite Swift's virtues, Johnson still resented his failure to secure the Dublin M.A., though Johnson himself noted that "the mode in which [Swift's] first degree was conferred [by want of merit and by special favor] left him no great fondness for the University" (3.191).

Swift and Johnson, in fact, had a great deal in common. Both were eccentric, nursed a sense of grievance, had an imperious manner, and suddenly turned on friends with savage arrogance and cruel contempt. Lifelong invalids, they were obsessed with death, often melancholy and terrified of insanity. In a telling anecdote, which appeared in "Young" rather than in "Swift" (and which Yeats used brilliantly in "Blood and the Moon"), Young described Swift pointing up at a noble elm, whose upper branches were withered and decayed. Foreseeing his own madness, he exclaimed, "I shall be like that tree, I shall die at the top" (4.138). When Johnson was touring Scotland, Lady MacLeod naïvely asked him if man was naturally good. Echoing Hobbes' *homo homini lupus* (man is a wolf to man) in *Leviathan,* he replied: "'No, madam, no more than a wolf.' Boswell. 'Nor no woman, sir?' Johnson. 'No, sir.' Lady MacLeod started, saying low, 'This is worse than Swift.'"

In his life of Swift, Johnson emphasized many details that suggested he was anatomizing himself instead of Swift. Johnson was also hard of hearing and, though nearsighted, refused to wear spectacles; he loved to eat fruit, and neither liked nor understood music; he was habitually idle; and he charitably supported a perpetually discontented household. At home, Swift "must necessarily offend more than he gratifies, because the preference given to one affords all the rest a reason for complaint" (3.197). Johnson told Hester that his own collection of misfits "made his life miserable from the impossibility he found of making theirs happy, when every favour he bestowed on one was wormwood to the rest."

Swift hated solitude and felt conversation was "the great softener of
the ills of life" (3.203). Anna Williams habitually stayed up till after
midnight to provide Johnson with tea and sympathy. Again like Johnson, whose "amorous inclinations were uncommonly strong," Swift
was "strongly excited by the amorous attention of a young woman"
(3.201). Johnson must have noticed that the real name of Swift's Stella
was Hester Johnson—the very name Hester Thrale would have assumed if she'd fulfilled Johnson's fantasies and married him after the
death of her husband.

Johnson did not discuss Swift's best poems: "A Description of a City
Shower," "Cadenus and Vanessa" or "Verses on the Death of Dr. Swift."
He admired the irreverent *Tale of a Tub* (which cost Swift a bishopric
under Queen Anne), yet rather absurdly told Boswell, when speaking of
Gulliver's Travels, "when once you have thought of big men and little men,
it is very easy to do all the rest." In "Swift" he also denied the greatness of
the satire by asserting that "the part which gave least pleasure was that
which describes the *Flying Island,* and that which gave most disgust must
be the history of the *Houyhnhnms*" (3.203). Johnson couldn't stomach
Swift's excremental vision, let alone the obscene poetry of "The Lady's
Dressing Room" ("Repeating in his am'rous Fits, / Oh! Caelia, Caelia,
Caelia, shits").[9] He fiercely concluded that Swift's "depravity of intellect
took delight in revolving ideas, from which almost every other mind
shrinks with disgust" (3.213).

Though mentally troubled and disease-ridden himself, Johnson displayed an astonishing lack of compassion, not only for Milton's psychological anguish, but also for Swift's Job-like agonies. He seemed to
relish the description of Swift's suffering in old age, and recorded his
torments with a certain morbid relish: "he had an inflammation in his
left eye, which swelled it to the size of an egg, with boils in other parts;
he was kept long waking with the pain, and was not easily restrained
by five attendants from tearing out his eye" (3.207–208).

In *The Vanity of Human Wishes* Johnson had coupled Swift with his old
enemy Marlborough and used him to exemplify the futility of personal
aspirations. But as Dr. William Wilde (Oscar's father) observed of those
lines: "supposing them to be true, what do they prove?—that a feeble

old man of seventy-eight, occasionally suffering the most excruciating torture, who had lost his memory and was labouring under paralysis, the result of disease of his brain . . . was a 'driv'ler and a show'!" Swift, his alter ego, terrified Johnson. By writing with clinical objectivity of his deafness and solitude, madness, disease and death, Johnson not only dissociated himself from Swift but also from all that he feared in Swift.

Ever procrastinating, Johnson took four years to complete his "Prefaces." He tended to write letters about writing instead of writing about what he wanted to write. He slyly suggested, in a deliberately jerky sentence that repeated "haste" and emphasized "vigour," the halting progress of his stop-and-go efforts: "I finished the lives of the Poets, which I wrote in my usual way, dilatorily and hastily, unwilling to work, and working with vigour and haste." Once more he could say, as he had said after completing the *Dictionary*: "I knew very well what I was undertaking,—and very well how to do it,—and have done it very well."[10]

VI

Though Johnson was justifiably pleased with the *Lives,* some of his readers were not. Friends of Lord Lyttleton, who'd died as recently as 1773, were outraged by Johnson's condescending treatment of an aristocrat and statesman who'd been admired for his benevolence and integrity. Lyttleton, like Johnson, was ugly and awkward; but Johnson offensively noted that "he had a slender uncompacted frame, and a meagre face" (4.188). His hostility, no doubt, went back to 1739 and to his unequal rivalry with the noble lord for the attention of the pious Hill Boothby.

When Johnson heard that the eminent lawyer William Pepys had criticized his portrayal of Lyttleton, he became dreadfully angry and caused a violent scene. Pepys, paling as Johnson reddened, but up to the occasion, wrote that in June 1781 he'd been forced into the argument, which lasted for several hours, by Johnson's public challenge to a verbal duel:

I met Johnson some time ago at Streatham, and such a Day did we pass in Disputation upon the Life of our dear Friend Lord Lyttleton as I trust it will never be my fate to pass again! The moment the [table] Cloth was removed, he challenged me to *come out* (as he called it) and to say what I had to object to his Life of Lord Lyttle-ton. This (you see) was a call which, however disagreeable to myself and the rest of the Company, I could not but Obey, and so *To it we went* for 3 or 4 hours without ceasing.

Fanny Burney was horrified by the spectacle of Johnson's aggressive ferocity. Echoing the biblical command "Come forth" and his biblical namesake—"The Lord called Samuel: and he answered, Here am I" (I Samuel 3:4)—Johnson thundered at poor Pepys:

Never before have I seen Dr. Johnson speak with so much passion; "Mr. Pepys," he cried, in a voice the most enraged, "I understand you are offended by my Life of Lord Lyttleton, what is it you have to say against it? Come forth, Man! Here am I. Ready to answer any charge you may bring." . . . He repeated his attack and his Challenge, and a violent disputation ensued, in which this great, but *mortal* man did, to own the truth, appear unreasonably furious and grossly severe: I never saw him so before.

When Hester Thrale reprimanded Johnson for his rudeness, he remained unrepentant and exclaimed: "I will defend myself in every part, and in every atom!"

William Cowper, ineligible as a living poet for inclusion in the *Lives,* composed an epitaph on Johnson after his death and praised his good sense, forcible expression and penetrating insight. "I allow him to be a man of Gigantic talents and most profound Learning," Cowper wrote, "nor have any doubts about the universality of his knowledge." But he'd been reluctant to send Johnson a volume of his poems lest he call down the wrath of the all-powerful Jehovah of criticism. Cowper told a friend, "I have no objection in the world to your conveying a Copy to Dr. Johnson, though I well know that one of his printed Sarcasms, if he should happen to be displeased, would soon find its way into all companies, and spoil the Sale. He writes indeed like a man that thinks a great deal, and that sometimes thinks religiously; but report informs me that he has been severe enough in his animadversions."[11]

Two far greater poets later expressed unrestrained admiration for the *Lives*. Byron thought Johnson possessed the "noblest critical mind." Matthew Arnold, in his edition of the *Lives*, concluded: "The more we study him, the higher will be our esteem for the power of his mind, the width of his interests, the largeness of his knowledge, the freshness, fearlessness, and strength of his judgments."[12]

LACERATED FRIENDSHIP
1781–1783

I

Henry Thrale had never recovered from the death of young Harry. He continued to eat so voraciously that Johnson felt obliged to tell him, "after the Denunciation of your Physicians this Morning, such eating is little better than Suicide." Despite these warnings, Henry continued to indulge his one remaining pleasure and suffered two strokes in 1779. In January his head sank onto the table, his speech was slurred and he was unable to recognize anyone. In October his speech was again inarticulate and he became comatose. Two years later he collapsed in the midst of a parliamentary campaign and, clearly unable to function, lost the election. Hester noted that he couldn't stay awake for more than four hours at a time and had become incontinent.

Johnson was deeply affected when Henry died, at fifty-two, in April 1781. He not only liked and admired his "Master," but also knew that his comfortable way of life in Thrale's household would come to an end. He regretfully told Bennet Langton, "how much soever I valued him, I now wish that I had valued him more." In an attempt to comfort Hester, he said that he too had been hit hard by the calamity (which touched him even more deeply than the loss of his mother) and that "no death since that of my Wife has ever oppressed me like this." Offering the traditional Christian consolation, he added, in convoluted diction that reflected his distress, "He that has given You happiness in marriage to a degree of which without personal knowledge, I should have thought the description fabulous, can give You another mode of happiness as a Mother." To Hester this was highly ironic. Her marriage had been miserably unhappy and, after a bitter quarrel, she would soon become estranged from all her daughters.

Since there were no male heirs in the family to inherit and run the business, the Anchor Brewery had to be sold. Johnson, as one of Henry's four executors, proved indispensable. An economic historian wrote that he had an expert knowledge of "such technical matters as coining, the trade of a butcher, granulating gunpowder, brewing spirits, tanning, malting, the various operations of processing milk for whey, cheese and butter." In Paris, he'd shown a strong interest in all aspects of manufacturing; and the inventor Richard Arkwright "pronounced him to be the only person who, on a first view, understood both the principle and powers of his most complicated piece of machinery."[1] While negotiating to sell the brewery, according to Boswell, "Johnson appeared bustling about, with an ink-horn and pen in his button-hole, like an excise-man; and on being asked what he really considered to be the value of the property which was to be disposed of, answered, 'We are not here to sell a parcel of boilers and vats, but the potentiality of growing rich, beyond the dreams of avarice.'" The Anchor Brewery was sold to the managers, only a month after Henry's death, for the gigantic sum of £135,000.

There was public speculation about whether Johnson might marry Hester. John Hawkins' daughter, retailing current rumors, wrote, "on the death of Mr. Thrale it was concluded by some that he would marry the widow; by others that he would entirely take up his residence in her house." Johnson liked domestic life, loved Hester and would have married her if he could. It would have been extremely convenient to have a capable, lively, wealthy woman take care of him in old age. But even if marriage were out of the question, he still hoped, at least, they could continue their old way of life at Streatham. He wanted to maintain their ritual of whippings; she was eager to break it. The forty-year-old

Hester admired Johnson as a father and friend, but had absolutely no romantic feelings for him. Denying the absurd gossip in the newspapers and emphasizing that neither of them seriously contemplated marriage, she noted, "it would be news to *him* perhaps that he & I are going to be married."[2]

Boswell, however, greatly amused by the prospect of Johnson's marriage, was moved to write a gossipy poetic lampoon. Like many authors, he felt a reckless desire to see his work in print, despite the harm it would do both to others and to himself. His scurrilous "Ode by Dr. Samuel Johnson to Mrs. Thrale: upon Their Supposed Nuptials," written in 1781 and published after Johnson's death, in 1788, was in excruciatingly bad taste. Like Garrick, Boswell portrayed Johnson as a ludicrous lover to repay him for all the numerous insults and humiliations he'd suffered over the years:

My dearest darling, view your slave,
    Behold him as your very scrub,
Ready to write as authour grave,
    Or govern well the brewing tub.

To rich felicity thus rais'd,
    My bosom glows with amorous fire;
Porter no longer shall be prais'd;
    'Tis I myself am Thrale's entire. . . .

Five daughters by your former spouse
    Shall match with nobles of the land;
The fruit of our more fervent vows
    A pillar of the state shall stand.

In Boswell's poem Johnson expressed his lustful feelings, "My bosom glows with amorous fire," in the most hackneyed and clichéd language. Hinting at his bewitchment and his low social status (considerably inferior to that of both Boswell and Hester), Johnson describes himself as her slave and as a "scrub," or "mean fellow," who could run the brewery as well as write his books. In several outrageous puns Boswell takes up the brewing metaphor and plays on "porter," Tetty's married name and the name of a dark brown ale; and on "entire," a kind of popular malt and the name of a stallion (as opposed to a gelding). The vast wealth of the brewery would enable Hester's daughters to marry into the aristocracy, and the aged Johnson, following the stallion image, would procreate sons who'd become leading politicians. Though the poem revealed the way contemporaries viewed Johnson's close relations with Hester, few readers were amused by Boswell's exercise in egoistic fatuity.

II

Henry Thrale's death and the upheaval it caused in his own life depressed Johnson and overwhelmed him with thoughts of loss and guilt. In *Rasselas* he had written, "no disease of the imagination is so difficult of cure, as that which is complicated with the dread of guilt," and for half a century he had brooded over a troubling incident in his youth. To earn a bit of extra money, his father used to set up a bookstall on market days in Uttoxeter, about fifteen miles north of Lichfield. In November 1731, when he was ill, he asked Sam either to go there with him or take his place. A lazy and contrary young man, Johnson thought tending the stall was beneath him and refused. A few weeks later his father died. Guilt-stricken when his mother died in 1759, he noted in his diary, "forgive me, O Lord, whatever my Mother has suffered by my fault, whatever I have done amiss, and whatever duty I have neglected." But his father's death tortured him forever. In November 1781, on the very same day and exactly fifty years later, the seventy-two-year-old Johnson took a post chaise from Lichfield and returned to the scene of the crime.

Johnson later evoked the mood of this episode:

Once, indeed I was disobedient; I refused to attend my father to Uttoxeter-market. Pride was the source of that refusal, and the remembrance of it was painful. A few years ago, I desired to atone for this fault; I went to Uttoxeter in very bad weather, and stood for a considerable time bareheaded in the rain, on the spot where my father's stall used to stand. In contrition I stood, and I hope the penance was expiatory.

Pride was the original sin in the Garden of Eden, and the source of all other sins. Johnson often dwelled on this scene in his imagination and confessed it to others. He portrayed himself as a latter-day St. Simeon Stylites, standing for hours bareheaded in wet weather on the guilty spot. As the astonished townsmen glanced at the trembling, soaking madman and began to hurry home out of the rain, he still wondered if—through the bitter wasteland of contrition and penance—he had finally achieved expiation. Like Coleridge's ancient mariner, "The man hath penance done, / And penance more will do."[3]

Johnson told the Reverend Richard Warner that he had been mocked by the crowd during his public self-abasement: "[I stood] exposed to the sneers of the standers-by and the inclemency of the weather; a penance by which I trust I have propitiated heaven for this only instance, I believe, of contumacy toward my father." In his second confession to a clergyman, he informed the son of his publisher, the Reverend George Strahan Jr., that "it was Market Day; I went to the Place where my poor Father's Stall stood: it was a rainy Day, Sir; I pulled off my Hat, my Wig, and I stood there for two Hours, drenched in Rain, and I hope the Penance was expiatory."[4] In old age—suffering from heart disease, emphysema and dropsy—he risked his life in the hope of easing, if not extinguishing, his lifelong guilt.

III

In January 1782, nine months after Henry's death, Johnson lost another close friend. At the age of seventy-six, Robert Levet died suddenly of a heart attack in Bolt Court. Johnson had known him for thirty-five years and had billeted him in his household since 1762. Thrale was rich, sybaritic, powerful and influential; Levet was poor, austere, insignificant and obscure. Johnson's moving elegy, "On the Death of Dr. Robert Levet" (August 1783), expressed the same heartfelt grief as his funeral sermon for Tetty. The poem, written in alternately rhyming eight-syllable lines, was arranged in quatrains:

Condemn'd to hope's delusive mine,
    As on we toil from day to day,

By sudden blasts, or slow decline,
  Our social comforts drop away.

Well tried through many a varying year,
  See LEVET to the grave descend;
Officious, innocent, sincere,
  Of ev'ry friendless name the friend.

Yet still he fills affection's eye,
  Obscurely wise, and coarsely kind;
Nor, letter'd arrogance, deny
  Thy praise to merit unrefin'd.

When fainting nature call'd for aid,
  And hov'ring death prepar'd the blow,
His vig'rous remedy display'd
  The power of art without the show.

In misery's darkest caverns known,
  His useful care was ever nigh,
Where hopeless anguish pour'd his groan,
  And lonely want retir'd to die.

No summons mock'd by chill delay,
  No petty gain disdain'd by pride,
The modest wants of ev'ry day
  The toil of ev'ry day supplied.

His virtues walk'd their narrow round,
  Nor made a pause, nor left a void;
And sure th' Eternal Master found
  The single talent well employed.

The busy day, the peaceful night,
  Unfelt, uncounted, glided by;
His frame was firm, his powers were bright,
  Tho' now his eightieth year was nigh.

Then with no throbbing fiery pain.
  No cold gradations of decay,

Death broke at once the vital chain,
　And free'd his soul the nearest way.

The thematic opening, where deluded man is forced to seek unobtainable hope, evokes yet again the vanity of human wishes. The "social comforts," suggesting not only the Thrales' household but also the comfort of friends, expire suddenly, like Levet, or slowly, like Anna Williams, who would die in September 1783. Johnson, as "mine" turns to "grave" and "drop away" to "descend," then focuses on Levet. He's "officious" in the sense of being helpful and (unlike the inimical Baretti) is a friend to those who have no other friend. Defending Levet's rough, even brutish demeanor, Johnson suggests that he was much wiser than he seemed, and that his humble yet meritorious service should not be disdained by his social superiors. The next three quatrains, as "darkest caverns" continues the underground imagery of "mine" and "grave," portray Levet's self-sacrificial work among the London poor.

　The vital core of the poem appears in the seventh quatrain, where Johnson praises Levet for "the single talent well employed." He alludes to the parable of the talents in Matthew 25:14–30, especially verse 26, in which the master berates the servant for burying the talent (or coin) he was given, instead of using it to the fullest. Milton had also alluded to this parable in the sonnet on his blindness, "When I Consider How My Light is Spent":

And that one Talent which is death to hide,
Lodg'd with me useless, though my Soul more bent
To serve therewith my Maker, and present
My true account, lest he returning chide.[5]

Johnson's penultimate quatrain is optimistic. Levet continued his medical work and, in his mid-seventies (a great age in the eighteenth century), seemed in good health. "Decay" in the final quatrain recalls "slow decline" in the first and also rhymes with "day" and "away" in the opening lines. In contrast to the menace of "hov'ring death" in line 14, the vital link between life and death is suddenly and painlessly broken in the final quatrain. Levet's soul ascends to heaven "the nearest way."

IV

Levet's death made Johnson think of his own. In August 1783, the month his elegy appeared and Anna Williams lay dying, he complained to Hester about his physical pain and mental despair: "I am now broken with disease, without the alleviation of familiar friendship, or domestick society." The sometime hypochondriac—seriously ill with insomnia, cough and asthma—sent her a depressing series of bulletins about his blisterings and bleedings. He also gave her a remarkably objective account of the minor stroke he suffered during the night of June 16, 1783. In this crisis, his fear of losing his mind, which he'd always thought might happen, was even greater than his fear of dying. But he found that his close brush with death was not as terrible as he had feared:

> I went to bed, and in a short time waked and sat up as has been long my custom when I felt a confusion and indistinctness in my head which lasted, I suppose about half a minute. I was alarmed and prayed God, that however he might afflict my body he would spare my understanding. This prayer, that I might try the integrity of my faculties, I made in Latin verse. The lines were not very good, but I knew them not to be very good, I made them easily, and concluded myself to be unimpaired in my faculties.
>
> Soon after I perceived that I had suffered a paralytick stroke, and that my speech was taken from me. I had no pain, and so little dejection in this dreadful state that I wondered at my own apathy, and considered that perhaps death itself when it should come, would excite less horrour than seems now to attend it.

Only Johnson, in extremis, could have had the moral strength to compose a Latin prayer and then make a critical judgment about its inadequacy. His prayer beseeched God to "spare my mind, and let it not be an offence in me to ask to please Thee with the only faculty with which I can do so."

Johnson could not escape pain by night in sleep or anxiety by day with friends. When tormented by insomnia he tried to drive the night along by translating Greek epigrams into Latin. During the day, he explained, not even conversation could alleviate his misery: "visitors are no proper companions in the chambers of sickness. They come when I could sleep, or read, they stay till I am weary, they force me to attend, when my mind calls for relaxation, and to speak when my powers will hardly actuate my tongue."[6] Hester's extraordinary sympathy encouraged Johnson's endless lamentations. But the more he complained to Hester and pleaded for her assistance, the more she wished to free herself from the intolerable burdens he now imposed upon her.

But Johnson had an unusual and unsuspected rival for Hester's affections: Gabriele Piozzi. Born in 1740 (a year before Hester) in the Veneto region of northeast Italy, he'd come to England in about 1776 as a singer, voice teacher, harpsichordist and minor composer. He met Charles Burney in musical circles, and in February 1778 Burney introduced him to Hester. As Piozzi was singing that evening, Hester, bored by the music, "mischievously slipped behind the panting tenor and mimicked his every gesture, with squared elbows, ecstatic shrugs of the shoulders, and languishing eyes." The nearsighted, self-absorbed Johnson didn't notice her behavior. But Burney, horrified by her rudeness to his guest, delivered a sharp rebuke, which she meekly accepted. In contrast to Henry Thrale, English, Protestant, a wealthy businessman and an MP, Piozzi was Italian, Catholic, an insignificant singer and musician. But Henry was egoistic, unfaithful and rather brutal; Gabriele charming, devoted and kind.

Hester continued to see Piozzi at musical events in friends' houses and invited him to perform at Streatham, where she used him to attract guests to her soirées. By August 1780 she no longer wanted to mock or tease him. In her diary she described the irresistible Piozzi as if he were caressing her with his music:

Piozzi is become a prodigious Favourite with me; he is so intelligent a Creature, so discerning, one can't help wishing for his good Opinion: his Singing surpasses every body's for Taste, Tenderness, and true Elegance; his Hand on the Forte Piano too is so soft, so sweet, so delicate, every Tone goes to one's heart I think; and fills the Mind with Emotions one would not be without, though inconvenient enough sometimes—I made him sing yesterday, &

tho' he says his Voice is gone, I cannot some how or other get it out of my Ears,—odd enough!

In January 1781, three months before Henry's death, the Thrales hired Piozzi as Queeney's singing teacher. Hester had fallen in love with the gentle, attractive Italian and, after Henry's death, despite violent opposition from family and friends, decided to marry him.

Johnson never suspected Hester's feelings for Piozzi. But he sensed, after she'd let Streatham to a tenant and had temporarily fled to Brighton, that he was no longer at the center of her life and was in danger of losing her. In 1755 he'd written emotional letters to Hill Boothby, whom he'd hoped to marry, declaring, "do not forget me. My heart is full of tenderness." In December 1781, sensing that Hester was trying to detach herself, he adopted a similar though more pleading tone with her: "do not neglect me, nor relinquish me. Nobody will ever love You better, or honour You more." Finally recognizing his rival four months later, he begged her, "do not let Mr. Piozzi nor any body else put me quite out of your head, and do not think that any body will love You like, Your humble servant, Sam. Johnson."[7]

Johnson knew how difficult it was to deal with an aged invalid like himself. In *Rambler* 162 he'd written, with considerable acuity, that a sick old man makes impossible demands on everyone. He wants "quickness in conjecturing his desires, activity in supplying his wants, dexterity in intercepting complaints . . . flexibility to his present humour, submission to hasty petulance, and attention to wearisome narrations." All this, and more, he asked of the infinitely obliging Hester. As he got older, more irascible and more entrenched in her household, he became increasingly selfish, unremittingly dictatorial and generally intolerable.

After Henry's death and before she ever thought of actually marrying Piozzi, Hester wrote that she desperately wanted to escape from and even get rid of Johnson. He'd turned her into a servant, took up all her time, made her conform to his strange schedule, and then criticized her dress and household management—without in the least realizing how much he hurt her. She therefore found it convenient to retire to Bath, where I knew Mr. Johnson would not follow me, and where I could for that reason command some little portion of time for my own use; a thing impossible while I remained at Streatham or at London, as my hours, carriage, and servants had long been at his command, who would not rise in the morning till twelve o'clock perhaps, and oblige me to make breakfast for him till the bell rung for dinner, though much displeased if my toilet was neglected, and though much of the time we passed together was spent in blaming or deriding, very justly, my neglect of oeconomy, and waste of that money which might make many families happy.

She now felt that Johnson had been exploiting her, and became much more critical of the personal habits she had tolerated for so long: "he cares more for my roast Beef & plumb Pudden which he now devours too dirtily for endurance: and since he is glad to get rid of me, I'm sure I have good Cause to desire the getting Rid of *him*."

Johnson was also a considerable obstacle to her long-desired trip to Italy, which she and her daughters hoped to take with Piozzi as their cicerone. But as she noted in her diary, "to leave Mr. Johnson shocked me, & to take him appear'd impossible."[8] In the end, it was also impossible to take her daughters, and she eventually escaped from all her problems on a romantic flight to Italy.

Despite his friendships with Psalmanazar and Baretti, Paoli and the Italian teacher Francesco Sastres, Johnson was generally hostile to foreigners and warned friends about the spiritual danger of reading books by Catholics. He also stated as axiomatic in *Adventurer* 74: "That the woman was undone who married below herself, was universally agreed." Yet many of his friends were involved with and even married foreigners. Boswell fell in love with a Dutch lady, Gibbon with a Swiss. Elizabeth Desmoulins married a French Huguenot refugee; Garrick a Viennese Catholic dancer; and Fanny Burney later wed a French Catholic émigré, M. D'Arblay.

There were also close parallels between Hester's situation and Johnson's own life. The widow Tetty Porter married Johnson when she was forty-five; the widow Hester Thrale married Piozzi when she was forty-three. The family and friends of both Tetty and Hester were strongly opposed to what they felt was an unsuitable union. Johnson, forty-two when Tetty died, had given up his sexual life; but Hester, forty when Henry died, refused to make that sacrifice. She had the happy second marriage that Johnson was never able to attain.

The opposition to Hester's marriage was formidable indeed. Piozzi, though a decent fellow with honorable intentions, was neither well born nor socially distinguished, and appeared to be an obvious fortune hunter. Queeney, now in her late teens, had always been cold and critical of her mother, and she now ruthlessly denigrated Piozzi and condemned her infatuation. Everyone agreed that Hester's degrading passion for a mere singer, already the cause of considerable scandal, would ruin her daughters' marriage prospects. George Steevens, for example, referred to her marriage to Piozzi as a "Disgrace" that raised "an obscure penniless Fiddler into sudden Wealth and awkward Notoriety."

Baretti, who felt he'd been driven away and left with nothing, was insanely jealous of his fellow countryman. Though Piozzi was no better than himself, he'd somehow managed to secure Hester's affection as well as her fortune. Baretti had stormed out of Streatham five years before Piozzi arrived. But he now claimed that she'd not only poisoned young Harry, but had also slept with Piozzi while Thrale was still alive: "Piozzi never turned his attentions but to money, and she hers to his battering ram." Horrified by his unremitting malice, Hester noted that Baretti "accuses me of Murder & Fornication."[9] Neither chastened after his murder trial nor subdued after the threat of death, he remained full of spite until he died in 1789, estranged from his companions and missed by very few.

In January 1783, yielding to persuasive arguments about her reputation and her daughters' prospects, Hester repressed her personal feelings. She begged Piozzi to return to Italy for two years, until Queeney came of age. He chivalrously agreed to sacrifice their happiness and surrender the wealthy widow to the prospect of an aristocratic husband. Hester operatically wrote that he "went home to Wigmore Street at [Queeney's] Command: brought all my Letters, Promises of Marriage &c put them into *her* Hand—& cried 'Take your Mama—and make her a Countess—It shall kill *me* never mind—but it shall *kill her too!*'" Two days later, the still emotional Hester, who seemed to have picked up Piozzi's dramatic expressions and hothouse Italian, exclaimed in her diary, "Adieu to all that's dear, to all that's lovely. I am parted from my Life, my Soul! my Piozzi: Sposo promesso! Amante adorato! Amico senza equale! [Betrothed! Adored lover! Friend without equal!]"

Just after this crisis, in mid-April 1783, Hester's youngest child, Henrietta Sophia, died at the age of four. Accustomed by now to the death of her children, she recorded the loss with less emotion than she'd felt after giving up Piozzi. But she was furious with Queeney, who'd not only ruined Hester's life, but was also quite indifferent to the death of her little sister: "Harriet is dead, my other Girls' Fortunes increased, their Insolence extream, and their hardness of Heart astonishing: When the Baby was to be moved to Streatham for the Air—it will kill her said I—She will be nearer the Church Yard replies the eldest, coldly."[10] Hester fell into a deep depression, followed in November by a nervous breakdown. Faced with yet another dangerous crisis, Queeney finally relented and recalled the faithful Piozzi from Italy. Wary about his future after he'd been sent packing and reluctant to cross the Alps in winter, he delayed his return to England and was not reunited with his fiancée until July 1.

V

At the end of his life Johnson wrote his greatest work, *The Lives of the Poets,* and had his most devastating quarrel. In October 1777 he'd told Hester how Mrs. Burney had been crushed when one of her daughters eloped: "there is in this event a kind of system of calamity, a conflagration of the soul. Every avenue of pain is invaded at once. Pride is mortified, tenderness is wounded, hope is disappointed." This is an apt description of his own intense feelings after his break with Hester in July 1784. As he sadly wrote in *Vanity:* "Now lacerated Friendship claims a Tear."

Johnson's twenty-year friendship with Hester came to a cataclysmic end five months before his death, when the egoistic desires of a moribund old man clashed with the passionate determination of a romantic widow. Hester had endured an unhappy marriage to an adulterous husband; twelve life-threatening childbirths, and the deaths of her beloved mother and eight of her children; and quarrels with the cold-hearted Queeney and with the venomous Baretti. She now wished, for the first time, to follow her heart, to love and be loved, and to lead her own life. The last thing she wanted, when she fell in love with Piozzi, was the burden of Johnson's illness, gloomy prognostications and ritualistic whippings. It was essential, if she were ever to achieve her long-sought happiness, to liberate herself from Johnson—the most serious impediment to her "choice of life."

Johnson's health deteriorated as Hester's love increased. Declining rapidly and approaching death, he'd recently lost the social comfort of Topham Beauclerk (who'd died in April 1780), Henry Thrale, Robert Levet and Anna Williams. Elizabeth Desmoulins, after yet another bitter fight with Williams, had left Bolt Court in May 1783, a month before Johnson's stroke. In his hour of need he couldn't bear to lose yet another close friend, as well as the coddled existence that enabled him to tolerate his wretched and now sadly depleted household.

Hester waited until the very last moment to tell Johnson that she'd decided to marry Piozzi. Johnson then wrote her a savage letter: the most selfish and discreditable act of his entire life. On July 2, 1784, with the same vitriolic anger he'd used to blast Chesterfield and Macpherson, he judged and condemned Hester for choosing Piozzi and love (the vainest of human wishes) over her country and children, her religion and reputation. He also expressed his feelings for her, which no longer mattered, and begged for a meeting in Bath or London (which she'd do anything to avoid), so he could use all the powers at his command to persuade her to change her mind:

> If I interpret your letter right, You are ignominiously married, if it is yet undone, let us once talk together. If You have abandoned your children and your religion, God forgive your wickedness; if you have forfeited your Fame, and your country, may your folly do no further mischief.
>
> If the last act is yet to do, I, who have loved you, esteemed you, reverenced you, and served you, I who long thought you the first

of humankind, entreat that before your fate is irrevocable, I may once more see You.

He'd revealed his secret to Hester and now reacted violently. As Katharine Balderston observed, he'd suffered a tremendous blow to his ego and had been deserted "by the woman to whom he had abjectly exposed his uttermost weakness."[11]

Rising brilliantly to the occasion, Hester responded with a letter, worthy of Johnson himself, that vigorously defended Piozzi's birth, character and talent:

I have this Morning received from You so rough a Letter, in reply to one which was both tenderly and respectfully written, that I am forced to desire the conclusion of a Correspondence which I can bear to continue no longer. The Birth of my second Husband is not meaner than that of my first, his sentiments are not meaner, his Profession is not meaner,—and his Superiority in what he professes—acknowledged by all Mankind.—It is want of fortune then that is *ignominious*, the Character of the Man I have chosen has no other Claim to such an Epithet. The Religion to which he has always been a zealous Adherent, will I hope teach him to forgive Insults he has not deserved—mine will I hope enable me to bear them at once with Dignity and Patience.

Impressed by Hester's response, on July 8 Johnson did a volte face and characteristically tried to mollify the person he'd provoked. He claimed he'd not been hurt by her decision, though he was deeply wounded, sent his heartfelt benediction and thanked her for all the help she'd given him: "What You have done, however I may lament it, I have no pretence to resent, as it has not been injurious to me. I therefore breathe out one more sigh of tenderness perhaps useless, but at least sincere. I wish that God may grant you every blessing. . . . Whatever I can contribute to your happiness, I am very ready to repay for that kindness which soothed twenty years of a life radically wretched." But the damage was done—the friendship was over.

Four days later Hester told Fanny Burney (who opposed her marriage, but had not told her so), "Dr. Johnson wrote me a most ferocious Letter in answer to that you saw the Copy of, but when he read my Reply to it, he softened at once; has sent Prayers and Wishes for mine and my Piozzi's happiness—and behaved with all the Tenderness you can imagine."[12] In late July, Hester married Piozzi, first in a Catholic and then in an Anglican service. Her judgment of his character proved accurate; their marriage was a great success and lasted until his death in 1809.

Despite the brave front he assumed in his recantation, Johnson was shattered by the loss of Hester. Writing to John Hawkins that summer, he expressed his bitter feelings: "Poor Thrale! I thought that either her virtue or her vice would have restrained her from such a marriage. She is now become a subject for her enemies to exult over, and for her friends, if she has any left, to forget or pity." When he saw Fanny Burney in November, he tried to be insouciant, but revealed the depth of his anguish by declaring: "I drive her quite from my mind. If I meet with one of her letters, I burn it instantly. I have burnt all I can find. I never speak of her, and I desire never to hear of her more. I drive her, as I said, wholly from my mind." In a letter to Charles Burney, the seventy-five-year-old Johnson described his mental state after the loss of his dearest friend: "wherever I turn the dead or the dying meet my notice, and force my attention upon misery and mortality."[13]

21

THE NIGHT COMETH
1783–1784

I

Johnson's bitter quarrel with Hester Piozzi and her departure for Italy in July 1784 deprived him of his most intimate friend and domestic comfort in the last months of his life. Johnson's manner of dying was completely in character. It was as contradictory, combative and violent as his life had been. He was courageous, yet filled with self-pity and lamenting his fate; fearful of dying, yet affirming his belief in a benign deity; furious at the betrayal of his body and taking savage risks to stay alive; hating to lose control of his life and dreading the loss of consciousness death would bring. His view of life as a struggle served him well at the end. Though death was inevitable, confrontation with it tested his character and prolonged his life. A weaker man would have given up long before Johnson did. He did not go quietly, but raged against the dying of the light. Though brave, he was not afraid to show his weakness and fear of divine judgment.

In the last years of his life Johnson reversed the precept from Ovid that he'd quoted in *Rambler* 32, "let pain deserv'd without complaint be borne," and complained about the pain he felt he'd *not* deserved. He well knew, as he wrote in *Rambler* 48, that it was futile for the sufferer to hope for a sympathetic response from those who were not in pain: "if the purpose of lamentation be to excite pity, it is entirely super-fluous for age and weakness to tell their plaintive stories; for pity pre-supposes sympathy . . . [and] those who do not feel pain, seldom think that it is felt."[1] Most of Johnson's letters became morbid bulletins of dis-tress. In March 1782 he wrote to his stepdaughter, Lucy Porter, describ-ing his despondent mood, "To be sick, and to see nothing but sickness and death is but a gloomy state."

He told another friend that Bolt Court had turned into a hospital for incurables: "This little habitation is now but a melancholy place, clouded with the gloom of disease and death. Of the four inmates one [Levet] has been suddenly snatched away, two [Williams and Desmoulins] are oppressed by afflictive and very dangerous illness; and I tried yesterday to gain some relief by a third bleeding from a disorder which has for some time distressed me." Later that year he wrote to Boswell that he was mightily depressed by thinking about his friends' illnesses as well as his own: "I have struggled through this year with so much infirmity of body and such strong impressions of the fragility of life, that death, wherever it appears, fills me with melan-choly."[2] Friends must have dreaded the arrival of these letters. The struggle to overcome adversity had become a losing battle.

Well aware of his negative effect on others, he often "bewailed his Animal infirmity" and said that "sickness had made him a peevish, self-ish, ungrateful, snarling Dog." Like the aged Jonathan Swift, he was also "Deaf, giddy, helpless, left alone, / To all my Friends a Burthen grown." Even Fanny Burney, after visiting him at Bolt Court, agreed with Hester's view that Johnson had become very difficult indeed: "I was really quite grieved to see how unamiable he appeared, and how greatly he made himself dreaded by all, and by many abhorred."[3]

All Johnson's friends could see that his health was rapidly deterio-rating. Echoing Alexander Pope's "this long Disease, my Life," he'd mentioned "the general disease of my life," and in his "Preface" to the *Dictionary* regretfully noted that "much of my life has been lost under the pressures of disease."[4] In his last years he suffered from stroke, gallstone, gout, arthritis, bronchitis, emphysema, asthma, tumor and dropsy. His strong will and self-confidence rarely faltered; and he took an active, perhaps overactive, role in his own treatment. Though surrounded by physicians, he liked to medicate himself and even wrote his own prescriptions. He ingested, at various times and for various ailments, a witch doctor's brew of valerian, musk, hartshorn, squills, terebinth, ipecacuanha, Spanish fly and his nostrum of choice: opium.

In the days before painkillers, a patient often took opium to induce sleep. At the end of his life Johnson became addicted to the drug, and consumed almost as much as Coleridge and De Quincey would take in the next century. Reynolds wrote that Johnson "sleeps half the day in consequence of a quantity of Opium which he [is] constantly taking." In a passage suppressed by Boswell, Johnson revealed that the narcotic had terrifying side effects, producing phantoms that haunted his dreams: "Opiates, though they ever lulled my bodily pains, yet they usually filled my imagination with horrors and visions that disturbed for several hours my clear judgment." Fanny Burney, alarmed by this walking pharmacopoeia, recorded that Johnson came close to killing himself, but somehow managed to survive: "he continues his strange discipline, starving, mercury, opium,—and though for a Time half demolished by its severity, he always, in the end, rises superior both to the disease and the *remedy*,—which is commonly the most alarming of the two."[5]

Johnson also tried other methods, both intellectual and sensual, to ease his chronic pain and insomnia. Like his hero Herman Boerhaave, he "often relieved and mitigated the sense of his torments by the recollection of what he had read, and by reviewing those stores of knowledge which he had reposited in his memory." Ignoring the fatal example of Henry Thrale, Johnson once gorged himself, Boswell wrote, on "a glorious haunch of venison at [John] Taylor's table. Dr. Johnson eat and eat again. [Taylor's neighbor John] Alsop, who did not like him, wickedly prest him to eat more—which he did. He grew so ill that it was feared he would have died of downright eating, and had not a Surgeon been got to administer to him without delay a Clyster ["injection into the anus"] he must have died." After this feast, he went to the other extreme and for a time drank only milk.

Johnson's primary physician, Thomas Lawrence, died in 1783. In addition to the faithful Frank Barber and a constant stream of visitors, he was now attended by four physicians and a surgeon: Richard Brocklesby, William Heberden, Richard Warren, William Butter and William Cruikshank. He also had a male nurse, hired for menial duties in the last days, whom Johnson described as "an idiot, as awkward as a turnspit just put into the wheel, and as sleepy as a dormouse."[6]

William Harvey had discovered the circulation of the blood as long ago as 1628, yet the favored treatment for most illnesses—following the ancient belief "let out the blood, let out the disease"—was still bloodletting. Johnson's doctors believed that if the patient had too little blood, he began to fade; if he had too much, after devouring a glorious haunch and drinking a few bottles of port, he might suffer a stroke. But they failed to realize that frequent and massive discharge of blood was dangerous. In March 1782, for example, after losing sixteen ounces (the amount given by a modern blood donor), he wrote Hester, "I think the loss of blood has done no harm; whether it has done good, time will tell. I am glad that I do not sink without resistance." He defiantly declared, the month before he died, "I will be conquered; I will not capitulate."

Johnson was just as willing to undertake surgery as he was to medicate himself and drain his blood. In the eighteenth century, before the discovery of anesthetics and antiseptics, the risks of infection, hemorrhage and trauma made invasive surgery extremely dangerous. In 1776 Henry Thrale had had a grossly swollen testicle, which he feared was cancerous and was relieved to discover was merely venereal. (In 1793 Edward Gibbon also had a hydrocele [accumulation of fluid] in his testicle, which, when punctured, drew off eight pints of water.) In September 1783 Johnson described his own dire condition, with cool and detailed objectivity, in a letter to the Plymouth physician John Mudge. After accidentally discovering that his left testicle was much larger than the right, he asked his doctors to pierce it with a trocar (an instrument used for withdrawing fluid from a cavity) and they discovered that he had a sarocele, or fleshy excrescence. A month later he wrote, with scrupulous particularity, "the tumor has increased both in surface and in weight, and by tension of the skin is extremely tender, and impatient of pressure or friction. Its weight is such as to give great pain, when it is not suspended, and its bulk such as the common dress does but ill conceal, nor is there any appearance that its growth will stop. It is so hot, that I am afraid it is in a state of perpetual inflammation."[7]

His doctors first thought the enormous, fast-growing tumor was cancerous and were prepared to use "fire and sword" to castrate him. Ready to face the terrifying consequences in order to save his life, he told Hester, "if excision should be delayed there is danger of gangrene. [I would not] for fear of pain perish in putrescence." The surgeon, though ready to perform the excision, had to take a short journey. In his absence, Johnson dealt with the problem himself, trying a last desperate puncture and breaking open the wound. In a letter, he proudly described the grisly details of his surgery: "by its discharge [it] reduced the tumour to half its bulk, and by abating the inflammation took away the soreness. I no longer feel its weight; and the skin of the scrotum which glistened with tension is now lax and corrugated."

Relieved of one illness, and still intact, Johnson soon lurched toward two others. He wrote Boswell that in December 1783, "I was seized with a spasmodick asthma so violent, that with difficulty I got to my own house, in which I have been confined eight or nine weeks. . . . The asthma, however, is not the worst. A dropsy gains ground upon me; my legs and thighs are very much swollen with water, which I should be content if I could keep there, but I am afraid that it will soon be higher. My nights are very sleepless and very tedious. And yet I am extremely afraid of dying."[8]

Johnson's physical distress was heightened by the mental anguish that prevented him from sleeping. In January 1783 he had told John Taylor, "I have been for some time labouring under very great disorder of Body, and distress of Mind." To another friend he described his agonizing insomnia: "My thoughts were disturbed, my nights were insufferably restless, and by spasms in the breast I was condemned to the torture of sleepyness without the power to sleep." Overwhelmed by illness and depression, Johnson responded eagerly to signs of encouragement and offers of relief. When an acquaintance told him "he saw health returning to his cheek, Johnson seized him by the hand and exclaimed, 'Sir, you are one of the kindest friends I ever had.'"[9]

Johnson believed that a warmer climate would improve his condition. He dreaded spending another winter in England and wrote that an invalid always thinks a change of locale will cure him: "a sick man wishes to be where he is not." Henry Fielding had gone to Lisbon in an attempt to recover his health, and Tobias Smollett had lived out the last three years of his life in Livorno. Johnson had always longed to visit Italy but missed several opportunities. In June 1784 Boswell and Reynolds, in a final effort, applied to the lord chancellor, Lord Thurlow, for a government grant to finance Johnson's journey to Italy. When Boswell told Johnson of their petition, he was deeply moved and said, "'This is taking prodigious pains about a man.' 'O! Sir, (said I, with most sincere affection), your friends would do every thing for you.' He paused, grew more and more agitated, till tears started into his eyes."[10] Though the application was unsuccessful, Thurlow himself offered to advance him £600 as a mortgage on his pension, but Johnson refused. He didn't want to sustain the obligation and had no friend to travel with him, though Frank Barber could have gone as his servant. His accounts later revealed that Johnson was much richer than he thought and could have paid his own way to Italy without the help of an official grant.

Instead of going to Italy, Johnson took his last trip to the Midlands, which lasted from mid-July to mid-November 1784. After he returned to London, except for a two-day visit to William Strahan's house in Islington, just north of the city, he was confined to his house. Knowing the end was near, he ordered his affairs with surprising energy. He saw many of his friends, wrote and translated poems and prayers, drew up his will and added a codicil, composed Latin epigraphs for his wife's tombstone and for those of his parents and brother. He took to his bed during his final week; wrote his last prayer on December 5 and last letter on the 10th.

A week before his death and after a particularly difficult night, he told Dr. Brocklesby that he was a dying man and dramatically quoted *Macbeth*: "Canst thou not minister to a mind diseas'd," to which the doctor answered, to fortify him with stoic resolution: "therein the patient / Must minister to himself" (5.3.40, 45–46). Johnson felt his doctors were too timid and feared giving him pain when he was fighting for his life. The day before his death, dreading neither punctures nor incisions, he reproached the surgeon for cowardice and exclaimed: "[Cut] deeper, deeper;—I will abide the consequence; you are afraid of your reputation, but that is nothing to me. . . . You all pretend to love me, but you do not love me so well as I myself do."

Commanding his own fate and trying to preserve his life, he ordered Frank to fetch him a case of lancets. He then put his hands under the bedclothes and plunged a lancet deep into the calf of each leg. When the instrument was taken from him, he seized a pair of scissors from the drawer next to his bed, jabbed it once again into his bloated legs and watched the bloody liquid gush out of his body. Boswell later explained: "imagining that the dropsical collection of water which oppressed him might be drawn off by making incisions in his body, he, with his usual resolute defiance of pain, cut deep, when he thought that his surgeon had done it too tenderly."[11]

II

In the last week of his life Johnson hastily burned a great many papers in his fireplace. The most precious were two quarto volumes containing a detailed and intensely personal account of his entire life. Boswell wrote Reynolds that he'd once read a great deal in those volumes and, seeking exoneration, asked Johnson "if he thought I could have resisted the temptation when I found them lying open? He said with one of his complacent Smiles, 'I believe you could not.' I told him that for once I was tempted to be a thief—to have carried them off and never seen him more and asked how this would have affected him. He said 'It would have made me mad.'"

Boswell's rival biographer, the upright magistrate John Hawkins, actually tried to steal the surviving diary that Boswell had merely been tempted to steal. Johnson noticed the book was missing and saw it in Hawkins' pocket. Obviously lying, Hawkins claimed that he was trying to keep it from George Steevens, who (he said) was intent on taking it. Emphasizing the need to protect his most private thoughts and repeating what he'd said to Boswell about going mad, Johnson angrily told Hawkins: "You should not have laid hands on the book; for had I missed it, and not known you had it, I should have roared for my book, as Othello did for his handkerchief, and probably have run mad." Boswell believed that Johnson was so upset by Hawkins' theft that he consigned that diary and many valuable papers to the flames.[12] The burned diary probably contained references to his darkest secrets: fear of insanity, lustful fantasies, sexual passions, marital infidelity, masturbation, chains and whips.

The death-obsessed Johnson, clearly aware that he was dying, saw his confrontation with death—decribed in Jeremy Taylor's greatly admired *Holy Dying* (1651)—as a personal challenge. In his life of Addison, he quoted the poet's remarkably tranquil and exemplary remark, *"I have sent for you that you may see how a Christian can die."* But Johnson's pessimism about this world was exceeded only by his gloom about the next. Asked by Boswell, "is not the fear of death natural to man?," he vehemently replied, with only slight exaggeration, "so much so, Sir, that the whole of life is but keeping away the thoughts of it." Associating sleep with death, Johnson quoted his favorite Sir Thomas Browne, who said that sleep was so like death "that I dare not trust it without my prayers." Johnson then added, "their resemblance is, indeed, apparent and striking; they both, when they seize the body, leave the soul at liberty."[13] Connecting death with damnation rather than salvation, he feared that if he died in his sleep, sinful and unprepared to meet God, he'd be in great danger of being damned.

Johnson was incredulous yet deeply disturbed by Boswell's report of seeing how a cool and rational atheist could die. "I told him," Boswell wrote, "that David Hume said to me, he was no more uneasy to think he should *not be* after this life, than that he *had not been* before he began to exist. Johnson. 'Sir, if he really thinks so, his perceptions are disturbed; he is mad.'" Johnson refused to believe that Hume could really deny the existence of the soul and ignore the divine judgment that must inevitably follow death. Unable to counter Hume's argument, he merely dismissed him as "mad." When Johnson withdrew from conversation, he would habitually and audibly recite the frightening lines from Shakespeare's *Measure for Measure* about the finality of death without religious faith:

> Ay, but to die, and go we know not where,
> To lie in cold obstruction and to rot,
> This sensible warm motion to become
> A kneaded clod.
> (3.1.118–121)

Shakespeare's lines expressed precisely what Hume believed would happen to him, but did not fear. The thought of rotting in the earth terrified Johnson, and he was not comforted by the idea that his awareness would cease when he became "a kneaded clod." Consciousness itself was so dear to him that the end of it was in itself a terrible fate.

Johnson fervently believed mere existence was so much better than nothing, or nothingness, that he preferred to endure agonizing pain than not exist at all. He was also despondently fond of quoting Milton's lines from *Paradise Lost* about permanent extinction:

> For who would lose,
> Though full of pain, this intellectual being,
> Those thoughts that wander through Eternity,
> To perish rather, swallow'd up and lost
> In the wide womb of uncreated night,
> Devoid of sense and motion?

Yet he was also capable of quite mundane thoughts about the reality of physical death. In late November, when Frank brought him a note, he was struck by an odd idea: he'd receive no more letters in the grave.

Johnson frequently thought and wrote about the Four Last Things: Death, Judgment, Heaven and Hell. In Sermon 15 he declared of the dying man, "when death comes upon him, he will recollect his broken resolves with unutterable anguish." In *Idler* 103, the final number of that periodical, he depressingly reflected, on the "last day, the hour at which probation ceases, repentance will be vain; the day in which every work of the hand, and imagination of the heart shall be brought to judgment, and an everlasting futurity shall be determined by the past." His fear of damnation was based on his conviction that his religious devotions, meditations and prayers, charitable acts and good works—in short, his exemplary Christian life—would count for nothing in the severity of the final reckoning. It was based on his literal belief in Hell and the absolute certainty that his doom was predestined. No wonder that Johnson wrote Hester, "I have much need of entertainment, spiritless, infirm, sleepless, and solitary, looking back with sorrow and forward with terrour."[14]

In December 1784, when Dr. Warren politely asked if he was better, Johnson responded with a blast of realism, "you cannot conceive with what acceleration I advance towards death." Visitors knew he was dying. John Wesley, who spent two hours with him, misleadingly described him as "sinking into the grave by a gentle decay." In December Hannah More also wrote a friend: "Poor dear Johnson! He is past all hope. The dropsy has brought him to the point of death, his legs have been scarified; but nothing will do."[15]

There are three variants of his last words. He supposedly told a hitherto unknown Miss Morris, who was somehow admitted to his deathbed, "God bless you my dear," which sounds like a conventionally pious remark. According to the Italian translator John Hoole, he muttered something about a cup of milk that was handed to him improperly, which seems too banal. Hawkins recorded, most convincingly, that his last words were in Latin: "*Jam moriturus*" ("I am dying now"). He finally died of congestive heart failure, with Barber and Desmoulins at his bedside, at 7:15 PM on Monday, December 13, 1784.

Since graves were often robbed and undertakers sold corpses for anatomical dissections, Johnson left specific instructions to Reynolds, Hawkins and the lawyer Sir William Scott to shield his dead body. "If my executors think it proper to mark the spot of my interment by a stone," he wrote, "let it be so placed as to protect my body from injury." Nevertheless, his wishes were ignored. In order to determine the exact cause of his death and to see if his internal organs were "uncommonly affected," his executors agreed to an autopsy. The surgeon found extensive pathology:

Two of the valves of the aorta ossified.
The air cells of the lungs unusually distended.
One of the kidneys destroyed by the pressure of the water.
The liver schirrous [hardened].
A stone in the gall bladder, of the size of a common gooseberry.

Only a titanic struggle enabled Johnson, despite the formidable assault of lethal diseases as well as his own medications, bloodletting and self-surgery, to survive until the age of seventy-five.

A week after Johnson's death his hearse, pulled by six horses and followed by thirteen coaches and thirteen carriages, left Bolt Court and proceeded down Fleet Street to Westminster Abbey. The pallbearers included Langton, Burke, Paoli, Sir Joseph Banks and the politician William Windham. John Taylor officiated at the funeral, which disappointed some spectators by omitting the anthem and choir service. Johnson was appropriately buried at the foot of Shakespeare's monument and near his two great companions: Garrick at his right hand and Goldsmith just opposite. Some friends were allowed to choose a volume from his library. Langton took the polyglot Bible; Reynolds, the 4th edition of the *Dictionary*; Hawkins, Holinshed's *Chronicles* (a major source for Shakespeare's plays).

Hawkins was furious that Johnson had made Frank Barber his principal heir and had left him a handsome annuity of £70 a year. Hawkins took the watch that Johnson had left to Frank, and recorded that "the impudent Negro said, 'he plainly saw there was no good intended for him' and in anger left me." Frank complained about this theft to Johnson's friends, who forced Hawkins to return the watch. Everyone was astonished that the unworldly Johnson, who never knew what he possessed, died worth nearly £3,000. His assets at death were:

£1,200—money left with friends who served as his bankers
1,054—invested in 3% annuities
100—in cash

235—the value of his family house in Lichfield
320—the value of his library

___

£2,909[16]

After his death, Johnson became his admirers and Boswell his leading acolyte. The critic Walter Raleigh, noting Boswell's limitations and Johnson's distinctive relations with each of his friends, wrote: "Boswell never knew him as Mrs. Thrale knew him—in the every-day round of domestic life; nor as Goldsmith and Sir Joshua Reynolds knew him— a fellow-craftsman to be treated on terms of equality and brotherhood; nor as Hannah More and Frances Burney knew him—playful, gentle, nonsensical, and protective. Least of all did he know him as Savage knew him." Boswell's *Life of Johnson,* published in 1791, has factual errors, huge gaps, structural flaws, notable prejudice and important suppressions. It portrays a fully formed rather than a changing, developing and maturing Johnson. But Boswell's compulsive searching out of original documents, attention to anecdote and minute detail, creation of a "Flemish picture," dramatization of crucial episodes—and denigration of his competitors and rivals—established the techniques and form of modern biography.

In a typically self-satisfied yet well-founded letter, Boswell was pleased to announce that he had successfully preserved Johnson's "minute particularities of conduct": "I am absolutely certain that *my* mode of Biography which gives not only a *History* of Johnson's *visible* progress through the World, and of his Publications, but a *View* of his mind, in his Letters, and Conversations, is the most perfect that can be conceived, and will be *more* of a *Life* than any Work that has ever yet appeared." Boswell, then Macaulay, emphasized Johnson's eccentric character, as Saul Bellow later observed in *Ravelstein*: "Macaulay's essay on Boswell's *Johnson* [1831]. . . put me into a purple fever. Macaulay exhilarated me with *his* version of the *Life,* with the 'anfractuosity' of Johnson's mind. . . . Thanks to him I still see poor convulsive Johnson touching every lamppost on the street and eating spoiled meat and rancid puddings."[17] These portrayals of Johnson were so vivid and so powerful that they obscured for many readers the importance of his writing, which was not fully appreciated until the midtwentieth century.

Johnson's portrait of his spiritual soul mate, the Renaissance humanist Desiderius Erasmus, provides the best account of his own moral character and intellectual achievement: "Compelled by want to attendance and solicitation, and so much versed in common life, that he has transmitted to us the most perfect delineation of the manners of his age; he joined to his knowledge of the world, such application . to books, that he will stand for ever in the first rank of literary heroes." The parliamentarian William Gerard Hamilton wrote one of the finest epitaphs on the original and authoritative writer who dominated his age: "He has made a chasm, which not only nothing can fill up, but which nothing has a tendency to fill up. Johnson is dead. Let us go to the next best:—there is nobody; no man can be said to put you in mind of Johnson."[18]

EPILOGUE:
JOHNSON'S INFLUENCE

I

Johnson's impact on later writers comes less from his work itself than from his extraordinary personality. He himself is one of the great characters in literature. His opinions and conversation were recorded in intimate detail in letters, journals and memoirs, and in Boswell's great biography; and his work has always been interpreted in the context of his life. Though deeply serious, he brought a sense of humor and sharp wit to illuminate his great subjects: the powerful claims of the individual conscience, the moral struggle inherent in life, the suffering in human existence, the sense of his own imperfections, the pain of religious belief.

Johnson created a moral and literary framework that in the nineteenth century influenced writers as different as Jane Austen, whose social comedies depend on Johnson's principles; Nathaniel Hawthorne, for whom Johnson embodied the tormented Puritan conscience; and A. E. Housman, who echoed Johnson's stoicism in his verse. In the twentieth century Johnson remained a key character and thinker. For Virginia Woolf, who used him in her novel *Orlando,* he was the noble archetype of the man of letters. Samuel Beckett, obsessed for years with Johnson's pessimism, wrote a play about him. In *Pale Fire* Nabokov's cunningly covert allusions to Johnson make the vague outlines of John Shade's character more vivid.

Jane Austen was devoted to both the character and the writing of "My dear Dr. Johnson," whose works were frequently and appreciatively read in her home. Her family valued Johnson's orthodox Toryism, Anglicanism, piety and moral rectitude. He emphasized not the formal tenets of religion, but the individual's striving for goodness and humility. Austen's intellectual worldview was permeated with Johnson. In *Northanger Abbey* (1818) she gently satirized the way people deferred to Johnson's judgments. Eleanor Tilney, advising Catherine Morland about how to please her brother, warns her that he will invoke Johnson's *Dictionary* as the absolute authority on usage: "The word 'nicest' as you used it, did not suit him; and you had better change it as soon as you can, or we shall be overpowered with Johnson . . . all the rest of the way." Austen also imitated the master, whose style she wittily adapted to the novel. In *Rambler* 115 Johnson's young narrator says, "I was known to possess a fortune, and to want a wife." Her most celebrated sentence, the opening of *Pride and Prejudice* (1813), is an elaboration of this line in Johnsonian style: "It is a truth universally acknowledged, that a single man in possession of a good fortune, must be in want of a wife." Johnson's essays were full of epigrams and wise pronouncements that Austen put into the mouths of her characters. He observed that all self-censure was oblique commendation: "this affectation of candour or modesty was but another kind of indirect self-praise, and had its foundation in vanity." In this novel the hero, Mr. Darcy, a rather pompous young man who talks in a deliberately Johnsonian manner, expresses that same belief to Elizabeth Bennet: "Nothing is more deceitful . . . than the appearance of humility. It is often only carelessness of opinion, and sometimes an indirect boast."[1]

In *Mansfield Park* (1814) Johnson is both a moral touchstone and a source of wit. Edmund Bertram, the serious clergyman who's endowed with Johnson's common sense and moral concerns, offers his cousin Fanny Price, the solemn heroine, copies of "Crabbe's *Tales,* and the *Idler.*" Later in the novel, when Fanny returns to her squalid home, Austen writes that she "was tempted to apply to them Dr. Johnson's celebrated judgment as to matrimony and celibacy, and say, that though

Mansfield Park might have some pains, Portsmouth could have no pleasures." Fanny refers to chapter 26 of *Rasselas* in which the widower Johnson, inspired by St. Paul's "It is better to marry than to burn" (I Corinthians 7:9), stated, "Marriage has many pains, but celibacy has no pleasures." The critic Robert Scholes has argued that Jane Austen adopted the moral philosophy of the *Rambler* and *Rasselas*. She agreed with Johnson's ideas about the "relationship of manners and morals, and assumptions about the nature of love and the qualities which make for a happy marriage. . . . The closeness—almost unity—of thought and attitude which exists between Jane Austen and Johnson on important matters . . . is certainly striking."[2]

For Nathaniel Hawthorne, the relationship of manners and morals was not as clear-cut, and his puritan sensibility drew him to Johnson's melancholy and anguished conscience. Again and again Hawthorne returned to the central act of contrition in Johnson's life, to his journey to the Uttoxeter market, where he stood in the rain as a penance for his youthful act of filial disobedience. Hawthorne dwelled on the episode in two essays and used the public exemplum in his fictional master-piece *The Scarlet Letter*. His chapter on Johnson in his didactic *Biographical Stories for Children* (1842) concentrated on the apparently trivial but irreverent act, early in life, which gnawed at Johnson's conscience. He embellished the incident by inventing Michael Johnson's response, and used it to teach American children to obey their parents and remain contrite before God: "But all his fame could not extinguish the bitter remembrance which had tormented him throughout life. Never, never had he forgotten his father's sorrowful and upbraiding look. . . . By thus expressing his deep repentance and humiliation of heart, he hoped to gain peace of conscience and the forgiveness of God."

After Hawthorne's Bowdoin College friend Franklin Pierce had been elected president, he was appointed American consul in Liverpool and in 1855 sedulously followed Johnson's footsteps in London, Lichfield and Uttoxeter. In his 1863 essay on the Midlands towns, he confessed that, apart from Johnson's poems, he preferred the man to the writer. He identified himself, in contrast to the down-to-earth Johnson, as the creator of a more ethereal literature: "considering that my native propensities were towards Fairy Land . . . I do not remember, indeed,

ever caring much about any of the stalwart Doctor's grandiloquent pro-
ductions, except his two stern and masculine poems, 'London' and
'The Vanity of Human Wishes'; it was as a man, a talker, and a hu-
morist, that I knew and loved him." Hawthorne then focused on the
aged Johnson in Uttoxeter. He'd always been deeply impressed by that
extraordinary incident, which he felt had atoned for a fundamental sin
in Johnson's life: "He stands bareheaded, a venerable figure, and a countenance extremely sad and woe-begone, with the wind and rain driving hard against him . . . to lighten his half-century's burden of
remorse."

Finally, Hawthorne made brilliant use of the Uttoxeter episode in
The Scarlet Letter (1850). The Reverend Arthur Dimmesdale (whose
name means shadowy valley) seduces the married Hester Prynne.[3]
Nobly keeping her guilty secret, Hester refuses to identify the father of
her illegitimate child. As punishment for her sin, and while Dimmesdale remains silent, she's forced to stand in the pillory and to wear the
scarlet "A" that brands her as an adulteress.

In two crucial scenes, separated by many tormented years, Dimmesdale mounts to the very place where Hester once stood. The emotional
power of these scenes is strengthened by the tacit allusion to Johnson:

> Mr. Dimmesdale reached the spot where, now so long since, Hes-
> ter Prynne had lived through her first hours of public ig-
> nominy. . . . Why, then, had he come hither? Was it but the
> mockery of penitence? . . . Had he been driven hither by the im-
> pulse of that Remorse which dogged him everywhere . . . the
> agony of heaven-defying guilt and vain repentance. . . . And thus,
> while standing on the scaffold, in this vain show of expiation, Mr.
> Dimmesdale was overcome with a great horror of mind, as if the
> universe were gazing at a scarlet token on his naked breast.

In this first scene it is midnight; the whole town is asleep and there
is no danger of discovery. In the second scene, seven years later,
Dimmesdale—after preaching a brilliant Johnsonian sermon on sin,
anguish and repentance—is ineluctably drawn to the very same scaffold

in the marketplace and makes his long-sought and long-repressed confession: "ye, that have loved me!—ye, that have deemed me holy!—behold me here, the one sinner of the world! At last!—at last!—I stand upon the spot where, seven years since, I should have stood; here, with this woman, whose arm, more than the little strength wherewith I have crept hitherward, sustains me, at this dreadful moment, from grovelling down upon my face." In Boswell's account Johnson remained silent during his solemn and dignified struggle with his tormented conscience. Dimmesdale, whose sin is more grievous, must publicly proclaim his intolerable guilt. His speech is filled with exclamation marks, rhetorical repetitions, awkward style ("wherewith I have crept hitherward") and operatic threats to grovel on the ground. The episode that captured Hawthorne's imagination revealed the essential reason for Johnson's torment: the lack of conviction that he could in fact be forgiven, and the religious doubt that drove him to melancholy and the fear of madness. Hawthorne the novelist understood the dramatic tension in the Protestant ethic: the constant striving to do good and constant dread of eternal damnation.

A. E. Housman, classicist and poet, was influenced by an altogether different aspect of Johnson. He attacked Johnson's critical judgments of Milton, Pope and William Collins in *The Name and Nature of Poetry* (1933), but imitated some of Johnson's poetry in his own verse. In his parodic "Lines on Thomas Warton's Poems," Johnson ironically claimed that alcohol could alleviate the pains and evils of the world:

> Smite thy bosom, sage, and tell,
>   Where is bliss? And which the way? . . .
> When the smiling sage reply'd—
>   Come, my lad, and drink some beer.

Addressing his own likely lad in similar quatrains, but in a more serious mood, Housman repeated his version of Johnson's last six words:

> The troubles of our proud and angry dust
>   Are from eternity, and shall not fail.

Bear them we can, and if we can we must.
  Shoulder the sky, my lad, and drink your ale.

In a similar fashion, the morbid melancholy and tragic view of life in Johnson's last poem, a translation of Horace's *Odes* (IV.vii):

But wretched Man, when once he lies
Where Priam and his sons are laid
Is nought but Ashes and a Shade,

was repeated by Housman, a great Latin scholar, in "For My Funeral":

We now to peace and darkness
  And earth and thee restore
Thy creature that thou madest
  And wilt cast forth no more.[4]

In *The Vanity of Human Wishes* Johnson wrote, with characteristic gloom:

Yet hope not Life from Grief or Danger free,
Nor think the Doom of Man revers'd for thee.

In *A Shropshire Lad* Housman expressed an equally grim view of human misery and ended with a crucial Johnsonian word:

Ay, look: high heaven and earth ail from the prime foundation;
All thoughts to rive the heart are here and all are vain.

Johnson believed "the change of old establishments is always an evil." Housman agreed with him and stated, "I . . . do not like changing anything without due reason."[5]

Norman Page noted that Housman, like Johnson, had a taste for invective and was master of the cruel condemnation and knockout blow.

He "is fond of the Johnsonian trick of ridicule by reductive metaphor or analogy: of the notes of the hapless Merrill's edition of Catullus, he declares that 'half the ship's cargo has been thrown overboard to save the bilge-water.'"[6] Johnson, ever the great example of the independent scholar and man of letters, inspired in Housman a vein of caustic wit and devotion to scholarship.

Virginia Woolf was also a great admirer of Johnson. She was strongly influenced by her father, Leslie Stephen, who wrote extensively about Johnson and popularized his biographical method in the last quarter of the nineteenth century.[7] Woolf collected her essays on Johnson's friends—Boswell, Charles Burney and Giuseppe Baretti—but published only one obscure, anonymous review about Johnson. In "Saint Samuel of Fleet Street" (1925), the usually sharp-tongued, hypercritical Woolf praised his impressive character and, echoing "such stuff / As dreams are made on" in *The Tempest*—remarked: "There can be no doubt . . . that Dr. Johnson has proved himself of the stuff that Saints are made of. . . . He is one of the very few human beings who love their kind."

Woolf begins *The Common Reader* (also 1925) by claiming that she wrote with the same sound intentions and for the same receptive audience as Johnson, and quotes the memorable final paragraph of *The Lives of the Poets*:

There is a sentence in Dr. Johnson's Life of Gray which might well be written up in all those rooms, too humble to be called libraries, yet full of books, where the pursuit of reading is carried on by private people. ". . . I rejoice to concur with the common reader; for by the common sense of readers, uncorrupted by [Johnson wrote "with"] literary prejudices, after all the refinements of subtilty and the dogmatism of learning, must be finally decided all claim to poetical honours." It defines their qualities; it dignifies their aims.

Three years later, in *Orlando: A Biography,* her protean heroine turns up in eighteenth-century England and observes several members of

Johnson's household (including Anna Williams) illuminated through a screen. Woolf's striking scene portrays some of Johnson's most famous idiosyncrasies: his twisted fingers (portrayed by Reynolds), his spasmodic movements, his insatiable thirst for tea and his grandiloquent conversation. It also alludes to a shadowy passage in the *Life of Savage* in which Savage, after discovering the identity of his real mother, would "walk in the dark evenings for several hours before her door, in hopes of seeing her as she might come by accident to the window, or cross her apartment with a candle in her hand."[8]

> She stood half an hour watching three shadows on the blind drinking tea together in a house in Bolt Court. . . . There was the Roman-looking rolling shadow in the big armchair—he who twisted his fingers so oddly and jerked his head from side to side and swallowed down the tea in such vast gulps. Dr. Johnson, Mr. Boswell, and Mrs. Williams,—those were the shadows' names. . . . The great Roman shadow now rose to its full height and rocking somewhat as he stood there rolled out the most magnificent phrases that ever left human lips.

A critic recently pointed out that in an unpublished version of Woolf's *The Waves* (1931), Bernard, the disappointed writer, connects Percival, who dies in his mid-twenties in India, to Johnson's most pessimistic poem: "In the second draft, Bernard pictures Percival in India, reading (appropriately) Johnson's poem on 'The Vanity of Human Wishes' 'with his legs over the arm of a camp chair,' soon after [T. S.] Eliot had sent the Woolfs his [1930] edition of that poem."

Woolf's use of Johnson was intellectual and aesthetic; Samuel Beckett's was intensely personal and emotional. He was born in 1906, and won the Nobel Prize for literature in 1969. Like Hawthorne, he strongly identified with the historical figure of Samuel Johnson (his namesake) and made a pilgrimage to Lichfield. But Beckett used Johnson's religious doubt, his melancholy and fits of insanity to emphasize his own sense of futility. Johnson once said, "If . . . I had no duties, and no reference to futurity, I would spend my life in driving briskly in a post-chaise with a pretty woman." Beckett twisted this famous comment to suit his own temperament. Leaving out the pretty girl and making the journey pointless rather than pleasant, he mentioned "Johnson's dream of happiness, driving happily to and fro nowhere."[9] Like Johnson, Beckett often sank into torpor and spent half the day in bed.

In 1937 Beckett planned to write a play about Johnson and read many books by and about him in the library of Trinity College, Dublin. His three manuscript notebooks, now in the Reading University Library, emphasize Johnson's dark side. His principal source was Johnson's *Prayers and Meditations* (1785 and many later editions), which revealed his morbid "obsession with mental and physical deterioration," with "melancholy, madness and death." Beckett's biographer Deirdre Bair, who discussed the unfinished play with him, wrote that Beckett and Johnson, whom he called a tragic, "spiritually self-conscious" figure who needed to suffer, had a great many personal and literary qualities in common:

He finds much that appeals to him, particularly the melancholy moods and depressions which characterized Johnson's later life. [Beckett said] "it's Johnson, always Johnson, who is with me. And if I follow any tradition, it is his." Johnson's life as well as his work has appealed to Beckett. Johnson had psychological problems of his own, and like Beckett, he was a late bloomer. Beckett may have identified his physical afflictions with Johnson's—i.e., his boils, with Johnson's scrofula. Most importantly, in both men there is a love of theory and abstraction, and an incredible erudition.

Beckett's drama, famous for its pared-down, elliptical style, seems quite different from Johnson's. But Beckett, like Jane Austen, was fascinated by Johnson's *Dictionary.* He too favored Latinate roots and philosophic diction, and used many polysyllabic words in *More Pricks Than Kicks* (1934) and *Murphy* (1938). He also quoted Johnson in *Watt* (1953) and, after a series of repetitions, wrote, "and so on, until all trace is lost, on account of the vanity of human wishes." Beckett's devotion to Johnson lasted throughout his life. His biographer Anthony Cronin reported that in his small Parisian writing room in the 1960s, "on the specially built shelves stood those books which he wanted to have near him when he was working. There were his own works and those of James Joyce [and] various early editions of the works of Samuel Johnson."[10]

Beckett had the same pessimistic worldview as Johnson, but was not sustained, even precariously, by his religious faith. Johnson's assertion in chapter 11 of *Rasselas* that in human life there is "much to be endured, and little to be enjoyed," is very close to Beckett's bleak outlook. Recent critics, noting their similarities, observed that Beckett "wrote so frequently and eloquently about that chasm between desire and fulfillment, expectation and realisation, hope and despair, which is the mark of Johnson in his periodical essays, in *Rasselas* and in *Vanity.*" The last chapter of *Rasselas*, "The conclusion, in which nothing is concluded," appealed to Beckett's nihilism. Beckett, who called *Rasselas* "a grand book," also described what Johnson expressed in his private diaries but repressed in his published work, and emphasized "the horror of annihilation, the horror of madness, the horrified love of Mrs. Thrale, and the whole mental monster ridden swamp."

Bair added that "Beckett's original idea was to write a play in four acts, called *Human Wishes,* after Johnson's poem. . . . He intended to explain Johnson's esteem for 'the imbecile Mr. Thrale' by concentrating on Mrs. Thrale's relationship to the mature Johnson, and his obsessive, unspoken love for her." Beckett told a friend, "it seems now quite certain that he was rather absurdly in love with her all the fifteen [actually, twenty] years he was at Streatham, though there is no text[ual authority] for the impotence." Nevertheless, he was obsessed with Johnson's supposed impotence and described it as "the fake rage to cover his retreat from her, then the real rage when he realizes that no retreat was necessary, and beneath both the despair of the lover with nothing to love with."[11] In a stroke of brilliant casting, he thought the married homosexual Charles Laughton could play Johnson.

Beckett planned to begin the play with Henry Thrale's funeral in 1781, which left Hester free to remarry, and to end it with Johnson's death three years later. The opening scene in Johnson's bizarre household (which also fascinated Virginia Woolf) would provide a contrast to his luxurious life with the Thrales at Streatham. But Beckett remained uncertain about whether to focus on Johnson's unreciprocated love for Hester or on the pathetic inmates of his radically discontented household: the blind Anna Williams, the sickly Elizabeth Desmoulins, the prostitute Poll Carmichael and the unlicensed Dr. Levet. As Johnson lamented to Hester, "Williams hates every body; Levett hates Desmoulins, and does not love Williams; Desmoulins hates them both; Poll loves none of them."

Beckett's ten-page fragment begins in Bolt Court on April 4, 1781, with the three hostile women on stage. Hodge, Johnson's beloved black cat, is asleep. The drunken Levet appears, belches loudly and leaves without saying a word. Johnson does not appear at all. There's no dramatic action, merely a few petulant women engaged in vituperative and slightly amusing dialogue. Desmoulins, for example, speaks Johnson's words about Hodge without providing either a meaningful context or the delightful anthropomorphic phrase "out of countenance." Boswell had reported that as he watched Johnson stroke Hodge and said that he was a fine cat, Johnson replied: "'why yes, Sir, but I have had cats whom I liked better than this'; and then as if perceiving Hodge to be out of countenance, adding, 'but he is a very fine cat, a very fine cat indeed.'" Beckett writes, in staccato style:

Desmoulins: Hodge is a very fine cat, a very fine cat indeed. . . . For his age, an uncommonly fine cat in all respects. . . .
Williams: I may be old, I may be blind, halt and maim, I may be dying of a pituitous defluxion [common cold], but my hearing is unimpaired. . . .
You say you are not merry. Very well. But who is merry in this house? You would not call me merry, Madam, I suppose? . . .
Nobody in this house is merry.
Desmoulins: I hope you are satisfied, Madam.[12]

The ladies are anxiously waiting for Johnson and eager for news about Thrale's funeral. They imitate his Latinate diction—"peevishness of decay," "recumbent scurrility," "hilarity of ebriety"—and Desmoulins quotes *Hamlet*: "that undiscovered country from whose [bourn / No traveler returns]." Poll quotes the theme of Beckett's dramatic fragment, "Death meets us everywhere," and gives examples from two of Johnson's favorite books, Jeremy Taylor's *Holy Living* (1650) and *Holy Dying* (1651). The decrepit old ladies reflect Johnson's own poor health and obsession with death. The dialogue is ironic, since the prostitute Poll, even if Johnson had encouraged her to consult this difficult text on the day of Thrale's funeral, would never have read or understood it.

The ladies also discuss three Irish playwrights—Arthur Murphy, Hugh Kelly and Oliver Goldsmith—and mention that the last two died in 1774. When Desmoulins states that Goldsmith's "debt to nature is discharged," Williams regrets that he died before repaying his debt to *her*. Desmoulins, contentious as always, rejects Williams' statement that Kelly is "dead and damned these last five [i.e., seven] years," by asserting, "Mr. Kelly may be poorly, but he is alive."[13]

Beckett seems to have misconceived the style as well as the setting and themes of the play. He misleadingly claimed that he abandoned the fragment because he was incapable "of putting it into the Irish accent as well as the proper language of the period. It would not do to have Johnson speaking proper language, after the manner of Boswell, while all the other characters speak only the impossible jargon I put into their mouths." But there was a more compelling reason for giving it up. Another critic noted that "the more of Johnson he recorded in these notebooks, the more preposterous was the amatory scenario that initially impelled his interest."[14] Yet the play was not a total loss. The fragment helped Beckett transform Johnson's pessimism into his characteristically bleak view of the world.

Beckett didn't mention *Human Wishes* to his official bibliographer, grew impatient when Bair tried to discuss it with him, brusquely refused to let his American director read it and finally gave the manuscript to a scholar, saying "he was glad to be rid of it." He hated the play, which was not only a failure, but also reflected his own sexual impotence, which he projected onto Johnson. Cronin reported that Beckett, like his Johnson, though not completely impotent, "had difficulty copulating with the women for whom he had real feeling."[15]

II

Johnson and Nabokov seem diametrically opposed. The quintessential Englishman, the epitome of the eighteenth-century "Age of Johnson," favored lofty abstractions, moralistic content and elaborate Latinate style. Modern readers mistakenly assume that his works are impenetrable: his criticism misguided, his poetry prosaic, his essays didactic. Nabokov, by contrast, is the embodiment of the witty, urbane and cosmopolitan modern writer. An uprooted victim of violent revolution, a scientist and scholar, he wandered across two continents and wrote, in two languages, subtly sophisticated, exquisitely stylish and teasingly elusive books. Yet Nabokov perceived the greatness of Johnson and was strangely drawn to the man whose appearance, character and writings profoundly influenced the creation of his tragicomic masterpiece, *Pale Fire* (1962).

The epigraph to *Pale Fire*, taken from Boswell's *Life of Samuel Johnson* (incorrectly cited by the pedantic Charles Kinbote as the *Life of Dr. Johnson*) immediately alerts readers to Johnson's monumental presence in the novel. The epigraph relates how Johnson told Bennet Langton that a crazy gentleman had been shooting cats: "then in a sort of kindly reverie, he bethought himself of his own favourite cat and said, 'But Hodge shan't be shot; no, no, Hodge shall not be shot.'"[16] Hodge may have inspired the appearance of two cats in *Pale Fire*. A black cat comes with Kinbote's rented house, but unlike Johnson, he reveals his defective character by neither loving it nor maintaining its proper diet: "it was a likable little creature but after a while its movements began to grate on my nerves and I farmed it out to . . . the cleaning woman" (61). When the depressive Kinbote considers committing suicide by gently rolling off a rooftop, he notes that "a cat may be trusted to flash out of the way" and shan't be hurt (157). Jakob Gradus, who accidentally murders Shade, is, like the shooter of cats in the epigraph, both mad and violent. But Kinbote shall not be shot.

John Shade is the son of Samuel. Shade's middle name, Francis, was the name of Johnson's black servant, Francis Barber. Francis, the main beneficiary of Johnson's will, married and had a son named Samuel. In *Pale Fire* the Negroes in art and life are both inspired by Francis Barber. Shade's childhood clockwork toy "was a little Negro [boy] of

painted tin with a keyhole in his side and no breadth to speak of,"
which he kept "as a kind of *memento mori*" (99). Kinbote's Negro gar-
dener, Jack, becomes a living *memento mori* when he hits Gradus over
the head with a spade (what else?) just after Gradus has accidentally
killed Shade. (Trotsky, Nabokov's bête noire, was killed by an ice pick
jabbed into the back of his skull.) Just as Johnson gave a notoriously
provocative toast at Oxford, "here's to the next insurrection of the negroes in the West Indies,"[17] so the equally humane Shade attacks "the
barbarous traditions of slavery" (155), a volatile issue in Johnson's time,
though not in Shade's.

Describing his own physical appearance, Shade tells Kinbote, "I
have been said to resemble . . . Samuel Johnson" (188). Both Johnson
and Shade are physically unattractive and plagued by chronic illness.
Johnson had a series of debilitating diseases and died of heart failure.
The unhealthy Shade calls himself "asthmatic, lame and fat" (26).
Kinbote—referring to Johnson's slightly older contemporary, the
satiric artist William Hogarth, and to Shade's secret drinking habit—
emphasizes the Johnsonian contrast between his decaying body and
brilliant intellect. Kinbote calls Shade "a fleshy Hogarthian tippler"
(like Johnson's cousin Cornelius Ford), and describes "his misshapen
body, that gray mop of abundant hair, the yellow nails of his pudgy
fingers, the bags under his lusterless eyes" (17).

Anatomizing Johnson's physical defects, Boswell noted that the scars
of his scrofula were deeply visible and that he had convulsive starts and
odd gesticulations. Fanny Burney described his rolling and twitching
motions. At first sight, Hogarth thought Johnson was actually an idiot.
Shade, age 61 and not as far gone as Johnson, has the same disheveled
"jerky shuffle" as well as "a wobbly heart, a slight limp, and a certain
curious contortion in his method of progress" (8, 13).

Despite these formidable disabilities Shade, like Johnson, has "an
inordinate liking for long walks" (13). Just as Johnson agreed to "frisk"
with his young friends Bennet Langton and Topham Beauclerk at three
in the morning, so Shade enthusiastically tells Kinbote, "Let's go for a
good ramble tonight" (183). Variations of Johnson's *Rambler,* the title of
his most impressive moral essays, echo through the novel. Kinbote
comes from a northern country called Zembla, a near anagram and

near homonym for the *Rambler.* Kinbote, referring to the Rambler car made by Nash Motors in the 1950s, twice mentions that he has a "powerful Kramler" (114, 200).

The characters of Johnson and Shade also have striking similarities. Both men married young and adored their wives. Johnson described his bitter years as a Grub Street hack in the *Life of Savage,* and Shade alludes to Johnson—Kinbote's notes also need annotation—when he writes of "the prosemongers of the Grubby Group" (191). Both men have (or have had) drinking problems. Johnson said, "Abstinence is as easy to me, as *temperance* would be difficult," but was annoyed when he had to stay sober as his friends drank and laughed.

Shade's daughter Hazel's obsessive investigation of poltergeists corresponds to Johnson's sometimes credulous investigations of supernatural phenomena: premonitory voices and the fraudulent Cock Lane ghost. Johnson and Shade have the same impressive intellect, prismatic conversation and gruff "dignity of the heart" (16). Both celebrated writers bewail the difficulties of their self-imposed literary tasks. As Johnson said in the "Preface" to his monumental work: "the *English Dictionary* was written . . . amidst inconvenience and distraction, in sickness and in sorrow."[18]

Most important, Shade, like Johnson, is an unusually kind man who has deep sympathy for the poor, the unfortunate and the outcast. Miserable people always had a claim on Johnson's compassion. Most of Johnson's contemporaries felt more abhorrence than tenderness for the starving masses, but he believed that "a decent provision for the poor is the true test of civilization." His own early poverty made him identify with the oppressed and inspired a lifelong effort to alleviate their sufferings. Boswell reported that he placed pennies in the hands of children sleeping in the streets and "frequently gave all the silver in his pocket to the poor."[19] When asked why he gave charity to beggars, he said that it enabled them to survive and continue to beg. Kinbote mentions that Shade was always "very kind to the unsuccessful" and that the core of his ethics was the concept of "pity" (168, 160). Though Nabokov does not give specific examples, he uses Johnson's humanity to give weight to Shade's compassion.

Shade's saturnine temperament also derives from Johnson. When composing his poetry, Shade seems "more forlorn than pensive" (203). In his "Pale Fire," Shade—whose name means ghost and is an anagram for Hades, the abode of the dead—wants to know "for sure what dawn, what death, what doom / Awaited consciousness beyond the tomb" (27). In that poem he "surveyed" (a word borrowed from the second line of Johnson's *The Vanity of Human Wishes*) "death's abyss" and—more sceptical yet more positive than Johnson—concludes his third canto by affirming: "I have returned convinced that I can grope / My way to some—to some—'Yes, dear?' Faint hope" (45). Brian Boyd, his biographer, noted that Nabokov, like Shade, "dedicated his art and his life to exploring and fighting death's abyss."

Nabokov alluded to Johnson when describing how Shade wrote poetry with unusual speed. Speaking of Johnson's major poem *The Vanity of Human Wishes,* Boswell exclaimed: "the fervid rapidity with which it was produced, is scarcely credible. I have heard him say, that he composed seventy lines of it in one day, without putting one of them upon paper till they were finished" in his mind. Shade, in a similar feat, wrote, with shrewd Johnsonian wit and common sense, 230 lines of Canto Two in less than 24 hours. Shade also writes in heroic couplets and likes parody. Johnson parodied Bishop Thomas Percy's *Hermit of Warkworth* by writing: "I put my hat upon my head / And walk'd into the Strand / And there I met another man / Whose hat was in his hand."[20] Shade confesses, "I have a certain liking, I admit, / For Parody, that last resort of wit" (190).

When Johnson published *London* anonymously in 1738, Pope famously predicted that the author "will soon be *déterré.*" Johnson's "Pope" was the last to be written and the best of *The Lives of the Poets.* Shade has also written a book on Pope whose title, *Supremely Blest,* comes from the *Essay on Man.* In that poem Pope ironically compares the transmutations of an alchemist and a poet: "The starving chemist in his golden views / Supremely blest, the poet in his Muse." Kinbote explains that Shade's "book is concerned mainly with Pope's technique but also contains pithy 'observations' [another word from the first line of Johnson's *Vanity*] on 'the stylized morals of his age'" (140). In this poem Pope refers to Boswell's country and to what Kinbote calls his "distant northern land" (224): "In Scotland, at the Orcades; and there, / At Greenland, Zembla, or the Lord knows where." Shade's poem is filled with echoes of Pope. In line 831, for example, the intimate command, "'Darling, shut the door,'" alludes to the colloquial injunction in the first line of the *Epistle to Dr. Arbuthnot* (1735): "Shut, shut the door, good John! fatigued, I said."

Kinbote describes Shade's poem as "an autobiographical . . . rather old-fashioned narrative in a neo-Popian prosodic style—beautifully written" (209). Shade confirms his descent from the Augustans, who loved to inhale powdered tobacco, by asserting, "Personally, I am with the old snuff-takers" (160). When he seeks relief from the intense pressures of poetic composition and entertains some academic guests, he considers the evening "devoted to what his favorite eighteenth-century writers have termed 'the Bustle and Vanity of the World'" (113).[21] Lady Bustle, a country housewife in *Rambler* 51, is obsessed with cooking and preserving; human vanity is the theme of Johnson's major poem.

Apart from references to the *Rambler,* there are several other, more subtle allusions to Johnson's works. His political satire *Marmor Norfolciense* has a pedantic commentator who, like Kinbote, tries to work out the meaning of a puzzling poem. Johnson published the first important *Dictionary of the English Language.* Shade, equally devoted to dictionaries, "kept a Bible-like Webster open at M" (119). That letter, halfway through the alphabet and conveniently dividing the two open halves of a massive tome, is also the Roman numeral for the final, unwritten line of his 999-line poem. Like the last sentence of Joyce's *Finnegans Wake,* the last line of *Pale Fire* circles back and connects to the first line: "slain" rhymes with "lane."

Kinbote, using several multilingual puns, alludes to the Happy Valley in *Rasselas* (1759). He rejects the invitation of a ferocious clubwoman and refuses "to speak on the subject of 'The Hally Vally' (as she put it, confusing Odin's Hall [Valhalla] with the title of a Finnish epic [Kalevala])" (16). In one of the most savage couplets in *Vanity,* Johnson foreshadowed Shade by alluding to the fact that Swift went mad at the end of his life. Swift's mercenary servants then exhibited him, drooling like an idiot, to the gaping public. In one of his finest variant lines, Shade, echoing Johnson, mentions writers who sank into senile imbecility before reaching the "Strange Other World":

> And minds that died before arriving there:
> Poor old man Swift, poor——, poor Baudelaire. (120)

Kinbote wonders what the dash might stand for, but doesn't suggest any possibilities. Nabokov challenges the curious reader to complete the line. Three mad poets with monosyllabic surnames were born between Swift and Baudelaire. Smart (Johnson's friend) alliterates with Swift; Clare provides an internal rhyme with Baudelaire. Kleist would add a German to the Englishman and Frenchman, and suggest the suffering of Christ.

Just as Johnson inspired many aspects of Shade's life and gave depth to his art, so the figure of Boswell influenced the character of Kinbote—a pale flickering imitation of Shade's incandescent flame. Indeed, Kinbote makes the comparison explicit. Kinbote, like Boswell, is a strenuous stenographer. In his black pocketbook he jots down "among various extracts that had happened to please me (a footnote from Boswell's *Life of Dr. Johnson* . . .) [and] a few samples of John Shade's conversation" (111). Like Boswell, Kinbote identifies with his subject and gets "accustomed to another life's running alongside" and often colliding with his own (130). Boswell was thirty-one years younger than Johnson, Kinbote seventeen years younger than Shade, and both have possessively filial feelings toward their heroes and alter egos. Boswell was an insatiable fornicator; Kinbote is a secret pederast. Boswell's psychopathology included obsessive gambling, drinking, priapism and voyeuristic attendance at public executions. Kinbote is a classic case history of pathological monomania, delusions and paranoia.

Like Boswell, Kinbote questions, pursues and even spies on his subject, vividly remembering and precisely recording Shade's conversations. Boswell deliberately drew Johnson's fire in order to create memorable scenes and hounded him with probing questions. Kinbote actually bursts into the room while Shade is shaving in his bath. Boswell managed to lure Johnson to his native Scotland, and both wrote books about their journey. Kinbote draws Shade's attention to *his* native country and supplies him with a lot of material about Zembla, which Shade has no interest in and firmly rejects.

When thinking of Johnson, Boswell felt a contagion of desire. Kinbote, ineluctably drawn to Shade "under the incubus of curiosity" (116), drenches "every nerve . . . in the romance of his presence." Sybil Shade, far less tolerant than her husband of his aggressive intrusions, calls Kinbote "the monstrous parasite of a genius" (123). Boswell was intensely jealous of Johnson's friends and consistently denigrated his rival biographers, especially Hester Thrale. Kinbote is jealous of Sybil and goes berserk at the very thought of the academic intrigues of Professor Hurley's despicable little clique. They spurt the thick venom of envy on his text of the poem, and invent malicious criticism "to asperse the competence, and perhaps honesty, of its present editor and commentator" (8). He is furious that their vindictive and grossly misleading obituary does not contain "*one reference* to the glorious friendship that brightened the last months of John's life" (73).

Boswell shared Johnson's melancholy, depression and guilt. When he confessed his agonies, Johnson felt threatened and warned him never to mention his own mental problems. Kinbote, in a lucid moment, describes himself as "a desponder in my nature, an uneasy, peevish, and suspicious man" (124). Like Boswell and Johnson (who often quoted Richard Burton's "be not solitary, be not idle"), Kinbote can't bear solitude and laments "the depths of [his] loneliness and distress" (69).

Pale Fire reveals how profoundly Nabokov identified with Johnson's personality. Brian Boyd's summation of Nabokov's essential character clarifies the striking parallels—"crystal on crystal"—between Johnson and Shade's creator: "For Nabokov, the ability to show 'staunch kindness' to others in the midst of one's own private agony is the highest of ethical principles."

Though Johnson's work seemed to go out of fashion soon after his death, his personality lived on. His strong, vivid character could not be directly transformed into fiction, but was most effective as an unseen presence in *The Scarlet Letter,* a shadowy figure in *Orlando* or Shade's shadow in *Pale Fire.* His authority as a moralist and humanist pervades the work of Jane Austen, A. E. Housman and Samuel Beckett. In *The Lives of the Poets* Johnson emphasized the dignity and worth of the man of letters, whose values he exemplified. For more than two centuries after his death, Johnson has also remained an enduring presence in the work of imaginative writers. As he wrote of Shakespeare, "the stream of time, which is continually washing the dissoluble fabricks of other poets, passes without injury by the adamant" of Johnson.[22]

NOTES

INTRODUCTION: THE STRUGGLE

1. Ford Madox Ford, *The March of Literature: From Confucius' Day to Our Own* (New York, 1938), p. 614; *Rambler* 48, in Samuel Johnson, *The Yale Edition of the Works of Samuel Johnson* (New Haven, 1958–2005), 3:260 (cited as "Yale"); Friedrich Nietzsche, *The Will to Power,* trans. and ed. Walter Kaufman (New York, 1967), p. 493.

2. James Boswell, *Life of Johnson,* ed. R. W. Chapman (1791; Oxford, 1961), p. 427 (I usually cite this more accessible edition as *"Life"*); Boswell, *Life,* p. 54; *Idler* 102, Yale 2:312.

3. Samuel Johnson, *The Letters of Samuel Johnson, 1731–1784,* ed. Bruce Redford (Princeton, 1992–94), 1:50; *Johnson on Shakespeare,* Yale 7:111; *Letters,* 4:160; *Rambler* 78, Yale 4:49.

4. *Letters,* 2:301; Boswell, *Life,* p. 1358; *Adventurer* 111, Yale 2:455 (Tennyson echoes this belief in "Ulysses": "To strive, to seek, to find, and not to yield"); Boswell, *Life,* p. 268; Fanny Burney, *Early Journals and Letters, Vol. 3: The Streatham Years, Part 1, 1778–1779,* ed. Lars Troide and Stewart Cooke (Oxford, 1994), p. 148.

5. Thomas Carlyle, *"Sartor Resartus" and "On Heroes and Hero-Worship"* (1841; London, 1959), p. 411; John Ruskin, *Praeterita,* intro. by Kenneth Clark (1889; Oxford, 1978), p. 210.

6. *Dr. Campbell's Diary of a Visit to England in 1775,* ed. James Clifford, intro. S. C. Roberts (Cambridge, England, 1947), p. 68; Marshall Waingrow, "Introduction" to *The Correspondence and Other Papers of James Boswell Relating to the Making of the "Life of Johnson,"* 2nd ed. (New Haven, 2001), p. xxxvi.

7. Boswell, *Correspondence Relating to "Life of Johnson,"* p. 278; *James Boswell's "Life of Johnson": An Edition of the Original Manuscript, in Four Volumes,* ed. Marshall Waingrow et al. (New Haven, 1994–98), 1:146–147; James Boswell, *Life of Johnson,* ed. George Birkbeck Hill, 1934; revised and enlarged by L.F. Powell (Oxford, 1971), 1:539; Boswell, *Life,* p. 143.

8. Christopher Hibbert, *The Personal History of Samuel Johnson* (1971; London, 1998), p. 214; John Wain, *Samuel Johnson: A Biography* (New York, 1974), p. 289; W. Jackson Bate, *Samuel Johnson* (New York, 1977), p. 388; Bernard Meyer, "On the Application of Psychoanalysis in W. Jackson Bate's Life of Samuel Johnson," *Journal of the Philadelphia Association for Psychoanalysis,* 6 (1979), 159; Robert DeMaria, *The Life of Samuel Johnson: A Critical Biography* (Oxford, 1993), p. 261.

ONE: LICHFIELD LAD

1. Boswell, *Life,* pp. 708; 775; *Letters,* 3:370; Boswell, *Life,* p. 707; James Boswell, *Journal of a Tour to the Hebrides,* ed. Frederick Pottle and Charles Bennett (New York, 1936), p. 39.

2. John Brewer, *The Pleasures of the Imagination: English Culture in the Eighteenth Century* (Chicago, 1997), pp. 591–592; *Letters,* 2:48–49; A. L. Reade, *Johnsonian Gleanings* (London, 1909–1952), 10:32.

3. Reade, *Gleanings* 3:95; 5:69; 5:70.

4. Boswell, *Life,* p. 445; *Diaries,* Yale 1:7; Liza Picard, *Dr. Johnson's London* (New York, 2000), p. 208.

5. *Diaries,* Yale 1:3; 5; 6.

6. Peter Chase, "The Ailments and Physicians of Dr. Johnson," *Yale Journal of Biology and Medicine,* 23 (April 1951), 375; Meyer, "Application of Psychoanalysis," p. 156; Samuel Johnson, "Life of Dr. Herman

Boerhaave," in *The Works of Samuel Johnson* (Oxford Authors), ed. Donald Greene (New York, 1984), p. 55.

7. T. B. Macaulay, *History of England* (1849–55; Chicago, 1886), 3:429–430; Crawfurd, in David Green, *Queen Anne* (New York, 1970), p. 269n; William Shaw, *Memoirs of the Life and Writing of the Late Samuel Johnson,* and Hester Lynch Piozzi, *Anecdotes of the Late Samuel Johnson,* ed. Arthur Sherbo (Oxford, 1974), p. 63; Reade, *Gleanings,* 1:1.

8. *Diaries,* Yale 1:14; Sir John Hawkins, *The Life of Samuel Johnson,* ed. Bertram Davis (New York, 1961), p. 4; Stephen Greenblatt, *Will in the World: How Shakespeare Became Shakespeare* (New York, 2004), pp. 26, 178.

9. Boswell, *Life,* pp. 34; 459; 33.

10. George Bernard Shaw, "Preface" to *Misalliance* (1914; New York, 1963), p. 21; Campbell, *Diary,* p. 79; *Poems,* Yale 6:343.

11. Hester Lynch Piozzi, *Thraliana: The Diary of Mrs. Hester Lynch Thrale (later Mrs. Piozzi), 1776–1809,* ed. Katharine Balderston (Oxford, 1942; revised 2nd ed. 1951), 1:1; James Boswell, *Note Book, 1776–1777,* ed. R. W. Chapman (London, 1925), p. 3; *Thraliana,* 1:181.

12. James Boswell, *London Journal, 1762–1763,* ed. Frederick Pottle (New York, 1950), p. 284; Boswell, *Life,* p. 302; *Diaries,* Yale 1:10; Piozzi, *Anecdotes,* p. 68.

13. Shaw, *Memoirs,* p. 8; *Thraliana,* 1:202; Miguel de Cervantes, *Don Quixote,* trans. Charles Jarvis (New York, 1995), p. 200; Boswell, *Life,* p. 36.

14. Samuel Johnson, "Barretier," in *Works, with an Essay by Arthur Murphy* (London, 1850), 2:157; Piozzi, *Anecdotes,* p. 65; Samuel Johnson, *The Lives of the Most Eminent English Poets,* ed. Roger Lonsdale (Oxford, 2006), 3:91; Samuel Johnson, *The Complete English Poems,* ed. J. D. Fleeman (New York, 1971), pp. 45; 188.

15. *The Iliad of Homer,* trans. Alexander Pope, ed. and intro. Reuben Brower and W. H. Bond (New York, 1965), p. 174; Johnson, *Complete Poems,* p. 31; Pat Rogers, *The Samuel Johnson Encyclopedia* (Westport, Conn., 1996), p. 442; Boswell, *Tour,* p. 378.

16. *Lives of the Poets,* 2: 179; Boswell, *Life,* p. 76; Reade, *Gleanings,* 3:118.

TWO: VILE MELANCHOLY

1. See Lynda Mugglestone, "Samuel Johnson at Pembroke College," p. 2, unpublished lecture, courtesy of Dr. Mugglestone, Pembroke College; *Lives of the Poets,* 4:126; Boswell, *Life,* p. 44.

2. G. M. Trevelyan, *History of England. Vol. 3: From Utrecht to Modern Times* (1926; Garden City, N.Y., 1954), p. 33; A. S. Turberville, *Johnson's England: An Account of the Life and Manners of His Age* (1933; Oxford, 1952), 2:236; 238; Mugglestone, "Johnson at Pembroke," p. 3.

3. *Idler* 33, Yale 2:105; Samuel Johnson, "Burman," in *Works,* 2:160; *Complete Poems,* p. 86; Charles Mallet, *A History of the University of Oxford* (Oxford, 1927), 3:74.

4. Alexander Pope, *Poems,* ed. John Butt (New Haven, 1963), p. 194; Hawkins, *Life of Johnson,* p. 9; Boswell, *Correspondence Relating to "Life of Johnson,"* p. 83.

5. Boswell, *Life,* p. 632; G. M. Trevelyan, "Dr. Johnson's England," *English Social History: A Survey of Six Centuries, Chaucer to Queen Victoria* (1942; London, 1967), p. 381; Edward Gibbon, *Autobiography,* ed. Dero Saunders (New York, 1961), pp. 73, 75, 79, 77.

6. *Rambler* 180, Yale 5:182; "Burman," *Works,* 2:161.

7. *Poems,* Yale 6:394; Piozzi, *Anecdotes,* p. 70; Boswell, *Life,* pp. 45; 46; Boswell, *Correspondence Relating to "Life of Johnson,"* p. 281.

8. Hawkins, *Life of Johnson,* p. 8. When Ezra Pound sent James Joyce a new pair of shoes in 1920, the impoverished Irishman was also offended and furious.

9. *Diaries,* Yale 1:26; Boswell, *Life,* p. 53.

10. Reade, *Gleanings,* 10.83; Douglas Macleane, "Johnson," *A History of Pembroke College, Oxford* (Oxford, 1897), p. 340; Mugglestone, "Johnson at Pembroke," p. 4.

11. Conor Cruise O'Brien, *Edmund Burke,* abridged edition (London, 2002), p. 15; Boswell, *Life,* p. 961.

12. Boswell, *Life,* pp. 1231; 50–51; 440; Gibbon, *Autobiography,* p. 45.

13. *Thraliana,* 1:421; Bate, *Samuel Johnson,* p. 103; Chester Chapin, *The Religious Thought of Samuel Johnson* (Ann Arbor, 1968), p. 39.

14. Boswell, *Tour,* p. 174; Frances Reynolds, in *Johnsonian Miscellanies,* ed. George Birkbeck Hill (Oxford, 1897), 2:257 and n1.

15. Boswell, *Life,* p. 47; *Rasselas,* Yale 16:149; *Lives of the Poets,* 1:408; 4:122.

16. "Review of Soame Jenyns' *A Free Enquiry into the Nature and Origins of Evil,*" in *Works,* ed. Greene, p. 528; *Thraliana,* 1:199; Piozzi, *Anecdotes,* p. 67.

17. Hawkins, *Life of Johnson,* p. 122; Boswell, *Life,* ed. Hill, 1:63n1; Boswell, *Correspondence Relating to "Life of Johnson,"* p. 71; *Letters,* 1:143.

18. Pope, in Reade, *Gleanings,* 6:98; Boswell, *Life,* pp. 68; 1398; Geoffrey Williamson, *The Ingenious Mr. Gainsborough* (London, 1972), p. 72; Boswell, *Life,* p. 107.

19. Campbell, *Diary,* p. 53; Burney, *Early Journals,* 3:73; Frances Burney, *Memoirs of Dr. Burney* (London, 1832), 2:91; Donald Greene, "The Making of Boswell's *Life of Johnson,*" *Studies in Burke and His Time,* 12 (1971), 1819–20.

THREE: PREPOSTEROUS UNION

1. Reade, *Gleanings,* 10.92; Boswell, *Life,* p. 61; *Rambler* 142, Yale 4:393.

2. *Letters,* 1:4; Boswell, *Life,* ed. Hill, 1:531; Reade, *Gleanings,* 6:46–48.

3. Boswell, *Life,* p. 62; "Preface" to *Voyage to Abyssinia,* Yale 15:3; 4–5.

4. *Boswell in Extremes, 1776–1778,* ed. Charles Weis and Frederick Pottle (New York, 1970), p. 180; Boswell, *Life,* p. 986; *Boswell in Search of a Wife, 1766–1769,* ed. Frank Brady and Frederick Pottle (New York, 1957), p. 167.

5. Boswell, *Life,* p. 1035; *Rasselas,* Yale 16:99; 98; 161.

6. *Sermons,* Yale 14:6; *Irene,* in *Poems,* Yale 6:152; *Thraliana,* 1:386.

7. Piozzi, *Anecdotes,* p. 145; Boswell, *Life,* p. 68; Boswell, *Life,* ed. Hill, 1:244n2; 4:57n3.

8. *Thraliana*, 1:224; Boswell, *Life*, p. 69; Shaw, *Memoirs of Johnson*, pp. 33–34.

9. Boswell, *Correspondence Relating to "Life of Johnson,"* p. 66; Garrick, in Boswell, *Life*, p. 71; Williams, in Cornelia Knight, *The Autobiography of Miss Cornelia Knight* (London, 1861), 1:314; *Thraliana*, 1:177.

10. Boswell, *Life*, p. 407; Boswell, *Correspondence Relating to "Life of Johnson,"* p. 66; Anna Seward, *The Swan of Litchfield; Being a Selection from the Correspondence of Anna Seward*, ed. Hesketh Pearson (London, 1936), pp. 87–88.

11. John Wilson Croker, in Reade, *Gleanings*, 6:23; Boswell, *Life*, p. 69; *Thraliana*, 1:177. Ernest Hemingway's third wife, Martha Gellhorn, also had a mania for cleanliness. Hemingway liked to have dinner while wearing his bloodstained fishing clothes. Martha, who called him none-too-affectionately "the Pig," wanted him to bathe more often, be well groomed and wear smart clothes. As with Johnson, this was a hopeless cause.

12. *Thraliana*, 1:178; *Boswell: Laird of Auchinleck, 1778–1782*, ed. Joseph Reed and Frederick Pottle (New York, 1977), pp. 142–143.

13. Donald Greene, *The Politics of Samuel Johnson*, 2nd edition (1960; Athens, Ga., 1990), p. 61; Ian McIntyre, *Garrick* (London, 1999), p. 25.

14. "Preface" to *Preceptor*, in *Works* (1850), 2:372; *Sermons*, Yale 14:92; *Lives of the Poets*, 1:248.

15. Turberville, *Johnson's England*, 2:213; "Preface" to *Preceptor*, in *Works* (1850), 2:377; Piozzi, *Anecdotes*, p. 133.

16. Boswell, *Tour*, p. 71; "Anecdote of Dr. Johnson," manuscript, April 11, 1803, Container List, p. 7b, Houghton Library, Harvard University; Boswell, *Life*, pp. 487–488.

17. Gibbon, *Autobiography*, pp. 58; 69; Boswell, *Life*, p. 71; James Clifford, *Young Sam Johnson* (New York, 1955), pp. 162–163.

18. *Lives of the Poets*, 3:75; Alexander Boswell, in Reade, *Gleanings*, 6:52; [John Jackson], *History of the City and County of Lichfield*, 2nd ed. (Lichfield, 1796), p. 85, Houghton Library; Thomas Kaminski, *The Early Career of Samuel Johnson* (New York, 1987), p. 207n5.

19. *Lives of the Poets*, 1:251; *Letters*, 2:199; Boswell, *Life*, ed. Hill, 1:532; George Stone and George Kahrl, *David Garrick: A Critical Biography* (Carbondale, Ill., 1979), p. 13.

FOUR: BENEVOLENT GIANT

1. Boswell, *Life*, pp. 280–281; Humphry, in *Johnson Miscellanies*, 2:401; James Northcote, *Memoirs of Sir Joshua Reynolds* (London, 1813), p. 41.

2. B. N. Turner, in Norman Page, ed., *Samuel Johnson: Interviews and Recollections* (Totowa, N.J., 1987), p. 119; Sir Walter Scott, *Lives of the Novelists* (London, 1887), p. 503; Walter Stanhope, in Thomas Curley, *Sir Robert Chambers: Law, Literature and Empire in the Age of Johnson* (Madison, 1998), p. 21.

3. *Boswell for the Defence, 1769–1774*, ed. W. K. Wimsatt and Frederick Pottle (New York, 1960), pp. 165–166; Boswell, *Life*, p. 331; Mrs. Harris, in A. Lytton Sells, *Oliver Goldsmith: His Life and Works* (London, 1974), p. 96.

4. Ian McIntyre, *Joshua Reynolds: The Life and Times of the First President of the Royal Academy* (London, 2003), p. 145; Boswell, *Life*, p. 1285; *Lives of the Poets*, 4:55; Boswell, *Life*, ed. Hill, 2:436n7; Boswell, *Life*, p. 1016.

5. Boswell, *Correspondence Relating to "Life of Johnson,"* p. 71; *Diaries*, Yale 1:77; More, in *Johnson Miscellanies*, 2:197; *Adventurer* 102, Yale 2:440; Boswell, *Life*, p. 746.

6. Johnson, in Northcote, *Memoirs of Reynolds*, p. 46; "Review of Hanway's *Journal*," in *Works*, ed. Greene, pp. 516; 509; Boswell, *Life*, p. 342; *Rambler* 60, Yale 3:321; Boswell, *Life*, p. 343.

7. Boswell, *Life*, ed. Hill, 5:511; H. D. Best, in *Johnson Miscellanies*, 2:391; 2:396.

8. Piozzi, *Anecdotes*, p. 98; Hawkins, *Life of Johnson*, p. 204; Piozzi, *Anecdotes*, p. 129.

9. *Adventurer* 74, Yale 2:398; Arthur Murphy, in *Johnson Miscellanies*, 2:424; Boswell, *Life*, p. 112; Piozzi, *Anecdotes*, p. 137.

10. *Adventurer* 131, Yale 2:485–486; James Northcote, *The Life of Sir Joshua Reynolds,* 2nd ed., revised and augmented (London, 1819), 1:75 (Northcote changed the title from *Memoirs* to *Life* in the later edition); Boswell, *Life,* p. 580.

11. *Thraliana,* 1:189; Boswell, *Life,* p. 580; *Rambler* 32, Yale 3:175.

12. *Sermons,* Yale 14:3; Boswell, *Life,* ed. Hill, 3:1n2.

13. *Lives of the Poets,* 3:91; Boswell, *Correspondence Relating to "Life of Johnson,"* p. 194. Aldous Huxley recalled that D. H. Lawrence was similarly self-sufficient: "He regarded no task as too humble for him to undertake, nor so trivial that it was not worth his while to do it well. He could cook, he could sew, he could darn a stocking." Aldous Huxley, "Introduction" to *The Letters of D. H. Lawrence* (New York, 1932), p. xxxi.

14. Piozzi, *Anecdotes,* pp. 138; 139; *Idler* 31, Yale 2:98; *Rambler* 199, Yale 5:272.

15. *Letters,* 3:284; Boswell, *Life,* p. 549.

16. Boswell, *Life,* p. 52; *Rambler* 122, Yale 4:289–290; *Rambler* 77, Yale 4:44.

17. *Adventurer* 120, Yale 2:469; Murphy, in *Johnsonian Miscellanies,* 1:412; Boswell, *Tour,* p. 7.

18. Boswell, *Life,* p. 1075; Gretchen Rubin, *Forty Ways to Look at Winston Churchill* (New York, 2003), p. 188.

FIVE: GRUB STREET

1. F. P. Lock, *Edmund Burke. Vol. I, 1730–1784* (Oxford, 1998), p. 65; Boswell, *Life,* p. 608. By 1922, as T. S. Eliot wrote in *The Waste Land* (I. 62–66), this lively crowd had been transformed, under the pressures of modern life, into a mass of mechanical robots:

A crowd flowed over London Bridge, so many,
I had not thought death had undone so many.
Sighs, short and infrequent, were exhaled,
And each man fixed his eyes before his feet.
Flowed up the hill and down King William Street.

2. Picard, *Johnson's London*, p. 129; A. R. Humphreys, *The Augustan World: Life and Letters in Eighteenth-Century England* (London, 1954), p. 8; *Idler* 28, Yale 2:89.

3. Casanova, in Picard, *Johnson's London*, pp. 26; 266; Johnson, in Joseph Wood Krutch, *Samuel Johnson* (New York, 1944), p. 37.

4. Jennifer Uglow, *Hogarth: A Life and a World* (New York, 1997), p. 7; *Johnsonian Miscellanies*, 2:11; Picard, *Johnson's London*, p. 226.

5. Roy Porter, *English Society in the Eighteenth Century* (New York, 1990), p. 2; Boswell, *Life*, p. 514; *Rambler* 53, Yale 3:284; "Considerations on Corn," in *Political Writings*, Yale 10.305; Boswell, *Life*, p, 446.

6. "On a Letter from a French Refugee," in *Political Writings*, Yale 10.175; "On the Fireworks," in *Political Writings*, Yale 10.115; Piozzi, *Anecdotes*, p. 89.

7. Sir John Fielding, in Dorothy Marshall, *Dr. Johnson's London* (New York, 1968), p. 221; Porter, *English Society*, p. 18; Henry Fielding, in Marshall, *Johnson's London*, p. 241; Basil Williams, *The Whig Supremacy, 1714–1760*, 2nd ed. (Oxford, 1962), p. 60.

8. Williams, *Whig Supremacy*, p. 135; *Idler* 38, Yale 2:118–121; Porter, *English Society*, p. 135; Ian Gilmour, *Riot, Risings and Revolution: Governance and Violence in Eighteenth-Century England* (London, 1992), p. 148.

9. Leon Radzinowicz, *A History of English Criminal Law and Its Administration from 1750* (London, 1948), p. 426; Blake Ehrlich, *London on the Thames* (London, 1966), p. 143; Roy Porter, *London: A Social History* (Cambridge, Mass., 1994), pp. 153–154; Gilmour, *Riot*, p. 169; Marshall, *Johnson's London*, p. 252; Porter, *London*, p. 152.

10. Boswell, *Life*, p. 1160; *Rambler* 114, Yale 4:242–244, 246; "Thoughts on Falkland's Islands," in *Political Writings*, Yale 10.370.

11. Hibbert, *Personal History of Johnson*, p. 52; Piozzi, *Anecdotes*, p. 100; Murphy, in *Johnsonian Miscellanies*, 1:380; Boswell, *Life*, p. 75 (two quotes); *Letters*, 1:6.

12. *Poems*, Yale 6:41; "Cave," in *Works* (1850), 2:174; John Nichols, *Literary Anecdotes of the Eighteenth Century* (London, 1812), 5:50, 55.

13. "Preface to *The Gentleman's Magazine*," in *Works* (1850), 2:415; Boswell, *Life*, ed. Hill, 1:163n1; *Letters*, 1:126.

14. *Johnsonian Miscellanies,* 2:11; *Letters,* 1:17; Burney, in Marshall, *Johnson's London,* p. 200. In *A Room of One's Own* (1929; London, 1945), p. 55, Virginia Woolf muddled the facts when she wrote: "Eliza Carter— the valiant old woman who tied a bell to her bedstead in order that she might wake early and learn Greek." According to Boswell's *Life,* p. 850, Carter learned Greek when she was young, not old, and was not wakened by a bell. She used a candle to burn a string, which released a weight that crashed to the floor and woke her up.

15. Boswell, Percy, Dyer and Reynolds in Boswell, *Life,* ed. Hill, 1:28n1; Burney, *Early Journals,* 3:76.

16. Jonathan Swift, "A Modest Proposal," in *"Gulliver's Travels" and Other Writings,* ed. Ricardo Quintana (New York, 1958), p. 492; Tobias Smollett, *The Expedition of Humphry Clinker,* ed. Robert Gorham Davis (New York, 1950), pp. 152–153; Boswell, *Life,* ed. Hill, 3:443; Piozzi, *Anecdotes,* p. 119.

SIX: LONDON OBSERVED

1. *Adventurer* 115, Yale 2:458; *Rambler* 71, Yale 4:11.

2. *Thraliana,* 1:173; *Lives of the Poets,* 4:16. A century and a half later Ernest Hemingway, when asked what things harm a writer's work, mentioned: "Politics, women, drink, money, ambition. And the lack of politics, women, drink, money and ambition" (*Green Hills of Africa,* New York, 1935, p. 28).

3. *Idler* 102, Yale 2:312; *Idler* 59, Yale 2:182–183; *Rambler* 155, Yale 5:63.

4. Boswell, *Life,* pp. 731; 144; *Lives of the Poets,* 4:180; 2:126, 1:239, 4:90.

5. Boswell, *Life,* pp. 52; 612–613; *Rambler* 184, Yale 5:201.

6. Johnson, *Letters,* 3:311; Boswell, *Tour,* p. 45; Boswell, *Life,* p. 528.

7. *Lives of the Poets,* 2:13; 1:266; John Paul Russo, *Alexander Pope: Tradition and Identity* (Cambridge, Mass., 1972), p. 90; *Johnsonian Miscellanies,* 2:215–216.

8. Nichols, *Literary Anecdotes,* 5:515; *Rambler* 208, Yale 5:318; Boswell, *Life,* pp. 145; 234.

9. Boswell, *Life*, p. 381; *Diaries*, Yale 1:225. In a strikingly similar way, the work-obsessed George Orwell, dying of tuberculosis, wrote in his diary in early 1949: "There has literally been not one day in which I did not feel that I was idling, that I was behind with the current job, & that my total output was miserably small. Even at the periods when I was working 10 hours a day on a book, or turning out 4 or 5 articles a week, I have never been able to get away from this neurotic feeling" (*Collected Essays, Journalism and Letters*, ed. Sonia Orwell and Ian Angus, New York, 1968, 4:510–511.)

10. *Rambler* 21, Yale 3:120.

11. *Rambler* 137, Yale 4:362; *Rambler* 154, Yale 5:58; "Review of *The General History of Polybius*," in *Works* (1850), 2:497; *Rasselas*, Yale 16:41.

12. Boswell, *Life*, p. 742; Peter and Julia Bondanella, eds., *Dictionary of Italian Literature* (Westport, Conn., 1979), p. 465; *Letters*, 1:13; 19; "Father Paul Sarpi," in *Works* (1850), 2:109–111.

13. *Lives of the Poets*, 4:40; Maynard Mack, *Alexander Pope: A Life* (New York, 1985), p. 737; Pope, *Poems*, p. 147; *Commentary*, Yale 17:74–75; Nichols, *Literary Anecdotes*, 2:552.

14. E. L. McAdam Jr., "Johnson's Lives of Sarpi, Blake and Drake," *PMLA*, 58 (June 1943), 470–471; "Blake," in *Works* (1850), 2:120; *Rambler* 114, Yale 4:242.

15. "Life of Boerhaave," in *Works*, ed. Greene, p. 67; Keith Crook, "The Development of Samuel Johnson's Idea of Imagination," Ph.D. dissertation, London University, 1975, p. 40, quoting *Works*, ed. Greene, p. 58; "Life of Boerhaave," in *Works*, ed. Greene, pp. 57; 69.

16. Gilbert Highet, *Juvenal the Satirist* (1954; New York, 1961), pp. x–xi; Moses Hadas, *A History of Latin Literature* (New York, 1952), p. 284; *Lives of the Poets*, 2:143; Niall Rudd, ed., *Johnson's Juvenal: "London" and "The Vanity of Human Wishes"* (Bristol, 1981), p. x.

17. Juvenalis, *Satirae*, ed. Arthur Maclean, 2nd. ed. (London, 1867), p. 68; John Dryden, *Poetical Works*, ed. George Noyes (Boston, 1950), p. 331; *Complete Poems*, p. 67; Dryden, *Poetical Works*, p. 327; *Complete Poems*, p. 61.

18. *Lives of the Poets*, 4:45; *Letters*, 1:16; John Cannon, *Samuel Johnson and the Politics of Hanoverian England* (Oxford, 1994), p. 47.

19. *Complete Poems,* p. 61; "Some Thoughts on Agriculture," in *Works* (1850), 2:403; *Rambler* 166, Yale 5:116; *Complete Poems,* p. 66.

20. Dorothy George, *London Life in the Eighteenth Century* (1925; New York, 1964), p. 269; Gilmour, *Riot,* p. 165; *Sermons,* Yale 14:237.

21. *Rambler* 40, Yale 3:216; *Rambler* 144, Yale 5:3–7.

22. Thomas Gray, *Correspondence,* ed. Paget Toynbee and Leonard Whibley (Oxford, 1935), 1:295; Tennyson, in J. P. Hardy, *Samuel Johnson: A Critical Study* (London, 1979), p. 51; Pope, in *Johnsonian Miscellanies,* 1:373.

23. Boswell, *Life,* pp. 94–95; 96.

24. *Lives of the Poets,* 3:189, 191; Jonathan Swift, *Correspondence,* ed. Francis Elrington Ball (London, 1910–14), 1:xxxvi–xxxvii; 4:151; 6:209.

25. Reade, *Gleanings,* 6:113; Boswell, *Tour,* p. 26; Boswell, *Life,* p. 212.

SEVEN: POLITICS AND PASSION

1. Boswell's *"Life of Johnson": Edition of the Original Manuscript,* 2:41; *The Letters and Prose Writings of William Cowper,* ed. James King and Charles Ryskamp (Oxford, 1979), 2:5; Piozzi, *Anecdotes,* pp. 113–114.

2. Clifford, *Young Sam Johnson,* p. 227; Piozzi, *Anecdotes,* p. 114; Seward. *Correspondence,* p. 128.

3. *Thraliana,* 1:538, and Piozzi, *Anecdotes,* p. 113; *Lives of the Poets,* 4:87; Piozzi, *Anecdotes,* p. 113: *Letters,* 1:22.

4. *Letters,* 1:24 (Tetty); 1:177 (Sarah); Piozzi, *Anecdotes,* p. 119 (Psalmanazar); Clifford, *Young Sam Johnson,* p. 186 (Birch); Boswell, *Life,* p. 732 (Ellis); p. 59 (Meynell); Piozzi, *Anecdotes,* p. 113 (Aston); Boswell, *Life,* p. 1278 (Lennox); Piozzi, *Anecdotes,* p. 66 (Bathurst); Boswell, *Life,* p. 1021 (Garrick); p. 845 (Langton); *Letters,* 3:231 (Beauclerk); Campbell, *Diary,* p. 77 (Goldsmith); Boswell, *Life,* p. 1069 (Reynolds); Piozzi, *Anecdotes,* p. 130 (Burke); Boswell, *Life,* p. 410 (Paoli); p. 384 (George III); Burney, *Early Journals,* 3:100 (Hester); *Thraliana,* 1:601 (Hester).

5. Williams, *Whig Supremacy,* pp. 26–27; Greene, "Introduction" to *Political Writings,* Yale 10.177; "Considerations on Corn," in *Political*

Writings, 10.311; *Adventurer,* 45, Yale 2:359; *Johnsonian Miscellanies,* 2:466.

6. *Complete Poems,* pp. 53; 67–68; Jeremy Lewis, *Tobias Smollett* (London, 2003), p. 69, and Gilmour, *Riot,* p. 126.

7. Boswell, *Life,* p. 304; Donald Greene, "The Double Tradition of Johnson's Politics," *Huntington Library Quarterly,* 59 (1996), 119, and Greene, *Politics of Johnson,* p. 240.

8. Cannon, *Johnson and the Politics of Hanoverian England,* pp. 6 and 113; Boswell, *Life,* pp. 1154–55 and 477; *Complete Poems,* p. 160; *Idler* 10, Yale 2:33.

9. Philip Magnus, *Edmund Burke: A Life* (London, 1931), p. 24; "Browne," in *Works* (1850), 2:193; *Political Writings,* Yale 10.51; 25.

10. *Complete Poems,* p. 62; *Political Writings,* Yale 10.52; 65; 73.

11. Williams, *Whig Supremacy,* p. 31; Lock, *Edmund Burke,* pp. 218–219; Boswell, *Life,* p. 1386; Murphy, in *Johnsonian Miscellanies,* 1:379.

12. Johnson in Hardy, *Samuel Johnson,* p. 42; *Works* (1787), 13:391; Johnson in Greene, *Politics of Johnson,* p. 120.

13. Murphy, in *Johnsonian Miscellanies,* 1:379; 378; *Works* (1850), 2:425; *Works,* ed. Greene, pp. 117; 123–124. Two hundred years later, George Orwell made exactly the same point: "Unlike a novel or a book of verse, a pamphlet has no assured channel by which it can reach the readers most likely to appreciate it. The pamphlets of Milton, Swift, Defoe, Junius and others were literary events, and they were also a recognised part of the political life of the period" ("Introduction" to *British Pamphleteers* [1948], in *The Complete Works of George Orwell,* ed. Peter Davison, London, 1998, 19:112).

14. Piozzi, *Anecdotes,* p. 137; Thomas Tyers, in *Johnsonian Miscellanies,* 2:347; *Lives of the Poets,* 4:50.

15. Clarence Tracy, *The Artificial Bastard: A Biography of Richard Savage* (Cambridge, Mass., 1953), p. 57; Pope, *Poems,* p. 751; Boswell, *Life,* p. 119.

16. *Rambler* 70, Yale 4:6; Tracy, *Artificial Bastard,* p. 147; Richard Holmes, "Biography: Inventing the Truth," in *The Art of Literary Biography,* ed. John Batchelor (Oxford, 1995), p. 21.

17. W. K. Wimsatt Jr., "Johnson's *Dictionary*," in *New Light on Dr. Johnson*, ed. Frederick Hilles (New Haven, 1959), p. 77; *Sermons*, Yale 14:207; Boswell, *Life*, pp. 1376, 1375.

18. Giacomo Casanova, *History of My Life*, trans. Willard Trask (1970; Baltimore, 1997), 9:173; Hawkins, *Life of Johnson*, p. 134; *Rambler* 107, Yale 4:209; *Rambler* 170, 5:139; *Rambler* 171, 5:144–145.

19. *Johnsonian Miscellanies*, 2:326 (two quotes). William Gladstone, when prime minister, also had a powerful urge to interview and redeem prostitutes. He would roam the streets, "often accost women himself, and suggest that they should accompany him home, where he told them that they would be treated with respect by his wife and by himself, and that they would be given food and shelter. . . . His object was to enable the women to escape from their profession" (Philip Magnus, *Gladstone: A Biography*, 1954; New York, 1964, p. 106). Gladstone's compulsion, like Johnson's, surprised and alarmed his friends.

20. James Boswell, *Life of Samuel Johnson*, ed. John Wilson Croker (London, 1890), pp. 835–836; Boswell, *Tour*, pp. 176–177; Boswell, *Life*, p. 845; Trevelyan, *English Social History*, p. 398; Edmund Burke, *A Philosophical Enquiry into our Ideas of the Sublime and Beautiful*, ed. James Boulton (1757; London, 1958), p. 155.

21. Boswell, *Tour*, p. 226; Reverend Baptist Turner, unpublished anecdote, in Peter Murray Hills, bookseller's catalogue 92 (June 1965), pp. 31–32, Donald Greene Archive.

22. Bernard Meyer, "Some Observations on the Rescue of Fallen Women," *Psychoanalytic Quarterly*, 53 (1984), 212; Porter, *English Society in the Eighteenth Century*, p. 286; James Boswell, *Boswell: The Applause of the Jury, 1782–1785*, ed. Irma Lustig and Frederick Pottle (New York, 1981), p. 291.

EIGHT: DOOM OF MAN

1. *Johnson on the English Language*, Yale 18:58; Boswell, *Life*, p. 135; *Johnson on Language*, 18:26; 57.

2. Baretti, in Allen Reddick, *The Making of Johnson's Dictionary, 1746–1773*, revised ed. (Cambridge, England, 1996), p. 62; *Letters*, 1:50.

3. Boswell, *Life*, p. 211; Albert Baugh, *History of the English Language* (New York, 1935), p. 385.

4. *Johnson on Language*, 18:107; *Johnson Miscellanies*, 2:390; Matthew Arnold, *Poetry and Criticism*, ed. Dwight Culler (Boston, 1961), p. 257.

5. Dryden, *Poetical Works*, p. 347; *Complete Poems*, p. 83–92; Lord Byron, *Letters and Journals, 1810–1812*, Vol. 2, ed. Leslie Marchand (Cambridge, Mass., 1973), p. 95; George Herbert, "The Church Porch," in *Poems*, ed. Arthur Waugh (London, 1907), p. 7.

6. *Rasselas*, Yale 16:43–44; Rudd, *Johnson's Juvenal*, pp. 56–57; "Essay on Epitaphs," in *Works*, ed. Greene, p. 97; Dryden, *Poetical Works*, p. 347.

7. Samuel Taylor Coleridge, *Essays and Lectures on Shakespeare* (London, 1907), p. 413; "Review of Du Halde's *History of China*," in *Works* (1850), 2:469.

8. John Milton, "Lycidas," in *Paradise Regained: The Minor Poems and Samson Agonistes*, ed. Merritt Hughes (New York, 1937), p. 295, and *Complete Poems*, p. 86; Pope, "Second Epistle of the Second Book of Horace Imitated," in *Poems*, p. 652, and *Complete Poems*, p. 90.

9. Dryden, *Poetical Works*, p. 352; Rudd, *Johnson's Juvenal*, p. 66; *Lives of the Poets*, 2:143. Johnson's emotive and menacing "darkling" resonated through the nineteenth century. It was adopted by John Keats in "Ode to a Nightingale" (1819): "Darkling I listen; and, for many a time / I have been half in love with easeful Death"; by Matthew Arnold in "Dover Beach" (1867): "And we are here as on a darkling plain / Swept with confused alarms of struggle and flight, / Where ignorant armies clash by night"; and by Thomas Hardy in the title of "The Darkling Thrush" (1900).

10. Jonathan Swift, *Collected Poems*, ed. Joseph Horrell (Cambridge, Mass., 1958), 2:502; W. B. Yeats, *Collected Poems* (New York, 1959), p. 233.

11. J. G. Lockhart, *Life of Sir Walter Scott* (1848; London, 1906), p. 213; Ezra Pound, *Guide to Kulchur* (New York, 1970), p. 179; *Lives of the Poets*, 4:80, and T. S. Eliot, "Poetry in the Eighteenth Century," in *The Pelican Guide to English Literature. Vol. 4: From Dryden to Johnson*, ed. Boris Ford (1930; London, 1957), pp. 276; 275.

12. George Kahrl, "Introduction" to *The Correspondence of James Boswell with David Garrick, Edmund Burke and Edmond Malone* (London, 1986), pp. 8–9; *Letters of Hannah More,* ed. R. Brimley Johnson (London, 1925), p. 110; Boswell, *Life,* p. 962.

13. Burney, *Early Journals,* 3:75; Gainsborough, in McIntyre, *Reynolds,* p. 170; *Thraliana,* 1:177; Boswell, *Life,* p. 863; *Thraliana,* 1:177.

14. Reverend Baptist Turner, in Hill Catalogue, p. 31, Greene Archive; *Rambler* 200, Yale 5:277–280; Sir Joshua Reynolds, *Portraits,* ed. Frederick Hilles (New York, 1952), pp. 97–98.

15. Hawkins, *Life of Johnson,* p. 185; Boswell, *Life,* p. 599; Stone and Kahrl, *David Garrick,* p. 636.

16. David Garrick, *Letters,* ed. David Little and George Kahrl (Cambridge, Mass., 1963), p. 778; Boswell, *Tour,* p. 93; *Lives of the Poets,* 2:179.

17. *Lives of the Poets,* 2:387; *Complete Poems,* p. 82; *Rambler* 122, Yale 4:290; Reade, *Johnsonian Gleanings,* 10.120; Leslie Marchand, *Byron: A Biography* (New York, 1957), 1:38.

18. Edward Gibbon, *The Decline and Fall of the Roman Empire* (1776–88; New York: Modern Library, n.d.), 2:1327; 1335 and note, quoting *Poems,* Yale 6:113; Steven Runciman, *The Fall of Constantinople* (Cambridge, England, 1965), pp. 58–59, 151–152; *Johnson on Shakespeare,* Yale 8:1047.

19. *Lives of the Poets,* 3:26, and *Johnson on Shakespeare,* Yale 7:84; Garrick, in Murphy, *Johnsonian Miscellanies,* 1:387; Boswell, *Life,* p. 140; *Johnson on Shakespeare,* Yale 7:140.

20. *Poems,* Yale 6:162, 169; 123; 152; 192; 179; Martin Booth, "Introduction" to *Eighteenth-Century Tragedy* (Oxford, 1965), p. xi.

21. Boswell, *Life,* pp. 1070; 1068; Boswell, *Life,* ed. Hill, 4:5n1; Boswell, *Life,* p. 142, and William Shakespeare, *Twelfth Night* (2.4.113–114).

22. Johnson's writings and sayings, even when falsely attributed to other people, have achieved a proverbial status. In *Irene* (6.211) Mahomet declares: "I came to heighten tortures by reproach, / And add new terrors to the face of death." The *Oxford Dictionary of Quotations*

(Oxford, 1979), pp. 321 and 569, mistakenly claims that two eminent lawyers, Baron Lyndhurst and Sir Charles Wetherell, speaking of Lord Campbell's *Lives of the Lord Chancellors* (1845–47), were the first to say that the biographer "has added new terror to death."

NINE: GREATEST GENIUS

1. Boswell, *Life,* pp. 143–144; Bate, "Introduction" to *Rambler,* Yale 3:xxv; Edward Bloom, *Samuel Johnson in Grub Street* (Providence, R.I., 1957), pp. 151–152; *Rambler* 192, Yale 5:239.

2. *Rambler* 20, Yale 3:115; *Idler* 70, Yale 2:217; *Rambler* 175, Yale 5:160; *Rambler* 4, Yale 3:25.

3. *Complete Poems,* p. 47; "Essay on Epitaphs," in *Works,* ed. Greene, p. 101; Edmund Wilson, "Reexamining Dr. Johnson," in *Classics and Commercials: A Literary Chronicle of the Forties* (New York, 1950), p. 249.

4. *Rambler* 165, Yale 5:112, 110; *Rambler* 143, Yale 4:395; François La Rochefoucauld, *Maxims,* trans. L. W. Tancock (London, 1959), p. 112; *Rambler* 52, Yale 3:283, 281. In a modern variant of this aperçu, Gore Vidal remarked, "It is not enough to succeed. Others must fail."

5. *Rambler* 56, Yale 3:303. When George Orwell took over as literary editor of the *Tribune,* he also mentioned finding his desk drawers "stuffed with letters and manuscripts which ought to have been dealt with weeks earlier, and hurriedly shutting it up again" (Orwell, "As I Pleased," January 31, 1947, in *Works,* 19:37).

6. *Rambler* 42, Yale 3:227; *Rambler* 23, Yale 3:129; *Rambler* 109, Yale 4:215–216.

7. *Rambler* 2, Yale 3:14, 13; *Rambler* 208, Yale 5:315; 316; 318; 319; Boswell, *Life,* ed. Hill, 1:210n1.

8. *Adventurer,* 74, Yale 2:396; *Adventurer,* 62, Yale 2:378; *Adventurer,* 120, Yale 2:466 (two quotes).

9. Charlotte Lennox, *The Female Quixote* (London, 1752), pp. 300, 302; Hawkins, *Life of Johnson,* p. 121.

10. Boswell, *Life,* p. 333; Crook, *Johnson's Idea of Imagination,* p. 178, quoting John Locke, *An Essay Concerning Human Understanding,* 2

vols., ed. A. C. Fraser (1690; Oxford, 1894), II.iv.6; George Steevens, in *Johnsonian Miscellanies*, 2:320.

11. *Rambler* 175, Yale 5:160; Trevelyan, *History of England*, p. 27; J. H. Plumb, *England in the Eighteenth Century* (1950; London, 1972), p. 44.

12. *Political Writings*, Yale 10.158; Reverend Baptist Turner, in Hill Catalogue, p. 31, Greene Archive; Boswell, *Life*, ed. Hill, 3:298n1; Boswell, *Life*, p. 724.

13. Owen Chadwick, "The Religion of Samuel Johnson," *Yale University Library Gazette*, 60 (1986), 130; Boswell, *Life*, pp. 314–315. Evelyn Waugh also used faith to control his evil urges. As he told his biographer, "You have no idea how much nastier I would be if I was not a Catholic. Without supernatural aid I would hardly be a human being" (Christopher Sykes, *Evelyn Waugh: A Biography*, Boston, 1975, p. 334).

14. Gray, "Introduction" to *Sermons*, 14:xliv, xlvii; James Gray, *Johnson's Sermons: A Study* (Oxford, 1972), p. 230.

15. *Sermons*, Yale 14:53; 112–113; 19; *Diaries*, Yale 1:64; 71; 133.

16. *The Book of Common Prayer* (New York, 1945), p. 604; Piozzi, *Anecdotes*, p. 127; *Diaries*, Yale 1:70; 76; 123.

17. Boswell, *Life*, p. 1296; Adam Smith, in *Johnsonian Miscellanies*, 2:423–424; Boswell, *Life*, p. 281.

18. William Cowper, "The Castaway," in *The Oxford Book of Eighteenth-Century Verse*, ed. David Nichol Smith (Oxford, 1926), pp. 592, 594; W. H. Auden, "The Protestant Mystics," in *Forewords and Afterwords* (New York, 1974), p. 75.

19. Boswell, *Life*, p. 169; from Anna Williams, in *Johnsonian Miscellanies*, 2:173–174; *Thraliana*, 1:178.

20. John Taylor, in Donald and Mary Hyde, *Dr. Johnson's Second Wife* (Princeton, 1953), n.p; Shaw, in *Memoirs of Johnson*, p. 33; Hydes, *Johnson's Second Wife*, n.p.

21. Boswell, *Applause of the Jury*, pp. 110–112. James Joyce, who used the *Life of Johnson* to teach English at the Berlitz School in Trieste, portrays a similar scene in *Ulysses* when Molly Bloom remembers Father Corrigan exciting himself in the confessional by closely questioning her about her sex life: "he touched me father and what harm if he did where

and I said on the canal bank like a fool but whereabouts on your person my child on the leg behind high up was it yes rather high up was it where you sit down yes O Lord couldn't he say bottom right out and have done with it" (*Ulysses*, 1922; ed. Hans Walter Gabler, New York, 1986, p. 610).

22. Madame D'Arblay [Fanny Burney], *Diary and Letters*, ed. Austin Dobson (London, 1904), 2:270; *Letters*, 1:59; Boswell, *Life*, p. 169; *Letters*, 1:61; Hawkins, *Life of Johnson*, p. 131.

23. *Sermons*, Yale 14:268–269; *Letters*, 1:45, 3:337; Jonathan Swift, "On the Death of Mrs. Johnson" (1728), in *The Works of Jonathan Swift*, ed. Herbert Davis (Oxford, 1962), 5:227; Izaak Walton, *Life of Dr. John Donne* (Oxford, 1956), p. 51.

24. Boswell, *Life*, p. 957; George Steevens, in *Johnsonian Miscellanies*, 2:317; Shaw, *Memoirs of Johnson*, p. 34; *Letters*, 1:90.

25. *Diaries*, Yale 1:127; 292; 319; *Letters*, 3:223.

26. *Diaries*, Yale 1:52; 53; Boswell, *Life*, p. 444; Boothby, in Chapin, *Religious Thought*, p. 57.

27. *Letters*, 1:117–118; 119–121. In *Hedda Gabler* (1890), Ibsen punctures the heroine's romanticism when Judge Brack tells her that Eilert Lövborg has "wounded himself mortally." She exclaims: "Through the heart!—Yes!" and Brack replies: "No—in the bowels" (Henrik Ibsen, *Six Plays*, trans. Eva Le Gallienne, New York, 1957, p. 424).

28. *Johnsoniana: Anecdotes of the Late Samuel Johnson*, ed. Robina Napier (London, 1884), pp. 133; 142; 152, Harvard; Piozzi, *Anecdotes*, p. 114.

TEN: INTELLECTUAL ENTERTAINMENTS

1. *Idler* 23, Yale 2:72; Boswell, *Life*, pp. 1358, 214; 1013.

2. Porter, *London*, p. 171; Nichols, *Literary Anecdotes*, 5:55; Boswell, *Life*, p. 545.

3. Lacy Collison-Morley, *Giuseppe Baretti; with an Account of His Literary Friendships and Feuds in Italy and England in the Days of Dr. Johnson* (London, 1909), p. 83; *Thraliana*, 1:164; *Letters*, 1:85, 83.

4. Boswell, *Life,* pp. 394–395; Baretti, in E. S. De Beer, "Johnson's Italian Tour," in *Johnson, Boswell and Their Circle: Essays Presented to Lawrence Fitzroy Powell,* ed. Mary Lascelles (Oxford, 1965), p. 162.

5. *Johnsonian Miscellanies,* 2:390; Boswell, *Life,* pp. 174; 176, 177; 574; 845.

6. Boswell, *Life,* p. 312; Carola Hicks, *Improper Pursuits: The Scandalous Life of Lady Di Beauclerk* (London, 2001), pp. 148, 151; Boswell, *Life,* p. 537.

7. Boswell, *Life,* pp. 175; 1018–1019; Boswell, *Laird of Auchinleck,* p. 83; Boswell, *Life,* p. 1072; *Letters,* 3:231.

8. Johnson, in Roger Lonsdale, *Dr. Charles Burney: A Literary Biography* (Oxford, 1965), p. 182; Burney, in Lonsdale, *Charles Burney,* p. 235; Fanny Burney, *Early Journals,* 3:245.

9. Boswell, *Life,* pp. 931, 932; *Letters,* 3:114.

10. Gavin de Beer, *Gibbon and His World* (London, 1968), pp. 34; 109; Boswell, *Life,* ed. Hill, 4:73n4; Boswell, *Life,* p. 615.

11. George Colman, *Random Records* (London, 1830), 1:122; Gibbon, in John Butt, edited and compiled by Geoffrey Carnall, *The Mid-Eighteenth Century* (Oxford, 1979), p. 234; *Journey to the Western Islands of Scotland,* Yale 9:40, and Gibbon, *Autobiography,* p. 154.

12. Malone, in McIntyre, *Joshua Reynolds,* p. 149; *Thraliana,* 1:382; Fanny Burney, *Early Journals,* 3:139; Malone, in Derek Hudson, *Sir Joshua Reynolds: A Personal Study* (London, 1958), p. 137.

13. *Thraliana,* 1:42; Johnson, in Northcote, *Memoirs of Reynolds,* pp. 316; 317; Piozzi, *Anecdotes,* p. 88.

14. Johnson, in Northcote, *Memoirs of Reynolds,* p. 40; *Letters,* 1:244; Reynolds, *Portraits,* p. 83, and Sir Joshua Reynolds, in *Johnsonian Miscellanies,* 2:233.

15. Reynolds, *Portraits,* p. 74; Sir Joshua Reynolds, *Discourses on Art,* ed. Stephen Mitchell (1797; Indianapolis, 1965), p. 93; John Courtenay (politician and MP), in McIntyre, *Joshua Reynolds,* p. 158.

16. McIntyre, *Joshua Reynolds,* p. 140; Reynolds, *Portraits,* p. 76. Robert Frost, an elderly widower, was also reluctant to retire and loved to protract his late-night talks. When a younger friend walked him home after midnight, Frost would insist on walking the friend home,

and the friend, of course, would then have to walk back home with Frost.

17. *Letters,* 4:188; Frances Reynolds, in *Johnsonian Miscellanies,* 2:299; McIntyre, *Reynolds,* p. 144. Neither R. W. Chapman nor Bruce Redford found the source of Johnson's italicized *"Mortal born to bear."* Nora Crook, in a letter to Jeffrey Meyers of January 10, 2007, suggested that Johnson was slightly misquoting two couplets in Book XXIV of Pope's translation of *The Iliad:*

A while they sorrow, then dismiss their Care;
Fate gives the Wound, and Man is born to bear.

Rise then: Let Reason mitigate our Care:
To Mourn, avails not: Man is born to bear.
Pope, *The Iliad of Homer,* pp. 539, 555.

18. Frances Reynolds, in *Johnsonian Miscellanies,* 2:274; Reynolds, *Portraits,* pp. 68, 78–79; *Thraliana,* 1:205; Piozzi, *Anecdotes,* p. 142.

19. Fanny Burney, in Stanley Ayling, *Edmund Burke: His Life and Opinions* (New York, 1988), p. 142; Lock, *Edmund Burke,* pp. 505, 185, 268; Ayling, *Edmund Burke,* p. 146.

20. Greene, "Double Tradition of Johnson's Politics," p. 117; Johnson, in Lock, *Edmund Burke,* p. 423; Boswell, *Life,* p. 485.

21. Edmund Burke, *Correspondence,* ed. Thomas Copeland (Chicago, 1958–78), 4:47; *Lives of the Poets,* 2:179; *Letters,* 1:265.

22. Boswell, *Life,* p. 1079; Piozzi, *Anecdotes,* p. 130; Boswell, *Life,* p. 696.

23. Lock, *Edmund Burke,* p. 48; Conor Cruise O'Brien, "Samuel Johnson and Edmund Burke," *Transactions of the Johnsonian Society,* ed. Peter Stockham (Lichfield, 1994), p. 1; Boswell, *Life,* p. 1385; Cannon, *Johnson and the Politics of Hanoverian England,* p. 296.

24. Johnson, in John Ginger, *The Notable Man: The Life and Times of Oliver Goldsmith* (London, 1977), p. 151; Boswell, *Life,* p. 293; Edmond Malone, in E. H. Mikhail, ed., *Goldsmith: Interviews and Recollections* (New York, 1993), p. 98.

25. Davies, in *Goldsmith: Interviews and Recollections,* p. 64; Murphy, in *Johnsonian Miscellanies,* 1:421; Richard Knowles, in *Goldsmith: Interviews and Recollections,* pp. 123–124.

26. Garrick, in Boswell, *Life,* ed. Hill, 1:413n6; Reynolds, *Portraits,* p. 55; Boswell, *Life,* pp. 527; 511.

27. Hawkins, *Life of Johnson,* p. 179; Boswell, *Life,* p. 293, and *Life of Johnson,* ed. Hill, 1:414n4; Boswell, *Tour,* p. 265; Boswell, *Life,* p. 524.

28. Boswell, *Life,* p. 400; Sells, *Oliver Goldsmith,* pp. 76; 108; *Lives of the Poets,* 3:2; Boswell, *Life,* p. 294.

29. Johnson, "Notice of *The Traveller,*" *Critical Review* (December 1764), 458–462; Johnson, in Campbell, *Diary,* p. 77; *Johnson on Shakespeare,* 7:70; *Complete Poems,* p. 160.

30. *Rambler* 59, Yale 3:314; Fanny Burney, *Early Journals,* 3:95; Boswell, *Life,* pp. 388–389.

31. Oliver Goldsmith, *Collected Letters of Oliver Goldsmith,* ed. Katharine Balderston (Cambridge, England, 1928), p. 156; *Goldsmith: Interviews and Recollections,* p. 85; Boswell, *Life,* p. 525.

32. *Goldsmith: Interviews and Recollections,* p. 127; *Letters,* 2:146, 147; *Lives of the Poets,* 2:192.

ELEVEN: SLUGGISH RESOLUTION

1. Stone and Kahrl, *David Garrick,* p. 394; *Johnson on Language,* Yale 18:xxxii; 100; 102; 93.

2. *Johnson on Language,* Yale 18:105; 79; 89–90; 92; 111–112.

3. *Letters,* 1:116; *Johnson on Language,* Yale 18:113; "Ascham," in *Works* (1850), 2:206.

4. *Lives of the Poets,* 3:20; Chesterfield-Johnson, in McIntyre, *David Garrick,* p. 33; *Johnson on Language,* Yale 18:55; Chesterfield, in James Boulton, ed., *Johnson: The Critical Heritage* (London, 1971), pp. 97; 102.

5. Boswell, *Tour,* p. 97; Thomas De Quincey, *Dr. Johnson and Lord Chesterfield* (New York, 1945), pp. 17; 14; *Rambler* 136, Yale 4:356–357; *Rambler* 163, Yale 5:100, 102.

6. *Letters,* 1:95–96; De Quincey, *Johnson and Chesterfield,* p. 13; Boswell, *Life,* p. 187 (two quotes).

7. Boswell, *Life*, pp. 188; 549; Chesterfield, in Isaac Reed, *The Early Biographies of Samuel Johnson*, ed. O. M. Brack Jr. and Robert Kelley (Iowa City, 1974), p. 17; *Complete Poems*, p. 87. George Orwell, the gloomy twentieth-century moralist most like Johnson, did not achieve fame until he published *Animal Farm*, at the age of forty-two, in 1945. For a comparison of Johnson and Orwell, see Jeffrey Meyers, *A Reader's Guide to George Orwell* (London, 1975), pp. 9–10.

8. Boswell, *Life*, p. 1034; *Letters*, 4:426; 1:103; *Johnson on Language*, Yale 18:375.

9. Adam Smith, in Boulton, *Critical Heritage*, p. 115; Samuel Taylor Coleridge, *Biographia Literaria*, ed. J. Shawcross, (1907; Oxford, 1965), 1:164n; James Sledd and Gwin Kolb, *Dr. Johnson's "Dictionary": Essays in the Biography of a Book* (Chicago, 1955), p. 111; *Complete Poems*, p. 149.

10. Linda Colley, *Britons: Forging the Nation, 1707–1837* (New Haven, 1992), p. 178; *Complete Poems*, p. 62; "Observations on the Present State of Affairs," in *Political Writings*, Yale 10.188; "The Patriot," in *Political Writings*, Yale 10.395; "Thoughts on Falkland's Islands," in *Political Writings*, Yale 10.370–371.

11. Johnson, "Review of Thomas Blackwell's *Memoirs of the Court of Augustus*," in *Works* (1825), 5:635; *Adventurer* 99, Yale 2:433; Boswell, *Correspondence Relating to "Life of Johnson*," p. 141.

12. Trevelyan, *English Social History*, p. 363; *Political Writings*, Yale 10.283; 281; 284. See John Milton, "Areopagitica," in *Milton's Prose*, ed. Malcolm Wallace (Oxford, 1949), p. 290: "Good and evil we know in the field of this World grow up together." Johnson also paraphrases this passage in *Rasselas*, Yale 16:67 and *Idler* 44, Yale 2:139.

13. Wesley, in *Political Writings*, Yale 10.285; 288–289; Dudley Pope, *At Twelve Mr. Byng Was Shot* (Philadelphia, 1962), p. xi.

14. *Political Writings*, Yale 10.219; 239–240; Voltaire, *Candide*, trans. Robert Adams (New York, 1966), p. 57.

15. Bloom, *Johnson in Grub Street*, pp. 186–187; Review of Jenyns' *"Free Enquiry*," in *Works*, ed. Greene, pp. 527 (two quotes); 535; Jenyns, in Clifford, *Dictionary Johnson*, p. 183.

16. See J. D. Fleeman, "The Revenue of a Writer: Samuel Johnson's Literary Earnings," in *Studies in the Book Trade: In Honour of Graham Pollard,* ed. R. W. Hunt (Oxford, 1975), pp. 211–230; *Letters,* 1:132; 158.

TWELVE: DANGEROUS IMAGINATION

1. *Letters,* 1:43; 176; 179. See Albert Camus, *The Stranger,* trans. Stuart Gilbert (1942; New York, 1954), p. 1: "Mother died today. Or, maybe, yesterday; I can't be sure."

2. *Letters,* 1:181–182; *Idler* 41, Yale 2:129; *Rasselas,* Yale 16:75–76; 155.

3. *Rasselas,* Yale 16:7. When Baretti found it difficult to translate the first sentence into French, Johnson thought for two or three minutes, urged him to take up his pen and said, "'if you can understand my pronunciation, I will see what I can do.' He then dictated the sentence to the translator, which proved admirable, and was immediately adopted: 'Mortels! Vous qui prêtez l'oreille à la douce voix d'une imagination séduisante et qui poursuivez vivement les fantômes de l'espoir. . . .'" James Clifford, "Johnson and Foreign Visitors to London: Baretti and Others," *Eighteenth Century Studies Presented to Arthur Wilson,* ed. Peter Gay (Hanover, N.H., 1972), p. 108.

4. During World War II, the name of Rasselas' Happy Valley was adopted by the scandalous upper-class enclave of English colonials living in the white highlands of Kenya. See James Fox, *White Mischief: The Murder of Lord Erroll* (1982).

5. *Rasselas,* Yale 16:54; 28; 119; 50.

6. *Rasselas,* Yale 16:8; 109; Boswell, *Life,* p. 480; *Rasselas,* Yale 16:157.

7. *Irene,* in *Poems,* Yale 6:165; *Rasselas,* Yale 16:16 (two quotes); 60; 132; 102.

8. Francisco Goya, *Los Caprichos* (1799; New York, 1969), plate 43; *Rambler* 8, Yale 3:43; *Rasselas,* Yale 16:150.

9. *Rasselas,* Yale 16:82; [Edmund Burke], in Boulton, *Critical Heritage,* p. 157; *Rasselas,* Yale 16:8; Samuel Taylor Coleridge, "Kubla Khan," in *Poetical Works,* ed. Ernest Hartley Coleridge (London, 1957), p. 297.

10. Turberville, *Johnson's England,* 1:138; *Idler* 58, Yale 2:181; Piozzi, *Anecdotes,* p. 151; Boswell, *Life,* p. 698.

11. *Idler* 58, Yale 2:182; *Letters,* 1:206; "Anecdote of Johnson," manuscript, [18??], Container List, p. 7a, Harvard.

12. *Letters,* 1:206, 285; *Lucy Porter to Dr. Johnson: Her Only Known Letter,* intro. by James Clifford (Stinehour Press, privately printed, September 21, 1979), p. 5, Greene Archive; Boswell, *Life,* p. 861.

13. *Idler* 31, Yale 2:97; *Idler* 35, 2:110, 109; *Idler* 84, 2:261, 263.

14. *Idler* 17, Yale 2:55; *Idler* 18, 2:57; *Idler* 22, 2:319–320.

15. Boswell, *Life,* pp. 287–288; 951, 900; Boswell, *Life,* ed. Hill, 1:408n3.

16. Boswell, *Life,* p. 265 (two quotes); *Letters,* 1:208; *Lives of the Poets,* 3:75; Charles Churchill, in Boulton, *Critical Heritage,* p. 359.

17. Horace Walpole, *Memoirs and Portraits,* ed. Matthew Hodgart (1822; New York, 1963), p. 238; James Boswell, *The Ominous Years, 1774–1776,* ed. Charles Ryskamp and Frederick Pottle (New York, 1963), p. 301; Boswell, *Life,* pp. 320; 304.

THIRTEEN: SOCIETY OF THE AFFLICTED

1. *Thraliana,* 1:184–185 (two quotes); Hawkins, *Life of Johnson,* p. 172.

2. Boswell, *Life,* p. 172; John Hawkins, in *Johnson Miscellanies,* 2:112; Boswell, *Life,* ed. Hill, 1:244n2; Burney, *Early Journals,* 3:76.

3. *Rambler* 19, Yale 3:106; "Proposal for *Essays,*" in *Works* (1825), p. 505; Boswell, *Life,* p. 736.

4. Hawkins, *Life of Johnson,* p. 175; B. N. Turner, in *Samuel Johnson: Interviews and Recollections,* p. 121; Laetitia Hawkins, in *Johnson Miscellanies,* 2:141; *Letters,* 4:203.

5. Burney, *Early Journals,* 3:146–147; *Letters,* 3:189; Marshall, *Johnson's London,* p. 235.

6. Burney, *Early Journals,* 3:148–149; Boswell, *Life,* p. 1144 (two quotes); Burney, *Early Journals,* 3:100; 103.

7. *Idler* 87, Yale 2:270; "Essay on Epitaphs," in *Works,* ed. Greene, pp. 101–102; Boswell, *Life,* p. 876.

8. *Johnsonian Gleanings,* 2:7; Piozzi, *Anecdotes,* p. 92; Letter from the Jamaican-born Nora Crook to Jeffrey Meyers, May 16, 2006.

9. *Thraliana*, 1:175; Piozzi, *Anecdotes*, p. 130; *Johnsonian Gleanings*, 2:75; *Samuel Johnson: Interviews and Recollections*, p. 117.

10. Boswell, *Tour*, p. 104, and Boswell, *Life*, p. 688; *Johnsonian Gleanings*, 2:12; *Letters*, 1:188.

11. Piozzi, *Anecdotes*, p. 131; Boswell, *Life*, p. 1217 (two quotes); Thomas Gray, *Poems of Gray and Collins*, ed. Austin Lane Poole (London, 1961), p. 23. See also John Keats, "To Mrs. Reynolds's Cat" (1818), *Poetical Works*, ed. H. W. Garrod (London, 1956), p. 422: "Gaze / With those bright languid segments green, and prick / Those velvet ears."

12. *Letters*, 3:140; 4:137.

FOURTEEN: CONTAGION OF DESIRE

1. *The False Alarm*, in *Political Writings*, Yale 10.332; Boswell, *Life*, pp. 277–279.

2. *Johnsonian Miscellanies*, 2:395; Boswell, *Life*, pp. 287; 297.

3. Boswell, *Life*, pp. 329; 334; *Lives of the Poets*, 3:175; *Boswell on the Grand Tour: Italy, Corsica, and France, 1765–1766*, ed. Frank Brady and Frederick Pottle (London, 1955), pp. 293–294.

4. Swift, "Verses on the Death of Dr. Swift," in *Collected Poems*, 2:723; *Boswell for the Defence*, p. 104; Boswell, *London Journal*, p. 84.

5. *Johnson on Shakespeare*, Yale 7:523; Peter Martin, *A Life of James Boswell* (New Haven, 2000), p. 86; *Letters*, 4:262, 3:232.

6. Frances Burney, *Memoirs of Dr. Burney*, 2:190; Boswell, *Correspondence Relating to "Life of Johnson,"* p. 185; *Letters*, 2:223; Boswell, *Life*, pp. 928, 756.

7. Boswell, *Life*, pp. 602–603; 302; 775.

8. Boswell, *Life*, p. 1235; Boswell, *Ominous Years*, p. 302; Boswell, *Life*, p. 1201.

9. *Rambler* 160, Yale 5:86; Boswell, *Tour*, pp. 78–79; Margaret Forbes, in Boswell, *Life*, ed. Hill, 2:486.

10. Fanny Burney, in Peter Thresher, *Pasquale Paoli: An Enlightened Hero, 1725–1807* (London, 1970), p. 171; *Johnsonian Miscellanies*, 2:16.

11. Garrick, *Letters,* p. 588; *Lives of the Poets,* 2:111; Henry Fielding, *Tom Jones,* ed. R. P. C. Mutter (1749; London, 1975), p. 510.

12. John Nichols, in *Johnson Miscellanies,* 2:411; Cornelia Knight, in *Johnsonian Miscellanies,* 2:175; Boswell, *Life,* p. 1141.

13. Boswell, *Life,* pp. 329–330; *Lives of the Poets,* 2:149; *Rambler* 45, Yale 3:245, *Rambler* 11, Yale 3:58.

14. Arthur Murphy, in *Johnsonian Miscellanies,* 1:383; Boswell, in Michael Joyce, *Samuel Johnson* (London, 1975), p. 133; Boswell, *Life,* p. 1084; Northcote, *Memoirs of Reynolds,* p. 130.

15. Joseph Cradock, in *Johnsonian Miscellanies,* 2:71; 2:69; "Anecdote of Dr. Johnson," manuscript [December 2, 1805], Container List, p. 6, Harvard; Frances Reynolds, in *Johnsonian Miscellanies,* 2:278.

16. Boswell, *Life,* p. 1148; Northcote, *Memoirs of Reynolds,* p. 303; Boswell, *Life,* p. 914, and Max Beerbohm, "A Clergyman," *"And Even Now" and "A Christmas Garland"* (1918; New York, 1960), p. 131.

17. *Rambler* 40, Yale 3:220; Boswell, *Life,* p. 1327.

FIFTEEN: BANDYING CIVILITIES

1. *Johnson on Shakespeare,* Yale 7:88; Greenblatt, *Will in the World,* p. 11; *Rasselas,* Yale 16:123; *Complete Poems,* p. 140. This Jacob Tonson was the great-nephew and namesake of the original publisher of Dryden and Pope.

2. *Johnson on Shakespeare,* Yale 7:51; Brian Vickers, *Shakespeare: The Critical Heritage,* Vol. 5 (London, 1979), p. 20; *Johnson on Shakespeare,* Yale 7:56; 7:95; Walter Raleigh, *Six Essays on Johnson* (Oxford, 1910), p. 76.

3. *Johnson on Shakespeare,* Yale 7:99; 110–111; W. K. Wimsatt Jr., "Introduction" to *Johnson on Shakespeare* (New York, 1960), p. xv; Turberville, *Johnson's England,* 2:163.

4. Garrick, *Letters,* 2:845; Bentley, in Mack, *Alexander Pope,* p. 348; Boswell, *Tour,* p. 207; Vickers, *Shakespeare: Critical Heritage,* 5:14.

5. *Johnson on Shakespeare,* 7:62; 65; 77; 69; W. H. Auden, "The Globe," in *The Dyer's Hand and Other Essays* (1962; New York, 1968), p. 175.

6. *Johnson on Shakespeare,* Yale 7:81; 71.

7. *Johnson on Shakespeare,* Yale 7:425 (*King John*); 8:881; 908 (both *Cymbeline*).

8. *Johnson on Shakespeare,* Yale 8:769–770 (*Macbeth*); 8:695; 703; 704 (*King Lear*); 8:1045 (*Othello*). Italics mine.

9. *Johnson on Shakespeare,* Yale 8:974 (*Hamlet*); 8:1047 (*Othello*); Charles Churchill, "*The Ghost,*" in *Poetical Works,* ed. Douglas Grant (Oxford, 1956), p. 126. See Roy Campbell, "On Some South African Novelists," in *Adamastor* (1930; New York, 1931), p. 98:

You praise the firm restraint with which they write—
I'm with you there, of course:
They use the snaffle and the curb all right,
But where's the bloody horse?

10. Boswell, *Life,* p. 1150; William Hazlitt, *The Characters of Shakespeare's Plays,* in Boulton, *Critical Heritage,* p. 199; J. Isaacs, in Harley Granville-Barker and G. B. Harrison, *A Companion to Shakespeare Studies* (Garden City, N.Y., 1960), p. 315.

11. *Rambler* 21, Yale 3:119; Marshall, *Johnson's London,* p. 145; Boswell, *Life,* pp. 380; 381; 383–384.

12. Baretti, in Duncan Robinson, "Guiseppe Baretti as 'A Man of Great Humanity,'" in Guilland Sutherland, ed., *British Art, 1740–1820: Essays in Honor of Robert Wark* (San Marino, Calif., 1992), pp. 84–85 (two quotes); Baretti, in Boswell, *Life,* ed. Hill, 2:97n1; Baretti, in McIntyre, *Joshua Reynolds,* p. 204.

13. *Thraliana,* 1:232; Baretti, in Collison-Morley, *Giuseppe Baretti,* pp. 55, 47; *Lives of the Poets,* 3:134; Johnson, in Collison, *Baretti,* p. 217.

14. *Complete Poems,* p. 61; Johnson, in McIntyre, *Joshua Reynolds,* p. 204, and Collison, *Baretti,* p. 218.

15. *Thraliana,* 1:176; Thomas Curley, "Introduction" to Sir Robert Chambers, *A Course of Lectures on English Law, 1767–1773* (Madison, 1986), pp. 10; 20; *Works,* ed. Greene, pp. 575–576.

16. Beer, *Gibbon and His World,* p. 45; Magnus, *Edmund Burke,* p. 61; McIntyre, *Joshua Reynolds,* p. 207.

17. Cannon, *Johnson and the Politics of Hanoverian England*, p. 297. For the origins of this nicely balanced sentence, see Wilfred Thesiger, *Arabian Sands* (New York, 1959), p. 20: "I craved for the past, resented the present, and dreaded the future"; and Malcolm Muggeridge on George Orwell, in *The World of George Orwell*, ed. Miriam Gross (London, 1971), p. 172: "he loved the past, hated the present and dreaded the future."

18. *Sermons*, Yale 14:245–246; Lonsdale, in *Lives of the Poets*, 1:368; Boswell, *Life*, p. 615.

19. *Political Writings*, Yale 10.343; 319, 327.

20. John Wilkes, *A Letter to Samuel Johnson* (London, 1770), pp. 33; 5; 49; 16; 34; 33, Harvard.

21. Boswell, *Life*, pp. 864; 769; 765; 767; 768.

22. *Political Writings*, Yale 10.350; 369; 371.

23. Britain never renounced its rights to the islands. Two centuries later, in April 1982, Argentina, which had inherited Spain's claim, suddenly occupied the Falklands. Intent on maintaining its sovereignty, and rejecting the argument that the islands were not worth a war, Britain, led by Margaret Thatcher, transported its troops across 8,000 miles and fought Argentina in an undeclared war that killed more than a thousand combatants. After a final attack on June 13, Argentina surrendered and Britain regained its futile "spots of earth in the deserts of the ocean."

SIXTEEN: DOMESTICK PLEASURES

1. *Idler* 59, Yale 2:182–183; *Letters*, 1:143; *Diaries*, Yale 1:73; 92.

2. *Rasselas*, Yale 16:149; *Diaries*, Yale 1:264; *Letters*, 2:75. In a similarly agonized fashion, Franz Kafka described himself, in a letter to his fiancée, as "a sick, weak, unsociable, taciturn, gloomy, stiff, almost hopeless man . . . quite incapable of human happiness." After seeing her in Berlin, he added: "It couldn't have been worse. Next thing will be impalement" (Franz Kafka, *Letters to Felice*, ed. Erich Heller and Jürgen Born, trans. James Stern and Elisabeth Duckworth [London, 1974], pp. 272, 283; 352).

3. Boswell, *Life,* p. 342; *Letters,* 1:77–78; 91; Boswell, *Life,* pp. 613–614.

4. Turberville, *Johnson's England,* 2:285; Boswell, *Life,* p. 635.

5. Murphy, in *Johnsonian Miscellanies,* 1:423; Piozzi, *Anecdotes,* pp. 102; 86; *The Letters of Samuel Johnson, with Mrs. Thrale's Genuine Letters to Him,* ed. R. W. Chapman (Oxford, 1952), pp. 331–332.

6. *Rambler* 74, Yale 4:27; Burney, in James Clifford, *Hester Lynch Piozzi (Mrs. Thrale),* (1941; 2nd ed. 1952; New York, 1968), p. 152; Katharine Balderston, "Introduction" to *Thraliana,* I.x; Boswell, *Correspondence Relating to "Life of Johnson,"* p. 114.

7. Williams, *Whig Supremacy,* p. 133; Peter Mathias, "Dr. Johnson and the Business World," in *The Transformation of England: Essays in the Economic and Social History of England in the Eighteenth Century* (London, 1979), pp. 310–311; *Samuel Johnson, 1709–1784,* exhibition catalogue, ed. K. K. Yung (London, 1984), p. 116; Hester Piozzi, *A Catalogue of Excellent and Genuine Household Furniture* (1816), p. 34, Harvard.

8. *Thraliana,* 1:185–186 (two quotes); Clifford, *Hester Piozzi,* p. 192; Piozzi, *Anecdotes,* pp. 155.

9. *Rambler* 39, Yale 3:213; *Thraliana,* 1:306; 52–53; 309; Clifford, *Hester Piozzi,* pp. 49–50.

10. Hester Thrale, in Burney, *Early Journals,* 3:303; *Thraliana,* 1:356; 432; Bate, *Samuel Johnson,* p. 550.

11. Frances (born 1765) lived for ten days, Henry Salusbury (1767–76) for nine years, Anna Maria (1768–70) for two years, Lucy Elizabeth (1769–73) for four years, Penelope (1772) for ten hours, Ralph (1773–75) for two years, Frances Anna (1775) for seven months and Henrietta Sophia (1778–83) for four years.

12. *Thraliana,* 1:401; Hester, in Clifford, *Hester Piozzi,* p. 79; *Rasselas,* Yale 16:95.

13. *Thraliana,* 1:178; Johnson, in Clifford, *Hester Piozzi,* pp. 112–113; *Rambler* 87, Yale 4:93, 95.

14. *Letters,* 1:412; Boswell, *Life,* p. 323; *Johnsonian Miscellanies,* 2:406.

15. Hawkins, *Life of Johnson,* p. 212; Letter on the heathen oracles from Christian Kopff to Jeffrey Meyers, June 6, 2006. Johnson's question may

have been prompted by the idea that at the birth of Christ the oracles ceased throughout the world and the impostures of paganism disappeared. Milton refers to this in *Paradise Regained*: "No more shalt thou by oracling abuse / The Gentiles; henceforth Oracles are ceased" (I.455–56).

16. Baretti, in Theodore Besterman, *Voltaire*, 3rd. ed. (Oxford, 1976), p. 146n. E. S. De Beer, quoting Baretti, in *Johnson, Boswell and Their Circle*, p. 161 (two quotes); Baretti, in *The French Journals of Mrs. Thrale and Doctor Johnson*, ed. Moses Tyson and Henry Guppy (Manchester, 1932), p. 247; *Letters*, 2:248.

SEVENTEEN: MIND DISEASED

1. Piozzi, *Anecdotes*, p. 85; Clifford, *Hester Piozzi*, p. 88; Swift, "Holyhead" and "Stella's Birth-day," in *Collected Poems*, 1:93; 159.

2. "To Mrs. Thrale on her Thirty-fifth Birthday," "On Hearing Miss Thrale Deliberate about her Hat," "A Short Song of Congratulation," in *Complete Poems*, pp. 132–133; 137; 138.

3. Piozzi, *Anecdotes*, p. 72. Playing the same sort of game and describing his friends in terms of food, Goldsmith wrote, "Burke shall be tongue, with a garnish of brains; Reynolds lamb"; and himself a "gooseberry fool" (Sells, *Goldsmith*, p. 186).

4. *Thraliana*, 1:167–168; 167; Burney, *Early Journals*, 3:120; *Thraliana*, 1:188.

5. *Thraliana*, 1:459; Piozzi, *Anecdotes*, p. 101; *Thraliana*, 1:184; Burney, *Early Journals*, 3:86.

6. Burney, *Early Journals*, 3:164–165; 152; Claire Harman, *Fanny Burney: A Biography* (New York, 2001), p. 70; Burney, *Early Journals*, 3:155; Burney, *Diary and Letters*, 1:247.

7. Burney, *Early Journals*, 3:150–151; 3:255–256, 4:430. After Johnson's death Fanny became keeper of the robes to Queen Charlotte, wife of George III, from 1786 to 1791. In 1793 she married the French émigré Alexandre d'Arblay and had one son, who predeceased her. During an operation for breast cancer, without anesthesia, that took place in 1811, she showed great courage and hair-raising powers of description. When

she suddenly realized that the doctor intended to sever her entire breast instead of excising only part of it, she resigned herself to the "terrour that surpasses all description, & the most torturing pain." See *Journals and Letters of Fanny Burney, 1803–1812*, ed. Joyce Hemlow (Oxford, 1975), 6:612.

8. *Thraliana*, 1:540; *Letters*, 4:343; *Thraliana*, 1:415n4; *Diaries*, Yale 1:140.

9. *Thraliana*, 1:415 and note 4; 1:384n4; Police report, in Ronald Hayman, *De Sade: A Critical Biography* (New York, 1978), p. 28; Giuseppe Tomasi di Lampedusa, *The Leopard*, trans., Archibald Colquhoun (1958; New York, 1961), p. 166. See Jeffrey Meyers, "The Literature of Pain," *Human Rights Review*, 8 (July–September 2007), 409–417.

10. *Thraliana*, 1:386 and note 2; Boswell, *Life*, p. 857; *Letters*, 2:38–39 (my translation).

11. *Letters of Johnson and Mrs. Thrale*, p. 332; *Thraliana*, 1:384; 1:415.

12. Katharine Balderston, "Johnson's Vile Melancholy," in *The Age of Johnson: Essays Presented to Chauncey Brewster Tinker*, ed. Frederick Hilles (New Haven, 1949), pp. 11–12; Richard von Krafft-Ebing, *Psychopathia Sexualis*, trans., Franklin Klaf (New York, 1965), p. 86; *Lives of the Poets*, 2:29.

EIGHTEEN: SAVAGE CLANS

1. Boswell, *Life*, p. 859; Boswell, *Life*, ed. Hill, 4:15n3; Trevelyan, *History of England*, p. 22.

2. *Letters*, 2:243; D. H. Lawrence, *Letters: Vol. II, 1913–1916*, ed. George Zytaruk and James Boulton (Cambridge, England, 1981), p. 330; *Letters*, 2:78; Boswell, *Life*, p. 742; *Letters*, 1:246–247; 2:276.

3. Murphy, in *Johnsonian Miscellanies*, 1:428; Martin Martin, *A Description of the Western Islands of Scotland*, ed. Donald McLeod (1703; Stirling, 1934), p. 270; James Thomson, *The Seasons*, ed. James Sambrook (Oxford, 1981), p. 178; J. D. Mackie, *A History of Scotland* (London, 1964), p. 277.

4. *Journey to the Western Islands of Scotland*, Yale 9:90; 97; 57; Tacitus, *Agricola*, section 30; Brewer, *Pleasures of the Imagination*, p. 656.

5. *Letters*, 2:96; *Journey*, Yale 9:28; 100–101; 156; *Letters*, 2:92.

6. *Journey,* Yale 9:148 (two quotes); 9:xxxiv; 164; 118.

7. "Browne," in *Works* (1850), 2:191; *Letters,* 2:168–169; 181; Edward Gibbon, *Letters, 1750–1794,* ed. J. E. Norton (London, 1956), 2:91.

8. Boswell, *Tour,* pp. 8; 22; 62; 291; 147.

9. Boswell, *Tour,* pp. 100; 110, 112; Joyce, *Samuel Johnson,* p. 139; Boswell, *Tour,* pp. 249–251.

10. Boswell, *Tour,* p. 215; *Letters,* 2:111; Boswell, *Life,* p. 554n1; "Anecdote of Mr. Johnson," manuscript, [18??], Container List, p. 7a, Harvard.

11. Boswell, *Tour,* pp. 370 (two quotes); 375.

12. *A Journey into North Wales in the Year 1774,* in Boswell, *Life,* ed. Hill, 5:429–452.

13. *Journey into Wales,* in Boswell, *Life,* ed. Hill, 5:450; 442 and note 3; 440n3.

14. *Letters,* 2:101; 149; 151; 4:172.

15. Boswell, *Life,* p. 442; James Gray, "Arras / Hélas!: A Fresh Look at Samuel Johnson's French," *Johnson after Two Hundred Years,* ed. Paul Korshin (Philadelphia, 1986), p. 87; Frances Reynolds, in *Johnsonian Miscellanies,* 2:290.

16. Boswell, *Life,* pp. 651; 657; 650; 659.

17. Boswell, *Life,* pp. 658–659; *Letters,* 2:274–275, 277.

18. *Letters,* 2:313; *Thraliana,* 1:319; Collison-Morley, *Baretti,* p. 297; *Letters,* 2:365–366.

19. *French Journals of Thrale and Johnson,* pp. 236; 246; 252; *Thraliana,* 1:487.

20. *Thraliana,* 1:48; John Wilson Croker, ed., *Johnsoniana; or Supplement to Boswell; Being Anecdotes and Sayings of Dr. Johnson* (London, 1836), pp. 341–342.

21. Garrick, *Letters,* p. 993; *Political Writings,* Yale 10. 414; 454. In his life of Milton, Johnson reaffirmed that "they who most loudly clamour for liberty do not most liberally grant it" (*Lives of the Poets,* 1:276).

22. *Political Writings,* Yale 10.405; 428; 448; 451–452.

23. Boswell, *Life,* p. 946; Campbell, in *Johnsonian Miscellanies,* 2:55–56; Magnus, *Edmund Burke,* pp. 80–81; Franklin, in Krutch, *Samuel Johnson,* p. 450.

24. James Basker, *Samuel Johnson in the Mind of Thomas Jefferson* (Charlottesville, Va., 1999), p. 5; Samuel Taylor Coleridge, *Specimens of the Table Talk* (London, 1835), 2:274; Lord North, in Cannon, *Johnson and the Politics of Hanoverian England,* p. 83.

25. Paul Langford, *A Polite and Commercial People: England 1727–1783* (Oxford, 1989), p. 491; O. M. Brack Jr., ed., *The Macaroni Parson* (Los Angeles, privately printed, 2004), pp. 8–9; 15, Loren Rothschild Collection.

26. Radzinowicz, "The Case of Dr. Dodd," in *History of English Criminal Law,* 1:455, 451; *Letters,* 3:25; Johnson, in A. D. Barker, "Samuel Johnson and the Campaign to Save William Dodd," *Harvard Library Bulletin,* 31 (1983), 168.

27. *Sermons,* Yale 14:309, 310; Paul Alkon, "Johnson's Condemned Sermon," in *The Unknown Samuel Johnson,* ed. John Burke Jr. and Donald Kay (Madison, 1983), p. 117; Boswell, *Life,* p. 849; John Bender, *Imagining the Penitentiary: Fiction and the Architecture of Mind in Eighteenth-Century England* (Chicago, 1987), p. 103.

28. "On the Fireworks for the Peace of Aix-la-Chapelle," in *Political Writings,* Yale 10.114–115; Boswell, *Correspondence Relating to the "Life of Johnson,"* p. 119.

29. William Butler Yeats, "No Second Troy," in *Collected Poems,* p. 89; Rogers, *Johnson Encyclopedia,* p. 164; *Letters,* 3:269; 303.

NINETEEN: ENCHAIN THE HEART

1. *Lives of the Poets,* 2:101; Boswell, *Life,* p. 301; *Idler* 84, Yale 2:261; *Rambler* 60, Yale 3:321.

2. *Works* (1850), 2:197; *Letters,* 3:237; Boswell, *Life,* pp. 4; 989.

3. Boswell, *Life,* ed. Hill, 4:36n3; Boswell, *Life,* pp. 474; 840.

4. *Rambler* 60, Yale 3:319; *Works* (1850), 2:198; T. S. Eliot, "The Metaphysical Poets," in *Selected Essays, 1917–1932* (New York, 1932), pp. 250; 243.

5. *Complete Poems,* p. 87; *Letters of Robert Burns,* ed. G. R. Roy, 2nd ed. (Oxford, 1985), 2:46; *Works* (1850), 2:423.

6. Earl of Rochester, *Poems on Several Occasions,* ed. James Thorpe (Princeton, 1950), p. 28; *Poems of Gray and Collins,* p. 247.

7. *Johnson on Language,* Yale 18:55–56; *Johnson on Shakespeare,* Yale 8:605; Pope, *Poems,* p. 701.

8. Milton, *Prose,* p. 290; *Adventurer* 126, Yale 2:475; R. W. Ketton-Cremer, *Thomas Gray: A Biography* (Cambridge, England, 1955), pp. 191; 248.

9. Boswell, *Tour,* p. 170; Piozzi, *Anecdotes,* p. 131; Boswell, *Life,* p. 595; Swift, *Collected Poems,* 1:246.

10. Sir William Wilde, *The Closing Years of Dean Swift's Life* (Dublin, 1849), p. 70; *Diaries,* Yale 1:303–304; Boswell, *Life,* p. 1034.

11. O. M. Brack Jr., ed., *Samuel Johnson in New Albion* (Los Angeles, privately printed, 1997), p. 34, Rothschild Collection; Burney, *Early Journals,* 4:367–368, 370; Cowper, *Letters and Prose Writings,* 2:8; 1:520.

12. Lord Byron, *Letters and Journals,* ed. R. E. Prothero (London, 1922–24), 5:564; Matthew Arnold, *The Six Chief Lives from Johnson's "Lives of the Poets"* (London, 1878), p. xxvi.

TWENTY: LACERATED FRIENDSHIP

1. *Thraliana,* 1:488; *Letters,* 4:23; 3:330; Mathias, "Johnson and the Business World," p. 298; Steevens, in *Johnsonian Miscellanies,* 2:325.

2. Boswell, *Life,* p. 1132 (Johnson was quoting Edward Moore's play *The Gamester,* 1753: "I am rich beyond the dreams of avarice"); Letitia Hawkins in *Johnsonian Miscellanies,* 2:140; Hester, in John Riely, "Johnson's Last Years with Mrs. Thrale: Facts and Problems," *Bulletin of the John Rylands University Library,* 57 (1974), 202.

3. James Boswell, "Ode by Dr. Samuel Johnson to Mrs. Thrale: upon Their Supposed Approaching Nuptials" (1788), Harvard; *Rasselas,* Yale 16:162; *Diaries,* Yale 1:69; Boswell, *Life,* p. 1357; Coleridge, *Poetical Works,* p. 202.

4. *Johnsonian Miscellanies,* 2:427; Boswell, *Correspondence Relating to "Life of Johnson,"* p. 300.

5. *Complete Poems,* pp. 139–140; Milton, *Minor Poems,* p. 379.

6. *Letters,* 4:186; 151; *Complete Poems,* p. 154; *Letters,* 4:265.

7. Clifford, *Hester Piozzi,* p. 159; *Thraliana,* 1:452; *Letters,* 1:120; 3:379; 4:32.

8. *Rambler* 162, Yale 5:97–98; Piozzi, *Anecdotes*, p. 156; Hester, in Riely, "Johnson's Last Years," p. 200; *Thraliana*, 1:540.

9. *Adventurer* 74, Yale 2:398; Steevens, in *Thraliana*, 2:629n2; Lyle Larsen, "Joseph Baretti's Feud with Hester Thrale," *Age of Johnson*, 16 (2005), 119; *Thraliana*, 2:615.

10. Clifford, *Hester Piozzi*, p. 218; *Thraliana*, 1:557; 563.

11. *Letters*, 3:86; *Complete Poems*, p. 90; *Letters*, 4:338; Balderston, "Johnson's Vile Melancholy," p. 14.

12. Hester Lynch Piozzi, *The Piozzi Letters. Vol. I, 1784–1791*, ed. Edward and Lillian Bloom (Newark, Del., 1989), pp. 81–82; *Letters*, 4:343; Piozzi, *Letters*, p. 86.

13. *Letters*, 4:351; D'Arblay, *Diary and Letters*, 2:271; *Letters*, 4:358.

TWENTY-ONE: THE NIGHT COMETH

1. *Rambler* 32, Yale 3:176; *Rambler* 48, 3:259.

2. *Letters*, 4:22; 9.

3. Boswell, *Correspondence Relating to "Life of Johnson,"* p. 30; Swift, "On His Own Deafness," in *Collected Poems*, 1:99; D'Arblay, *Diary and Letters*, 2:108.

4. Pope, *"Epistle to Dr. Arbuthnot,"* in *Poems*, p. 602; *Diaries*, Yale 1:142; *Johnson on Language*, Yale 18:109–110.

5. Reynolds, *Letters*, p. 124; Boswell, *Correspondence Relating to "Life of Johnson,"* p. 29; Burney, *Early Journals*, 4:476.

6. *Works*, ed. Greene, p. 64; Boswell, *Correspondence Relating to "Life of Johnson,"* p. 81; Hawkins, *Life of Johnson*, p. 274.

7. *Letters*, 4:19; Boswell, *Life*, p. 1358; *Letters*, 4:197.

8. *Letters*, 4:205; 223; 285.

9. *Letters*, 4:405; 125; Boswell, *Life*, p. 1375.

10. *Letters*, 4:414; Boswell, *Life*, p. 1324.

11. Boswell, *Life*, p. 1379; Hawkins, *Life of Johnson*, p. 275; Boswell, *Life*, p. 1379.

12. James Boswell, *Correspondence of James Boswell with Certain Members of the Club*, ed. Charles Fifer (New York, 1976), pp. 175–176; Hawkins, *Life of Johnson*, p. 272. Several other writers followed Johnson's

unfortunate example. Lord Byron's papers were burned by his executors; Thomas Hardy, Henry James, Somerset Maugham and W. H. Auden burned their own papers.

13. *Lives of the Poets*, 3:19; Boswell, *Life*, pp. 416; *Adventurer* 39, Yale 2:351.

14. Boswell, *Life*, p. 426; Milton, *Paradise Lost*, p. 44; *Sermons*, Yale 14:165; *Idler* 103, Yale 2:316; *Letters*, 4:266.

15. Boswell, *Life*, p. 1388; John Wesley, *Journals* (New York, 1963), p. 389; Hannah More, *Letters*, p. 101.

16. Hawkins, *Life of Johnson*, pp. 273; 276; Hawkins, in *Johnsonian Miscellanies*, 2:83; Fleeman, "Revenue of a Writer," p. 223.

17. Raleigh, *Six Essays on Johnson*, p. 72; Boswell, *Correspondence Relating to "Life of Johnson,"* p. 208; Saul Bellow, *Ravelstein* (New York, 2000), p. 6. In *Dubin's Lives* (1979; New York, 1980), p. 14, Bernard Malamud also paid tribute by writing that Johnson "inspired men to reason and courage. He had learned from life."

18. *Rambler* 108, Yale 4:214; Boswell, *Life*, pp. 1394–1395.

EPILOGUE: JOHNSON'S INFLUENCE

1. Jane Austen, *Selected Letters, 1796–1817*, ed. R. W. Chapman (Oxford, 1955), p. 81 (February 8, 1807); Jane Austen, *Northanger Abbey*, ed. R. W. Chapman (1818; London, 1954), p. 108; *Johnsonian Miscellanies*, 2:153; Jane Austen, *Pride and Prejudice*, ed. R. W. Chapman (1813; London, 1959), p. 48.

2. Jane Austen, *Mansfield Park*, ed. R. W. Chapman (London, 1960), pp. 156; 392; Robert Scholes, "Dr. Johnson and Jane Austen," *Philological Quarterly*, 54 (1975), 381, 389.

3. Nathaniel Hawthorne, "Samuel Johnson," *Biographical Stories for Children* (1842), in *Tales, Sketches and Other Papers* (Boston, 1882), pp. 175–176; Nathaniel Hawthorne, "Lichfield and Uttoxeter," *Our Old Home* (Boston, 1882), pp. 150; 162. Thomas Curley, "Johnson's America," *The Age of Johnson*, 6 (1994), 31, noted that Hawthorne fictionalized "Bowdoin College as a Johnsonian 'Happy Valley of Abyssinia' in his first novel, *Fanshawe* (1828)." The first word in the title of his *Blithedale Romance* (1852) means Happy Valley.

4. Nathaniel Hawthorne, *The Scarlet Letter* (1850; New York, 1959), pp. 152–153; 267; *Complete Poems*, pp. 132 and 141; A. E. Housman, *Collected Poems* (New York, 1971), pp. 108; 210. In the last line Housman also echoes Charles Doughty's *Adam Cast Forth* (1908).

5. *Complete Poems*, p. 87; Housman, *Poems*, p. 72; "Considerations on Corn," in *Political Writings*, Yale 10.311; A.E. Housman, *Letters*, ed. Henry Maas (London, 1971), p.120.

6. Norman Page, *A. E. Housman: A Critical Biography* (New York, 1983), p. 140. In "Dr. Johnson and A. E. Housman," *Harvard Studies in Classical Philology*, 88 (1984), 241–257, R. Renehan concluded that Johnson's "Preface" to *The Plays of William Shakespeare* (1765) and Housman's *The Name and Nature of Poetry* show their kindred spirits.

7. See Leslie Stephen, "Dr. Johnson's Writings." *Hours in a Library* (London, 1876); *History of English Thought in the Eighteenth Century* (London, 1876); *Samuel Johnson* (London, 1878); entry on Johnson in the *Dictionary of National Biography* (1892); review of Reade's *Johnsonian Miscellanies*, in *Studies of a Biographer* (London, 1898); and *English Literature and Society in the Eighteenth Century* (London, 1904).

8. Virginia Woolf, "Saint Samuel of Fleet Street," *Nation and Athenaeum*, Literary Supplement, 38 (November 14, 1925), 248 (see B. J. Kirkpatrick and Stuart Clarke, *A Bibliography of Virginia Woolf*, 4th edition, Oxford, 1997, p. 279); Virginia Woolf, "Preface" to *The Common Reader* (New York, 1925), p. 1; *Lives of the Poets*, 3:124.

9. Virginia Woolf, *Orlando: A Biography* (1928; London, 1945), p. 128 (the subtitle of this unusual book is a subtle tribute to Johnson's favorite genre); Julia Briggs, *Virginia Woolf: An Inner Life* (New York, 2005), p. 251; Boswell, *Life*, p. 845; James Knowlson, *Damned to Fame: The Life of Samuel Beckett* (New York, 1996), p. 243.

10. Quoted in Stephen Dilks, "Samuel Beckett's Samuel Johnson," *Modern Language Review*, 98 (April 2003), 294, 298; Deirdre Bair, *Samuel Beckett: A Biography* (New York, 1978), pp. 256–257; Samuel Beckett, *Watt* (London, 1953), p. 60; Anthony Cronin, *Samuel Beckett: The Last Modernist* (1997; New York, 1999), p. 501.

11. Lionel Kelly, "Beckett's *Human Wishes*," in *The Ideal Core of the Onion: Reading Beckett*, ed. John Pilling and Mary Bryden (Bristol, 1992), p. 36; Knowlson, *Damned to Fame*, p. 250; Bair, *Samuel Beckett*, p. 253; Cronin, *Samuel Beckett*, p. 255.

12. Boswell, *Life*, pp. 1007; 1217; Samuel Beckett, "*Human Wishes*," *Disjecta: Miscellaneous Writings and a Dramatic Fragment*, ed. Ruby Cohn (New York, 1984), pp. 155, 156, 158, 160.

13. Beckett, *Human Wishes*, pp. 161–163. The style, content and wit of this scene is taken straight from the "Cyclops" chapter of *Ulysses*, p. 247:

—Paddy Dignam dead! says Alf.
—Ay, says Joe.
—Sure I'm after seeing him not five minutes ago. . . . He's no more dead than you are.
—Maybe so, says Joe. They took the liberty of burying him this morning anyhow. . . .
—He paid the debt of nature.

14. Bair, *Samuel Beckett*, p. 255; Kelly, "Beckett's *Human Wishes*," p. 31.

15. Bair, *Samuel Beckett*, p. 257; Cronin, *Samuel Beckett*, p. 255.

16. Vladimir Nabokov, *Pale Fire* (1962; New York, 1968), p. 111; Boswell, *Life*, p. 1217.

17. Boswell, *Life*, pp. 876.

18. Hannah More, in *Johnsonian Miscellanies*, 2:197; *Johnson on Language*, Yale 18.111–112.

19. Boswell, *Life*, pp. 446; 437.

20. Brian Boyd, *Vladimir Nabokov: The American Years* (Princeton, 1991), p. 439; Boswell, *Life*, p. 137; *Complete Poems*, p. 128.

21. Boswell, *Life*, p. 92; Pope, *Poems*, pp. 523; 524. This condemnation of vanity, which originates in Ecclesiastes (1:2) and was repeated by Bunyan, Johnson and Thackeray, first appeared in the anonymous *Life of St. Sebastian:* "He forsook the bustle and vanity of the world and withdrew to a monastery."

22. Boyd, *Vladimir Nabokov*, p. 448; *Johnson on Shakespeare*, Yale 7.70.

Bibliography

WORKS BY SAMUEL JOHNSON

Samuel Johnson. *A Dictionary of the English Language.* London: Bohn, 1850.

————. *The Letters of Samuel Johnson, 1731–1784.* Ed. Bruce Redford. 5 vols. Princeton: Princeton University Press, 1992–94.

————. *The Lives of the Most Eminent English Poets.* Ed. Roger Lonsdale. 4 vols. Oxford: Oxford University Press, 2006.

————. *Prefaces and Dedications.* Ed. Allen Hazen. New Haven: Yale University Press, 1937.

————. *Works.* Ed. Robert Lynam. 6 vols. London: George Cowie, 1825.

————. *Works, with an essay by Arthur Murphy.* 2 vols. London: Bohn, 1850.

————. *Works* (Oxford Authors). Ed. Donald Greene. Oxford: Oxford University Press, 1986.

————. *The Yale Edition of the Works of Samuel Johnson* New Haven: Yale University Press:

Vol. 1. *Diaries, Prayers, and Annals.* Ed. E. L. McAdam Jr. with Donald and Mary Hyde. 1958.

Vol. 2. *"The Idler" and "The Adventurer".* Ed. W. J. Bate, John Bullitt and L. F. Powell. 1963.

Vols. 3–5. *The Rambler.* Ed. W. J. Bate and Albrecht Strauss. 1969.

Vol. 6. *Poems*. Ed. E. L. McAdam Jr. with George Milne. 1964.

Vols. 7–8. *Johnson on Shakespeare*. Ed. Arthur Sherbo. 1968.

Vol. 9. *A Journey to the Western Islands of Scotland*. Ed. Mary Lascelles. 1971.

Vol. 10. *Political Writings*. Ed. Donald Greene. 1977.

Vol. 14. *Sermons*. Ed. Jean Hagstrum and James Gray. 1978.

Vol. 15. *A Voyage to Abyssinia*. Ed. Joel Gold. 1985.

Vol. 16. *"Rasselas" and Other Tales*. Ed. Gwin Kolb. 1990.

Vol. 17. *A Commentary on Mr. Pope's Principles of Morality, or Essay on Man*. Ed. O. M. Brack Jr. 2004.

Vol. 18. *Johnson on the English Language*. Ed. Gwin Kolb. 2005.

OTHER WORKS

Alkon, Paul. *Samuel Johnson and Moral Discipline*. Evanston, Ill: Northwestern University Press, 1967.

Bate, Walter Jackson. *The Achievement of Samuel Johnson*. New York: Oxford University Press, 1955.

———. *Samuel Johnson*. New York: Harcourt Brace Jovanovich, 1977.

Boswell, James. *Journal of a Tour to the Hebrides*. Ed. Frederick Pottle and C. H. Bennett. New York: Literary Guild, 1936.

———. *Life of Johnson*. Ed. R. W. Chapman. London: Oxford University Press, 1961.

———. *Life of Johnson*. Ed. George Birkbeck Hill, 1934; revised and enlarged by L. F. Powell. 6 vols. Oxford: Clarendon Press, 1971.

———. *The Correspondence of James Boswell with Certain Members of the Club, including Oliver Goldsmith, Bishops Percy and Barnard, Sir Joshua Reynolds, Topham Beauclerk and Bennet Langton*. Ed. Charles Fifer. New York: McGraw-Hill, 1976.

———. *The Correspondence of James Boswell with David Garrick, Edmund Burke and Edmond Malone*. Ed. Thomas Copeland. London: Heinemann, 1986.

———. *The Correspondence and Other Papers of James Boswell Relating to the Making of the "Life of Johnson"*. Ed. Marshall Waingrow. 2nd ed. New Haven: Yale University Press, 2001.

Boulton, James, ed. *Johnson: The Critical Heritage.* London: Routledge & Kegan Paul, 1971.

Brack, O. M. Jr., and Robert Kelley, eds. *The Early Biographies of Samuel Johnson.* Iowa City: University of Iowa Press, 1974.

Brewer, John. *The Pleasures of the Imagination: English Culture in the Eighteenth Century.* Chicago: University of Chicago Press, 1997.

Brownell, Morris. *Samuel Johnson's Attitude to the Arts.* Oxford: Clarendon Press, 1989.

Burney, Fanny. *Early Journals and Letters, Vol. 3: The Streatham Years. Part 1, 1778–1779.* Ed. Lars Troide and Stewart Cooke. Oxford: Clarendon Press, 1994.

———. *Early Journals and Letters, Vol. 4: The Streatham Years. Part 2, 1780–1781.* Ed. Betty Rizzo. Montreal: McGill-Queen's University Press, 2003.

Clifford, James. *Hester Lynch Piozzi (Mrs. Thrale).* 1941; 2nd ed. 1952. New York: Columbia University Press, 1968.

———. *Young Sam Johnson.* New York: McGraw-Hill, 1955.

———. *Dictionary Johnson.* New York: McGraw-Hill, 1979.

Fleeman, J. D. *A Bibliography of the Works of Samuel Johnson.* 2 vols. Oxford: Oxford University Press, 2000.

Fussell, Paul. *Samuel Johnson and the Life of Writing.* New York: Norton, 1971.

Greene, Donald. *The Politics of Samuel Johnson.* 1960; 2nd ed. Athens: University of Georgia Press, 1990.

———. *The Age of Exuberance: Backgrounds to Eighteenth-Century Literature.* New York: Random House, 1970.

———. *Samuel Johnson.* 1970; updated edition. Boston: Twayne, 1989.

———. "Samuel Johnson's *Life of Richard Savage.*" *The Biographer's Art: New Essays.* Ed. Jeffrey Meyers. London: Macmillan, 1989. pp. 11–30.

———. *Selected Essays.* Ed. John Abbott. Lewisburg, Pa.: Bucknell University Press, 2004.

Hawkins, Sir John. *The Life of Samuel Johnson.* Ed. Bertram Davis. New York: Macmillan, 1961.

Hibbert, Christopher. *The Personal History of Samuel Johnson.* 1971; London: Pimlico, 1998.

Hill, George Birkbeck, ed. *Johnsonian Miscellanies*. 2 vols. Oxford: Clarendon Press, 1897.

Hilles, Frederick, ed. *The Age of Johnson: Essays Presented to Chauncey Brewster Tinker.* New Haven: Yale University Press, 1949.

———. *New Light on Johnson.* New Haven: Yale University Press, 1959.

Holmes, Richard. *Dr. Johnson & Mr. Savage.* New York: Pantheon, 1993.

Kaminski, Thomas. *The Early Career of Samuel Johnson.* New York: Oxford University Press, 1987.

Korshin, Paul, ed. *Johnson after Two Hundred Years.* Philadelphia: University of Pennsylvania Press, 1986.

Krutch, Joseph Wood. *Samuel Johnson.* New York: Henry Holt, 1944.

Lascelles, Mary, ed. *Johnson, Boswell and Their Circle: Essays Presented to Lawrence Fitzroy Powell.* Oxford: Clarendon Press, 1965.

Lipking, Lawrence. *Samuel Johnson: The Life of an Author.* Cambridge, Mass.: Harvard University Press, 1998.

Meyers, Jeffrey. "The Sermons of Swift and Johnson," *Personalist,* 47 (January 1966), 61–80.

———. "Johnson, Boswell and Modern Biography," *New Rambler* (2001–2002), 50–59.

———. "Shade's Shadow: Samuel Johnson in Nabokov's *Pale Fire,*" *New Criterion,* 24 (May 2006), 31–35.

———. "Samuel Demands the Muse: Johnson's Stamp on Imaginative Literature," *Antioch Review,* 65 (Winter 2007), 39–49.

———. "Samuel Johnson's Writer's Block," *London Magazine* (December 2006–January 2007), 28–35.

———. "Review-Essay of Samuel Johnson's *Lives of the Poets,*" *Yale Review,* 95 (January 2007), 144–158.

Novak, Maximillian. "James Boswell's *Life of Johnson.*" *The Biographer's Art: New Essays.* Ed. Jeffrey Meyers. London: Macmillan, 1989. pp. 31–52.

Page, Norman, ed. *Samuel Johnson: Interviews and Recollections.* Totowa, N.J.: Barnes & Noble, 1987.

Picard, Liza. *Dr. Johnson's London.* New York: St. Martin's, 2000.

Piozzi, Hester Lynch. *Anecdotes of the Late Samuel Johnson* and William Shaw. *Memoirs of the Life and Writings of the Late Samuel Johnson.* Ed. Arthur Sherbo. London: Oxford University Press, 1974.

————. *Thraliana: The Diary of Mrs. Hester Lynch Thrale (later Mrs. Piozzi), 1776–1809.* Ed. Katharine Balderston. 2 vols. Oxford: Oxford University Press, 1942; revised 2nd ed., 1951.

Porter, Roy. *English Society in the Eighteenth Century.* New York: Penguin, 1990.

Reade, A. L. *Johnsonian Gleanings.* 11 vols. London: Francis, 1909–52.

Rogers, Pat. *The Samuel Johnson Encyclopedia.* Westport, Conn.: Greenwood Press, 1996.

Wain, John. *Samuel Johnson: A Biography.* New York: Viking, 1974.

Watkins, W. B. C. *Perilous Balance: The Tragic Genius of Swift, Johnson and Sterne.* 1939; Cambridge, Mass.: Boar's Head, 1960.

INDEX